# OECD Competition Assessment Reviews: Greece 2017

OECD
BETTER POLICIES FOR BETTER LIVES

This work is published under the responsibility of the Secretary-General of the OECD. The opinions expressed and arguments employed herein do not necessarily reflect the official views of OECD member countries.

This document and any map included herein are without prejudice to the status of or sovereignty over any territory, to the delimitation of international frontiers and boundaries and to the name of any territory, city or area.

**Please cite this publication as:**
OECD (2017), *OECD Competition Assessment Reviews: Greece 2017*, OECD Publishing, Paris.
*http://dx.doi.org/10.1787/9789264088276-en*

ISBN 978-92-64-26637-7 (print)
ISBN 978-92-64-08827-6 (PDF)

**Photo credits:** Cover © lian_2011/iStock/Thinkstock

Corrigenda to OECD publications may be found on line at: *www.oecd.org/about/publishing/corrigenda.htm*.

# *Foreword*

After suffering one of the longest and most serious economic crises ever experienced by any European country, which resulted in a severe drop of real GDP and major losses in employment and incomes, the Greek economy is projected to improve in 2016-2017. Progress has been made in balancing the budget and implementing significant labour market and fiscal reforms.

Despite these recent reforms, Greece's product markets remain among the most heavily regulated in the OECD. These structural flaws adversely affect the ability of new firms to enter markets and hamper innovation, efficiency and productivity. Weak competition and barriers to entry result in less choice and higher prices for Greek consumers, less investment for the Greek economy and fewer jobs. Enhancing competition is critical to Greece's prosperity.

Against this background, the OECD was asked to conduct a third assessment of Greece's competition laws and regulations, focusing on five sectors: e-commerce; construction; media; wholesale trade; and a number of manufacturing sub-sectors such as chemicals and pharmaceuticals. These sectors together represent 11.2% of GDP and 16.7% of employment.

The OECD Competition Assessment Project, carried out in close communication with the Greek government and with the support of the European Commission, examined about 1 290 items of legislation, identified 577 potential restrictions to competition and submitted 356 recommendations for reform in the sectors covered by the study. When fully implemented, these recommendations are expected to improve the functioning of these sectors and thus bring tangible benefits to consumers and to the economy, in the form of lower prices for the former and increased turnover and competitiveness for the latter.

This assessment provides the Greek government with detailed policy solutions for addressing persistent structural malfunctions in specific sectors. As such, it constitutes a valuable contribution to reform efforts aimed at getting the Greek economy back on a sustainable growth path by enhancing its competitiveness, encouraging investment and creating more and better jobs.

I congratulate the Greek government and the European Commission for their determination to continue on this path and for their combined efforts to reinforce the business environment in the selected sectors as a necessary stage in leading Greece to design, develop and deliver better policies for better lives.

Angel Gurría

Secretary-General, OECD

# *Acknowledgments*

This report is the result of the 2016 project on Competition Assessment of Laws and Regulations in five economic sectors in Greece, conducted under the auspices of the Minister of Economy, Development and Tourism, HE Georgios Stathakis.

This project was organised in the context of the technical assistance provided by the European Commission's Structural Reform Support Service (SRSS).

This document was produced with the financial assistance of the European Union. The views expressed herein can in no way be taken to reflect the official opinion of the European Union.

Our thanks go to Kaspar Richter, Head of Unit, Alessandra Budello and Theodoros Galanis, all of the Growth and Business Environment Unit, Structural Reform Support Service (SRSS) for providing support and contributing to the task of co-ordinating a project of this complexity. In addition, we are grateful to the many European Commission officials who have responded to our queries and have commented on our report.

Our particular thanks go to the Hellenic Competition Commission (HCC), which supported the project from its inception and contributed full-time staff on secondment to work with the project team. In addition to the seconded HCC staff members, Fotis Papadopoulos, Economist, and Giannis Stefatos, Economist, we would like to thank Dimitris Loukas, Vice-Chairman, Lefkothea Nteka, Commissioner-Rapporteur, Dionysia Xirokosta, Director-General, Kelly Benetatou, Director, Pantelis Boronas, Director, and Lila Katsereli, Head of Advocacy Unit, for all their preparatory work and for the follow-on support by the HCC throughout the project. We would also like to thank Assimakis Komninos, former Commissioner-Rapporteur, for initially supporting the competition assessment work in Greece that ultimately began in 2013.

We are grateful to Ilias Xanthakos, Secretary General of the Ministry of Economy, Development and Tourism and Chair of the High-level Committee (HLC), for ensuring the necessary inter-ministerial co-ordination structure. We would like to thank the members of the HLC who participated in meetings to discuss the findings of the project. The members were as follows: Antonios Papaderakis, Secretary General of Commerce and Consumer Protection, Ministry of Economy, Development and Tourism; Efstratios Zafiris, Secretary General of Industry, Ministry of Economy, Development and Tourism; Nikolaos Antonoglou, Secretary General of the Ministry of Rural Development and Food; George Dedes, Secretary General of the Ministry of Infrastructure, Transport and Networks; Christina Baritaki, Secretary General of the Ministry of Environment and Energy; Eirini Klabatsea, Secretary General of Physical Planning and Urban Environment, Ministry of Environment and Energy; Petros Giannoulatos, Secretary General, Ministry of Health; Ioannis Baskozos, Secretary General of Public Health, Ministry of Health; Eleni Papadopoulou, Secretary General of Economic Policy, Ministry of Finance; Eleftherios Kretsos, Secretary General of Information and Communication; Dimitrios Papagiannakos, Secretary General of Government Co-ordination; Dimitrios Tzanakopoulos, Secretary General of the Prime

Minister's Office and Dimitrios Tzortzis, former Secretary General of Telecommunications and Post, Ministry of Infrastructure, Transport and Networks.

We would also like to thank Michail Verroiopoulos, Secretary General of Energy and Mineral Resources, Ministry of Environment and Energy; Nikolaos Mantzoufas, Secretary Special for Public Private Partnerships, Ministry of Economy, Development and Tourism; Aikaterini Antoniou, President of EOF; Ioannis Kaplanis, General Director of OBI; Charalambos Kasimis, Secretary General of Agricultural Policy and Management of European Funds, Ministry of Rural Development and Food; Vassilis Maglaras, Secretary General of Communications, Ministry of Infrastructure, Transport and Networks; Theopisti Perka, Secretary General of the Ministry of Infrastructure, Transport and Networks and Maria Vlazaki, Secretary General of the Ministry of Culture and Sports, for their support.

For his help with the project organisation and co-ordination we would like to extend our thanks to Loudovikos Kotsonopoulos, special advisor to the Minister of Economy, Development and Tourism. In addition we would like to thank Panagiotis Markatselas, Manolis Patsourakis, Dimitra Sakareli and Konstantinos Vrettos, from the Co-ordination Unit for Strategic Development Planning, Ministry of Economy, Development and Tourism. For their help with co-ordination with the other authorities, our thanks go to Ioanna Gkergki and Stavroula Angelidi, Secretariat General of Government Co-ordination.

In addition, we acknowledge the input from government experts who participated in the project by providing information, advice and feedback throughout the project from the following departments of the involved ministries:

- Ministry of Economy, Development and Tourism: Secretariat General of Commerce and Consumer Protection, Secretariat General of Industry, Secretariat of Public and Private Partnerships, General Directorate of Foreign Economic and Trade Policies, Directorate of Coordination of Trade, Department of Exports, Directorate of Quality Policy, Directorate of Institutional Settings and Market Supervision of Products and Services, Directorate of Technical Industrial Legislation, Directorate of Technical Professions and Security Facilities, Directorate of Licensing of Businesses and Business Parks, Directorate of Commerce Policy, Organisation of Central Markets of Athens (OKAA);
- Ministry of Environment and Energy: Secretariat General of Regional Planning and Urban Development, Secretariat General of Energy and Mineral Resources, General Directorate for the Environmental Policy, Directorate for the Protection of Biodiversity, Soil and Waste Management;
- Ministry of Finance: General Secretariat of Economic Policy, General Directorate of Customs and Excise Duties, General Directorate of Tax Administration, Directorate of Alcohol and Foods of the General Directorate of Chemical State Laboratory, Directorate of Energy, Industrial and Chemicals Products of the General Directorate of Chemical State Laboratory;
- Ministry of Health: National Organisation for Medicines (EOF) – Product Assessment Division, Division of Validation of Applications and Issue of Market Authorisations, Manufacturing and Market Surveillance Division, Health Procurement Committee (EPY), National Organisation for the Provision of Health Services (EOPYY) – Directorate of Medicine, Independent Legal Department;
- Ministry of Infrastructure, Transport and Networks: Secretariat General of Public Works, Directorate of Broadband, Network Infrastructure and ICT Projects, Secretariat General of Transport;

- Ministry of Interior and Administrative Reconstruction; Secretariat General of Public Order; Hellenic Police, Directorate of State Security, Department of Weapons and Explosives, Secretariat of Citizen Protection;
- Ministry of Rural Development and Food: General Secretariat of Ministry of Rural Development and Food; Directorate General of Sustainable Plant Production, Directorate General of Animal Production and Veterinary Services, Directorate of Land Reclamation, Water and Soil Resources and Fertilisers, Directorate of Animal Nutrition, Feed and Pastureland, Directorate of Cultivating Systems, Hellenic Food Authority (EFET), Directorate of Strategy, Rural Development, Evaluation and Documentation;
- Ministry of Labour, Social Insurance and Solidarity, Directorate of Safety and Health at Work;
- Ministry of Culture and Sports;
- Hellenic Telecommunications and Post Commission (EETT);
- Greek National Council for Radio and Television (NCRTV);
- Hellenic Copyright Organisation (OPI);
- Hellenic Industrial Property Organisation (OBI); and
- Single Public Procurement Authority.

We would also like to thank the Hellenic Federation of Enterprises (SEV), its Business Environment Observatory and its member companies for their constructive collaboration and help. We would like to convey our thanks to the Hellenic Confederation of Commerce & Entrepreneurship (ESEE), the Hellenic Confederation of Professionals, Craftsmen & Merchants (GSEVEE), the Technical Chamber of Greece (TEE), the Hellenic Association of Chemical Industries (HACI), the Greek e-Commerce Association (GRECA), the Hellenic Start-up Association, the Hellenic Association of Mobile Application Companies (HAMAC), Consumers' Association "Quality of Life" (EKPIZO), the Association of the Greek Manufacturers of Packaging & Materials (AGMPM), the Panhellenic Union of Pharmaceutical Industry (PEF), the Panhellenic Association of Pharmaceutical Wholesalers and Qualified Pharmacists (PAPW), the Hellenic Fertiliser Association (SPEL), the Hellenic Federation of Printing Media Communication (SEMEE), the Hellenic Crop Protection Association (HCPA), the Association of Greek Contracting Companies (SATE), Athens University of Economics and Business (AUEB), the Greek Mobile Operators Association (EEKT), the Association of the Greek Industry of Detergents and Soaps (SEVAS), the Hellenic Association of Pharmaceutical Companies (SFEE), the Panhellenic Association of Engineers Contractors of Public Works (PEDMEDE), the Hellenic Association of Consulting Firms (HELLASCO), the Hellenic Association of Petrol Station Owners (POPEK), the Greek Association of Industries and Processors of Olive Oil (SEVITEL), the Hellenic Association of Industries and Packers of Olive Oil (ESVITE), the Association of the Technical Companies of the Highest Classes (STEAT), the Association of International Freight Forwarders & Logistics Enterprises of Greece (SYNDDEL), the Hellenic Aerosol Association (HAA), the Central Market & Fishery Organisations (CFMO), the Greek Seed Trade Association (EEPES), the Panhellenic Association of Private Radio Stations, the Association of Companies of Broadly Used Pharmaceuticals (EFEX), the Hellenic Association of Private National TV Broadcasters (EITISEE), the Hellenic Petroleum Marketing Companies Association (SEEPE), the Association of the Greek Tobacco Industries, and the Association of Privately Owned Radio Stations in Attika.

We are also grateful to the many companies that have voluntarily contributed their experiences and knowledge.

The opinions expressed in the report do not necessarily reflect the views of the above-mentioned organisations or individuals.

The Competition Assessment Toolkit was developed by Working Party No. 2 of the Competition Committee with the input of members of many delegations to the OECD, both from member and non-member jurisdictions. The materials were drafted at the OECD Secretariat under the leadership of Sean F. Ennis, Senior Economist in the Competition Division of the OECD Directorate for Financial and Enterprise Affairs.

The OECD project team in Athens consisted of Panagiotis Barkas, Economist, Elli Filippopoulou, Lawyer, Christos Genakos, Economist, Konstantinos Gloumis-Atsalakis, Lawyer, Panagiota Makri, Lawyer, Domna Michailidou, Economist, Avgi Oikonomidou, Economist, Spyros Pappas, Senior Liaison Officer, Eleni Rentouka, Lawyer, Euclides Sakellarios, Senior Communications Officer, Panoraia Spiliopoulou, Lawyer, Matt Tavantzis, Economist, Athina Vounatsou, Lawyer, all OECD Competition Division, and Fotis Papadopoulos, Economist, and Giannis Stefatos, Economist, both Hellenic Competition Commission. The project team was led by Federica Maiorano, Senior Competition Expert, with office support from Christina Anagnostopoulou, OECD Competition Division.

The project team in Paris consisted of Sean Ennis, Acting Head of Division, Despina Pachnou, Competition Expert, both at the OECD Competition Division, and John Davies, former Head of the OECD Competition Division. Comments on the report were provided by Michael Saller, James Mancini, Pedro Caro de Sousa, Chris Pike and Pedro Gonzaga, all OECD Competition Division. Special thanks go to the OECD colleagues who provided their input and offered useful comments and feedback. These include Valérie Paris, Health Division; Raimonds Aronietis, International Transport Forum; Michael Donohue and Brigitte Acoca, Consumer Policy Division; Piritta Sorsa, Christine de la Maisonneuve, Falilou Fall, Christine Lewis, Vassiliki Georgokopoulou, all Economics Department – Country Studies Branch; Bálazs Égert, Economics Department – Structural Studies Department; Sam Paltridge and Verena Weber, Communication Infrastructure and Services Policy Division; Anne Gourmelon, Environment, Health and Safety Division; Stéphane Buydens, Consumption Taxes Unit. Our thanks go to Alain de Serres, Head of the Structural Studies Department, Economics Department, and Antonio Capobianco, Senior Competition Expert, Competition Division, for their presentations in our workshops.

We would also like to thank Vasileios Stelianidis, Dimitris Ypsilantis, Knud Erik Skouby, Anders Henten, Reza Tayadoni and Iliana Giannouli for their contributions.

The report was edited for publication by Tom Ridgway, and prepared for publication by Erica Agostinho, Communications Assistant, OECD Competition Division and Edward Smiley, Publications Officer, OECD Directorate for Financial and Enterprise Affairs.

# *Table of contents*

Preface by HE Georgios Stathakis ........ 15

Preface by Maarten Verwey ........ 17

Abbreviations and acronyms ........ 19

Executive summary ........ 23

*Chapter 1.* Assessment and recommendations ........ 27

1.1. The benefits of competition ........ 28
1.2. Main recommendations from the Competition Assessment project ........ 29
1.3. Horizontal findings ........ 34
1.4. Benefits of lifting barriers and prioritisation of recommendations ........ 36
Notes ........ 39
References ........ 40

*Chapter 2.* E-commerce ........ 43

2.1. Definition and economic overview ........ 44
2.2. Overview of the legislation ........ 46
2.3. Monitoring obligations of internet intermediary service providers ........ 49
2.4. Definition of consumer ........ 50
2.5. Legal and commercial guarantees ........ 53
2.6. Definition of supplier ........ 54
2.7. Commercial guarantees ........ 55
2.8. Identification logo for online pharmacies ........ 57
Notes ........ 57
References ........ 64

*Chapter 3.* Construction ........ 65

3.1. Definition and economic overview ........ 66
3.2. Sector overview ........ 68
3.3. The system of registries: Categories of works and classification of companies ........ 70
3.4. Individual restrictions in the system of registries ........ 76
3.5. Pricing and budgeting ........ 79
3.6. E-Systems (Public procurement and e-monitoring of public works and designs) ........ 82
Notes ........ 83
References ........ 86
*Annex 3.A1.* Public procurement for construction works and designs ........ 88

*Chapter 4.* Media ........ 95

4.1. Definition and economic overview ........ 96
4.2. Overview of the legislation ........ 98
4.3. Publishing activities ........ 99
4.4. Audio-visual production and content ........ 104
4.5. Free-to-air media ........ 111
4.6. Pay TV ........ 123
Notes ........ 130
References ........ 138

*Chapter 5.* Chemicals and rubber, electrical equipment, paper and printing ........ 141

5.1. Chemicals and rubber products ........ 142
5.2. Electrical equipment ........ 164
5.3. Paper and paper products ........ 168
5.4. Printing and reproduction of recorded media ........ 169
Notes ........ 172
References ........ 177

*Chapter 6.* Pharmaceuticals ........ 179

6.1. Definition and economic overview ........ 180
6.2. Overview of the legislation ........ 184
6.3. Licensing ........ 185
6.4. Marketing and promotion ........ 189
6.5. Pricing and reimbursement ........ 194
6.6. Wholesale trade ........ 200
Notes ........ 200
References ........ 205

*Chapter 7.* Wholesale trade ........ 209

7.1. Definition and economic overview ........ 210
7.2. Overview of the legislation ........ 212
7.3. Agricultural, meat and fishery products ........ 214
7.4. Wholesale trade of solid, liquid and gaseous fuels and related products ........ 223
7.5. Transportation of goods ........ 232
Notes ........ 237
References ........ 241

*Annex A.* Methodology ........ 243

*Annex B.* Legislation screening by sector ........ 249

## Tables

1.1. Summary of the legal provisions analysed by sector ........ 29
1.2. Summary of estimated impacts by sector ........ 36
1.3. E-commerce ........ 37
1.4. Construction (public works and designs) ........ 37
1.5. Media ........ 37
1.6. Manufacturing and wholesale trade of chemicals and rubber products, electrical equipment, paper and paper products, and printing and reproduction of recorded media ........ 38

1.7. Manufacturing and wholesale trade of pharmaceuticals ........ 38
1.8. Wholesale trade of other products ........ 38
3.1. General statistics, construction, EUR, 2013 ........ 66
3.2. Construction sector in Greece, general description, 2013 ........ 67
3.3. Registry of Contractors (MEEP) – tender value thresholds by class ........ 72
3.4. Minimum gross turnover, equity and fixed assets per class registered in the Registry of Contractors (MEEP) ........ 74
3.5 Number of companies registered in each class of the Registry of Contractors (MEEP), August 2016 ........ 75
3.A1.1. Summary statistics – Greece ........ 89
3.A1.2. Project size, number of offers and discounts – Greece ........ 91
3.A1.3. Summary statistics – EEA, FYROM and Switzerland ........ 92
3.A1.4. Project size, number of offers and discounts – EEA, FYROM and Switzerland ........ 93
4.1. Public aid to the Greek press, 2009-2012 (€ million) ........ 100
4.2. Number of subscribers, 2013-2015 ........ 123
5.1. Withdrawal decisions for detergents and cleaning products by the GCSL (2013-2015) ........ 149
5.2. Competent authorities for biocides ........ 152
5.3. Income from excise duty imposed on isopropyl alcohol (2005-2015) ........ 163
6.1. The distribution of price difference in wholesale price of affected medicinal products ........ 197

## Figures

2.1. Share of e-commerce value to total turnover in EU Member States, 2014-2015 ........ 44
2.2. Percentage of enterprises selling via internet and/or networks other than internet in Greece and EU28, 2015 ........ 45
2.3. Level of internet access (at household level), and share of internet purchases by individuals in Greece and EU28, 2004-2015 ........ 46
3.1. Turnover and employment by firm size, 2013 ........ 67
3.2. Turnover by firm size, 2009-2013 ........ 68
3.3. Registry of contractors (MEEP) – tender value thresholds by class ........ 72
3.A1.1. Number of competing offers and discount of winning bid in tenders for public works and design projects – Greece ........ 90
4.1. Contribution to media sector's total turnover – Greece ........ 97
4.2. Breakdown of total employment in the media sector – Greece ........ 98
5.1. Value added as a percentage of manufacturing for chemicals and rubber products (2008-2013) ........ 143
5.2. Turnover of manufacturing chemicals and rubber products in Greece (2008-2014) ........ 143
5.3. Share of manufacturing chemicals and rubber products turnover per category in Greece (2008-2014) ........ 144
5.4. Share of decision-making process in the correct use of a plant protection product (2014, 2016) ........ 154
5.5. Share of professional users with training on use of plant protection products (2014, 2016) ........ 154
5.6. Structure of poisonings from plant protection products by cause (2012-13, 2014) ........ 155
5.7. Value added as a percentage of manufacturing for electrical equipment (2008-2013) ........ 165
5.8. Turnover of manufacturing electrical equipment in Greece (2008-2014) ........ 165

5.9. Share of manufacturing of electrical equipment turnover per category in Greece (2008-2014) ... 166
5.10. Value added as a percentage of manufacturing for paper and paper products (2008-2013) ... 168
5.11. Turnover of manufacturing paper and paper products in Greece (2008-2014) ... 169
5.12. Value added of printing and reproduction of recorded media as a percentage of manufacturing (2008-2013) ... 170
5.13. Turnover of printing and reproduction of recorded media in Greece (2008-2014) ... 171
6.1. Economic activity in the manufacturing of pharmaceuticals ... 180
6.2. Economic activity in the wholesale trade of pharmaceuticals ... 181
6.3. Number of pharmaceutical warehouses in Greece ... 182
6.4. Expenditure on health as a percentage of GDP, 2015 ... 182
6.5. Pharmaceutical spending as a percentage of total health spending ... 183
6.6. Share of generics in the total pharmaceutical market, 2015 (or nearest year) ... 195
6.7. Price ratio of generics vs. all pharmaceuticals, 2015 (or nearest year) ... 196
6.8. Calculating the consumer welfare effect of the 15% maximum price reduction cap ... 197
7.1. Value added of wholesale trade (2008-2013) ... 210
7.2. Percentage changes of value added of wholesale trade and GDP (2008-2013) ... 211
7.3. Share of value added of wholesale trade per category in Greece (2008-2013) ... 211
7.4. Turnover of wholesale trade per category in Greece (2008-2014) ... 212
A.1. Changes in consumer surplus ... 247

## Boxes

1.1. What is regulatory quality? ... 35
2.1. The estimated consumer benefits from reforms on e-commerce ... 48
2.2. Example of consumer definitions in selected EU Member States ... 52
3.1. Requirements for participation in tenders for public works ... 73
4.1. International media-ownership rules, ... 114
5.1. Umbrella branding ... 151
5.2. Storage requirements of plant protection products ... 157
5.3. Cosmetics notification fee in Sweden ... 161
5.4. The estimated consumer benefits from removing the tax on isopropyl alcohol ... 163
6.1. OECD Health Policy in Greece ... 183
6.2. Marketing authorisation in the European Economic Area ... 190
6.3. Codes and regulations of ethical pharmaceutical promotion and communications worldwide ... 192
6.4. Maximum price decrease in re-pricing procedure for generics ... 197
6.5. Use of External Reference Pricing (ERP) in Europe ... 199
7.1. Examples of similar facilities in other OECD countries ... 219
7.2. Type ST licences ... 225
7.3. Consumer survey on fuel ... 230
A.1. OECD Competition Checklist ... 244
A.2. Measuring changes in consumer surplus ... 247

**Follow OECD Publications on:**

http://twitter.com/OECD_Pubs

http://www.facebook.com/OECDPublications

http://www.linkedin.com/groups/OECD-Publications-4645871

http://www.youtube.com/oecdilibrary

OECD Alerts http://www.oecd.org/oecddirect/

# *Preface*

*by* HE Georgios Stathakis,
Minister for Economy, Development and Tourism

The aftershock of the global crisis in 2008 struck hard the Greek economy, which suffered an eight-year long recession and lost 26 % of its GDP. Since taking office, the current government's top priority has been to secure the country's return to sustainable and inclusive economic growth that will alleviate the inequalities incurred by the crisis and boost employment. A key element in this direction is to create a proper institutional framework that will boost investment and innovation, which are the drivers of a competitive economy. In this regard, product market reforms pursued in the context of the current OECD Competition Assessment Review are crucial, as they secure equal rules for all market stakeholders and promote the restriction of bottlenecks in their operation. The current project focused on five key sectors, namely, wholesale trade, manufacturing, e-commerce, media, and construction.

It is the firm belief of the Greek government that competition policy is not about extensive market deregulation, but rather about smart regulation. In that sense, the aim of smart regulation is to ensure the orderly and efficient functioning of markets through the design of fine-tuned and encompassing rules that meet current economic conditions and societal concerns. While attaining this goal, our emphasis is on achieving greater growth potential for established and new business ventures, and encouraging higher employment and employability for the workforce. Both these aims ought to be observed within the general framework of the unobstructed functioning of supply chains, without endangering the imperative of maintaining safety, health and environmental standards.

The government shall use the conclusions of the current Competition Assessment Review within this framework; in other words, not a competition assessment for the sake of deregulation, but one that aims at a fair and strategic reform of the legislation. This strategic reform shall serve the protection of public interest, the promotion of development goals within their current social and economic context, and the furtherance of the critical supporting role of Public Administration. The output of the project, some 356 recommendations, ensures efficient and fair market sharing and the prevention of monopolistic or quasi-monopolistic phenomena, supports the maximisation of consumer benefit, and provides assistance to the Greek government's ongoing attempts to reshape the Greek economy's overall outlook.

Regarding the review procedure, both our and our OECD partners' main concern was to reassure stakeholder engagement in the overall project. This essentially required facilitating, and most importantly encouraging, interaction between the OECD's research team and public -service experts, as well as with all relevant producer organisations and sectoral associations. This practice aimed to enhance the methodology of the assessment with the inclusion of the valuable experiences of regulators and market actors, while taking into account the real market conditions that quite often form the subject of complex or obscure regulations.

This approach has definitely borne fruit. Overall more than 120 meetings took place throughout the project. Cooperation with the civil service and consultation with market stakeholders have been extensive and actively sought throughout the project, ensuring that a variety of aspects and concerns were taken into account in forming the end result. Furthermore, ministerial experts, via their involvement with the project's proceedings, gained valuable experience on evaluating policy design and implementation through the lens of competition law and economics. This active involvement of public servants in the overall project constitutes an institutional legacy that the OECD project bequeathed to the Greek administration, in this way helping to develop a state capacity to address competition issues.

I would like to express my sincere gratitude to the OECD team, to SRSS and to all those from the civil -service sector who were involved in the project, and for carrying out successfully and in a balanced way this Competition Assessment Review within such a short time frame. I strongly believe that their contribution to our project of "putting Greece back to work" has been essential.

Georgios Stathakis

Minister for Economy,
Development and Tourism Greece

# *Preface*

*by* Maarten Verwey
Director General of the Structural Reform
Support Service of the European Commission

While Greece's economy is slowly moving towards recovery, many people in Greece remain doubtful about the future. After the long years of economic adjustment, they are wondering whether this economy will be for everyone or just for the lucky few.

This question is important. After all, closed markets and feeble innovation have held back the Greek economy for a long time. Barriers to competition, often put in place to favour vested interests, have contributed to this weakness.

Competition is an essential part of a more sustainable economy. For consumers, it makes the pay check last longer and widens their choice range. For businesses, it spurs innovation. As prices fall, more people can afford to buy the products, and well-run businesses can take a bigger slice of the market, leading to expansion and generation of new jobs.

Competition also supports a level playing field. It allows everyone to have their fair share of the benefits of growth. Removing barriers to competition and ensuring that everyone plays by the same rules show that public authorities are taking care of the interests of people, and not just of big business.

This is important in both Greece and the rest of Europe. Competition policy is a key tool in our collective efforts to boost growth and jobs, which is the first priority of the European Commission. As President Juncker highlighted in his 2016 State of the Union speech, Europe stands for a fair playing field, where consumers are protected against cartels and abuses by powerful companies.

This report makes an important contribution to this agenda in Greece. Based on the collaborative effort of a large team of experts from the public administration, the Hellenic Competition Commission, the OECD and the Structural Reform Support Service, it lays out actions to remove barriers to competition in e-commerce, construction, media, manufacturing and wholesale trade. For example, strengthening consumer protection legislation, rendering public tendering procedures more transparent, ensuring legal certainty in the legal framework for radio stations, reforming the pricing policy for pharmaceuticals and removing geographic obstacles to competition in wholesale markets can provide a level playing field in these key economic sectors and support the recovery.

I would like to express my great appreciation for the fruitful and rewarding cooperation with the Greek national authorities and the OECD. The Structural Reform Support Service stands ready to assist the Greek authorities in reaping the benefits of this important project.

Maarten Verwey

Director General of the Structural Reform Support Service
of the European Commission

# Abbreviations and acronyms

| | |
|---|---|
| AEPO | Approval of environmental conditions |
| AESGP | Association of the European Self-Medication Industry |
| AFI | Alternative fuels infrastructure |
| AGMPM | Association of the Greek Manufacturers of Packaging & Materials |
| art. | Article (of law) |
| ASMR | Added therapeutic value (Amélioration du service médical rendu) |
| AUEB | Athens University of Economics and Business |
| CE | Conformité Européenne |
| CEN | European Committee for Standardization |
| CENELEC | European Committee for the Electrotechnical Standardization |
| CEPS | French Economic Committee for Health Care Products (Comité Economique des Produits de Santé) |
| COCO | Company owned, company operated |
| CODO | Company owned, dealer operated |
| CP | Centralised Procedure for Market Authorisation of Pharmaceutical Products |
| CPMP | Committee for Proprietary Medical Products |
| CPNP | Cosmetic Product Notification Portal |
| DIEPPY | Rules for trading of products and rendering of services |
| DODO | Dealer owned, dealer operated |
| DP | Decentralised Procedure for Market Authorisation of Pharmaceutical Products |
| EC | European Community |
| ECR | Efficient Consumer Response Association |
| EEA | European Economic Area |
| EEKT | Greek Mobile Operators Association |
| EEPES | Greek Seed Trade Association |
| EETT | Hellenic Telecommunications & Post Commission |
| EFET | Hellenic Food Authority |
| EFEX | Association of Pharmaceutical Companies of Non-prescription Medicines |
| EITISEE | Hellenic Association of Private National TV Broadcasters |
| E.K.PI.ZO | "Quality of Life" consumers' association |

| | |
|---|---|
| ELOT | Hellenic Organisation for Standardisation |
| EL.STAT. | Hellenic Statistical Authority |
| EMA | European Medicines Agency |
| EOF | National Organisation for Medicines |
| EOPYY | National Organisation for the Provision of Health Services |
| EPY | Health Procurement Committee |
| ERP | External Reference Pricing |
| ESEE | Hellenic Confederation of Commerce & Entrepreneurship |
| ETEP | National Technical Specifications |
| ETSI | European Telecommunications Standards Institute |
| EU | European Union |
| EYSED | Special Co-ordination and Implementation Office for Co-founded Actions in the Field of Commerce. |
| FEK | Government Gazette |
| GCSL | General Chemical State Laboratory |
| GDP | Gross domestic product |
| GE.DI.FA | General Sale Medicines (Γενικής Διάθεσης Φάρμακα - ΓΕ.ΔΙ.ΦΑ.) |
| G.E.M.I | General Electronic Commercial Registry |
| GMP | Good manufacturing practices |
| GRECA | Greek E-commerce Association |
| GSEVEE | Hellenic Confederation of Professionals, Craftsmen and Merchants |
| GVA | Gross value added |
| HAA | Hellenic Aerosol Association |
| HACI | Hellenic Association of Chemical Industries |
| HCC | Hellenic Competition Commission |
| HCPA | Hellenic Crop Protection Association |
| HELLASCO | Hellenic Association of Consulting Firms |
| HLC | High-level committee |
| HTA | Health technology assessment |
| IFPMA | International Federation of Pharmaceutical Manufacturers and Associations |
| IKE | Private company |
| IME GSEVEE | Small Enterprises' Institute of the Hellenic Confederation of Professionals, Craftsmen and Merchants |
| ISO | International Organization for Standardization |
| JMD | Joint Ministerial Decision |
| KATH | Central Market of Thessaloniki Organisation |
| L | Litre |
| LD | Legislative Decree |

| | |
|---|---|
| L.L.C | Limited liability company |
| LPG | Liquefied petroleum gas |
| MD | Ministerial Decision |
| MAH | Market authorisation holder |
| MEEP | Registry of Constructors |
| MEK | Registry of Acquired Experience |
| MFP | Multi-factor productivity |
| MM | Registry of Designers and Design Offices |
| MRP | Mutual recognition procedure |
| MT | Metric tonnes |
| NACE | Statistical Classification of Economic Activities in the European Community |
| NCRTV | Greek National Council for Radio and Television (ΕΣΡ) |
| NGV | Natural gas vehicle |
| NHS | National Hellenic Standard |
| OBI | Hellenic Industrial Property Organisation |
| OKAA | Central Markets and Fishery Organisation |
| OPI | Hellenic Copyright Organisation |
| OTC | Over-the-counter (medicines) |
| par. | Paragraph (of article of law) |
| PAPW | Panhellenic Association of Pharmaceutical Wholesalers and Qualified Pharmacists |
| PD | Presidential Decree |
| PEDMEDE | Panhellenic Association of Engineers Contractors of Public Works |
| PEF | Panhellenic Union of Pharmaceutical Industry |
| PGEU | Pharmaceutical Group of the European Union |
| PMR | Product Market Regulation (index) |
| RD | Royal Decree |
| R&D | Research and development |
| RIA | Regulatory impact assessment |
| RMS | Reference member state |
| RPM | Retail price maintenance |
| S.A. | Société Anonyme |
| SATE | Association of Greek Contracting Companies |
| SEEPE | Hellenic Petroleum Marketing Companies Association |
| SEMEE | Hellenic Federation of Printing Media Communication |
| SEV | Hellenic Federation of Enterprises |
| SEVAS | Association of the Greek Industry of Detergents and Soaps |
| SEVT | Federation of Hellenic Food Industries |

| | |
|---|---|
| SFEE | Hellenic Association of Pharmaceutical Companies |
| SMPA | Swedish Medical Products Agency |
| SMR | Therapeutic value (Service médical rendu) |
| SPC | Supplementary Protection Certificate |
| SPEL | Hellenic Fertiliser Association |
| STEAT | Association of Technical Companies of the Highest Classes |
| SYNDDEL | Association of International Freight Forwarders and Logistics Enterprises of Greece |
| TEE | Technical Chamber of Greece |
| VAT | Value added tax |
| WUWM | World Union of Wholesale Markets |

# Executive summary

The OECD was asked to carry out an independent policy assessment to identify rules and regulations that may hinder the competitive and efficient functioning of markets in five sectors of the Greek economy: e-commerce, construction, media, wholesale trade, and selected sub-sectors of manufacturing, such as chemicals and pharmaceuticals.

The project proceeded in five stages. Stage 1 defined the exact scope of all sectors. A list consisting of about 1 290 sector-relevant legislation was made with the help of government experts. In Stage 2, this legislation was screened, using the OECD's Competition Assessment methodology, to identify potential competition barriers. The review included both national provisions and pieces of legislation transposing EU directives. In Stage 3, we researched the policy makers' objectives for each provision. An in-depth analysis was carried out qualitatively. In Stage 4, we developed draft recommendations for those provisions that were found to restrict competition, taking into account EU legislation and equivalent provisions in comparable countries, notably other EU Member States. In the final stage, recommendations were finalised. At the same time, several workshops with ministerial experts were held to build the Greek administration's competition assessment capabilities.

As a result of this work, the report makes 356 recommendations on specific legal provisions that should be abolished or amended. In some cases, the restrictive provision was removed or modified during the course of the project following OECD comments on draft legislation, and hence no recommendation was made in the final report. All final recommendations are detailed in Annex B.

**Summary of the legal provisions analysed by sector**

| | E-commerce | Construction | Media | Pharmaceuticals | Other manufacturing | Wholesale trade | Total |
|---|---|---|---|---|---|---|---|
| **Pieces of legislation** | 71 | 251 | 251 | 155 | 268 | 292 | 1 288 |
| **Potential restrictions identified** | 15 | 61 | 68 | 88 | 80 | 265 | 577 |
| **Recommendations made** | 10 | 42 | 68 | 54 | 48 | 134 | 356 |

Throughout the project, we have sought to identify the sources of the benefits brought by the recommendations and, where possible, provide quantitative estimates. Our estimates were based either on a bottom-up quantification of specific regulations, where possible; or on conservative estimates of efficiency gains and an expansion of the business activity affected. If the restrictions identified in the project are lifted, the OECD conservatively estimates a positive impact on the Greek economy of around EUR 414 million. This amount is the total of the estimated positive effects on consumer surplus and higher turnover in all the sectors, as a result of removing current regulatory barriers to competition.

In addition, the rationalisation of the body of legislation in these sectors – if the recommendations are fully implemented – will also positively affect the ability of businesses to compete in the longer term. As a result, we consider that the cumulative, long-term impact on the Greek economy of lifting all the restrictions identified as harmful will be significant. In this report we do not attempt to estimate this effect.

### Key recommendations

- Repeal the obsolete and outdated legislation identified, a task which the public administration began before the end of our project.
- Abolish barriers to entry for the sectors analysed. These barriers include strict licensing requirements in the wholesale trade of fuel, such as minimum capital requirements and minimum requirements for storage.
- The regulation of exclusive contracts between fuel wholesalers and retailers should be reviewed to ensure that the duration of the agreements cannot be extended beyond the legal terms, to encourage more competition among wholesalers.
- Simplify the rules and lift restrictions on the operation of pharmaceutical warehouses to reduce costs and administrative burden for wholesalers.
- In the construction sector, bidders should be able to participate in a tender irrespective of their classification within the Registries provided they satisfy the criteria described in the call for tenders.
- Engineers and designers should be allowed the flexibility to register in a greater number of categories than currently allowed.
- In the construction sector, guidelines or standardised documents should be issued to provide guidance to contracting authorities and encourage more uniform implementation.
- Regarding e-procurement and e-monitoring of public works and designs, authorities should apply e-procurement processes and consider the introduction of e-monitoring mechanisms that consolidate all the information on each contract, either in a single integrated system or easily accessible through interoperable systems.
- The legal framework for the advertisement of over-the-counter (OTC) medicines should be updated and clearly aligned with recent amendments in the liberalisation of the distribution channels of commonly used medicines (Γενικής Διάθεσης Φάρμακα – ΓΕΔΙΦΑ / General Sale Medicines – GEDIFA) as a special category of OTCs.
- The pricing rules for pharmaceuticals impose a maximum price reduction for generics and foresee price equation between off-patent and generic medicines in certain cases. This deprives generics of their price advantage compared to the original branded product, leaving no room for competition or for generics' further penetration in the market. The rule should be amended to preserve the price difference between generic and branded products.

- The licensing and regulatory framework for radio stations is fragmented and largely not implemented in practice. The Greek authorities should ensure that economic operators have legal certainty and can make informed business choices based on a clear regulatory framework.

- The regulatory framework for pay TV should be reviewed and made more flexible, specifically on licence fees, corporate structure and cross-ownership rules. The report does not include the assessment of Law 4339/2015 and of Joint Ministerial Decision 7577/2016 in relation to digital free-to-air TV licences, due to the administrative and legal procedures ongoing during the project.

- The definition of independent audiovisual producer should be reviewed in line with the EU Audiovisual Media Services Directive and the provisions regarding production and supply of media content should be streamlined.

- Remove the excise duty on isopropyl alcohol, which forces economic operators to incur complex and costly processes.

- Streamline the legislation on consumer protection, including the provision of a uniform definition of consumer and the clarification of the framework on guarantees.

- The authorities should allow trading detergents in bulk at wholesale level, enabling companies to save on packaging and potentially lowering prices of detergents for final consumers.

- The legal framework on cosmetics and biocides should be aligned with the relevant EU regulatory framework in order to recognise the primary and secondary functions of borderline products.

- The restrictions identified on freight transport by road, such as constrains on business operation and differential treatment between transport operators, should be removed. This reform would benefit wholesalers and the transport sector.

*Chapter 1*

# Assessment and recommendations

*This assessment identifies distortions to competition in the Greek legislation. It proposes recommendations for the removal of regulatory barriers to competition in five sectors of the Greek economy: e-commerce, construction, media, wholesale trade, and selected sub-sectors of manufacturing. Five hundred and seventy-seven potential regulatory restrictions were identified and analysed, and this report makes 356 specific recommendations to remove potential barriers and increase competition. The resulting benefits will include lower prices and greater choice for consumers as new, more efficient firms enter the market or existing firms adopt innovative forms of production. This report identifies the sources of those benefits and, where possible, provides quantitative estimates. If the particular quantified restrictions are lifted and the expected effects are realised, the OECD estimates that the positive impact on the Greek economy will be around EUR 414 million.*

Laws and regulations are key instruments in achieving public-policy objectives, such as consumer protection, public health and environmental protection. When they are overly restrictive or onerous, however, a comprehensive review can help identify problematic areas and develop alternative policies that still achieve government objectives without harming competition.

The Competition Assessment of Laws and Regulations project aims to identify regulatory barriers, including those that restrict entry to a market; constrain firms' ability to compete (e.g. by regulating prices or limiting advertising); treat competitors differently (e.g. by favouring incumbents); facilitate co-ordination among competitors; or restrict consumers' ability to change suppliers. The methodology followed in this systematic exercise is summarised in Annex A, which also describes the stages of the project and provides full references to the OECD Competition Assessment methodology. This report has identified and evaluated market regulations in the sectors of electronic commerce (e-commerce), construction, media, wholesale trade, and certain manufacturing sub-sectors, such as chemicals and pharmaceuticals.[1]

## 1.1. The benefits of competition

The main benefits of competition include lower consumer prices, greater consumer choice, better quality of products and services, higher employment, greater investment in R&D, and faster innovation adoption. Consumers' ability to choose between different providers of goods benefits not only consumers themselves, but also the economy as a whole. When customers can choose and shop around for products and services, firms are incentivised to compete with each other, innovate more and be more productive (Nickell, 1996; Blundell et al., 1999; Aghion et al., 2004). Industries in which there is greater competition experience faster productivity growth. These conclusions have been confirmed by a wide variety of empirical studies, as summarised in OECD (2014c). The primary reason that competition stimulates productivity is that it allows more efficient firms to enter the market and gain share at the expense of less efficient firms.

In addition to the evidence that competition promotes growth, there are many studies that have shown the positive effects of more flexible product market regulation, the area most closely relevant for this project.[2] These studies analyse the impact of regulation on productivity, employment, R&D and investment, among other variables. Differences in regulation also matter and can significantly reduce both trade and foreign direct investment (FDI) (Fournier et al., 2015; Fournier, 2015).[3]

There is a particularly large body of evidence on the productivity gains from more flexible product market regulation. At firm and industry level, restrictive product market regulation is associated with lower multifactor productivity levels (e.g. Nicoletti and Scarpetta, 2003; Arnold et al., 2011).[4] The result has been shown to hold also at aggregate level (Égert, 2016b). Anti-competitive regulations have an impact on productivity that goes beyond the sector in which they are applied and this effect is more important for the sectors closer to the productivity frontier (Bourlès et al., 2013).[5] Specifically, a large part of the impact on productivity goes through the channel of investment in R&D (Cette et al., 2013).

Innovation and investment in knowledge-based capital, such as computerised information and intellectual property rights, are also affected by stricter product market regulation (Andrews and Criscuolo, 2013; Andrew and Westmore, 2014). Pro-competition reforms to product market regulations are associated with an increase in the number of patents (Westmore, 2013). In addition, lifting barriers enables innovative firms to combine more efficiently the resources needed to market new ideas and products. More generally, more stringent product market regulations are shown to be associated with less investment (lower capital stock) and to amplify the negative effects of a more stringent labour market (Égert, 2016a).[6]

Greater flexibility can also lead to higher employment. Cahuc and Kamarz (2004) find that after deregulating the road -transport sector in France, employment levels increased at a faster rate than before deregulation.[7] A recent OECD study (Criscuolo et al., 2014) finds that small firms that are younger than five years on average contribute to about 42% of job creation.[8] As noted in OECD (2015), "such a disproportionately large role by young firms in job creation suggests that reducing barriers to entrepreneurship can contribute significantly to income equality via employment effects". The impact of lifting anti-competitive regulations on income inequality is unclear, however. On one hand, greater flexibility leads to higher employment; on the other, deregulation is also associated with greater wage dispersion.[9] Recent work (OECD, 2015c) investigates the relationship between competition and inequality. The authors calibrate a model to assess the redistributive effects of market power in eight countries.[10] They find that market power benefits the wealthiest households and that the share of wealth of the top 10% of households deriving from market power is between 10% and 24%.

In summary, anti-competitive regulations that hinder entry and expansion in markets may be particularly damaging for the economy because they reduce productivity growth, limit investment and innovation, and harm employment creation. Removing regulatory barriers to competition was the overall aim of the project carried out by the OECD with the support of the Hellenic Competition Commission. The rest of the chapter outlines the main findings from the project.

## 1.2. Main recommendations from the Competition Assessment project

The five sectors[11] covered in the Competition Assessment of Laws and Regulations project accounted for about 11.2% of Gross Value Added and 16.7% of employment of the Greek economy as a whole in 2014.[12] Lifting barriers to competition in these sectors could potentially have a significant economic impact on the Greek economy.

The recommendations discussed in this section were developed after a thorough analysis of the legislation and its impact on competition. Overall, the review has identified 577 potential regulatory barriers in the 1 288 legal texts collected for the purposes of this assessment. In total, the report makes 356 specific recommendations to mitigate harm to competition. These are set out in detail in Annex B to the report.

Table 1.1. **Summary of the legal provisions analysed by sector**

| | E-commerce | Construction | Media | Pharmaceuticals | Other manufacturing | Wholesale trade | Total |
|---|---|---|---|---|---|---|---|
| **Pieces of legislation** | 71 | 251 | 251 | 155 | 268 | 292 | 1 288 |
| **Potential restrictions identified** | 15 | 61 | 68 | 88 | 80 | 265 | 577 |
| **Recommendations made** | 10 | 42 | 68 | 54 | 48 | 134 | 356 |

*Source*: OECD analysis.

### *E-commerce*

E-commerce was designated as a priority sector within the context of the OECD Competition Assessment project in Greece. Consequently, the review of the relevant legislation and the analysis of potential barriers to competition were expedited; and ensuing recommendations were delivered earlier than those in other sectors. A few recommendations have already been implemented by the authorities.

The OECD recommends adopting a uniform definition of consumer across consumer-protection legislation. At the moment, the legislation incorporates a number of different definitions. This may prevent e-commerce providers from, for example, applying automated processes, drafting the terms and conditions of use, or offering standardised contracts, given that rights and obligations vary depending on various factors, such as whether the customer is an individual or a legal entity.

The Greek authorities should also clarify the definitions and distinction between legal and commercial guarantees, define the rights of consumers connected to each in the core consumer-protection Law 2251/1994, and consider adopting a shorter duration of the legal guarantee for second-hand goods.

Similar to the case on the definition of consumer, there are alternative definitions of supplier found in the law on consumer protection. Moreover, the Greek legislation has the unintended consequence of burdening local (e-commerce) sellers with additional obligations, in relation to commercial guarantees, compared to their competitors abroad.

Implementing these recommendations is expected to create legal certainty and increase transparency, while at the same time reducing compliance costs for Greek businesses.

More generally, streamlining and codifying Law 2251/1994 would resolve to a large extent the confusion and inconsistency resulting from fragmented legislation. Given the horizontal nature of consumer-protection legislation and its application beyond e-commerce, this streamlining should follow a broader consultation with market operators.

The main recommendations for the e-commerce sector are described in Chapter 2 and listed analytically in Annex B.

### *Construction*

A number of recommendations in the sector are aimed at increasing participation in tenders for public works and designs.

In order to participate in public tenders for works and designs, individuals and companies are required to belong to registries register in categories depending on the nature of the activities, e.g. road works and hydraulic projects. In addition, they are classified according to their experience, staffing and financial standing. OECD recommends that bidders be able to participate in tenders, provided that they fulfil all participation criteria, irrespective of their classification within the registries.

More flexibility should be granted to individuals and companies to operate in the markets both for public works and designs. We recommend that simultaneous registration of individuals and companies as designers and contractors should be allowed. However, they should not be allowed to bid for the construction of a project that they have designed – unless explicitly provided for in the call for tenders. In public designs, while individuals are currently allowed to register in a maximum of 2 categories out of 28 in total, they should be allowed to register in a greater number of categories consistent with their university degrees, i.e. specific disciplines of engineering, such as civil or mechanical engineering.

These recommendations will eliminate artificial barriers to participation and allow individuals and companies to compete on more tenders. The expected benefits include more competition in tenders and greater synergies in works and designs.

Price lists for public works and designs are published and binding for all contracting authorities across the country. In the standard format for tenders, participants are required to offer discounts with respect to these published price lists. However, these lists have not been updated recently. According to the OECD Guidelines on fighting bid rigging in public procurement, "contracting authorities should use maximum reserve prices only if based on thorough market research and if officials are convinced they are very competitive". The price lists currently in force should be updated to reflect market conditions.

Some legal provisions allow broad discretion to contracting authorities. For instance, for works that are separate in time and nature from the main project (i.e. preliminary works) guidelines should be issued to clarify the definition of these works in order to ensure a consistent approach is followed by contracting authorities.

Contracting authorities should enhance good governance and reinforce integrity in public procurement by implementing e-procurement and introducing e-monitoring of public works and designs. This needs to encompass all stages, ranging from assessing the need for procurement of works or designs, to contract management and final payment. Good management, prevention of misconduct and e-monitoring of public works and design contracts can promote fair and equitable treatment for potential suppliers, and improve tendering procedures, supervision and further planning of public works. OECD recommends that authorities consider electronic archiving of consolidated data and e-monitoring of public works.

The Greek authorities have already incorporated into Law 4412/2016 on public procurement a number of OECD comments on the draft version. For instance, some articles of the initial version of the law restricted bidders' business choices. The OECD also commented on the importance of limiting the use of direct award and of ensuring sufficient transparency. For instance, an article of the draft law was modified following OECD comments to ensure that the invitation for consultation with economic operators is disseminated as widely as possible prior to issuing a tender.

The main recommendations for the construction sector are described in Chapter 3 and listed analytically in Annex B.

### *Media*

The legislation sets the criteria newspapers and magazines need to meet to be eligible for publishing state announcements and benefitting from reduced postal rates. In both cases, the criteria should be reviewed to ensure that new entrants and incumbents benefit from a level playing field.

The licensing and regulatory framework for radio stations is fragmented and largely not implemented in practice. The Greek authorities should ensure that economic operators have legal certainty and can make informed business choices based on a clear regulatory framework.

The OECD recommends reviewing the definition of independent audiovisual producer in line with the European Audiovisual Media Services Directive. In addition, the compulsory registration of producers and production companies in Registries of Professional Chambers should be abolished.

The licensing and regulatory framework for pay-TV/radio should be updated so as to reflect new technological developments. Further, various regulatory restrictions on pay-TV/radio content need to be relaxed. The recommendations aim at facilitating investment choices in a wider range of technologies and, as a result, to increase choices for consumers. Moreover, reducing business costs for pay-TV/radio broadcasters and for suppliers of programmes may lead to lower prices.

The present draft does not include the assessment of Law 4339/2015 and of Joint Ministerial Decision 7577/2016 in relation to digital free-to-air TV licences, due to ongoing administrative and legal procedures.

The main recommendations for the media sector are described in Chapter 4 and listed analytically in Annex B.

***Manufacture and wholesale trade of chemicals***

Isopropyl alcohol is subject to an excise duty in Greece. This yields only limited tax revenues. In addition, in case of exemption for industrial purposes, Greek producers are forced to incur the complex and costly process of denaturation foreseen by the law, which adds to their costs. Savings could be made and prices lowered if the final industrial product was not burdened either with excise duty or with the cost of the denaturation procedure.

The authorities should allow trading detergents in bulk at wholesale level, enabling companies to save on packaging and potentially lowering prices of detergents for final consumers. Moreover, decisions on withdrawal of detergents should be made public, in order to foster consumer protection, transparency and competition.

The legislation on plant protection products, fertilisers and seeds is scattered across different legal texts and has changed many times in the last few years. This creates additional complexity and uncertainty for economic operators, especially new entrants and smaller firms. We recommend abolishing restrictive storage requirements, which can increase costs and act as a barrier to entry, and simplifying the requirements for the sale to take place under the supervision of a suitable professional. These recommendations will reduce costs for economic operators, while still achieving the policy objective of sustainable and safe use.

Innovation in cosmetics has led to "borderline" products that combine cosmetic and biocidal characteristics and so cannot be easily categorised. The National Organisation for Medicines should comply with EU soft law on borderline products, recognising their primary and secondary functions. This recommendation will remove the uncertainty currently faced by suppliers and, in consequence, lower a possible barrier to entry and help increase product variety for consumers.

EOF applies pharmaceutical provisions to the licensing of the biocidal products that fall under its competence. In particular, umbrella branding would not be allowed for these products. As a result, operators would not be able to market biocidal products with different qualitative chemical composition in terms of active ingredients under the same brand name. Umbrella branding economises on the costs of creating a new brand, leading to lower expenses such as advertising costs, trade deals and promotions. At the same time, it makes it easier to launch new products and therefore increases product variety for consumers. We recommend that these restrictions on umbrella branding, designed for pharmaceutical products, should not apply to biocides.

The main recommendations for the chemicals sector are described in Chapter 5 and listed analytically in Annex B.

***Manufacture and wholesale trade of pharmaceuticals***

The pricing rules for pharmaceuticals foresee a maximum price reduction for generics in repricing procedures. In case the revised price exceeds that of the reference product the price of the latter shall be adjusted upwards so that the two be equated. This deprives generics of their price advantage compared to the original product, leaving no room for competition or their further penetration in the market. The OECD recommends that the maximum price reduction rule is revised so that it always allows for a certain price difference between generic and off-patent products.

The legal framework for the advertisement of over-the-counter (OTC) medicines should be updated and clearly aligned with recent amendments in the liberalisation of the distribution channels of commonly used medicines (Γενικής Διάθεσης Φάρμακα – ΓΕΔΙΦΑ / General Sale Medicines – GEDIFA) as a special category of OTCs. In addition, more flexibility should be allowed in the promotion of OTCs, including the advertisement of benefits to the public. Given that from January 2017 the prices of OTC medicines will be no longer regulated, conveying this information through advertisement in all points of sale could result in enhance competition and ultimately lower prices to the benefit of patients. The presence of pharmacists and quantity restrictions in points of sale sufficiently ensure public-health protection.

The authorities should review the regulatory framework of promotions, including the ex-ante approval of scientific events and conferences by the National Organisation for Medicines. A notification accompanied by an ex -post control mechanism by National Organisation for Medicines could achieve the policymaker's objectives without affecting the firms' marketing strategies.

Restrictions on the operation of warehouses should be lifted to enable economic operators to achieve economies of scale. The legal framework on the operation of warehouses should be made more flexible to allow for the establishment of more than one economic unit within the same prefecture and supporting storage areas outside it. The resulting economies of scale and more intense competition among pharmaceutical wholesalers would allow more efficient use of resources and better coverage of the market.

The main recommendations for the pharmaceuticals sector are described in Chapter 6 and listed analytically in Annex B.

### *Wholesale trade*

The authorities should simplify and make the licensing framework for the wholesale trade of fuel more flexible in order to make entry into the market easier for new wholesalers. For instance, requiring that storage spaces have a certain minimum capacity or that fuel wholesalers should own a minimum number of bottles for liquid gas can create barriers to entry into this market.

The duration of exclusivity agreements between wholesalers and retailers is regulated by law. The legislation should be clarified to ensure that the duration of the agreements cannot be extended beyond the legal term, thus encouraging more competition among wholesalers each time the term of the agreement lapses.

The legal framework for central wholesale markets allows for only one wholesalers' market in Athens, one in Thessaloniki and one in Patras. This framework is outdated, given market developments, and should be relaxed to enable wholesalers, possibly in combination with other market players, to set up competing private wholesale markets.

The Greek authorities should review the framework for the transportation of goods on own account to make it easier for wholesalers to transport goods using their own trucks. In addition, the grandfathering rights granted to transport businesses operating under the earlier framework should be phased out. The conditions for obtaining a road-transport operator licence should not favour certain company types, such as sociétés anonymes (SA), at the expense of other types typically chosen by smaller operators.

The main recommendations for the wholesale trade sector are described in Chapter 7 and listed analytically in Annex B.

## 1.3. Horizontal findings

### *Obsolete legislation*

Frequently, provisions superseded by more recent legislation have not yet been explicitly removed from the body of legislation. In its overview of Greece, the OECD notes that "repealing old laws which are no longer necessary is not common practice" (OECD, 2015b). Among the 356 recommendations in this project, almost 90 were about obsolete provisions.

Obsolete, inactive or redundant legislation can act as a regulatory barrier by creating legal uncertainty and potentially raising regulatory and compliance costs facing suppliers and market players, notably legal costs.

The OECD recommends that superseded legislation be explicitly abolished. By removing obsolete legislation from the body of legislation and the online legal libraries of competent authorities, market participants and potential entrants face a more transparent, less complex and more certain business environment, ensuring that both operation and entry are facilitated. Streamlining legislation should be done preferably in the context of codification of the sectoral legislation.

The provisions identified by the OECD team as obsolete are included in the recommendations listed in Annex B for each of the sectors.

### *Regulatory quality*

The regulations reviewed in this project are often scattered across many different pieces of legislation. In order for businesses and consumers to have a comprehensive understanding of the legislation applicable to a specific economic activity, they need to identify the relevant provisions in many separate texts and understand how these provisions interact with each other. In addition, subsequent modifications to core pieces of legislation result in further fragmentation and a lack of clear rules.

The streamlining and codification of the legislation would be particularly beneficial to new entrants, who are less familiar with the legislation, and smaller competitors, for whom compliance costs are likely to be relatively more important than for larger companies. A previous OECD project focusing purely on the administrative burden of regulations,[13] a subset of compliance costs, estimated they cost Greek businesses in 13 areas[14] about EUR 3.28 billion (OECD, 2014a).

The implementation of regulation in a transparent way is one of the key tenets of regulatory quality (see Box 1.2 below). Transparency and accountability are among the requirements for sound governance of regulators (OECD, 2014). Transparency enhances the regulator's accountability; instils confidence in the regulator; and helps regulated firms understand regulators' policies and expectations, and anticipate how these policies will be monitored and enforced. Transparency also helps consumers – for instance, decisions on product recalls can affect consumers and public health, so it is beneficial to the public for such decisions to be published. Regulators sometimes publish decisions as a matter of best practice (for instance, the National Organisation for Medicines), but this is not always the case.

Box 1.1. **What is regulatory quality?**

Regulations are the rules that govern the everyday life of businesses and citizens. They are essential but they can also be costly in both economic and social terms. In that context, "regulatory quality" is about enhancing the performance, cost effectiveness and legal quality of regulatory and administrative formalities. The notion of regulatory quality covers process, i.e. the way regulations are developed and enforced, which should follow the key principles of consultation, transparency and accountability, and be evidence-based. The concept of regulatory quality also covers outcomes, i.e. regulations that are effective at achieving their objectives, efficient (do not impose unnecessary costs), coherent (when considered within the full regulatory regime), and simple (regulations themselves and the rules for their implementation are clear and easy to understand for users).

Building and expanding on the *Recommendation of the Council on Improving the Quality of Government Regulation* (OECD, 1995), it is possible to define regulatory quality by regulations that:

1. serve clearly identified policy goals, and are effective in achieving those goals;
2. are clear, simple, and practical for users;
3. have a sound legal and empirical basis;
4. are consistent with other regulations and policies;
5. produce benefits that justify costs, considering the distribution of effects across society and taking economic, environmental and social effects into account;
6. are implemented in a fair, transparent and proportionate way;
7. minimise costs and market distortions;
8. promote innovation through market incentives and goal-based approaches; and
9. are compatible as far as possible with competition, trade and investment-facilitating principles at domestic and international levels.

*Source*: Reproduced from Box 1.1, OECD (2015), OECD Regulatory Policy Outlook 2015, OECD Publishing, Paris, *http://dx.doi.org/10.1787/9789264238770-en*.

### *Grandfather clauses*

Grandfather clauses refer to situations in which existing businesses (i.e. incumbents) are allowed to continue operations under older rules, while new entrants are subject to new and usually stricter ones. These clauses are often implemented to allow existing firms to depreciate their previous investments, made in compliance with the old regulations. To achieve this objective, grandfather clauses should be time-limited rather than permanent.

Grandfather clauses raise new suppliers' costs relative to incumbents. As a result, they can act as a disincentive for entry and, even if entry does take place, lead to asymmetric regulatory treatment of similar firms. Such restrictions have been identified in the sectors examined and include:

- road-transport operators are subject to different requirements for proving their financial standing, depending on when their licences were issued;
- commercial exhibition spaces are subject to different minimum requirements, if they were already operating at a certain date; and
- the legislation on radio and TV licensing considers that legally operating broadcasters are those that are licensed before certain pieces of legislation came into force.

The grandfather clauses identified by the OECD team are included in the recommendations listed in Annex B for each of the sectors.

## 1.4. Benefits of lifting barriers and prioritisation of recommendations

The Competition Assessment project focuses on laws and regulations relevant for the sectors under analysis. Its focus is on legislation and not its enforcement. This matters because changes in regulation can only have an impact if regulation is enforced. There are many reasons why regulation in practice may be less growth friendly than intended (O'Brien, 2013). The business environment is also important. Complementary to this analysis, there are other measures of administrative burden and ease of doing business that capture these broader issues. These include the OECD's Indicators of Product Market Regulation and the World Bank's Ease of Doing Business Index.

The recommendations address specific restrictions identified in the legislation: their impact is directly linked to lifting those restrictions and the consequent positive effect on competition in the relevant sectors. It was not possible to quantify the effects of all the individual restrictions identified, either because of lack of data or the nature of the regulatory change. Where possible, we have provided detailed estimates in the report. This is the case for the tender system for public works (Chapter 3), the tax on isopropyl alcohol (Chapter 5) and the removal of the cap on price reductions in the pharmaceutical sector (Chapter 6).

For some other recommendations, the OECD has considered whether recommendations would be expected to have an impact on either consumer benefit, through lower prices, or on economic activity, in terms of greater efficiency and additional revenue. In the former case, the framework described in Annex A was applied; in the latter, we have made a conservative assumption on an overall improvement in the efficiency of operation.[15] More specifically, if a number of restrictions identified in the project are lifted, we estimate a conservative benefit for the Greek economy of around EUR 414 million. This amount is the total of the estimated positive effects on consumer surplus, improved efficiency and higher turnover in the sectors analysed as a result of removing current regulatory barriers to competition.

Table 1.2. **Summary of estimated impacts by sector**

| Sector / restriction | Benefit | Number of corresponding recommendations |
|---|---|---|
| **E-commerce** | EUR 3.8 million | 6 |
| **Construction** | EUR 18 million | 14 |
| **Chemicals** | EUR 17 million | 20 |
| **Of which excise duty on isopropyl alcohol** | EUR 3.6 million | 3 |
| **Pharmaceuticals** | EUR 177 million | 12 |
| **Of which restriction on 15% cap on price reduction of generics** | EUR 34 million | 1 |
| **Wholesale trade of other products** | EUR 198 million | 43 |

*Source*: OECD analysis.

Full implementation of the recommendations set out in this report is expected to deliver positive long-term effects on employment, productivity and growth. The cumulative and long-term impact of lifting the restrictions identified on the Greek economy should not be underestimated. The rationalisation of the body of legislation in these sectors, which some authorities have suggested they will undertake, will positively affect the ability of businesses to compete in the longer term – provided that the recommendations are implemented fully.

Final recommendations have been prioritised based on their likely impact, considering a combination of the scale of the activity they affect (in terms of turnover) and the expected likely benefit from lifting the restriction. In a number of cases, recommendations have been subsequently grouped by product / activity, since this is the relevant reference for the scale of the activity they affect, and ranked within each sector. The tables below list the prioritised recommendations within each sector, along with an indication of the legal texts that need to be amended.

The rest of the report describes the outcome of the assessment in each of the sectors.

**Annex A** to the report describes in detail the methodology followed, both in screening the laws and regulations and in assessing the harm to competition.

**Annex B** provides the full list of all the potential barriers identified and the recommendations, by sector.

Table 1.3. **E-commerce**

| Recommendation | Feasibility (legal text) |
|---|---|
| Streamlining consumer protection law | Law |
| Definition of consumer | Law |
| Clarification of legal and commercial guarantees; definition of supplier | Law |
| Obligatory commercial guarantee | Law |

Table 1.4. **Construction (public works and designs)**

| Recommendation | Feasibility (legal text) |
|---|---|
| Updating price lists | Law / secondary legislation<br>Design and implementation of update mechanism, if needed |
| Registries for public works and designs (disconnect classification and tender qualification; lift restriction on dual registration for companies) | Law / secondary legislation<br>Design and development of electronic systems, if needed |
| Expand registration of designers by category | Ministerial Decision |
| Allow professionals to belong to the registry of designers (MM) and the registry of acquired experience (MEK) | Law |
| Implementation of electronic systems* | Law / secondary legislation<br>Design and development of systems |
| Provide guidance to contracting authorities (e.g. clarification of preliminary works, most advantageous offer as tender criterion) | Circular / standardised documents |

* Recommendations on the establishment and operation of e-procurement, and especially e-monitoring of public works and designs, are included in Annex B of this report. Recommendations on e-monitoring of public works are general in nature thus they include/pertain to, but are not limited to, the amendment of any relevant provisions. The OECD recommends the adoption of all legal and/or technical tools necessary for the effective operation of e-monitoring of public works and designs.

Table 1.5. **Media**

| Recommendation | Feasibility (legal text) |
|---|---|
| Overall framework for radio licensing | Law and secondary legislation |
| Pay TV licensing restrictions and costs | Law |
| Requirements on TV programme suppliers | Law |
| Broadcasters' obligation to invest in cinema production | Law |
| Independent producers of audio-visual works | Law |
| Ownership / cross-ownership rules (free-to-air media) | Assessment and law |

Table 1.6. **Manufacturing and wholesale trade of chemicals and rubber products, electrical equipment, paper and paper products, and printing and reproduction of recorded media**

| Recommendation | Feasibility (legal text) |
|---|---|
| Excise duty on isopropyl alcohol | Law and two Ministerial Decisions |
| Restrictions on plant protection products (e.g. minimum requirements) | Presidential Decree and Ministerial Decision |
| Manufacturing requirements for detergents | Ministerial Decision |
| Duration of licences and requirements on the responsible scientist for fertilisers | Law and Ministerial Decision |
| Patent application procedure (horizontal) | Presidential Decree and Ministerial Decision |
| Definition of primary and secondary use of cosmetics | Circular |
| Umbrella branding for biocides | Legislative Decree and Joint Ministerial Decision |

Table 1.7. **Manufacturing and wholesale trade of pharmaceuticals**

| Recommendation | Feasibility (legal text) |
|---|---|
| Advertisement of over-the-counter (OTC) medicines (e.g. advertisement of price discounts) | Circular |
| Requirements for establishing warehouses and operational restrictions, e.g. geographical | Law |
| Maximum price reduction of generics (15%) | Ministerial Decision |
| Use of own fleet for transportation | Law |
| New entrant's ability to co-locate with other manufacturers | Law |

Table 1.8. **Wholesale trade of other products**

| Recommendation | Feasibility (legal text) |
|---|---|
| Minimum capital requirements for fuel wholesalers | Law |
| Minimum storage requirements for fuel wholesalers | Law |
| Exclusive contracts between fuel wholesalers and retailers | Law |
| Agricultural products (e.g. central markets, letters of guarantee) | Law and Joint Ministerial Decision |
| Restrictions on freight transport by road (e.g. ownership of maximum two trailers per tractor) | Law |
| Obligation to rely on registered stevedores (Type A) | Law and Ministerial Decision |
| Recommendations on seeds (e.g. intra-EU trade) | Joint Ministerial Decision |

## Notes

1. These sectors were identified in the Memorandum of Understanding for a stability support programme signed by the Hellenic Republic in August 2015.

2. The methodology followed in this project is consistent with the product market regulations (PMR) developed by the OECD, see OECD (2014b), Box 2.1, p. 67. To measure a country's regulatory stance and track reform progress over time, the OECD developed an economy-wide indicator set of product market regulations (PMR) in 1998 (Nicoletti et al., 1999). The indicator was updated in 2003, 2008 and 2013.

3. Fournier et al. (2015) find that national regulations, as measured by the economy-wide PMR index, have a negative impact on exports and reduce trade intensity (defined as trade divided by GDP). Differences in regulations between countries also reduce trade intensity. For example, convergence of PMR among EU member states would increase trade intensity within the EU by more than 10%. Fournier (2015) studies the impact of heterogeneous PMR in OECD countries. He finds that lowering regulatory divergence by 20% could increase FDI by about 15% on average across OECD countries. The paper investigates specific components of the PMR index and finds that command-and-control regulations and measures protecting incumbents (antitrust exemptions, entry barriers in networks and services) are especially harmful in reducing cross-border investments.

4. Arnold et al. (2011) analyse firm-level data in 10 countries from 1998 to 2004 using the PMR index at industry-level, and find that more stringent PMR reduces firms' MFP.

5. The study of 15 countries and 20 sectors from 1985 to 2007 estimate the effect of regulation of upstream service sectors on downstream productivity growth.

6. The author investigates the link between product and labour market regulations with investment (capital stock) using a panel of 32 OECD countries from 1985 to 2013.

7. Employment growth increased from its level of 1.2% per year between 1981 and 1985 to 5.2% per year between 1986 and 1990. Between 1976 and 2001, total employment in the road transport sector doubled, from 170 000 to 340 000.

8. The sample includes 18 countries over a 10-year period.

9. Using the OECD's summary index of PMR in seven non-manufacturing industries in the energy, telecom and transport sectors, Causa et al. (2015) find stringent PMR has a negative impact on household disposable income. This result holds both on average and across the income distribution, and leads to greater inequality. The authors note that lower regulatory barriers to competition would "tend to boost household incomes and reduce income inequality, pointing to potential policy synergies between efficiency and equity objectives".

10. These are Australia, Canada, Germany, France, United Kingdom, Japan, Korea, and USA.

11. The sub-sectors of manufacturing covered in the project were pharmaceuticals, chemicals, rubber products, electrical equipment, paper and paper products, printing and reproduction of recorded media. The manufacture of paints, varnishes and similar coatings, printing ink and mastics (NACE code 20.3), as well as the manufacture of plastic products (NACE code 22.2), were not part of this project, as their regulatory framework was examined during the 2013 OECD Competition Assessment of Laws and Regulations in Greece project ("Building materials").

12. Due to low data granularity, manufacture of paints, varnishes and similar coatings, printing ink and mastics, and plastics are included in the figure, even though these products are not covered by this assessment.

13. OECD (2015b) defines administrative burdens as "the costs involved in obtaining, reading and understanding regulations, developing compliance strategies and meeting mandated reporting requirements, including data collection, processing, reporting and storage, but not including the capital costs of measures taken to comply with the regulations, nor the costs to the public sector of administering the regulations".

14. These were as follows: agriculture and agricultural subsidies; annual accounts/company law; energy; environment; fisheries; food safety; pharmaceutical legislation; public procurement; statistics; tax law (VAT); telecommunications; tourism; working environment/employment relations.

15. Throughout the report, when a recommendation is expected to have a likely impact on prices or the overall market, for instance through efficiency gains, the following assumptions are used: 1) low impact – 0.5%; 2) medium impact – 1%; and (iii) high impact – 1.5%. All revenue data is taken from Eurostat.

## References

Aghion, P., Blundell, R., Griffith, R., Howitt, P. and S. Prantl (2004), "Entry and Productivity Growth: Evidence from Microlevel Panel Data", *Journal of the European Economic Association*, 2(2-3): 265-276.

Andrews, D. and C. Criscuolo (2013), "Knowledge-Based Capital, Innovation and Resource Allocation", *OECD Economics Department Working Papers*, No. 1046, OECD Publishing, Paris, *http://dx.doi.org/10.1787/5k46bj546kzs-en.*

Andrews, D. and B. Westmore (2014), "Managerial capital and business R&D as enablers of productivity convergence", *OECD Economics Department Working Papers*, No.1137, OECD Publishing, Paris.

Arnold, J.M., G. Nicoletti and S. Scarpetta (2011), "Does Anti-Competitive Regulation Matter for Productivity? Evidence from European Firms", *IZA Discussion Paper*, No. 5511, *http://ssrn.com/abstract=1765677.*

Blundell, R., R. Griffith and J. van Reenen (1999), "Market Share, Market Value and Innovation in a Panel of British Manufacturing Firms", Review of Economic Studies, Vol. 66, 529-554.

Bourlès, R., G. Cette, J. Lopez, J. Mairesse and G. Nicoletti (2013), "Do Product Market Regulations in Upstream Sectors Curb Productivity Growth: Panel Data Evidence for OECD Countries", *Review of Economics and Statistics*, 95(5): 1750-1768.

Cahuc, P. and F. Kramarz (2004), "De la précarité à la mobilité : vers une Sécurité sociale professionnelle", report to the Ministre de l'Économie, des Finances et de l'Industrie et au ministre de l'Emploi, du Travail et de la Cohésion sociale, France.

Causa, O., A. de Serres and N. Ruiz (2015), "Structural Reforms and Income Distribution", *OECD Economic Policy Paper Series*, No. 13, *www.oecd-ilibrary.org/economics/structural-reforms-and-income-distribution_5js3777lbxzn-en.*

Cette, G., Lopez, J. and J. Mairesse (2013), "Upstream product market regulations, ICT, R&D and productivity", *NBER Working Paper*, No. 19488.

Criscuolo, C., P.N. Gal and C. Menon (2014), "The Dynamics of Employment Growth: New Evidence from 18 Countries", *OECD Science, Technology and Industry Policy Papers*, No. 14, OECD Publishing, Paris, *http://dx.doi.org/10.1787/5jz417hj6hg6-en.*

Égert, B. (2016a), "Regulation, Institutions, and Productivity: New Macroeconomic Evidence from OECD Countries", *American Economic Review*, Vol.106(5), May, pp.109-13.

Égert, B. (2016b), "Regulation, Institutions and Aggregate Investment: New Evidence from OECD Countries", *OECD Economics Department Working Papers*, forthcoming.

Fournier, J.-M. (2015), "The Negative Effect of Regulatory Divergence on Foreign Direct Investment", *OECD Economics Department Working Paper*, No. 1268, OECD Publishing, Paris, *http://dx.doi.org/10.1787/5jrqgvg0dw27-en.*

Fournier, J.M., A. Domps, Y. Gorin, X. Guillet and D. Morchoisne (2015), "Implicit Regulatory Barriers in the EU Single Market: New Empirical Evidence from Gravity Models", *OECD Economics Department Working Papers*, No. 1181, OECD Publishing, Paris, *http://dx.doi.org/10.1787/5js7xj0xckf6-en.*

Nickell, S. (1996), "Competition and Corporate Performance", *Journal of Political Economy*, 104/4: 724-746.

Nicoletti, G. and S. Scarpetta. 2003. "Regulation, productivity and growth: OECD evidence", *Economic Policy*, 18(36): 9-72.

O'Brien, P. (2013), "Policy Implementation in Italy: Legislation, Public Administration and the Rule of Law", *OECD Economics Department Working Papers*, No. 1064, OECD Publishing, Paris, *http://dx.doi.org/10.1787/5k44sssdmgzs-en.*

OECD (2016), *OECD Economic Surveys: Greece 2016*, OECD Publishing, Paris, *http://dx.doi.org/10.1787/eco_surveys-grc-2016-en.*

OECD (2016), Economic Policy Reforms 2016: Going for Growth Interim Report, OECD Publishing, Paris, *http://dx.doi.org/10.1787/growth-2016-en.*

OECD (2015), *Economic Policy Reforms 2015: Going for Growth*, OECD Publishing, Paris, *http://dx.doi.org/10.1787/growth-2015-en.*

OECD (2015a), Business and Finance Outlook 2015, OECD Publishing, Paris, *http://dx.doi.org/10.1787/9789264234291-en.*

OECD (2015b), *OECD Regulatory Policy Outlook 2015*, OECD Publishing, Paris, *http://dx.doi.org/10.1787/9789264238770-en.*

OECD (2015c), Market Power and Wealth Distribution, Working Paper by the Secretariat, DAF/COMP(2015)10, *www.oecd.org/officialdocuments/publicdisplaydocumentpdf/?cote=DAF/COMP(2015)10&docLanguage=En*

OECD (2014), *The Governance of Regulators*, OECD Publishing, Paris, *http://dx.doi.org/10.1787/9789264209015-en*.

OECD (2014a), Measurement and Reduction of Administrative Burdens in Greece: An Overview of 13 Sectors, OECD Publishing, Paris, *http://dx.doi.org/10.1787/9789264213524-en*.

OECD (2014b), Economic Policy Reform 2014: Going for Growth Interim Report, OECD Publishing, Paris, *http://dx.doi.org/10.1787/growth-2014-en*.

OECD (2014c), Factsheet on how competition policy affects macro-economic outcomes, *www.oecd.org/daf/competition/factsheet-macroeconomics-competition.htm.*

Westmore, B. (2013), "R&D, Patenting and Growth: The Role of Public Policy", *OECD Economics Department Working Papers*, No. 1047, OECD Publishing, Paris. http://dx.doi.org/10.1787/5k46h2rfb4f3-en

# Chapter 2

# E-commerce

*Much of the legislation related to e-commerce is governed by or reliant upon EU legislation. Both EU and national laws in the relevant areas are currently under review, principally within the framework of the EU's Digital Single Market strategy. The assessment of this sector looked at the core law on e-commerce, as well as other legislation directly or indirectly affecting it. Potential barriers to competition were found principally in the area of consumer protection, which is currently fragmented, with conflicting definitions and unclear provisions. Simplifying, streamlining and codifying consumer-protection legislation will remove legal uncertainty and compliance costs; better serve e-commerce providers, who rely on automated and standardised processes; level the playing field with foreign providers; and boost consumer confidence in making online purchases – and so remove impediments to growth in the sector.*

## 2.1. Definition and economic overview

Electronic commerce ("e-commerce") includes a range of activities that cuts horizontally across the economy, in sectors including retail, wholesale and services. In that sense, it enables and facilitates trade, and mirrors many of the activities and sectors of the offline economy.

For the purposes of the present assessment, e-commerce is defined as business-to-business (B2B), business-to-consumer (B2C), consumer-to-business (C2B) or consumer-to-consumer (C2C) commercial transactions of products, services and data provided in principal against remuneration, at a distance, at the individual request of a recipient of goods and services, and conducted over computer-mediated networks. While distance selling is the key differentiating element of e-commerce transactions, each of those characteristics is important when considering whether a transaction falls within the scope of e-commerce. The sector includes orders made over the web (independently of the medium used to access the web), an extranet or an electronic data interchange. Orders made by telephone, facsimile or manually typed e-mail are not part of the sector.

In Greece, e-commerce appears to be less advanced than in other EU Member States. According to the most recent data from Eurostat, only 6% of Greek firms with 10 or more employees made online sales in 2015 (9% in 2014).[1] The value of e-commerce sales of similarly sized firms accounted for 1% of their total turnover.[2] The corresponding rates in the EU were 17% (15% in 2014), both in terms of number of firms and share of turnover.

Figure 2.1. **Share of e-commerce value to total turnover in EU Member States, 2014-2015**

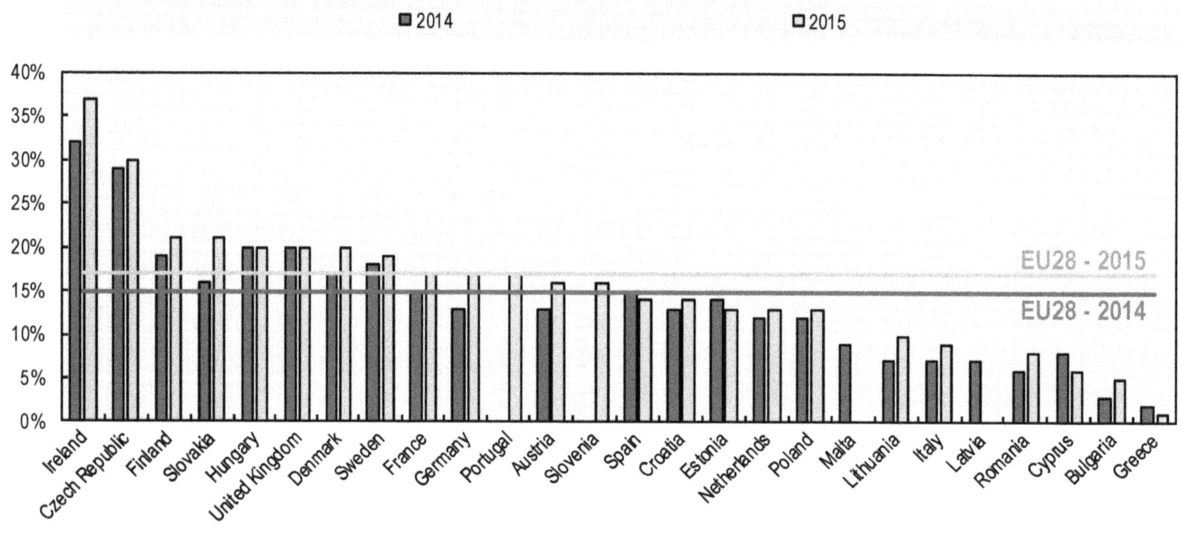


*Notes*: Percentage of turnover from e-commerce for all enterprises (excluding financial sector) with 10 employees or more.

*Source*: Eurostat, Information Society database (isoc_ec_evaln2).

The fact that e-commerce is less developed in Greece is also confirmed by comparing the importance of e-commerce in each sector,[3] as illustrated in Figure 2.2. The percentage of firms making online sales in the EU is 2.3 to 6 times larger than in Greece.

Figure 2.2. **Percentage of enterprises selling via Internet and/or networks other than Internet in Greece and EU28, 2015**

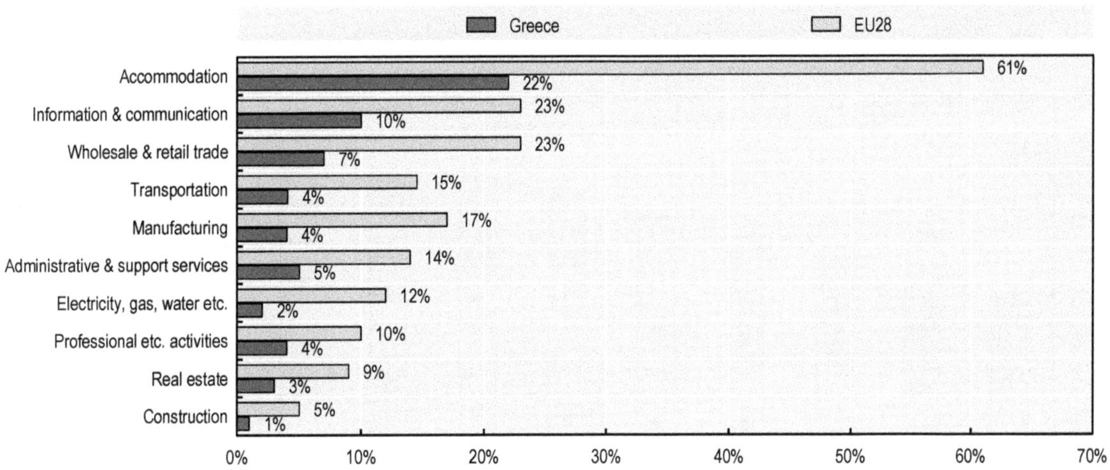


*Notes*: Percentage of enterprises (excluding financial sector) with 10 employees or more, selling at least 1% of turnover online.

*Source*: Eurostat, Information Society database (isoc_ec_eseln2).

E-commerce appears to have potential for growth in Greece, with underlying factors trending upwards, as discussed below. According to the annual survey on Greek B2C e-commerce conducted by the E-Business Research Center of the Athens University of Economics and Business,[4] 25% of online buyers made more than half of their purchases online (9% in 2014), with an average spend up by 10% on 2014. Moreover, 65% of online purchases by Greek buyers were made on Greek websites (60% in 2014).

E-commerce is affected by a number of factors, exogenous to the sector itself, which are however critical to its development. For example, on the demand side, consumer culture (the propensity to make purchases online) and trust (for example, in using electronic payment systems[5]) are identified as critical determinants in the sector's growth.

Access to computer networks is also a critical factor, and Eurostat data shows a substantial increase in Internet penetration in Greece: 68% of households had Internet access in 2015, up from 46% in 2010. The percentage of Internet users making online purchases also increased from 27% in 2010 to 47% in 2015. These statistics on increasing Internet penetration, coupled with the relatively low penetration of e-commerce, suggest considerable untapped growth potential in the sector.

Figure 2.3. **Level of Internet access (at household level), and share of Internet purchases by individuals in Greece and EU28, 2004-2015**

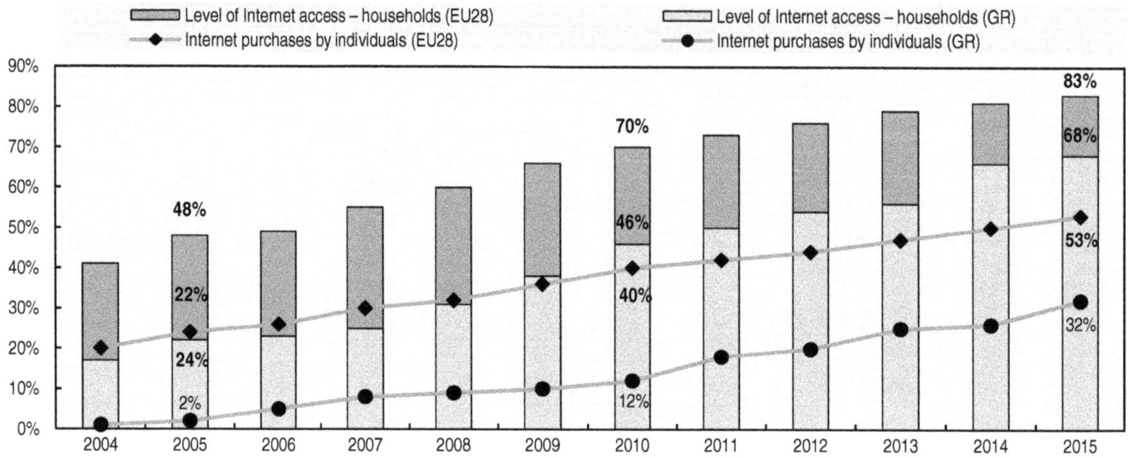


*Notes*: Individuals who have purchased online in the 12 months, as a percentage of total population.

*Source*: Eurostat, Information Society database (isoc_ci_in_h and isoc_ec_ibuy).

On the supply side, factors include sellers' ease of access to, and use of, the Internet, as well as costs – monetary or otherwise – associated with their operations (for example, in relation to parcel delivery and payment systems).

## 2.2. Overview of the legislation

E-commerce was designated as a priority sector within the context of the OECD Competition Assessment project in Greece. Consequently, the review of the relevant legislation and the analysis of potential barriers to competition were expedited, and ensuing recommendations were delivered earlier than those in other sectors. This prioritisation partly reflects the importance and potential positive contribution of e-commerce to the Greek economy. E-commerce is also considered a priority for the European Commission, as reflected in its Digital Single Market strategy,[6] which aims to "allow better access for consumers and business to online goods and services across Europe [and so] remove the key differences between online and offline worlds".

OECD mapping of legislation for the sector found 71 laws and regulations. As previously discussed, the sector mirrors offline economic activities and sectors, so many of the laws reviewed also apply horizontally to other sectors. This is also reflected in the OECD's recommendations, most of which are best implemented in the context of wider review and consultation.

The mapped legislation includes:

- horizontal legislation **on e-commerce**: product- and service-related laws (applicable both to traditional trade and e-commerce) have largely been reviewed in previous OECD Competition Assessment projects, or they are being reviewed in other chapters of the present assessment;

 

- legislation **directly or indirectly affecting** e-commerce in such areas as: 1) consumer protection; 2) digital signatures; 3) protection of personal data and electronic communications; 4) payment services; 5) domain names; 6) intellectual-property rights; 7) accounting rules targeting electronic commercial transactions; and 8) taxation targeting electronic sales of products and provision of services.

***EU legislation***

Much of the legislation related to e-commerce is largely governed by or is heavily reliant on EU legislation, which has been transposed into Greek laws.[7] In most cases, other than those identified in the following sections, national implementing laws do not introduce changes to EU Regulations and Directives that would impede competition in e-commerce. Moreover, both EU and national legislation relating to e-commerce are currently under review and revision, mainly within the framework of the Digital Single Market strategy. For example, at the EU level, legislative proposals have been formulated on the portability of online-content services,[8] parcel delivery,[9] geo-blocking,[10] contract rules for distance sales,[11] and VAT.[12] Adoption of that legislation will significantly affect the development of e-commerce. Greek authorities are party to the ongoing reviews, and are or will be implementing new legislation as it comes into force.

***National legislation***

The core legislation on e-commerce is Presidential Decree 131/2003, which is largely in line with the EU Directive it transposes (Directive 2000/31/EC, the "E-commerce directive").[13] A review of this Presidential Decree did, however, highlight a provision relating to intermediary service providers that needs to be amended.

Other potential barriers to competition were found principally in the area of consumer protection.[14] The main piece of legislation in this area is Law 2251/1994 on consumer protection: it has been amended multiple times since 1994 to bring it into line with EU Directives in this area, but the Greek legislator has made use of the discretion afforded to national legislators in various areas that affect e-commerce.

Law 2251/1994 has seen a number of revisions and amendments over the past 22 years. This practice of bringing amendments to the core consumer-protection law – including by legally authorised ministerial decisions[15] – without codifying them results in legal uncertainty and costs for suppliers and consumers. Both suppliers and consumers need to conduct extensive research in order to understand which regulations are in force and which are not.[16] Streamlining and codification of Law 2251/1994 would resolve to a large extent the confusion and inconsistency resulting from fragmented legislation.[17] Given the horizontal nature of consumer-protection legislation and its application beyond e-commerce, any streamlining should follow a broader consultation with market operators.

Simplification of the relevant legislation, which currently contains complex, obsolete and contradictory provisions, will better serve the needs of e-commerce providers, who rely on automated processes, including online contracts, terms and conditions, and communications. Such processes will be facilitated if based on clear, high-standard and transparent consumer-protection legislation. Furthermore, consolidating and streamlining this legislation will reduce legal uncertainty and compliance costs for e-commerce providers.

Such simplification will also boost consumer confidence in making online purchases,[18] which has been identified by market participants as a significant impediment to e-commerce growth.

Lastly, to the extent that Greek consumer-protection law imposes heavier obligations and restrictions on local e-commerce providers relative to internationally based e-commerce ones, it has the potential to disadvantage the former. For example, some C2C transactions are, perhaps unintentionally, regulated – with sellers having to provide guarantees over and above those required in other countries. Amending the relevant provisions will lift such potential barriers facing e-commerce providers based in Greece.

The main restrictions identified in e-commerce, as traced in the Greek legislation, are described in detail in the following sections. Their harm to competition, together with international comparisons where applicable, and recommendations are set out. The benefits of the recommendations are estimated at about EUR 4 million, assuming a conservative combined effect of 0.1% from all recommendations.[19]

Box 2.1. **The estimated consumer benefits from reforms on e-commerce**

An increase in the use of e-commerce as a means of facilitating trade has the potential to bring significant changes to demand- and supply-side fundamentals; and shift market outcomes.

A large body of empirical research supports a prediction that e-commerce leads to lower prices in various product markets. For example, Brynjolfsson and Smith (2000)[1] and Clay, Krishnan and Wolff (2001)[2] find that prices dropped following the establishment of online book markets. Scott Morton, Zettelmeyer, and Silva-Risso (2001)[3] document that consumers who used an online service to search for and purchase a car paid – on average – 2% less than those who did not. Brown and Goolsbee (2002)[4] estimate that the use of price comparison websites has resulted in the price of term life insurance policies falling by 8%-15%. Sengupta and Wiggins (2006)[5] find that airline tickets purchased online cost approximately 11% less than those purchased offline (controlling for ticket and flight characteristics).

The recommendations set out in this chapter are aimed at removing obstacles to furthering the adoption of e-commerce by businesses, and boosting consumer confidence in making online purchases. Removing obstacles and lowering the cost of e-commerce activity can foster growth in the sector: an increase in e-commerce turnover by 0.5% equates to an increase of €19million in the sector's turnover.[6] Moreover, on the basis of the evidence cited above, the (average) prices consumers pay are likely to fall. If prices were to fall by 1% (a range between 0.5% and 1.5%), the methodology outlined in Annex A suggests a consumer benefit[7] of €38.4 million (ranging between €19.1 and €57.9 million respectively).[8]

An additional benefit, not reflected in these figures, will likely come from wider consumer choice and improved access to markets – whether this concerns consumers' access to more distant Greek providers or providers based outside Greece. Similarly, Greek firms may benefit from a much wider, geographical pool of customers.

1. Brynjolfsson, E. and Michael D. Smith, (2000), "Frictionless Commerce? A Comparison of Internet and Conventional Retailers", *Management Science*, 46(4): 563-585.
2. Clay, K., Krishnan, R. and E. Wolff (2001), 'Prices and Price Dispersion on the Web: Evidence from the Online Book Industry" *Journal of Industrial Economics*, 49(4): 521-539.
3. Scott Morton, F., Florian Zettelmeyer and Jorge Silva-Risso (December 2001), "Internet Car Retailing", *Journal of Industrial Economics*, 49 (4): 501-519.
4. Brown, Jeffrey R. and Austan Goolsbee (2002), "Does the Internet Make Markets More Competitive? Evidence from the Life Insurance Industry", *Journal of Political Economy*, 110(3): 481-507.
5. Sengupta, A. and Steven N. Wiggins (February 2014), "Airline Pricing, Price Dispersion and Ticket Characteristics On and Off the Internet", *American Economic Journal: Economic Policy*, 6 (1).
6. E-commerce Europe estimates that the turnover of B2C sales of goods and services in Greece in 2015 was €3.8 billion. Ecommerce Europe (2016), *European B2C E-commerce Report 2016*.
7. Assuming an elastic demand, with elasticity $|\varepsilon| = 2$.
8. These estimates are based on the turnover of B2C sales. Consequently they underestimate the magnitude of the potential effect, given that B2B, C2B, and C2C transactions are not taken into account.

 

*Parcel Delivery*

There is a close relationship between postal services and e-commerce;[20] in particular with respect to parcel and commercial express deliveries. Barriers to effective competition in postal services may affect e-commerce to the extent that delivery cost is passed on to consumers (either directly or indirectly, if borne by the supplier); and/or service quality (for example, the speed or security of deliveries) is reduced. If price and quality of postal services were affected, this may hinder growth in e-commerce. This issue is of particular importance to Greece given its geographical location and morphology.

Prices for (cross-border) parcel deliveries within the European Union are under review by the European Commission.[21] In Greece, the National Telecommunications and Post Commission (EETT) has launched Pricescope, an electronic observatory of prices for telecommunication and postal services. This platform aims to increase price transparency by giving consumers easily accessible and reliable price-comparison information about postal services, including parcel delivery.[22]

The Competition Assessment of e-commerce legislation included a review of targeted and self-contained laws and regulations related to parcel delivery. [23] One issue potentially seen as a hindrance to more efficient parcel-delivery services in Greece is the postal-code system, designed and maintained by Hellenic Post.[24] It is acknowledged that many addresses have incomplete (or inadequate) details to allow for easy and timely deliveries, and postal codes cover areas that are too broad. The make-up of rural areas in Greece and street naming and numbering both appear to play a role. A more efficient postal - code file, made available in a timely manner[25] to all market participants, may facilitate parcel deliveries. The inefficiency of the current framework may indeed have an impact on parcel delivery, but the magnitude of possible effects on price and quality of this service and the consequences for e-commerce remain unclear.

## 2.3. Monitoring obligations of Internet intermediary service providers

***Description and objective of the provisions***

Presidential Decree 131/2003 implements the EU Directive on electronic commerce[26] and addresses the liability of service providers who act as intermediaries in transmitting information, in the context of information -society services, such as, for example, Internet service providers (ISPs). The relevant provisions[27] limit the liability of service providers and their duty to act, on the condition that they:

- act as a “mere conduit”, i.e. they transmit information or provide access to a network, but they do not themselves initiate the transmission of information, select its receiver, or select/modify the information;
- perform “caching” services, i.e. they temporarily store information for the purpose of making its transmission more efficient, but they do not modify the information or obtain data on its usage, and they comply with conditions on access to information and rules regarding updating it, and disable access to it if required; or
- provide a “hosting” service, i.e. they store information at the request of a service recipient, but they are not aware that this information is illegal and they revoke access to it if they become aware of it.

In harmonisation with the Directive, the Presidential Decree further intends to relieve intermediary service providers of the obligation to monitor the legality of information they transmit or store. It includes a separate provision to that effect, with direct reference to the activities outlined above.[28]

***Harm to competition***

The exemptions described above are designed to cover intermediary service providers whose sole involvement is giving access to a communication network and facilitating the transmission of information, and so encourage such activities. The Presidential Decree, however, contains erroneous numbering in its text that constitutes wrongful implementation of Directive 2000/31/EC.[29] This error means that providers' obligations to monitor information when acting as hosts are not lifted.

This has the effect of imposing on intermediary service providers (for example, ISPs) the *unconditional* requirement to monitor the information they store. This requirement is in direct conflict with the Directive's intent to limit liability and lift the monitoring requirement under certain conditions, in line with its objective of encouraging the development of information -society services, in particular electronic commerce. It also directly affects (e-commerce) platforms, networks and applications hosting (e-commerce) traders, inadvertently imposing a general obligation that they monitor the content placed and transactions conducted upon their platforms, and actively seek indications of illegal activities.

These extended monitoring obligations of Greek ISPs/platforms, mistakenly introduced into Greek law, create legal uncertainty, as well as extra regulatory and compliance costs for local e-commerce providers.

***Recommendation and benefit***

The OECD recommends that the references in the text of Article 14 of the Presidential Decree 131/2003 be amended to point to Articles 11, 12 and 13, instead of Articles 10, 11 and 12. Correcting the erroneous cross references in the Law will align the text with the Directive it implements and achieve the legislator's intended purpose.

## 2.4. Definition of consumer

***Description of the relevant provisions***

As mentioned above, Law 2251/1994 is the core law concerned with consumer protection and consumer rights in Greece. Since it first came into force, it has been amended and extended multiple times to incorporate new provisions and transpose EC Directives in relevant areas.[30]

This patchy implementation of amendments has left the law unclear and, in some cases, inconsistent.[31] In particular, the law contains varying definitions of the consumer: firstly, as an individual or legal entity that is the intended final recipient of products and services, including advertising message recipients or guarantors;[32] and secondly, as an individual acting for purposes that are outside that individual's trade, business, craft or profession.[33] The narrow latter definition was introduced and used by EC Directives; the wider former definition pre-dated relevant EC Directives and has survived subsequent amendments to the Law.[34]

Which of these conflicting definitions is used depends on the area of consumer protection that the provision pertains to. For example, the wider definition applies to general transaction terms; the sale of consumer goods and guarantees; a manufacturer's liability for defective goods; consumer health and safety; and the liability of service providers.[35] The narrow definition is explicitly applicable in the case of contracts (including those for sale of goods or provision of services at a distance); the provision of financial services at a distance; and unfair commercial practices.[36]

Moreover, there are instances where it is unclear and a matter of interpretation which definition is applicable; for example, in the case of comparative advertising.[37]

The result is that the level of consumer protection is different in each of the above cases,[38] resulting in confusion and legal uncertainty.

***Harm to competition***

The existence of multiple definitions of "consumer" within the same core law on consumer protection results in real costs for suppliers, caused by the need to understand and comply with the legislation. Also, this lack of clarity in conjunction with potentially extended liability in certain areas of consumer protection harms competition and provides disincentives to enter into the relevant market(s). These effects are magnified in the case of e-commerce where the need for standardisation and certainty is greater, given that transactions are made at a distance without extensive communication between suppliers and their customers.[39]

More specifically, the confusion around multiple definitions:

- creates legal uncertainty concerning rights and obligations of consumers and suppliers: this necessitates a case-by-case approach and leaves the provision(s) open to interpretation as both suppliers and consumers may need to seek legal advice to interpret the law and clarify which provision is relevant;
- prevents e-commerce providers from applying automated processes, drafting terms and conditions of use, offering standardised contracts etc., given that rights and obligations vary depending on whether their customers are individuals or legal entities and whether they are acting for purposes that are inside or outside their business or profession;[40] and
- leads to regulatory and compliance costs, such as the cost of seeking legal advice and legal expenses for cases tried before the courts: there exists extensive case law, including Supreme Court decisions, on an issue that should not be contentious.[41]

In addition, the legacy definitions of consumer found in the law have the – unintended, in the case of certain transactions – effect of defining businesses as consumers and so affording them the protection and compensatory measures otherwise reserved for individuals. Extensively widening the scope of consumer-protection laws:

- extends the liability facing (e-commerce) suppliers in the context of consumer rights in certain areas and imposes an additional burden on suppliers;
- may act as a disincentive for new entry in the B2B market, given that provisions intended for B2C may apply in the case of B2B transactions; and
- puts local e-commerce suppliers at a competitive disadvantage, to the extent that other Member States (or other countries outside the EU) have adopted a narrower and less onerous definition of consumer.

Box 2.2. **Example of consumer definitions in selected EU Member States**

The definition of consumer has been "revisited" by national legislators in other EU Member States, often as a result of a legislative streamlining and consolidation exercise undertaken following the transposition of EU Directives. In certain areas of consumer protection, some countries extend the protection given to consumers to additional persons by virtue of explicit legal provisions.

***Cyprus.***[1] The current consumer-protection law, which explicitly references Directive 2011/83/EC, uses the narrow definition of consumer as "an individual acting for purposes that are outside that individual's trade, business, craft or profession".[2] A similar definition was found in the pre-existing law on abusive terms in consumer contracts.[3]

***France.*** The March 2014 law on consumer rights similarly adopts as a principle the narrow definition of a consumer as "any individual acting for purposes that are outside that individual's trade, business, craft or profession".[4] Until this law came into force, the consumer had not been defined, and it had been left to the courts to decide, on a case-by-case basis.

***Italy.*** All consumer-protection legislation has been consolidated into a single law, Codice del Consumo (Consumer Code), which collects and synthesises all existing consumer-protection provisions. Consumer issues (advertising, accuracy of information, consumer contracts, product safety, access to justice and consumer organisations) were previously covered by specific regulations that were adopted on an ad hoc basis, mostly to implement EU Directives.[5] Under the Code, a consumer is "a natural person acting for purposes that are unrelated to that person's trade, business, craft or profession".[6]

***Spain.*** The provisions on consumer protection are found in Royal Decree 1/2007. The law, as amended in 2014, defines a consumer or user as "a natural person acting for purposes that are unrelated to that person's trade, business, craft or profession". It extends this protection to "legal entities or institutions that act in a non-profit capacity in a field unrelated to their trade or business", thus adopting a definition that is wider than the one found in the European Directives.[7] Spanish law provides for certain exceptions to the above uniform definition, such as civil liability for defective products and services. It also clearly distinguishes the definition used in the context of travel packages, whereby a consumer is "any person that is the principal contractor, beneficiary or assignee".[8]

***United Kingdom.*** Until the Consumer Rights Act came into force in 2015, each instrument transposing different EC Directives had its own definition of consumer. Under the Consumer Rights Act, which consolidates key consumer rights covering contracts for goods, services and digital content, and unfair terms in consumer contracts, a consumer is "an individual acting for purposes that are wholly or mainly outside that individual's trade, business, craft or profession".[9]

1. *Note by Turkey:* The information in this document with reference to "Cyprus" relates to the southern part of the Island. There is no single authority representing both Turkish and Greek Cypriot people on the Island. Turkey recognises the Turkish Republic of Northern Cyprus (TRNC). Until a lasting and equitable solution is found within the context of the United Nations, Turkey shall preserve its position concerning the "Cyprus issue".
   *Note by all the European Union Member States of the OECD and the European Union*: The Republic of Cyprus is recognised by all members of the United Nations with the exception of Turkey. The information in this document relates to the area under the effective control of the Government of the Republic of Cyprus.
2. Law 133(I)/2013 on consumer rights. See Art.2(1): "«καταναλωτής» σημαίνει κάθε φυσικό πρόσωπο το οποίο, όσον αφορά τις συμβάσεις που καλύπτει ο παρών Νόμος, ενεργεί για λόγους οι οποίοι δεν εμπίπτουν στην εμπορική, επιχειρηματική, βιοτεχνική ή ελεύθερη επαγγελματική του δραστηριότητα."
3. Law 93(I)/1996 on abusive terms in consumer contracts.
4. Law 344/2014 Consumer code. See Art.3: "est considérée comme un consommateur toute personne physique qui agit à des fins qui n'entrent pas dans le cadre de son activité commerciale, industrielle, artisanale ou libérale".
5. See *www.codicedelconsumo.it.*
6. Legislative Decree 206/2005 Consumer Code, as amended and in force. See, for example, Art.3(1)a: "si intende per [...] consumatore o utente: la persona fisica che agisce per scopi estranei all'attività imprenditoriale, commerciale, artigianale o professionale eventualmente svolta".
7. Royal Decree 1/2007 approving the amended text of the general law for the protection of consumers and users and other complementary laws, as amended and in force. See Art.3: "A efectos de esta norma y sin perjuicio de lo dispuesto expresamente en sus libros tercero y cuarto, son consumidores o usuarios las personas físicas que actúen con un propósito ajeno a su actividad comercial, empresarial, oficio o profesión. Son también consumidores a efectos de esta norma las personas jurídicas y las entidades sin personalidad jurídica que actúen sin ánimo de lucro en un ámbitoajeno a unaactividad comercial o empresarial."
8. See Art.151 par.1 rec.g: "'Consumidor o usuario': cualquier persona en la que concurra la condición de contratante principal, beneficiario o cesionario" in Royal Decree 1/2007 ibid.
9. Consumer Rights Act 2015. See Art.2(3): "'Consumer' means an individual acting for purposes that are wholly or mainly outside that individual's trade, business, craft or profession". This definition is wider than the one adopted by the EC Directive, stipulating that for individuals to be defined as consumers they need act wholly or mainly outside their trade, business, craft or profession."

More generally, the lack of clarity weakens the effectiveness of consumer-protection law, especially for individuals who are the intended recipients of its protection, and burdens the enforcement system with the task of clarifying definitions on a case-by-case basis.[42]

### *Recommendation and benefit*

The OECD recommends that a uniform definition of consumer applicable across Law 2251/1994 on Consumer Protection be adopted. This should be done in the context of a broader review of, and consultation on, the law, given that consumer-protection legislation is horizontal and applies beyond e-commerce.

A uniform definition of consumer (with or without explicit exceptions in relation to specific areas of consumer protection) will create legal certainty and increase transparency. It will also ensure that protection is targeted at, and clearly reserved for, those persons and entities that are the weaker party in transactions, thus fulfilling the intent of the law without extending cover beyond its scope.

## 2.5. Legal and commercial guarantees

### *Description of the relevant provisions*

EC Directive 1999/44[43] regulates the guarantees offered for the sale of consumer goods, including both commercial guarantees and lack-of-conformity rights, also known as a "legal guarantee". It has the intention of ensuring "a uniform minimum level of consumer protection in the internal market" through the harmonisation of laws and regulations in Member States in the above field.

The Directive provides a common framework for legal guarantees and grants extended rights to consumers in relation to sellers, i.e. right of repair, replacement, reduction in price, or contract rescission in cases of non-conformity of goods with the contract or advertised properties; the legal guarantee is compulsory, extends over a period of two years as from the delivery of goods and burdens the final seller, who has, in turn, the right to seek redress from liable persons in the contractual chain.

The Directive also harmonises, to a lesser extent, the legal framework for commercial guarantees, i.e. additional optional warranties offered by the guarantor, be it the manufacturer, importer or seller.

The relevant provisions have been transposed in Greece in the form of amendments to:

- pre-existing articles of the Greek Civil Code,[44] to cover legal guarantee rights, thus applying not only to consumer goods, but also to all movable (and immovable) goods; and
- Law 2251/1994[45] on Consumer protection, to cover commercial guarantee rights.

Lastly, when implementing the EU Directive's provisions, the Greek legislator has not considered and/or made use of the discretion afforded to Member States to provide for shorter legal guarantees on second-hand goods, on the basis of the contractual terms or agreements between the seller and the buyer.

### *Harm to competition*

The fragmentation of provisions on guarantees, scattered through the consumer-protection law and the Civil Code, creates legal uncertainty with regards to the rights and obligations of consumers and suppliers. The complexity of the law, which has been open to interpretation, prevents e-commerce providers from providing clear communications to their customers and applying automated processes in relation to legal and commercial guarantees, while raising regulatory and compliance costs for e-commerce providers.

Moreover, implementing the legal guarantee in the Civil Code has the unintended consequence of making the relevant provisions applicable not only to B2C transactions, but also B2B and C2C transactions.[46] This results in a potential barrier to C2C sales of goods on e-commerce platforms, including second-hand goods, the main platforms for such transactions. Such transactions, via e-commerce platforms, were not that common at the time of the EU Directive's implementation. Differential treatment of second-hand goods, given their nature, could help boost their sales on e-commerce platforms, which are most suitable for such transactions.

The complexity of the provisions and the fragmented legal framework create a lack of understanding and unclear communication of the rights and obligations stemming from commercial and legal guarantees. For example, the fact that a legal guarantee is in force irrespective of any commercial guarantees offered by the supplier/seller is often not advertised or communicated clearly.[47] As a result, consumers are left ill informed, with reduced confidence, and the legislator's objective – for e-commerce, in particular – is not achieved.

***Recommendation and benefit***

The OECD recommends that the definitions and distinction between legal and commercial guarantees be clarified and streamlined; the rights of consumers connected to each of the above are clearly defined in Law 2251/1994; and a shorter duration of the legal guarantee for second-hand goods be considered.[48]

This should be done in the context of a broader review of and consultation on the law, given that consumer-protection legislation is horizontal in nature and applies beyond e-commerce.

It is also recommended that a review of the Civil Code provisions is launched, which will take into account the specificities of C2C and B2B transactions, and the relevant legislative developments at EU level.

A clear and well-defined framework on the rights and obligations arising from legal and commercial guarantees will allow suppliers to better understand, organise and communicate the terms of sale and after-sale obligations. This will in turn boost consumer confidence in purchasing, especially online.

## 2.6. Definition of supplier

***Description of the relevant provisions***

Law 2251/1994 on consumer protection also contains varying definitions of supplier.

The section concerned with the rights and obligations of consumers and suppliers in relation to retail sale of goods and associated guarantees[49] defines a supplier as "the manufacturer and/or importer and/or any person purporting to be a producer by placing his name, trademark or other distinctive sign on consumer goods".[50]

This definition, though, is different to other definitions in the same law, which treat suppliers as "the legal entity or individual that supplies goods or services to the consumer, acting within his business or profession";[51] or as "the individual or legal entity (whether governed by private or public law) that acts, even if through an intermediary acting in its name or on its behalf, for purposes related to its trade, business, manufacture or profession".[52] Further, the first definition is different to the definitions found in Directive 1999/44/EC,[53] which distinguishes between a producer and a seller;[54] and clearly links legal guarantees to the latter and commercial guarantees only to the entity that offers them (be it the producer or the seller).

***Harm to competition***

As with the different definitions of consumer, the lack of a uniform definition of supplier creates legal uncertainty and confusion; leads to regulatory and compliance costs for e-commerce providers; and complicates the use of automated processes.

Moreover, the fact that the Greek law bundles together sellers and producers within the definition of a supplier in relation to guarantees has implications for their respective liability, and burdens local (e-commerce) sellers with additional obligations.[55]

***Recommendation and benefit***

The OECD recommends that conflicts regarding the definition of supplier be resolved: a uniform definition of supplier applicable across Law 2251/1994 be adopted; and the definitions of producer and seller be clarified, in line with Directive 1999/44/EC. A uniform definition of supplier will create legal certainty and increase transparency.

This should be done in the context of a broader review of, and consultation on, the law, given that consumer-protection legislation is horizontal in nature and applies beyond e-commerce.

## 2.7. Commercial guarantees

***Description of the relevant provisions***

Article 5 of Law 2251/1994[56] describes consumers' and suppliers' rights and obligations in relation to the retail sale of goods and guarantees for such sales.

The Greek legislator made use of the discretion afforded to Member States in transposing the corresponding EC Directive into this law and created extended obligations for suppliers to ensure additional consumer protection. For example, a commercial guarantee, offered by the "supplier", is compulsory for durable goods – and should be made available in writing, in Greek.[57] This obligation is an additional requirement introduced in national legislation and is not part of the corresponding EC Directive,[58] which only requires that such guarantees, when voluntarily provided by specific "offerers", be communicated to consumers under specific conditions.

Law 2251/1994 also stipulates that "suppliers" (according to the broad definition of the law, which includes both producers and sellers) are required to inform consumers in writing about the expected lifetime of a product,[59] and, in the case of durable goods, to offer a guarantee of such a duration that is reasonable and proportional to that expected lifetime, irrespective of guarantees given by the manufacturer.[60]

Finally, there is also the requirement that final "suppliers" repair, at their own cost, the product while it is covered by a commercial guarantee. This requirement applies to the final seller even in cases where the manufacturer and/or producer do not offer such a commercial guarantee. Moreover, this obligation may be more burdensome for local final e-commerce suppliers – who are often importers of products – since they also need to cover the cost of shipping products abroad for repair.[61]

### *Harm to competition*

As discussed above, the law obliges suppliers (as widely defined above and in practice including e-commerce providers) to provide an array of rights connected to commercial guarantees. These obligations are binding not only for the "offerer" of the commercial guarantee – as foreseen by the Directive – but also for any final local supplier, importer or seller, even if the original manufacturer might have not provided a guarantee.

Not only do these provisions impose certain requirements on the final sellers (rather than the manufacturer/producer) but, most importantly, they directly regulate and remove elements of the competitive interaction among market participants, notably in relation to commercial guarantees for durable products. In contrast with legal guarantees, which intend to offer a minimum level of consumer protection, commercial guarantees are part of the competitive offering for consumers. Indeed, they are typically offered on most durable goods, as a result of the competitive process.[62]

The costs of these rights to suppliers are obvious. They include the provision of additional communications connected to the life cycle of products; repairs related to the obligatory commercial guarantee for durable goods; the duration of the guarantee linked to products' lifetimes; and transportation and mailing costs related to the free repairs.

As the cost of a guarantee can in certain cases be reflected in the final price that consumers pay, imposing the above requirements reduces consumer choice by not allowing suppliers to offer lower-priced products to less risk-averse consumers willing to trade off a guarantee for a lower upfront cost. In that respect, these obligations limit their ability to offer products targeting different consumer groups.

The obligations placed on Greek suppliers (again, as widely defined above and in practice including e-commerce providers) in relation to commercial guarantees are also more burdensome than the provisions of Directive 1999/44/EC. Local e-commerce providers need to bear the cost of these commercial guarantees and associated repairs, for prolonged periods of time. Moreover, the effect on cost can potentially be exacerbated given that the guarantees and associated rights may be offered not only to individual consumers, but also legal entities (if they are the final recipients of the goods, in line with the wider definition of consumer)[63] that have significantly higher product-usage rates.

To the extent that similar requirements are not imposed on competitors abroad, there is also the potential that these requirements can hinder the ability of local providers to compete effectively in the Greek market.

### *Recommendation and benefit*

The OECD recommends that the requirement that commercial guarantees have to be offered for durable products be abolished. Further, it is recommended that obligations linked to commercial guarantees only be imposed on the *offerer*, in line with the EC Directive. This should be done in the context of a broader review of and consultation on the law, given that consumer-protection legislation is horizontal and applies beyond e-commerce.

These recommendations should be read in conjunction with the recommendation on clarifying the rights and obligations relating to legal guarantees, as set out in Section 2.5 above.

Aligning Greek law with the European Directive 1999/44 will relieve the unintended burden placed on local suppliers and increase transparency.

## 2.8. Identification logo for online pharmacies

### *Description and objective of the provisions*

The European legal framework[64] regulating the sale of medicinal products by means of information-society services and the conditions required for such sale to take place allows Member States a degree of discretion about authorising the sale of medicinal products at a distance.[65] As part of this framework, a common Europe-wide logo has been established, which online pharmacies are required to display. This logo enables the identification of those offering medicinal products; and serves as a means of containing the illegal sale of such products.[66]

A recent Joint Ministerial Decision[67] introduces the certification process of legally operating e-pharmacies in Greece, i.e. granting the common logo to identify persons offering medicinal products for sale at a distance. The Joint Ministerial Decision designates the Panhellenic Pharmaceutical Association (PPA)[68] as the competent body for issuing the common logo to e-shops selling medicinal products and sets out the information required for the logo to be issued.[69] The same provision stipulates that applications to the PPA for the common logo must be submitted by pharmacists.

### *Harm to competition*

This provision does not afford the PPA any discretion in its decision to accept or reject an application for issuing the common logo of the EU Regulation 699/2014 to (legally operating) online pharmacies in Greece.

However, in contrast with references in other articles of the Joint Ministerial Decision and with requirements for the licensing of brick-and-mortar pharmacies,[70] the text only explicitly allows pharmacists themselves (and not pharmacies as businesses) to submit such applications. While it appears that the legislator's intention is to allow the persons responsible for the operation of online pharmacies and not only pharmacists to apply for and obtain the common logo,[71] the language is ambiguous, open to interpretation and creates legal uncertainty. As a consequence, it potentially restricts access to the process and to online trading, as permitted by the law in force.

### *Recommendation and benefit*

The OECD recommends that the wording of Article 4 of Joint Ministerial Decision Γ5(β)/Γ.Π. οικ. 20293/2016 be amended and/or clarified as regards the persons responsible for submitting an application for the common-logo of the EU Regulation 699/2014 for online pharmacies. It should be clarified that the persons responsible for the operation of online pharmacies can submit an application and not only pharmacists.

## Notes

1. Percentage of firms (excluding financial sector) with 10 employees or more selling online at least 1% of their turnover.

2. Percentage of turnover from e-commerce for all enterprises (excluding financial sector) with 10 employees or more.

3. According to the annual survey of Greek B2C e-commerce conducted by the E-Business Research Center of the Athens University of Economics and Business, the top categories of online purchases by Greek consumers in 2015 were for travel services; accommodation; IT hardware; event tickets; and apparel.

4. Press release, including key findings, available at *www.eltrun.gr/wp-content/uploads/2015/12/ΗλΕμποριο2015-1.pdf.*

5. It has been put to the OECD that the imposition of capital controls in Greece in June 2015 resulted in more electronic transactions being made. However, it is not clear whether this has boosted e-commerce sales (or indeed led to any change in consumer behaviour as regards making online purchases) or simply substituted other forms of payment for online transactions, such as cash on delivery.

6. See Communication from the Commission to the European Parliament, the Council, the European Economic and Social Committee and the Committee of the Regions on A Digital Single Market Strategy for Europe (06.05.2015).

7. Review of and recommendations on EU legislation are outside the scope of the OECD Competition Assessment project, except where EU Directives have been transposed into Greek laws and regulations, including areas where discretion is allowed to national legislators.

8. See Proposal for a Regulation of the European Parliament and of the Council on ensuring the cross-border portability of online content services in the internal market (09.12.2015); and Communication from the Commission to the European Parliament, the Council, the European Economic and Social Committee and the Committee of the Regions, Towards a modern, more European copyright framework (09.12.2015).

9. See Proposal for a Regulation of the European Parliament and of the Council on Cross-border parcel delivery services (25.05.2016).

10. See Proposal for a Regulation of the European Parliament and of the Council on Addressing geo-blocking and other forms of discrimination based on customers' nationality, place of residence or place of establishment within the internal market and amending Regulation (EC) No 2006/2004 and Directive 2009/22/EC. (25.05.2016).

11. See Communication from the Commission to the European Parliament, the Council and the European Economic and Social Committee on Digital contracts for Europe – Unleashing the potential of e-commerce (09.12.2015).

12. See Communication from the Commission to the European Parliament, the Council and the European Economic and Social Committee on an Action Plan on VAT – Towards a single EU VAT area – Time to decide (07.04.2016).

13. Directive 2000/31/EC of the European Parliament and of the Council of 8 June 2000 on certain legal aspects of information society services, in particular electronic commerce, in the Internal Market ("Directive on electronic commerce") (Official Journal L178, 17.07.2000).

14. EU legislation on consumer protection is also under partial review within the Digital Single Market agenda. See Proposal for a Regulation of the European Parliament and of the Council on Cooperation between national authorities responsible for the enforcement of consumer protection laws (25.05.16).

15. See Art 14 par.4 of Law 2251/1994 on Consumer Protection (Government Gazette A'37/16.11.1994) as amended and in force.

16.. On 30 June 2016, the online legal library of the General Secretariat for Commerce and Consumer Protection at the Ministry of Development and Economy, the competent public authorities on consumer protection, included many regulations that are no longer in force, as well as an unofficial "codified" version of Law 2251/1994 ibid that does not include all the modifications and abolition of pre-existing provisions in the law. For example, the OECD team has identified two Ministerial Decisions, from 2001, superseded by more recent legislation, but not explicitly removed from the body of legislation and the website of the competent authorities. Firstly, Joint Ministerial Decision Z1-178/ 2001 on transactions by cards – harmonisation with Recommendation 1997/489/EC regarding transactions made by electronic payment instruments etc. (Government Gazette B'255/09.03.2001) has been largely explicitly abolished by Law 3862/2010: Art.2-4 were abolished by Art.82(β) of Law 3862/2010 Harmonisation with Directives 2007/64/EC, 2007/44/EC and 2010/16/EU – Government Gazette A'113/13.07.2010 on payment services etc.; Art.5 has been de facto abolished since it amends JMD Φ1-983/91 on consumer credit, which has been repealed and replaced by Art. 24 JMD 699/2010 on consumer-credit contracts; while Art.1 and Art.6 referring to objective and entry into force have not been explicitly repealed. Secondly, Joint Ministerial Decision Z1-404/2001 on the indication of prices on products offered to consumers – Harmonisation with Directive 1998/6/EC on Consumer protection regarding the indication of prices on products offered to consumers (Government Gazette B'827/28.06.2001) has been superseded by provisions in the Code on Marketing and Trading of Products and Services (see Art.2 and Art.6 of Ministerial Decision A2-718/ 2014 Code on Marketing and Trading of Products and Services – ΔΙ.Ε.Π.Π.Υ. – Government Gazette B'2090/31.07.2014).

17. Such codification is foreseen by the Greek legislator in Presidential Decree 116/2014 Organogram of the Ministry of Development and Competitiveness (Government Gazette A'185/03.09.2014), see Art.62 par.3 rec.α, γγ.

18. The OECD Council has recently revised its recommendations on how consumer protection should be applied in e-commerce. According to these recommendations, "Consumers who participate in e-commerce should be afforded transparent and effective consumer protection that is not less than the level of protection afforded in other forms of commerce". See OECD (2016), *Consumer Protection in E-commerce: OECD Recommendation*, OECD Publishing, Paris, *http://dx.doi.org/10.1787/9789264255258-en.*

19. Turnover estimates for 2015 were taken from E-commerce Europe (2016) and include B2C transactions only. Assuming price elasticity equal to 2%.

20. This link is recognised in several reports. For example, see Report from the Commission to the European Parliament and the Council on the Application of the Postal Services Directive (Directive 97/67/EC as amended by Directive 2002/39/EC and 2008/6/EC) (17.11.2015).

21. See Proposal for a Regulation of the European Parliament and of the Council on Cross-border parcel delivery services (25.05.2016). The sector has been identified by the European Commission as one critical to its Digital Single Market strategy, and is thus under review. The review encompasses improvements in parcel delivery, consultations opened by the European Commission and its Green Paper. Moreover, the European Commission has identified significant cross-country issues. Large areas of related laws (for example, VAT) are under the European Commission and the European Court of Justice remit. Related themes, such as the Universal Service Obligations and the call for transparency, are also being discussed at a European level.

22.. See EETT Decision ΑΠ 743/014/2014 on the establishment and operation of postal services' retail-pricing monitoring system (Government Gazette B'83/2014).

23. Parcel delivery is linked with other postal services (including Universal Service Obligations), which fall outside the scope of the current review. For example, there are issues relating to the interaction between incumbent operators and private companies; preferential treatment awarded to the former to attain

public-policy objectives; blurred boundaries between various product definitions, e.g. what constitutes a service falling under Universal Service Obligation provisions; and the multiplicity of value-added services offered to customers in terms of traceability and speed or proof of delivery.

24. See Administrative Agreement οικ.55102/1727/2010 (4IHN1-Π) between the Greek State and Hellenic Post, based on Art.19 par. 9 of Law 2688/1998. The agreement has expired but it has not been replaced and is still in force. It is common practice for the postal-code system be maintained by the formerly nationally owned/incumbent postal-service operator in each country, under monitoring by a competent regulator. The database is then made available to other providers or commercially traded, typically upon payment of a regulated fee. This is the case of example in France (see Les droits d'accès des opérateurs autorisés aux installations ou informations postales détenues par le prestataire du service universel at *http://arcep.fr/index.php?id=12332*); Germany (see *www.postdirekt.de*); Ireland (see *www.eircode.ie* and *www.irishstatutebook.ie/eli/2011/act/21/section/66/enacted/en/html*, where the relevant law stipulates that "The Minister may, with the prior consent of the Minister for Public Expenditure and Reform, enter into a contract with one or more than one person for the development, implementation and maintenance of a system ... for the allocation, dissemination and management of postcodes for the purposes of, or relating to, the provision of postal services and the use of the national postcode system by other persons for such other purposes as the Minister considers appropriate"); Italy (see *www.poste.it/postali/cap.shtml*); and the United Kingdom (see Ofcom, *Postcode Address File – Review*, 7 February 2013; and the online registry found at *www.poweredbypaf.com*).

25. Regulations state that the National Telecommunications and Post Commission (EETT) must provide access to the database at a reasonable cost. They do not stipulate, however, that this be done within a certain time frame. Hellenic Post is in the process of making the database available in electronic form, which will likely make updates faster.

26. Directive 2000/31/EC ibid.

27. See Art.11-13 of Presidential Decree 131/2003 harmonisation with Directive 2000/31 of the European Parliament and of the Council on certain legal aspects of information society services, in particular electronic commerce, in the Internal Market (Government Gazette A'116/16.05.2003).

28. See Art.14 par.1 of Presidential Decree 131/2003.

29. "Οι φορείς παροχής υπηρεσιών δεν έχουν, για την παροχή υπηρεσιών που αναφέρονται στα **άρθρα 10, 11 και 12** του παρόντος γενική υποχρέωση ελέγχου των πληροφοριών που μεταδίδουν ή αποθηκεύουν ούτε γενική υποχρέωση δραστήριας αναζήτησης γεγονότων ή περιστάσεων που δείχνουν ότι πρόκειται για παράνομες δραστηριότητες." (Emphasis added), Presidential Decree 131/2003.

30. See, for example, Directive 97/7/EC of the European Parliament and of the Council of 20 May 1997 on the Protection of consumers in respect of distance contracts (Official Journal L144, 04.06.1997); Directive 97/55/EC of European Parliament and of the Council of 6 October 1997 amending Directive 84/450/EEC concerning misleading advertising so as to include comparative advertising (Official Journal L290, 23.10.1997); Directive 1999/44/EC of the European Parliament and of the Council of 25 May 1999 on certain aspects of the sale of consumer goods and associated guarantees (Official Journal L171, 07.07.1999); Directive 2002/65/EC of the European Parliament and of the Council of 23 September 2002 concerning the distance marketing of consumer financial services and amending Council Directive 90/619/EEC and Directives 97/7/EC and 98/27/EC (Official Journal L271, 09.10.2002); Directive 2005/29/EC of the European Parliament and of the Council of 11 May 2005 concerning unfair business-to-consumer commercial practices in the internal market and amending Council Directive 84/450/EEC, Directives 97/7/EC, 98/27/EC and 2002/65/EC of the European Parliament and of the Council and Regulation (EC) No 2006/2004 of the European Parliament and of the Council (Official Journal L149, 11.06.2005); Directive 2011/83/EU of the European Parliament and of the Council of 25 October 2011 on consumer rights, amending Council Directive 93/13/EEC and Directive 1999/44/EC of the European

Parliament and of the Council and repealing Council Directive 85/577/EEC and Directive 97/7/EC of the European Parliament and of the Council (Official Journal L304, 22.11.2011).

31. The codification of consumer-protection legislation is foreseen in Presidential Decree 116/2014 Organogram of the Ministry of Development and Competitiveness (Government Gazette A'185/03.09.2014), see Art.62 par.3 rec.α, γγ).

32. See Art.1 par.4 of Law 2251/1994 ibid.: "Καταναλωτής [νοείται] κάθε φυσικό ή νομικό πρόσωπο ή ενώσεις προσώπων χωρίς νομική προσωπικότητα για τα οποία προορίζονται τα προϊόντα ή οι υπηρεσίες που προσφέρονται στην αγορά και τα οποία κάνουν χρήση των προϊόντων ή των υπηρεσιών αυτών, εφόσον αποτελούν τον τελικό αποδέκτη τους. Καταναλωτής είναι και: αα) κάθε αποδέκτης διαφημιστικού μηνύματος, ββ) κάθε φυσικό ή νομικό πρόσωπο που εγγυάται υπέρ καταναλωτή, εφόσον δεν ενεργεί στο πλαίσιο της επαγγελματικής ή επιχειρηματικής δραστηριότητας του" ("The consumer is defined as any individual or legal entity or association of individuals who is the intended recipient of goods or services offered on the market and who is the user of those goods or services, when he is the final recipient; the consumer is also any advertising message recipient and any individual or legal entity who acts as a guarantor on behalf of a consumer, when he does not act in a professional or business capacity.")

33. See Art.3 rec.1, Art.4θ par.1δ and Art. 9α rec.α of Law 2251/1994 ibid.: "[Ως] καταναλωτής [ορίζεται] κάθε φυσικό πρόσωπο το οποίο [...] ενεργεί για λόγους οι οποίοι δεν εμπίπτουν στην εμπορική, επιχειρηματική, βιοτεχνική ή ελευθέρια επαγγελματική του δραστηριότητα."

34. This definition of consumer was introduced in Art.1 par.4 rec. a of Law 2251/1994 ibid. and complemented by Art.1 par.5 of Law 3587/2007 amending and complementing Law 2251/1994 as in force and transposing Directive 2005/29 of the European Parliament and Council (Government Gazette A'152/10.07.2007). This Directive itself recites the narrow definition of consumer, see Art. 2(a) of Directive 2005/29/EC of the European Parliament and of the Council of 11 May 2005 concerning unfair business-to-consumer commercial practices in the internal market and amending Council Directive 84/450/EEC, Directives 97/7/EC, 98/27/EC and 2002/65/EC of the European Parliament and of the Council and Regulation (EC) No 2006/2004 of the European Parliament and of the Council (Official Journal L149, 11.06.2005).

35. See Art.2 and Art.5-8 of Law 2251/1994 ibid., respectively.

36. See Art.3 and Art.4α-η, Art. 4θ, and Art.9α of Law 2251/1994 ibid., respectively.

37. Art. 9 of Law 2251/1994 ibid.

38. For example, professionals who purchase insurance or undertake a loan online, in their professional capacity, are not considered consumers, but may be considered consumers if they make the same transaction offline. Professionals who purchase a durable product (e.g. a printer) online or at a bricks-and-mortar shop in their professional capacity are treated as consumers when they wish to exercise rights stemming from the commercial guarantee the supplier is obliged to provide them. Should they wish to withdraw from the purchase contract, however, they are not treated as consumers.

39. See paragraph 1 in *Consumer Protection in E-commerce: OECD Recommendation,* ibid.: "Consumers who participate in e-commerce should be afforded transparent and effective consumer protection that is not less than the level of protection afforded in other forms of commerce."

40. See paragraph 34 in *Consumer Protection in E-commerce: OECD Recommendation,* ibid.: "Businesses should provide consumers with a clear and full statement of the relevant terms and conditions of the transaction."

41. This is evident in a number of court decisions that have treated businesses as consumers in their capacity as final recipients of goods or services. See, for example, decision 1343/2012 of the Supreme Court of

Greece (consumer definition is wide and includes any person who is the final recipient of a product or service, irrespective of whether it is intended for personal or professional use); decision 733/2011 of the Supreme Court of Greece (annulling the decision of a lower Court dismissing a liability for assets destined for professional use); decision 72/2011 of the Court of Appeals of Piraeus (extension of consumer protection to ship owner who agreed maritime insurance); decision 52/2011 of the Court of Appeals of Piraeus (extension of consumer protection to guarantor of third-party-trader debt); decision 118/2010 of the Court of First Instance of Corfu (consumer is the final recipient, irrespective of intended use, and the guarantor for contracts); decision 155/2008 of the Court of Auditors (municipal authorities are considered consumers in terms of protection rights). The fact that certain of these cases were decided by the Supreme Court for Greece shows the law's complexity and the potential costs involved.

42. See in *Consumer Protection in E-commerce: OECD Recommendation*, ibid., p.9: "Recognising the value to governments, businesses and consumers of clear guidance as to the core characteristics of effective consumer protection in e-commerce, which can be supplemented by additional measures for the protection of consumers in e-commerce."

43. Directive 1999/44/EC of the European Parliament and of the Council of 25 May 1999 on Certain aspects of the sale of consumer goods and associated guarantees (Official Journal L171, 07.07.1999).

44. Law 3043/2002 amended Art.534-561 of the Civil Code. The OECD understands that at the time a committee of experts, including civil-law expert academics, considered this the appropriate vehicle for incorporating the relevant provisions into Greek legislation with minimal intervention.

45. Law 3857/2007 (Art.6) and Law 3043/2002 (Art.3) amended Art.5 of Law 2251/1994 ibid., which describes the rights and obligations of consumers and suppliers in relation to retail sale of goods and guarantees for such sales.

46. The OECD understands that this was not the intention of the legislator, but rather a formulation resulting from the fact that C2C transactions at the time of drafting were less common and not projected to increase at the pace they did once facilitated by online transactions.

47. The OECD team was told about this uncertainty in the market by both consumer-protection associations and the competent authorities. For example, in March 2013, the General Secretariat for Consumer Protection performed a sweep of 13 e-shops selling durable goods online, and found that 55% of them did not explicitly mention the legal guarantee; and where they did, such references were either not made in tandem with the commercial guarantee or were not clear.

48. This would make use of the discretion allowed pursuant to Art.7 of Directive 1999/44/EC ibid.

49. Article 5 of Law 2251/1994 ibid.

50. See Art.5 par.1 of Law 2251/1994 ibid.: "[Π]ρομηθευτής είναι και ο κατασκευαστής καταναλωτικού προϊόντος, ο εισαγωγέας του σε κράτος μέλος της Ευρωπαϊκής Ένωσης (Ε.Ε.), καθώς και κάθε πρόσωπο που παρουσιάζεται ως παραγωγός καταναλωτικού προϊόντος, θέτοντας σε αυτό το όνομα του, το σήμα του ή άλλο διακριτικό σημείο."

51. See Art.1 par.4 of Law 2251/1994 ibid.: "Προμηθευτής, [είναι] κάθε φυσικό ή νομικό πρόσωπο το οποίο, κατά την άσκηση της επαγγελματικής ή επιχειρηματικής δραστηριότητας του, προμηθεύει προϊόντα ή παρέχει υπηρεσίες στον καταναλωτή. Προμηθευτής νοείται και ο διαφημιζόμενος."

52. See Art.3 par.2 of Law 2251/1994 ibid.: "[Προμηθευτής είναι] κάθε φυσικό πρόσωπο ή κάθε νομικό πρόσωπο, ανεξάρτητα από το εάν διέπεται από το ιδιωτικό ή δημόσιο δίκαιο, το οποίο ενεργεί, ακόμη και μέσω κάθε άλλου προσώπου ενεργούντος εξ ονόματος του ή για λογαριασμό του, για σκοπούς οι οποίοι σχετίζονται με τις εμπορικές, επιχειρηματικές, βιοτεχνικές ή επαγγελματικές δραστηριότητες του."

53. Directive 1999/44/EC ibid.

54. See Art.1 par.2 rec.(c) and (d) of Directive 1999/44/EC ibid: "**[S]eller** shall mean any natural or legal person who, under a contract, sells consumer goods in the course of his trade, business or profession; [whereas] **producer** shall mean the manufacturer of consumer goods, the importer of consumer goods into the territory of the Community or any person purporting to be a producer by placing his name, trade mark or other distinctive sign on the consumer goods." (Emphasis added.)

55. See further in Section 2.7.

56. Law 2251/1994 ibid.

57. See Art.5 par.4 of Law 2251/1994 ibid.: "**Σε περίπτωση προμήθειας καινούργιων προϊόντων με μακρά διάρκεια ζωής (διαρκή καταναλωτικά αγαθά), η παροχή γραπτής εγγύησης είναι υποχρεωτική**. Η εγγύηση πρέπει να περιλαμβάνει, με απλή, ευανάγνωστη και κατανοητή διατύπωση στην ελληνική γλώσσα, τουλάχιστον την επωνυμία και τη διεύθυνση του εγγυητή, το προϊόν στο οποίο αναφέρεται η εγγύηση, το ακριβές περιεχόμενο της, τη διάρκεια της και την έκταση της εδαφικής ισχύος της." (Emphasis added.)

58. See Art.6 of Directive 1999/44/EC ibid. on "Guarantees".

59. See Art.5 par.3 of Law 2251/1994 ibid.: "Κατά την πώληση, ο προμηθευτής **οφείλει να ενημερώνει τον καταναλωτή για την πιθανή διάρκεια ζωής του προϊόντος**. Πιθανή διάρκεια ζωής του προϊόντος είναι ο εύλογα αναμενόμενος χρόνος κατά τον οποίο το προϊόν θα μπορεί να χρησιμοποιείται σύμφωνα με τον προορισμό του, έστω και έπειτα από επισκευή ή αντικατάσταση ανταλλακτικών, εωσότου η φθορά από την τακτική χρήση καταστήσει το προϊόν άχρηστο ή την περαιτέρω χρήση του οικονομικά ασύμφορη." (Emphasis added.)

60. See Art.5 par.4 of Law 2251/1994 ibid.: "Η διάρκεια της εγγύησης πρέπει να είναι **εύλογη σε σχέση με την πιθανή διάρκεια ζωής του προϊόντος**. Ειδικά, για τα προϊόντα τεχνολογίας αιχμής, η διάρκεια της εγγύησης πρέπει να είναι εύλογη σε σχέση με το χρόνο κατά τον οποίο τα προϊόντα αυτά αναμένεται ότι θα παραμένουν σύγχρονα από τεχνολογική άποψη, αν ο χρόνος αυτός είναι συντομότερος από την πιθανή διάρκεια ζωής τους." (Emphasis added.)

61. See Art.5 par.3 of Law 2251/1994 ibid.: "**Κάθε φυσικό ή νομικό πρόσωπο που διαθέτει**, στο πλαίσιο της επαγγελματικής, εμπορικής ή επιχειρηματικής δραστηριότητας του, **απευθείας στον καταναλωτή καταναλωτικά προϊόντα**, υποχρεούται, με επιμέλεια του και χωρίς καμία επιβάρυνση του καταναλωτή, στην επισκευή του προϊόντος, εντός των ορίων της εγγύησης που παρέχεται γι' αυτό, συμβατικά ή από το νόμο." (Emphasis added.)

62. See, for example, Rec.21 of Directive 1999/44/EC ibid.: "[F]or certain categories of goods, it is **current practice for sellers and producers to offer guarantees** on goods against any defect which becomes apparent within a certain period … **[T]his practice can stimulate competition … [W]hile such guarantees are legitimate marketing tools,** they should not mislead the consumer." (Emphasis added)

63. See Art.1 par.4 of Law 2251/1994 ibid..

64. Art. 85c of Directive 2001/83/EC of the European Parliament and of the Council of 6 November 2001 on the Community code relating to medicinal products for human use (Official Journal L311, 28.11.2001) as amended by Directive 2011/62/EU of the European Parliament and of the Council of 8 June 2011 amending Directive 2001/83/EC on the Community code relating to medicinal products for human use, as regards the prevention of the entry into the legal supply chain of falsified medicinal products (Official Journal L174, 01.07.2011); Commission Implementing Regulation (EU) No 699/2014 of 24 June 2014 on the design of the common logo to identify persons offering medicinal products for sale at a distance to the public and the technical, electronic and cryptographic requirements for verification of its authenticity (Official Journal L184, 25.06.2014).

65. Relevant laws and regulations were reviewed and assessed by the OECD in *OECD Competition Assessment Reviews: Greece* (OECD Publishing, Paris 2014); see Annex B.2, p.321.

66. *Op. cit.* note 64.

67. Joint Ministerial Decision Γ5(β)/Γ.Π. οικ.20293/2016 designating the competent authority for the accreditation of electronic pharmacies (Government Gazette B'787/23.03.2016).

68. Πανελλήνιος Φαρμακευτικός Σύλλογος (Π.Φ.Σ.).

69. Art.4 of Joint Ministerial Decision Γ5(β)/Γ.Π. οικ.20293/2016, ibid. The application needs to include information on the trading name, VAT registration and location of the pharmacy connected to the online store; the date when online operations commence; and the address of the online site, which should display links to and contact details for the PPA and the National Organization of Medicines (Εθνικός Οργανισμός Φαρμάκων, Ε.Ο.Φ.).

70. See Joint Ministerial Decision Γ5(β)/Γ.Π.οικ.82829/2015 regulating the profession of a pharmacist and establishing a pharmacy (Government Gazette B'2330/29.10.2015); and Joint Ministerial Decision Γ5(β)/Γ.Π.οικ. 6915/ 2016 amending and complementing joint ministerial decision Γ5(β)/Γ.Π.οικ.82829/2015 regulating the profession of a pharmacist and establishing a pharmacy (Government Gazette, B'138/29.01.2016).

71. This interpretation has been confirmed by services within the Ministry of Health.

## References

*Annual E-Commerce Survey 2015*, E-Business Research Center, Athens University of Economics and Business. Press release available at *www.eltrun.gr/ecommerce_survey_2015.*

Greek Ministry of Economy, Development and Tourism; information provided by officials in ministry.

Greek Ministry of Economy, Development and Tourism, General Secretariat for Commerce and Consumer Protection, General Secretariat for Consumer Protection; information provided by officials and the General Secretariat website, *www.efpolis.gr* (accessed 30 June 2016).

Hellenic Consumers' Ombudsman; information provided by officials.

National Telecommunications and Post Commission (EETT); information provided by officials.

Online Dispute Resolution (ODR) platform of the European Union, webgate.ec.europa.eu/odr (accessed 19 May 2016).

OECD (2016), *Consumer Protection in E-commerce: OECD Recommendation*, OECD Publishing, Paris, *http://dx.doi.org/10.1787/9789264255258-en.*

### Databases

Eurostat, Information Society (database), *ec.europa.eu/eurostat* (accessed 30 March 2016).

## Chapter 3

# Construction

*The construction sector includes construction of buildings and civil engineering works, and numerous categories of economic activity, such as new works, repairs, additions and alterations. Recent legislative reforms, in particular, in the area of public procurement, have aimed to simplify and codify the regulatory framework. Despite these efforts, issues remain, including reform of the registry-based classification system for market operators and eligibility for tenders, and the need to ensure that the price-list system – which forms the basis of tenders for public works – is functioning correctly and is regularly updated. E-procurement and e-monitoring of public works are expected to have a long-term positive effect both on the cost of public works and on public revenue, yet the necessary integrated or interoperable electronic information systems are still to be introduced.*

## 3.1. Definition and economic overview

The construction sector covers several categories of economic activity. This study focuses on activities related to the design of works, as well as on construction activities for buildings and civil engineering works. The construction of buildings encompasses new works, repairs, additions, alterations and demolition works. The construction of civil engineering works covers mostly infrastructure works, such as roads, motorways, bridges, tunnels, railways and utility projects. The definition adopted is based on the European standard classification system (NACE), which groups core construction activities under group F.[1]

Construction activity is of great importance to the Greek economy. In 2013, a total of 85000 construction companies were operating in Greece, directly employing more than 193000 workers or 5.6% of the Greek labour force; the corresponding figure for the European Union is on average 5.5%. The Greek construction sector has a gross turnover of EUR 11.3 billion and contributes around EUR 4.3 billion in Gross Value Added (GVA) accounting for 3% of GDP in 2013, compared with an average of 5.3% for the European Union[2] (see Table 3.1).

Table 3.1. **General statistics, construction, EUR, 2013**

| | Greece | EU-28 |
|---|---|---|
| **Number of firms** | 85 000 | 3 280 000 |
| **Employment** | 193 000 | 12 730 000 |
| **Gross turnover (€ m)** | 11 250 | 1 545 000 |
| **GVA (%)** | 3 | 5.3 |

*Sources*: ELSTAT and Eurostat's Construction Statistics Database.

The construction industry has strong upstream and downstream links with other economic activities and can contribute to the development of, for example, public and private investment projects, trade and manufacturing. Despite the significant contraction of the sector during and following the financial crisis in Greece (see Figure 3.2), its contribution to the Greek economy remains substantial. Given the positive spillover effects of the sector it is calculated that in 2013 it contributed around EUR 20 billion to the Greek economy, or 11% of GDP, 22% of which is estimated to correspond to taxes and charges levied by the state.[3] In terms of employment, the Greek Foundation for Economic and Industrial Research (IOBE) has estimated that for each job created in the construction industry a total of three jobs are created throughout the entire economy.[4] Taking into account these significant multiplier effects, the overall contribution of construction activity in Greece was estimated in 2015 at around 500 000 jobs. It should be noted, however, that despite the sector's significant multiplier effects, labour productivity when compared to the rest of the EU is particularly low.[5]

In the EU, the construction sector is dominated by micro enterprises, which are firms that employ fewer than 10 persons. In 2010, micro and small-sized (employing 10 to 49 persons) enterprises employed more than half of the sub-sector's workforce in nearly all of the EU member states. Data from Greece suggest that the make-up of the sub-sector in Greece is similar.[6] Table 3.2 and Figures 3.1 and 3.2 demonstrate the structure and composition of the domestic construction sector with regards to firms' turnover, value added and employment positions according to their size. It is clear that in Greece micro enterprises dominate the construction market in both their share of total employment and turnover. It is interesting to note how the prevalence of large and very large enterprises is expressed in the Greek construction market. Specifically, while large and very large firms employ 12% of the total construction employees, they make up for 24% of the market's total turnover.

Table 3.2. **Construction sector in Greece, general description, 2013**

| | Micro and small enterprises (0-49 employees) | Large and very-large enterprises (>50 employees) |
|---|---|---|
| **Employment** | 88.0% | 12.0% |
| **Turnover** | 76.0% | 24.0% |
| **Value added** | 66.5% | 33.5% |

*Source*: Eurostat, Construction Statistics, epp.eurostat.ec.europa.eu, accessed April 2016.

Figure 3.1. **Turnover and employment by firm size, 2013**

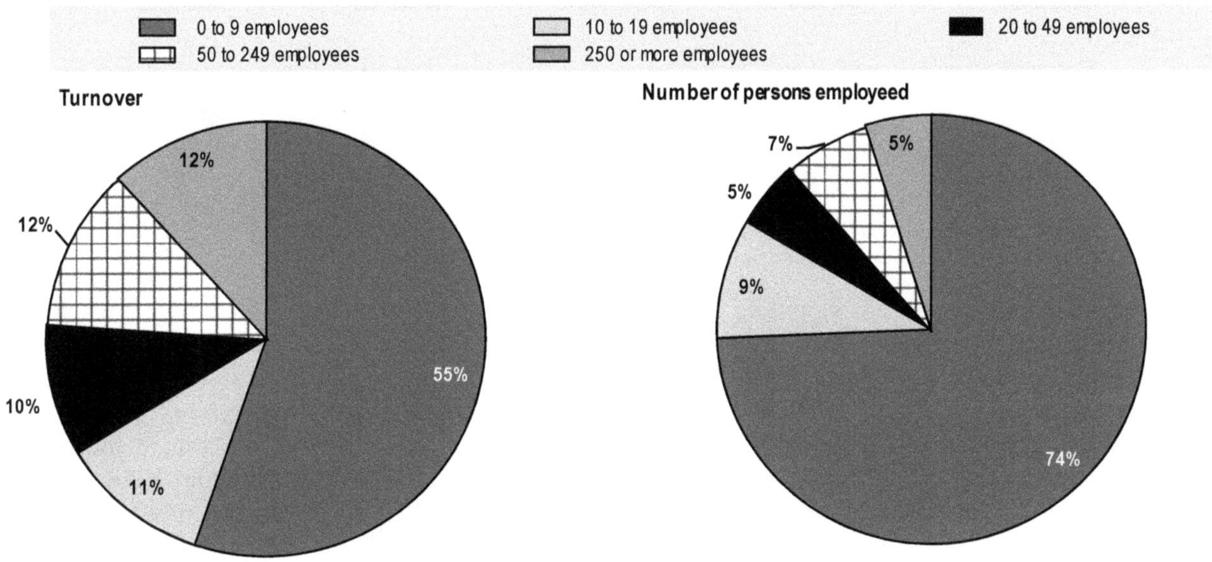


*Source:* Eurostat, Construction Statistics, epp.eurostat.ec.europa.eu, accessed April 2016.

Following the NACE definition, the construction sector can be broadly divided into two sub-sectors: the construction of buildings and the construction of civil engineering works. Across the EU, there are significant differences in the relative importance of these two sub-sectors within the construction sector: buildings account for nearly three quarters of total construction activity in Member States.[7]

### *Impact of the financial crisis on construction activity*

The construction sector, and the construction of buildings subsector in particular, has a highly pro-cyclical character. The financial crisis that started in 2008 has had profound effects on the sector across the EU: according to data from Eurostat, the level of total construction activity in the EU was in constant decline during the six-year period between 2008 and 2013.[8] In Greece, the financial crisis prompted a significant drop in domestic construction activity. As depicted in Figure 3.2, the construction sector's total turnover declined by 32% between 2009 and 2013, while the total number of enterprises active in the industry fell by 25%. Firm closures and bankruptcies have significantly increased in the past few years, weakening economic activity. The downturn further consolidated the market as it was mostly felt by small and medium-sized firms: throughout the 2009-2013 period: two thirds of enterprises employing between 20 and 249 employees stopped their operations.[9]

Figure 3.2. **Turnover by firm size, 2009-2013**

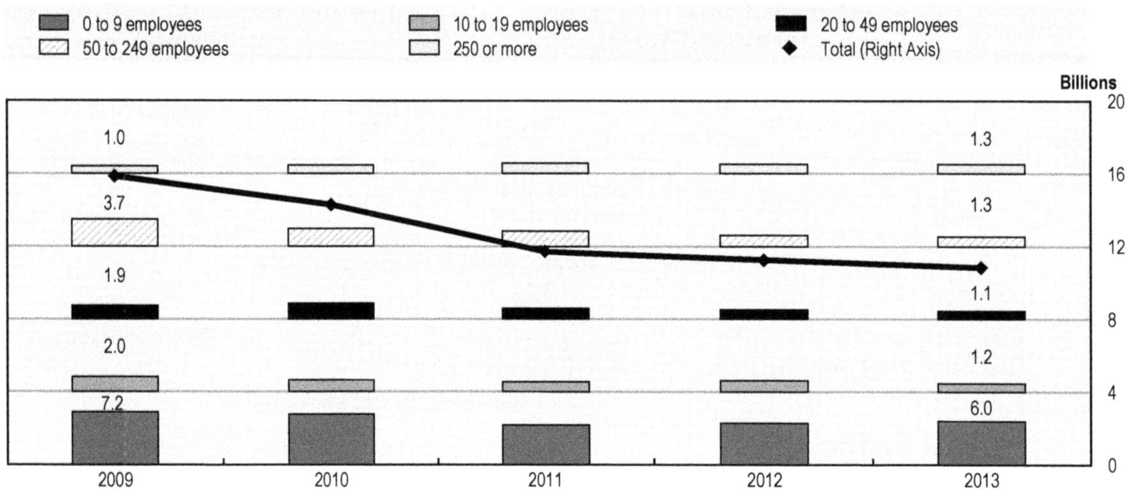


*Source*: Eurostat, Construction Statistics, epp.eurostat.ec.europa.eu, accessed April 2016.

Infrastructure investment in public works has also been significantly affected by the economic crisis. According to a recent PwC report,[10] the total value of new infrastructure projects in Greece decreased by 75% in the 10 years between 2006 and 2015. This corresponds to a compound decline in new infrastructure investments of EUR 50 billion (equivalent to about 3% of the Greek GDP) over this period. When compared with the EU average, the same report estimates that the gap in infrastructure investment ranges between 0.8% and 1.3% of GDP – a share that translates to about EUR 2 billion a year. The Greek Centre of Planning and Economic Research (KEPE) has estimated that investments in infrastructure have an economic multiplier of approximately two.[11] As such, investment in public infrastructure can generate and boost demand in a significant number of other sectors such as tourism, manufacturing and commerce, as well as overall urban development. The contraction in infrastructure investment during the past decade has therefore had wide-ranging effects, particularly considering its potential for creating direct growth and employment opportunities, as well as its positive spillover effects for the entire economy.

## 3.2. Sector overview

The mapping of the relevant regulatory framework for the construction of buildings and civil engineering works included 250 sector-related laws, presidential decrees, ministerial decisions and circulars. At the time of the mapping process, the legislation covering public designs and public works included two core (codifying) laws, which were accompanied by numerous ministerial decisions and circulars. These ministerial decisions and circulars were mostly concerned with the following: operation of registries of designers and contractors; pricing; technical specifications; and standardised documents for procurement of public designs and public works. In addition, the core law on public-private partnerships (PPPs) was screened. Finally, other legislation governing both public and private designs and works, including provisions on urban planning, spatial planning, and the environment, was also reviewed.

Until 2016, the regulatory framework for all public designs and works, concessions and PPPs incorporated the provisions foreseen in the relevant EU legislation, but was only partly codified. This incomplete codification meant laws remained largely fragmentary and included numerous exceptions in the form of special tendering regulatory framework. Law 4281/2014[12] aimed to simplify and codify the existing regulatory framework, abolished special regimes, and harmonised the regulatory framework with EU rules on public procurement for public tenders valued below EU thresholds for public procurement. Apart from a number of provisions, however, this legislation never came into force and it was ultimately repealed.[13]

The Greek Government, in line with its EU membership obligations, introduced Law 4412/2016[14] in order to harmonise national legislation with EU Directives 2014/24/EU[15] and 2014/23/EU.[16]

The new bill (now Law 4412/2016) on public procurement was brought before the Greek Parliament and was eventually voted in August 2016 during the drafting of the OECD's Competition Assessment report. The OECD was invited to comment on potential competition concerns arising from certain provisions of the law and the outcome of this consultation is reflected in the law's final version. More specifically, the OECD addressed and commented on 24 provisions of the draft law; these comments were assessed and/or implemented by the Greek authorities. More specifically, the OECD commented, among others, on: the categories of public designs (as defined by the national regulatory framework) and emphasised that these should not be any more restrictive than the list provided in the Directive 2014/24/EU; advised for a clear and uniform approach as to the definition of preliminary works; recommended that technical specifications should focus on functional performance (namely on what is to be achieved, rather than on how it is to be done) in order to attract the highest number of bidders in tenders; suggested that the authorities should issue guidelines on the application of the criterion of the most advantageous offer in order to improve the quality of designs and avoid the award of a contract without any technical evaluation of the offer; and emphasised the importance of clarifying time limits and the liability of designers – after the delivery of their design and during their acting as technical advisors to this same work.

Law 4412/2016 aims to codify the existing framework on public designs and public works. Yet it recites and retains in force almost all pre-existing provisions concerning registries of public works contractors and designers, pricing for construction works, and the execution and monitoring of public works. These provisions were also examined in the context of the Competition Assessment, together with the draft law as provided at the time by the Greek authorities,[17] and taking into account the recital and general provisions of the new law. With respect to the design of public procurement, the provisions carried over from pre-existing legislation were reviewed alongside the provisions introduced by Law 4412/2016, mainly concerning preliminary works, the participation of the designer in the execution of the main work, and the maturity of works.[18]

More specifically the new Law has introduced a number of provisions regarding the procurement of mature works, as well as provisions relating to preliminary works, with a view to making the procurement of designs and the execution of works more effective. However, the organisation of tender processes, an issue closely connected to the maturity of works, remains largely unchanged in the new law. The legislation grants the contracting authority discretion when launching a tender.

The decision on the tendering process for works, concessions or PPPs is left to the contracting authority or reserved for special committees. The decision-making process itself does not appear to follow standardised procedures, nor are there any rules requiring that the relevant information be made publicly available.

With the exception of a few provisions, the new law does not provide a standardised procurement method. However, it does foresee the publication of standardised documents for various categories of works, with uniform terms and criteria for works falling within each category. These documents would be binding for contracting authorities.

## Overview of current legislation

Registries of public works contractors and designers have had an important function in organising procurement for public works and designs: all Greek economic operators participating in tenders for such works are registered in the corresponding registries. Provisions on registries were found scattered in various laws and their amendments, and ministerial decisions.

Contracting authorities are required to use price lists established by ministerial decisions to compile budgets for public works. Price lists are similarly used to update the prices and costs of works for the duration of the contract. Currently, they appear not to be consolidated and, more importantly, not regularly updated.

In the area of electronic procurement (e-procurement) and monitoring (e-monitoring), the new law relies on and recites the previous legal framework. More specifically, provisions concerning the execution and monitoring of works, such as provisions on measurements and the "diary of works", were found unchanged in Law 4412/2016.

Public-private partnerships (PPPs) are mainly governed by a single piece of legislation, Law 3389/2005[19]. The terms included in the PPP contract award describe the specific terms pertaining to each partnership. The private partner to the partnership forms a special -purpose vehicle, which is made liable under the terms of the contract and assumes the risk for the effective execution and operation of the project. PPP contracts were, initially, not made publicly available; however, by virtue of early amendments to the corresponding law, they are now published in the Electronic Registry for Public Procurement (KHMDHS). Recently adopted laws 4412/2016 and 4413/2016[20] , also include provisions regulating PPPs.

The regulatory framework on spatial and urban planning is not codified, with relevant provisions scattered across various types of legislation. The general framework for spatial planning has been revised several times. Recent varied amendments to building regulations and the supervision mechanisms reflect efforts by the legislator to create a more coherent regulatory framework. At the time of writing of this report, a public consultation has been launched for a new draft law establishing a mechanism for identifying environmental interventions related to construction works. Finally, the general and regional frameworks concerning urban planning and sustainable development have also been revised, to take into account the current urban status quo.

Environmental provisions mostly incorporate EU legislation, while standardised environmental commitments follow equivalent EU rules. Provisions on environmental licensing (i.e. the approval of environmental terms for the execution of works) can mainly be found in Law 4014/2011,[21] as well as in various ministerial decisions. Terms and procedures may differ depending on the specific characteristics of the work in question and the potential impact on the environment. Exceptions are foreseen (for example, in the case of EU co-funded projects, or waste-management projects) to allow for more flexibility in executing certain works, while taking into account compliance with environmental standards and ensuring the least environmental impact.

## 3.3. The system of registries: categories of works and classification of companies

### *Description and objective of the provisions*

The participation of economic operators in tenders for public works and designs is governed by rules and procedures that aim to ensure that contractors and designers[22] who are awarded the contract are capable of completing the works and designs, respectively, according to the provisions in the call for tenders. The remainder of this section reviews the relevant provisions, namely Articles 92-107 of Law 3669/2008[23] and Article 75 of Law 4412/2016 for public works; Article 39 of Law 3316/2005[24] and Article 76 of Law 4412/2016 for designers.

To participate in tenders for public works, individuals are required to be registered in the Registry of Acquired Experience (MEK). Construction companies must register with the Registry of Contractors (MEEP).

Registration in MEK is reserved for those individuals whose academic qualifications enable them to execute the works in question. They are registered in the categories of works in which they specialise (for example, road works, hydraulic works, green projects). Their registration and certificate also reflects their specialisation and professional experience, the latter being determined by the number of years since the award of their university degree, the projects they have executed in the public or private sector, or a combination of the two.

Companies are registered in MEEP by categories and classes. They can register in one or more categories of works, depending on their specialisation (see further below); and they are assigned one class, on the basis of criteria set out by the law, principally their financial viability (see Box 3.1),the number of personnel they employ and their fields of specialisation. A company may only be registered in one class for each category of works. There are currently 14 categories of works and seven primary classes. Small companies with specific minimum staffing and financial capacity or fixed assets can be registered in two lower additional classes.

Company registration in MEEP and registration of individuals in MEK are linked. Companies demonstrate their experience (a classification criterion) and the categories of works they can execute based on the qualifications and corresponding certificates of the MEK-registered individuals they employ. Individuals registered in MEK may use their certificate/degree on behalf of one company only – in other words they must "declare' their association with a single firm. Companies are also obliged to keep their personnel unchanged for two years following their first registration in a class. A company's classification is subject to review in the event of personnel changes.

The categorisation and classification of a company is reflected in the call for tenders and the company's eligibility to participate in such tender. More specifically, a company is only allowed to bid in tenders for those categories of works in which they are registered. Moreover, each class is associated with certain contract -value ranges; companies in a certain class (or classes) can participate in a tender for works of a given budget as described below.

Up until 2014, companies were only allowed to participate in tenders with a budget that fell within the range defined for their respective class; in other words, a call for tenders would invite bids from companies belonging to one class of MEEP only. In August 2014, lower thresholds for the participation of a company in a tender were abolished[25] so that a call for tenders could invite bids from companies belonging to a specified class of MEEP, as well as all classes above it. Upper thresholds were set to be abolished with the issuance of a presidential decree detailing the terms under which companies would be allowed to participate in tenders above their class. This presidential decree, however, has never been issued and, consequently, upper thresholds are still not abolished.

According to Law 4412/2016 companies are obliged to register in specific categories of works and specific classes; however, the law does not seem clear as to whether class registration still serves as a participation criterion in the sense that a company would be prohibited from participating in a tender if not registered in the specific class (classes) associated with certain contract value, provided that it can prove that it satisfies the criteria set by the call for tenders.

The thresholds for participation in tenders differ in the case of partnerships between firms. Economic operators are allowed to form a joint venture (JV) and participate in tenders on the condition that they only partner with operators registered in the same class. In such cases, companies belonging to classes up to the fifth class can bid for tenders with a budget of up to 25% of the difference between the upper threshold of their class and the upper limit of the class above, provided the parties to the JV each take at least a 30% share of profits or losses.[26] For companies belonging to the sixth class, the upper threshold is EUR 60 million and each company's required share of profit and damages is 25%.

Table 3.3 and Figure 3.3 below show how the classes and participation of economic operators are formed according to the estimated budget of works, together with how participation thresholds are amended in cases where firms participate in JVs.

Table 3.3. **Registry of Contractors (MEEP) – tender value thresholds by class**

| Class | Lower limit (€) | Upper limit (€) | Upper limit – adjusted for JVs (€) |
|---|---|---|---|
| **7** | 35 000 000 | | |
| **6** | 10 500 000 | 44 000 000 | 60 000 000 |
| **5** | 3 500 000 | 22 000 000 | 27 500 000 |
| **4** | 1 400 000 | 7 500 000 | 11 125 000 |
| **3** | 500 000 | 3 750 000 | 4 687 500 |
| **2** | 175 000 | 1 500 000 | 2 062 500 |
| **1** | | 750 000 | 937 500 |
| **A2** | | 300 000 | 412 500 |
| **A1** | | 90 000 | 142 500 |

*Note*: Lower limits were abolished in August 2014.

*Source*: Based on Article 102 of Law 3669/2008 and Article 76 of Law 4412/2016.

Figure 3.3. **Registry of contractors (MEEP) – tender value thresholds by class**

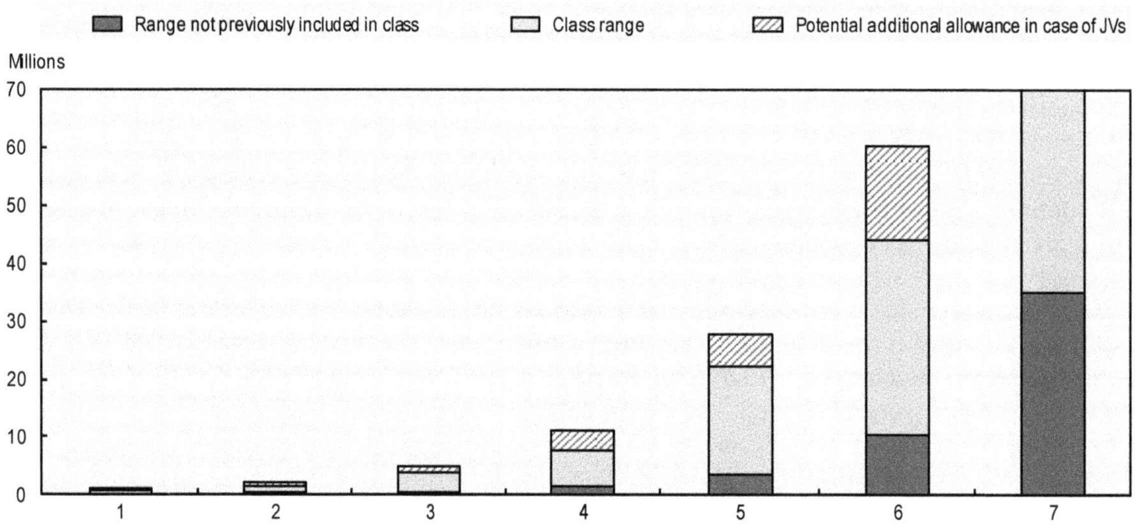


*Source*: Based on Article 102 of Law 3669/2008; and Article 76 of Law 4412/2016.

The MEEP Committee is responsible for accepting or rejecting applications by companies for registration in the Registry of Contractors. Once registered, companies are obliged to notify the MEEP Committee of any change in their structure. Information on the classification of companies and individuals is included in the electronic registry of the Directorate for Registries of the Ministry of Infrastructure, Transport and Networks.

For public -works designers, individuals and companies are obliged to register with the Registry of Designers Design Offices (MM). Participation in tenders for designs of public works is conditional on registration. Also, design companies must primarily engage in the design of works: neither registered design companies nor their affiliates are permitted to engage in non-design activities, such as the execution of public works.

Designers can be registered only in a limited number of categories (see below); their registration reflects their level of professional qualifications and their experience. Similarly to MEK-registered individuals, designers are only permitted to register with one design company.

***Harm to competition***

All the registries outlined above – Registry of Designers and Design Offices (MM), Registry of Acquired Experience (MEK) and Registry for Contractors (MEEP) – serve as a pre-selection process tool, filtering individuals and companies that wish to participate in tenders according to their professional skills, experience and financial capacity, and classifying them accordingly. The contracting authority, when initiating a call for tenders, matches the budget and nature of the project being procured with the relevant classes in question. This means that the pool of potential participants for any tender is known in advance.[27]

OECD best practices[28] (2011) suggest that procuring authorities should avoid unnecessary restrictions that may reduce the number of qualified bidders. Moreover, any minimum requirements should be established in respect of the size and content of the procurement contract rather than the size, composition or nature of firms that are eligible to submit bids.[29]

The way the Registries are organised in the context of procurement of public works and designs can produce three effects that potentially reduce competition, both directly and indirectly.

First, making class registration a requirement for participation in a tender creates direct barriers to entry. Compulsory tendering according to registries' classes may limit the number and range of qualified suppliers by granting exclusive participation rights to companies belonging to the designated classes; excluding those economic operators that are not included in the class summoned in the call for tenders.[30] Limiting eligible operator participation hinders competition and may result in worse pricing outcomes. This is empirically analysed in detail in Annex 3.A1 of this report: based on data for all complete tenders awarded through an open procedure for the eight years between 2009 and 2016 in Greece, an additional offer is shown to result in a 14.7% increase in the level of discount offered by the winner.

Box 3.1. **Requirements for participation in tenders for public works**

A company wishing to be registered into a specific class in the Registry of Contractors (MEEP) must meet a number of technical and financial criteria, including:

- experience of similar works and gross turnover in the previous three years (e.g. Table 3.4., column 1);
- financial viability, such as equity, bank deposits and fixed assets (e.g., Table 3.4, columns 2 and 3);
- minimum staffing, such as number and qualifications of technicians in the contractors' acquired experience registry (MEK).

Table 3.4. **Minimum gross turnover, equity and fixed assets per class registered in the Registry of Contractors (MEEP)**

| Class | Minimum gross turnover (in EUR thousands) | Minimum equity (in EUR thousands) | Minimum fixed assets (in EUR thousands) |
|---|---|---|---|
| **3** | 2 025 | 750 | 150 |
| **4** | 4 125 | 1 500 | 300 |
| **5** | 11 250 | 4 500 | 900 |
| **6** | 22 500 | 9 000 | 1 800 |
| **7** | 135 000 | 90 000 | 18 000 |

*Source: www.ypexd15.gr* (accessed August 2016) and Law (3669/2008).

Registration in a class allows a company to bid for public tenders of a budget not exceeding the upper limit specified by Greek legislation for that class (see Table 3.2). For example, if a contracting authority issues a tender with a budget of EUR 10 million, only companies belonging to classes 5, 6 and 7 could participate in the tender (operators in class 4 could not participate as the upper limit for that category is EUR 7.5 million). Since 2014, lower class thresholds have been abolished, so operators belonging to higher classes can now participate in tenders for lower ones (in our previous example, firms in classes 6 and 7 could participate in the tender alongside operators in class 5).

It is important for this Competition Assessment to establish whether this system of registries "artificially" restricts firms' participation in public-works tenders, and so whether it has an impact on competition. This means first looking at any alternative systems.[31]

One alternative system would completely abolish any system of registries and give contracting authorities complete freedom to define which criteria to use and their level at each call for tenders. For example, in our previous example, the contracting authority could issue a call for tender with a budget of EUR 10 million specifying that only companies with a minimum turnover of EUR 11 million and a certain level of minimum staffing could participate, without specifying a company's obligatory minimum equity and fixed assets. Although such a system could be less restrictive in theory than the current one, there are a number of concerns as to whether it would actually be more effective in practice. One of the aims of the current system of registries is to achieve a minimum level of standardisation and homogenisation to speed up the pre-qualification stage and eliminate the contracting authorities' incentives to manipulate the criteria in an arbitrary way. The added flexibility of a system where contracting authorities would have complete freedom to set the criteria for each tender needs to be balanced against: 1) the danger that criteria could be set by the contracting authorities in a way that restricts, instead of increasing, participation relative to the current system; 2) the possibility of an increased number of disputes from operators about preferential or unequal treatment for tenders for similar types of works; and 3) that the whole tender process would become more complicated and require more demanding monitoring.

A second alternative system would maintain the current system of registries, but allow contracting authorities to set levels for a number of existing criteria. For example, continuing our previous example, the contracting authority could issue a tender with a budget of EUR 10 million specifying that only companies with a minimum turnover of EUR 13 million could participate. Clearly such a system would be more restrictive than the current one, as some companies belonging to class 5 (with a minimum turnover of EUR 11.25 million) and placed between the minimum threshold and the new minimum of EUR 13 million would be excluded.[32]

Analogously, a contracting authority could be allowed to set a level on a number of existing criteria *below* the current minimum levels as specified in the registry system. For example, the contracting authority could issue a tender with a budget of EUR 10 million specifying that any company with a minimum turnover of EUR 9 million (below the minimum turnover of EUR 11.25 million for class 5) could participate. Such a system would implicitly allow near full flexibility to the contracting authority and be closer in spirit to the first scenario. But again, any added flexibility needs to be balanced against the danger of disputes from operators for preferential or unequal treatment for tenders for similar types of works.

Hence, it would appear extremely difficult to make clear improvements in the tendering mechanism within the class registry system that would increase participation, while maintaining its current benefits (e.g. process standardisation and fast pre-qualification). The current system's flexibility could be increased, however, to allow eligible firms to participate in tenders independent of their class participation. For example, being registered in a specific class should not prohibit economic operators from participating in tenders in higher classes on the condition that they fulfil the requirements of tender. In this manner, economic operators would be able to avoid various direct and indirect costs such as upgrading class, and the associated rigidities and resulting opportunity costs of class change. In addition, such as an amendment would set domestic operators on an equal footing with foreign competitors, which can already participate in a tender on the condition that they satisfy the participation criteria.

Second, the system of Registries, as currently organised, increases predictability in the market since, once a tender's budget is known, the pool of potential competitors is also known. Predictability and repeated interactions may facilitate co-ordination among bidders, especially in higher MEEP classes, which are populated by a smaller number of economic operators, as shown in Table 3.5.

Table 3.5. **Number of companies registered in each class of the Registry of Contractors (MEEP), August 2016**

| Class | Number of companies listed | Upper budget limit (EUR) |
|---|---|---|
| 7 | 6 | No upper limit |
| 6 | 32 | 44 000 000 |
| 5 | 47 | 22 000 000 |
| 4 | 134 | 7 500 000 |
| 3 | 237 | 3 750 000 |
| 2 | 1 487 | 1 500 000 |
| 1 | 2 134 | 750 000 |

*Source*: *www.ypexd15.gr* (accessed August 2016); and Law 3669/2008.

Third, there are rigidities inherently built in the system of registries given that, for example, contractors need to be part of a class for at least two years before applying for a class upgrade. All these factors potentially raise the opportunity cost of economic operators, as the time and resources committed to registration and/or class upgrade may hinder their ability to engage in other (more productive) activities. These costs do not symmetrically burden firms of all sizes; they tend to be greater for smaller ones.[33]

The current paper-based organisation of registries could be associated with higher administrative costs, which may further restrict participation. There are both time and monetary costs involved. Companies need to pay a fixed fee to be listed in the Registries and to renew their registration in a specific class. Initial registration and/or renewal requires the submission of documentation proving the relevant criteria have been met or that they continue to be met, e.g. proof that the company's personnel has remained unchanged for two years since the previous registration. Moreover, there is an additional indirect, but important cost involved: the time required for a company to register in class or to upgrade to a higher one might result in a provider not being able to participate in a tender until its registration is finalised.

However, the OECD acknowledges that the Registries aim to: 1) help economic operators establish their compliance with tender requirements without incurring the costs of submitting comprehensive documentation for each bid; and 2) facilitate the evaluation by contracting authorities of the bidder's professional and technical capabilities, as well as its financial standing in a unified and transparent way.

***Recommendation and benefit***

The OECD recommends that class registration no longer be a requirement for participation in tenders. Rather, participation should be conditional on the economic operator fulfilling the criteria, requirements and qualifications specified in the call for tenders.[34] However, the OECD acknowledges that a degree of standardisation is beneficial. These benefits could be attained by the publication of binding standardised documents [35]and the provision of technical specifications which focus on functional performance in order to increase participation. Overall, disconnecting class registration and tender participation widens the pool of potential eligible participants and fosters competition at a tender level.

## 3.4. Individual restrictions in the system of registries

In addition to the overall assessment of the system of registries, its operation, and its potential harm to competition, a number of specific provisions should be considered and addressed separately. These include provisions that restrict market participation, segment the market, and/or result in differentiated costs and preferential treatment for certain (groups of) suppliers.

***Dual registration in the Registry of Designers and Design Offices (MM) and the Registry of Acquired Experience (MEK) for individuals and the Registry of Designers and Design Offices (MM) and the Registry of Contractors (MEEP) for companies***

*Description and objective of the provision*

According to Article 39 of Law 3316/2005, still in force by virtue of Article 377 of Law 4412/2016, for individuals to register in the Registry of Designers and Design Offices (MM) they should not be contemporaneously registered in either the MEK or the MEEP.[36] Additionally, such individuals are not allowed to be employed by companies registered in the MEEP (Article 39, paragraph 2, subparagraph b, d and e). Similarly, according to Article 39, paragraph 3, subparagraph a and b subsection 2, design companies are prohibited from being affiliated with or being controlled – in any form – by companies registered in the MEEP.

Also, design companies are not allowed to have activities other than design. More specifically, design companies are prohibited from having within their scope the execution of public works and thus cannot register in the MEEP. The objective of these restrictions is to avoid the possibility of emerging moral hazard in the context of design and public works. For example, in the case of companies, a company participating both in a design tender and a tender for the execution of this design could have incentives to tailor the design it produces to benefit its own construction arm.

*Harm to competition*

While the concern that a design/constructing company may face conflicts of interest, as outlined above, could be valid, the OECD finds that the way the relevant provision attempts to remedy it – by imposing a blanket prohibition – is potentially restrictive.

As far as the prohibition on the contemporaneous registration to the MM and the MEK for individuals is concerned, the provision could be restrictive. Not allowing engineers to register contemporaneously in both the MEK and the MM makes switching more difficult (or costly) and decreases the flexibility individuals enjoy in building their specialisation and experience. The same is also valid with regards to the ability of individuals to obtain experience when working for a company registered in the MEEP or the MM. Allowing this contemporaneous registration of individuals as well as allowing them to work for construction or design companies registered in the MM or the MEEP could enhance the experience and specialisation in both design and construction.[37]

Moreover, prohibiting design companies to engage in construction activities, and thus register in MEEP, negates the creation of possible complementarities in the design and execution of public works and can also restrict firms' capacity to develop economies of scale and scope.

*Recommendation and benefit*

The OECD recommends that individuals be allowed to register contemporaneously in the Registry of Acquired Experience (MEK) and the Registry of Designers and Design Offices (MM); companies engaging in the construction or design of public works should be allowed to register in the both Registries. However, in order to avoid potential moral hazard and conflicts of interest, economic operators should not be allowed to bid (either directly or indirectly, relying on sub-contraction or lent experience) for the construction of a project that they have designed – unless explicitly provided for in the call for tenders.[38]

Particular attention needs to be paid here to the manner in which experience is gained and reported on an engineer's professional degree. Laws 3669/2008 and 3316/2005 specify how engineers' experience is reported in their Registry of choice (MEK or MM) according to, among others, the number of years since the award of their university degree. This could, potentially, be manifested in professional degrees with high scores deriving from the age of an engineer who could have however been inactive in his respective professional field.[39] Given the proposal of the OECD to allow dual membership in both MEK and MM the authorities should closely consider, and if necessary proceed into the respective legal adjustments, in order to ensure that an engineer does not, for example, concurrently gain experience in both Registries by the mere passage of time when he is in fact inactive in either construction or design activity.

***Registry of Designers and Design Offices (MM)***

*Description and objective of the provision*

Article 2 of Law 4412/2016 defines 28 categories for public designs, depending on their nature, e.g. urban, architectural, hydraulic designs. The same provision stipulates that individuals must be registered in certain categories, and assigned a class within each category.

According to Article 39 of Law 3316/2005, still in force by virtue of Article 377 of Law 4412/2016, designers are only allowed to register in a maximum of two categories, based on their specialised scientific and technical knowledge, as demonstrated by their university degree, field of study and experience. Moreover, designers are assigned a class within each category on the basis of a number of criteria: field of study, experience in preparing public and private projects; experience in supervising design studies; and years since obtaining their degree. This provision aims to ensure public designs are undertaken by qualified designers.

*Harm to competition*

The manner in which designers are allowed to register in the Registry of Designers is restrictive,[40] limits the range of suppliers in the market, and so potentially restricts competition in price, quality and innovation. The current regulatory framework does not align classification to categories of designs and services with designers' professional rights. This is contrary to empirical evidence that designers are, in principle, capable of participating in more than two categories, as per their university-degree qualifications.

*Recommendation and benefit*

The OECD recommends that the provision allowing designers to register in a maximum of two categories of designs – on the basis of their specialised scientific and technical knowledge but irrespective of the professional qualifications their university degree entitles them to – should be revisited. The categories in which designers are allowed to participate should increase taking into account their professional rights. This will remove the artificial delineation of the market introduced by this provision, and allow competition between designers to determine the appropriate degree of specialisation (and any resulting advantages).

### *Regional Registries*

*Description and objective of the provision*

Construction companies not registered in the Registry of Constructors may participate in small-scale public works only if they are registered in a Regional Registry. Registration is valid for three years. It is the OECD's understanding that the legislator's intention was to allow smaller, less qualified firms and individuals who could not qualify for registration in the main Registry of Contractors to perform public works, while ensuring effective execution of public works by qualified contractors.

According to Article 105 of Law 3669/2008, still in force by virtue of Article 380 of Law 4412/2016, companies are allowed to register in one Regional Registry only. Companies registered in Regional Registry are limited to execute works in the catchment area of their own registry and a single neighbouring area only. Registration in Regional Registries and in the Registry of Contractors (MEEP) is mutually exclusive. Further, partnerships between companies registered in MEEP and companies registered in the Regional Registries are not permitted.

*Harm to competition*

This provision places unnecessary restrictions on business strategies by, for example, disallowing partnerships and therefore limiting the capacity of smaller, locally registered firms to compete on the basis of their proven capabilities. As a result, it constitutes a likely impediment to competition. Moreover, geographic restrictions attached to registration in Regional Registries artificially segment the market and restrict participation.

*Recommendation and benefit*

Although the OECD cannot comment on the technical qualification criteria that allow firms to be classified in each type of registry, the mutual exclusiveness of the Regional and National Registries is found to be restrictive. The OECD recommends that Regional Registries be abolished; and the Registry of Contractors be amended, if necessary, for former Regional registrants to be accommodated. This will create one unified Registry, free from any unnecessary restrictions on firms' ability to participate in tenders (if they satisfy the corresponding selection criteria).

### *Legal form of companies registered in the Registry of Contractors (MEEP)*

*Description and objective of the provision*

Article 100 of Law 3669/2008, still in force by virtue of Article 380 of Law 4412/2016, prescribes that companies belonging to the third class of the registry or above are required to be incorporated as a société anonyme (SA).This requirement is in place to ensure that shareholders are known, allowing the committee of the Registry to validate each contractor's shareholding structure in the interest of transparency in public procurement.

*Harm to competition*

This requirement may be restrictive, given that there are certain criteria (such as minimum capital requirements, management board criteria and legal documentation) attached to the legal form of the company described in the provision. Satisfying such criteria is not necessarily related to the ability of a contractor to complete a project, so this requirement is deemed not to satisfy the proportionality objective for criteria in tender participation. Instead these criteria limit the range of potential suppliers, raise their cost of entry and, thereby, restrict their ability to compete. This creates disproportionate costs for those firms that would otherwise satisfy the financial and technical requirements for registration in the third class of the Registry of Contractors – a particular burden for companies on the lower end of the third class. This could constitute a disincentive to grow for public procurement-focused businesses, potentially resulting in less intense competition in higher classes and lower participation in higher-value tenders.

*Recommendation and benefit*

The OECD recommends abolishing the requirement that a company be an SA in order to be registered in the third class of the Registry of Contractors and above. This will enhance the incentives of firms, particularly the smaller ones, to compete and develop within the Registry's class system. The OECD suggests that, while this particular obligation should be abolished, the legal obligation for firms bidding for a tender to register shares to a natural person should be maintained. This would preserve the level of transparency initially sought by lawmakers.

## 3.5. Pricing and budgeting

### *Description of the framework*

Legislation on procurement of public works and designs contains a series of provisions on how tenders are organised; how budgets are compiled on the basis of binding price lists; the way offers are submitted evaluated, and priced (e.g. the normality of discounts or fixed pre-determined profit rates); and price/cost revisions after a contract has been awarded. In addition, provisions relating to the supervision of works after the awarding of a contract regulate the redesign of projects, replacement of a contractor, and rules in respect of complementary works if any are required.

The objective of this set of provisions is to manage potentially excessively low offers (i.e. winning bids offering excessively high discounts) and so minimise the risk of a contractor's subsequent failure to execute the project.

To that end, the law stipulates that a ministerial decision should be regularly issued to establish and update price lists both for works and designs. The lists are compiled on the basis of unit prices for and volumes of materials, rates and number of working hours, etc. Price lists for public works are binding and are issued for each category of works, for example, road infrastructure or hydraulic works; similar price lists are issued for public designs.

Price lists are used by the contracting authorities in preparing budgets for works being procured; and they are binding in nature – i.e. the contracting authority is obliged to base its budget on the price list current at the time of issuing a call for tenders. Participants then submit their tender offers expressed as percentage discounts of the budget as compared to the published price list – either submitting a single discount or individual discounts for each category of works, depending on the terms of each call for tenders. Contracting authorities then evaluate the bids they receive on the discounts offered.

The manner in which a tender is organised highlights the key role played by price lists in public procurement for works and designs. Price lists currently exist for the majority of works' categories, but not all. For example, there is no price list for most electromechanical works. Moreover, even though the law stipulates that price lists should be regularly updated, the most recent update of price lists in some categories dates back to 2013.

Finally, the law provides that, in the case of public works, the pricing (i.e. cost) of certain works has to be updated in line with price developments. In other words, after the award of the contract, contracting authorities regularly revise the pricing of certain works. These updates occur every three months, using a formula that takes into account, among other criteria, the time elapsed between the commencement of works and their execution. Updates can both increase and reduce prices.

*Harm to competition.*

Organising tenders on the basis of discounts to price lists is an alternative to systems in which bidders freely submit an offer to undertake a contract. Both systems are found in EU countries – for example, Italy and Germany also base their procurement on discounts. Given the reliance of this system on price lists and budgets, contracting authorities are required to disclose the budget for each call for tenders.

In its 2011 Report on Competition and Procurement,[41] the OECD notes that auction design plays a significant part in an effective procurement policy. It further suggests that the budget and underlying unit prices should not be disclosed, but rather used by contracting authorities for reference only. This could mitigate the risk that reference prices function as a focal point for bidders and facilitate collusive behaviour between suppliers. Moreover, according to OECD guidelines for fighting bid rigging in public procurement,[42] contracting authorities should use maximum reserve prices only if they are based on thorough market research and if officials are convinced they are competitive.

Predetermined price lists may facilitate bid rigging; and limit the freedom of structuring the offer and costing the items the way the bidder prefers. A large body of evidence from markets such as cement (Albæk, 1998), and fruits and vegetables (Genakos et al., 2011) suggests that publicly available prices have been used as focal points upon which suppliers co-ordinate on price.

However, past practice suggests that this mechanism is not an issue for the public procurement of works and designs in Greece: the risk of co-ordination does not appear to have materialized as economic operators participating in tenders for both public works and designs tend to compete with high discounts on reference prices. Based on data for 653 works, designs and service contracts tendered in an open procedure since 2006, the average discount offered by the winner was 34.4% (see Annex 3.A1 for more detailed information).

In fact, procuring authorities are often faced with the opposite problem – that of excessively high discounts ("excessively low offers"). It is often observed that unrealistically high discounts are offered in order to secure a contract in question. This may ultimately delay the execution of the works or lead to incomplete execution, incurring high direct and indirect costs to both the procuring authority and society as a whole.

The OECD considers that an alternative system, without reference price lists and (publicly available) budgets, may not be an improvement on the current one. If public works and designs were auctioned without reference budgets, the offers put in could be (well) above the contracting authority's undisclosed budget, resulting either in significant additional costs or in projects not being executed on time. An alternative system in which the budget for public construction projects is not published would also complicate the funding of works financed or co-financed by the EU, since according to EU rules, the budget for co-financed projects must be publicly available.

It is interesting to note that within the current system of unit price lists, price lists are not regularly updated in several categories of works and materials. Categories such as electromechanical works, high-pressure hydraulic works and certain heavy -industry categories of works are in practice not fully incorporated into the central system of unified pricing. Consequently, price updates in such categories occur neither as regularly nor as homogenously (with regards to covering all the materials and works included in each category) as in other categories of works. This could further limit competition in the market, as it could create a system of differing incentives depending on whether a contractor's costs fall within a price list or not. For instance, suppliers could offer different prices in different categories of works depending on whether they can place an offer as an absolute price per unit, or if they are instead required to bid based on a discount of a pre-set price.

Following the discussion above, the OECD has identified specific provisions – within the current system of price lists and discounts – that may impede competition between firms and limit their ability to formulate their (pricing or other) business strategies.

***Discount normality***

Contracting authorities using price lists to compile budgets generally detail prices for each sub-group of works. Offers are then submitted with reference to discounts for each of those sub-groups, unless the call for tenders dictates otherwise.

Article 95, paragraph 2 of Law 4412/2016 imposes the additional requirement that the discounts offered for the various categories (sub-groups) of public works are not significantly different. This "normality" between discounts in different categories is guaranteed by a formula that essentially requires that discounts between categories do not vary by more than 10%.

*Harm to competition*

Limiting the variation in discounts submitted by bidders restricts business strategies and removes a potential element of competition at the bidding stage. For instance, a bidder might be able to offer a bigger discount in one category (benefiting from economies of scale, bulk purchasing, lower transportation costs), but it is prevented from doing so. This could lead to cross-subsidization across different categories and limit the intensity of competition among bidders for specific sub-categories.

However, the OECD acknowledges that the provision is designed to deter bidders from submitting excessively low offers (excessive discounts), shifting the budget between categories of works, strategic bidding and limiting any potential need for complementary works or project redesigns.

*Recommendation and benefit*

The policy maker's objectives could be achieved in alternative ways, including effective supervision, a well-functioning pricing system and ex-post mechanisms. Given that the pricing system is being reviewed and that it may address the phenomenon of abnormally low offers, the OECD recommends that the need for this restriction should be assessed by the authorities.

***Price list updates***

According to Article 52 of Law 4412/2016, price lists for public works and designs should be regularly updated. This requirement was also found in the law in force until August 2016. However, the OECD understands that price lists for many categories of public works have not been updated since 2013.

*Harm to competition*

Price lists play a key role in the tendering process. They form the basis upon which budgets are compiled and discounts are (in turn) offered, and so directly affect an element of competition upon which the contract award is decided. Therefore, it is imperative that price lists are current and that they are a true reflection of market prices.

Overall, the methodology of updating price lists by issuing ministerial decisions carries a significant administrative burden that can inflate prices and limit firms' strategies. This has led to delays and rigidities in price lists being updated.

*Recommendation and benefit*

The OECD recommends that updates to price lists take place regularly, as stipulated in the law. It is also recommended that the competent authorities explore alternative means to set, update and publish price lists other than via ministerial decisions. A more efficient framework for updating and communicating price lists will ensure that they are aligned with true market conditions and will allow suppliers to submit accurate offers.

### 3.6. E-Systems (Public procurement and e-monitoring of public works and designs)

The current legislation provides for the use of e-procurement and the interoperability of e-systems related to public -procurement processes. Specific provisions also refer to the e-monitoring of public works and designs in particular; for example, contracting authorities are obliged to keep an electronic file of the contract for those public contracts which exceed certain financial thresholds. However, the operation of e-procurement for public works is provided for April 2017, while monitoring procedures, besides the electronic file obligation mentioned above, do not follow a consolidated electronic process.

The OECD acknowledges that effective on-site supervision is a key factor for the efficient execution of works, both by contracting authorities and economic operators. Equally, the lack of such supervision is seen as a major deficiency of the current system; and although Law 4412/2016 includes provisions aimed at enhancing the technical capability of contracting authorities to supervise works, a complete system of supervision still remains incomplete. Specifically, legislation is still not geared towards the electronic monitoring of public contracts. A number of important issues that still need to be addressed include, among others: the electronic monitoring of awarded contracts as well as the electronic recording of on-site supervision results (the "diary of works"), contract annulments, contract terminations and legal sanctions.

In order to support the effective allocation of public resources, the e-monitoring of public works and designs could provide a strategic tool to mitigate risks resulting from inefficiencies and corruption often met in major infrastructure and other complex public work and public design projects.

According to the OECD recommendations on public procurement,[43] authorities should "employ recent digital technology developments that allow integrated e-procurement solutions covering the public procurement cycle. Information and communication technologies should be used in public procurement to ensure transparency and access to public tenders, increasing competition, simplifying processes for contract award and management, driving cost savings and integrating public procurement and public finance information". The supervision and effective execution of public works can be enhanced by either the e-monitoring and maintenance of all information included in each contract consolidated into a single integrated system or by the enhanced availability and accessibility of such information through interoperable systems.

Moreover, the visibility and accessibility of information relevant to all stages of a public contract (from its initial procurement to its final payment) in the form of electronic consolidated data ensure transparency and promote "fair and equitable treatment for potential suppliers by providing an adequate and timely degree of transparency in each phase of the public procurement cycle".[44]

Electronic consolidated data could employ effective impact assessment methodologies to measure the effectiveness of the awarded public contract (e.g. benchmarks, monitoring results) and "allow (i) stakeholders to understand government priorities and spending, and (ii) policy makers to organise procurement strategically".[45]

*Recommendation and benefit*

The OECD recommends that the contracting authorities consider the introduction of e-monitoring mechanisms for public works and public designs contracts by keeping all the information on each contract consolidated, either in a single integrated system or easily accessible through interoperable systems. This will allow for higher transparency, access and participation in the market to be achieved.

## Notes

1. For the purposes of this assessment, NACE codes F41 (construction of buildings) and F42 (civil engineering works) were selected, while F43 (specialised construction) was considered to fall outside the scope of this assessment.

2. Eurostat (2016), Construction Statistics, epp.eurostat.ec.europa.eu (accessed March-September 2016).

3. IOBE (2015), *The Significance of Growth, the Barriers and the Future of the Construction Sector*, iobe.gr/docs/research/res_05_f_31032015_rep_gr.pdf (accessed on July 2013).

4. IOBE (2015), *The Significance of Growth, the Barriers and the Future of the Construction Sector*, ibid.

5. In general, the wage-adjusted labour productivity ratio [defined by Eurostat as "value added divided by personnel costs subsequently adjusted by the share of paid employees in the total number of persons employed" [Eurostat (2013), Glossary: Wage-adjusted labour productivity ratio, *http://ec.europa.eu/eurostat/statistics-explained/index.php/Glossary:Wage-adjusted_labour_productivity_ratio* (accessed April 2016)] for the EU 28 demonstrates that value added per person employed in the construction sector was equivalent to around 120% of the average personnel costs per employee. The Greek construction sector seems to suffer particularly from low levels of labour productivity with a wage-adjusted labour productivity ratio of 53%, the lowest in the European Union [Eurostat (2016), Construction Statistics, epp.eurostat.ec.europa.eu (accessed April 2016)]. This low level of labour productivity is a result of the average value added generated per person employed being significantly less than average personnel costs.

6. ELSTAT (2013), Basic Economic Magnitudes in the Construction Sector,, *www.statistics.gr/en/statistics/-/publication/SIN21/2013* (accessed on July 2013).

7. In 2012, according to Eurostat data, the construction of buildings sub-sector accounted for around 78% of total construction in the EU, while the construction of civil engineering works accounted for the remaining 22%. Eurostat (2016), Construction Statistics, epp.eurostat.ec.europa.eu (accessed March-September 2016).

8. Eurostat (2016), Construction Statistics, epp.eurostat.ec.europa.eu (accessed April 2016).

9. It is interesting to note here that, unlike all other categories of firms, very large enterprises were in fact the sole ones to increase their gross turnover during the 2009-2013 period.

10. PwC (2016), *Infrastructure: Funding the future – Greece,* March 2016, available at *www.pwc.com/gr/en/publications/assets/infrastructure-funding-the-future-2015-en.pdf.*

11. KEPE (2014), A Development Vision for Greece in 2020: Forecasts, Development Conditions and Finance Mechanisms, Athens.

12. Law 4281/2014 Government Gazette A 160/8.08.2014 on Support and development measures for the Greek Economy, organisational issues of the Ministry of Finance and other provisions.

13. Law 4412/2016 Government Gazette A 147/8.08.2016 on Public procurement of works, goods and services (adjustments to Directives 2014/24/EU and 2014/23/EU).

14. Law 4412/2016 ibid.

15. Directive 2014/24/EU of the European Parliament and of the Council of 26 February 2014 on public procurement and repealing Directive 2004/18/EC, Official Journal L 94, 28.3.2014.

16 Directive 2014/23/EU of the European Parliament and of the Council of 26 February 2014 on the award of concession contracts, Official Journal L 94, 28.3.2014.

17. In late September, at the time of the drafting of the current report, the Greek government released for public consultation a draft law on registries, pricing, and the e-monitoring of public works.

18 Maturity of works is the stage when all preparatory works required for a project to be procured are complete. More specifically, the term is used to describe the completion of all works related to general planning of the works; completion of the required designs; and acquisition of the necessary licences e.g. environmental licencing.

19. Law 3389/2005 Government Gazette A 232/22.9.2005 on Public-private partnerships.

20. Law 4413/2016, Government Gazette A'148/08.08.2016 on Procurement and execution of concession contracts – Harmonisation with Directive of 24 February 2014 of the European Commission and of the European Council (Official Journal L94/1/28.3.2014) for the procurement and execution of concessions – and other provisions.

21. Law 4014/2011 Government Gazette A 209/21.09.2011 on Environmental licencing of works and activities, regulation of arbitrary constructions in relation to the environmental balance and other provisions under the competence of the Ministry of Environment and Energy.

22. Designers are qualified engineers who according to their specialisation may design e.g. spatial planning, architectural, geotechnical designs which serve as the basis for the execution of public works.

23. Law 3669/2008 Government Gazette A 116/18.6.2008 on the Codification of legislation on the execution of public works.

24. Law 3316/2005 Government Gazette A 42/22.2.2005, correction of errors Government Gazette A 85/7.4.2005 on Procurement and execution of public designs and provision of related services and other provisions.

25. Law 4278/2014 Government Gazette A 157/4.08.2014 on Lighthouses, soldier recruitment and other provisions.

26. This acts as a safeguard against 'ghost' JVs formed solely for the purpose of by passing the value thresholds corresponding to a company's registration in MEEP.

27. Since Law 4278/2014 came into force and the lower thresholds for tender participation were abolished, all firms belonging to a certain class and the classes above it can participate in a tender.

28. OECD (2011), *Competition and Procurement,* OECD Publishing, Paris, *www.oecd.org/daf/competition/sectors/48315205.pdf.*

29. "Effective competition can be enhanced if a sufficient number of credible bidders are able to respond to the invitation to tender and have an incentive to compete for the contract. For example, participation in the tender can be facilitated if procurement officials reduce the costs of bidding, establish participation requirements that do not unreasonably limit competition, allow firms from other regions or countries to participate, or devise ways of incentivising smaller firms to participate even if they cannot bid for the entire contract" Specifically the OECD recommends to "Avoid unnecessary restrictions that may reduce the number of qualified bidders. Specify minimum requirements that are proportional to the size and content of the procurement contract. Do not specify minimum requirements that create an obstacle to participation, such as controls on the size, composition, or nature of firms that may submit a bid" (OECD, 2011, p.83).

30. Economic operators that fulfill class criteria would benefit from this provision, as they would now be eligible for participation in the call for tenders. Such operators could include firms, which could make use of lent experience (i.e. the use of one's financial or technical capability in order to execute the work), or which have applied already for a review of their classification but fall in the interim of the 2 years required for their class review.

31. Due to the technical nature of the criteria, OECD does not take a stance on the selection or the level of criteria required. Our comments pertain only to the design of the tendering mechanism.

32. Note that the law already allows for additional criteria to be included by the procuring authorities in each call for tenders, if considered necessary.

33. An electronic system could reduce some of these costs and equalize costs for all firms irrespective of their size.

34. According to OECD recommendations on public procurement, "in order to facilitate access to procurement opportunities for potential competitors of all sizes authorities should deliver clear and integrated tender documentation, standardised where possible and proportionate to the need, to ensure that: specific tender opportunities are designed so as to encourage broad participation from potential competitors, including new entrants", OECD (2015), *Recommendation of the Council on Public Procurement,* http://acts.oecd.org/Instruments/ShowInstrumentView.aspx?InstrumentID=320.

35. Standardised documents take the form of a model call for tenders approved by the competent body namely the Single Public Procurement Authority (SPPA); they provide, for common and repeated use, rules, guidelines, or technical specifications for procurement of designs and works; they are binding for contracting authorities.

36. Registration in the MEEP refers to the situation in which an individual is a sole trader, i.e. has a "personal company".

37. See also Hellenic Competition Commission (2014), *Opinion 34/2014 in plenary session,* p.23, *www.epant.gr/gnomo_details.php?Lang=gr&id=31&nid=31.*

38. The same rule seems to apply in Italy, according to the relevant Italian regulatory framework (Gazzetta Ufficiale della Repubblica Italiana (18 Aprile 2016), *Decreto Legislativo,* No. 250, Rome, Italy).

39. This could also affect a company's classification (under the current system) given the fact that this classification is determined, among others, by the noted experience of the company's minimum staffing. This could potentially influence the firm's ability to bid for works of higher budget. It should be noted here that in a system where class registration is not a requirement for participation the same issue could arise.

40. See also Hellenic Competition Commission (2014), *Opinion 34/2014 in plenary session,* p.23, available at *www.epant.gr/gnomo_details.php?Lang=gr&id=31&nid=31* (accessed on August 2016).

41. OECD (2011), *Competition and Procurement*, ibid.

42. OECD (2012), *Guidelines for Fighting Bid Rigging in Public Procurement*, OECD, available at *www.oecd.org/competition/cartels/42851044.pdf* (accessed on August 2016).

43. OECD, *Recommendation of the Council on Public Procurement*, ibid.

44. OECD, *Recommendation of the Council on Public Procurement*, ibid.

45. OECD, *Recommendation of the Council on Public Procurement*, ibid.

## References

Albæk, Svend, H. Peter Møllgaard and Per B. Overgaard, *"The Danish Competition Act and Barriers to Entry",* in S. Martin, ed. (1998), *Competition Policies in Europe*, Elsevier, New York.

ELSTAT, Construction database, *www.statistics.gr* (accessed March-September 2016).

ELSTAT (2013), *Basic Economic Magnitudes in the Construction Sector*, *www.statistics.gr/en/statistics/-/publication/SIN21/2013* (accessed July 2016).

Eurostat (2013), Glossary:Wage-adjusted labour productivity ratio, *http://ec.europa.eu/eurostat/statistics-explained/index.php/Glossary:Wage-adjusted_labour_productivity_ratio* (accessed April 2016.)

Eurostat (2016), Construction Statistics, epp.eurostat.ec.europa.eu (accessed March-September 2016).

Eurostat, NACE Codes, ec.europa.eu/eurostat/statistics-explained/index.php/File:Key_indicators,_construction_(NACE_Section_F),_EU-28,_2012.png (accessed March-September 2016).

Gazzetta Ufficiale della Repubblica Italiana (18 Aprile 2016), *Decreto Legislativo,* No. 250, Rome, Italy.

Genakos, C., P. Koutroumpis, & M. Pagliero, (2014), "*The impact of maximum markup regulation on prices*", *www.aueb.gr/users/cgenakos/Research.files/GKP_Markup%20regulation%20and%20prices.pdf.*

Hellenic Competition Commission (2014), *Opinion 34/2014 in plenary session*, *www.epant.gr/gnomo_details.php?Lang=gr&id=31&nid=31.*

IOBE (2015), *The Significance of Growth, the Barriers and the Future of the Construction Sector*, iobe.gr/docs/research/res_05_f_31032015_rep_gr.pdf.

KEPE (2014), *A Development Vision for Greece in 2020: Forecasts, Development Conditions and Finance Mechanisms*, Athens.

Ministry of Infrastructure, Transport and Networks, General Secretariat of Public Works, Directorate General for Public works, Directorate 15, *www.ypexd15.gr*.

OECD (2011), *Competition and Procurement*, OECD Publishing, Paris, *www.oecd.org/daf/competition/sectors/48315205.pdf.*

OECD (2012), *Guidelines for Fighting Bid Rigging in Public Procurement*, OECD Publishing, Paris, *www.oecd.org/competition/cartels/42851044.pdf.*

PwC (2016), Infrastructure: Funding the Future – Greece, www.pwc.com/gr/en/publications/assets/infrastructure-funding-the-future-2015-en.pdf.

# *Annex 3.A1*

# Public procurement for construction works and designs

In this Annex, we present the data, methodology and results of an analysis of the tendering process for public construction works and designs in Greece over the past decade. More specifically, we use data on publicly procured projects to assess the impact of the design of the competitive process on the outcome of the corresponding tenders. The following questions – partly guided by data availability and the extent to which the relevant information can be gleaned from the data – have been addressed in our analysis:

- the impact of the procurement procedure on the outcome of the tendering process;
- whether higher-value projects attract more bidders; and
- the significance of the degree of competition for a project, as measured by the number of offers submitted in the context of each tender, for the final outcome.

The analysis is based on data compiled by the competent Directorates in the Ministry of Infrastructure, Transport and Networks.[1] We have also relied on data submitted to the Tenders Electronic Daily (TED) database, maintained by the European Commission, to validate the results of our analysis and perform cross-country comparisons.

## Data from the Ministry of Infrastructure, Transport and Networks

### *Description of the data*

In response to a request from the OECD, all the Directorates within the Directorate General for Transport Infrastructure and the Directorate General for Hydraulic and Building Works of the General Secretariat for Infrastructure reported data on all the tenders they conducted and/or oversaw.

The data contains, among other things and to varying degrees of completeness, information on:[2] the tender date, the procedure followed,[3] its status,[4] the nature of the work involved,[5] the budget/expected value of the project, the number of offers submitted, the winning bid and corresponding discount offered, and final value after revisions (e.g. due to a change in VAT rate) and additional expenses (e.g. due to unforeseen works). It covers the period since 2009 for projects relating to public works; and the period since 2006 for designs, services, consulting services, and other projects.[6] Most tenders are concentrated in the years 2006-2009: the data contain over four times more records in the four-year period, 2006-2009, than any four-year period between 2010-2016. There is also some cyclicality, in that there are typically fewer tenders in the December/January and July/August periods.

An overview of the key variables of interest is set out in Table 3.A1.1. Other than the relative weight of various categories of projects and tender procedures, and their respective average and range, the table confirms a priori expectations. In particular, open tendering procedures – which are, by design, more competitive in nature – attract more participants and appear to secure higher discounts. An open procedure attracts, on average, 3.5 times more bids than other procedures; in turn, this results in discounts that are over 4 times greater on average. It follows that, absent non-price considerations, open procedures yield better pricing outcomes for contracting authorities.

Table 3.A1.1. **Summary statistics – Greece**

| Variable | Category | Observations | Mean | Standard deviation | Minimum | Maximum |
|---|---|---|---|---|---|---|
| **Budget / Expected value (€ '000)** | All | 747 | 5 149 | 16 009 | 16 | 147 600 |
| | Works | 286 | 12 055 | 24 292 | 25 | 147 600 |
| | Designs | 407 | 729 | 877 | 18 | 5 949 |
| | Other | 54 | 1 878 | 3 168 | 16 | 18 430 |
| **Winning bid (€ '000)** | All | 2 571 | 1 040 | 6 065 | 4 | 129 053 |
| **Number of (suitable) offers** | All | 787 | 7.9 | 5.4 | 1.0 | 30.0 |
| | Open | 692 | 8.7 | 5.4 | 1.0 | 30.0 |
| | Negotiated procedure | 81 | 2.7 | 1.7 | 1.0 | 12.0 |
| | Direct award | 10 | 1.0 | 0.0 | 1.0 | 1.0 |
| | Other | 4 | 3.0 | 0.8 | 2.0 | 4.0 |
| **Discount of winning bid (%)** | All | 737 | 31.4 | 21.6 | 0.0 | 91.2 |
| | Open | 653 | 34.4 | 21.0 | 0.0 | 91.2 |
| | Negotiated procedure | 79 | 7.8 | 9.0 | 1.5 | 47.1 |
| | Direct award | 1 | 3.2 | 0.0 | 3.2 | 3.2 |
| | Other | 4 | 15.6 | 5.8 | 8.7 | 20.7 |

*Notes:* The above table provides summary statistics for *completed* tenders only, i.e. for those contracts that have been awarded to the winner of the tender. Variables are reported where available and where it is meaningful to do so (e.g. the contract's expected value is not shown when it matches the winning bid by construction, in the case of direct awards). The number of offers shows the number of final bids found acceptable and admitted in the tender. The discount has been calculated by the authors on the basis of expected project value and winning bid; using the discount recorded in the original data does not result in any substantial changes to the statistics reported in the table.

*Source*: Authors' calculations based on data compiled by the General Secretariat for Infrastructure of the Ministry for Infrastructure, Transport and Networks.

### *Results and discussion*

We use these data to empirically examine two important relationships. Firstly, we examine the impact of the expected value (budget) of a project on the number of competitors participating in the tendering process. Our empirical analysis is based on the following specification:

$$(1)\quad \ln(Number\ of\ offers)_i = \alpha + \beta \ln(Expected\ value)_i + \gamma_{it} D_{it} + \varepsilon_{it}$$

The dependent variable in (1) is the logarithm of the number of offers accepted in tender $i$. The main explanatory variable of interest is the size of the project, as indicated by its expected value, whereas $D_{it}$ is a matrix of control variables and $\varepsilon_{it}$ is a random shock. The matrix of control variables includes joint year and month indicator variables to capture the varying (economic) conditions across time, as well as type and nature of work-indicator variables, which aim to control for the heterogeneity across projects. Equation (1) was estimated using fixed-effects panel data techniques and robust standard errors were calculated to account for heteroscedasticity across the various works.

The analysis is conducted on all *complete* tenders, decided after an *open* procedure. The sample for works used in the estimation has been restricted to tenders with a budget up to €44 million, which is the threshold above which only construction firms of the highest class can participate – there is a small number of firms registered in this class.[7]

Table 3.A1.2 reports our main results. Both in column (1) that examines the data on works and in column (2) that looks at the data on designs, we find a positive and statistically significant relationship: the higher the expected value (budget) of a project the more competitors participate in the tender. A 1% increase in the budget of a project leads to 0.12% more offers for works and 0.27% more offers for designs. Hence, it is advisable that contracting authorities do not split large works or designs into smaller pieces since the bigger the contract the more competitors it attracts.

The second empirical relationship we test, using the same data on completed open tenders, is whether the increased competition at tender level (as measured by the number of offers submitted) results in lower prices (in the form of large discounts). Figure 3.A1.1 shows a positive relationship between the number of (suitable) offers submitted in a tender and the final pricing outcome, i.e. the discount of the winning bid, for both works and designs. The positive relationship is clearly stronger for works than for designs. However, the less-pronounced relationship in the case of designs is partly driven by a high level of concentration of discounts at or around the 20% mark,[8] which reflects a cap on discount for design works previously imposed by regulation.

Figure 3.A1.1. **Number of competing offers and discount of winning bid in tenders for public works and design projects – Greece**

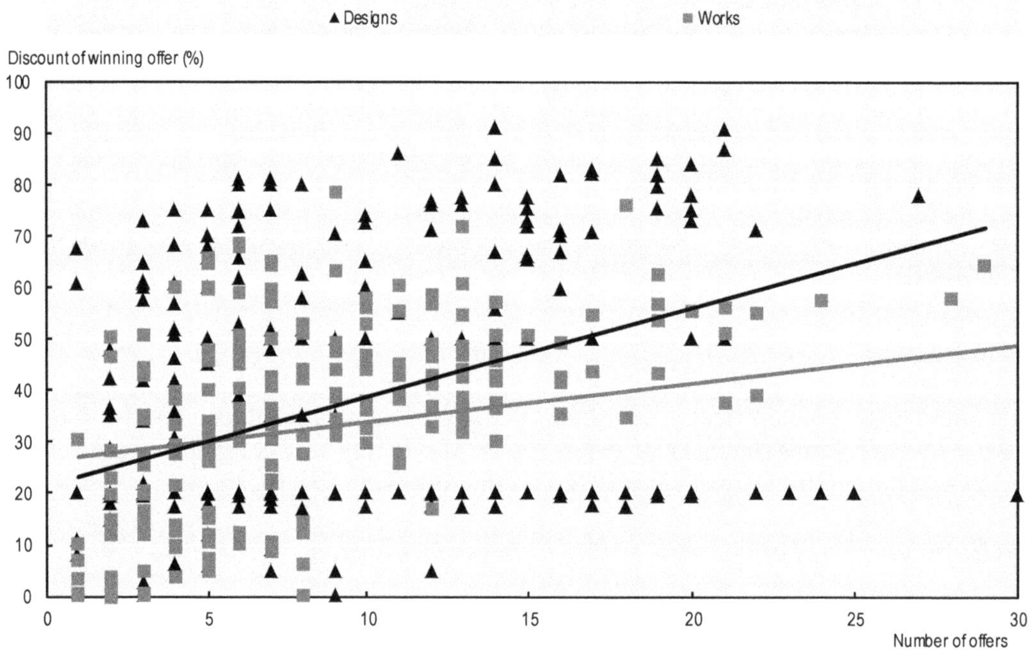


*Notes:* Completed tenders awarded after an open procedure. Discount calculated on the basis of expected value of each project and value of winning offer, where both were available. Linear fitted lines are an approximation only.

*Source*: OECD calculations based on the data compiled by the General Secretariat for Infrastructure of the Ministry for Infrastructure, Transport and Networks.

To formally test this relationship, we use the following empirical framework:

$$(2)\ \ln(Discount\ of\ winning\ offer)_i = \alpha + \beta(Number\ of\ offers)_i + \gamma_{it}D_{it} + \varepsilon_{it}$$

The dependent variable in (2) is the logarithm of the discount offered by the winner of tender $i$. The main explanatory variable of interest is the intensity of competition, as indicated by the number of offers submitted, whereas $D_{it}$ is a matrix of control variables and $\varepsilon_{it}$ is a random shock. The matrix of control variables includes joint year and month indicator variables, to capture the varying (economic) conditions across time, and also work- and project-type indicator variables that aim to control for the heterogeneity across projects. Equation (2) was estimated using fixed-effects panel data techniques and robust standard errors were calculated to account for heteroscedasticity across the various works.

The results are reported in the last three columns of Table 3.A1.2.[9] Column (3) aggregates the data for both works and designs and reveals a strong and positive relationship between the number of participants and the final discount offered. However, while a positive relationship is also found when works and designs are considered separately – columns (4) and (5) respectively, as depicted in Table 3.A1.1 – it is clearly stronger and statistically significant in the case of works.

Table 3.A1.2. **Project size, number of offers and discounts – Greece**

| | (1) | (2) | (3) | (4) | (5) |
|---|---|---|---|---|---|
| Project type | Works | Designs | All | Works | Designs |
| Expected value | less than €44m | All | All | All | All |
| Dependent variable | log (Number of offers) | log (Number of offers) | log (Discount) | log (Discount) | log (Discount) |
| log(Expected value) | 0.118 *** | 0.271 *** | | | |
| | (0.039) | (0.047) | | | |
| Number of offers | | | 0.050 *** | 0.137 *** | 0.015 |
| | | | (0.01) | (0.034) | (0.011) |
| Year/month dummies | yes | yes | yes | yes | Yes |
| Project type dummies | no | no | yes | no | No |
| Work type dummies | yes | yes | yes | yes | Yes |
| Observations | 193 | 392 | 650 | 216 | 388 |

*Notes:* Robust standard errors are reported in parentheses.
* signifies estimates significant at 10%,
** significant at 5%, and
*** significant at 1% level respectively.

Analysis based on *completed open* tenders. *Year/month* corresponds to month/year combinations. *Project type* distinguishes work and design projects. *Work type* identifies the nature of the work involved. The specifications include a constant, which is not reported in the table.

*Source*: OECD calculations based on the data compiled by the General Secretariat for Infrastructure of the Ministry for Infrastructure, Transport and Networks.

The results are also economically significant. In the case of public works, we find that an additional offer leads to a 14.7%[10] increase in the level of discount offered from the winner.[11] In other words, a hypothetical discount of 35%[12] would (on average) increase to 40% if an additional offer was accepted as part of the tendering process.[13] Hence, making the registry system more flexible and encouraging higher participation in a tender procedure can lead to more aggressive bidding and consequently higher discounts (lower prices) with significant benefits to public finance and consumer welfare.[14]

## Data from the European Commission's Tenders Electronic Daily (TED) database

### *Description of the data*

The European Commission collects information on public procurement, including public works and designs, from contract award notices (and contract notices)[15] issued by contracting authorities in the European Economic Area (EEA), Former Yugoslav Republic of Macedonia (FYROM) and Switzerland, between 2006-2015 (inclusive). In principle, the data consist of notices above the procurement thresholds established by EU Directives, although notices below the relevant thresholds are also found in the data. Information includes year of publication, contract authority, type of contract,[16] estimated value of the contract, type of procedure,[17] award criteria,[18] number of offers, and final value of the contract (winning bid) at tender level is included in the database.

We use a subset of this dataset, which relates to construction projects with complete data; and focus on construction works[19] awarded after an open tender. Summary statistics for the key variables of interest are set out in Table 3.A1.3 below.

Table 3.A1.3. **Summary statistics – EEA, FYROM and Switzerland**

| Variable | Observations | Mean | Median | Standard deviation |
|---|---|---|---|---|
| **Budget/Expected value (€ '000)** | 39 439 | 27 200 000 | 798 | 5 410 000 000 |
| **Winning bid (€ '000)** | 39 439 | 4 443 | 582.2 | 21 100 |
| **Number of offers** | 39 439 | 8.3 | 6 | 9.0 |
| **Discount of winning bid (%)** | 39 439 | 24.7 | 21.5 | 19.2 |

*Notes:* The above table provides summary statistics for construction work projects in the EEA, FYROM and Switzerland, awarded following an open tender procedure. There exist some outliers (abnormally high values) in the data: for this reason, maximum values are not reported; medians are shown instead. The discount has been calculated by the OECD on the basis of estimated contract value and award value; the table shows statistics for positive discounts only.

*Source*: OECD calculations based on the TED data supplement to the Official Journal of the European Union.

### *Results and discussion*

We use these data on public-work projects in a panel of 33 countries to establish whether the relationships outlined in the case of tenders for works in Greece are evident in the much richer pool of tenders in the TED data. Our empirical analysis is based on specifications equivalent to those used in the previous section:

$$(3)\quad \ln(Number\ of\ offers)_{ic} = \alpha + \beta\ln(Expected\ value)_i + a_t + a_c + \varepsilon_{itc}$$

$$(4)\quad \ln(Discount\ of\ winning\ offer)_{ic} = \alpha + \beta(Number\ of\ offers)_i + a_t + a_c + \varepsilon_{itc}$$

The dependent and explanatory variables are similar to the ones used in (1) and (2), i.e. the (logarithm of the) expected value of each contract, number of offers, and discount of winning bid. We control for combined year and month ($a_t$) and country ($a_c$) fixed effects, which control for time-dependent and country-specific characteristics. Both equations were estimated using fixed-effects panel data techniques and robust standard errors were calculated to account for heteroscedasticity across the various works.

The results are reported in Table 3.A1.4. The first two columns present the results for equation (3) both without (column 1) and with all the fixed effects (column 2). Again, there is statistically strong and positive relationship between the expected value of the work and the number of participants: a 10% increase in the value of the work increases participation by 0.5%. Similarly, the last two columns present the results for equation (4) both without (column 3) and with all the fixed effects (column 4). The number of offers has a positive effect on the discount (price) of the winning bid: an additional offer translates into a 3% increase in the level of discount offered from the winner.[20] Therefore, both relationships are qualitatively the same across the 33 countries as in Greece, although the economic magnitude of the results appears stronger in Greece.

Table 3.A1.4. **Project size, number of offers and discounts – EEA, FYROM and Switzerland**

| | (1) | (2) | (3) | (4) |
|---|---|---|---|---|
| **Dependent variable** | log(Number of offers) | log(Number of offers) | log(Discount) | log(Discount) |
| **log(Expected value)** | 0.091 *** | 0.052 *** | | |
| | (0.002) | (0.002) | | |
| **Number of offers** | | | 0.027 *** | 0.030 *** |
| | | | (0.001) | (0.002) |
| **Year/month dummies** | no | yes | no | Yes |
| **Country dummies** | no | yes | no | Yes |
| **Observations** | 39 439 | 39 439 | 39 439 | 39 439 |

*Notes:* Robust standard errors are reported in parentheses. * signifies estimates significant at 10%, ** significant at 5%, and *** significant at 1% level respectively. *Year/month* corresponds to month/year combinations. *Country* identifies the country where the tender took place. The specifications include a constant, which is not reported in the table.

*Source*: OECD calculations based on the data compiled by the General Secretariat for Infrastructure of the Ministry for Infrastructure, Transport and Networks.

## Notes

1. A full list of the competent Directorates can be found in the Database sources.

2. The data has been consolidated and cleaned, e.g. the classification of projects and categorisation of works has been made uniform across all groups of tenders.

3. Whether the contract was awarded following an open procedure, negotiated procedure, direct award, or other means (such as, for example, oral, closed, or restricted procedures). This broad categorisation follows more detailed classification of tender processes, e.g. an open procedure could be based on a system of itemised discounts, single discount and most advantageous offers.

4. A tender may be completed, not completed/cancelled, pending/in final stages etc.

5. For example, road works, ports, airports, electromechanical works, environmental works and hydraulic works

6. Classification of the project is inferred by the grouping of tenders by the competent Directorates. The "other" category includes services of consultants, design/consultant projects, supervision services, and those works projects that are identified as services or legal services.

7. Other than joint ventures, and firms outside Greece.

8. For example, over half of the design projects procured by Egnatia (a public company procuring infrastructure projects) on the basis of the most advantageous offer in an open procedure resulted in a discount of exactly 20%.

9. We use the discount rate as calculated from the expected value of the tender and the value of the winning bid. The results are substantially the same when the discount reported in the original data is used instead.

10. With $\beta = 0.137$, the increase in *Discount* from a unit increase in the *Number of offers* is $e^{\beta} = 1.147$.

11. Note that this is the percentage increase in the level of discount and *not* the size of the increase itself.

12. The average discount of winning bids after an open procedure for works projects is 34.6%.

13. 35% x (100% + 14.7%) = 40%.

14. It is possible that tenders with a higher budget attract larger companies that are, on average, more efficient and benefit more from economies of scale. Those companies are consequently able to offer higher discounts. This suggests a correlation between higher budgets and higher discounts, partly explained by efficiencies related to firm size. However, the fact that larger firms are *able* to offer higher discounts does not necessarily give them an *incentive* to do so: such an incentive is provided by the level of competition for each tender, as indicated by the number of participating bidders.

15. The data is extracted from standard public-procurement forms filled in by contracting bodies.

16. Works, supplies and services.

17. For example, competitive dialogue, negotiated procedure, open and restricted.

18. Lowest price, or most economically advantageous tender.

19. Filtering done using CPV codes 45000000 (NACE code 45).

20. With $\beta = 0.030$, the increase in *Discount* from a unit increase in the *Number of offers* is $e^{\beta} = 1.030$. As explained in note 10 above, this is the percentage increase in the level of discount and *not* the size of the increase itself.

## Databases

Tender data provided by the Ministry of Infrastructure, Transport and Networks, Directorate General for Transport Infrastructure (Directorates for Road Infrastructure; Safety of Road Infrastructure; Port Infrastructure; Airport Infrastructure; Operation, Maintenance and Exploitation of Concession Infrastructures; Public Works – Construction and Maintenance of Transport Infrastructure; Public Works – Construction of Concession Works – Peloponnese and Northern Greece; Public Works – Construction of Concession Works – Central and Western Greece; Metro; Cretan Development Organisation; Egnatia) and Directorate General for Hydraulics and Building Infrastructure (Directorates for Water, Drainage and Waste Management; Flood Prevention and Land Improvement Works; Buildings Infrastructure; Public Works – Construction and Maintenance of Hydraulics Infrastructure).

TED csv dataset (2006-2015), Tenders Electronic Daily, supplement to the Official Journal of the European Union. DG Internal Market, Industry, Entrepreneurship, and SMEs, European Commission, Brussels, *https://open-data.europa.eu/cs/data/dataset/ted-csv*. Version 2.1 (accessed on 29 July 2016).

*Chapter 4*

# Media

*Particular regulatory barriers to competition in the media sector were identified in publishing activities, programme production, radio and pay-TV broadcasting activities. These are often created by the non-implementation of legislation that is both outdated and fragmented. For example, the most recent legal framework for radio licensing has been in force since 2007, yet the relevant tenders have never been issued. The legal framework should be codified and various obsolete provisions should be removed. Restrictions regarding years of previous operation or circulation for radio licences, and public subsidies for the printed press have also been addressed. Limitations to the selection of programme suppliers to pay-TV broadcasters, as well as outdated licensing procedures and costs, reduce incentives to invest and adopt new technologies. Finally, the production of audio-visual content only by producers fulfilling specific requirements constitutes a barrier to entry in the profession and to the development of independent audiovisual producers. The following recommendations should contribute to simplifying the business environment and increasing consumer choice.*

## 4.1. Definition and economic overview

Today, "information" or "information goods" encompass anything that can be digitised. This means that all types of printed, audio, visual or audiovisual content are considered to be information goods, and therefore part of the media sector. For these information goods to be supplied on a one-to-many basis, a distribution channel of some kind is needed, be it a book, newspaper, radio, television or the Internet. It is therefore generally possible to draw a distinction between the information good itself and its method of distribution.

However, many of the markets across the media sector have experienced, and continue to experience, rapid change. The main aspect of that change related to this project is the phenomenon of convergence, or the coming together of media, telecommunication and information technologies into unified platforms and networks.

For this reason, the relevant legislation for media covered in the project includes the following activities:

- **Publishing activities** (NACE 58): "This division includes the publishing of books, brochures, leaflets, dictionaries, encyclopaedias, atlases, maps and charts; publishing of newspapers, journals and periodicals; directory and mailing list and other publishing, as well as software publishing."[1]

- **Motion picture, video and television programme production, sound recording and music publishing activities** (NACE 59): "This division includes production of theatrical and non-theatrical motion pictures whether on film, video tape or disc for direct projection in theatres or for broadcasting on television; supporting activities such as film editing, cutting, dubbing etc.; distribution of motion pictures and other film productions to other industries; as well as motion picture or other film productions projection. Buying and selling of motion picture or other film productions distribution rights is also included."[2]

- **Programming and broadcasting activities** (NACE 60): "This division includes the activities of creating content or acquiring the right to distribute content and subsequently broadcasting that content, such as radio, television and data programs of entertainment, news, talk, and the like. Also included is data broadcasting, typically integrated with radio or TV broadcasting. The broadcasting can be performed using different technologies, over-the-air, via satellite, via a cable network or via Internet."[3]

- **Computer programming, consultancy and related activities** (NACE 62): "This division includes the following activities of providing expertise in the field of information technologies: writing, modifying, testing and supporting software; planning and designing computer systems that integrate computer hardware, software and communication technologies; on-site management and operation of clients' computer systems and/or data-processing facilities; and other professional and technical computer-related activities."[4]

- **Information service activities** (NACE 63): "This division includes the activities of web search portals, data processing and hosting activities, as well as other activities that primarily supply information."[5]

Media accounted for 1.1% of GDP in Greece in 2013, compared with a figure of 3.5% for the European Union on average. When measured in terms of employment, the sector represents 1.5% of the Greek economy, while the corresponding figure for the European Union is on average 2.1%. According to the latest data from Eurostat,[6] in 2013[7] the media sector in Greece had a total turnover of about EUR 3 billion, and 11,438 enterprises employing 51,126 people. Figure 4.1 shows data on the breakdown of turnover into each sub-sector .

Figure 4.1. **Contribution to media sector's total turnover – Greece**

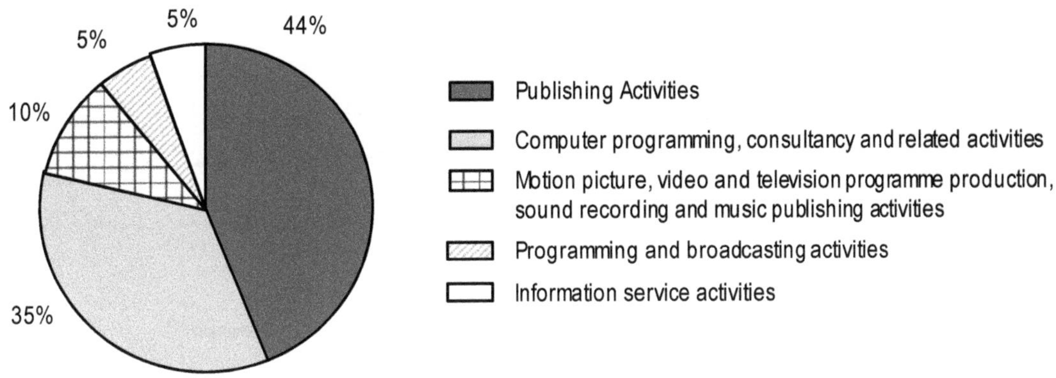


*Source*: Eurostat, Annual detailed enterprise statistics for services (NACE Rev. 2, H-N and S95), Database [sbs_na_1a_se_r2], *http://ec.europa.eu/eurostat* (accessed 4 April 2016).

Not all sub-sectors share the same importance in terms of turnover. Almost 80% of the total turnover is produced by publishing activities and computer programming, consultancy and related activities, while the remaining 20% is accounted for by the other three sub-sectors. While prominent in public discourse and heavily regulated,[8] programming and broadcasting activities only account for 5% of the media sector's total revenue.

The economic crisis since the 2008 financial crisis has undoubtedly had substantial effects on the sector. From 2008 to 2013, the number of active enterprises fell cumulatively by 10% in Greece. The relevant figures regarding employment and turnover are more striking: the former declined cumulatively by 33%, the latter by 49.5%. In other words, income in the media sector has been declining over the six-year period of 2008-2013 by 10.7% a year on average.

Since Eurostat data for 2014 are available only for the total number of persons employed, Figure 4.2 presents the breakdown of total employment across the five subsectors over the 2008-2014 period. The picture regarding the total number of enterprises and total turnover is quite similar.

The make-up of employment across the media sector largely mirrors that of revenue and has fallen in recent years (Figure 4.2)

Figure 4.2. **Breakdown of total employment in the media sector – Greece**

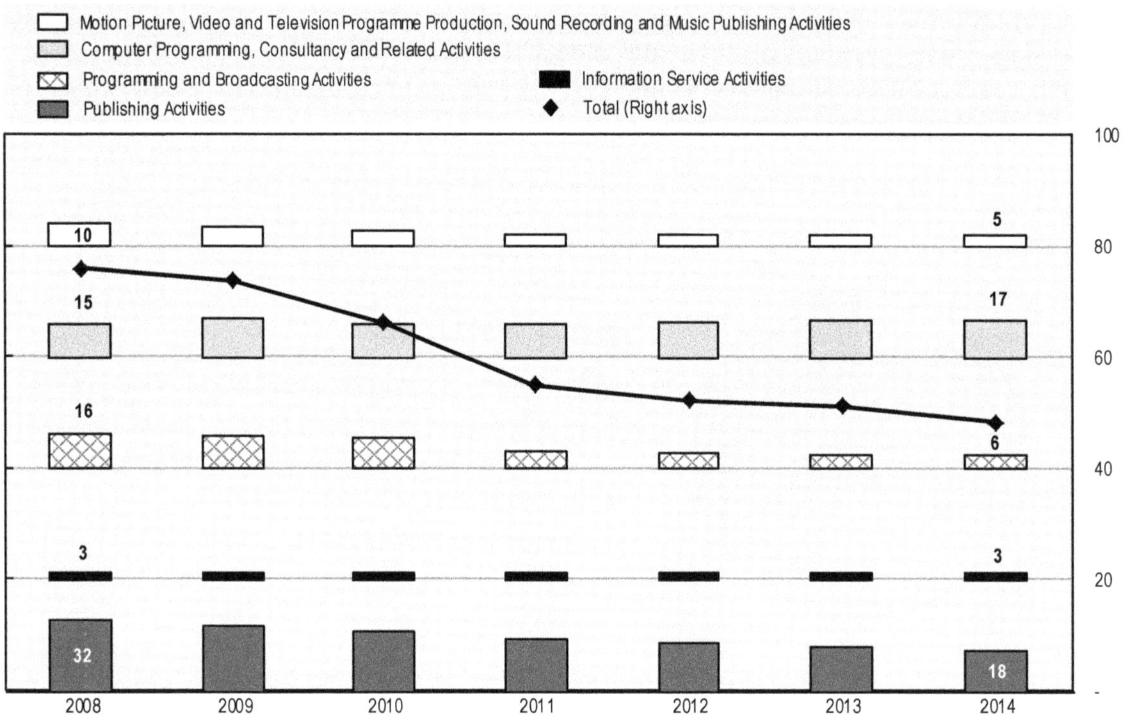


*Source*: Eurostat, Annual detailed enterprise statistics for services (NACE Rev. 2, H-N and S95), Database [sbs_na_1a_se_r2], *http://ec.europa.eu/eurostat* (accessed 4 April 2016).

The total number of persons employed in the five sub-sectors has declined by 37%. The largest decreases have taken place in programming and broadcasting (-64%) and publishing (-44%). On the other hand, the computer programming and consultancy, as well as information services have seen increases in employment by 8% and 6% respectively (over the same six-year period).

## 4.2. Overview of the legislation

Legislation mapping for the sector in Greece took in 251 laws and regulations. European Union (EU) legislation in this sector is limited and mainly concerns TV content, advertising and production.

Out of these 251 pieces of legislation, the following subcategories of legislation were identified.

- About 100 regulations deal with free-to-air TV and radio licensing, as well as pay TV/radio. This regulatory framework is extremely complex, fragmented and in some cases, outdated. Law 2328/1995[9] was the first law to set out the criteria for the tendering of the licensing procedure for free-to-air radio and TV broadcasters. However, it has been implemented only once, in relation to radio licensing in Attica. Law 3592/2007[10] on the licensing of media was promulgated without explicitly abolishing the provisions of Law 2328/1995. More recently, Law 4339/2015[11] regulating TV licensing came into force without having explicitly amended Law 3592/2007. Law 2644[12] regarding pay TV/radio came into force in 1995 and is still valid as slightly amended, although it clearly does not reflect the significant technological developments that have happened since 1995.

- With regard to publishing activities, many regulations have been identified that date back to the 1930s and 1940s, and that, although superseded and/or not enforced, were never explicitly abolished. The few applicable regulations in this subcategory concern state subsidies for the printed press.

- The mapping of legislation also includes laws and regulations on audiovisual productions, TV advertising and film-making. While TV advertising is mainly regulated by EU law transposed into the Greek legislation (Presidential Decree 109/2010[13]), the main laws for film-making and production of audiovisual works are Law 3905/2010[14] and Law 2328/1995 and stem from the national legislator.

- There are few regulations for computer programming, consultancy and related activities, mostly dealing with personal-data protection, domain names and copyright. The same applies in relation to information -service activities.

- Lastly, there are many administrative decisions by the National Council for Radio and Television (NCRTV) and the National Telecommunications and Post Commission (EETT), the competent regulatory authorities in the media sector, which interpret or implement in detail the relevant legislation.

## 4.3. Publishing activities

### ***Public announcements in Greek newspapers***

Greek newspapers publish public-interest publications/announcements paid by the state. There are specific criteria with which the newspapers should comply in order to be eligible for these publications/announcements.

More specifically, Article 2, Paragraph 1 of Law 3548/2007[15] provides that daily newspapers need to be published for at least two years and weekly newspapers need to be published for three years with the same title to be eligible to publish public announcements. Moreover, a minimum number of copies of the newspapers must be printed and sold per print: at least 500 copies for regions with populations of over 80 000 inhabitants; 350 copies a year for regions with populations under that figure. Other criteria, including that the eligible newspapers have sufficient and original content written by their journalists, also apply.

According to the official recital, the provisions are necessary to demonstrate that a newspaper is known to the public, as well as the sustainability of the company that publishes it, and its independence. The ultimate aim is the widest possible publicity for state-paid announcements and the widest possible distribution of information.

#### *Harm to competition*

Criteria for selecting which newspapers can publish public announcements should be implemented because not all newspapers can serve the policy objective. As mentioned, these requirements are necessary for achieving the biggest possible distribution of public announcements, as well as providing solid newspapers with financial support. Although the criteria on the minimum number of copies that need to be sold and on the minimum number of pages are restrictive, they are justified in light of the policy maker's objective of securing the widest possible publicity and transparency of state announcements. However, some criteria are harmful in terms of competition.

Restrictions on years of operation (two or three years) pose a direct barrier to entry by favouring incumbent businesses against new entrants. If new entrants can issue and sell the number of copies of the newspapers required by the law, as well as fulfil the other requirements, there is no sufficient justification for excluding them from this indirect subsidy.[16] A time period over which the minimum number of copies printed and sold is calculated should be introduced, however, to avoid cases of newspapers that reach the minimum number of copies only for a couple of days or one month. Given that the decision regarding which newspapers are eligible for publish public announcements is issued once a year, the minimum number of copies required by the law can be calculated on the basis of the previous year or the previous six months.

*Recommendation*

The requirement for previous years of circulation (two years for daily newspapers and three years for weekly newspapers) should be abolished. Instead of this requirement, the necessary time for calculating the minimum number of printed and sold copies should be provided, a period that could range from six months to one-year maximum.

***Preferential postal rates***

As in other European countries, Greek newspapers receive indirect public support due to the public-interest value of information. Subsidies to newspapers, from reduced telecommunication tariffs and air-transport charges, were abolished in Greece in 2011,[17] but preferential postal rates still act as indirect subsidies.

Press -subsidy schemes exist across Europe, most frequently taking the form of tax breaks. For example, in Belgium, Denmark, Norway and the UK, newspaper sales are completely exempt from VAT.[18] An example of increased indirect and direct newspaper support is France. In 2009, the total budget for subsidies for the private press was increased by EUR 600 million. Specifically, EUR 70 million were set aside to fund home delivery.[19]

As a result of new eligibility criteria in Joint Ministerial Decision 16682/2011,[20] public funding for special postal rates for the printed press (both newspapers and magazines) has dramatically decreased, as shown in Table 4.1.

Table 4.1. **Public aid to the Greek press, 2009-2012 (€ million)**

| Year | Postage | Telephones | Air transport in Greece | Air transport outside Greece |
|---|---|---|---|---|
| **2009** | 32.7 | 0.77 | 5.48 | 0.62 |
| **2010** | 27.8 | 0.65 | 5.95 | 0.47 |
| **2011** | 16.9 | 0.31 | 1.79 | 0.16 |
| **2012** | 5.7 (estimate) | Abolished | Abolished | Abolished |

*Sources*: Secretariat-General of Mass Media; Papathanassopoulos, 2014b

According to the aforementioned Joint Ministerial Decision 16682/2011, special postal rates apply only for the distribution of Greek printed press in Greece and only for newspapers issued at least once a month and magazines issued at least every three months.

Apart from the aforementioned prerequisites, newspapers or magazines must also meet at least one of the following criteria:

- they are eligible and selected for state announcements;
- their owners are members of the Hellenic Union of Editors of Periodical Press (HUEPP); or
- their owners are qualified to be members of the Union, but have not registered while at the same time they 1) exercise the profession of editor; 2) have the status of journalist; and 3) their newspapers[21] and/or magazines have been on the market for at least two years.

The official recital states that the criteria are necessary for excluding advertising brochures or other commercial documents from taking advantage of the special postal pricing. Setting specific and strict criteria is considered the only way to stop the distortions that occurred prior to the amendment of the Joint Ministerial Decision. In the OECD's understanding, preferential postal rates constitute indirect and steady public support to the printed press, which is struggling to compete with newer media outlets, such as TV/radio broadcasting and Internet, in terms of revenue and popularity. The fact that advertising revenues are increasingly absorbed by Internet platforms, such as social networks or sharing economy databases, has an even greater impact on newspapers.[22]

*Harm to competition*

Although the minimum frequency of circulation of the newspapers and magazines could be characterised as restrictive, it is justified in light of the policy maker's objective to financially support indirectly the printed press with a regular and serious presence in the market.

However, the compulsory direct link of the preferential postal rate to the membership or the potential membership of the owners to a particular professional union; the practice of specific professions (editor *and* journalist) by the owner; and the minimum two-year presence of their newspapers/magazines in the market, all pose a direct barrier to entry not only to new entrants that have not yet been in the market for two years, but also to printed-press owners who do not want to or who cannot join the specific union stated in the law. It should be noted that there are also other unions for printed-press owners[23] whose members do not have the privilege of preferential postal rates.

Moreover, as was mentioned, the criterion of years of previous circulation excludes newspapers and/or magazines issued by viable and successful companies simply because they have been in the market for less than two years. Finally, the requirement for the owner to be an editor and journalist prohibits other professionals from running print-media businesses, even if they could secure the minimum quality of their newspaper/magazine by employing professional editors and journalists.

*Recommendation*

OECD recommends abolishing the requirements regarding an owner of a newspaper/magazine's membership or potential membership of the Hellenic Union of Editors of Periodical Press; the number of years of prior circulation before becoming eligible for preferential postal rates; and the compulsory requirement that the owner of a newspaper also be an editor and journalist.

***Ownership Rules***

According to Article 13, paragraphs 10 and 11 of Law 2328/1995 strict ownership rules apply to newspapers. The provisions lay down that any person (legal entity or individual) can own, participate or hold stocks in a company that owns or controls in any way or participates in another company that owns or controls: 1) up to two daily news newspapers, published in Athens or Piraeus or Thessaloniki, distributed through press distribution agencies, one of which is published in the morning and the other in the afternoon; 2) up to one daily financial newspaper and up to one daily sports newspaper published in Athens, Piraeus or Thessaloniki; 3) up to two daily regional newspapers, but in different prefectures; 4) up to two not -daily regional newspapers, but in different prefectures; and 5) only one Sunday edition of a daily newspaper either with the same or similar title or as an independent newspaper (news or financial or sports).

The same restrictions apply also for the spouse and the relatives up to fourth degree of any individual who has any of the capacities mentioned above as long as they do not have and they do not prove that they are independent from a financial or business point of view. It should be noted that restrictions regarding relatives' ownership apply also for TV and radio (Law 3592/2007), but applies only to relatives up to third degree. The competent authority to supervise the implementation of the above rule is the National Council for Radio and Television (NCRTV).

These ownership restrictions regarding newspapers are still included in Law 2328/1995, in which TV and radio ownership rules also used to be included. Article 5 of Law 3592/2007 inserted new, less restrictive rules, regarding rules for TV and radio ownership and these are now in force. Yet those found in Law 2328/1995 have not been explicitly abolished. Following the legal principle that a newer law takes precedence over an older one, Article 5 of Law 3592/2007 should be applicable. However, the fact that Article 5 includes neither specific provisions regarding ownership rules for newspapers nor any provision explicitly abolishing Article13, paragraphs 10 and 11 of Law 2328/1995 creates legal uncertainty about whether the restrictions on newspaper ownership are still in force or not. In a 2011 study,[24] it is noted that press ownership restrictions have been abolished and that the authority charged with implementing them (NCRTV) has not contested them. Yet the Secretariat General for Information and Communication states that the provisions are in force.

Ownership restrictions on the number of newspapers aim to enhance and protect media pluralism and transparency. In principle, media plurality has an important contribution to make to a well-functioning democratic society, ensuring the diversity of viewpoints that are available and consumed. The restrictions on spouses and relatives aim to prevent existing players from controlling the market and threatening pluralism through the use of surrogates or family members as nominal owners.

It should be noted, that there are no Europe-wide media ownership rules. In the early 1990s the European Commission tried to assess whether extensive concentration could damage media pluralism. In the Green Paper (EC, 1992)[25] the European Commission stated that the safeguard of pluralism falls under the member states' competencies and that they should design the national ownership rules. The Commission's role is limited to protecting the proper functioning of the internal market.[26]

Nevertheless, a 2007 European Commission Staff Working Document[27] regarding regulations of media ownership, shows that no other member states, except Greece, apply a priori specific ownership restriction rules on print media. In other words, the regulatory frameworks of other member states do not include rules providing the specific number of printed -media outlets that an investor or his/her spouse or relatives can own or participate in without combining these rules with others.

More specifically, to ensure that the media operates in the public interest by promoting plurality and preventing undue influence by any media owner, other member states' rules require a case-by-case examination of the country's market conditions, and especially the power of influence of each newspaper and its circulation. More specifically, relevant rules (for instance, in Italy,[28] France,[29] Ireland,[30] the Netherlands,[31] Poland,[32] Slovenia,[33] and United Kingdom[34]) call the competent authorities to test the real impact of multiple ownerships on the market at the moment of the circulation of the new newspaper and/or whether this results in distortion of competition in the market and in harm to plurality. In other words, relevant rules restrict media concentration in a particular market and aim to hinder the creation of an enormous opinion-forming power.

Similar rules about media concentration based on market share that corresponds to 12-month total advertisement expenses, as well as to sales revenues are also in force for newspapers in Greece and are included in Article 3 of Law 3592/2007. The Hellenic Competition Commission (HCC), the competent authority to oversee the rules, acts independently of NCRTV, which is in charge only of the implementation of ownership rules. Any potential investor who wants to enter the media market must comply with both ownership and media -concentration rules.

*Harm to competition*

There is legal uncertainty as to whether the provisions of Law 2328/1995 are obsolete or not. While the majority of ownership and concentration rules regarding the media market are included in Law 3592/1997, restrictions on ownership of newspapers are found also in Law 2328/1995, as well as several provisions that are obsolete or not in force. This difficulty in identifying the applicable law means potential entrants to the printed-press market face legal and compliance costs and business uncertainty.

Similarly, the compulsory use of the press distribution agencies for the distribution of newspapers has been abolished.[35] Reference to press distribution agencies may therefore cause further legal uncertainty and related costs for clarifying its validity.

It is not clear if Article 13, paragraph 10 of Law 2328/1995 concerning the core ownership rule has a net negative or a net positive effect on competition in the newspaper market. On the one hand, investment choices of potential investors are limited by particular restrictions to the number and type of newspaper ownership. On the other hand, the provisions on ownership rules may prevent *a priori* situations of over-concentration in the market. The objective of freedom of entrepreneurship, however, should be counterbalanced by the objective of pluralism.

It should be taken into account that the implementation of both a priori ownership and media-concentration rules by both NCRTV and HCC, acting in parallel and independently, creates extra cost for potential investors.

Finally, regarding the restrictions on spouses and relatives (Article 13, paragraph 11 of Law 2328/1995), the competent authorities admit that although this rule targets problematic cases in terms of pluralism and transparency, it cannot be efficiently enforced because there are no specific criteria to define “financial and business independency”. The lack of specific criteria that act as the basis upon which a competent authority and/or the Court can issue decisions, the wide discretion given to authorities, as well as the lack of significant case law on this issue,[36] all result in legal uncertainty. They also constitute a barrier to entry for potential investors who wish to invest in a particular market, but are relatives of an already operating player.

*Recommendations*

Streamline the provisions of Article 13, paragraphs 10 and 11 of Law 2328/1995 and Articles 3 and 5 of Law 3592/2007. As part of this exercise, the correlation between a priori newspaper ownership restrictions in Law 2328/1995 and the media concentration rules of Article 3 of Law 3592/2007 should be reviewed with the objective of seeing if they can be combined and so focus more on the real impact of newspaper acquisition in the market and in the shaping of public opinion (i.e. apply criteria such as market share, daily circulation, share of newspaper supply in the market).

Specific criteria for the proof of financial and business independency of spouses and relatives before the competent administrative authorities and the courts should be provided.

References to press distribution agencies should be abolished.

## 4.4. Audiovisual production and content

***Limits to the outsourcing of TV-programme production***

Apart from ownership of media enterprises, media content and its production also affect the plurality in media.[37]

Article 1, paragraph 12 of Law 2328/1995 stipulates that licensed TV broadcasters have to manage and run TV broadcasting businesses themselves. Article 10 of the same law allows broadcasters to outsource the production of specific programming to independent producers of audiovisual works up to a level of 30%.

Article 11, paragraph 5 of Law 3592/2007, however, reiterates that both TV and radio broadcasters should operate the channel themselves, but that they can outsource the production of their programming to companies within the same group, as well as assign the production of specific programmes to production companies or the production of "specific broadcasts (emissions)" to independent producers. In this provision, there is no reference to a specific percentage of programming that can be outsourced. Yet Article 1, paragraph 12 of Law 2328/1995 has never been explicitly abolished.

Recently, Article 14, paragraph 4 of Law 4339/2015 provided that content providers (TV broadcasters) cannot assign the management or the use of their programmes or of their company to third parties. However, they can outsource the production of their programming to companies that belong to the same group. The outsourcing of the production of specific programming to production companies and of the production of "specific broadcasts (emissions)" to independent producers is also permitted.

It appears that all these provisions aim to forbid cases where the licensed TV broadcasters serve as nominal owners and in practice all ownership and concentration rules are contravened by using others to control the programming and content broadcast. These provisions can therefore be seen as aiming to enhance pluralism and transparency.

Nevertheless, the overlapping provisions result in legal uncertainty on the crucial issue of whether TV programmes may be outsourced, to whom, and up to what percentage of programming.

*Harm to competition*

Overlapping and partially conflicting provisions – namely Article 1, paragraph 12 of Law 2328/1995, Article 11, paragraph 5 of Law 3592/2007, and Article 14, paragraph 4 of Law 4339/2015 imposing restrictions on TV broadcasters outsourcing their programming – create legal uncertainty and confusion that may increase compliance and operating costs for TV broadcasters.

Extra costs and limitations on the ability of TV broadcasters to choose their suppliers may also be caused by the fact that the terms "programme" and "specific broadcasts (emissions)" used in the provisions have not been clarified. Similarly, the difference between production companies and independent producers has not been clarified. Rules, such as the fact that specific programmes can be assigned to production companies and specific broadcasts (emissions) to independent producers, result in restrictions on TV broadcasters' choices that are not clear and could also create barriers to entry in the market of audiovisual content production.

Once again, a balance needs to be found. On the one hand, restrictions on the sources of programming limit the freedom of TV broadcasters to outsource their programming according to their choices and business plan, and so limit their ability to invest their money in what they consider the most efficient way. On the other hand, the objective of protecting pluralism and transparency could counterbalance such restrictions, a position that becomes more obvious in cases such as news production.[38]

Finally, the requirement of broadcasters to outsource a minimum of 10% of their transmission time to independent audiovisual producers, as provided in the relevant Audiovisual Media Services Directive (AVMS Directive, 2010/13/EU)[39] and in the Greek legislation of Article 18 of Presidential Decree 109/2010[40] that transposed it, should also be taken into account (also see next paragraph "Independent producers of audiovisual works").

*Recommendations*

Consolidate and streamline rules of Article 1, paragraph 12 of Law 2328/1995, Article 11, paragraph 5 of Law 3592/2007 and Article 14, paragraph 4 of Law 4339/2015, while defining which programming can be freely outsourced and to whom; any restrictions should be maintained only on the grounds of pluralism and transparency, and the requirements of EU law, notably the AVMS Directive.

***Independent producers of audiovisual works***

Directive 89/552/EEC[41] – the "Television without Frontiers" directive – promoted the compulsory proportion of broadcasts for independent production in Europe. Although, the Directive did not contain a definition of independent producer, Recital 31 of its revised version in 1997 states that the definition should take account of criteria such as "the ownership of the production company, the amount of programming supplied to the same broadcaster and the ownership of secondary rights". Therefore, it was left to member states to define what was meant by "independent producer".[42]

This Directive was transposed into Greek legislation by Presidential Decree 100/2000[43] in which independent producers were defined as producers independent of broadcasters, as they are defined in Article 10 of Law 2328/1995.

The AVMS Directive that replaced the "Television without Frontiers" directive also has no definition of an independent producer. Only Recital 71 states that, "When defining 'producers who are independent of broadcasters' as referred to in Article 17, Member States should take appropriate account notably of criteria such as the ownership of the production company, the amount of programming supplied to the same broadcaster and the ownership of secondary rights".[44]

Presidential Decree 109/2010 transposed the new Directive into Greek legislation. Article 18 of that decree does not repeat that the independent producer is the same as defined in Article 10 of Law 2328/1995 and given that the relevant provision of Presidential Decree 100/2000 has been abolished, the term independent producer is now only defined in Article 10 of Law 2328/1995 under "Independent Producers of Audiovisual Works".

More specifically, paragraph 1 of that article stipulates that independent producers of audiovisual works have the exclusive right to sign contracts between intellectual-property rights (IPR) holders and

TV broadcasters, advertising companies, cinema companies or other relevant companies for the production of films, advertisements or audiovisual works longer than two minutes.

In addition, according to paragraph 2 of that article, the definition of independent producer is also linked to the definition of the producer of audiovisual works in Law 2121/1993[45] on Intellectual Property Rights. Article 47, paragraph 2(b) of Law 2121/1993[46] stipulates that the producer of audiovisual works is any natural or legal person who initiates and is responsible for the realisation of a first fixation of a series of images with or without sound. This definition is further broadened with a phrase in paragraph 2 of Article 10 of Law 2328/1995, which states that the independent producer prepares and realises audiovisual works, takes care of the supply of all essential means of production, undertakes the responsibility of technical and financial issues that are linked with the production, signs all the contracts and makes all the agreements with regards to the production. An extremely wide range of professional and economic activities are therefore defined as “producers of audiovisual works”, particularly, as the title of the relevant article suggests, as “independent producers”. Furthermore, paragraph 3 of Article 10 stipulates that independent audiovisual producers must register and pay the relevant fees before the relevant professional chamber.

Paragraph 3 of Article 10 also provides for specific and strict criteria that a person must fulfil in order to be accepted for registration. These qualifications include among others, relevant academic titles, any criminal record, a certificate of non-bankruptcy, previous experience of at least two consecutive years or three years in total as an independent producer or as employee of a production company, and having worked on the production of at least one feature film or eight TV programmes of a specific duration, or similar productions as evaluated by a committee convened by the Minister in Charge of Media and Press Issues.

Paragraph 4 of Article 10 provides that the producer of audiovisual works or the person who is a shareholder in a production company or a member of a production company’s governing body cannot be a public servant or have any contractual relation to the public sector as widely defined in Greek law or be an owner, shareholder or member of the governing body or employee of an advertising company. It has not been possible to identify the objective of this provision.

Audiovisual production companies should be signed up to a special section of the professional registry, according to Article 10, paragraph 5 of Law 2328/1995. Also, the unlimited liability partner/manager of personal-liability production companies, the manager of limited-liability audiovisual production companies (ΕΠΕ) who signs audiovisual production agreements on behalf of the company, and the CEO of société anonyme (SA) audiovisual production companies, should be also registered with the professional chamber and fulfil the relevant requirements. Moreover, the shares of audiovisual production companies with the structure of an SA should be registered (Article 10, paragraph 5(c), Law 2328/1995).

According to the official recital of Law 2328/1995, these provisions aim to protect the existence of the profession of the producer of audiovisual works and therefore promote the interests of those who fulfil the qualifications necessary to belong to the profession.

*Harm to competition*

Article 10, paragraphs 1 and 2, of Law 2328/1995 does not define independent audiovisual producer on the basis of criteria related to the ownership of the production company and the broadcasters or the amount of programming supplied to the same broadcasters (see Recital 71 of the AVMS Directive), but on the basis of specific tasks and activities they undertake. This creates legal uncertainty regarding the definition of independent audiovisual producer, which is crucial also for the application of rules relating to restrictions facing broadcasters in outsourcing TV programmes.

Article 10, paragraph 1 of the same law provides for the exclusive competence of independent audiovisual producers, as restrictively defined, to act as intermediaries between the IPR holders and any organisations concluding contracts related to the production of audiovisual works (broadcasters, film or advertising companies and any other organisation/company of the public or private sector). This compulsory intermediation restricts competition at various levels. It also limits IPR holders' chances of finding potential investors themselves, as well as deciding on the terms and conditions of use, development and production of their works.

Paragraphs 3, 4 and 5 of Article 10 limit competition in the market of audiovisual productions by creating entry barriers to the profession of producers of audiovisual works and the economic activity of audiovisual productions and as a result hamper innovation and the development of new content. Barriers include registration before the relevant professional chamber, fulfilment of strict requirements and a submission of numerous supportive documents that limit the access to the profession and economic activity without sufficient justification for the necessity of such restrictions. These restrict the chances for new talented creators who wish to enter the market as individuals. Indeed, as the Greek Council of State stated in Decision 1667/2012, recital 7, registration with a professional chamber cannot be compulsory for prominent professionals who exercise tasks of a scientific or artistic nature.[47]

The prohibition on audiovisual producers or members, shareholders or managers of audiovisual production companies owning, participating or working for an advertising company (in Article 10, paragraph 4 of Law 2328/1995) is considered as another unjustified restriction to entry to the profession. While it might be argued that such a restriction is put forth in order to prevent vertical integration between advertising and audiovisual production companies, there is no real justification for stricter regulations of this particular market than for other sectors of the economy, which are regulated by the general laws of competition.

Regarding the restriction on audiovisual production companies and their producers, members, shareholders or managers being employed under whatever contractual relation with the public administration and the wider public sector, as defined by the Greek law, we note that the relevant provisions of the Code of Public Servants constitute the prominent legal framework for the employment status of public servants. According to Article 31 of Law 3528/2007 ratifying the Code of Conduct for Public Administrative Employees,[48] public servants can exercise private remunerated activities as long as a special committee confirms that there is no conflict with their activities in the administration. Applying stricter rules for audiovisual production activity creates an unnecessary barrier to entry in the market.

Finally, obliging SA audiovisual production companies to register their shares may further increase administrative costs and hinder entry in the market. However, it can be characterised as proportionate to the wider objective of transparency in the media sector without being particularly harmful to competition.

*Recommendations*

Define the term "independent producer" of audiovisual works in line with the AVMS Directive on the basis of criteria related to the ownership of the production company, as well as the amount of programming supplied to the same broadcasters. Any restrictions, such as the compulsory registration of company's shares, provided in Article 10, paragraph 5(c) of Law 2328/1995 should be treated within the said definition.

Abolish the provision of Article 10, paragraph 1 of Law 2328/1995.

Abolish compulsory registration for audiovisual producers, audiovisual production companies and their members, shareholders and/or managers with a professional chamber in order to exercise the relevant profession or activity.[49]

The ban on audiovisual producers participating in advertising and/or being employed in the public sector, as set out in Article 10, paragraph 4 of Law 2328/1995, should be explicitly abolished. Any eventual conflicts of interest may be treated within existing regulations such as Article 31 of the Code of Conduct for Public Administrative Employees.

***Broadcasters' obligation to invest in cinema production***

According to Article 8 of Law 3905/2010, both public and private television broadcasters have an obligation to invest in the production of Greek cinematographic films as defined in Article 3[50] of the same law.

Public broadcaster ERT is obliged to invest 1.5% of its annual revenue in cinema production. Similarly, private free-to-air TV broadcasters have the legal obligation to invest 1.5% of their annual advertisement income in cinema production. Lastly, pay-TV broadcasters, as well as providers of IPTV and VOD, now have the legal obligation to invest 1.5% of their annual total revenue in film production.

According to the same provisions of Article 8 of Law 3905/2010, ERT and free-to-air private TV broadcasters may legally substitute half of this financial investment with "in-kind" investment in the promotion of Greek films. Pay -TV broadcasters, as well IPTV and VOD, are not provided with this alternative. (Pay TV with advertising time available was given this option until the end of 2014, in accordance with the same provisions.) More specifically, free-to-air public and private TV broadcasters may reduce by half their obligation for direct financial investment in film production by granting to the Hellenic Film Centre free advertising time for the advertisement and promotion of cinematographic works of a total value that equals half of the amount they are obliged to invest in production.

Non-compliance with these provisions entails the imposition of an administrative fine equalling the amount that should have been invested. The fine must be paid to the Ministry of Culture and is ultimately passed to the Greek Film Centre by the ministry, essentially becoming a third-party levy.

According to the official recital, this provision aims to support Greek cinema production, which is considered to be an important cultural asset. In addition, private funding for film production stemming from big companies will be increased and different sources of funding will be used, contributing to pluralism.

*Harm to competition*

Enforcement of the above legal obligations has not been consistent in the case of public broadcasters and very limited in the case of private TV broadcasters who have refused to pay owed amounts and repeatedly challenged the provisions.[51] On the other hand, pay-TV broadcasters have regularly invested significant amounts in the production of Greek films.

From a competition-assessment point of view, the amount due to be paid (which turns into a levy if not invested in cinema production in any given year) is a significant cost for broadcasters. It may distort the audiovisual market against TV broadcasters and in favour of film producers by violating the freedom of the former to choose how to invest and distribute their resources.

However, the objectives of the provision regarding the support of Greek film and the promotion of Greek culture are important and justify the harm caused to TV broadcasters. The support of film production is a common policy in almost all EU countries,[52] despite there being no EU regulation that imposes the obligation to support film production. Countries with mandatory investment in film production by TV broadcasters include Belgium, Spain, France and Italy. It should be mentioned that these mandatory obligation on linear and non-linear services are national and apply only on services that originates in the given country.[53]

The "in-kind" investment given to public and private free-to-air broadcasters for the promotion of Greek films, which takes the form of granting free airtime to the Hellenic Film Centre for the advertisement and promotion of Greek films, as implemented after 2015, is discriminatory against pay-TV broadcasters as it increases their costs and limits their investment choices. Moreover, in an era of financial crisis, given the extreme circumstances that companies face in managing their cash flows, this alternative should apply to all TV broadcasters, particularly in the face of difficulties not only in collecting the money due for direct investment in film production, but also in finding productions in which they can profitably invest. More flexible methods for complying with the legal requirement of compulsory investment in film production should therefore be implemented.

In addition, the equal treatment between free-to-air TV broadcasters and pay-TV broadcasters requires that they are both obliged to invest according to their financial standing. Yet the amounts due are calculated differently between free-to-air and pay-TV broadcasters. For the former, the calculation is based upon their advertising revenues (an amount equal or less than their total gross revenues), while for the latter, it is based on total gross revenues. This discrepancy between the two amounts can lead to increased costs for pay-TV providers, while their free-to-air counterparts are left with more resources to allocate to investments of their choice. In order to keep a level playing field for all businesses in the sector the calculation of the amount due should be based upon the same criteria, whether this is total gross revenue, net revenue or any other amount directly comparable between the two different business models.

*Recommendations*

The OECD has no recommendation on the obligation to invest in film production.

The OECD recommends that pay-TV broadcasters also be allowed to opt to grant the Hellenic Film Centre free airtime for the advertisement and promotion of works of a total value that equals half the amount they are obliged to invest in the production of Greek films, thus reducing by half their obligation to invest directly in film production, similar to free-to-air TV broadcasters. Also, that both pay-TV broadcasters and free-to-air TV broadcasters' film-investment contributions be calculated on the same basis according to their financial standing.

***Presumption regarding the competences of collecting societies (IPR law)***

According to Article 55, paragraph 2 of Law 2121/1993, copyright -collecting societies[54] are presumed to have the competence to administer and/or protect the rights in all works or in respect of all authors about which or whom a written declaration of transfer to the society has been effected, or for which it has been granted power of attorney. In particular, where a collecting society exercises the specific right to a single equitable remuneration as described in Article 49, Paragraph 1 of the same law,[55] it is presumed that such a collecting society represents without exception all beneficiaries, both national and foreign, and all their works (independently of any written declaration effected by the collecting society concerning the rights holders and/or the works represented by the latter). In such a case, the same is presumed where, for each category of beneficiaries there are more collecting societies, given that the rights are exercised by the competent collecting societies altogether (as added with article 46 of Law 3905/2010). Regardless of whether its authorisation rests on a transfer of rights or on power of attorney, a collecting society shall in all circumstances be entitled to initiate judicial or extrajudicial action in its own name and to exercise in full legitimacy all the rights transferred to it, or for which it holds power of attorney.

It is our understanding that this provision aims 1) to facilitate the protection of beneficiaries, their rights and the collection of royalties through collecting societies, and 2) to further facilitate the specific right of collection of equitable remuneration provided in Article 49 of Law 2121/1993. It further helps collecting societies representing various categories of rights to exercise in common their rights and negotiate together with users/radio-TV broadcasters about the determination and the collection of remuneration.

Moreover, while collecting societies need a written declaration of transfer of rights to them in order to be presumed to have the competence to administer and/or protect the relevant rights holders and works, there is no such requirement regarding collecting societies collecting equitable remuneration. For the latter, it shall be presumed that the relevant collecting society represents without exception all beneficiaries and all their works without any written declaration needed.

In the same context, Article 55, Paragraph 4 of Law 2121/1993, as amended by Article 46 of Law 3905/2010 regarding the liability of collecting societies, states: "If a rights holder disputes a collecting society's competence over a work which is assumed to be included under the declaration referred to in paragraph (2)[56] and which has, accordingly, on the basis of that declaration, been included in a contract concluded by the collecting society with a user, the collecting society shall defend the case of the user and offer all possible assistance in any court action which may follow. If the collecting society is adjudged not to have competence over the work, it shall, in addition to any penalty imposed upon it, be liable for the payment of compensation to the user with which it signed the contract, the amount of which shall be determined pursuant to the special safeguarding measures." This does not apply for the collection of equitable remuneration.

*Harm to competition*

The provisions have resulted in legal uncertainty, including conflicting case-law,[57] on whether users (including radio and TV broadcasters) should pay equitable remuneration in respect of audio, visual and/or audiovisual works of rights holders who are not members of collecting societies and who do not wish to receive fees from them; and whether the presumption provided in Article 55, paragraph 2.2 is rebuttable or non-rebuttable for users and rights holders given that it is presumed that the relevant collecting society represents without exception all beneficiaries and all their works without any written declaration needed.

The legal uncertainty regarding the fees users (including radio and TV broadcasters) have to pay to collective societies creates disincentives to enter the market and freely choose works to broadcast. In other words, given that the provision states that the collecting society represents without exception all beneficiaries and all their works, but that there is uncertainty whether this is a rebuttable presumption or not, users who choose to broadcast works not represented by the collecting society do not know whether they have to pay equitable remuneration and whether they can prove that they have not .

In addition, it should be taken into consideration that the costs for users increase further if they have to prove that they are not obliged to pay the collecting society. The only way to defend themselves is to go before the courts, and relevant court proceedings in Greece are extremely time-consuming and costly.

*Recommendations*

It should be clarified either in the law or in a circular that the legal presumption of Article 55, paragraph 2.2 of Law 2121/1993 is rebuttable, so that users who opt to broadcast specific works that are not represented by collecting societies (i.e. their rights holders do not wish to receive the equitable remuneration) are not obliged to pay the relevant fees to collecting societies.

An independent alternative dispute-resolution mechanism could be established (see also the option provided by Article 34 of Directive 2014/26/EU[58]) to give users, collecting societies and rights holders the option to settle their disputes in a less time-consuming and costly manner than the courts.

## 4.5. Free-to-air media

***Ownership/ cross-ownership rules***

The important role that the media play in shaping public opinion serves as a basis for special regulations that aim to secure media pluralism (the presence of a number of different and independent voices) and diversity (the presence of different political opinions and representations of culture). Under Article 10 of the European Convention on Human Rights[59], states should take all measures, including restrictions or penalties, necessary in a democratic society to ensure freedom of expression and freedom to hold opinions.[60] Therefore, merger and acquisition activity can give power to media outlets and thus may endanger media pluralism.[61]

In Greece, Law 1866/1989[62] abolished the state monopoly in the television sector by allowing the operation of private TV stations. [63] It attempted to limit concentration of media ownership, providing that shareholding in television companies could not exceed 25% of the company's capital. Law 2328/1995 introduced more restrictive rules, prohibiting participation in more than two different categories of media (press, radio, TV). The "two out of three" model was supplemented by provisions precluding ownership of more than one TV and radio station and press-ownership restrictions. Shareholding in a television enterprise was kept to a maximum of 25% of the company's capital and a similar ceiling was introduced for foreign ownership in electronic media. However, despite of the enactment of a strict regulatory framework, concentration of media ownership occurred.[64]

In the Greek state's latest attempt to create a less restrictive regulatory approach to both media ownership (Article 5) and media concentration (Article 3) is Law 3592/2007, a potential investor should comply with both set of rules (Article 5, paragraph 9) in order to enter the media market. NCRTV is the competent authority for supervising compliance with ownership and cross-ownership restrictions, while HCC is competent for the compliance with concentration rules.

The provisions regarding ownership rules are included in Article 5 of Law 3592/2007. According to paragraph 1, the control of more than one electronic media of the same type (TV and radio) is prohibited. According to paragraph 3 of Article 5, control is the exercise of substantive influence over media management and operation. Being the owner, executive director, manager or member of the board of directors in more than one electronic media automatically denotes control. This is also the case with partners and shareholders who hold at least 1% of the capital of more than one electronic media and figure among the 10 most important partners or shareholders of the media concerned in terms of shares or voting rights; or who enjoy the right to appoint at least one member of the board of directors of the media involved. Media control can also be established via "intermediaries" (i.e. spouses and relatives up to third degree), provided that "unfair influence", determined by a final judicial decision, is exercised over media management to the detriment of pluralism and competition. This rule applies only for spouses or relatives of individuals with Greek nationality as long as they are shareholders of companies not registered in stock markets in EU and OECD member states.

Paragraph 2 permits sole ownership up to 100% of a licensed TV and of a licensed radio broadcaster of informative content.[65] Paragraph 6(a) also allows participation (shareholding) in an electronic media of the same type of informative content unless control, as defined above, is established.

Paragraph 6(b) limits participation in media enterprises of non-informative content to:

- one TV broadcaster of non-informative content (national or regional) and one (national or regional) of informative content or two of non-informative content (national or regional);
- 15% of the total number of radio licences of non-informative content (regional) and a maximum of three radio broadcasters in total.

Media concentration rules in Article 3 of Law 3592/2007 insert special provisions regarding the concentration of informative-content media so as to control the impact on media diversity. For media of non-informative content (paragraphs 1 and 2), the general competition rules set out in Law 3959/2011 apply. To avoid the creation of dominant positions of media of informative content, the Greek legislator has established specific "dominance thresholds", ranging from 25% to 35%, depending on the number of the media markets under examination.[66]

However, according to Article 5, paragraph 10 of Law 3592/2007, these restrictions on the participation (shareholding) in TV and radio broadcasters of informative and non-informative content, as defined in paragraph 6 of Article 5,[67] and the concentration thresholds of Article 3 with which the potential investor should comply, apply for owners, shareholders, managers or members of the board of directors of companies that operate in Greece under the condition that these companies are not registered in stock markets of EU or OECD member states.

Finally, paragraph 14 of Article 5 stipulates that all restrictions regarding media ownership rules apply only for natural or legal entities that own or participate in media enterprises in Greece and only for their domestic business activity.

As mentioned above, the overall objective of these provisions is to protect pluralism and diversity of opinion in the media, as well as to enhance transparency and competition among media enterprises. It was not possible to identify the specific objective of each one of the provisions described above.

*Harm to competition*

The state's aims are to accommodate economic competition, the freedom of doing business and economic efficiency in general, while at the same time fortifying pluralism by promoting transparency in the ownership of media enterprises. So while this may limit potential investors' investment choices, it prevents situations of over-concentration and allows the objective of pluralism, diversity and transparency to be achieved.

It might still be argued that the cut-off point of ownership of 1% of the capital of a media enterprise in paragraph 3 of Article 5 is too strict for investors to exercise real control over a particular media company. And assessing control in this way is certainly not common practice in other sectors of the economy, where more conventional criteria (such as shareholder majority) are followed.

 

As discussed, paragraph 3(b) aims to prevent cases that may affect pluralism and diversity and so extends media ownership rules to the spouse and relatives up to the third degree. It cannot be efficiently enforced, however, because there are not specific criteria to define "unfair influence". The result is legal uncertainty as competent authorities and the courts are unable to justify their decisions; there is also a lack of significant caselaw on the issue.[68] Together this constitutes a barrier to entry for potential investors who want to enter and invest. Moreover, the fact that this rule applies only to Greek shareholders of companies not registered in stock markets in EU or OECD member states distorts competition and raises costs of these firms, without obvious justification by favouring foreigners and Greek shareholders registered in foreign stock markets. The aim of this kind of provision is to protect pluralism and diversity and to promote competition, which such an exception undermines, while creating an uneven playing field.

The exception inserted into paragraph 10 of Article 5 regarding the application of ownership rules and concentration thresholds only on owners, shareholders, managers or members of the board of directors of media companies operating in Greece, only if not registered in stock markets of EU or OECD member states, is not justified. As a result, potential harm to competition cannot be counterbalanced by a valid public -policy objective. The provision not only favours owners, shareholders and managers of companies that are registered in stock markets against those that are not, but also it jeopardises the aim of this set of rules to protect pluralism, diversity, transparency and to enhance competition.

In Greece, according to the literature (Anagnostou et al., 2010), "Scholars have also drawn attention to the fact that the exclusive use of economic criteria for the establishment of a dominant position, based on advertising expenditure and sales income, is inappropriate. They have claimed that the assessment of whether a media enterprise enjoys a dominant position in the market or not must also be based on criteria related to the influence it exerts on the public, usually reflected in audience shares… The endorsement of a pure economic approach, coupled with the fact that concentration control follows and does not precede operators' merging plans, could substantially undermine the ability of competition law and policy to support citizen access to a wide range of media outlets and voices".[69]

Finally, to promote diversity of media ownership, all adequate information about media ownership structures should be made available and accessible by interested parties and the civil society.[70]

*Recommendations*

Competent administrative authorities and the courts should be given specific criteria for the proof of unfair influence and abolish the exception currently in Article 5, paragraph 3(b) of Law 392/2007 that provides for foreigners and Greek shareholders of companies registered in stock markets of EU and OECD member states.

Article 5, paragraph 10 of Law 3592/2007 should be abolished since it favours companies registered in stock markets of EU and OECD member states.

Ownership and cross-ownership rules should be reviewed in combination with media concentration rules (as is done with newspapers), so as to conclude whether they can be updated to focus more on the real impact of media in the market and the shaping of public opinion (for instance, apply the criterion of audience share).

Box 4.1. **International media-ownership rules**

Media pluralism and freedom of expression is supported by the European Union, but there are no specific EU rules concerning limits on media ownership and cross-ownership. The regulation of media ownership is subject to national regulations influenced by the history and the cultural background of each country.

**France**

In broadcasting, the Conseil Supérieur Audiovisuel (CSA, Higher Audiovisual Council) enforces ownership limits based on three criteria: capital share, number of licences and audience share. Nobody can hold – either directly or indirectly – more than 49% of any national broadcast licence holder whose average annual audience share exceeds 2.5%. A national broadcaster is defined as having a potential reach of over 10 million people (around 15% of the national population) and includes radio, cable and satellite. Shareholders must inform the competent authority when their holding exceeds 10% in any given company. These limits apply to both analogue and digital television, but there are other analogue-only restrictions. A "15/15" rule means that nobody holding an interest of over 15% in a national analogue licensee can hold over 15% in any other; a "5/5/5" rule prevents anyone from holding an interest of over 5% in more than two. In addition, no entity can hold more than one licence for national analogue television, more than seven for digital television, or more than two for satellite television.

Finally, there are restrictions based on audience share:

- no one can own both a national TV licence (analogue or digital) with an audience share of over 2.5% *and* a licence for local analogue TV;
- no one can hold local analogue TV licences with a cumulative reach over 12 million people, or digital TV licences with the same cumulative reach, and these limits do not work in combination;
- no one can hold more than one local TV licence (analogue or digital) in the same broadcast area.

**Germany**

Media regulation in Germany falls to individual state governments, but in the 1990s they mutually established the Kommission zur Ermittlung der Konzentration im Medienbereich (KEK, Commission on Concentration in the Media). KEK can intervene in TV or radio markets if a company's combined media holdings (including newspapers) comprise more than 30% of annual viewer (or circulation) share. A 25% holding of the television market can also trigger intervention. Germany has a complex approach to measuring audience share across mediums, and KEK applies different weightings to shares in different formats, on the basis that different kinds of media exert varying influence on the public sphere.

**United Kingdom**

The British Parliament has over the years put in place rules related to media ownership. These include:

- the national cross-media ownership rule, which prohibits a newspaper operator with a market share of 20% or more circulation from holding a Channel 3 licence or a stake in a Channel 3 licensee greater than 20%;
- regulator Ofcom's public interest test, which allows the secretary of state to intervene in a merger involving a broadcaster and/or a newspaper enterprise if certain conditions are met;* the secretary of state may decide to issue an intervention notice that triggers a review of whether the merger might result in harm to the public interest;
- the disqualified persons restrictions, which prevent certain bodies or persons from holding any broadcast licences, others from holding certain kinds of broadcast licences, and still others from holding broadcast licences, unless Ofcom has determined that it is appropriate for them to do so.

* The Secretary of State may intervene if the enterprises cease to be distinct; the value of the enterprise being taken over exceeds GBP 70 million; and/or the merger results in at least a 25% share of supply of goods or services in the UK (or substantial part of the UK), or involves an enterprise that has a 25% share of supply of newspapers or broadcasting. Ofcom (2015), ibid.

*Sources*: France and Germany - "The elephant next door: a survey of international media ownership regulations", Media Reform Coalition (2015), www.mediareform.org.uk/wp-content/uploads/2015/11/The_Elephant_Next_Door-A_Survey_of_International_Media_Ownership_Regulations.pdf.

UK - Ofcom (2015), "Report to the Secretary of State on the operation of the media ownership rules listed under Section 391 of the Communications Act 2003, http://stakeholders.ofcom.org.uk/binaries/research/media-literacy/media-ownership/morr_2015.pdf.

### *Radio licensing*

*Overview of radio licensing*

The state's radio-broadcasting monopoly was abolished with Law 1730/1987,[71] which allowed the establishment and operation of local radio stations following administrative authorisation based on criteria provided by the law, without the provision of a prior tender procedure.

Pursuant to this law and Presidential Decree 25/1988, radio licences were issued by the administration. However, from 1989 several private radio stations began operating without any administrative authorisation. This uncontrollable situation of illegal establishment and operation of radio stations[72] led to the introduction of Law 2328/1995. This new law contained a set of provisions regarding the licensing procedure that introduced a competitive process, criteria for rating bidders, a four-year period of validity of licences, and the possibility of their renewal. Once in force, calls for radio licences were issued only in the prefecture of Attica and Thessaloniki. In 2001, 20 radio licences were finally granted in Attica[73] and in 2002, 15 additional licences were added.[74] In the prefecture of Thessaloniki, the procedure stayed pending and no licences have yet been granted. In other regions, the licensing procedure never even began.

In 1999, Article 53, paragraph 1 of Law 2778/1999[75] came into force. It provided that: "Radio stations which were in operation on 1 November 1999, are considered as legally operating until the decision of the Minister of Press and Media provided in Article 7, paragraph 2 of Law 2328/1995 regarding the launch of the tender for licensing radio stations is issued." By virtue of this provision, all radio stations that could prove by any means that they had been operating since at least that date applied to the NCRTV to obtain a certificate of a legally operating radio station.

A tender was in progress in Attica and so radio stations operating there at that time could not take advantage of this provision. However, when radio licences in Attica expired, Article 15, paragraph7(a) of Law 3444/2006 was enacted to extend them until 30 June 2006, when a new tender for radio licences was to have been issued. Instead, over the following years several provisions[76] delayed the launch of the tender process for radio licences and so in effect extended the validity of existing radio licences. Even in the new Law 3592/2007, regarding the criteria for radio licensing, whose provisions abolished de facto but not explicitly the relevant provisions of Law 2328/1995, Article 5, paragraph 7 (b) stated that all radio stations (licensed according to Presidential Decree 25/1988 or after a tender, such as in Attica, or those that are considered as legally operating) could continue their operation until tenders that followed the new criteria set out by Law 3592/2007 were issued. In the same law, Article 20, paragraph 5 provided an extension until 31 December 2007 for radio licensing.

In 2009, Article 50 of Law 3801/2009 provided the possibility for radio stations owned by political parties represented in parliament, which had been broadcasting before the promulgation of Law 3592/2007 and which fulfilled its criteria, to continue their operation and be considered as legally functioning until the launch of the tender process for radio licensing. It was not possible to identify the objective of this provision, but in our understanding, these radio stations were not able to prove their operation before 1 November 1999.

Despite the existence of a new legal framework (i.e. Law 3592/2007) for radio licensing that could be applied and which is still in force, consecutive provisions for extension of the deadline for launching a tender were regularly enacted.[77] The most recent was Article 86, paragraph 1 of Law 4313/2014, which provided a deadline for radio licence tenders of 31 December 2015.

Since this date, the licences of radio stations in Attica, the validity of which depend on the launch of the tender for radio licensing, have typically expired. Nevertheless, all radio stations in Attica continue broadcasting without any action taken by the administration to stop their operation. Radio stations operating in all other Greek prefectures, besides Attica, can continue to broadcast legally as long as they have or can get the certificate of legally operating radio broadcasters as laid out in Law 2778/1999.[78] It is not clear though whether the expiration of the extension of the tender deadline has had an impact on the validity of their certificates.

The Council of State has already ruled that the indefinite tolerance of the operation of radio stations that started their operation illegally, but are now considered as legally operating just because they were broadcasting before 1 November1999 runs contrary to the Constitution. This is justified in two ways. First, the provisions are not in conformity with the constitutional principle that the state has to ensure the applicability of laws in force, and second, they violate the principle of equality because they establish a differential treatment between individuals who wanted to and could have afforded to run a radio station but did not because it was illegal, and those who illegally occupied a radio frequency and simply started broadcasting.[79]

In addition to the indefinite extensions of the radio-licence tender process, other provisions show the administration's inaction in establishing a consistent legal framework regarding the operation of radio stations and their licences.

More specifically:

- Article 6, paragraphs 3 and 4 of Law 4279/2014 allows radio broadcasters with an informative-content licence to change their content category to non-informative simply by submitting a declaration to NCRTV, and then continue operating under the same licence;

- Article 8, paragraph 9 (στ) of Law 3592/2007 allows the licence of a radio station to be recalled from the licensee and directly granted to its employees by virtue of a decision of the Minister of Press and Media if it ceases or suspends operations for a period of at least six months or delays payment during at least four months of one third of its employees or one third of its personnel's total salaries.

*Harm to competition*

The above legal framework severely limits competition in the radio-broadcasting market. These provisions are damaging competition because the market is essentially sealed from new entrants: no new licences are currently available and incumbent broadcasters have their expired licences continuously renewed on a temporary basis.[80] Therefore, the only way for a potential new entrant to invest in the market is to acquire one of the existing firms holding a temporary licence.

Furthermore, the fact that these licences are only renewed on a temporary basis creates uncertainty in the market and limits competition, because it is very likely that under these circumstances, potential investment plans by incumbent and new-entrant businesses are put on hold until a proper licensing procedure is launched and the rules are clearly stated.

More specifically, the provision of Article 8, paragraph 9 (στ) of Law 3592/2007 that enables the employees of a bankrupt radio station to gain control of the company and therefore of the radio licence, distorts market conditions. In general, in other industries, a bankrupt company is driven into liquidation and in this way resources are released from an unsuccessful business for a new venture in the market.

This way resources released back onto an open market (e.g., a radio frequency) would be purchased by the most efficient purchaser. On the contrary, the provision in this case distorts the market by allowing bankrupt radio stations to operate on different terms to those of their non-bankrupt competitors with dubious results with regards to economic efficiency and consumer welfare.

Article 6, paragraphs 3 and 4 of Law 4279/2014 enables radio stations of informative content to switch to non-informative content simply by submitting a declaration to NCRTV. As the limited number of analogue radio frequencies means that only a fixed set of radio stations may be licensed in any given prefecture, the state wants to optimally distribute those frequencies between informative and non-informative content. If a company is not able to operate by providing the content for which it is licensed, then the licence should be returned to the state and re-auctioned. This will keep a level playing field between all broadcasters and retain the desired ratio between informative and non-informative radio stations, and so maximise consumer welfare.

*Recommendations*

After completing the relevant technical analysis and issuing a map of frequencies, the authorities should launch tenders for each prefecture with a specific number of licences both for radio stations of informative and non-informative (music, sports) content.[81] This will establish a stable investment environment with legal certainty and specific conditions known to all participants from the outset. All other provisions that insert derogations to the licensing procedure should be abolished.

Article 6, paragraphs 3 and 4 of Law 4279/2014 should be abolished.

Article 8, paragraph 9 (στ) of Law 3592/2007 should be abolished.

***Specific criteria for licensing***

*Overall legal framework*

Law 3592/2007, the legal framework for launching a tender for radio licensing, has been in force since 2007, but it has never been properly applied and no tenders for radio licensing have been published. It de facto replaced (according to the legal principle that a newer law overrides a predecessor if they regulate the same issue) the relevant articles of Law 2328/1995, without specifically abolishing them. As a result, there is legal uncertainty regarding the validity of provisions included in Law 2328/1995.

*Harm to competition*

Legal uncertainty raises legal and compliance costs and may act as a disincentive to enter or remain in the relevant market.

*Recommendation*

Law 2328/1995 and Law 3592/2007 should be streamlined, so as to establish a definitive legal framework for radio licensing.

*Corporate structure*

Article 6, paragraph 6(a) of Law 2328/1995 provides that: "If the shares of an SA which is a radio licence holder are owned by another SA, the shares of the latter should be registered and owned by an individual. There is no possibility of an SA being owned by another SA." This obligation for company structures is not repeated in Law 3592/2007 and it is therefore unclear whether it has been abolished or not.

Assuming that it is still in force, radio stations that want to hold a licence have to fulfil this requirement, raising an issue about obligatory company structure.

The OECD's understanding is that this provision's objective is to enhance transparency of the ownership of licence-holding radio stations, allowing the public the possibility of knowing who is broadcasting. However, given that all shareholders in an SA with a radio licence have to be registered, the aim of transparency could be achieved even if there were more than two SAs among the owners.

*Harm to competition*

As long as the rules for registering shareholders of all holding companies of media enterprises remain in place, there is no justification to enforce a particular corporate structure on a media group. Transparency can still maintained by applying the same rules to all holding companies and to the persons who own them.

*Recommendation*

The requirement that all shares be registered is justified by the policy maker's objective of protecting pluralism and objectivity in the media sector. If this condition is met, however, it removes any necessity to dictate the exact corporate structure of media organisations. This restriction should therefore be abolished.

*Minimum staff requirements*

Article 8, paragraph 14 of Law 3592/2007 provides that radio stations should employ a minimum number of full-time staff calculated according to the population of the region and the kind of the radio licence (informative/non-informative) they hold.

- In regions where the population is more than 2 million inhabitants, radio stations of informative content must have at least 20 employees, and non-informative stations must have 5.
- In regions where the population is less than 2 million inhabitants, radio stations of informative content must have at least 12 employees, and non-informative stations must have 5.
- In regions where the population is less than 1 million and more than 500 000: radio stations of informative content must have 9 employees and non-informative stations must have 5.
- In regions where the population is less than 500 000 and more than 150 000: radio stations of informative content must have 7 employees and non-informative stations must have 4.
- In regions where the population is less than 150 000 and more than 100 000: radio stations of informative content must have 6 employees and non-informative stations must have 4.
- In regions where the population is less than 100 000: radio stations of informative content must have 5 and non-informative stations must have 3.

According to the official recital of the law, this provision aims to protect pre-existing jobs in the case of new radio licences, while providing radio-licence holders with the minimum staff required for their smooth and efficient operation.

*Harm to competition*

A state-imposed minimum staff requirement can be acceptable in cases of services of high social importance, such as hospitals or childcare facilities,[82] where providers must provide sufficient numbers of suitably qualified, competent, skilled and experienced staff to meet the needs of service users. These are cases where quality is difficult to monitor/observe and respond to, hence providers may cut costs and endanger quality with potentially serious consequences. However, as a general rule, state intervention in employee numbers in a private company cannot be justified in terms of public interest.

Setting minimum employment requirements can be extremely restrictive to competition and to business freedom. Due to this restriction, radio stations have extremely similar employment structures and are unable to manage their resources optimally. Eventually this may lead radio broadcasters to suffer higher variable costs, which in turn may lead to higher prices in the upstream market of advertising and less innovation in the market.

*Recommendation*

Abolish the minimum-staff requirement for radio-licence holders.

*Grandfathering clauses*

The licensing procedure for radio stations contains a set of provisions where radio licensing is based on a points system that favours radio stations already operating during the procedure. Article 9(a) of Law 3592/2007 states that a radio broadcaster receives half a point for each year of its operation with a renewed licence or as a "legally operating" radio station. An incumbent radio station can get up to 120 points through this criterion. Article 9(a.4) decreases this bonus by up to half for radio stations wishing to receive a licence in a prefecture different to the one in which they had been operating. In other words, incumbent radio stations are given preferable treatment over prospective entrants to the market. This restriction also works horizontally with radio stations that remain in the same region given favourable treatment in any potential licensing procedure over those that choose to move from another region.

Although it was not possible to identify the objective of these provisions, it is the OECD's understanding that they aim to protect existing stations' investments, as well as jobs.

*Harm to competition*

Both these provisions have been recognised[83] as creating obstacles to new entrepreneurs. They greatly distort competition by treating incumbent businesses more favourably than potential entrants to the market (the so-called grandfather clause). The regulation may discourage new players entering the market, and as a result reduce the overall number of participants in the market or may reduce the costs of inefficient incumbents keeping them in the market when they should not be.

*Recommendation*

These provisions should be explicitly abolished.

*Prior experience and operation*

Articles 9(b) and 9ΣΤ of Law 3592/2007 also focus on the existing market presence of radio stations as part of the criteria for licensing radio stations. Article 9(b), for example, provides that during the competitive process, existing radio stations that have been fined for breaches of operations provisions have points docked at a level dependent on the seriousness of the violation and the fine. Article 9ΣΤ I/II states that existing radio stations are given extra points for the quality and variety of their programming, as reviewed by the NCRTV.

These provisions aim to improve the quality and variety of programming and create incentives for existing radio stations to follow both legal and content-related rules. Indeed, according to the official recital of Article 9ΣΤ, the provision aims to guarantee the qualitative level of radio stations' programming and the fulfilment of radio broadcasting's social mission.

While this evaluation system raises the chances of a good player capable and willing to obey the rules and offer good services, it also takes in existing radios that have been operating for many years without proper licensing and control by NCRTV; given that the NCRTV cannot be in plenary and exercise its powers [84] regarding the regulation and supervision of the radio market (and not only) for more than one year, these provisions cannot be equally implemented for all existing radio stations. Moreover, it should be noted that both negative and positive criteria provided in the law are not sufficiently defined.

The points deducted for each radio station in case of fines and sanctions are calculated proportionally and based upon the number of fines or sanctions imposed on other radio stations participating in the licensing procedure. The evaluation of the quality and variety of programming gives NCRTV wide discretion in awarding 75 points to the best in terms of quality and variety programme and proportionally fewer points to the programme of other radio stations. Despite this, the law does not actually provide specific criteria for assessing programming quality and variety.

This means that participants cannot know how many points will be deducted/added before the start of the licensing procedure and so cannot assess whether it is worth their participating or not.

*Harm to competition*

It is not harmful to competition if, in a licensing procedure of a limited public resource such as the analogue radio frequencies, the state reserves the right to evaluate that resource's previous usage (positive or negative), as long as the evaluation criteria are clear, known and applicable to all players in the market.

*Recommendation*

The state should define and publish in advance all proportionally awarded positive and negative criteria that are applicable to all players in the market (both incumbent and new entrants).

***TV***

> The present draft does not include the assessment of Law 4339/2015 and of Joint Ministerial Decision 7577/2016 in relation to digital free-to-air TV licences, due to ongoing administrative and legal procedures.

*TV network provider*

*Removal of multiplexes*

Article 80(ιη) of Law 4070/2012, as amended by Article 19 of Law 4339/2015 on the licensing of digital-TV broadcasting, stipulates that the Minister of Infrastructure, Transport and Networks reserves the right, following a substantiated opinion by the competent regulator (EETT), to issue a Ministerial Decision that withdraws from a network provider the usage and exploitation of any multiplex that has not been sufficiently used for four months in total, provided that the content of the multiplex can be broadcast by the remaining multiplexes managed by the network provider of digital terrestrial broadcasting. "Non-sufficient use" is further explained as the situation where the multiplex does not contain a minimum of four standard-definition (SD) digital broadcasts or a smaller number of high-definition (HD) digital broadcasts. By virtue of the same Ministerial Decision, the exploitation of a recalled multiplex can then be assigned to a new network provider for broadcasting digital content regionally or nationally.

According to the official recital, the removal of a multiplex can be done only for public-interest reasons and the better exploitation of public frequencies.

*Harm to competition*

The provision is aimed at encouraging the full use of the spectrum by network providers. It is very difficult to define the meaning of "use", however, and therefore to identify the conditions under which a spectrum may be taken away. In particular, the unclear and potentially broad definition of "public interest" may lead to a wide variety of reasons why the State might remove an underused multiplex. Article 10, paragraphs 2 and 5 and Article 14 of Directive 2002/20/EC on licensing electronic communications networks and services, provide the legal framework under which national regulatory authorities may trigger a suspension or withdrawal of usage rights: first, if the undertaking is infringing the conditions of its licence, and second, as a last resort of repeated breaches.

Without further clarification of the situations that can trigger such a unilateral action from the state, the provision creates legal uncertainty and disincentives for potential investors to enter the market in the future or for current players to invest in infrastructure.

Moreover, there may be legitimate reasons why the spectrum holder is not using its resources fully. This provision should also be viewed in the light of the number of licensed TV broadcasters in the (national and regional) market. A limited number of licences, for example, will inevitably result in the network provider having unused frequency bandwidth due to limited demand.

*Recommendations*

The provision should be abolished or amended in order to provide a restrictive reference of the public-interest criteria that can trigger such unilateral action from the state, in accordance with Directive 2002/20/EC on licensing electronic communications networks and services. It should also be made clear that limited usage of multiplexes should be directly attributed to the network providers, such as cases of technical inefficiencies by the network provider or non-compliance with its licensing conditions.

*ERT SA as a network provider*

Article 2, paragraph 11 of Law 4173/2013 provides that the Greek public broadcaster ERT is a network provider for its own programming, as well as for third-party content providers. For these functions, ERT is exempt from any kind of licensing procedures. Additionally, the competent ministers provide it with the frequencies it needs without charge.

It was not possible to identify the objective of this provision. However, OECD understands that it allows ERT as a network provider to carry and broadcast third-party content and thus to enhance pluralism and to supply the public with information that meets a level of quality, and standards of completeness and versatility.

*Harm to competition*

This provision may be harmful to competition if ERT by virtue of its capacity as a network provider is allowed to broadcast the commercial content of private third-party content providers. ERT's network is provided by the state for free and is exempt from licensing, creating an uneven playing field for commercial network providers, who pay the state for their marketed frequencies (multiplexes) and have to go through costly licensing procedures. Differential treatment between companies offering the same service for commercial purposes is discriminatory and an obstacle to competition. ERT must comply with all the regulations relating to commercial broadcasters if it wishes to compete with them, otherwise ERT may act only as a network provider to carry public interest content (usually provided by other public owned broadcasters).

*Recommendation*

The phrase "third party" should be deleted, otherwise it should be further clarified in the law, in order to make sure that ERT cannot use its state-subsidised frequencies and premises to compete with commercial network providers.

*TV advertising*

Article 23(1) of Directive 2010/13/EC provides that the proportion of television advertising spots and teleshopping spots within a given clock hour shall not exceed 20%. This hourly limit on admissible advertising protects the integrity of programming.[85]

According to Article 23(2) of Directive 2010/13/EC, announcements made in connection with a broadcaster's own programmes, including ancillary products directly derived from them, are exempt from Article 23(1)'s limits.[86] In order to avoid distortions of competition, this derogation should be limited to announcements concerning products that fulfil the dual condition of being both ancillary to and directly derived from the programmes concerned. The term "ancillary" refers to products intended specifically to allow the viewing public to benefit fully from, or to interact with, these programmes.[87]

This Directive was transposed into Greek law by Presidential Decree 109/2010, and the initial version of the relevant provision regarding the derogation (Article 23, paragraph 3) was in line with the Directive.[88] However, following an amendment of the decree by virtue of Article 6, paragraph 8 of Law 4279/2014, the provision was amended and new derogations were added. This meant that what is not considered as advertising time was extended to cover announcements made by the broadcaster in connection with the rest of its activities, as well as the activities of other enterprises belonging to the same media group, such as informative or entertainment services offered over the Internet, the production and distribution of audio and/or audiovisual works, and technical training for providing services in the above sectors. These derogations do not meet the dual condition of being both ancillary to, and directly derived from, the programmes as defined by the Directive. They are not indeed products intended specifically to allow the viewing public to benefit fully from, or to interact with, the programmes of the TV broadcaster.

 

Similarly, Article 5, paragraph 16 of Law 3592/2007, as amended by Article 6, paragraph 2 of Law 4279/2014, provides that TV and radio broadcasters belonging to the same media group and having the same management control, can promote their programmes, services, activities through self-promoting announcements set out in Article 23, Paragraph 3 of Presidential Decree 109/2010.

*Harm to competition*

The derogations added by the Greek legislator implicitly raise advertising costs for purchasers of advertising time that are not part of a particular media group compared to those that are. The latter take advantage of free advertising that is extra to the permitted time for advertising in a given clock hour. As a result, these companies have a cost advantage over their competitors, while the ability of new entrants (not belonging in a media group) to inform potential customers of their market presence is restricted.

*Recommendation*

The amendment of Article 23, paragraph 2 of Presidential Decree 109/2010 made by Article 6, Paragraph 8 of Law 4279/2014 should be abolished and the first version of the provision should be revived in line with Article 23, paragraph 2 of Directive 2010/13/EC. Accordingly, Article 5, Paragraph 16(b) of Law 3592/2007 should be abolished.

## 4.6. Pay TV

The presence of pay TV in Greece has increased significantly over the past few years, and by 2015, total subscribers exceeded 1 million. In 2011, penetration of pay TV was measured at 9%; in 2013 at 18%; and in 2014 at 23%.[89] The main players in the market are NOVA, OTE TV, Cyta and Vodafone TV. The first two are the dominant players in terms of market share, based on subscriber numbers, followed by Cyta and Vodafone, which have a total of 100 000 subscribers.

Table 4.2. **Number of subscribers, 2013-2015**

| | 2013 | 2014 | 2015 |
|---|---|---|---|
| NOVA | 452 000 | 507 261 | 494 643 |
| OTE TV | 255 000 | 353 000 | 450 000 |

*Source*: Companies' annual financial statements.

Law 2644/1998, which constitutes the main legal framework for the supply of subscription broadcasting services and so regulates pay-TV services regardless of their platform (digital or analogue) or delivery system (terrestrial, cable or satellite), dates back to 1998.

While the law has been amended for particular issues since its promulgation, it has not been updated. Its provisions do not therefore reflect the new technology and innovative media products that have appeared since 1998. For example, content and services have been digitalized and over-the-top (OTT) services[90] such as non-linear content have arrived and replaced some traditional pay-TV services.[91] In the United Kingdom, for example, recent market research shows that revenues from subscription video on demand (SVoD) services, which are dominated by OTT services, have grown substantially in recent years. Netflix, for example, accounts for almost half of total SVoD revenues, and this share is expected to rise further in the future.[92]

At a European level these new challenges are currently under discussion in the context of the Digital Single Market (DSM) policy. A recent report to the European Parliament found that: "applying the notion of 'imposing similar obligations on OTT services to those imposed on equivalent traditional services' is exceedingly challenging in practice. To what degree are the services in fact equivalent? Does the OTT service in fact raise the same issues as those to which regulation of the corresponding traditional service seeks to respond? Given the implementation differences between traditional versus online services, to what degree is it proportionate or realistic to impose equivalent obligations?"[93]

### *Corporate Structure*

Article 2, paragraph 1 of Law 2644/1998 stipulates that licences are granted only to particular business entities (SA), whose shares must be registered. If the holder of the shares of the licensed SA is another SA, then these shares should be owned by individuals and be registered. A corporate structure featuring another SA as a licence holder is prohibited.

Article 2, paragraph 2 then states that this obligatory share registration does not apply to non-Greek SAs as long as, 1) they can prove they have high solvency; 2) they have been in the market of media or telecommunications for at least three years; and 3) they do not have to declare registered shares in the law of their country of origin. Moreover, the obligation of registered shares does not apply to shares held in stock markets of EU or OECD member states.

According to the official recital, share registration enhances transparency and pluralism in the media sector. The policy maker's objective for foreign companies with market experience of at least three years is to attract companies that are reliable, solid and responsible in doing business. The required participation in stock markets confirms that a company has complied with strict rules and requirements of operations that should guarantee transparency.

#### *Harm to competition*

As long as the rules for registering shareholders of all holding companies of media enterprises remain in place, there is no justification in continuing to enforce a particular corporate structure on a media group. Transparency can still be maintained by applying the same rules to all holding companies and to the persons who own them.

The exclusion of Article 2, paragraph 2 regarding companies that participate in the stock market from the obligation to register shares, is reasonable since it is indeed the case that stock -market regulations require that a company complies with strict rules and conditions of operation, which also meet the requirements of transparency.

It is not clear how the high-solvency criterion affects the market. On one hand, it is vague and results in higher costs for the foreign company (which has the burden of proof). On the other hand, it may favour foreign companies against local ones, which have no other option but to enter the market by declaring registered shares. In either case, it provides the administration with wide discretion to interpret and implement the criterion *ad hoc*.

The obligation of foreign companies to have at least three years' presence in a media or telecommunications market is unnecessary. It hinders competition by creating barriers to entry to the relevant market, especially for new formed companies that may otherwise have the financial capacity to invest in the industry. There is no such restriction in the licensing procedures of free-to-air TV broadcasters and new companies may enter that market.

 

*Recommendation and benefits*

The policy maker's objective to protect pluralism and objectivity in the media sector justifies the restrictions on share registration. If this condition is met, however, there is no reason in going a step further and dictating the exact corporate structure of media organisations. The obligation to register shares easily allows regulators to trace ownership of media groups, if needed.

The high-solvency criterion for foreign companies should be abolished.

The requirement for foreign companies to have at least three years' previous presence in a media or telecommunications market should be abolished.

***Licensing restrictions and costs***

According to Article 2, paragraph 3(a) of Law 2644/1995, an SA can be granted one licence for one delivery system (terrestrial, cable or satellite), and then hold one more licence for broadcasting the same services through another delivery system. The competent Minister decides the number of licences for terrestrial distribution and the scarcity of the resources/frequencies means they are granted through a competitive procedure.[94] For satellite and cable services, licences are granted upon application to SAs that fulfil all the requirements provided by the law.[95]

On top of other requirements, Article 9, paragraph 7 of Law 2644/1998 states that an SA has to pay a one-off fee of almost EUR 44 000 per 24 hours of the total daily programming (in the law the amount of money is still in drachmas: 15 million) and almost EUR 8 000 (3 million drachmas) for 24 hours of radio programming. Moreover, an annual fee corresponding to a percentage of the annual revenue of the pay-TV provider using satellites or cable is applied. This percentage begins at 0.5% for the first two years and increases gradually throughout the following 10 years until it reaches 3%. For terrestrial delivery systems, the annual fee amounts to 3.5% of the revenues starting from the first year.

According to the official recital, the first provision aims to the avoidance of horizontal concentration in the field of broadcasting services, while the second helps fund NCRTV in its supervisory role and to develop services provided by public broadcaster ERT.

*Harm to competition*

In an effort to avoid the creation of dominant positions, the law limits the number of licences that one party can hold.[96]

A party can have only one pay-TV/radio licence for each method of distribution (e.g. satellite, cable, terrestrial). This can be justified for terrestrial distribution on the basis of scarcity of resources, but for satellite and cable distribution, it limits freedom of business and harms competition. It is therefore difficult to justify the prohibition on holding more than one satellite licence, particularly as pay-TV services have been chosen explicitly by consumers who pay for the product, and that pay-TV content in Greece is non-informative and therefore cannot be seen as influencing public opinion.

The restriction on the number of distribution methods a party can use to broadcast harms competition by limiting the freedom of businesses to adopt new technologies and by providing disincentives for innovation. Due to the advent of new technologies, it should be left to the businesses to choose the means by which they broadcast their content, particularly given that, as mentioned above, pay-TV services constitute commercial products that require consumers' explicit willingness to buy and use. It is understood that the policy maker's aim here is to avoid a "spill-over" of a possible dominant position into neighbouring technologies. To go as far as limiting the number of technological distribution methods, however, may severely hinder competition intensity in any given distribution channel by forcing companies to focus on one particular technological field, and so limit competition in others.

The lack of an updated and streamlined definition of the term "delivery system/means of distribution" also causes barriers to entry for businesses that want to invest in pay TV/radio and offer new subscription services such as non-linear services and subscription VOD through new technologies such as broadband networks (IPTV) or free Internet (OTT). Although Article 15 of Law 3592/2007 describes a licensing procedure for providers of radio and television services through broadband networks (IPTV), the competent authority, NCRTV, does not apply it to web television/radio services.[97]

More specifically, Article 15 of Law 3592/2007 stipulates that radio and television services through broadband networks (IPTV) should be licensed by NCRTV in terms of their content, unless the same content has been already authorised for broadcast through another platform. To broadcast this content, the network provider can be the same company as the content provider and should have been "granted a General Authorisation"[98] by EETT. Television over the Internet (OTT) does not fall under this regulatory framework and in general, it is not regulated.

As a result, there are currently three parallel systems offering similar products. Although they cannot yet be characterised as direct substitutes, in the near future, as Internet penetration progresses, they will be increasingly addressed to the same consumers. Pay TV has to fulfil all the requirements concerning company structure, capital, ownership rules provided by Law 2644/1998; IPTV delivered over broadband networks is licensed by EETT for the network and by NCRTV for content, but the requirements are much more relaxed than for pay TV; and finally, TV programming over the Internet, one type of so-called OTT services, can be freely broadcast without a license, control or authorisation.

It should also be noted that each system has different licensing fees. For pay TV, they are provided by the law and amount to almost EUR 44000 for every 24 hours of daily programming, plus 3% (or less depending on the years of operation) of the company revenues. Fees for networks used by IPTV are paid to EETT and are comparatively less[99] than those paid by pay TV, while OTT services pay no licence fees.

Having different regulatory regimes creates an uneven playing field for businesses and thus distorts competition, while considerably raising business costs; this is likely to feed through into prices.

The one-off licence fee that pay-TV/radio service providers have to pay to obtain their licence and the annual fee based on their revenues is collected for public-interest purposes (funding the regulatory authority and contributing to the development of ERT's services). Moreover, licence fees often exist in other European countries such as the Netherlands, Sweden and the United Kingdom.

However, the fact that the size of the fee is set out in a law dating back to 1998, and in the meantime, the economy, business environment and technology have all changed, may create uncertainty and give the impression of an unreliable market. This may in turn deter new entrants from investing in the pay-TV/radio market. Furthermore, the law should be updated so as to take into account all technological distribution methods used by the different various subscription-TV products currently available in the market and so allow licensing procedures and fees to converge and be reviewed to reflect the current economic and financial circumstances. This should create a more level playing field.

*Recommendations*

The restriction on the number of licences that a party using other technological methods of distribution than terrestrial can hold should be abolished.

The restriction on the number of delivery systems/means of distribution that a licensed pay-TV/radio broadcaster can use for transmitting its programming should be abolished.

The distribution means of pay-TV/radio broadcasters should be streamlined to create a level playing field for pay TV, IPTV and OTT (where possible, and especially for the last).

Update the one-off licence fee and annual fee paid by pay TV/radios, so as to correspond to new market conditions including IPTV and, if possible, OTT.

***Cross-ownership rules***

According to Article 2, paragraph 4 of Law 2644/1998, the licence holder of pay TV/radio services cannot simultaneously own a free-to-air broadcasting licence (taken out under Law 2328/1995). On the contrary, it can participate in a company that holds a free-to-air broadcasting licence, as long as there is no harm to competition, dominant position is not abused and pluralism is protected. Besides, the shareholders of licence-holding company can own or participate in a company that owns free-to-air licence only if the previous requirements are met.

Article 2, paragraph 5 of Law 2644/1998 stipulates that pay TV/radio licence holders, its shareholders as well as the shareholders of its shareholders, are prohibited from participating in more than two categories of media (any kind of television, radio, newspapers).[100]

According to the official recital, both provisions are an attempt to avoid the creation of horizontal concentration in broadcasting services.

Yet, more recent legislation on cross-ownership rules (Article 5, Law 3592/2007) regulates the same issues differently, without explicitly abolishing these provisions. More specifically, this article states that a licensed television broadcaster may own only one television licence and one radio licence (of informative content), but places no restriction on newspaper ownership. These licence holders may also participate in a company that holds a television licence, as long as they do not control it. (The term "control" is defined in great detail by the law.)

*Harm to competition*

Article 2, paragraphs 4 and 5 of Law 2644/1998 may constitute a barrier to new entrants. Moreover, there is legal uncertainty regarding their validity, resulting in legal and compliance costs for both companies already in the market and new entrants.

If the provisions are still in force, then they regulate the same issues in a completely different and far stricter way than those the Greek legislator decided to adopt in Law 3592/2007.

There is no obvious reason for having stricter cross ownership rules for pay-TV/radio services than for free-to-air TV/radio services, particularly as they create barriers to potential investors. While protecting pluralism and transparency is important and should be taken into account, pay TV/radio constitutes a product that consumers consciously decide to buy and it is often of purely entertainment (e.g. music, films, sports) content. Therefore it may have less of an impact on plurality in terms of its influence on civic engagement.[101]

*Recommendation*

Amend the provisions of Article 2, paragraphs 4 and 5 of Law 2644/1998 so as to provide the same cross-ownership restrictions as those set out in Law 3592/2007.

### *Suppliers of programming*

Article 3, paragraph 1 of Law 2644/1998 provides that pay-TV/radio broadcasters can either produce their own programming or buy in content from managers or suppliers[102] (each of those defined in detail in the law and hereinafter referred to jointly as "supplier"). Suppliers must have the form of an SA with registered shares

Each supplier can provide up to 30% of a pay-TV/radio licence holder's monthly programming. If the supplier or its shareholders participate in the share capital of another supplier of the pay TV/radio licence holder, total programming time for the two suppliers jointly cannot exceed 40% (Article 3, paragraphs 2 and 3 of Law 2644/1998).

The spouse or the relatives up to the fourth degree of an individual who holds a pay -TV/radio licence or is a shareholder in a licensed pay -TV/radio company or is a supplier of a pay -TV/radio company or participates in similar companies (licence holders or suppliers), cannot participate in a supplier's company structure unless they can prove their financial and business independence (Article 3, paragraph 4 of Law 2644/1998).

Finally, the suppliers, their shareholders and the shareholders of the latter, are not allowed to participate in licensed free-to-air radio broadcasters and newspaper publishers if they supply programmes to pay TV, and vice versa, i.e. supplying programming to pay radio prohibits participation in free-to-air licensed TV broadcasters and newspaper publishers (Article 3, paragraph 6 of Law 2644/1998).

Contracts signed between pay-TV/radio licence holders and suppliers, according to Article 4, paragraph 1 of Law 2644/1998, are invalid if they are not submitted and certified by the Minister in Charge of Press and Media (or NCRTV, if competence has been transferred).

All the aforementioned provisions constitute an extremely detailed legal framework for regulating the supply of programmes to pay-TV/radio broadcasters. According to the official recital, their purpose is to avoid interdependencies between pay-TV/radio licence holders and suppliers, and so to safeguard pluralism and impartiality. For the detailed rules concerning the participation in another supplier's company, the official recital argues that it is essential for avoiding the use of surrogates who breach the rule in practice. Moreover, in order to justify the restrictions on cross-ownership, the official recital points out the equal importance of both the license holder and the supplier of programme in protecting pluralism and transparency. Thus ownership restrictions are introduced in order to avoid horizontal and vertical concentration in the media market. Finally, it is argued that the contracts between suppliers and licensed pay -TV operator should be checked to ensure enforcement of the aforementioned provisions.

*Harm to competition*

The restrictions provided by the law on the supply of pay -TV/radio programming cannot be sufficiently justified on the basis of transparency, pluralism and content impartiality. As already noted, pay TV/radio is a product that consumers buy consciously after having examined its content and qualities. Restrictions on who supplies this programming limit pay -TV/radio broadcasters' investment choices and optimal allocation of resources. They also raise operational costs and may result in higher prices and limited choices for consumers.

More specifically, the supplier's obligation to have a particular corporate structure (SA) with registered shareholders hinders competition and raises costs, as companies that have chosen another structure cannot participate in this market. The transparency required can be achieved through other corporate structures – as long as all participants are required to be disclosed and registered.

The limit on the supply of programming by one particular supplier limits pay-TV/radio broadcasters' choices and subsequently, consumer choice. Moreover, it deters suppliers from producing more programming as, a small Greek pay-TV/radio market could leave them without a buyer.

The unclear definition of financial and business independence creates legal uncertainty and barriers to entry since its exact meaning cannot be known in advance and it is left to the competent authority's discretionary power to check it case by case.

The restrictions on participation in free-to-air broadcasters go beyond the relevant ownership restrictions provided in Law 3592/2007 for free-to-air broadcasters. It should therefore be clarified whether they have been updated or not. If they are still in force, they create entry barriers and restrict potential entrants in both markets (free-to-air and pay TV) and cannot therefore be justified.

Finally, there exists legal uncertainty about who is the competent authority to verify the contracts signed between suppliers and pay-TV/radio broadcasters, as well as under which terms such a verification takes place. The obligation to have a contract verified is also extremely restrictive and increases administrative costs for all affected businesses.

*Recommendations*

The compulsory corporate structure of an SA for suppliers should be abolished as other corporate structures can also guarantee the transparency required as long as they have to disclose their participants (Article 3, paragraph 1 of Law 2644/1998).

The limit on the hours of programming that can be supplied by one supplier should be abolished (Article 3, paragraphs 2 and 3 of Law 2644/1998).

The competent authorities should be provided with clear criteria so they can examine the "financial and business independence" of relatives in accordance with Article 3, paragraph 4 of Law 2644/1998.

Restrictions on the participation of suppliers in free-to-air broadcasters should be abolished (Article 3, paragraph 6 of Law 2644/1998).

The compulsory verification of contracts between suppliers and pay-TV/radio licence holders should be abolished (Article 4, paragraph 1 of Law 2644/1998).

***Taxation on the bills of pay TV/radio***

A recent provision, Article 54 of Law 4389/2016, imposes a tax of 10% on consumers' monthly bills for pay -TV/radio services in Greece.

*Harm to competition*

As mentioned, the advent of new technologies has resulted in new distribution channels for pay TV/radio, as well as new products not included in the legal framework of Law 2644/1998. Therefore, this taxation affects only the companies (and subsequently their consumers) that fall under Law 2644/1998, whereas companies offering similar products (e.g. pay TV on demand) are not similarly regulated.

*Recommendation*

Streamline the provision (either expand or abolish) so as to create a level playing field for all competitors.

## Notes

1. Division as defined by United Nations Statistics Division, *http://unstats.un.org/unsd/cr/registry/regcs.asp?Cl=27&Lg=1&Co=58*

2. Division as defined by United Nations Statistics Division, *http://unstats.un.org/unsd/cr/registry/regcs.asp?Cl=27&Lg=1&Co=59*

3. Division as defined by United Nations Statistics Division, *http://unstats.un.org/unsd/cr/registry/regcs.asp?Cl=27&Lg=1&Co=60*

4. Division as defined by United Nations Statistics Division, *http://unstats.un.org/unsd/cr/registry/regcs.asp?Cl=27&Lg=1&Co=62*

5. Division as defined by United Nations Statistics Division, *http://unstats.un.org/unsd/cr/registry/regcs.asp?Cl=27&Lg=1&Co=63*

6. Eurostat, Annual detailed enterprise statistics for services (NACE Rev. 2, H-N and S95), Database [sbs_na_1a_se_r2], *http://ec.europa.eu/eurostat* (accessed 4 April 2016).

7. 2014 data were available only for the number of persons employed.

8. About 40% of the total legal documents that consist the legal mapping of the media sector, regulate issues of the programming and broadcasting activities; this is in direct contrast to the 5% that this particular sub-sector contributes to the total turnover of the sector.

9. Official Gazette A'159/3.8.1995

10. Official Gazette A'161/19.7.2007

11. Official Gazette A'133/29.10.2015

12. Official Gazette A'233/13.10.1995

13. Official Gazette A'190/5.11.2010

14. Official Gazette A'219/23.12.2010

15. Official Gazette A'68/20.3.2007

16. See Legal Opinion 241/2011 of the Greek Legal Council of State (Νομικό Συμβούλιο του Κράτους) in which it is mentioned that a newspaper that entered the daily market after previously circulating on a weekly basis could not publish state announcements, although it was well known and it fulfilled the other requirements of the law, simply because it did not have daily circulation for two years.

17. Article 48, Law 3986/2011.

18. Schweizer, C., M. Puppis, M. Künzler, S. Studer, (2014), "Public Funding of Private Media", *Media Policy Brief 11*, LSE Media Policy Project, March 2014.

*www.lse.ac.uk/media@lse/documents/MPP/LSE-MPP-Policy-Brief-11-Public-Funding-Private-Media.pdf,* p.5.

19. Article 19 (2012), Regulation on State Aid to Print Media,. *www.article19.org/data/files/medialibrary/3554/State-subsidies-press.pdf,* p.5.

20. Official Gazette B'2032/13.9.2011

21. Newspapers and magazines should be issued periodically at least once every month for newspapers and three months for magazines

22. Schweizer, C., et al, (2014), ibid, p.8

23. See *http://media.gov.gr/index.php/εποπτεια-των-μ-μ-ε/επαγγελματικές-ενώσεις-μμε* (accessed 26.09.2016).

24. Anagnostou D., E. Psychogiopoulou & A. Kandyla (2011), "Does media policy promote media freedom and independence? The case of Greece", MEDIADEM, *www.mediadem.eliamep.gr/wp-content/uploads/2012/01/Greece.pdf,* p.21

25. Pluralism and Media Concentration in the Internal Market - An Assessment of the Need for Community Action. Green Paper. COM (92) 480 final, 23 December 1992

26. Iosifidis, P. (2014), "Pluralism, Media Mergers and European Merger Control", The Palgrave Handbook of European Media Policy, London, *http://dx.doi.org/10.1057/9781137032195_25,* pp.461-475.

27. European Commission (2007), Commission Staff Working Document: "Media Pluralism in the Member States of the European Union" ({SEC(2007)32}), Brussels, 16 January 2007, *http://ec.europa.eu/information_society/media_taskforce/doc/pluralism/media_pluralism_swp_en.pdf.*

28. In Italy, no one owner may control more than 20% of the total daily newspaper circulation or more than 50% of a total regional or inter-regional circulation. Any purchase which breaches these limits is liable to be declared void in court, but the limits may be exceeded in the normal course of organic business growth. See, EC (2007), ibid.

29. In France, companies are not allowed to acquire a new newspaper if the acquisition pushes their total daily national circulation to over 30%. See, EC (2007), ibid.

30. No specific limit, but the Minister for Enterprise and Employment has the power to refer any proposed takeover, merger or investment to the Competition Authority to determine whether such an action would lead to a distortion in trade or lessening of commercial competition. See, EC (2007), ibid.

31. The Competition Authority must be notified of any merger in which participating companies have a combined turnover of over EUR 113.5 million and at least two of them have a turnover within the Netherlands of minimum EUR 30 million. See, EC (2007), ibid.

32. Dominant market position is defined as a company's ability to prevent effective competition and conduct business independently of its competitors and customers to a significant extent. A dominant position is when its share of the market exceeds 40%; there are not separate circulation thresholds at local, regional and national level. See, EC (2007), ibid.

33. If any publisher controls over 50% of the market, it has to be reported to the authorities. Source: EC (2007), ibid.

34 In the UK, "The Media Public Interest Test" allows the Secretary of State to intervene in a merger involving a broadcaster and/or a newspaper enterprise if certain conditions are met. The Secretary of State may intervene if 1) the enterprises cease to be distinct; 2) the value of the enterprise being taken over exceeds GBP 70 million; and/or 3) the merger results in at least a 25% share of supply of goods or services in the UK (or substantial part of the UK) or involves an enterprise that has a 25% share of supply of newspapers or broadcasting. See Ofcom (2015) "Report to the Secretary of State on the operation of the media ownership rules listed under Section 391 of the Communications Act 2003, *http://stakeholders.ofcom.org.uk/binaries/research/media-literacy/media-ownership/morr_2015.pdf.*

35. The compulsory distribution of newspapers through press distribution agencies was abolished by virtue of Art.1 ΙΔ.4 of Law 4093/2012 (A'222/12.11.2012).

36. See the Decision of the Greek Council of State, No. 2952/2004.

37 EC (2007), ibid.

38. For instance, the appointed news provider rule in UK, which provides that the channel 3 licence holder needs to source its news from a single news provider that is suitably well-funded and independent of the BBC. See Ofcom (2009), Media Ownership Rules Review, Ofcom, London, *www.ofcom.org.uk/__data/assets/pdf_file/0026/38375/Media-Ownership-Rules-Review.pdf*, p.74.

39. Directive 2010/13/EU of the European Parliament and of the Council of 10 March 2010 on the coordination of certain provisions laid down by law, regulation or administrative action in Member States concerning the provision of audiovisual media services (Audiovisual Media Services Directive), Official Journal L 95, 15.4.2010, p. 1–24

40. Official Gazette A'190/5.11.2010

41. Council Directive 89/552/EEC of 3 October 1989 on the coordination of certain provisions laid down by Law, Regulation or Administrative Action in Member States concerning the pursuit of television broadcasting activities (Official Journal L298, 17.10.1989).

42 See Graham D. et al. (2005), "Impact Study of Measures (Community and National) Concerning the Promotion of Distribution and Production of TV Programmes Provided under Article 25(a) of the TV Without Frontiers Directive: Final Report", David Graham and Associates for The Audiovisual, Media and Internet Unit Directorate-General Information Society and Media European Commission, *www.pedz.uni-mannheim.de/daten/edz-du/gda/05/TV_Progr_25a_finalrep.pdf.*

43. Official Gazette A'98/17.3.2000

44. Recital 71 of AVMS Directive states "When defining 'producers who are independent of broadcasters' as referred to in Article 17, Member States should take appropriate account notably of criteria such as the ownership of the production company, the amount of programmes supplied to the same broadcaster and the ownership of secondary rights." Directive 2010/13/EU, ibid.

45. Official Gazette A'25/4.3.1993

46 An amendment of Art.47 of Law 2121/1993 made after the promulgation of Law 2328/1995 changed the numbers of the paragraphs in Article 47. However, the reference that is made in Art.10, par.1 of Law 2328/1995 to par.2(b) has not been accordingly corrected to reflect that par.2(b) corresponds to par.3(b).

47. According to the Decision of the Greek Council of State, the professional chambers are addressed to professionals whose activity is purely commercial and their main aim is to enter the market and make profit.

 

48. Law 3528/2007 ratifying the Code of Conduct for Public Administrative Employees (Official Gazette A'26/26.09.2007).

49. See also OECD recommendation in row 65 of Media Recommendations Table to explicitly abolish Ministerial Decision 84148/1376//1402/2005 on the exercise of the professions of technicians in the film and TV industry. This administrative regulation provided for compulsory licensing by the Culture Ministry of anyone who wished to work in the film and TV industry, including production manager, director, photographer, editor, on the basis of strict requirements. The regulation is considered abolished since its enactment was based on authorisation of Art.1 of Law 358/1976, which provided the legal framework of the licensing of such professions, and which was abolished by Art. 1, par.H(2) of Law 4254/2014.

50. Article 3 of Law 3905/2010 states that:

*"A 'Greek film work' is a film work that meets the requirements of Article 4 and two of the three following criteria: (A) the original version is in proportion at least 51% in Greek language, (B) at least 51% of the shooting to having been carried out on Greek territory (C) at least 51% of the budget to having been spent on the Greek territory. [...] In exceptional cases, a movie production which does not meet the criteria A, B and C of Article 3, but is related to Greece because of copyright and its content, or special production conditions, may be considered as Greek, after a special decision of the Greek Film Centre."*

Article 4 of Law 3905/2010 provides a detailed point system for different film categories (fiction, documentaries, animated). Films should meet the minimum points required by the law. The point system is related to the citizenship of members of a film's creative team, its actors and technical crew, as well as filming and post-production locations. More specifically, members are required to be Greek citizens or citizens of another member state of the European Union and/or a state included in the Council of Europe European Convention on Transfrontier Television and/or nations included in Council of Europe European Convention for the Cinematographic Co-production ratified by Law 3004/2002 (Official Gazette A'76/08.04.2002) and/or states outside Europe with which Greece has signed bilateral agreement related to film co-production, or they must be a permanent resident of Greece if they come from a country outside the European Union; the legal person is required to have its head office or branch in Greece or in one of the member states of the European Union; the location of shooting shall lie within the Greek territory.

51. See Opinion of the Legal Council of State 54/2016

52. The four main sources of public financing for the film and audiovisual sector in Europe are: 1) public funding; 2) fiscal incentives; 3) mandatory obligations for broadcasters to invest in film and audiovisual production; 4) guarantee facilities (facilitation of access to finance). For instance, there is a mechanism of direct funding that takes the forms of: own production; co-production; direct funding and of indirect funding that include payments to film funds (or similar bodies); payments to film distribution funds; active participation in film funding institutes; taxes (used by the state to support film); broadcasting fees (indirectly used to support film); media services (provision of advertising time, active publicity for films, etc); provision of technical equipment or personnel; special access to picture archives; purchase of rights to films (including presales). See European Audiovisual Observatory (2016), "Funding for film and TV content in Europe rocketed by 13.4% between 2010 and 2014", *www.obs.coe.int/en/-/funding-report-pr-2016*; and EAO (2006), Broadcasters' Obligations to Invest in Cinematographic Production, Iris Special, European Audiovisual Observatory, Strasbourg.

53. Cabrera Blázquez F., M. Cappello, C. Grece, S. Valais (2015), *Territoriality and its impact on the financing of audiovisual works*, IRIS Plus, European Audiovisual Observatory, Strasbourg, 2015,, *www.obs.coe.int/documents/205595/8261963/IRIS+plus+2015en2.pdf/ad5c5a8f-4e85-4e3c-b763-9c763895da1e*, p.47.

54. Copyright collecting societies or collective rights management organisations are: “a type of licensing body which grants rights on behalf of multiple rights holders in a single (‘blanket’) licence for a single payment. Generally speaking, rights holders will join a CMO as members and instruct it to license rights on their behalf. The CMO charges a fee for the licence, from which it deducts an administrative charge before distributing the remainder as royalties. They are typically not for profit organisations and are owned and controlled by their members, the right holders.” UK Intellectual Property Office, *www.gov.uk/guidance/licensing-bodies-and-collective-management-organisations*.

55. Art.49, par.1 provides: “When audio recordings (or visual or audio/visual recordings) are used for a radiotelevision broadcast by any means, such as wireless waves, satellite or cable, or for communication to the public, the user shall pay a single and equitable remuneration to the performers whose performances are carried on the recordings and to the producers of the recordings. This remuneration shall be payable only to collecting societies. The said collecting societies shall be responsible for negotiating and agreeing the remuneration levels, raising the claims for the payment and collecting the remuneration from the users. Where there is a dispute between the users and the collecting societies, the level of the equitable remuneration and the terms of payment shall be determined by the single-member court of first instance pursuant to the cautionary measures procedure at the request of collecting societies (as amended with Art. 46 of L.3905/2010). The final judgment concerning the remuneration shall be rendered by the competent court.”

56. Article 55 of Law 2121/1993.

57. See the interpretation of Article 49 of L. 2121/1993, Vagena, E. et al (2012) “Law of Intellectual Property Rights,”, Sakkoulas Publications, Athens-Thessaloniki, pp.883-884; Mpampetas G., (2015), “‘Legitimation’ of collective societies based on the presumption of article 46§3 of L. 3905/2010”, Chronica Idiotikou Dikaiou IE/2015, pp.164-172, argues that the presumption regarding the collection of the equitable remuneration is irrebuttable.

58. Directive 2014/26/EU of the European Parliament and of the Council of 26 February 2014 on collective management of copyright and related rights and multi-territorial licensing of rights in musical works for online use in the internal market (Official Journal L84/20.3.2014).

59. ARTICLE 10 of ECHR, "Freedom of expression". 1. Everyone has the right to freedom of expression. This right shall include freedom to hold opinions and to receive and impart information and ideas without interference by public authority and regardless of frontiers. This Article shall not prevent States from requiring the licensing of broadcasting, television or cinema enterprises. 2. The exercise of these freedoms, since it carries with it duties and responsibilities, may be subject to such formalities, conditions, restrictions or penalties as are prescribed by law and are necessary in a democratic society, in the interests of national security, territorial integrity or public safety, for the prevention of disorder or crime, for the protection of health or morals, for the protection of the reputation or rights of others, for preventing the disclosure of information received in confidence, or for maintaining the authority and impartiality of the judiciary.

60. Leandros N. (2010), “Media Concentration and Systemic Failures in Greece”, International Journal of Communication, 4(2010), pp.886-905. The European Parliament, the Commission and the Council of Europe have all underlined, in many reports and resolutions, the special democratic role of the media and the related need for pluralism, tolerance, and openness (European Parliament, 2008, 1994; European Commission, 2005a; Council of Europe, 2003).

61. Iosifidis, P. (2014), ibid.

62. Official Gazette A’222/6.10.1989

63. Iosifidis, P. & I. Katsirea (2014), "Public service broadcasting in the Era of Austerity", *International Journal of Digital Television*, 5(1), *http://dx.doi.org/10.1386/jdtv.5.1.103_7,* pp.103-106.

64. In 2001 an ex-member of the National Council for Radio and Television revealed that the Council examined the shareholders lists of the television stations of national range and discovered a number of infringements; see Iosifidis, P. & D. Boucas (2015), "Media Policy and Independent Journalism in Greece", Open Society Foundations, *www.opensocietyfoundations.org/sites/default/files/media-policy-independent-journalism-greece-20150511.pdf.*

65. According to Art.5, par.5 of L. 3592/2007, media of informative content have daily programming that includes frequent and original news, political commentaries and programmes with analysis regarding the actual political and economic situation. Media of non-informative content have programming that exclusively concerns entertainment; for instance, music, sports, films, documentaries, and children's programming. The latter can broadcast non-original news lasting a maximum of one minute an hour.

66. Any natural or legal entity is deemed dominant if active, 1) in media undertakings of the same type, when it has obtained at least 35% market share in the relevant market of each medium in the same range; 2) in media undertakings of different types, when it has obtained either at least 35% market share in the relevant market of each medium or at least 32% market share in the aggregate of two markets, when active in two different media undertakings in the same range; 3) at least 28% market share in the aggregate of three markets, when active in three different media undertakings in the same range; 4) at least 25% market share in the aggregate of four markets, when active in four different media undertakings in the same range.

67. Art.5, par.6 states that: "a) The participation (shareholding) in media of informative content (TV, radio) is permitted without limits regarding the percentage, under the restrictions of paragraphs 2 and 3; b) the participation in media of non-informative content is permitted under the condition that it does not go beyond: a) one TV broadcaster of non-informative content (national or regional) and one (national or regional) of informative content or two of non-informative content (national or regional); b) the percentage of 15% of the total number of radio licences of non-informative content (regional) and maximum 3 radio broadcasters in total."

68. See the Decision of the Greek Council of State No. 2952/2004.

69. Anagnostou D., E. Psychogiopoulou & A. Kandyla (2010), "Media policies and regulatory practices in a selected set of European countries, the EU and the Council of Europe: The case of Greece", MEDIADEM, *www.mediadem.eliamep.gr/wp-content/uploads/2010/05/Greece.pdf,* p.23; and Iosifidis, P. (2014), ibid.

70. Transparency of Media Ownership in Europe: A report for the High-Level Group on Media Freedom and Pluralism, Open Society Media Programme (2012), summary at *www.opensocietyfoundations.org/sites/default/files/Transparency_Media_Ownership_Europe_20121217_0.pdf.*

71. L.1730/1987 (Official Gazette A'145/18.08.1987); see, Karakostas I. (2012), *Media Law*, Nomiki Vivliothiki, Athens, p.136.

72. See the explanatory report of Law 2328/1995 (*http://www.hellenicparliament.gr/Nomothetiko-Ergo/Anazitisi-Nomothetikou-Ergou?law_id=292c430b-f747-4f6c-a560-920bfce9151b*).

73. Official Gazette B'631/25.5.2001.

74. Official Gazette B'304/14.3.2002.

75. The explanatory report of art. 53 of L. 2778/1999 states that the frequency maps and relevant tenders for certain prefectures of the country have been issued and in a short time the relevant procedures in all prefectures will have been completed so as the effort to establish legitimacy and transparency in the radio landscape in the country to be achieved.

76. L. 3444/2006, Art.15, par.7(b): extension until 30.06.2006; Law 3548/2007 art.9, par.2: extension until 30.06.2007.

77. After L. 3592/2007, which is the legal framework in force for radio licencing, nine provisions added in several laws with irrelevant content have been promulgated.

| Legal provisions | Extension of the deadline for launching a tender |
|---|---|
| Law 4313/2014 art.86, par.1 | Until 31.12.2015 |
| Law 4279/2014 art.6, par.4(a) | Until 31.12.2014 |
| Law 4208/2013 art.17 | Until 31.12.2013 |
| Law 4038/2012 art.8, par.4 | Until 31.12.2012 |
| Law 3905/2010 art.49, par.8 | Until 31.12.2011 |
| Law 3838/2010 art. 29 par. 4 | Until 31.12.2010 |
| Law 3775/2009 art.38 | Until 31.12.2009 |
| Law 3723/2008 art.9 | Until 30.06.2009 |
| Law 3640/2008 art.2, par.1 | Until 31.10.2008 |

78. The provision of L. 2778/1999 regarding the possibility of radio stations to be recognised as legally operating just because they have started their operation before 1.11.1999 is still in force.

79. See Decisions 1206/2012 and 3315/2014 of the Greek Council of State.

80. The same remark was made by the Greek Council of State under the constitutional principle of equality (see endnote 86).

81. According to Art.8, par.3 of L. 3592/2007, the Minister of Infrastructure, Transport and Networks together with the Minister in Charge of the Media Sector, based upon the opinion of the national regulator for networks (EETT), should issue a joint ministerial decision (JMD) with the map of frequencies for radio broadcasting. More specifically, the map of frequencies defines the technical requirements for radio broadcasting including ERT SA, the restrictions with which the broadcast centre should comply, the prefecture/ geographic coverage area of each broadcast centre and thus the map of frequency for each prefecture / geographical area is formed, according also to the International Telecommunication Convention and the Radio Regulation attached to it as well as the International Conventions for assignment frequencies in radio stations. Finally, in the JMD the procedures for the periodic inspection of the restrictions above are included.

82. See "For instance, English nurseries can look after up to four two-year-olds for every member of staff, compared to six two-year-olds per member of staff in the Netherlands and Ireland, and eight two-year-olds in France. Other countries – such as Denmark, Germany and Sweden – do not set national mandatory ratios for children of any age," UK Department of Education (2013), "More great childcare: Raising quality and giving parents more choice", Department of Education, London, *www.gov.uk/government/uploads/system/uploads/attachment_data/file/219660/More_20Great_20Childcare_20v2.pdf, p.8.*

83. "Generally, from the standpoint of standard theory, there are at least four ways in which regulation may create obstacles to entrepreneurs seeking to enter an industry with service-improving innovations: (i) By increasing the overall cost of doing business within an industry; (ii) by explicitly treating incumbents more favorably than new entrants, (iii) by implicitly imposing a regulatory risk on new entrants that is greater than that faced by incumbents; (iv) By creating regulatory complexity that favors incumbents

who have already worked their way down "compliance learning curves," Auerswald P.E. (2015), "Enabling Entrepreneurial Ecosystems", Kauffman Foundation, Arlington, p.14.

84. A brief presentation of NCRTV and its powers is available at *www.esr.gr/arxeion-xml/pages/esr/esrSite/list_docs?section=1a6156445e291e7983571826e98263e5&categ=3d4eee4d84a11e7d83571826e98263e5&last_clicked_id=link2.*

85. See Recital 85 of Directive 2013/13/EC , *http://eur-lex.europa.eu/LexUriServ/LexUriServ.do?uri=OJ:L:2010:095:0001:0024:en:PDF.*

86. According to the Directive's recitals, daily transmission time allotted to announcements made by the broadcaster in connection with its own programmes and ancillary products directly derived from these, or to public service announcements and charity appeals broadcast free of charge, should not be included in the maximum amounts of daily or hourly transmission time that may be allotted to advertising and teleshopping. See Recital 97 of Directive 2013/13/EC.

87. Recital 98 of Directive 2013/13/EC.

88. "Ανακοινώσεις που γίνονται από τηλεοπτικό οργανισμό για τα δικά του προγράμματα και δευτερεύοντα προϊόντα που παράγονται απευθείας από τα προγράμματα αυτά, κοινωνικά μηνύματα, ανακοινώσεις χορηγίας και τοποθέτηση προϊόντος, δεν προσμετρώνται στον ως άνω διαφημιστικό χρόνο."

89. See "Pay TV: Content, mobile apps and commercial policy define the scene", Marketing Week Online (23.09.2015), *www.marketingweek.gr/default.asp?pid=9&la=1&cID=3&arID=56037* (accessed on 10.09.2016).

90. An over-the-top service is digital content bought by end-users from a third party and for which an ISP's only role is to transport the data.

91. See Digital TV Europe (2015), "Friend or foe: OTT and Pay-TV services", *www.digitaltveurope.net/410341/friend-or-foe-ott-and-pay-tv-services/* (accessed 11.9.2016).

92. See Ofcom (2015), The Communications Market Report, *www.ofcom.org.uk/research-and-data/cmr/cmr16.*

93. Directorate-General for Internal Policies of the European Parliament (2015), Over -the-Top players (OTTs), Study for the IMCO Committee, 2015, *www.europarl.europa.eu/RegData/etudes/STUD/2015/569979/IPOL_STU(2015)569979_EN.pdf*

94. Art. 5 of L. 2644/1998.

95. Art 6 of L. 2644/1998.

96. OECD, Competition issues in television and broadcasting, Contribution from Greece, DAF/COMP/GF/WD(2013)44, 28/02/2013.

97. The official NCRTV website mentions that Article 15 applies to broadband networks, but not web TV/radio. See, *www.esr.gr/arxeion-xml/pages/esr/esrSite/view?section=e5f2cfb3c0aa1e7683571826e98263e5&categ=87af05904c851c7b83571826e98263e5.*

98. Administrative Regulation EETT 676/41 (B'298/14.02.2013) "Regulation for General Authorisation", *www.eett.gr/opencms/export/sites/default/admin/downloads/telec/apofaseis_eett/kanonistikes_apofaseis_eett/AP676-041.pdf.*

99. "B. Annual Fees. 1. All persons operating under a General Authorisation regime and providing public communication networks or publicly available electronic communication services shall have to pay an annual administrative fee, calculated as a percentage of the total gross income derived from the provision of public communication networks or publicly available electronic communication services under a General Authorisation regime as follows:

| Zone of total annual income (E) in EURO million | Administrative fee factor per zone |
|---|---|
| E ≤ 0.15 | 0 |
| 0.15 < E ≤ 250 | 0.0025 |
| 250 < E ≤ 750 | 0.004 |
| 750 < E | 0.0005 |

"For each calendar year, the annual administrative fee, which shall be calculated based on the above table, shall be paid no later than 30 June of the following calendar year, and shall necessarily be accompanied by the Declaration of Payment of Fees (Annex C) without requiring any relevant prior written notification by EETT". See Administrative Regulation EETT 676/41, ibid.

100. This provision is in line with the rule "two out of three" provided by Law 2328/1998, updated by Law 3592/2007, which includes the same rule.

101. This statement is not necessarily true in other countries, but in Greece almost all available subscription-TV products are entertainment content (such as films and sport) and not informative content (such as news and political talk shows).

102. According to Art.3, the distinction between managers (διαχειριστής) and suppliers (προμηθευτής) of the programme is based on the duration of the supplied programme and the logo used during its broadcasting. Manager is the company that either supplies at least 20 hours of programme a day and in this case the use of its logo is compulsory or uses its logo even if the programme is less than 20 hours. In all other cases, the company is called supplier.

## References


Anagnostou D., E. Psychogiopoulou & A. Kandyla (2010), Media policies and regulatory practices in a selected set of European countries, the EU and the Council of Europe: The case of Greece, MEDIADEM, *www.mediadem.eliamep.gr/wp-content/uploads/2010/05/Greece.pdf.*

Anagnostou D., E. Psychogiopoulou & A. Kandyla (2011), "Does media policy promote media freedom and independence? The case of Greece", MEDIADEM, *www.mediadem.eliamep.gr/wp-content/uploads/2012/01/Greece.pdf.*

Article 19 (2012), Regulation on State Aid to Print Media, *www.article19.org/data/files/medialibrary/3554/State-subsidies-press.pdf.*

Auerswald P.E. (2015), "Enabling Entrepreneurial Ecosystems", Kauffman Foundation, Arlington.

Cabrera Blázquez F., M. Cappello, C. Grece, S. Valais (2015), Territoriality and its impact on the financing of audiovisual works, IRIS Plus, European Audiovisual Observatory, Strasbourg, 2015, *www.obs.coe.int/documents/205595/8261963/IRIS+plus+2015en2.pdf/ad5c5a8f-4e85-4e3c-b763-9c763895da1e*.

David Graham and Associates (2005), "Impact Study of Measures (Community and National) Concerning the Promotion of Distribution and Production of TV Programmes Provided under Article 25(a) of the TV Without Frontiers Directive: Final Report", David Graham and Associates for the Audiovisual, Media and Internet Unit Directorate-General Information Society and Media European Commission, *www.pedz.uni-mannheim.de/daten/edz-du/gda/05/TV_Progr_25a_finalrep.pdf*.

Directorate-General for Internal Policies of the European Parliament (2015), Over -the-top players (OTTs), Study for the IMCO Committee, 2015, *www.europarl.europa.eu/RegData/etudes/STUD/2015/569979/IPOL_STU(2015)569979_EN.pdf*.

European Commission (1992), "Pluralism and Media Concentration in the Internal Market: An Assessment of the Need for Community Action", Green Paper, COM (92) 480 final, 23 December 1992.

European Commission (2007), Commission Staff Working Document: "Media Pluralism in the Member States of the European Union" ({SEC(2007)32}), Brussels, 16 January 2007, *http://ec.europa.eu/information_society/media_taskforce/doc/pluralism/media_pluralism_swp_en.pdf*.

EAO (2006), Broadcasters' Obligations to Invest in Cinematographic Production, Iris Special, European Audiovisual Observatory, Strasbourg.

European Audiovisual Observatory (2016), "Funding for film and TV content in Europe rocketed by 13.4% between 2010 and 2014", *www.obs.coe.int/en/-/funding-report-pr-2016*.

Iosifidis, P. (2014), "Pluralism, Media Mergers and European Merger Control", The Palgrave Handbook of European Media Policy, London, *http://dx.doi.org/10.1057/9781137032195_25*, pp.461-475.

Iosifidis, P. & D. Boucas (2015), "Media Policy and Independent Journalism in Greece", Open Society Foundations, *www.opensocietyfoundations.org/sites/default/files/media-policy-independent-journalism-greece-20150511.pdf*.

Iosifidis, P. & I. Katsirea (2014), "Public service broadcasting in the era of austerity", International Journal of Digital Television, 5(1), pp.103-106, *http://dx.doi.org/10.1386/jdtv.5.1.103_7*.

Leandros N. (2010), "Media Concentration and Systemic Failures in Greece", International Journal of Communication, 4(2010), pp.886-905.

Media Reform Coalition (2015), "The elephant next door: a survey of international media ownership regulations", *www.mediareform.org.uk/wp-content/uploads/2015/11/The_Elephant_Next_Door-A_Survey_of_International_Media_Ownership_Regulations.pdf*.

OECD (2013), "Competition issues in television and broadcasting, Contribution from Greece", DAF/COMP/GF/WD(2013)44, 28/02/2013.

Ofcom (2009), Media Ownership Rules Review, Ofcom, London, *www.ofcom.org.uk/__data/assets/pdf_file/0026/38375/Media-Ownership-Rules-Review.pdf.*

Ofcom (2015), Report to the Secretary of State on the operation of the media ownership rules listed under Section 391 of the Communications Act 2003, *http://stakeholders.ofcom.org.uk/binaries/research/media-literacy/media-ownership/morr_2015.pdf.*

Ofcom (2015), The Communications Market Report, *www.ofcom.org.uk/research-and-data/cmr/cmr16.*

Open Society Media Programme (2012), "Transparency of Media Ownership in Europe: A report for the High-Level Group on Media Freedom and Pluralism", summary at *www.opensocietyfoundations.org/sites/default/files/Transparency_Media_Ownership_Europe_20121217_0.pdf.*

Schweizer, C., M. Puppis, M. Künzler, S. Studer (2014), "Public Funding of Private Media", Media Policy Brief 11, LSE Media Policy Project, March 2014, *www.lse.ac.uk/media@lse/documents/MPP/LSE-MPP-Policy-Brief-11-Public-Funding-Private-Media.pdf.*

UK Department of Education (2013), "More great childcare: Raising quality and giving parents more choice", Department of Education, London, *www.gov.uk/government/uploads/system/uploads/attachment_data/file/219660/More_20Great_20Childcare_20v2.pdf.*

Βαγενά Α., Δεσποτίδου Α., Ζάννος Γ.Α., Κανελλοπούλου-Μπότη Μ., Κοτσίρης Λ.Ε., Κυπρούλη Κ., Παπαδοπούλου Α., Παπαδοπούλου Μ.Δ., Σαραφιανός Δ., Σινανίδου Μ.Γ., Σταματούδη Ε., Συνοδινού Τ.Ε. (2009), «Νόμος για την Πνευματική Ιδιοκτησία», Εκδόσεις Σάκκουλα, Αθήνα-Θεσσαλονίκη [Vagena, E. et al (2012) "Law of Intellectual Property Rights", Sakkoulas Publications, Athens-Thessaloniki]

Καράκωστας Ι. (2012), "Το δίκαιο των Μ.Μ.Ε.", Νομική Βιβλιοθήκη, Αθήνα [Karakostas I. (2012), Media Law, Nomiki Vivliothiki, Athens]

Μπαμπέτας Γ. (2015) "Η Νομιμοποίηση των οργανισμών συλλογικής διαχείρισης βάσει του τεκμηρίου του άρθρου 46 παρ. 3 του Ν. 3905/2010", Χρονικά Ιδιωτικού Δικαίου, ΙΕ 2015, σελ. 164-172 [Mpampetas G., (2015), "'Legitimation' of collective societies based on the presumption of article 46§3 of L. 3905/2010", Chronica Idiotikou Dikaiou IE/2015, pp.164-172]

**Databases**

Eurostat, Annual detailed enterprise statistics for services (NACE Rev. 2, H-N and S95), Database [sbs_na_1a_se_r2], *http://ec.europa.eu/eurostat* (accessed 4 April 2016).

*Chapter 5*

# Chemicals and rubber, electrical equipment, paper and printing

*Manufacture and wholesale trade of chemicals and rubber products, electrical equipment, paper and paper products, and printing and reproduction of recorded media are covered in this chapter. Regulatory barriers to competition are identified in the detergents and biocides industries, especially in terms of product trading (i.e. selling in bulk, prevention of umbrella-branding) and the licensing of manufacturing facilities. For cosmetics, products' primary and secondary functions should be recognised by Greek legislation in line with EU guidance, helping suppliers and enhancing product mix. Abolishing excise duty on isopropyl alcohol would result in lower prices and in an increase of the competitiveness of Greek manufacturers that use it as a raw material. The alignment of the administrative registration and conformity marks of sockets and plugs will facilitate suppliers' operations and enhance consumer protection. The cumulative effect of the recommendations will be to make markets more open and competitive, to the benefit of consumers.*

This chapter covers the manufacture of chemicals and rubber products, electrical equipment, paper and paper products, and printing and reproduction of recorded media in Greece. It describes the sectors' findings of the competition assessment, as well as the sectors' overview. It is noted that the assessment of the legislation covered both manufacturing and wholesale trade activities.

The aforementioned sectors[1] accounted for 1.2% of GDP in Greece in 2013, compared with a figure of 3.2% for the European Union on average. When measured in terms of employment, the sector represents 1.4% of the Greek economy; the corresponding figure for the European Union is 2.7% on average.

The main restrictions identified in the manufacturing sectors assessed in this project, as traced in the Greek legislation, are described in detail in the following sections. Their harm to competition and recommendations are also set out. The benefits of these recommendations are estimated to amount to EUR 17 million. This includes an estimated consumer benefit of EUR 3.6 million, as a result of abolishing excise duty on isopropyl alcohol, passed onto the final price; see the analysis outlined in Box 5.4. The OECD has considered whether recommendations would be expected to have an impact on either consumer benefit, through lower prices, or on economic activity, in terms of greater efficiency and additional revenue. In the former case, the framework described in Annex A was applied; in the latter, we have made a conservative assumption on an overall improvement in the efficiency of operation.[2]

## 5.1. Chemicals and rubber products

The sub-sectors examined in this section include the following codes:

- Manufacture of basic chemicals, fertilisers and nitrogen compounds, plastics and synthetic rubber in primary forms (NACE code 20.1)
- Manufacture of pesticides and other agrochemical products (NACE code 20.2)
- Manufacture of soap and detergents, cleaning and polishing preparations, perfumes and toilet preparations (NACE code 20.4)
- Manufacture of other chemical products (NACE code 20.5)
- Manufacture of man-made fibres (NACE code 20.6)
- Manufacture of rubber products (NACE code 22.1)

It is also noted that manufacture of paints, varnishes and similar coatings, printing ink and mastics (NACE code 20.3), as well as manufacture of plastics products (NACE code 22.2), were not part of this project, as their relevant regulatory framework was examined during the first OECD Competition Assessment of Laws and Regulations in Greece project in 2013[3].

Although the review of the legislation has covered chemicals and rubber products both at manufacturing and at wholesale trade level, due to data limitations the sector overview that follows deals only with the manufacturing level.

### *Economic overview*

Chemicals as primary raw materials are mostly imported in Greece. Manufacturing companies operating in the domestic market mostly deal with processing them into end products.

Figure 5.1 compares the value added of chemicals and rubber products as a percentage of the total manufacturing in Greece and in the EU[4] for the six-year period of 2008-2013. During this time, the sub-sector's contribution to the overall manufacturing sector amounts to 4.5% on average in Greece, compared to 7.2% at EU level.

Figure 5.1. **Value added as a percentage of manufacturing for chemicals and rubber products (2008-2013)**

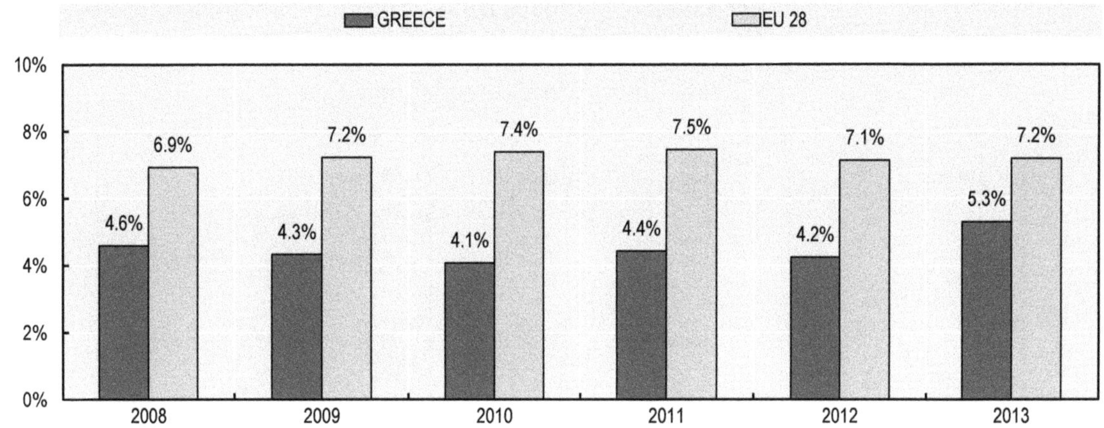


*Note*: Value added at factor cost

*Source*: Eurostat, Annual detailed enterprise statistics for industry (NACE Rev. 2, B-E), Database [sbs_na_ind_r2], *http://ec.europa.eu/eurostat* (accessed 24 August 2016).

Figure 5.2 depicts the turnover of manufacturing of chemicals and rubber products and total manufacturing for Greece, for the period 2008-2014. The sector's turnover amounts to EUR 2 062 million in 2014, showing gradual increase over the three-year period of 2012-2014 (14.0%), despite the recession, which has affected the manufacturing sector as a whole (-4.9% during the same period).

Figure 5.2. **Turnover of manufacturing chemicals and rubber products in Greece (2008-2014)**

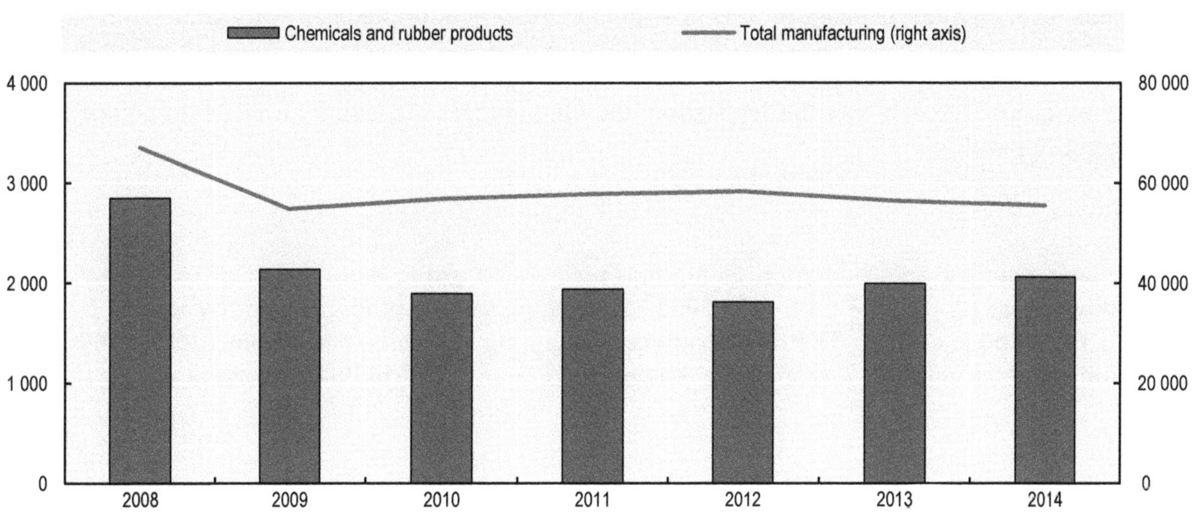


*Note*: Turnover in EUR millions

*Source*: Eurostat, Annual detailed enterprise statistics for industry (NACE Rev. 2, B-E), Database [sbs_na_ind_r2], *http://ec.europa.eu/eurostat* (accessed 24 August 2016)

Figure 5.3 shows the structure of the turnover of manufacturing of chemicals and rubber products per category. Manufacture of basic chemicals, fertilisers and nitrogen compounds, plastics and synthetic rubber in primary forms and manufacture of soap and detergents, cleaning and polishing preparations, perfumes and toilet preparations cover more than 70% of total turnover during the seven-year period 2008-2014.

Figure 5.3. **Share of manufacturing chemicals and rubber products turnover per category in Greece (2008-2014)**

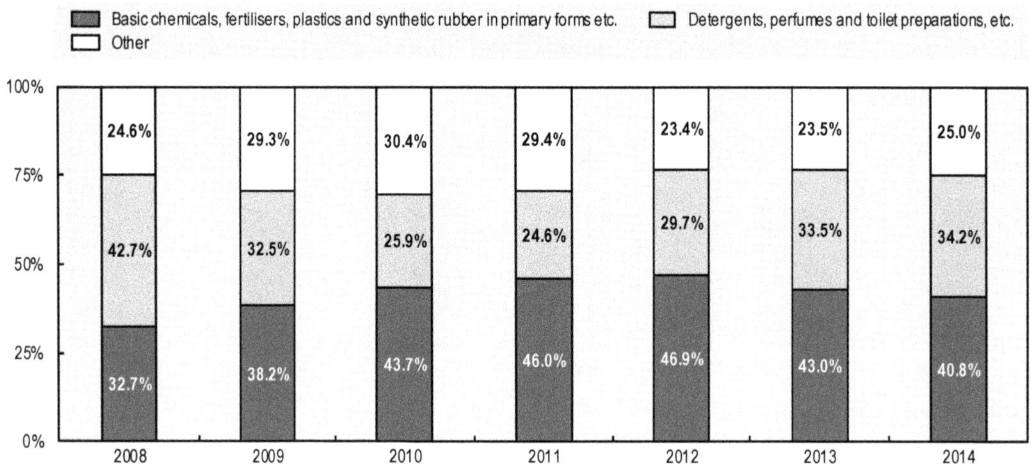


*Source*: Eurostat, Annual detailed enterprise statistics for industry (NACE Rev. 2, B-E), Database [sbs_na_ind_r2], *http://ec.europa.eu/eurostat* (accessed 24 August 2016).

The number of manufacturing companies in the sector has fallen from 1001 companies in 2008 to 686 companies in 2014, of which one third operates in the soap and detergents, cleaning and polishing preparations, perfumes and toilet preparations sub-sector.[5]

Employment has shrunk from 13 288 in 2008 to 10 636 persons in 2014. The soap and detergents, cleaning and polishing preparations, perfumes and toilet preparations sub-sector ranks first in terms of employment, with an average share of 39.1% of total employment in the chemicals sector over the same period.

After extensive screening of the legislation, the OECD team identified obstacles to competition in the following sub-sectors.

*Detergents*

The detergents sub-sector (NACE code 20.41) generated gross value added of EUR 79.0 million in 2013, down from EUR 239.8 million in 2008.[6] During the same period, turnover contracted by 72.6% overall, to EUR 256.9 million. The number of manufacturing enterprises fell from 225 in 2008 to 164 in 2013 and the total number of employees was reduced from 2 827 to 1 705 workers during the same period.

*Pesticides*

The pesticides[7] sub-sector (NACE code 20.20) generated gross value added of EUR 29.4 million in 2013, remaining stable overtime, and a total turnover of EUR 151.2 million, increased by 5.6% on an annual basis since 2008.[8] The number of manufacturing enterprises was 21 in 2013, employing a total of 552 workers.

*Fertilisers*

The fertilisers sub-sector (NACE code 20.15) generated gross value added of EUR 50.6 million in 2013, losing over half of its value since 2008 (EUR 113.0 million).[9] Total turnover amounted to EUR 282.7 million in 2013, a decline of 2.9% on an annual basis since 2008. The number of operating enterprises in the sub-sector rose from 36 in 2008 to 41 companies in 2013; total employment, however, decreased from 1 032 workers in 2008 to 831 in 2013.

*Cosmetics*

The cosmetics sub-sector (NACE code 20.42) generated gross value added of EUR 180.9 million in 2013, an increase of 10.4% on an annual basis since 2008.[10] Total turnover amounted to EUR 412.4 million in 2013, while previous years averaged around EUR 270 million. Despite the fall in the number of operating enterprises in the sub-sector (from 105 in 2008 to 72 in 2013), total employment increased from 2 269 in 2008 to 2 963 in 2013.

***Overview of the legislation***

The mapping of the legislation for the sector included 137 sector-specific laws and regulations, as well as framework and horizontal legislation covering manufacturing as a whole. Out of the 137 regulations:

- 17 pieces of regulations are framework legislation and concern the classification, packaging and labelling of dangerous substances and preparations;
- 69 laws and regulations are relevant to agricultural inputs, of which 3 regulations are applicable to all relevant goods, 50 applicable to plant protection products and 16 applicable to fertilisers;
- 38 regulations are relevant to different categories of chemical products, such as detergents, biocidal products, dispersants, cosmetics, explosives, pyrotechnics and tyres;
- 8 laws and regulations concern taxation issues, mainly excise duties on alcohol products used by the chemical industry as raw materials (e.g. isopropyl alcohol), as well as regulations that include provisions on the establishment and function of tax warehouses;
- 5 pieces of laws and regulations are relevant to chemicals, mainly the bottling of compressed (pressurised) gas.

With regard to detergents, the core legislative framework originates from the EU, consisting mainly of EU Regulation 648/2004.[11] Regarding national legislation, Presidential Decree 111/2014,[12] setting out the organisational structure of the Ministry of Finance and, subsequently the competencies of the General Chemical State Laboratory (GCSL), assigns the latter as the competent authority for the control of detergents. The control mechanisms, the fees and the penalties for the violation of the relevant legislation are left to Ministerial Decisions. More particularly, Ministerial Decisions 1233/1991 and 172/1992[13] provide the legal framework for the licensing of manufacturing facilities of detergents and Joint Ministerial Decision 381/2005[14] introduces the necessary national provisions for the implementation of EU Regulation 648/2004.

The legislative framework for biocides is more complex, due to recent legislative changes on national and EU level. EU Regulation 528/2012[15] introduced new licensing procedures for biocidal products whose active ingredients have been approved at an EU level, yet national implementing measures were issued only in May 2016, through Joint Ministerial Decision 4616/52519/2016.[16] Until

EU Regulation 528/2012 covers all active ingredients included in biocides, the products are regulated under Law 721/1977[17] for those falling under the competency of the Ministry of Rural Development and Food, and under Ministerial Decision 7723/1993[18] for those falling under the competency of the National Organisation for Medicines (EOF).

As far as agricultural chemical inputs are concerned, Law 4036/2012[19] and Presidential Decree 159/2013[20] constitute the core legislation for plant protection products, regulating their production, usage, control and circulation. Concerning fertilisers, Law 1565/1985[21] sets the basic legal framework. Both plant protection products and fertilisers are intensely regulated, with substantive part of the legislation having EU origin. However, EU Regulations and Directives leave room for important national interventions, many of which impose restrictions that have been identified.

The core legislation for cosmetics that are placed and circulated in the EU market consists of EU Regulation 1223/2009, which provides for a centralised notification procedure before the circulation of the products in the market and further streamlines the framework for all operators in the sector. In addition, under the Greek legislative framework, Ministerial Decision A6/2880/1980 provides for specific rules on good manufacturing practices and control of cosmetics specifying the requirements cosmetic manufacturers shall comply with.

As regards isopropyl alcohol (also called isopropanol), the imposition of excise duty and its exemption procedure, the National Customs Code and Ministerial Decisions 811/337/2008[22] and 812/338/2008[23] constitute the main regulatory framework. These regulations set out the terms and conditions for the denaturation establishment and function of tax warehouses of isopropyl alcohol either domestically produced or coming from EU countries.

***Detergents***

*Selling detergents in bulk*

*Description of the provisions*

According to Article 84 paragraph 3 of Ministerial Decision A2/718/2014 on Rules for the supply and distribution of products and the provision of services,[24] selling detergents and cleaning products in bulk is forbidden and is subject to penalties (see paragraph 5 of Article 84). Since there is no clarification in the Ministerial Decision or in any other piece of relevant legislation, this prohibition seems to cover both wholesale and retail trade of detergents.

*Objective of the provisions*

There is no official recital. However, following communication with the GCSL, it is OECD's understanding that this provision aims to facilitate the control of detergent quality on grounds of consumer protection and traceability, since it is more difficult to control the composition and quality of chemical products traded in bulk. Additionally, packaged goods are easily classified and labelled.

*Harm to competition*

In general, the prohibition of wholesale trade of detergents in bulk restricts the ability of companies to exploit economies of scale and raises the cost of operations, potentially leading to higher consumer prices. Moreover, EC regulations do not forbid the trading of detergents in bulk, but introduce provisions in order to safeguard consumer protection. In particular, Regulation 648/2004, when referring to the necessary information that has to be labelled on the packaging, indicates that the same information must appear on all documents accompanying detergents transported in bulk.[25] It is, therefore, evident that the EU legal framework does not restrict the selling of detergents in bulk, as long as the necessary conditions are met. The national legislation may therefore create regulatory uncertainty.

*Recommendation and benefits*

Given the considerations above, we recommend **abolishing the restriction of trading in bulk** for the case of wholesale trade, as long as accompanying documentation is available. As a result, suppliers will be able to exploit economies of scale and benefit from reduced costs.

*Licensing of detergent manufacturers*

*Description of the provisions*

The legal framework for manufacturing facilities of detergents is regulated by Ministerial Decisions 1233/1991 and 172/1992 on the Registration System for detergents and cleaning products. These Ministerial Decisions introduce the obligation for manufacturers of detergents to obtain a special licence from the GCSL and set out the conditions for the issuance of such a licence. The justification for such restriction is public health and the protection of the environment.

In the relevant legislation the following restrictive provisions have been identified.

- Article 6 paragraph 4 of Ministerial Decision 1233/1991 and 172/1992 regulates minimum square metres of the premises of the industries or professional laboratories where the manufacture of detergents takes place. More specifically, this provision requires a surface of at least $100m^2$ for each establishment, as a prerequisite for the operator to be granted the necessary operation licence.

- Article 6 paragraph 6 of Ministerial Decisions 1233/1991 and 172/1992[26] sets out that the special licence granted by the GCSL will be abolished or revoked if the ownership status of the manufacturing facility changes.

The objective of these provisions is not clear, since there are no official recitals. However, following communication with the GCSL, the OECD has concluded that:

- Article 6 paragraph 4: the minimum surface guarantees an adequate space where all activities can take place for health and safety reasons, as well as to guarantee the quality of the product;

- Article 6 paragraph 6: the objective is to safeguard against the illegal operation of a manufacturing facility by any legal or natural person who is not the owner.

*Harm to competition*

From a competition point of view, a minimum -surface requirement imposes an extra cost and may discourage potential entrants, thus acting as a barrier to entry in the market, especially for small-scale operators. Even if this minimum requirement is not that restrictive, since the threshold is low, the provision does not appear necessary. The operator's liability is sufficient to ensure all health and safety requirements, and these can be safeguarded by other means. For example, the authorities have the power to inspect premises ex post and so ensure that health and safety requirements are met.

The revocation of licences in the case of ownership changes may cause harm to competition, since it restricts entrepreneurship and business strategies. In particular, it may discourage operators from entering or exiting the market, in their search for profitable investments. The obligation to re-issue the special licence in case of change of ownership status is disproportionate, as the production facilities are not altered.

*Recommendations and benefits*

The OECD recommends:

- abolishing minimum dimensions, in order to give greater flexibility to potential investors, and possibly encourage entry;
- abolishing the ownership rule since it goes beyond what is necessary to achieve the policy maker's objective. However, a notification procedure to the competent authority in case of change in the ownership status of an enterprise could be established. As a result, operators will avoid unnecessary costs and procedures.

*Withdrawal of detergents from the market*

*Description of the provisions*

According to Article 1 paragraph 1 of Joint Ministerial Decision 381/2005 on the Determination of competent authority and of the control mechanisms, fees and penalties for the application of EU Regulation 648/2004 on detergents,[27] the Directorate of Raw Materials and Industrial Products of the GCSL is the competent authority for the application of Regulation 648/2004 on detergents. Article 3 paragraph 4 foresees that if a detergent is not in compliance with the provisions of Regulation 648/2004, the Directorate of Raw Materials and Industrial Products should withdraw from the market the detergent in question. Therefore, seizure and withdrawal decisions concerning detergents are issued by the Directorate of Raw Materials and Industrial Products.

There is no official recital for this provision. However, it is the OECD's understanding that it aims to protect public health and the environment by allocating responsibility of controls of detergents circulating in the market to the competent Directorate of the GCSL. Compliance with the European and Greek legislative framework is ensured through market inspections implemented by the competent national authorities.

*Harm to competition*

Following communication with the Directorate of Raw Materials and Industrial Products of the GCSL, the OECD understands that decisions about the withdrawal of detergents from the market are currently not published or made public, and only the company that produces or imports the product in question is notified. This limits information available to consumers, as well as their ability to decide from whom to purchase. This is especially important when products are withdrawn on the grounds of protecting public health. Finally, publication of product-withdrawal decisions is extremely important, since it promotes transparency and fosters competition.

Table 5.1 shows that both withdrawal decisions and non-compliant samples of detergents and cleaning products have been reduced, in absolute terms, during the period 2013-2015.

Table 5.1. **Withdrawal decisions for detergents and cleaning products by the GCSL (2013-2015)**

| | 2013 | 2014 | 2015 |
|---|---|---|---|
| **Samples** | 205 | 172 | 118 |
| **Non-compliant samples** | 78 | 41 | 36 |
| **Percentage of non-compliant samples** | 38.0% | 23.8% | 30.5% |
| **Inspections** | 162 | 172 | 129 |
| **Products checked** | 587 | 799 | 586 |
| **Withdrawal decisions** | 73 | 36 | 27 |

*Source*: Annual Activity Reports, GCSL of Greece.

*Recommendation and benefit*

The OECD recommends that decisions of the Directorate of Raw Materials and Industrial Products of the GCSL on withdrawal of detergents should be made public, in order to foster consumer protection, transparency and competition. Other national bodies and authorities competent for the circulation of products in the market, which carry out inspections and have the authority to withdraw tested products if not found appropriate to circulate, already publish their decisions, either on their websites, i.e. National Organisation for Medicines (EOF) or as press releases, i.e. National Food Authority (EFET). In all cases, the objective is consumer protection and better comparative decision making between products, by delivering the information consumers would value.

***Biocides***

*Introduction*

Annex V of EU Regulation 528/2012[28] concerning the making available on the market and use of biocidal products, distinguishes between 22 product-types of biocides. According to Article 81 of that Regulation, Member States shall designate a competent authority, or competent authorities, responsible for its application. They should have a sufficient number of suitably qualified and experienced staff so that the obligations laid down in the Regulation can be carried out efficiently and effectively.

Greece has divided the competency for biocides between two national authorities, the National Organisation for Medicines and the General Directorate of Sustainable Plant Production of the Ministry of Rural Development and Food. This is mainly due to historical reasons. Disinfectants or personal and pet hygiene products, which under the current EU legislation are categorised as biocidal products, have fallen under the competency of the National Organisation for Medicines since its establishment in 1983,[29] while the Ministry of Rural Development and Food has been responsible for the licensing and control of pest-control products (rodenticides, vermicides, insecticides, etc.), since 1977, as introduced by Law 721/1977.

*Description of the provisions*

Both national and EU legislation require an authorisation procedure for making biocides available on the market and their use. Biocides that fall under the jurisdiction of the National Organisation for Medicines are authorised pursuant either to Regulation 528/2012 or Ministerial Decision 7723/1994,[30] whereas those that fall under the jurisdiction of the Ministry of Rural Development and Food are authorised in accordance with either to Regulation 528/2012 or Law 721/1977.[31]

All these procedures require an application accompanied by supporting documents, e.g. identification and contact details of the person responsible for the circulation of the product; chemical and technical characteristics of the product; and trade name of the product, etc. It should also be noted that neither the EU nor the Greek legal framework for biocides sets any restrictions on the use of the trade name of the product in relation to the active ingredient it contains.

When considering applications for the authorisation of biocides, the National Organisation for Medicines does apply a combination of pharmaceutical provisions, in order to prevent producers from marketing products with different qualitative chemical composition in terms of active ingredients under the same brand name ("umbrella branding" or "family branding"[32]). Specifically, the National Organisation for Medicines applies Article 10 paragraph 2 of Legislative Decree 96/1973[33] on the marketing of pharmaceutical products to biocides, according to which the brand name of a pharmaceutical product must mandatorily change upon any amendment in the active substance. Moreover, the National Organisation for Medicines applies Joint Ministerial Decision Δ.ΥΓ3α/Γ.Π.32221/2013[34] on the production and circulation of medicinal products for human use when evaluating dossiers for authorisation of biocides and more specifically the following provisions:

- Article 2 recital 23 on the name of the medicinal product, according to which the name given to a medicinal product may be either an invented name or a common or scientific name, together with a trademark or the name of the manufacturer; the invented name shall not be liable to confusion with the common name; and
- Article 9 paragraph 3 on the application for authorisation, according to which the application shall be accompanied by the following particulars and documents, among others: "(b) name of the medicinal product".

According to the National Organisation for Medicines, since the authorisation is unique for each product, the trademark accompanying the product, as part of its authorisation documents, is also unique. Therefore, biocidal products with different qualitative chemical composition in terms of active ingredients cannot circulate under the same brand name. The OECD team understands that this is a new interpretation of the legislation and that new products are not being authorised under the same brand name.

*Objective of the provisions*

It was not possible to identify the objective of these specific provisions through the official recital. However, following communication with the National Organisation for Medicines, the OECD understands that the objective of these provisions is to avoid consumer confusion over different biocidal products circulating under the same brand name, and so to protect public health.

*Harm to competition*

If these provisions are interpreted as completely preventing umbrella branding, then they could hamper suppliers' ability to compete and prevent them from exploiting economies of scope in advertising. Developing a brand name usually involves significant advertising expenses, so if a company cannot use the same brand name on slightly different products with small additions (such as the clarification that the product is to be used for hands or for the floor), it will have to invest more in brand development.

In addition, products authorised until recently were allowed to bear the same brand, despite their different chemical composition. The new interpretation of the provisions would block the entry of new products and possibly discriminate against some suppliers over others.

Box 5.1. **Umbrella branding**

Umbrella branding, also known as family branding, is a type of marketing tactic which involves the use of one brand name for the sale of several related products. For example, a company may use one brand to market soap, lotion, hair shampoo and nail polish, instead of creating a different brand name and identity for every product.

Extending brands beyond the original product category is perceived to have various advantages.

First, it is considered to be more profitable, as it requires lower expenses such as advertising costs, trade deals, and price promotions. Umbrella branding is a form of economies of scope, as it economizes on the costs of creating a new brand (Cabral, 2007). At the same time, it also lowers the risk for firms in introducing new products, increasing product variety for consumers.

Second, umbrella branding tends to incentivise the brand owner to sustain consistent quality, alleviating producer moral hazard issues (Andresson, 2002; Cabral, 2007). Firms may hesitate to offer low-quality products as these may harm the brand's overall image.

Third, umbrella branding can help consumers in their decision-making for new products when quality information is missing. Consumers make inferences from the characteristics observed in one product, particularly with respect to quality, to form their expectations of the characteristics of others products under the same umbrella brand (Hakenes and Peitz, 2008).

Fourth, umbrella branding can have pro-competitive effects and result in lower prices, under certain conditions. The main intuition behind this result is that if switching costs are relatively low, the strategic effect of attracting and retaining customers in a competitive market can outweigh the "harvest" incentive that firms may have to extract a larger consumer surplus from consumers of a product under the umbrella brand (Dube, Hitsch and Rossi, 2009).

*Sources*: *http://definitions.uslegal.com/f/family-branding/.* Andersson, F. (2002), "Pooling Reputations," International Journal of Industrial Organization, 20(5), 715-730. Dube, J.P., G.Hitsch and P.Rossi (2009), "Do Switching Costs Make Markets Less Competitive?", Journal of Marketing Research, Vol. 46, No. 4, p. 435. Cabral L. M. B. (2007), "Optimal brand umbrella size. Technical report", New York University. Hakenes H. and M. Peitz (2008), "Umbrella branding and external certification", Preprints of the Max Planck Institute for Research on Collective Goods, Bonn.

Furthermore, these provisions create differential treatment between biocides authorised by the National Organisation for Medicines and those authorised by the Ministry of Rural Development and Food, since the latter body does not apply these provisions or any other regulation that impedes the authorisation of biocides with different qualitative chemical composition in terms of active ingredients under the same brand name.

The differential treatment of biocidal products depending on the competent authority can also be observed in other issues, such as control mechanisms, manufacturing practices, and duration of the approval procedure.

The European legal framework on biocides leaves it up to member states to decide whether competencies are best split or exercised by one competent authority. However, best practice suggests that there should be a single supervising authority for biocides, instead of responsibilities being split between two different authorities.

Table 5.2 shows that 22 out of 31 member states of the European Chemicals Agency have only one competent national authority for the application of the Regulation on biocidal products and that only nine member states, among them Greece, have more than one competent national authority. In these cases, the combination of competent national authorities varies; for example, in Lithuania, Portugal and Spain, competency is split between Ministries of Health and Agriculture.

Table 5.2. **Competent authorities for biocides**

| | Member states | Number |
|---|---|---|
| **One competent authority for biocides** | AT, BE, BG, CH, CY, CZ, DK, EE, FI, FR, HR, IE, IS, IT, LV, MT, NO, PL, SE, SI, SK, UK | 22 |
| **More than one competent authority for biocides** | DE, EL, ES, HU, LT, LU, NL, PT, RO | 9 |

*Source*: European Chemicals Agency, *https://echa.europa.eu/contacts-of-the-member-state-competent-authorities.*

*Recommendation and benefit*

The National Organisation for Medicines should halt applying these provisions to biocidal products and allow suppliers to use the same brand name for different products, if their specific uses are clearly shown. As a result, suppliers will be able to reduce marketing and advertising costs and have more efficient positioning of their products. This could lead to increased competition between suppliers, as well as lower prices and greater choice and variety for consumers.

***Plant protection products***

*Requirement for responsible scientist and prescription system*

*Description of the provisions*

Provision (a): According to Article 35 paragraph 1a of Law 4036/2012, wholesale and retail trade of plant protection products can take place following a notification procedure only in specialised stores that comply with specific requirements set out in the law and which operate with a "responsible scientist". Paragraph 1b of the same article sets special requirements for the "responsible scientist" (e.g. he or she must hold a university degree in a relevant specialisation obtained from an EU or third-country university). Moreover, paragraph 1c foresees that the sales of plant protection products can be executed by either the "responsible scientist" or an "employee-salesperson"; the latter should either comply with the requirements of responsible scientist or be the holder of a professional certificate for trading on plant protection products, according to EU regulatory requirements (i.e. EU Directive 2009/128, Article 5). Finally, according to paragraph 4 of this Article, either the "responsible scientist" or the "employee-salesperson" should be present at the time of selling of plant protection products (in line with EU Directive 2009/128, article 6 par. 1).

Provision (b): Article 35, paragraph 5 of Law 4036/2012 sets out the prescription as a prerequisite for the selling of plant protection products. The prescription is issued by a scientist/professional who meets the criteria to become a "responsible scientist", but is not necessarily the one notified for the trading store that sells the products in question. Also, responsible for the proper execution of the prescription at the trading store is the "responsible scientist" and/or the "employee-salesperson" (Article 35 paragraph 1 d of Law 4036/2012). It is noted that Ministerial Decision 9497/104760/2014[35] provides the legal framework for the prescription for the use of plant protection products and, in particular, Article 3 foresees an electronic system. However, this system is not yet in force.

Provision (c): Article 7 of Presidential Decree 159/2013, provides for the requirements for notification of wholesale trade enterprises of plant protection products, which to a great extent coincide with the requirements for notification for retail enterprises (Articles 5 and 6). More precisely, for the case of both natural and legal persons, this article foresees that the "responsible scientist" can be notified for no more than one store and physical and continuous presence at the establishment is required. Moreover, concerning legal persons, the "responsible scientist" notified, if not an employee, must participate in the capital share of the company with a minimum share of at least 20%.

*Objective of the provisions*

Provision (a): According to the official recital, the objective of the provision is to set requirements for the wholesale and retail trade of plant protection products. Following further communication with the Ministry, the OECD understands that another objective is the secure sustainable use and storage of plant protection products, so as to reduce the risks and impact on human health and the environment, as stated by EU Directive 2009/128. These products should therefore be traded with caution and the notification of a "responsible scientist", as well as the presence of the latter or an "employee-salesperson" at the time of selling in specialised stores guarantees their proper use. This provision is also in line with EU Directive 2009/128.[36]

Provision (b): The provision introduces a prescription system in order to assure the proper use of plant protection products. This provision is also in line with Articles 1, 3 and 14 of EU Directive 2009/128 on sustainable use of pesticides.[37]

Provision (c): There is no official recital. However, following communication with the Ministry, these requirements were introduced in order to secure the sustainable use of plant protection products, thus reducing the risks and impact on human health and the environment, as EU Directive 2009/128 dictates. The notification of a "responsible scientist" guarantees that these products are traded with caution. Furthermore, the requirement for participation in the capital share of the company with a minimum share of at least 20% is introduced for control purposes, in order to ensure responsible scientist's active involvement in the company and the trading of plant protection products. The provision also foresees an alternative; an employment contract between the "responsible scientist" and the undertaking that also serves control purposes and guarantees physical and continuous presence of the "responsible scientist" at the establishment.

The importance of appropriately educated or trained personnel being involved in the trading of plant protection products can also be supported by the data.

Figure 5.4 shows that more than 80% of professional users follow the advice of a scientist on the use of plant protection products.

Participation of professional users in training programmes has improved over time, but over 50% of farmers have still not yet received any kind of training with respect to plant protection products (Figure 5.5).

Lastly, according to data from the Ministry of Rural Development and Food, there were 922 poisonings from plant protection products in 2012 and 2013 (combined) and 387 poisonings in 2014. Figure 5.6 depicts that the majority of poisonings occur during professional use.

Figure 5.4. **Share of decision-making process in the correct use of a plant protection product (2014, 2016)**

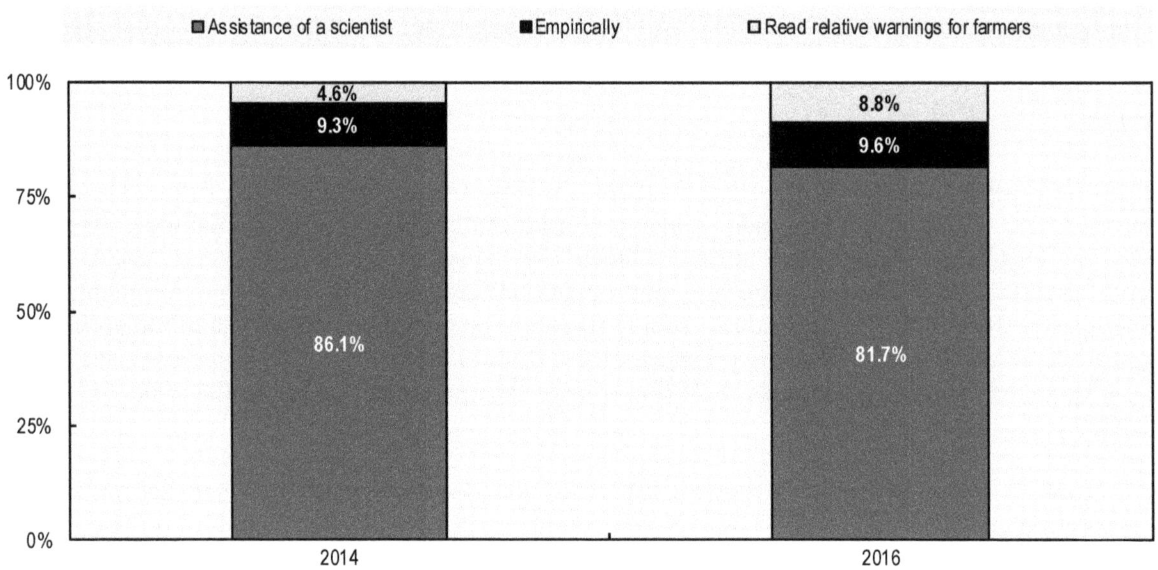


*Notes*:
"Assistance of a scientist" includes employee at a specialised store, consultant, or other. Percentages may not always add up due to rounding.
Annual survey conducted by the Ministry of Rural Development and Food. In 2014, sample size was 2 815 professional users; in 2016, it was 3 190 professional users. *www.minagric.gr/index.php/el/for-farmer-2/crop-production/fytoprostasiamenu/elenxoifitoprostateytikonmenu/540-statistika-fytorosta.*

*Source*: Annual survey on sustainable use of plant protection products, Ministry of Rural Development and Food.

Figure 5.5. **Share of professional users with training on use of plant protection products (2014, 2016)**

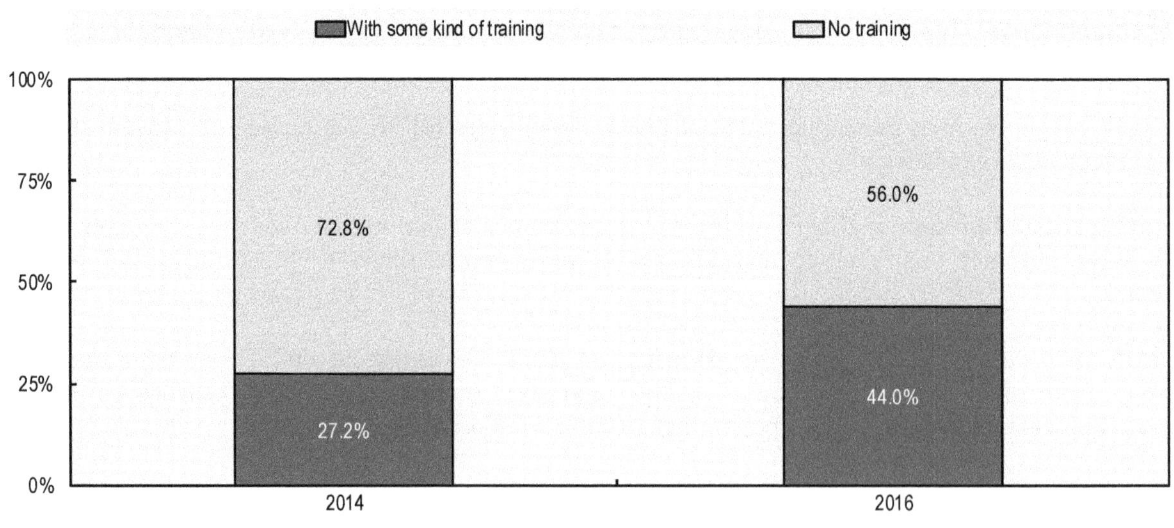


*Note:* Annual survey conducted by the Ministry of Rural Development and Food. In 2014, sample size was 2 815 professional users; in 2016, it was 3 190 professional users. *www.minagric.gr/index.php/el/for-farmer-2/crop-production/fytoprostasiamenu/elenxoifitoprostateytikonmenu/540-statistika-fytorosta.*

*Source*: Annual survey on sustainable use of plant protection products, Ministry of Rural Development and Food.

Figure 5.6. **Structure of poisonings from plant protection products by cause (2012-13, 2014)**

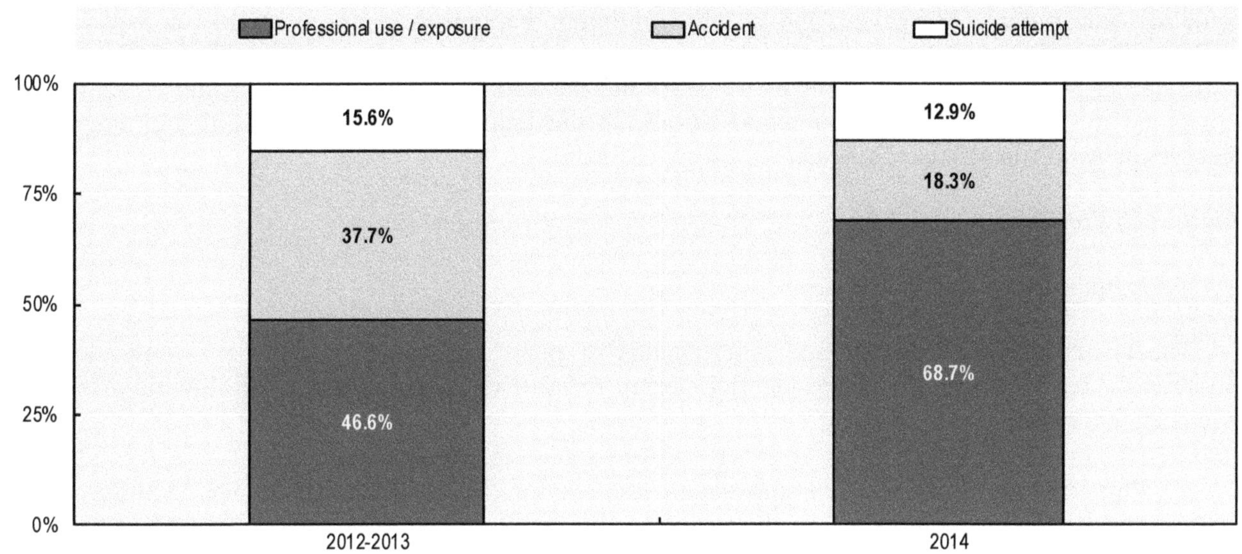


*Note*: Percentages may not always add up due to rounding.

*Source*: Ministry of Rural Development and Food, *www.minagric.gr/images/stories/docs/agrotis/Georgika_Farmaka/elenxoi/ENHMERWSH_KOINOY_OXEIA_DHLHTHRIASH220416.pdf.*

### *Harm to competition*

Provision (a): No harm to competition has been identified, since the requirements set are proportionate to the objective of safeguarding proper distribution and use of plant protection products.

Provision (b): This provision causes no harm to competition. The implementation of the prescription system, as well as the requirement for a scientist/professional, in order to prescribe plant protection products, is justified.

Provision (c): The provision that restricts the ability of notifying the "responsible scientist" in more than one store is superseded, since the previous regime, according to which the sales of plant protection products could only be executed by a "responsible scientist", was abolished. More specifically, Law 4036/2012 was amended in 2014 (Article 44, paragraph of Law 4235/2014[38]), allowing for an employee-salesperson to also execute sales. Therefore, the provision that demands the notification of a "responsible person" for each trading store, in order to ensure his/her presence at the time of sales, goes beyond what is necessary. In addition, the requirement for the participation of the responsible scientist with at least 20% capital share in the trading company restricts business practices. Finally, the provisions on physical and continuous presence of the responsible scientist both for natural and legal persons are also inactive, since the employee-salesperson that can also execute sales was introduced in 2014.

### *Recommendation and benefits*

Provision (a): No recommendation for change is made for the specific provisions.

Provision (b): Recommendation to start enforcing use of the electronic prescription system, which is expected to guarantee safe and sustainable use of plant protection products.

Provision (c): Abolish the requirement of the notification of a responsible scientist for not more than one store, since it is superseded by the current legislative framework, and thus eliminate sources of regulatory uncertainty. Moreover, abolish the minimum capital share requirement, as well as the requirement for the physical and continuous presence of the responsible scientist. The partnership or work relationship between the responsible scientist and the trading company should be more flexible and correspond to the needs of the contractual parties, in the light of the introduction of the "employee-salesperson" who can also execute sales.

*Storage requirements*

*Description of the provisions*

The legal framework for storage requirements of plant protection products by wholesale trade enterprises is set by Article 11 of Presidential Decree 159/2013.[39] In particular, the following provisions have been identified.

- Paragraph 1a sets out minimum square metres for the premises of storage facilities. More specifically, it requires that each storage facility has a surface of at least $100m^2$ and be located only on the ground floor.
- Paragraph 1e states that extra storage can only be established in a basement or a half-basement.

In addition, other requirements in Presidential Decree 159/2013 focus on the characteristics of the ventilation systems; fireproofing and safety; construction materials of floor and shelves; special storage rooms for unsuitable products; separate and secure storage (classified by category) to other agricultural inputs; and proper labelling.

The provision aims to meet the conditions set out in Article 13 of Directive 2009/128, which states that, "Member States shall ensure that storage areas for pesticides for professional use are constructed in such a way as to prevent unwanted releases; particular attention shall be paid to location, size and construction materials", taking into account that plant protection products are chemicals and flammable.

*Harm to competition*

Restrictive surface and floor building requirements may act as barriers to entry and constrain suppliers' strategy and business practices, discouraging potential entrants and possibly reducing the number of suppliers. While the OECD understands from the competent authorities that the requirements are not considered restrictive for current participants, they may limit future entry.

Based on international practice, the OECD understands that other Member States do not impose minimum surface requirements. The same applies to floor requirements; e.g. in Italy,[40] a provision states that the trading store must not be located in underground or basement floors (the contrary to Greek legislation).

Generally, other Member States and accepted international practice place the emphasis on other qualitative characteristics for securing safe and proper storage of products, and *not* on surface area and floor building requirements.

*Recommendation and benefit*

Abolish minimum dimensions and floor restrictions for both operation and extra storage to allow new entrants to freely choose their locations, on the condition that all other qualitative characteristics of wholesale-trade facilities are met (e.g. ventilation system, fireproofing and safety, separate and secure storage). More emphasis should be placed on targeted controls.

Box 5.2. **Storage requirements of plant protection products**

**Ireland**

There are a number of general building-related requirements (e.g. stores can be adjacent to buildings, be attached to other buildings or comprise compartments within buildings, but must either have separate entrances or exits to the exterior, and stores must not have residential accommodation over storage areas). In addition, other requirements exist in relation to site selection, storage capacity, storage cabinets and cages, design and construction of floors, walls, roofs, rainwater systems, bunds, doors, emergency exits, windows, lighting, heating and electrical fittings, and ventilation facilities.

**United Kingdom**

Stores may range from major buildings or stores within buildings to small self-contained or prefabricated stores including suitable chests, bins or vaults, or vehicles used for storage. In all cases, stores should be:

- suitably sited;
- of adequate capacity;
- soundly constructed of fire-resistant materials;
- provided with suitable access and exits (this excludes chests bins and vault-type storage);
- capable of containing 110% of the total amount of pesticides likely to be stored at any time (or 185% in "pollution risk or environmentally sensitive areas");
- dry and protected from frost;
- well-lit and ventilated;
- marked with appropriate warning signs and secured against theft and vandalism;
- equipped, organised and staffed to accommodate intended contents.

**Belgium**

A checklist form is used to control the following characteristics: separate and locked storage of plant protection products, proper ventilation, good condition and cleanness of storage room, as well as proper warning signalling.

*Sources*: Ireland, Irish Agricultural Supply Industry Standards (2013), "Requirements for the Design and Construction of Pesticides Stores", *www.pcs.agriculture.gov.ie/sud/pesticidedistributors/distributionstoresandsalesdisplayareas;* UK, Department for Environment, Food and Rural Affairs, "Code of Practice for suppliers of pesticides to agriculture, horticulture and forestry", *www.hse.gov.uk/pesticides/resources/Y/yellow_code.pdf,* p. 28-29; Belgium, Agence fédérale pour la sécurité de la chaîne alimentaire, "Détention de pesticides, pulvérisateurs" *www.favv-afsca.be/checklists-fr/_documents/FAVVChecklist-2438v1fr.pdf.*

***Fertilisers***

*Responsible scientist*

*Description of the provisions*

According to Article 47 of recent Law 4384/2016[41], trading enterprises of fertilisers are required to employ a responsible scientist, who must meet specific requirements, on a full-time dependent work contract at each of its establishments.

The objective of this provision is that the responsible scientist ensures the correct use of fertilisers (which not only are chemical products, but can also have potentially explosive properties, such as those of ammonium nitrate) and minimises the risk of environmental burden and degradation (e.g. nitrate pollution, eutrophication).

Under the provisions of Law 4152/2013,[42] which was previously in force, micro[43] or small fertiliser trading enterprises could employ responsible scientists on a part-time basis to reduce labour costs. In addition, Joint Ministerial Decision 4166/51687/2014[44] and Presidential Decree 159/2014[45] specified the details of part-time employment in these cases and the appropriately trained personnel who should be employed additionally.

This was preceded by Hellenic Competition Commission Opinion 19/VI/2012,[46] which considered that the full-time employment of the responsible scientist was disproportionate to the objective in the case of small and micro size enterprises, and suggested part-time employment.

*Harm to competition*

The presence of a responsible scientist during the operation hours of the business is justified to achieve the policy objective. However, a full-time dependent work contract may raise the cost of operation (labour cost) for smaller firms, which may not operate full-time; thus this requirement may act as a barrier to entry for smaller operators, while not necessarily achieving the policy maker's objective.

*Recommendations and benefits*

Abolish the requirement of the full-time dependent work contract for the responsible scientist, and explicitly repeal obsolete provisions. The responsible scientist is important and should remain as a prerequisite for the notification of operation, in order to ensure proper use of fertilisers and protection of the environment. Nevertheless, suppliers should have the flexibility to decide on the type of employment (i.e. part-time employment), as long as safety objectives are fulfilled.

*Permit of operation*

*Description of the provisions*

Law 1565/1985[47] and Joint Ministerial Decision 9748/100747/2012[48] state that the necessary permit of operation for trading enterprises of fertilisers is renewable and has a duration of five years for Type A enterprises (retail traders) and three years for Type B trade enterprises (wholesale and retail traders). According to the relevant Registry[49] of the Ministry of Rural Development and Food, 2,450 Type A enterprises and 220 Type B enterprises are currently in operation. The provisions' objective is to set specific durations of operation, so that the necessary thorough and periodical checks of enterprises' operational requirements can be undertaken.

*Harm to competition*

These provisions create differential treatment between the two types of trading enterprises, as both can make retail sales, but have different durations for their operational permits. As a result, these provisions may discourage operators to enter the market, particularly as Type B enterprises.

*Recommendation and benefits*

Align the duration of both permits to five years to remove differential treatment.

## *Cosmetics*

### *Harmonisation with EU rules*

#### *Description of the provisions*

EU provides for harmonised rules in the sector of cosmetic products. EU Regulation 1223/2009[50] is the main regulatory framework for the centralised notification procedure[51] (which must be followed before cosmetics can enter the market) and streamlines the framework for all operators in the sector. The National Organisation for Medicines is the competent authority for market surveillance at national level, monitoring compliance with the requirements laid down in the Regulation.

Before the Regulation entered into force in July 2013, the main legislation governing the sector was Directive 76/768/EEC.[52] This Directive was transposed into Greek legislation by Joint Ministerial Decision ΔΥΓ3α/ΓΠ. 132979/2005,[53] which was later updated several times in order to incorporate the amendments of the EU Directive. The Ministerial Decision was last amended in 2011, and so is not in line with Regulation 1223/2009.

In addition, within the Greek legislative framework, Ministerial Decision A6/2880/1980 provides for specific rules on good manufacturing practices and control of cosmetics, which specify the requirements with which cosmetic manufacturers must comply. However, under the EU Regulation, it is ISO 22716 on Good Manufacturing Practices (GMP) – Guidelines on Good Manufacturing Practices, published in 2007, that provides for the relevant European harmonised standard for the GMP requirements of the Regulation.[54]

#### *Harm to competition*

Since EU Cosmetics Regulation is now applicable, existing Ministerial Decisions are not applicable in practice and may cause uncertainty as to the regulatory framework governing good manufacturing practices of cosmetics. These provisions therefore could deter new entrants and act as a barrier to entry.

#### *Recommendation*

Both Ministerial Decisions should be explicitly abolished, in order to eliminate sources of regulatory uncertainty. Any new Ministerial Decision issued in the context of the national framework should be in line with the provisions of EU Regulation 1223/2009.

### *Borderline products*

#### *Description of the provisions*

According to Circular 92428/2009[55] issued by the National Organisation for Medicines regarding the legal circulation of cosmetic products, labelling and packaging leaflets of cosmetic products must not include claims on antibacterial, antimicrobial or antiseptic use. Any such terms should be removed from the labelling and package leaflets of cosmetics. In case suppliers wish to market their products with antibacterial, antimicrobial or antiseptic claims, they must apply for a market authorisation pursuant to the biocides regulatory framework. The Circular refers to and interprets the requirements set out in Ministerial Decision ΔΥΓ3α/ΓΠ.132979/2005.

Innovation in cosmetics has led to “borderline” products that combine cosmetic and biocidal characteristics and so cannot be easily categorised. Drawing a clear borderline and defining a classification of products falling into the scope of Cosmetic Products Regulation 1223/2009 or the

Biocidal Products Regulation 528/2012 is crucial for the proper implementation of Regulations by the competent national authorities. After several cases of borderline products were identified, the EU Commission has provided guidance documents on the relevant applicable framework.[56] According to Commission guidance, the categorisation can be accomplished through the detailed definition of the products under classification, with emphasis given on the purposes of their use.

The definitions of cosmetic and biocidal products are provided in the relevant EU frameworks governing each sector. The EU Cosmetics Regulation states that products with a mainly or exclusively cosmetic purpose should be classified as cosmetic products and so fall under the requirements of the Cosmetic Products Regulation 1223/2009. This allows for secondary biocidal claims in cases where the primary function of the product is cosmetic, but clearly states that the assessments of whether a product is a cosmetic product has to be made on a case-by-case basis, taking into account each product's characteristics.[57] Accordingly, the EU Biocides Regulation recognises that where a product's biocidal function is inherent to its cosmetic function, or where that biocidal function is considered to be a secondary claim of a cosmetic product, the function and the product should remain outside the scope of this Regulation.[58]

Therefore, within the EU framework, a cosmetic product with secondary claims about additional functions of its ingredients not necessarily related to the primary function of the product can circulate in the market. National competent authorities must assess on a case-by-case basis whether a product falls within the scope of the Cosmetics Products Regulation or the Biocides Regulation.

Circular 92428/2009 is intended to help companies intending to market cosmetic products by reminding them of the different market-authorisation procedures to be followed in cases of products classified as cosmetics or biocides.[59] It results, however, in a strict classification of products without taking into consideration the cases of borderline products.

*Harm to competition*

According to the EU Cosmetics Regulation, a biocidal claim is permitted for cosmetic products provided that the biocidal function is secondary to the cosmetic function. Circular 92428/2009 has the effect of treating interchangeable cosmetic products circulating in the market differently. Greek legislation, unlike EU regulation, does not recognise products' primary and secondary functions, resulting in regulatory uncertainty with regard to their legal circulation in the market. The provision may constitute a barrier to entry for new suppliers wishing to place their products in the Greek market and so limit the variety of cosmetic products available to consumers.

*Recommendation*

Circular 92428/2009 issued by the National Organisation for Medicines should be rephrased to bring it into line with the EU legislative framework. The primary and secondary functions of products should be recognised as foreseen in the EC Note for Guidance CA-Jul 13-Doc.5.1.h and relevant EU documents concerning borderline products. In addition, any references to the Ministerial Decision ΔΥΓ3α/ΓΠ. 132979/2005 should be eliminated from Greek legislation.

*Levy of 1% on the wholesale price of cosmetics*

*Description of the provisions*

Law 1316/1983 assigned the responsibility of the market surveillance of cosmetic products to the National Organisation for Medicines. To cover the associated costs, it imposes a levy of 1% on the wholesale price of cosmetics, payable by companies operating in the sector and based on the value of their sales.[60] The National Organisation for Medicines Circular 13898/2011 provides practical guidance on the relevant legal provisions. The levy must be paid on a monthly basis to the National Organisation for Medicines by persons in Greece or abroad (another Member State or in a third country) responsible for placing cosmetic products on the Greek market.

Compliance with EU Cosmetics Regulation is controlled by national competent authorities in EU Member States. It is accepted that legislation may levy fees intended to cover the costs of the tasks carried out by these agencies. According to the National Organisation for Medicines, the 1% levy is used to fund the costs of market surveillance and so must be directly related to the specific verification procedures undertaken by the Organisation for products circulating in the Greek market.

Box 5.3. **Cosmetics notification fee in Sweden**

The Swedish Medical Products Agency's (SMPA) provisions on cosmetic products (*Läkemedelsverkets föreskrifter (LVFS 2013:10) om kosmetiska produkter*) specify the procedure and the costs related to the circulation of cosmetics products in Sweden. It states that fees payable to the Agency are used to cover the costs incurred by its surveillance of cosmetic products.

For the purposes of fee payment, the SMPA categorises the companies operating in the cosmetics sector into two categories. The first includes the manufacturers of cosmetics, importers, distributors changing cosmetics or other designated responsible persons. These companies are obliged to notify to the Cosmetic Product Notification Portal (CPNP) their products and pay two fees: a lump-sum annual fee of SEK 4 000 (€427) and an annual fee for each product of SEK 600 (€63) (up to 200 products). The second category includes only distributors that do not have to alter the product to fulfil Swedish labelling requirements. These companies are not obliged to notify to the CPNP, but they are required to pay an hourly fee of SEK 750 (€79) for the actual surveillance work. Alternatively, they are given the option of joining the first category (and its fee structure) on the condition that the product is voluntarily notified to the SMPA at the time surveillance work begins.

The notification of cosmetics to the SMPA became optional and voluntary from the 11 July 2013. The possibility of notifying cosmetics described above is voluntarily and may be alternatively done directly in the CPNP.

Exchange rate: EUR 1 = SEK 9.538, *www.ecb.europa.eu/stats/exchange/eurofxref/html/eurofxref-graph-sek.en.html* (accessed 13 September 2016).

*Source*: Swedish Medical Products Agency (2016), *https://lakemedelsverket.se/english/product/Cosmetic-products/Legislation/* (accessed 24 August 2016).

*Harm to competition*

The levy on cosmetics aims to finance the National Organisation for Medicines' work of quality checks and market supervision. Such a levy should be set in a way that does not create perverse incentives for firms' marketing and pricing strategies. The current scheme, requiring companies to pay a fee proportional to their revenues, benefits from the marketing and brand building of the firms. For example, a company that sells a few units of a very expensive cosmetic will pay the same levy as a company that markets various products sold at a low price. Given the market surveillance purpose of the levy, the latter company imposes a much higher burden than the former, as random checks need to be performed across its multiple product lines. The relative higher burden on the more expensive cosmetics (holding sales constant) may distort firms' advertising and pricing strategies as an unintended consequence. Instead, if the levy is proportional to the number of products marketed by each firm and the number of units sold, this would be proportional to the burden imposed on the surveillance authority without affecting the way companies compete in the market.

*Recommendation*

The administration should consider the introduction of an alternative scheme based on the number of products marketed by each firm and the number of units sold. This way the burden on suppliers will not impact upon their price strategy. The new scheme should be designed in a way that is revenue neutral for the National Organisation for Medicines (i.e. its revenues remain unchanged under the new scheme).

***Excise duty on isopropyl alcohol***

*Introduction*

Over the past 20 years, revenues from excise duties in OECD countries have been relatively stable, accounting for about 8% of total tax revenue in 2011 (OECD 2014). OECD notes that there is great divergence between member countries, with excise accounting for 2.8% of total tax revenue in New Zealand and 17.8% in Turkey. In Greece, this percentage is more than 10% of total tax revenue.

While the main characteristics and objectives ascribed to excise duties are approximately the same across EU and OECD countries, their implementation gives rise to significant differences between countries. The aforementioned divergence concerns not only the tax rate imposed on goods, but also the choice of goods on which each member country imposes excise duties. Pursuant to Council Directive 2008/118/EC[61] concerning the general arrangements for excise duty, which repealed Directive 92/12/EEC,[62] EU Member States have the possibility of imposing excise duty on products other than the ones mentioned in the Directive. Based on this discretionary power, Greece chose to impose excise duty on isopropyl alcohol (also known under its chemical name, isopropanol).

*Description of the provision and objective*

Law 2960/2001,[63] the National Customs Code, introduces an excise duty on isopropyl alcohol of EUR 2.93 per kilogram of net weight whether produced domestically or imported from EU Member States or third countries. Ministerial Decision 811/337/2008[64] elaborates upon this provision and sets down the terms and conditions for the denaturation procedure, as well as the exemption from excise duty of isopropyl alcohol if used as a raw material for industrial purposes. Moreover, Ministerial Decision 812/338/2008[65] concerns the establishment and function of tax warehouses of isopropyl alcohol whether domestically produced or coming from EU countries.

There is no official objective for these particular provisions. In principle, "while the original reason for introducing excise duties was to raise revenue, they are also used to discourage consumption of certain products because they are considered harmful to health or the environment" (OECD 2014). Moreover, the imposition of excise duties on goods reflects countries' policies and governmental objectives. With reference to this specific excise duty, it is the OECD's understanding that the objective is the general legal practice according to which excise duties are imposed on alcohols, except when they are used as raw material for industrial purposes and so denatured.

In particular, alcohol not intended for human consumption is exempt from excise duties (European Commission 2016). However, in order to benefit from this exemption, the alcohol must be denatured in accordance with methods laid down by Ministerial Decisions. Denaturation[66] of alcohol is therefore an important anti-fraud measure that helps prevent the criminal circumvention of excise duties. Denaturation must take place in tax warehouses in order to ensure proper oversight of the process and prevent isopropyl alcohol on which excise duty has not been paid from being released into circulation and illegally sold for consumption.

Box 5.4. **The estimated consumer benefits from removing the tax on isopropyl alcohol**

Isopropanol is mainly used for industrial purposes, typically as raw material for detergents and cleaning products, and is unfit for human consumption. Despite that, legislation in Greece imposes an excise duty on isopropanol. Firms can be exempt only if they follow a specific procedure, called denaturation, in accordance to methods laid down by Ministerial Decisions. It is the OECD's understanding that some firms choose to follow the exemption procedure, which is a costly, administrative complex and cumbersome process, whereas others prefer to bear the cost of the excise duty than follow the exemption procedure. Hence, this excise duty unnecessary raises the marginal cost for the whole industry.

Based on data provided by the Ministry of Finance, Table 5.3 depicts the income from the excise duty imposed on isopropyl alcohol for the years 2005-2015 in Greece. The average annual cost per operator amounts to EUR 4 425, ranging from EUR 1 590 in 2007 to EUR 8 927 in 2015. The fact that some firms prefer to pay the excise duty cost instead of following the exemption procedure indicates that this procedure is significantly more costly than the excise duty cost itself. In what follows, we use the excise duty as a conservatively lower bound of the cost incurred by firms.

Table 5.3 depicts the income from the excise duty imposed on isopropyl alcohol for the period 2005-2015 in Greece. The average annual cost per operator amounts to EUR 4 424.74.

Table 5.3. **Income from excise duty imposed on isopropyl alcohol (2005-2015)**

| Year | Income from excise duty imposed (in EUR) | Number of operators that attribute the excise duty |
|---|---|---|
| 2005 | 97 695.49 | 34 |
| 2006 | 106 772.03 | 37 |
| 2007 | 49 294.91 | 31 |
| 2008 | 70 468.77 | 26 |
| 2009 | 82 719.23 | 23 |
| 2010 | 139 344.32 | 36 |
| 2011 | 148 390.03 | 29 |
| 2012 | 119 454.96 | 22 |
| 2013 | 118 601.83 | 23 |
| 2014 | 149 858.23 | 23 |
| 2015 | 178 531.02 | 20 |

*Source*: General Secretariat of Customs and Excise Duties, Ministry of Finance.

The OECD recommends abolishing the provision that introduces excise duty on isopropyl alcohol. Abolishing this provision would lower the marginal cost for all firms. Based on the work of Weyl and Fabinger (2013), the absolute pass-through of an industry-wide marginal cost change *t* can be expressed as:

$$\frac{dp}{dt} = \frac{1}{1 + \theta(1 + \varepsilon_s)}$$

where $\varepsilon_s$ is a measure of the demand curvature (technically the elasticity of slope of the inverse demand)* and $\theta$ is the conduct parameter that measures the intensity of competition ($\theta$ ranges from 0 for the case of perfect competition to 1 in the case of monopoly). Hence, assuming constant marginal costs, a reduction in the tax would translate to a reduction in prices that would range from 100% in the case of perfect competition to 50% in the case of monopoly, with a mid-point of 75% in the case of oligopoly.

The marginal cost reduction, following the excise duty abolition, is assumed at 1%. Following from the above, in the case of perfect competition this would translate into a 1% drop in final prices. In the case of monopoly, this would translate into a 0.5% drop in final prices. In the perhaps more realistic case of oligopoly, the corresponding price drop would be 0.75%.

For the benefit with reference to detergents, one of the main products for which isopropyl alcohol is used, in 2015, detergents manufacturers' sales were EUR 477.4 million. In the case of perfect competition, based on the methodology outlined in Annex A (Box A.2) and assuming an elasticity of demand equal to 2, the change in consumer benefit is estimated to be EUR 4.8 million. In the more conservative case of oligopoly, the consumer benefit is estimated to be EUR 3.6 million (i.e. a 0.75% price drop – assuming a 1% cost reduction and based on a 75% pass-through rate, as explained above).

* This elasticity captures the percentage change in the slope of demand arising from a 1% increase in quantity. It equals zero for linear, positive for concave and negative for convex demand. For our calculations here we assume a linear demand.

*Source*: Weyl, E. G., and M. Fabinger (2013), "Pass-Through as an Economic Tool: Principles of Incidence under Imperfect Competition", *Journal of Political Economy*, Vol.121, No.3, pp.528-583. Eurostat, Prodcom Annual Data 2015, http://ec.europa.eu/eurostat/web/prodcom/data/excel-files-nace-rev.2 (accessed 24 August 2016).

However, since isopropyl alcohol is already unfit for human consumption and mainly used for industrial purposes, usually as a raw material for detergents and cleaning products, it should not be subject to excise duty in the first place. Particularly as isopropyl alcohol cannot be substituted by other alcohols and cannot be used as consumable alcohol. Therefore, since this substance is mostly used by industry, these provisions introduce an excise on a good that is generally exempt from excise duty.

*Harm to competition*

From an economic perspective, an excise duty raises the marginal cost of the raw material. The higher cost of the raw material hurts consumers in multiple ways, mostly resulting in higher consumer price and possibly leading to reduction of output for producers and restriction of the market.

The legal framework for the excise duty on isopropyl alcohol provides for an exemption procedure – through denaturation – for industrial users of isopropyl alcohol. Due to the complexity of the denaturation procedure, however, there are manufacturers that prefer to bear the cost of the excise duty rather than follow the exemption procedure. Bigger manufacturers can absorb the cost of the denaturation and exemption procedure and can benefit from the exemption possibility provided by the legislation, whereas smaller manufacturers with less steady production schedules are forced to pay the excise duty. This leads to differential treatment, since it raises costs for some market participants but not others.

Furthermore, domestic Greek manufacturers that use isopropyl alcohol as raw material are at a disadvantage compared to other EU-based manufacturers who are not faced with the excise duty. Another reason is that the denaturation process introduces other components into the isopropyl alcohol (e.g. smelling agent, foul-tasting agent or analytical marker), which changes the composition of the final product. This means that Greek products with isopropyl alcohol domestically produced are not the same as the equivalent ones produced in other EU countries, and that manufacturers operating both in Greece and other EU countries have to alter their international products in order to comply with the Greek legislation on excise duty.

*Recommendation and benefits*

As well as abolishing the provision that introduces excise duty on isopropyl alcohol, the OECD recommends abolishing the Ministerial Decisions that provide for an exemption, the denaturation procedure, and regulate the function of tax warehouses of isopropyl alcohol. Abolishing this excise duty should result in lower prices as the final industrial product will not be burdened either with excise duty or the cost of the denaturation procedure. It will also lower production costs and increase of the competitiveness of Greek manufacturers using isopropyl alcohol as a raw material. In addition, lowering costs may encourage the entry of more suppliers. The consumer benefit from abolishing this provision is estimated to be EUR 3.6 million annually.

## 5.2. Electrical equipment

The sub-sector of electrical-equipment products (NACE code 27) includes the manufacture of products that generate, distribute and use electrical power. Examples of such products include electric motors, generators, transformers, electricity distribution and control apparatus, batteries and accumulators, wiring and wiring devices, electrical-lighting equipment, and domestic appliances.

The review of the legislation covered electrical equipment both at manufacturing and at wholesale trade level. Due to a lack of data, the sector overview deals only with the manufacturing level.

## *Economic overview*

Figure 5.7 compares the value added of electrical equipment as a percentage of the total manufacturing in Greece and in the EU[67] for the years 2008-2013. The sub-sector's contribution to the overall manufacturing sector averages 2.7% in Greece, compared to 5.3% at the EU level, during the six-year period 2008-2013.

Figure 5.7. **Value added as a percentage of manufacturing for electrical equipment (2008-2013)**

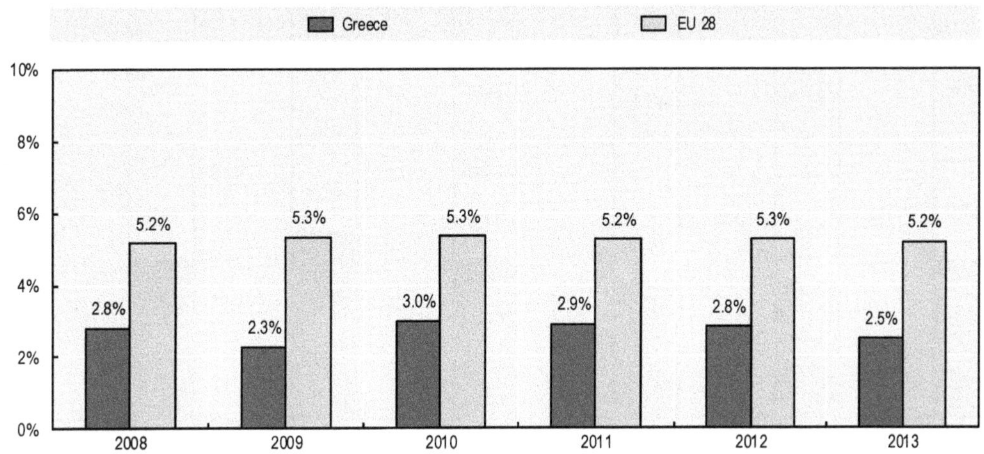


*Note*: Value added at factor cost

*Source*: Eurostat, Annual detailed enterprise statistics for industry (NACE Rev. 2, B-E), Database [sbs_na_ind_r2], *http://ec.europa.eu/eurostat* (accessed 24 August 2016).

Figure 5.8 shows the turnover of manufacturing of electrical equipment and manufacturing as a whole for Greece for the seven-year period 2008-2014. The sub-sector's turnover amounts to EUR 1 248 million in 2014, down from EUR 1 911 million in 2008.

Figure 5.8. **Turnover of manufacturing electrical equipment in Greece (2008-2014)**

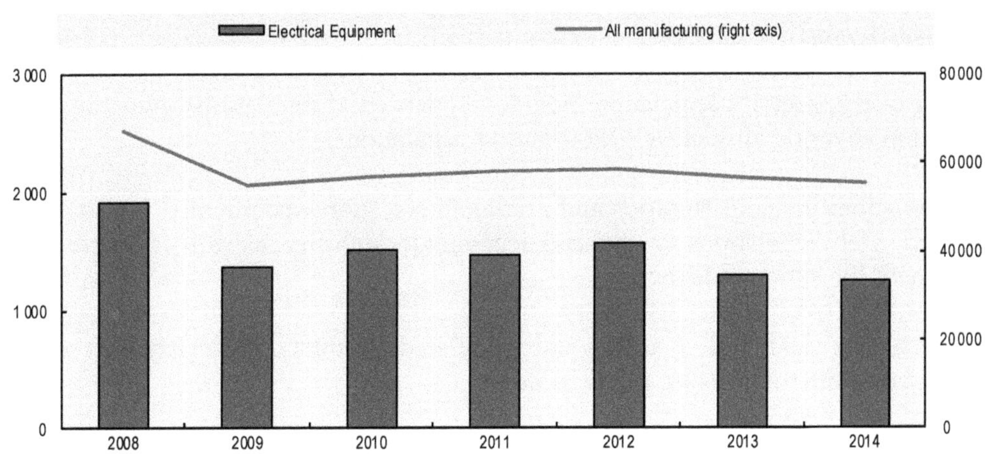


*Note*: Turnover in EUR millions.

*Source*: Eurostat, Annual detailed enterprise statistics for industry (NACE Rev. 2, B-E), Database [sbs_na_ind_r2], *http://ec.europa.eu/eurostat* (accessed 24 August 2016).

The majority of total turnover of manufacturing of electrical equipment comes from two sub-categories: "Manufacturing of domestic appliances" and "Manufacturing of wiring and wiring devices" (Figure 5.9). Together they account for more than 55% of total turnover throughout the period 2008-2014.

Figure 5.9. **Share of manufacturing of electrical equipment turnover per category in Greece (2008-2014)**

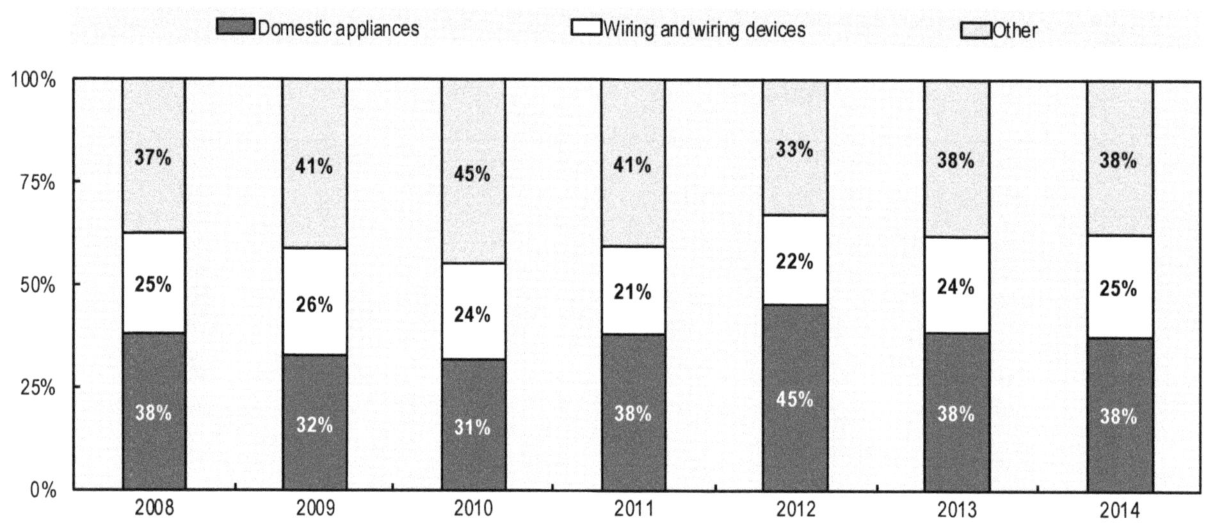


*Note*: Percentages may not always add up due to rounding.

*Source*: Eurostat, Annual detailed enterprise statistics for industry (NACE Rev. 2, B-E), Database [sbs_na_ind_r2], *http://ec.europa.eu/eurostat* (accessed 24 August 2016).

The number of manufacturing companies fell from 1446 companies in 2008 to 953 companies in 2014, while employment dropped from 10400 to 6498 workers[68] over the same time period. In terms of number of manufacturing companies, the highest share belongs to the category of electric lighting equipment (33.7% in 2014), whereas the domestic appliances category ranked first in employment (30.4% in 2014).

### *Overview of the legislation*

The mapping of this sector's legislation includes 11 laws and regulations, plus the framework and horizontal legislation covering all sectors. Out of the 11 regulations:

- three regulations concern batteries and accumulators, more specifically, legislation introducing health and safety regulations for the lead-accumulator industry, as well as distribution and waste management for these products;
- two regulations deal with marking energy-related products, their labelling and eco-design requirements, both transposing EU legislation;
- one Ministerial Decision refers to the making available in the market and the installation of sockets and plugs; and

- five regulations deal with various issues regarding electrical equipment, such as alternative management of electrical and electronic waste, low -voltage electrical equipment, electrical installations, and electromagnetic compatibility.

From a legal point of view, the electrical equipment sector is mostly an EU harmonised sector. The only field for divergence is in sockets and plugs, since member states follow different technical standards and harmonisation would be extremely difficult.

***Main recommendations***

*Sockets and plugs*

*Description of the provision*

According to Article 3 of Ministerial Decision 529/2000,[69] sockets and plugs can circulate in the market only if they:

- are registered at the designated Registry of the General Secretariat of Industry; and

- have acquired a conformity mark proving they meet the standards of the Hellenic Organisation for Standardisation (ELOT) or any other technically equivalent international standard.

In addition, pursuant to Article 6 of the aforementioned Ministerial Decision, the duration of the registration of these products in the Registry of the General Secretariat of Industry lasts three years and is renewable for another three years upon application by the supplier before the competent authority. The technical standards of the conformity marks are usually renewed by the Standardisation Organisation every five years, a renewal necessary to keep pace with technological progress. Therefore, the conformity mark based on each certificate should also be renewed by the supplier, so that the products in question are in conformity with the valid (renewed) certificate.

The objective of this provision is to monitor effectively the trade of sockets and plugs, via a registration process, so that the safety of internal electrical installations is guaranteed.

*Harm to competition*

The obligation to renew the registration of sockets and plugs at the Ministry's Registry every three years is an administrative procedure that calls for an additional cost for each type of registered socket and plug and therefore may discourage new entrants or smaller operators.

In addition, it is noted that conformity marks (granted either by the Hellenic Organisation for Standardisation or by any other international organisation) may be valid for a shorter or a longer time period than the three-year registration, depending on their renewal. For example, should a product still comply with the standardisation-certificate requirements after three years and the registration is not renewed, there is no threat to public safety. On the contrary, if the three-year registration obligation has not lapsed, but the product circulates in the market without being compliant with a conformity mark, public safety will not be protected.

*Recommendations and benefits*

The Ministry should review this provision to align the respective durations of the registration and the conformity mark granted by the Hellenic Organisation for Standardisation (ELOT) or any other technically equivalent international standardisation organisation. The Ministry should also introduce an updated electronic Registry for this purpose, to follow any changes in the approved standardisation certificates. As a result, suppliers' operation will be facilitated and the administration will profit from easier and more efficient monitoring, safeguarding consumer protection.

## 5.3. Paper and paper products

The manufacture of paper and paper products sub-sector (NACE code 17) includes the manufacture of pulp, paper and paperboard, as well as a wide variety of converted paper products (e.g. household and personal hygiene paper products, paper stationery, and wallpaper).

The review of the legislation has covered paper and paper products both at manufacturing and at wholesale trade level. Due to data limitations, the sector overview deals only with the manufacturing level.

### *Economic overview*

Figure 5.10 compares the value added of paper and paper products as a percentage of the total manufacturing in Greece and in the EU[70] for the six-year period 2008-2013. The sub-sector represents a small, relatively constant, percentage of the manufacturing sector, both in Greece and at the EU level.

Figure 5.10. **Value added as a percentage of manufacturing for paper and paper products (2008-2013)**

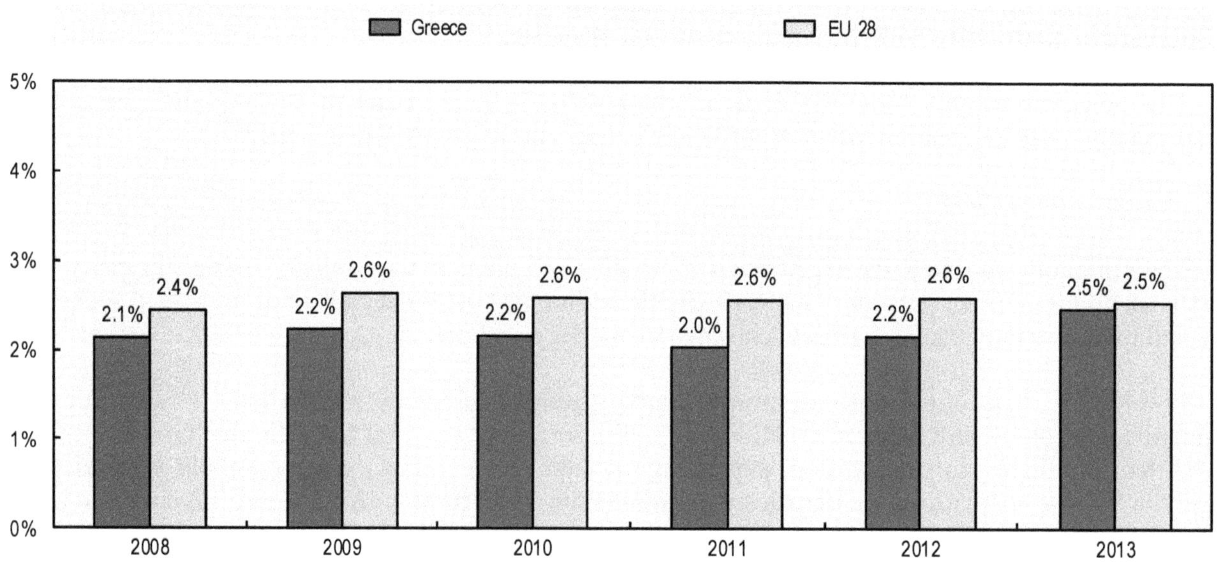


*Note*: Value added at factor cost

*Source*: Eurostat, Annual detailed enterprise statistics for industry (NACE Rev. 2, B-E), Database [sbs_na_ind_r2], *http://ec.europa.eu/eurostat* (accessed 24 August 2016).

A comparison of the turnover of the paper and paper products and those of the manufacturing sector as a whole is presented in Figure 5.11. The sub-sector's turnover amounts to EUR 1184 million in 2014, showing gradual increase over the four-year period 2011-2014 (15.5%), despite the recession, which has affected the manufacturing sector as a whole (-4.1% over the same time period).

Figure 5.11. **Turnover of manufacturing paper and paper products in Greece (2008-2014)**

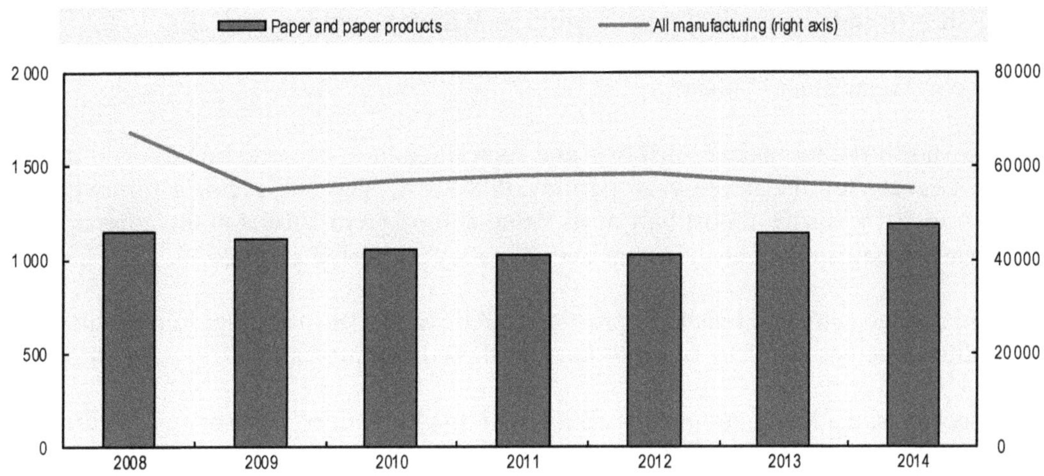


*Note*: Turnover in EUR millions

*Source*: Eurostat, Annual detailed enterprise statistics for industry (NACE Rev. 2, B-E), Database [sbs_na_ind_r2], *http://ec.europa.eu/eurostat* (accessed 24 August 2016).

The sector is made up mostly of small and medium-sized enterprises. They have been negatively affected by the recession of the last few years in Greece, in terms of number of operating companies and employment. In particular, during the seven-year period 2008-2014, the number of manufacturing companies fell from 878 to 646 companies and employment was reduced from 9503 to 7094 workers.[71]

### *Overview of the legislation*

No sector-specific legislation has been identified. However, it is noted that the general legal framework on the establishment of industrial activities, as part of the horizontal legislation, applies to paper and paper-products manufacturing enterprises.

### *Recommendations*

No specific competition problems have been identified following the review of the legislation.

## 5.4. Printing and reproduction of recorded media

The printing and reproduction of recorded media sub-sector (NACE code 18) includes printing of products (e.g. newspapers, books, periodicals, business forms, greeting cards), as well as associated support activities (e.g. bookbinding, plate-making services, and data imaging). It also includes the reproduction of recorded media (e.g. compact discs, video recordings, software on discs or tapes, records). This sub-sector excludes publishing activities.

The review of the legislation has covered printing and reproduction of recorded media both at manufacturing and at wholesale trade level, where applicable. Due to a lack of data, the sector overview deals only with the manufacturing level.

***Economic overview***

Figure 5.12 depicts the value added of printing and reproduction of recorded media companies, as a percentage of the overall manufacturing sector in Greece and in the EU[72] for the six-year period 2008-2013. The sub-sector's share is small (less than 3% over time) and also follows a downward trend, similar to conditions at an EU level.

Figure 5.13 shows the turnover of printing and reproduction of recorded media and manufacturing as a whole for Greece, for the seven-year period 2008-2014. The sub-sector's turnover amounts to EUR 521 million in 2014, losing almost half of its value compared to 2008. On the contrary, turnover of total manufacturing remains relatively constant over the six-year period 2009-2014.

Printing and service activities related to printing (NACE code 18.1) amount to more than 95% of the total turnover value, whereas the share of reproduction of recorded media (NACE code 18.2) is limited.

This sub-sector is made up of mostly small and medium-sized enterprises. Their number has decreased from 3393 companies in 2008 to 2318 companies in 2014.[73] Average employment in each company during this period is four people.

Figure 5.12. **Value added of printing and reproduction of recorded media as a percentage of manufacturing (2008-2013)**

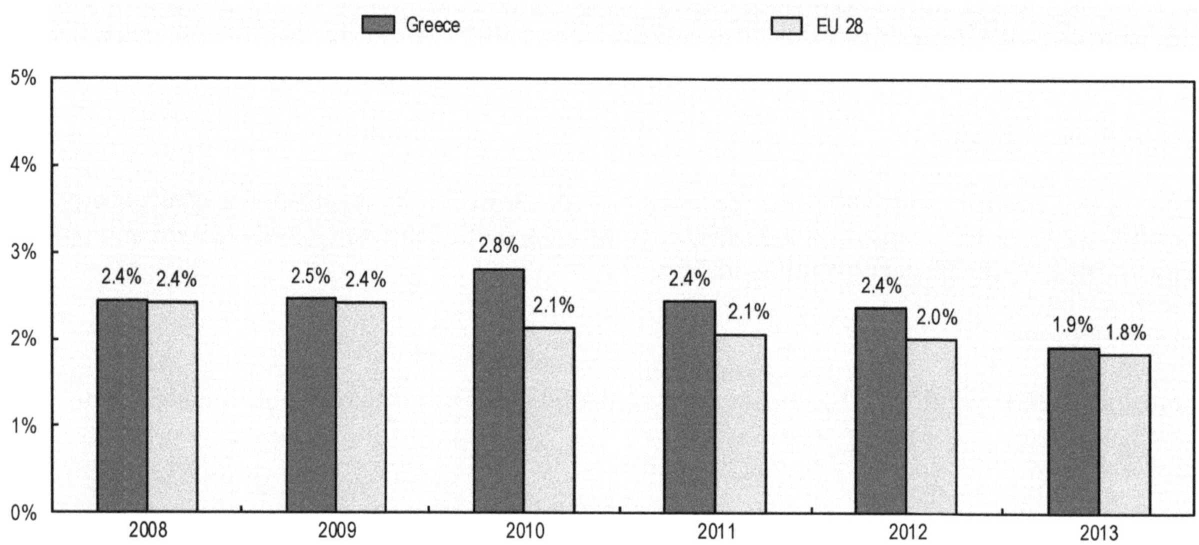


*Note*: Value added at factor cost

*Source*: Eurostat, Annual detailed enterprise statistics for industry (NACE Rev. 2, B-E), Database [sbs_na_ind_r2], *http://ec.europa.eu/eurostat* (accessed 24 August 2016).

Figure 5.13. **Turnover of printing and reproduction of recorded media in Greece (2008-2014)**

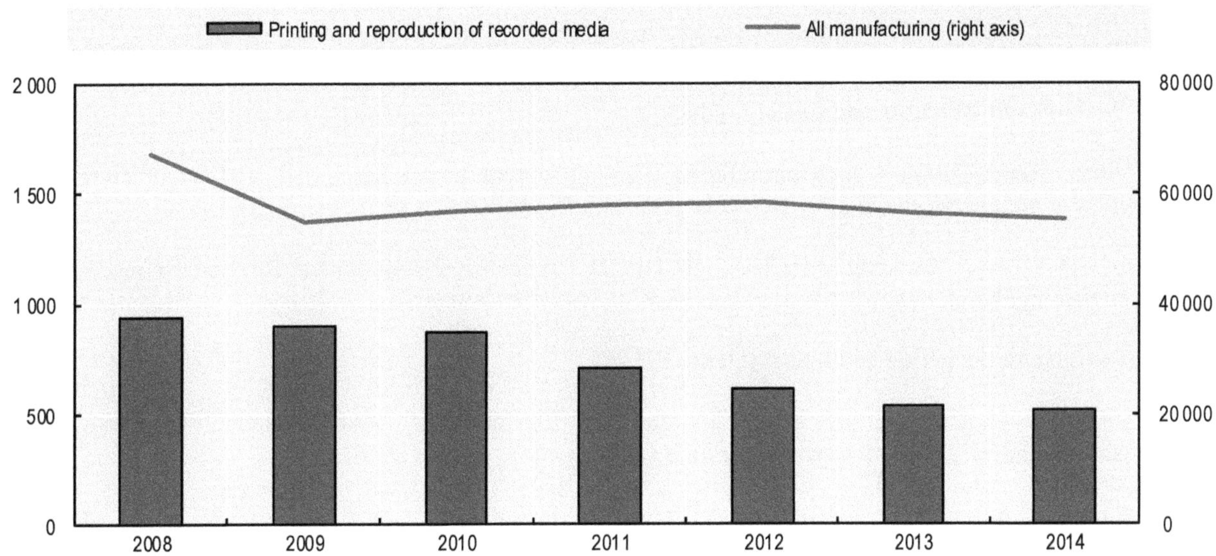


*Note*: Turnover in EUR millions

*Source*: Eurostat, Annual detailed enterprise statistics for industry (NACE Rev. 2, B-E), Database [sbs_na_ind_r2], *http://ec.europa.eu/eurostat* (accessed 24 August 2016).

## *Overview of the legislation*

The mapping of the legislation for the sector included four sector-specific regulations.

- Joint Ministerial Decision 1110/1988[74] and Decision of the Supreme Chemical Council of the General Chemical State Laboratory 1196/1989[75] on the classification, packaging and labelling of paints, varnishes, printing inks, adhesives and similar products, both transposing European legislation.
- Royal Decree 464/1968[76] introducing a Regulation for health and safety at printing facilities.
- Circular 1244/2015 of the Ministry of Finance on VAT on printing of books, newspapers and journals along with their delivery.[77]

In addition, the OECD has identified a provision in Law 2121/1993,[78] setting out the basic legal framework for Intellectual Property Rights, according to which a fair remuneration is imposed, in favour of intellectual -property collecting societies, on the value of photocopying machines, scanners and photocopy paper, whether produced domestically or imported. Due to the fact that this provision derives from Directive 2004/48/EC, however, no further analysis was executed. Apart from this provision, no other restriction has been identified.

## *Recommendations*

No specific competition problems have been identified following the review of the legislation.

## Notes

1. Data refer to "Manufacture of paper and paper products", "Printing and reproduction of recorded media", "Manufacture of electrical equipment", "Manufacture of chemicals and chemical products" and "Manufacture of plastic and rubber products".

2. When recommendations are expected to have an impact both on wholesale trade and manufacturing, their effect is split between the affected levels of the supply chain.

3. OECD (2014), "Building materials", in OECD Competition Assessment Reviews: Greece, OECD Publishing, Paris. *http://dx.doi.org/10.1787/9789264206090-9-en*,

4. The data for the period 2008-2010 refer to EU 27.

5. Eurostat, Annual detailed enterprise statistics for industry (NACE Rev. 2, B-E), Database [sbs_na_ind_r2], *http://ec.europa.eu/eurostat* (accessed 24 August 2016).

6 Eurostat, Annual detailed enterprise statistics for industry (NACE Rev. 2, B-E), Database [sbs_na_ind_r2], *http://ec.europa.eu/eurostat* (accessed 24 August 2016).

7. The term "pesticide" is often used interchangeably with "plant protection product"; however, pesticide is a broader term that also covers non plant/crop uses, for example biocides. See *http://ec.europa.eu/food/plant/pesticides/index_en.htm*

8. Eurostat, Annual detailed enterprise statistics for industry (NACE Rev. 2, B-E), Database [sbs_na_ind_r2], *http://ec.europa.eu/eurostat* (accessed 24 August 2016).

9. Eurostat, Annual detailed enterprise statistics for industry (NACE Rev. 2, B-E), Database [sbs_na_ind_r2], *http://ec.europa.eu/eurostat* (accessed 24 August 2016).

10. Eurostat, Annual detailed enterprise statistics for industry (NACE Rev. 2, B-E), Database [sbs_na_ind_r2], *http://ec.europa.eu/eurostat* (accessed 24 August 2016).

11. See Regulation (EC) No 648/2004 of the European Parliament and of the Council of 31 March 2004 on detergents (Official Journal L104/08.04.2004).

12. See Presidential Decree 111/2014 on Organisational structure of the Ministry of Finance (Official Gazette, A'178/29.08.2014).

13. See Ministerial Decision 1233/1991 and 172/1992 on Registration System for detergents and cleaning products (Official Gazette, B'277/20.04.1992).

14. See Joint Ministerial Decision 381/2005 on Determination of competent authority and of the control mechanisms, fees and penalties for the application of Regulation 648/2004 on detergents (Official Gazette, B'539/02.05.2006).

15. See Regulation (EU) No 528/2012 of the European Parliament and of the Council of 22 May 2012 concerning the making available on the market and use of biocidal products (Official Journal L 167, 27.6.2012).

16. See Joint Ministerial Decision 4616/52519/2016 on Supplementary measures for the application of Regulation 528/2012 on marketing and use of biocidal products (Official Gazette, B'1367/16.5.2016).

17. See L. 721/1977 on Circulation approval and control of plant protection products and relevant issues (Official Gazette, A'298/07.10.1977).

18. See Ministerial Decision 7723/1993 on Circulation of disinfectants (Official Gazette, B'961/23.12.1994).

19. As amended by L. 4351/2015 (Art.18) and 4235/2014 (Art.44).

20. See Presidential Decree 159/2013 on Trading and store functionality requirements of plant protection products (Official Gazette, A'251/18.11.2013).

21. As amended by Laws 2040/1992 (Art.17), 2326/1995 (Art.1), 2732/1999 (Art.6), 2945/2001 (Art.35), 3147/2003 (Art.32), 4235/2014 (Art.49) and 4351/2015 (Art.33).

22. Ministerial Decision 811/337/2008 (Official Gazette, B'1380/15.07.2008).

23. Ministerial Decision 812/338/2008 (Official Gazette, B'1380/15.07.2008).

24. See Art.84 par.3 of Ministerial Decision A2/718/2014 on Rules for the supply and distribution of products and the provision of services (Official Gazette, B'2090/31.07.2014).

25. See Art.11 par.2 of Regulation (EC) 648/2004 of the European Parliament and of the Council of 31 March 2004 on Detergents (Official Journal, L104/08.04.2004).

26. The MD also provides for abolishing or revoking the special licence granted by the GCSL, in case of termination of production, or relocation of production facilities, or alteration in meeting the required terms of operation. This provision is proportionate to the objective of safeguarding proper production process.

27. See Art.1 par.1 of Joint Ministerial Decision 381/2005 on Determination of competent authority and of the control mechanisms, fees and penalties for the application of Regulation 648/2004 on detergents (Official Gazette, B'539/02.05.2006).

28. See Regulation (EU) No 528/2012 of the European Parliament and of the Council of 22 May 2012 concerning the Making available on the market and use of biocidal products (Official Journal L167, 27.6.2012); EU biocides regulation entered into force in September 2013.

29. See Art.2 par.2 of L. 1316/1983 on the Establishment of the National Organisation for Medicines: "The following products fall under the competency of the Organisation: [...] (ιστ) Disinfectants, antiseptics and air fresheners" (Official Gazette, A'11/11.1.1983).

30. See Ministerial Decision 7723/1994 on Circulation of disinfectants (Official Gazette, B'961/1994).

31. See L. 721/1977 on Circulation approval and control of plant protection products and other relevant provisions (Official Gazette, A'298/07.10.1977).

32. Umbrella branding involves the same brand being associated with various products in various markets (e.g. Yamaha, Virgin, Palmolive), which enables firms to make scale savings, as all their products and all their communications contribute to their notoriety. See OECD (2009), *Trademarks as an Indicator of Product and Marketing Innovations*, OECD Publishing, Paris. *www.oecd-ilibrary.org/science-and-technology/trademarks-as-an-indicator-of-product-and-marketing-innovations_224428874418.*

33. See Legislative Decree 96/1973 on Trade of pharmaceutical products (Official Gazette, A'172/3-8.8.1973).

34. See Joint Ministerial Decision Δ.ΥΓ3α/Γ.Π.32221/2013 on Harmonisation of Greek legislation with EU legislation in the sector of production and circulation of medicinal products for human use in compliance with Directive 2001/83/EC on the Community Code relating to medicinal products for human use as amended by Directive 2011/62/EU as regards the prevention of the entry into legal supply chain of falsified medicinal products (Official Gazette, B'1049/29.04.2013).

35. See Ministerial Decision 9497/104760/2014 on the Prescription of plant protection products (Official Gazette, B'2310/28.08.2014).

36. According to Art.6 par.1 of Directive 2009/128/EC of the European Parliament and of the Council of 21 October 2009 establishing a framework for Community action to achieve the sustainable use of pesticides: "Member States shall ensure that distributors have sufficient staff in their employment holding a certificate referred to in Article 5(2). Such persons shall be available at the time of sale to provide adequate information to customers as regards pesticide use, health and environmental risks and safety instructions to manage those risks for the products in question". See (Official Journal, L309/24.11.2009).

37. Art.14 of Directive 2009/128/EC ibid. states that, "Member States shall take all necessary measures to promote low pesticide-input pest management, giving wherever possible priority to non-chemical methods, so that professional users of pesticides switch to practices and products with the lowest risk to human health and the environment among those available for the same pest problem".

38. See L.4235/2014 on Food, animals, animal feed, plant protection products etc (Official Gazette, A'32/11.02.2014).

39. See L.4235/2014 on Food, animals, animal feed, plant protection products etc (Official Gazette, A'32/11.02.2014).

40. Italy's National Action Plan for the Sustainable Use of Plant Protection Products, *http://ec.europa.eu/food/plant/pesticides/sustainable_use_pesticides/nap/index_en.htm.*

41. See Law 4384/2016 on Agricultural Cooperatives, forms of collective organisation of rural areas and other provisions (Official Gazette, A'78/26.04.2016).

42. See Section E.10 par. 1 of Law 4152/2013 on Implementing measures for Laws 4046/2012, 4093/2012 και 4127/2013 (Official Gazette, A'107/09.05.2013).

43. According to the EU Recommendation 2003/361 (Official Journal L124, 20.05.2003), a micro enterprise is defined as "an enterprise which employs fewer than 10 persons and whose annual turnover and/or annual balance sheet total does not exceed EUR 2 million" and a small enterprise is defined as "an enterprise which employs fewer than 50 persons and whose annual turnover and/or annual balance sheet total does not exceed EUR 10 million".

44. According to the EU Recommendation 2003/361 (Official Journal, L124/20.05.2003), a micro enterprise is defined as "an enterprise which employs fewer than 10 persons and whose annual turnover and/or annual balance sheet total does not exceed EUR 2 million" and a small enterprise is defined as "an enterprise which employs fewer than 50 persons and whose annual turnover and/or annual balance sheet total does not exceed EUR 10 million".

45. See Art.2 of Presidential Decree 159/2014 on Part-time employment of responsible scientist in small and micro enterprises of production and trade of seeds and propagating material and trade of fertilisers (Official Gazette, A'241/05.11.2014).

46. See paragraph 3 of Opinion 19/VI/2012 of the Hellenic Competition Commission (Official Gazette, B'3114/26.11.2012).

47. See Art.4 par.3β of L.1565/1985 on Fertilisers (Official Gazette, A'164/25-26.09.1985).

48. See Art.3 par.5 of Ministerial Decision 9748/100747/2012 on Determining the requirements and procedure for getting a licence for type A and B trade of fertilisers (Official Gazette, B'2692/ 04.10.2012).

49. Ministry of Rural Development and Food, registry database, wwww.minagric.gr/pol_yliko/py_companies_lipasmata.aspx, (accessed 4 September 2016).

50. Regulation (EC) No.1223/2009 of the European Parliament and of the Council of 30 November 2009 on cosmetic products (Official Journal, L342/22.12.2009). The "EU Cosmetics Regulation" entered into force in July 2013.

51. According to Art.13 of the Regulation (EC) No 1223/2009 ibid., all cosmetic products marketed in the EU must be registered in the Cosmetic Products Notification Portal (CPNP) before being placed on the market. See https://webgate.ec.europa.eu/cpnp/faq/?event=faq.show (accessed 4 September 2016). After a product has been registered in the CPNP, no further notification at national level is required.

52. Council Directive 76/768/EEC of 27 July 1976 on the approximation of the laws of the Member States relating to cosmetic products (Official Journal, L262/27.9.1976, p.169). The Directive had been amended several times and was recast in a single text into Regulation (EC) No.1223/2009 ibid.

53. See Joint Ministerial Decision ΔΥΓ3α/ΓΠ. 132979/2005 on the Adaptation of Greek legislation to Community Directives in cosmetics sector (Official Gazette, B'352/18.03.2005).

54. Compliance with the requirements of EU Regulation is presumed if ISO 22716:2007 is applied.

55. See National Organisation for Medicines Circular 92428/28.12.2009 on the Legal circulation of cosmetic products.

56. EC Guidance documents, available at http://ec.europa.eu/growth/sectors/cosmetics/products/borderline-products.

57. See recitals 6 and 7 of the Preamble of EU Regulation 1223/2009, ibid.

58. See recital 20 of the Preamble of EU Regulation 528/2012, ibid.

59. It was not able to identify the objectives of the Circular. The objective as described is based on the OECD's understanding of an exchange with the National Organisation for Medicines.

60. See Art. 11, par.1ζ of L.1316/1983 ibid.

61. Council Directive 2008/118/EC of 16 December 2008 concerning the General arrangements for excise duty and repealing Directive 92/12/EEC (Official Journal L9, 14.1.2009).

62. Council Directive 92/12/EEC of 25 February 1992 on the General arrangements for products subject to excise duty and on the holding, movement and monitoring of such products (Official Journal L076, 23.03.1992).

63. See National Customs Code, Law 2960/2001, Art.81 par.4 (Official Gazette, A'265/22.11.2001).

64. See Ministerial Decision 811/337/2008 ibid.

65. See Ministerial Decision 812/338/2008 ibid.

66. Denaturation of alcohol is a process that renders alcohol unfit for human consumption. Three components are commonly used to prevent the product from being consumed either accidentally (for example by children) or on purpose: (1) a smelling agent, (2) a foul-tasting agent, and (3) an analytical marker, which remains present (even in trace quantities) even if fraudulent attempts are made to remove agents 1 and 2.

67. The data for the period 2008-2010 refer to EU-27.

68. Eurostat, Annual detailed enterprise statistics for industry (NACE Rev. 2, B-E), Database [sbs_na_ind_r2], *http://ec.europa.eu/eurostat* (accessed 24 August 2016).

69. See Ministerial Decision 529/2000 on Circulation in the market and installation of sockets and plugs (Official Gazette, B'67/28.01.2000).

70. The data for the period 2008-2010 refer to EU-27.

71. Eurostat, Annual detailed enterprise statistics for industry (NACE Rev. 2, B-E), Database [sbs_na_ind_r2], *http://ec.europa.eu/eurostat* (accessed 24 August 2016).

72. The data for the period 2008-2010 refer to EU-27.

73. Eurostat, Annual detailed enterprise statistics for industry (NACE Rev. 2, B-E), Database [sbs_na_ind_r2], *http://ec.europa.eu/eurostat* (accessed 24 August 2016).

74. See Joint Ministerial Decision 1110/1988 on Classification, packaging and labelling of paints, varnishes, printing inks and related products (Official Gazette, B'733/05.10.1988).

75. See Decision of the Supreme Chemical Council of the General Chemical State Laboratory 1196/1989 on Classification, packaging and labelling of paints, varnishes, printing inks and related products (Official Gazette, B'51/30.01.1990).

76. See Royal Decree 464/1968 on Regulation on health and safety of workers in printing industries or graphic arts and paper processing industries (Official Gazette, A'153/28.06-12.07.1968).

77. Circular 1244/2015 of the Ministry of Finance on VAT on printing of books, newspapers and journals along with their delivery, issued on 03.11.2015.

78. See Art.18 par.3 of L. 2121/1993 on Copyright, Related Rights and Cultural Matters (Official Gazette, A'25/04.03.1993).

## References

Andersson, F. (2002), "Pooling Reputations," International Journal of Industrial Organization, 20(5), p. 715-730.

Cabral L. M. B. (2007), "Optimal brand umbrella size: Technical report", New York University, New York.

Dube, J.P., G.Hitsch and P.Rossi (2009), "Do Switching Costs Make Markets Less Competitive?", Journal of Marketing Research, Vol. 46, No. 4, p. 435.

European Commission, Taxation and Customs Union, "Alcohol Not For Human Consumption" information page, *https://ec.europa.eu/taxation_customs/business/excise-duties-alcohol-tobacco-energy/excise-duties-alcohol/alcohol-not-human-consumption_en* (accessed 05.09.2016).

Eurostat (2008), NACE Rev.2: Statistical classification of economic activities in the European Community, *http://ec.europa.eu/eurostat/documents/3859598/5902521/KS-RA-07-015-EN.PDF* (accessed 05.09.2016).

General Chemical State Laboratory of Greece, Annual Activity Reports, *www.gcsl.gr/index.asp?a_id=22.*

Hakenes H. and M. Peitz (2008), "Umbrella branding and external certification", Preprints of the Max Planck Institute for Research on Collective Goods, Bonn.

OECD (2009), "Trademarks as an Indicator of Product and Marketing Innovations", OECD Science, Technology and Industry Working Papers, No. 2009/06, OECD Publishing, Paris, *http://dx.doi.org/10.1787/224428874418.*

OECD (2014), Consumption Tax Trends 2014: VAT/GST and excise rates, trends and policy issues, OECD Publishing, Paris, *http://dx.doi.org/10.1787/ctt-2014-en.*

Weyl, E. G., and M. Fabinger (2013), "Pass-Through as an Economic Tool: Principles of Incidence under Imperfect Competition", Journal of Political Economy, Vol. 121, No. 3, pp.528-583.

**Databases**

Eurostat, Annual detailed enterprise statistics for industry (NACE Rev. 2, B-E), Database [sbs_na_ind_r2], *http://ec.europa.eu/eurostat* (accessed 24 August 2016).

Eurostat, Prodcom Annual Data 2015, *http://ec.europa.eu/eurostat/web/prodcom/data/excel-files-nace-rev.2* (accessed 24 August 2016).

*Chapter 6*

# Pharmaceuticals

*The pharmaceutical industry makes a significant contribution to GDP, employment and economic health, and constitutes a prominent and growth-enhancing area of economic activity in Greece. Its regulatory framework is apt to significant state involvement with the critical objective of public-health protection. The economic and social importance of this sector increases the need for consistently applied rules and regulations, which must find a balance between efficiency, effectiveness and inclusive growth. Currently, competition appears hindered by legislation restricting various aspects of pharmaceuticals, creating differential treatment of economic agents and legal uncertainty. These include pricing mechanisms that do not allow generics to exploit their price advantages; an advertising framework for over-the-counter medicines (OTCs) that may lead to price rigidities; limitations on scientific events that burden marketing strategies; and operational restrictions on pharmaceutical warehouses that may lead to wholesale trade inefficiencies. The implementation of these recommendations would enable the achievement of health-protection policy objectives, while strengthening economic activity through fairer and more efficient practices and mechanisms.*

## 6.1. Definition and economic overview

This chapter examines the competition effects of legislation related to the manufacturing and wholesale trade of pharmaceutical products and preparations.[1] For the purposes of the present assessment, the definition of pharmaceuticals includes medicines for human use, veterinary products, food supplements and foodstuffs intended for particular nutritional uses, dietary foods for special medical purposes, and foods intended for use in energy-restricted diets for weight reduction. The competition assessment looks at licensing, pricing, reimbursement, trade, marketing, storage, distribution, and other areas that affect the behaviour of economic agents involved in this market.

Besides analysing the main economic characteristics and impact of the sector on the Greek economy, it endeavours to shed light on the key obstacles to competition identified in the four main thematic categories, into which the sector legislation has been broken down. The recommendations are aimed at achieving the policy maker's objective with the least possible distortion to market competition.

Research and official data estimate the overall contribution of the sector to be around 4% of the country's GDP or about EUR 7.55 billion (SFEE, 2016)[2]. In the four years between 2011 and 2014, economic activity in the manufacturing of pharmaceuticals sector has accelerated both in the EU and in Greece, despite the protracted economic recession. Turnover increased in the EU-28 by 5%; in Greece, Eurostat data show a turnover increase for the sector of more than 60%. Unlike the EU, where the value added of pharmaceuticals saw a decline of 7%, in Greece it increased by more than 50%. This was accompanied by a parallel 58% increase in the number of persons employed to almost 10 000 people. The number of pharmaceutical companies also increased from 87 to 94, outpacing the respective 6% increase across the EU-28. Figure 6.1 shows that the sharpest increase in all four aspects of the economic activity took place between 2012 and 2013.

Figure 6.1. **Economic activity in the manufacturing of pharmaceuticals**

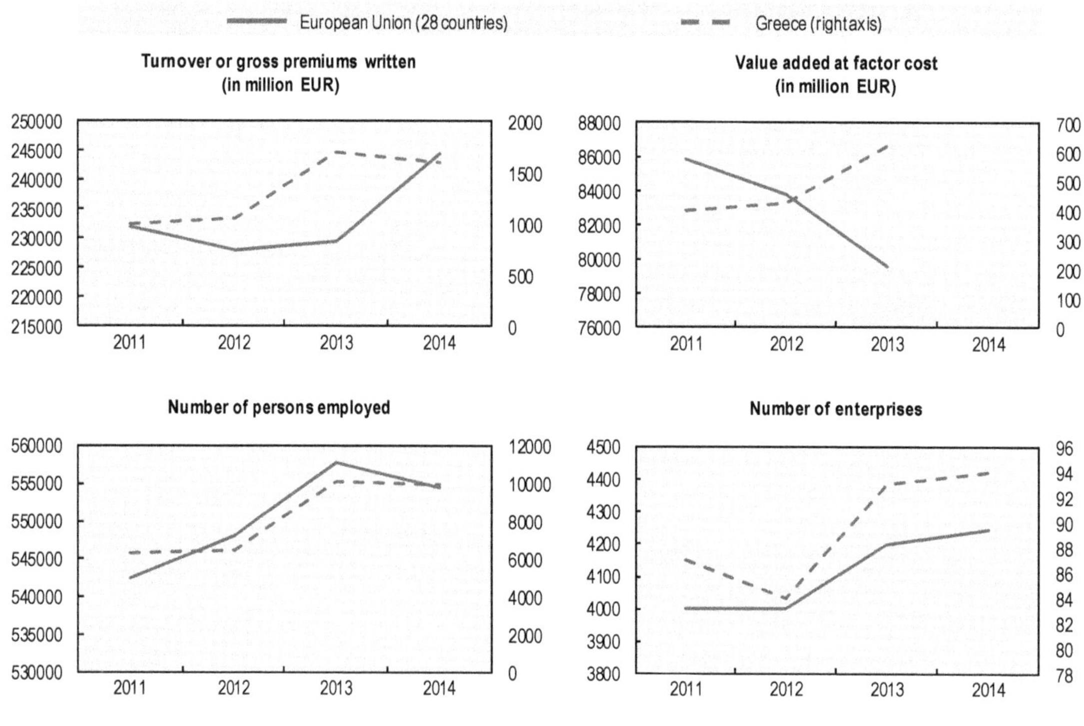


*Source*: Eurostat, Annual detailed enterprise statistics for industry (NACE Rev. 2), Database [sbs_na_ind_r2], *http://ec.europa.eu/eurostat* (accessed 4 April 2016).

In the three years between 2011 and 2013, the economic performance of pharmaceutical wholesalers in Greece showed mixed results. OECD estimations based upon Eurostat data show that the country accounted for 2% of the turnover and value added of the EU-28, 3% of the number of persons employed, and 4% of the number of enterprises of the sector. Moreover, the turnover saw a marginal increase of 0.3% in the EU-28 between 2011 and 2013, whereas in Greece it declined by 14%. The number of pharmaceutical wholesalers in Greece dropped by 4% with a larger decrease in the number of persons employed (14%). The corresponding figures in the EU-28 show a 3% increase in the number of enterprises and a 2% decline in employment. All these developments resulted in a 5% decline in the value added of the pharmaceuticals' wholesale trade. This drop was milder that the average one in the EU-28 where the total value added declined more significantly (-7%).

Figure 6.2. **Economic activity in the wholesale trade of pharmaceuticals**

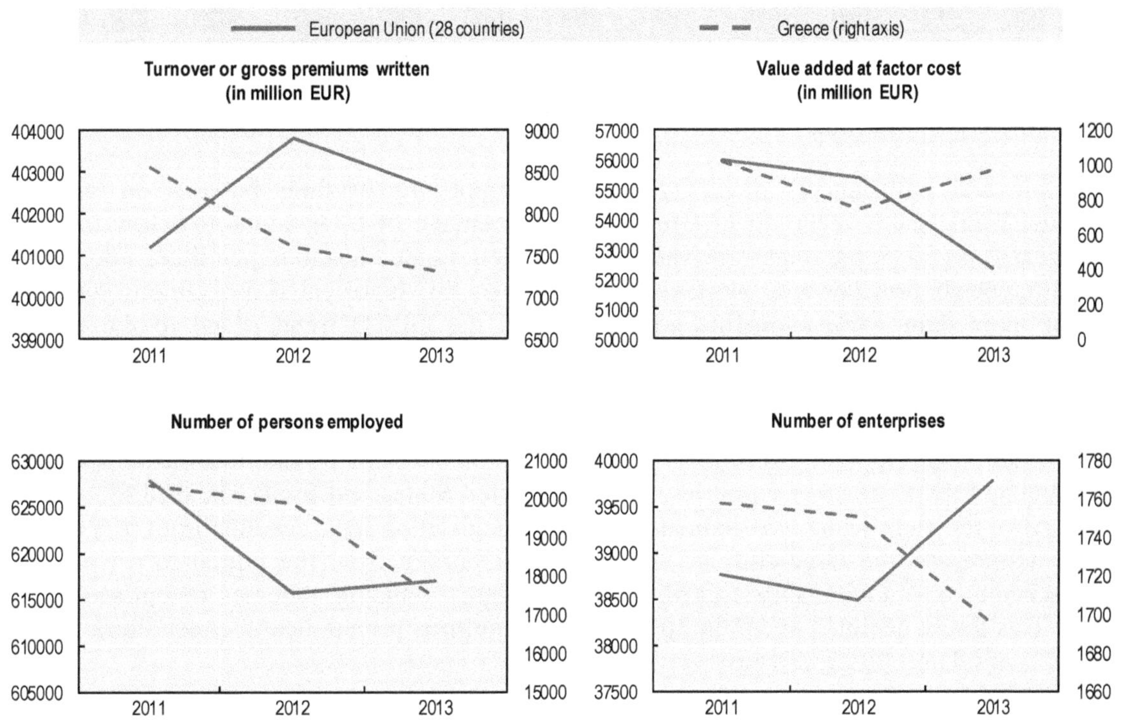


*Source*: Eurostat, Annual detailed enterprise statistics for services (NACE Rev. 2), Database [sbs_na_dt_r2], *http://ec.europa.eu/eurostat*(accessed 4 April 2016).

According to Article 103 of the Joint Ministerial Decision Δ.ΥΓ3α/Γ.Π.32221/2013,[3] wholesale trade of pharmaceuticals has to be authorised by the National Organisation for Medicines. The relevant licence defines the details about the facilities, where the wholesale trade shall take place. The duration of the licence shall not exceed five years. It may be subsequently renewed an unlimited number of times for the same duration. Pharmaceutical wholesale may be conducted by producers, their representatives or importers of pharmaceutical products (including the Market Authorisation Holders or MAHs), pharmaceutical warehouses, warehouses of supply cooperatives of pharmacists, cooperatives of pharmacists and third -party logistics enterprises. One hundred and twenty-eight, or about 7.6%, of the 1 695 enterprises engaged in wholesale trade of pharmaceuticals in 2013, were pharmaceutical warehouses. This number declined to 100 warehouses in 2014. As seen in Figure 6.3, the number of pharmaceutical warehouses operating in Greece declined during the last decade by more than 40%.

Figure 6.3. **Number of pharmaceutical warehouses in Greece**

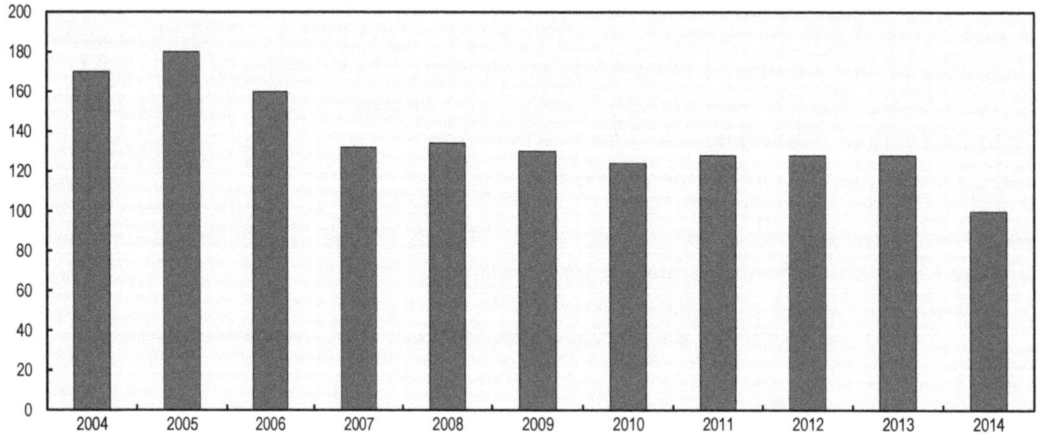


*Note*: Provisional data for 2010.

*Source*: Panhellenic Pharmaceutical Association – ELSTAT business registry.

Both people and governments devote significant proportions of their budgets on health and pharmaceuticals. Total health spending in Greece as a percentage of GDP remains below the OECD average (Figure 6.4). In 2015, the total of privately and publicly funded health expenditure stood at about EUR 14.4 billion, or about 8.2% of GDP. Compared to 2009, this represented a decline in total health expenditure of more than 35%, a decline which exceeds the OECD trend.[4] Due to the economic deceleration of the Greek economy that occurred in parallel, the share of health expenditure to GDP also declined, but at much slower pace. About 60% of total spending, or the equivalent of about 5% of Greek GDP, consisted of government and compulsory contributory healthcare financing schemes (OECD, 2015). This, in turn, suggests that Greece has the third highest level of private-healthcare spending to GDP (3.2%) among OECD member countries, after the United States and Switzerland (8.6% and 3.7% respectively). Also, the significant and frequent changes in legislation have resulted both in a reduction of health expenditure and the large shift of the health-cost burden from the public to private sector. Government schemes and compulsory contributory healthcare financing schemes comprised 6.9% of GDP in 2010. This figure declined to 5% in 2015. In the meantime, private health expenditure increased from 3% to 3.2% of GDP (OECD, 2016c).

Figure 6.4. **Expenditure on health as a percentage of GDP, 2015**

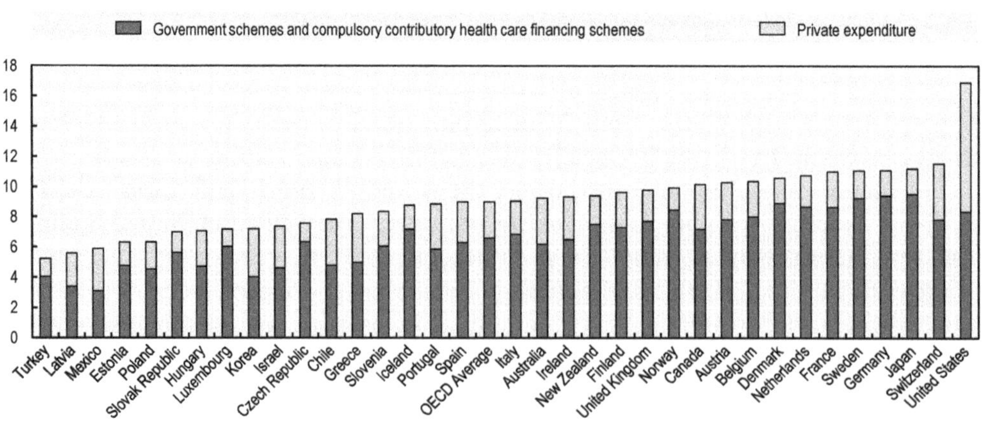


*Source*: OECD (2016c), "Health expenditure and financing: health expenditure indicators", *OECD Health Statistics* (database), *http://dx.doi.org/10.1787/data-00349-en* (accessed on 1 August 2016).

OECD data show that health expenditure, both private and public, declined significantly in the past few years of the economic crisis. On the other hand, the share of pharmaceutical expenditure in total health spending was relatively high. In 2014, it stood more or less at the same levels with 2009. In this respect, Greece ranked second among OECD member countries, only surpassed by Hungary. Pharmaceutical expenditure reached a peak in 2011 (34.8% of total health expenditure) and has been on a downward trend since, accounting for 28.4% of total health expenditure in 2014. Nevertheless, this remains well above the OECD average (16.3%) and the EU average (17.1%), reinforcing the fact that a relatively high fraction of health expenditure is captured by pharmaceutical products (Figure 6.5).

Figure 6.5. **Pharmaceutical spending as a percentage of total health spending**

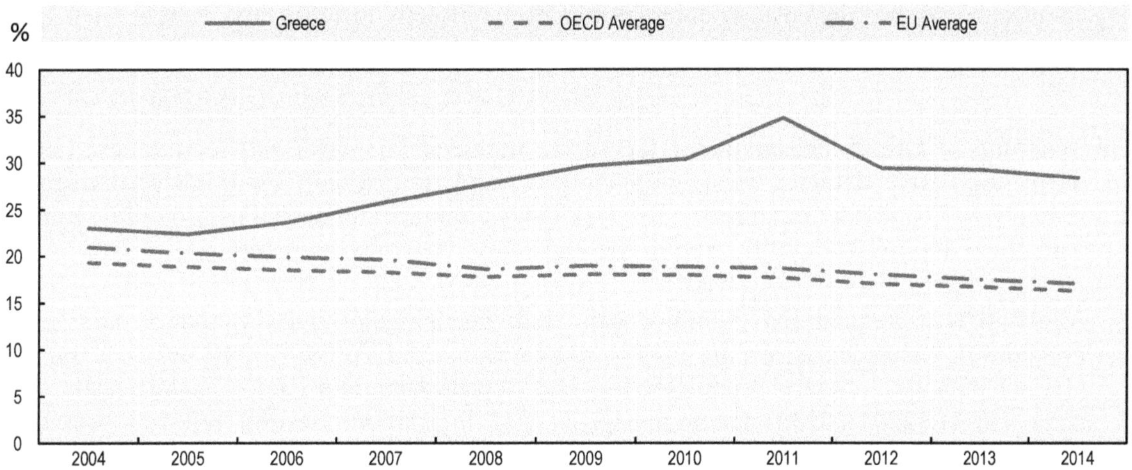


*Note*: 2008 data for Greece are missing.

*Source*: OECD (2016b), Pharmaceutical spending (indicator), http://dx.doi.org/10.1787/998febf6-en (accessed on 18 August 2016).

Pharmaceutical spending in Greece stood at 2.35% as a share of GDP in 2014. This was the highest share among OECD country members. In other OECD countries it ranged from 0.53% in Luxembourg to 2.17% in Hungary. Pharmaceutical expenditure and the issue of generics penetration have featured prominently in the policy agenda in Greece, with adopted measures including external reference pricing, generic substitution and international non-proprietary name (INN) prescribing. However, further efforts are needed in this direction. The OECD has provided health-policy recommendations aimed at rationalising and optimising health and pharmaceutical policy in Greece (Box 6.1).

Box 6.1. **OECD Health Policy in Greece**

The OECD Health Division concluded its latest review of the health system in Greece in 2016. The main proposals included in the *2016 OECD Health Policy in Greece* are a need for:

- further plans to rationalise pharmaceutical spending and reorganise hospital care;
- decisions on drug coverage to become more rational and be based on health technology assessments (HTA);
- effective programmes and awareness campaigns to educate health-care personnel and prevent excessive use of antibiotics.

*Source*: OECD (2016a), Health Policy in Greece, *www.oecd.org/greece/Health-Policy-in-Greece-January-2016.pdf*.

## 6.2. Overview of the legislation

Pharmaceuticals is one of the most regulated sub-sectors of both manufacturing and wholesale trade. This is due to the need to meet wide-ranging policy objectives, including rewarding innovation, ensuring equal access to medicines for patients, controlling public expenditure, and, most importantly, protecting public health. This means the sub-sector is subject to significant state intervention and has a great variety of stakeholders along the entire value chain. The National Organisation for Medicines (EOF) is the key competent authority for regulating the sector.

Pharmaceutical legislation is extensive and fragmentary: framework provisions are dispersed across numerous laws and ministerial decisions, which have been repeatedly revised over the past five years, resulting in many overlaps. The ensuing complexity affects, directly or indirectly, market participants. In addition, fragmentation of legislation in the sector can lead to legal uncertainty and lapses in implementation.

The mapping of Greek legislation for the sector included 155 laws and regulations. Legislation included laws, legislative decrees, presidential decrees, and ministerial/joint ministerial decisions. A significant number of National Organisation for Medicines circulars and decisions providing guidance on the proper practical interpretation of the applicable legislation were also assessed.

- About 40% of regulations examined deal with licensing, product circulation and inspection procedures. Licensing issues are mainly regulated by Legislative Decree 96/1973[5] on trade of pharmaceuticals, dietary supplements and cosmetics and Joint Ministerial Decision Δ.ΥΓ3α/Γ.Π.32221/2013,[6] which transposes EU legislation. Several relevant provisions on licencing and market surveillance are laid down in Law 1316/1983[7] on the establishment of the National Organisation for Medicines, the competent authority for granting market authorisations and carrying out market inspections.

- About 30% of regulations form the relevant legislation on pharmaceutical pricing and reimbursement. Pricing legislation, which includes among others the rebate and claw-back mechanisms, is mainly governed by laws passed by the Greek parliament after 2010. This was done in an effort to control public pharmaceutical expenditure, especially following its boost in the 2004-2010 period.[8]

- About 10% of regulations concern the marketing and promotion of medicinal products.

- About 20% of regulations constitute the framework of the pharmaceuticals wholesale trade.

The sector is largely governed by EU regulation. The requirements and procedures for the market authorisation for medicinal products for human use, as well as the rules for the constant supervision of products after they have been authorised, are harmonised provisions primarily laid down in Directive 2001/83/EC[9] and in Regulation (EC) No 726/2004.[10]

Pricing and reimbursement rules for medicines are not harmonised within the internal market and remain a national policy issue. The current national legal framework on pricing is laid down in Legislative Decree 96/1973, Law 4336/2015, 4337/2015,[11] and Ministerial Decision 28408/2016.[12] Screening of the relevant legislation revealed that a number of ministerial decisions on pharmaceutical pricing and related processes have been issued since late 2013. These decisions have decreased clarity for businesses about the processes to be followed in different cases. This lack of regulatory certainty is likely to have increased administrative costs for businesses as they spend time identifying the applicable rules and processes.

Approximately 25% of provisions initially identified as problematic from a competition perspective were found to be inactive and obsolete. New legislation has often not explicitly abolished antecedents, causing legal uncertainly. An example is Legislative Decree 96/1973, which contains several out-of-date provisions that could have been replaced rather than merely amended. In addition, references to the Market Code were found in several provisions despite the fact that the Market Code was abolished by Article 48, paragraph 2 of Law 4177/2013.[13] These references create regulatory uncertainty regarding the relevant applicable framework and may cause confusion among potential investors.

The main restrictions identified in the manufacturing and wholesale trade of pharmaceuticals, as traced in the Greek legislation, are presented in detail in the following sections. Their harm to competition is also presented, while international comparisons are drawn where applicable and further analysis is conducted and presented in the following sections in order to provide recommendations that lift unnecessary burden and allow for more competition. The benefits of the recommendations for the manufacturing and wholesale trade of pharmaceuticals are estimated at EUR 177 million. In particular, the recommendation on lifting the maximum price reduction of generics (Section 6.5) is expected to increase consumer welfare by EUR 34 million. This estimate is obtained using the methodology described in Annex A, incorporating an average price reduction of 14% from Box 6.5. The combined effect of the remaining recommendations, apart from the cap on price reductions, is estimated at EUR 143 million. For the other recommendations, the OECD has considered whether recommendations would be expected to have an impact on either consumer benefit, through lower prices, or on economic activity, in terms of greater efficiency and additional revenue. In the former case, the framework described in Annex A was applied; in the latter, a conservative assumption was made based upon an overall improvement in the efficiency of operation. When recommendations are expected to have an impact both on wholesale trade and manufacturing, their effect is split between the affected levels of the supply chain.

## 6.3. Licensing

### *Description of the legal framework*

The Legislative Decree 96/1973[14] on the trade of pharmaceuticals, dietary supplements and cosmetics is the main legislation defining the framework of licensing and trading pharmaceutical products in Greece. Since its introduction, the law has undergone numerous and significant amendments. Additions were also specified in new laws and ministerial decisions. This has resulted in many of its provisions becoming obsolete and not implemented. In practice, more recent provisions and European directives have replaced them. For example, Article 6, paragraphs 2 and 4 state that pharmaceutical products are granted market authorisation for a period of two to five years in Greece; the same for the renewal of that authorisation. However, following the adoption of the European Directive 2001/83/EC and its transposal in the national legislation by the Joint Ministerial Decision 32221/2013,[15] all pharmaceutical products, be they locally produced or imported, are granted market authorisation for a five-year period.

According to Law 1316/1983,[16] the main law on the establishment of the National Organisation for Medicines, the responsibility of granting market authorisation rests with this organisation. It is also the responsible agency for the proposal of prices to the Ministry of Health, which is in turn the authority in charge of publishing medicine price bulletins twice a year. National Organisation for Medicines procedures concerning market authorisations are generally aligned with EU legislation and practices. Following EU practice, market authorisations may be granted through the national procedure, the decentralised authorisation, the mutual-recognition procedure, and the centralised European authorisation from the European Medicines Agency (EMA). The last is automatically valid in all EU countries (ÖBIG, 2006).

According to Article 10 of Directive 2001/83/EC, the two main categories of licensed products are reference medicinal products (patented medicines) and generic medicinal products (generics).[17] The production of generics may only start after the expiry of patented medicines' data-protection period.[18] Furthermore, once the patent of a reference medicinal product and its supplementary protection certificate (SPC)[19] expire, a generic version containing the active ingredient may be released in the market. This renders the originator and the generics potential competitors, while having different and independent commercial strategies and conduct (UNCTAD, 2015).

***Description of the relevant provisions***

Various obstacles to competition were identified in the legislation concerning licensing of pharmaceuticals. An indicative list of obstacles found is outlined below. The corresponding harm to competition is described in the following subsection.

- According to Article 8, paragraph 1 of Legislative Decree 96/1973, market authorisation for imported pharmaceutical products is granted to companies' legal representatives, who must be permanently resident in Greece.

- Unlike medicinal products, food supplements, foodstuffs intended for particular nutritional uses, dietary foods for special medical purposes, and foods intended for use in energy-restricted diets for weight reduction do not need market authorisation. In such cases, a circulation notification and a notification fee payable to the National Organisation for Medicines is sufficient for market access. The two main pieces of legislation on food supplements and special nutrition food are the Joint Ministerial Decisions 127962/2004[20] and A2E/5478/1999.[21] They aim to harmonise Greek legislation with Directives 2002/46/EC, 89/398/EEC and 96/84/EC.[22] Article 6, paragraph 3στ of Joint Ministerial Decision 127962/2004 requires that food supplement labels show a National Organisation for Medicines notification number. Moreover, the same article obliges companies to state on product labels that products do not have market authorisation from National Organisation for Medicines, even though the law does not require them to be authorised. The statement aims to protect public health from the excessive consumption of food supplements and to raise awareness that these products do not have National Organisation for Medicines authorisation.

- According to Article 5.9 of National Organisation for Medicines decision 6206/2009,[23] the weighing and sampling of raw materials in factories manufacturing food supplements and foodstuffs intended for particular nutritional uses should be carried out in separate rooms designed for that specific purpose. Carrying out those procedures in the same area is prohibited in order to ensure quality control.

- Another operational requirement defined by law is found in the procedures of licensing mergers of pharmaceutical companies. Pursuant to Article 27, paragraph 5 of Law 1316/1983, production in the factories of merged companies is permitted only if each of them functions under the supervision of production managers and quality-control personnel. The same paragraph establishes that the National Organisation for Medicines has to authorise production transfer between merged factories and establish the necessary conditions for quality control.

These provisions aim at the protection of public health through the establishment of necessary quality control.

- Parallel imports of pharmaceutical products also encounter several restrictions in the Greek legislation. Articles 2, 3 and 6 of Ministerial Decision A6/4171/1987[24] require that parallel-imported products be identical to their equivalent pharmaceutical products already circulating in the Greek market. Despite the partial alignment with the recommendations of OECD (2014),[25] the requirement for identical rather than similar products remains under Article 2, paragraph 3. This creates legal uncertainty. In addition, Article 3 establishes that the licence of the imported product is valid throughout the defined five-year period in both Greece and the import country. If market authorisation expires in the country of origin or if, for any reason, the company there decides to withdraw it from the market, it should also be withdrawn from the Greek market.

- Another restriction on the operation of pharmaceutical companies is identified in Article 9 of Law 1965/1991.[26] Paragraphs 8 and 9 of this Article establish that only pharmaceutical industries or laboratories that have already been legally functioning for at least five years may be co-located in the same industrial area. This is permitted after a previous decision of National Organisation for Medicines and on condition that each of them functions independently under its own responsible producers and quality controls. Importers, producers and representatives are allowed to import, store, trade and distribute pharmaceuticals and diagnostic products produced or imported by them or on behalf of third parties only by using their own use trucks according to the provisions set in the law.

***Harm to competition***

- The law's requirement that the legal representative of a foreign pharmaceutical company be a permanent resident in Greece for it to obtain market authorisation for its products could prevent legal representatives from covering more than one country, and so reduce economies of scale. Centrally authorised market -authorisation holders are not required by the EMA to appoint a local representative.[27]

- Requiring food supplements to bear a statement on their label that they are not authorised by the National Organisation for Medicines may create the impression that these products are risky and act as a counter incentive for their market share expansion.

- The limitation regarding spaces for weighing and sampling of raw materials could limit the choices of suppliers. General operational requirements are already established in the good manufacturing practices for pharmaceutical companies, to which companies must adhere.

- The permission implied in Article 27, paragraph 5 of Law 1316/1983 concerning the operations and production transfer between merged factories could limit the incentives of firms to move towards more efficient forms of production and better management practices. The production quality of pharmaceuticals is ensured on a European level by Good Manufacturing Practice (GMP) certificates, which pharmaceutical companies are required to possess. Moreover, any change in the production of pharmaceutical products has to be reflected in the capability of a production licence. Given this existing system of quality control, this provision could create confusion and legal uncertainty as to whether it is necessary for a firm to have an extra authorisation in order to proceed with a merger decision.

- Linking the circulation of parallel-imported pharmaceutical products with the validity of licence in their origin country is a stricter rule than that defined by the European Commission.[28] This could limit the number of suppliers, especially among those less informed concerning the potential validity of a long-term licence in the origin country. Limiting the number of suppliers may lead to a smaller range of products circulating in the market. By allowing only "identical", rather than "sufficiently similar" products to be eligible for parallel import, this provision is deemed to restrict the choices of patients and health practitioners as it raises the barriers to entry in the Greek market and limits the availability of medicines. Taking into account the implementation of previous OECD recommendations with regard to this topic, the remaining reference to the requirement of identical products in the provision may also lead to legal uncertainty.

- The provisions about the co-location of pharmaceutical companies and the transport of pharmaceutical products exclusively through their own trucks are found to restrict competition in at least two ways. First, Article 8 of Law 1965/1991 grants preferential treatment to incumbent firms to the detriment of the more recently established. Given the policy maker's objective of protecting public health and ensuring quality, co-location based on the years of existence of the firm rather than its safety and quality features seems to restrict free -market operations of more recently established pharmaceutical companies. Second, limiting companies' freedom to choose optimal means of transportation by imposing the use of their own trucks does not seem to be adequately justified on public-safety grounds. Again, better functional rather than technical requirements could allow for more flexibility in managerial choices and give more degrees of freedom to the state to exercise its quality-control duties.

***Recommendation and benefits***

Pharmaceutical legislation is extremely complex, partly because of the frequent changes in national legislation demanded by a fast-changing sector. In response to this, the World Health Organization has produced basic principles concerning general pharmaceutical legislation, which may constitute a good starting point for any revision of Greek pharmaceutical legislation. For example, it is recommended that where *an out-of-date general drug law exists it should be , "replaced rather than merely amended. Determining the extent to which existing laws and regulations contribute to attaining the national policy objectives is essential. Because concepts of pharmaceutical policy are modern, legislation more than* 20 *years old may not be relevant; starting over may be simpler." (WHO, 2012:105)*

- It is recommended that Article 8, paragraph 1 of Legislative Decree 96/1973 be revised so the legal representatives of pharmaceutical companies wishing to obtain market authorisation for imported products no longer need to be permanent residents. This would align Greek law with European Directive 2001/83/EC and allow for a wider variety of products to enter the market, resulting in more competition.

- Concerning food supplements, the OECD recommends that the current labelling requirement is replaced by a more transparent version stating that the product is not subject to market authorisation, and is not required to obtain one from the National Organisation for Medicines.

- Article 5.9 of National Organisation for Medicines decision 6206/2009 should become less restrictive by lifting the requirement for separate designated rooms for weighing and sampling of raw materials, all while ensuring quality control. This would in turn allow for better and freer choice among management practices. Various quality controls from GMP are already in place concerning the establishments, buildings and production facilities of pharmaceutical companies.

- Establishing functional rather than the technical requirements in licensing legislation could stimulate innovation and the best use of management skills. Freeing up their choices while maintaining the requirements ensuring quality control, and most importantly exercising it by the relevant bodies, could allow a more efficient allocation of resources and allow for more competition. It is recommended that Article 27, paragraph 5 of Law 1316/1983 be rephrased in order to state clearly that both parts of it refer to the necessary amendments that need to be made in the capability of production licence and not another separate approval or licence by National Organisation for Medicines.

- Going forward and towards a more competitive market, it is recommended that Ministerial Decision A6/4171/1987 on the issue of parallel imports of pharmaceutical products be aligned with the European Commission Communication COM(2003)839. The latter allows imported products to be "sufficiently similar" to the ones already circulating in the domestic market, rather than identical. Moreover, the OECD, in line with the EC Communication, recommends lifting the requirement that the licence be valid both in the member state of origin and in Greece.

- The OECD also recommends the abolishment of the five-year threshold for firms to be eligible for co-location in the same industrial area. This would stop the differential treatment of firms based on their incumbent or long-standing position in the market and create a level playing field. Moreover, the requirement for pharmaceutical companies to use exclusively their own trucks, as defined in Article 9, paragraph 9 of Law 1965/1991, should be lifted and replaced by a more flexible version. It is recommended that the new law establishes the safety criteria that trucks have to meet, as well as the requirements for the transport of pharmaceutical products.

## 6.4. Marketing and promotion

### *Description of the relevant provisions*

The assessment of the legislation has identified two main restrictions in this area.

*OTC advertising*

Until the end of 2016, all over-the-counter medicines (OTC) are subject to price regulation.[29] Following OECD (2014) recommendations and the adoption of relevant reforms by the Greek government, their liberalisation will begin in 2017, with a newly established sub-category of OTCs, named General Sale Medicines (GEDIFA – ΓΕ.ΔΙ.ΦΑ.), which can be sold to the public outside pharmacies.

While this new category of OTCs will be sold in outlets other than pharmacies, there remain restrictions on their advertising. Paragraph Γ of National Organisation for Medicines Circular 49393/2011 stipulates that OTCs aimed at the general public cannot be advertised in clinics, hospitals, health centres, diagnostic centres or anywhere health services are provided. Advertisements for OTCs are allowed in pharmacies (which provide health services, but also conduct retail sales), but only under certain conditions and guidelines (as defined in Circular 49393/2011).

Box 6.2. **Marketing authorisation in the European Economic Area**

Authorisation for marketing a medicine within the European Economic Area (EEA) is granted through the competent authority of any EEA country – national authorisation which is valid within the particular country – or through one of the recognised procedures for obtaining authorisation in more than one EEA country. The holder of a marketing authorisation valid within the EEA must have an established presence within the EEA. The London-based **European Medicines Agency (EMA)** was established in 1995 to coordinate the evaluation and European market authorisation for both human and animal medicinal products. The EMA operates under the aegis of the European Commission's Directorate-General Enterprise, to which it forwards its opinions for approval for final marketing authorisation in all member states.

There exist three procedures for obtaining marketing authorisation in more than one EEA country: the centralised procedure, the mutual-recognition procedure, and the decentralised procedure.

The **centralised procedure (CP)** grants a marketing authorisation valid in all EEA countries. The procedure is mandatory for, but not limited to, biotechnology, AIDS, cancer, diabetes, and neurodegenerative disorder medicines, as well as orphan drugs. Applications submitted to the EMA by manufacturers are evaluated by the Committee for Proprietary Medical Products (CPMP), comprised of two experts nominated by each member state. The CPMP subcontracts the assessment to two rapporteurs selected from a pool of 3 500 drug-evaluation specialists in national regulatory agencies. The CPMP has 210 days from the receipt of a dossier to provide a recommendation to the European Commission for final approval; however, the clock can be stopped if rapporteurs request additional information from the applicant. Total accumulated time during which the clock is stopped generally should not exceed six months.

The decentralised and mutual-recognition procedures are based on the principle that first approval granted by the authorities of one member state is then recognised by other member states.

Through the **mutual-recognition procedure (MRP)**, manufacturers can apply for marketing authorisations in designated concerned member states (CMS) by validating the marketing authorisation previously granted in another member state, known as the reference member state (RMS). The competent authority in each CMS has 90 days in which to agree or not with the RMS's marketing-approval decision. In case of disagreement, the RMS sends its concerns to the CPMP; if a consensus is not reached after a further 60 days, the procedure moves into arbitration by the CPMP.

The **decentralised procedure (DP)**, introduced in 2005, increases the EMA's facilitating role in the harmonisation of marketing approvals. Manufacturers of new products not yet marketed in one of the EEA member states (and not obliged to use the CP), as well as generic versions of original products authorised through the CP, designate a RMS to undertake the assessment. Identical dossiers are submitted to the CMS where approval is also sought. The RMS steers the approval process, seeking agreement on elements that must be harmonised in the CMS and provides a decision. The RMS and the CMS are granted a maximum of 210 days (including a maximum of three months for clock-stops to allow applicants to respond to objections raised during evaluation) to come to an agreement on the full dossier. If agreement is not forthcoming then an additional 90 days are granted for arbitration, with a final decision by the CPMP. The recommendation is then forwarded to the European Commission for final decision on granting or refusing a marketing authorisation valid in all Concerned Member States.

The main difference between the MRP and the DP is that the latter is sought in cases where no marketing authorisation has been granted in an EEA country. Under the RMS and DP, manufacturers have greater control over the choice of RMS than with the centralised procedure.

A manufacturer can apply for a **national marketing authorisation** for products not obliged to go through the centralised procedure. This is done if the manufacturer intends to market a pharmaceutical in only one EEA country, or as a first step in the Mutual Recognition Procedure. Recent legislation to increase transparency requires that national regulatory bodies make marketing authorisations available "without delay" and publicly release clinical documentation, assessment reports and reports on the reasons that underlie the decision. Generic manufacturers often seek approval through national procedures for two reasons: (1) expiry dates of patents and supplementary protection certificates differ from one country to another, and (2) original products may have different forms, strengths, and labelling across countries, necessitating different studies to prove bio-equivalence.

*Notes:* The EEA is composed of the 28 European Union member countries, plus Norway, Iceland and Liechtenstein. It allows these last three to be part of the EU's single market.

*Source*: Reproduced from Pharmaceutical Pricing and Reimbursement Policies in Slovakia (Kaló, et al., 2008:7-8), Box 1, page 9.

Advertisements for OTCs may take the form of stands, screen displays, brochures and windows materials, and use material of a clear advertising nature, upon which guidelines on the proper use of medicine must be included. However, the circular has not been changed in order to take into account the new category of General Sale Medicines (GEDIFA) that will be traded outside pharmacies. Based on existing legislation, advertising these medicines remains banned in the new points of sale. The objective of advertising restrictions on medicines is to limit their use. The legislation also prohibits any OTC advertising to be associated with the provision of benefits to the public, even of low pecuniary advantage, without excluding the samples and virtual samples of medicines. This in turn derives from the consumer protection objective of the legislation.

*Scientific events*

All scientific events organised or funded by pharmaceutical companies should receive prior approval from the National Organisation for Medicines. This was initially foreseen in Article 16, paragraph 6 of Legislative Decree 96/1973.[30] According to National Organisation for Medicines Circular 17702/2016, the objective of this regulatory framework is to ensure compliance with ethical standards between health professionals and pharmaceutical companies, to control pharmaceutical expenditure and to assess the scientific nature of the events along with the proper implementation of their budget. Restrictions concerning the organisation of scientific events consist of specific and detailed requirements that usually aim to double-check the quality of information disseminated at these events. All detailed organisational and budget information should be submitted to the National Organisation for Medicines for prior approval. According to the National Organisation for Medicines, more than 6 500 medical practitioners went abroad in the first half of 2016 to attend conferences and scientific events.

***Harm to competition***

The limitations on the advertisement of OTCs have the potential to distort firms' promotion strategies. The liberalisation of GEDIFA supply channels, if not followed by a liberalisation of advertising rules, may not have a significant effect on market entry. This may lead to less competition and higher prices, especially after the end of 2016, when price deregulation will apply for GEDIFAs. The second provision of paragraph Γ of National Organisation for Medicines Circular 49393/2011 as it stands also restricts the ability of firms to advertise their price discounts and promotions. Given that GEDIFAs will be sold in outlets other than pharmacies from 2017, the restrictions on displaying discounts and promotions may limit the amount of information available to patients and their ability to make well-informed and rational choices about both the product and its price. There is no equivalent EU legislation and the circular was found not to be in line with Joint Ministerial Decision Δ.ΥΓ3α/Γ.Π.32221/2013,[31] transposing EU Directive 2001/83/EC.

The imposed limitations concerning the organisation of scientific events for the promotion of scientific knowledge may result in distorted marketing strategy of firms. The requirement for prior approval creates extra work for the National Organisation for Medicines and potential delays for conference organisers. As described in Box 6.3, the usual practice in other EU countries is that promotion and communications events are subject to codes of conduct and ethics rather than excessive regulation. Taking into consideration that the framework for the disclosure of transfers[32] between pharmaceutical companies and medical practitioners is currently not enforced, the regulation of scientific events aiming at achieving the objective of limiting these transfers is deemed to be justified. However, given that the maximum percentage of turnover that companies may devote to promotional expenses is regulated and explicitly defined in the Joint Ministerial Decision 28403/01/2012,[33] an ex post check of the scientific character and actual cost of those events in tandem with penalties already provided in the relevant provisions could achieve the policy maker's objective without affecting firms' marketing strategies.

### *Recommendation and benefits*

It is recommended that the provision on the advertisement of OTCs be extended in order to allow for the advertisement of GEDIFAs in their points of sale. These are already defined by MD Γ5(α)51194/2016[34], and this definition should be reflected in the provision. Moreover, the second provision of paragraph Γ of the National Organisation for Medicines Circular 49393/2011 should be reworded in order to allow the advertisement of price promotions and discounts, as a special category of benefits to the public. This change would allow more price competition among firms and could result in lower final prices for patients. However, free samples of pharmaceutical products may only be provided to healthcare professionals and with the aim of enhancing patient care (Directive 2001/83/EC and IFPMA, 2012). The presence of pharmacists and quantity restrictions at other points of sale ensure the protection of public health.

For scientific events organised in Greece, it is recommended that the prior approval by National Organisation for Medicines[35] of scientific events be abolished and replaced by a simple notification to the Organisation. An ex-post control mechanism should be foreseen in law in order to complement the notification requirement. This would free up National Organisation for Medicines resources, as well as allow for more competition in pharmaceutical companies' promotion through scientific events. It also has the potential to develop a new type of economic activity, as foreign firms may be attracted to Greece in order to organise their events.

Box 6.3. **Codes and regulations of ethical pharmaceutical promotion and communications worldwide**

While it is absolutely crucial for patients and medical practitioners to be informed about the latest developments and findings in the pharmaceutical research, the rules of ethical pharmaceutical promotion and communication aim to simultaneously achieve the dissemination of knowledge and truthful, scientifically accurate and fairly communicated content.

**Control systems**

Four general categories of control systems govern pharmaceutical companies' communications relating to prescription products: industry codes of practice; internal company standards; laws; and regulations.

Effective control mechanisms should apply to all interacting parties: pharmaceutical companies, healthcare professionals, government officials, patient groups, and others. Applying codes of practice, laws and regulations to all parties involved provides additional safeguards that discourage wrongdoing. For example, in Europe, if an inappropriate payment or gift is given or offered by a company or requested or accepted by a healthcare professional, both parties can be penalized. Similar laws exist in the United States.

**Laws and regulations**

European Union member states are required to apply a baseline set of laws relating to pharmaceutical communications, but individual countries may promulgate additional laws. In addition, general business-practice laws apply to pharmaceutical companies as they do to all business sectors. In recent years, anti-bribery and anti-corruption laws have significantly impacted pharmaceutical companies' interactions with healthcare professionals. For example, the Foreign Corrupt Practices Act in the US or the UK's Bribery Act can affect firms' activities beyond their respective domestic markets, making companies accountable for wrongdoing abroad.

At the same time, pharmaceutical companies that are members of the International Federation of Pharmaceutical Manufacturers and Associations (IFPMA) apply national association codes of practice and the IFPMA Code of Practice worldwide, in every market in which they operate, even in the absence of legal or regulatory controls.

Box 6.3. **Codes and regulations of ethical pharmaceutical promotion and communications worldwide** (cont.)

**Scope of activities covered by codes of practice**

At a national level, the requirements of codes of practice and legislation usually overlap extensively. A promotional claim or an activity that is illegal will also generally breach the local code of practice. In many countries, code requirements are broader than those in legislation and/or provide more detail on exactly what is and is not acceptable. In other countries, notably the United States, competition or antitrust law may limit the ability of companies or national associations to dictate joint marketing rules.

Generally speaking, the IFPMA Code of Practice and national codes require that product claims relating to prescription medicines be accurate, balanced and up to date. Material must be truthful and not misleading, including misleading by omission and half-truths. For example, claims must give a full account of available evidence and not provide only "half the picture". If challenged, a company is obliged to provide data to substantiate its claims.

One issue covered by most national codes is whether companies are able to support healthcare professionals' attendance at medical conferences. While codes in many countries deem it acceptable to sponsor attendance of healthcare professionals at scientific meetings, and cover associated costs such as reasonable travel, accommodation and meals, they also include a number of caveats. In particular, the main purpose of the meeting must be scientific and professional in nature and any refreshments provided must be incidental to that purpose. The venue must be conducive to the scientific or educational purpose, and international travel must be justified by the international nature of the meeting or other logistical or security reasons.

Banning sponsorship altogether could deny healthcare professionals who are without access to sufficient funding the opportunity to hear and interact with world leaders in their chosen field, unless alternative funding arrangements are developed or digitally based specialist educational services are expanded and feasible in their country. This is particularly important for healthcare professionals from developing counties, where alternative sources of funding may not be available.

The IFPMA Code was again expanded in 2012. A new title, the IFPMA Code of Practice (omitting earlier reference to marketing practices), reflected the extended scope beyond marketing activities.

***Guiding principles of the 2012 IFPMA Code of Practice.***

1. The health-care and well-being of patients are the first priority for pharmaceutical companies.
2. Pharmaceutical companies will conform to high standards of quality, safety, and efficacy as determined by regulatory authorities.
3. Pharmaceutical companies' interactions with stakeholders must at all times be ethical, appropriate and professional. Nothing should be offered or provided by a company in a manner or on conditions that would have an inappropriate influence.
4. Pharmaceutical companies are responsible for providing accurate, balanced and scientifically valid data on products.
5. Promotion must be ethical, accurate, balanced, and must not be misleading. Information in promotional materials must support proper assessment of the risks and benefits of the product and its appropriate use.
6. Pharmaceutical companies will respect the privacy and personal information of patients.
7. All clinical trials and scientific research sponsored or supported by companies will be conducted with the intent to develop knowledge that will benefit patients and advance science and medicine. Pharmaceutical companies are committed to the transparency of industry-sponsored clinical trials in patients.
8. Pharmaceutical companies should adhere to applicable industry codes in both the spirit and the letter. To achieve this, pharmaceutical companies will ensure that all relevant personnel are appropriately trained.

*Source*: Francer et al. (2014), IFPMA Code of Practice (2012).

## 6.5. Pricing and reimbursement

### *Description of the legal framework*

Despite EU harmonisation of rules governing the procedures for market authorisation of medicinal products circulating within the internal market, price setting falls within the exclusive competence of member states. They are free to develop their national pricing policies according to various price-setting criteria and mechanisms (Vogler, 2012).

The European Commission Pharmaceutical Forum's Working Group on Pricing and Reimbursement (European Commission, 2008) urges Member States to implement national pricing and reimbursement practices that achieve three overall objectives.

1. Optimal use of resources to maintain sustainable financing of healthcare.
2. Access to medicines for patients.
3. Reward for valuable innovation.

When designing their national pharmaceutical pricing framework and overall approach for balancing these three objectives, Member States must ensure that any national measure to control the prices of medicinal products or restrict the range of medicinal products covered by their national health-insurance systems complies with the requirements of Council Directive 89/105/EEC (the so-called Transparency Directive).[36] This harmonised legal framework lays down procedural requirements setting specific time limits for pricing decisions and calling for the application of objective and verifiable criteria in pricing and reimbursement procedures.

Under Greek legislation, the prices of all medicinal products are explicitly regulated.[37] The National Organisation for Medicines issues a biannual price bulletin, which sets the prices of all medicines. The manufacturer's maximum price level is fixed, but market authorisation holders are free to ask for a lower price than the set maximum price.[38]

Research has shown that market entry of generic competitors and price competition is negatively correlated with the degree of market regulation (Simoens, 2012). Optimal pricing policies should be designed in such a way that competition may still take place, even within the strict national regulatory framework on pharmaceuticals.

Different techniques are deployed separately or combined to regulate maximum prices. These include external reference pricing, internal reference pricing, economic evaluation, cost plus pricing and profit ceilings (OECD, 2008). Greece applies a combination of techniques in setting price limits. In the context of the national legal framework currently in force (Legislative Decree 96/1973, Law 4336/2015, 4337/2015 and Ministerial Decision 28408/2016),[39] external price referencing[40] is applied to define the prices of originator[41] pharmaceutical products. Generics entering the market receive a price by reference to the originator product (so-called generic price linkage).[42]

Pursuant to the national pricing framework, the expiration of the 10-year or possible 11-year data-protection period[43] is the trigger for a price change of originator pharmaceutical products, what are called, for pricing purposes, reference products. During the data-protection period, the maximum manufacturer's price (ex-factory price) of reference products is defined as the average of the three EU lowest prices for the same pharmaceutical product in terms of the active substance, pharmaco-technical form, strength and packaging. After the expiration of the data-protection period, on condition that the first respective generic has appeared in the Greek market, the ex-factory price of the reference product is automatically decreased, either by 50% of the last price received within the data-protection period or at a price equivalent to the average of the three EU lowest prices, depending each time on which is the lowest.

The price of generic medicinal products is set at 65% of the price of the corresponding reference medicinal products after the expiration of their data-protection period.[44] Initially, the National Organisation for Medicines attempts to link a generic to a reference product already circulating in the Greek market. In a second stage, it seeks to establish a link to a reference product marketed in other EU member states.

### *Re-pricing procedure for generics*

According to the biannual price-revision procedure laid down in Article 8, paragraph 3 of Ministerial Decision 28408/2016, with regard to the generic medicinal products, a price revision cannot result in a price drop exceeding 15% of the previously set wholesale price. If the revision of a generic price results in a price higher than the price of the respective reference product whose protection period has expired, then the price of the reference product shall be defined as equal to the revised generic price. In addition, price reviews resulting in reductions[45] apply solely to medicinal products with a retail price over EUR 7.80 and those with a daily treatment cost exceeding EUR 0.26 (price floors).[46]

As stated in the provision, these specific pricing rules have been introduced to promote the use of less expensive treatments and protect public health in order not to jeopardise the supplies of medicines following price revision in the Greek market. As regulators seek to balance an array of objectives not limited to cost-containment, it seems that this safety net of 15% maximum reduction, along with the introduction of the abovementioned price floors, aims to prevent severe reductions of generics' prices. This aims to provide stimulus to the generics pharmaceutical industry in view of implementing the national policy for increased generics' penetration in the market.

Figure 6.6. **Share of generics in the total pharmaceutical market, 2015 (or nearest year)**

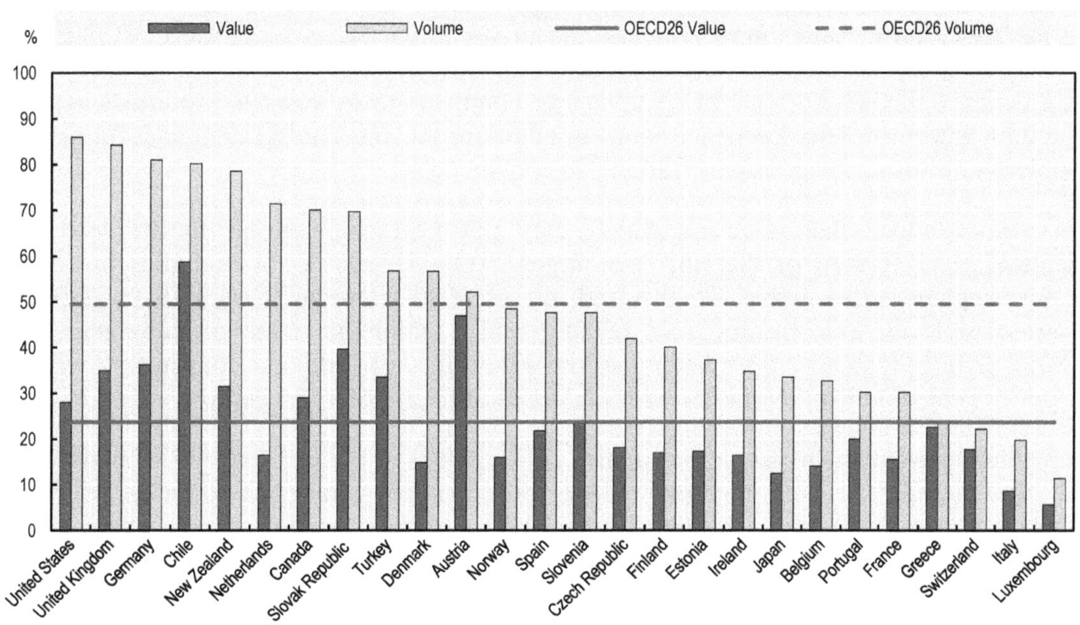


*Notes:* 1. Reimbursed pharmaceutical market data for the United Kingdom, Germany, New Zealand, the Netherlands, Denmark, Austria, Spain, Ireland, Belgium, France, Greece and Luxembourg; 2. Community pharmacy market data for the United States, Chile and Slovenia.

*Source*: OECD Health Statistics 2015, (OECD Publishing, Paris, 2015).

Figure 6.7. **Price ratio of generics vs. all pharmaceuticals, 2015 (or nearest year)**

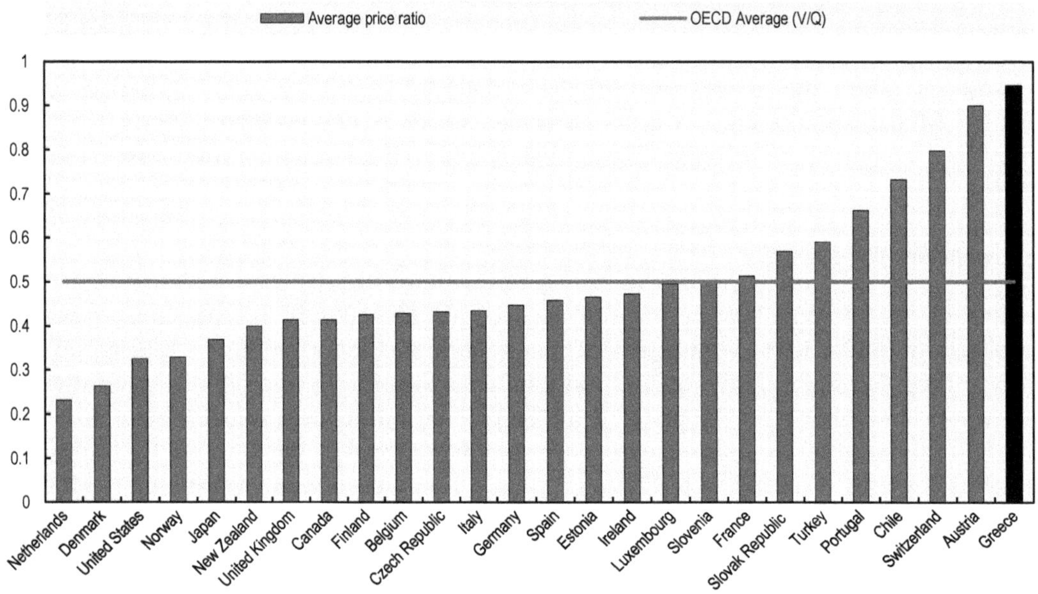


*Notes:* 1. Reimbursed pharmaceutical market data for the United Kingdom, Germany, New Zealand, the Netherlands, Denmark, Austria, Spain, Ireland, Belgium, France, Greece and Luxembourg; 2. Community pharmacy market data for the United States, Chile and Slovenia.

*Source:* OECD calculations[47] based on *OECD Health Statistics 2015*, (OECD Publishing, Paris, 2015).

## *Harm to competition*

Article 8, paragraph 3 of Ministerial Decision 28408/2016 artificially distorts competition between off-patent and generic medicines. Instead of serving the objective of achieving higher volume use of generics, the provision actually limits patients' incentives to choose generics over off-patent products already circulating in the market. Since the law enforces equal prices for off-patent products and generics, it deprives the latter of their price advantage compared to the original product, leaving no room for competition and further market penetration. In addition, this mechanism also undermines the policy maker's objective of using generics penetration[48] to contain costs.

It is acknowledged that price regulation may not necessarily result in the lowest possible pharmaceutical prices in view of attaining several goals (OECD, 2008), not excluding the safeguarding of sufficient supplies in the market. To that end, the provision introduces price floors defining which generics are eligible for a downward price revision and a maximum reduction percentage of 15% to avoid severe price reductions. The latter has the side-effect of reducing consumers' willingness to purchase generics by aligning their prices with the prices of their direct competitors.

Due to the nature and special characteristics of its products, the pharmaceutical market is heavily regulated. However, strong state intervention does not mean that there are no cases where substitute products compete strongly with each other for potential customers, as in the case of generic and off-patent drugs available for the same illness. For this reason, legislation should avoid creating unnecessary price distortions and introduce complementary measures to incentivise competition with the aim of keeping public expenditure under control.[49]

### *Recommendation and benefit*

Given the considerations above, we recommend that the maximum price reduction rule apply only when the resulting price of the generic is below that of the respective off-patent.

Box 6.4. **Maximum price decrease in re-pricing procedure for generics**

Generic medicinal products are priced at 65% of their reference product according to the Greek legislation, whereas off-patent originator medicines follow a reference pricing scheme and they are priced based on the three lowest prices in the EU. However, based on Ministerial Decision 28408/2016 (Article 8, paragraph 3), in the bi-annual price revision procedure for generic medicinal products, any price revision cannot result in a price drop exceeding 15% of the previous wholesale price. In case the revision of a generic price results in a price higher than the price of the respective reference product whose protection period has expired (off-patent drug), then the price of the reference product shall be defined as equal to the revised generic price. In addition, as explained in the text, the same Ministerial Decision provides for price floors as a further safeguard against sudden price drops.

This provision was introduced with the aim of promoting the use of generic products and to secure the supply of medicines in the Greek market. However, the provision artificially distorts competition between off-patent and generic medicines with a cost to the Greek state. First, the provision creates a welfare loss for consumers. Second, it reduces the scope for competition between generics and off-patent drugs. These arguments are described below.

By placing a cap (15%) on the price reduction of generics and, in some cases, by increasing the prices of the reference off-patent products, their prices are higher than what would otherwise be based on the reference-pricing scheme. Based on the latest price revision (22 August 2016) 2 489 prescription drugs (out of a total of 9 523) are affected by this provision or by the price floors, or roughly 26% of the total number. If the final wholesale price assigned to these products is compared to the wholesale price that would have prevailed given the 65% reference-pricing rule, then the mean difference across all products would be EUR 5.58 (with a range from 0.15 in the 5th percentile to EUR 12.53 in the 95th percentile, as shown in row 1 in Table 6.1 below).

Table 6.1. **The distribution of price difference in the wholesale price of affected medicinal products**

| | Mean | Standard deviation | Percentile 5% | Percentile 10% | Median | Percentile 90% | Percentile 95% | N |
|---|---|---|---|---|---|---|---|---|
| Price difference | 5.58 | 29.96 | 0.15 | 0.26 | 1.14 | 7.83 | 12.53 | 2 489 |
| Price difference weighted by quantity sold | 1.63 | 1.85 | 0.05 | 0.06 | 0.72 | 4.06 | 5.89 | 1 330 |
| Quantity (2015) | 19 963 | 56 854 | 23 | 85 | 4 547 | 49 928 | 83 088 | 1 330 |

Figure 6.8. **Calculating the consumer welfare effect of the 15% maximum price reduction cap**

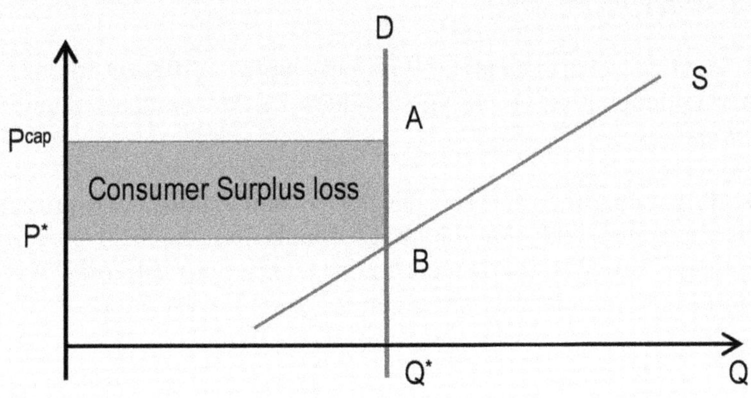

Box 6.4. **Maximum price decrease in re-pricing procedure for generics** (cont.)

To calculate the effect on consumer welfare of the 15% maximum price reduction cap and the price floors, we approximate the market as in Figure 6.8. The current equilibrium is given in point A. The demand is vertical as these are prescription drugs and we make the simplifying assumption that demand is driven by doctors' prescriptions and is not responsive to price in the short run. At the current market equilibrium the wholesale price is $P^{cap}$ and, based on this price, the quantity is Q*. If the 15% maximum price reduction cap and the price floors were to be abolished the new equilibrium would have been at point B, where the average regulated price would have fallen to P*, whereas the quantity would have remained constant at Q*. The grey shaded area indicates the loss in consumer surplus due to the maximum price-reduction cap and the application of price floors.

To calculate the impact on consumer welfare we also obtained detailed (drug-barcode level) information on the sales of the affected products in 2015 by QuintilesIMS. As shown in row 2 of Table 6.1, which contains the price difference weighted by quantity sold, many of the affected drugs had no sales in 2015 and hence their sales weighted mean difference across all products is lower than shown in row 1. The weighted price difference is EUR 1.63, with a range from 0.05 in the 5th percentile to EUR 5.89 in the 95th percentile. At the same time, average sales for these drugs were 19 963 units ranging from 23 in the 5th percentile to 83 088 in the 95th percentile as shown in row 3 of Table 6.1. Using these two numbers we can calculate the consumer welfare loss (as shown in Figure 6.8) for each affected drug assuming that the demand and the supply will be unaffected, at least in the short run. The total consumer loss due to maximum price reduction cap, including price floors, is estimated to be EUR 34 million. This calculation is an upper bound on the harm, since it is based on the comparison between the current provision and the removal of the 15% maximum price reduction.

In addition, by placing a restriction on the price reduction of the generic drug and by equating them to the off-patent products, the provision deprives the former of their price advantage compared to the original product, leaving little room for competition.

*Source:* OECD calculations based on latest price revision of medicines (EOF price bulletin, 22 August 2016) and barcode level data for 2015 provided by QuintilesIMS.

### *Co-marketing agreements*

Co-marketing agreements are common practice in the pharmaceutical industry as an instrument of commercial cooperation among competitors (European Commission, 2009)[50] and are permitted under EU regulations. Article 82, paragraph 1 of EC Regulation 726/2004[51] states that an applicant can submit "*more than one application for the same medicinal product when there are objective verifiable reasons relating to public health regarding the availability of medicinal products to* healthcare *professionals and/or patients or for co-marketing reasons*".

Co-marketing of identical pharmaceutical products under different brand names is aimed at enhancing products' market penetration by taking advantage of the commercial and promotional services of both co-operating companies.[52]

In Greece, Article 1, paragraph 5 of Ministerial Decision 28408/2016 provides that, when a co-marketing agreement is registered with the National Organisation for Medicines by all the respective market authorisation holders, original pharmaceutical products with different brand names circulating under a co-marketing agreement mandatorily are given the same lowest price.

### *Harm to competition*

When the maximum prices for the co-marketed products determined by the National Organisation for Medicines differ, the provision eliminates this difference and removes any residual price competition between co-marketed products. Setting a unique price for co-marketed products should not be an obligation imposed by the legal framework. According to the national pricing framework, market-authorisation holders are allowed to ask for a price lower to the maximum price set by the National Organisation for Medicines.[53] The mandatory equation of the prices of co-marketed medicines by National Organisation for Medicines is a non-justified restriction imposed by the legislation.

### *Recommendation*

We recommend the provision to be abolished.

Box 6.5. **Use of External Reference Pricing (ERP) in Europe**

The World Health Organization defines external reference pricing (ERP) as: "the practice of using the price of a pharmaceutical product (generally ex-manufacturer price, or other common point within the distribution chain) in one or several countries to derive a benchmark or reference price for the purposes of setting or negotiating the price of the product in a given country."[54]

Out of the 29 countries using ERP, it is the sole or main pricing policy in 20. In some countries, however, ERP is limited to specific sectors and/or medicines. In **Denmark**, for example, it was reintroduced in 2009 as a result of an agreement between the Danish Association of the Pharmaceutical Industry (*Lægemiddelindustriforeningen, LIF*), the Danish regions and the Ministry of Health stipulating that ERP should act as price ceiling for new medicines in the hospital sector and so contribute to cost-containment. In the out-patient sector in Denmark, the prices of medicines are still set by the pharmaceutical manufacturer (free pricing). In **Slovenia**, the price of medicines determines how ERP is applied: ERP is the main policy for setting maximum allowed prices, but is only a supportive policy for setting extraordinary higher prices or for lower prices agreed between the Market Authorisation Holder and the purchaser/payer. In **Ireland**, ERP is used as a supporting policy to set prices for new single source on-patent medicines, whereas it is the main criterion for realignment of existing prices.

In **10 countries** ERP is used as a **supportive criterion** in the decision process, and prices in other countries are considered together with other criteria. In these countries pricing authorities often take a broad range of factors into account when determining the prices for medicines that should be "reasonable". Other factors which are taken into account include: 1) the cost of the therapy cycle; 2) benefits to be gained for the patient from the medicine's use; 3) relative benefits compared to alternative treatments; 4) budget impact, i.e. analysis of the effects on the healthcare system; 5) funds available for reimbursement; 6) reward for innovation (provided that sufficiently detailed information about the research and development cost structure of the manufacturer has been submitted). The measurement of absolute benefits is done in gained quality-adjusted life years (QALY). The level of threshold values differs from country to country, often reflecting economic differences and the ability to pay.

Price applications may undergo thorough assessment. In France, for instance, if the pharmaceutical manufacturer wants to launch a medicine in the reimbursement market, then the product is evaluated by the Comité Économique des Produits de Santé (CEPS, Economic Committee for Healthcare Products). If accepted, and before a price is set, the transparency commission of the Haute Autorité de Santé (HAS, High Authority for Health) assesses the therapeutic value or *service médical rendu* (SMR) and the added therapeutic value or *amélioration du service médical rendu* (ASMR) of the medicine compared to treatment alternatives. The ASMR is rated on a scale ranging from ASMR I (major improvement, new therapeutic area, reduction of mortality) to ASMR V (no improvement). Based on this evaluation, CEPS enters into price negotiations with the MAH. However, only medicines with ASMR I-III are eligible for ERP and they are subject to health technology assessments (HTA) evaluation.

The countries most often cited as reference countries are France (20), Denmark, Belgium and Spain (18), Italy, and UK (17) and Austria, Germany and Slovakia (16).

*Source*: European Commission (2015a), "Study on enhanced cross-country coordination in the area of pharmaceutical product pricing".

## 6.6. Wholesale trade

### *Restrictions on establishments of pharmaceutical warehouses*

Article 2, paragraph 1 of Presidential Decree 88/2004[55] on the organisation and operation of pharmaceutical warehouses, provides that pharmaceutical warehouses may establish at most one supplementary supporting storage area to facilitate their activities; this supporting storage area may be only established within the same prefecture. The provision introduces two types of restrictions in warehouse facilities. Firstly, it foresees a limit in terms of the number of supporting storage units allowed; and secondly, it sets a geographic restriction as regards the establishment of these supporting units.

Presidential Decree 88/2004 provides for specific geographical areas of operation for pharmaceutical warehouses. It seems that this *geographical monopoly*[56] has its roots in Greece's particular geographical characteristics (its mountainous mainland and numerous islands). The OECD understands that the policy maker's objective is to safeguard product safety and protect patient health, especially with regard to susceptible pharmaceuticals.[57]

Such geographical restrictions in wholesale activities are not observed in the majority of EU countries where wholesalers are allowed to operate at national or regional level in case they choose to operate in a specific geographical area.[58]

### *Harm to competition*

The provision creates a geographical barrier to pharmaceutical warehouses establishing a supporting unit in a different prefecture. In addition, it prevents warehouses from establishing more than one economic unit within the same or in a different prefecture. Given that transportation and infrastructure developments allow for effective pharmaceutical distribution that safeguards medicines' good condition and safety, national legislation unduly limits warehouses' freedom to operate and function in a way that they deem appropriate and more profitable. This could reduce the number of suppliers, limit patient options and potentially access to medicines. Taking into account that pharmaceutical warehouses not only sell pharmaceutical products, but also other products, such as cosmetics,[59] the provision may cause artificial scarcity of such products in the market, potentially increasing prices. Moreover, since the number of economic units is limited, economic operators cannot develop economies of scale and are discouraged from engaging in vigorous competition.

### *Recommendation*

We recommend the provision to be abolished.

## Notes

1. NACE codes 21 and 46.46.

2 This includes an estimated direct impact of the industry on GDP at EUR 1.52 billion, an indirect impact at an additional EUR 2.18 billion and an induced impact at about EUR 3.8 billion (SFEE, 2016).

3. Joint Ministerial Decision Δ.ΥΓ3α/Γ.Π.32221/2013 on Harmonisation of Greek legislation with EU legislation in the sector of production and circulation of medicinal products for human use in compliance with Directive 2001/83/EC on the Community Code relating to medicinal products for human use as amended by Directive 2011/62/EU as regards the prevention of the entry into legal supply chain of falsified medicinal products (Government Gazette B'1049/29.04.2013).

4. OECD (2016b), Pharmaceutical spending (indicator). doi: 10.1787/998febf6-en.

5. Legislative Decree 96/1973 on trade of pharmaceuticals, dietary supplements and cosmetics (Government Gazette A'172/8.08.1973).

6. Joint Ministerial Decision Δ.ΥΓ3α/Γ.Π.32221/2013, ibid.

7. Law 1316/1983 on the Establishment of the National Organisation for Medicines (Government Gazette A' 3/11.01.1983).

8. According to the OECD (2016b), pharmaceutical expenditure increased from 1,8% to about 3% of GDP between 2004 and 2010.

9. Directive 2001/83/EC of the European Parliament and of the Council of 6 November 2001 on the Community code relating to medicinal products for human use (Official Journal, L311/28.11.2001, p.67)).

10. Regulation No. 726/2004 of the European Parliament and of the Council of 31 March 2004 laying down Community procedures for the authorisation and supervision of medicinal products for human and veterinary use and establishing a European Medicines Agency (Official Journal, L136/30.04.2004, p.1).

11. Legislative Decree 96/1973, ibid, Law 4336/2015 on Ratification of the draft agreement on the financial assistance by the European Stability Mechanism (ESM) regarding the implementation of the financing agreement (Official Gazette A'94/14.08.2015), 4337/2015 on Measures for the implementation of the agreement on budgetary targets and structural reforms (MoU) (Official Gazette A'94 129/17.10.2015).

12. Ministerial Decision 28408/2016 on Provisions on pharmaceuticals pricing (Official Gazette B'1102/19.04.2016).

13. Law 4177/2013 on Rules regulating the purchase of products and provision of services (Government Gazette A'173/8.08.2013).

14. Legislative Decree 96/1973, ibid.

15. Joint Ministerial Decision Δ.ΥΓ3α/Γ.Π.32221/2013, ibid.

16. Law 1316/1983, ibid.

17. Directive 2001/83 ibid, Art.10, par.2(b), defines generics as pharmaceutical products which display the "same qualitative and quantitative composition in active substances and the same pharmaceutical form as a reference medicinal product" and whose "bioequivalence with the reference medicinal product has been demonstrated by appropriate bioavailability studies". Generics are classified as branded generics (generics with a specific "invented" trade name) and unbranded generics, which use the international non-proprietary name and the name of the company.

18. The data-protection period is provided for by Art.11, par.1 of the Joint Ministerial Decision ΔΥΓ3α/Γ.Π.32221/2013 transposing Directive 2001/83/EC, ibid. According to Art.10 of the Directive,

generic products must not be placed on the market until 10 years have elapsed from the initial authorisation of the reference product. This 10-year period may be extended to 11 if "during the first eight years of those ten years, the marketing authorisation holder obtains an authorisation for one or more new therapeutic indications which, during the scientific evaluation prior to their authorisation, are held to bring a significant clinical benefit in comparison with existing therapies" (Art.10, par.1). After eight years applications for generic products can be submitted and lead to the granting of a market authorisation. The period of 10 years from initial authorisation of the reference product provides a period of so-called market protection after which generic products can be placed on the market (EC, 2015b).

19. The European Commission (2016) defines supplementary protection certificates (SPCs) as: "an intellectual property right that serve as an extension to a patent right. They apply to specific pharmaceutical and plant protection products that have been authorised by regulatory authorities. The EU wishes to provide sufficient protection for these products in the interest of public health and to encourage innovation in these areas to generate smart growth and jobs. Supplementary protection certificates aim to offset the loss of patent protection for pharmaceutical and plant protection products. This is due to the compulsory lengthy testing and clinical trials these products require prior to obtaining regulatory marketing approval. An SPC can extend a patent right for a maximum of five years."

20. Joint Ministerial Decision Υ1/Γ.Π127962/2004 on Harmonisation of the Greek legislation with the Directive 2002/46/EC on the approximation of the laws of the Member States relating to food supplements (Government Gazette B' 395/27.02.2004).

21. Joint Ministerial Decision A2E/5478/1999 harmonising the national legislation to the relevant EU legislation on the sector of special nutrition food according to provisions of EU 89/398 EC and EU 96/84 EC of the European Parliament and the Council (Government Gazette B' 189/5.03.1999).

22. Directive 2002/46/EC of the European Parliament and of the Council of 10 June 2002 on the approximation of the laws of the Member States relating to food supplements (Official Journal L 183/51), Council Directive of 3 May 1989 on the approximation of the laws of the Member States relating to foodstuffs intended for particular nutritional uses (Official Journal L 186/27), and Directive 96/84/EC of the European Parliament and of the Council of 19 December 1996 amending Directive 89/398/EEC on the approximation of the laws of the Member States relating to foodstuffs intended for particular nutritional uses (Official Journal L 48/20).

23. National Organisation for Medicines decision 6206/2009 on Standards for production of food supplements and foodstuffs intended for particular nutritional uses (Government Gazette B' 199/6.02.2009).

24. Ministerial Decision A6/4171/1987 on Parallel imports of medicinal products from EU member states (Government Gazette B' 361/9.06.-13.07.1987).

25. Recommendation 183 of Retail Trade section of OECD (2014), *OECD Competition Assessment Reviews: Greece*, OECD Publishing, Paris, p.319.

26. Law 1965/1991 Amending and completing the provisions on the National Organisation for Medicines and other provisions (Government Gazette A' 146/26.09.1991).

27. Pursuant to Article 2 of Regulation 726/2014, ibid, market authorisation holders must be established in the European Union and be responsible for the placing on the market of those medicinal products, whether they do it themselves or via one or more persons designated to that effect.

28. European Commission Communication COM(2003)839/F1 (30.12.2003).

29. According to Law 4254/2014 (Official Gazette A'85/07.04.2014), para.ΣΤ΄, subpara.ΣΤ.1, price controls on OTC medicines will be lifted in January 2017.

30. Legislative Decree 96/1973, ibid.

31. Joint Ministerial Decision Δ.ΥΓ3α/Γ.Π.32221/2013, ibid.

32. According to Art.66, par.7 of Law 4316/2014 (Government Gazette A'270/24.12.2014), pharmaceutical companies are obliged to disclose any benefit granted by them to healthcare professionals, including but not limited to grants, donations, registration fees for scientific conferences and events, travelling and accommodation costs and any other benefit related to the promotion of the prescribed medicines.

33. Joint Ministerial Decision Υ6α/28403/2001 on Expenditure of pharmaceutical firms related to promotion of pharmaceuticals (Government Gazette B' 684/31.05.2002).

34. Ministerial Decision Γ5(α)51194/2016 on Determination of terms and conditions for the creation of the sub-category of General Sale Medicines (GEDIFA), within the category of over-the-counter medicines (OTC) (Government Gazette B'2219/18.07.2016).

35. See Art. 16, par. 6 of the Legislative Decree 96/1973, ibid.

36. See Art. 1 of Council Directive 89/105/EEC of 21 December 1988 relating to the Transparency of measures regulating the pricing of medicinal products for human use and their inclusion in the scope of national health insurance systems (Official Journal L40, 11.02.1989), p.8-11. On 18 March 2013, the Commission adopted the amended Proposal for a Directive of the European Parliament and of the Council to replace the Transparency Directive providing among others for shorter timeframes in decision-making procedures, COM(2013) 168 final/2.

37. See endnote 30.

38. See Art.2, par.5 of Ministerial Decision 28408/2016, ibid.

39. See endnotes 11 and 12.

40. External price referencing or external price benchmarking is defined as the practice of comparing pharmaceutical prices across countries (OECD, 2008).

41. Original medicines are defined as the "first version of a medicine developed and patented by an originator pharmaceutical company, which has exclusive rights to marketing the product in the European Union for 20 years. An original product has a unique trade name for marketing purposes, the so called brand name" (WHO Collaborating Centre for Pharmaceutical Pricing and Reimbursement Policies, 2013:67).

42. This is an internal reference pricing technique to regulate the price of generics' market entrance. Through this practice, the generic is priced at market entry at a discount in relation to the price of the original product (OECD, 2008). For domestically produced medicinal products, Greece applies cost-plus pricing as set out in Article 10 of the Ministerial Decision 28408/2016, ibid, in accordance with the conditions provided therein.

43. See endnote 18.

44. See Art.8, par.1 of Ministerial Decision 28408/2016, ibid.

45. Currently, any price revision for all medicinal products cannot result in higher prices; see Art.8, par.1 of Ministerial Decision 28408/2016, ibid.

46. For generics with a retail price exceeding EUR 12, dynamic pricing will be implemented. More specifically, for each increase in sales corresponding to EUR 250,000 in wholesale prices in the year before the publication of the Price Bulletin, the prices defined shall be reduced, from 1% up to 15%; see Art.8, par.4 of Ministerial Decision 28408/2016, ibid.

47. For the calculation of the ratio of average prices, we have used the OECD data on the share of generics in terms of value (V) and in terms of volume (Q) in each country. We decompose the value share of generics (VG/VT), where $VG = QG * \overline{P}G$, $VT = QT * \overline{P}T$. Then by dividing this ratio by the volume share of generics (QG/QT), we get: $(VG/VT) / (QG/QT) = (QG * \overline{P}G / QT * \overline{P}T) / (QG/QT) = \overline{P}G / \overline{P}T$ where VT and QT are the value and volume of all pharmaceuticals in the pharmaceutical market in 2015. Values (V) are decomposed as quantities sold (Q) multiplied by the average price ($\overline{P}$).

48. According to Law 4336/2015, ibid, par.2.5.2, by December 2016, the authorities will take concrete measures to increase the share of generic medicines by volume to 60%. Also see the Memorandum of Understanding between the European Commission acting on behalf of the European Stability Mechanism and the Hellenic Republic and the Bank of Greece (EC, 2015c: 15-16)

49. For example, by providing incentives to pharmacists to promote generic over off-patent medicines. Indicatively, France has introduced different discount levels to stimulate pharmacists to dispense generic medicines (PPRI, 2008). Also, Portugal very recently (2016) approved a remuneration system for pharmacists linked to their contribution in reducing the retail price of the medicines (Cuatrecasas Gonçalves Pereira, 2016). In addition, pharmacists could be given incentives in the form of different retail margin levels for dispensing generics. In this regard, see the recent judgment of the European Court of Justice C-148/15 on prescription medicines, according to which price competition at retail level in the form of maximum, as opposed to fixed, pharmacy margins could be ultimately capable of benefiting the patients (Judgment of 19 October 2016, Deutsche Parkinson Vereinigung eV v, Zentrale zur Bekämpfung unlauteren Wettbewerbs eV, C-148/16, EU:C:2016:776).

50. EC (2009:425-426). Pharmaceutical Sector Inquiry.

51. Regulation No. 726/2004 of the European Parliament and of the Council, ibid.

52. Pitruzzella G. and G. Muscolo G (2016), *Competition and Patent Law in the Pharmaceutical Sector: An International Perspective*, Kluwer Law International, p.156.

53. See Art.2, par.5 of Ministerial Decision 28408/2016, ibid.

54. WHO (2015: 2). *WHO Guidelines on Country Pharmaceutical Pricing Policies.*

55. Presidential Decree 88/2004 on Organisation and operation requirements for pharmaceutical warehouses (Government Gazette B' 68/3.03.2004).

56. Kanavos P. et al. (2011), *The pharmaceutical distribution chain in the European Union: Structure and impact on pharmaceutical prices*, European Commission, Brussels, *http://eprints.lse.ac.uk/51051*, p.66.

57. It was not possible to identify the exact objective of the provision, so the version described is based on the OECD understanding after communication with the Ministry of Health.

58. Kanavos P. et al. (2011), ibid, p.24.

59. See Art.1 of Presidential Decree 88/2004, ibid. Pharmaceutical warehouses may further sell products of general medical use; veterinary medicinal products; cosmetics; dietary products; milk and infant foods; sanitary products for infants, pregnant women or who have recently given birth; orthopaedic equipment; and medical devices machinery and aids.

## References

Cuatrecasas, Gonçalves Pereira (2016), Compensation granted to pharmacies for the sale of the generics, *http://goo.gl/Vp3yFR* (accessed on 13 October 2016).

European Commission (2016), *Supplementary protection certificates for pharmaceutical and plant protection products*, European Commission, Brussels, *https://ec.europa.eu/growth/industry/intellectual-property/patents/supplementary-protection-certificates_en.*

European Commission (2015a), *Study on enhanced cross-country coordination in the area of pharmaceutical product pricing*, European Commission and Gesundheit Österreich Forschung und Planungs, Publications Office of the European Union, Luxembourg, *http://ec.europa.eu/health/systems_performance_assessment/docs/pharmaproductpricing_frep_en.pd.*

European Commission (2015b), *The Rules Governing Medicinal Products in the European Union: Volume 2A: Procedures for marketing authorisation, Chapter 1: Marketing Authorisation*, European Commission, Brussels, *http://ec.europa.eu/health/files/eudralex/vol-2/a/vol2a_chap1_201507.pdf.*

European Commission (2015c), Memorandum of Understanding between the European Commission acting on behalf of the European Stability Mechanism and the Hellenic Republic and the Bank of Greece, Athens-Brussels, 19 August 2015, *http://ec.europa.eu/economy_finance/assistance_eu_ms/greek_loan_facility/pdf/01_mou_20150811_en.pdf.*

European Commission (2009), "Pharmaceutical Sector Inquiry", European Commission, Brussels, *http://ec.europa.eu/competition/sectors/pharmaceuticals/inquiry/staff_working_paper_part1.pdf.*

European Commission (2008), *Guiding principles for good practices implementing a pricing and reimbursement policy,* Brussels, *http://ec.europa.eu/DocsRoom/documents/7584?locale=en.*

European Commission (2003), *Commission Communication on parallel imports of proprietary medicinal products for which marketing authorisations have already been granted*, Commission of the European Communities, Brussels, *http://eur-lex.europa.eu/LexUriServ/LexUriServ.do?uri=COM:2003:0839:FIN:en:PDF.*

European Commission (2001), Directive 2001/83/EC of the European Parliament and of the Council of 6 November 2001 on the Community code relating to medicinal products for human use (Official Journal, L311/28.11.2001), *http://ec.europa.eu/health/files/eudralex/vol-1/dir_2001_83_consol_2012/dir_2001_83_cons_2012_en.pdf.*

Francer, J., J. Zamarriego Izquierdo, T. Music, K. Narsai, C. Nikidis, H. Simmonds, & P. Woods (2014), "Ethical pharmaceutical promotion and communications worldwide: codes and regulations" in *Philosophy, Ethics, and Humanities in Medicine*, 9(7), *http://dx.doi.org/10.1186/1747-5341-9-7.*

Gruda, S., & L. Milo (2010), *SMEs development and competition policy in Albania*, Portal on Central Eastern and Balkan Europe, Bologna, *www.pecob.eu/flex/cm/pages/ServeBLOB.php/L/EN/IDPagina/2794.*

IFPMA (2012), *IFPMA Code of Practice,* International Federation of Pharmaceutical Manufacturers & Associations, Geneva, *www.ifpma.org/wp-content/uploads/2016/01/IFPMA_Code_of_Practice_2012_new_logo.pdf.*

Kaló, Z., E. Docteur and P. Moïse (2008), "Pharmaceutical Pricing and Reimbursement Policies in Slovakia", OECD Health Working Papers, No. 31, OECD Publishing, Paris. *http://dx.doi.org/10.1787/244264621247.*

Kanavos P. et al. (2011), *The pharmaceutical distribution chain in the European Union: structure and impact on pharmaceutical prices*, European Commission, Brussels, *.http://eprints.lse.ac.uk/51051.*

Luniku, R. (2014), *The Effects of Competition Policy Changes on International Trade And Export Flows: Canada Case Estimates.* Wayne State University Dissertations, *http://digitalcommons.wayne.edu/oa_dissertations/901.*

Management Sciences for Health (2012), *Managing Access to Medicines and Health Technologies.* Management Sciences for Health, Arlington, *www.msh.org/sites/msh.org/files/mds3-jan2014.pdf.*

MPA (2016), *Swedish Cosmetic Product Legislation.* Swedish Medical Products Agency, *https://lakemedelsverket.se/english/product/Cosmetic-products/Legislation.*

ÖBIG (2006), *Surveying, Assessing and Analysing the Pharmaceutical Sector in the 25 EU Member States: Country Profiles.* Österreichisches Bundesinstitut für Gesundheitswesen (ÖBIG). Luxembourg: Office for Official Publications of the European Communities, *http://ec.europa.eu/competition/mergers/studies_reports/oebig.pdf.*

OECD (2016a), *OECD Health Policy Overview: Health policy in Greece*, *www.oecd.org/greece/Health-Policy-in-Greece-January-2016.pdf*OECD Publishing, Paris, .

OECD (2016b), Pharmaceutical spending (indicator), http://dx.*doi*.org/*10.1787/998febf6-en* (accessed on 18 August 2016).

OECD (2016c), "Health expenditure and financing: Health expenditure indicators", *OECD Health Statistics* (database), *http://dx.doi.org/10.1787/data-00349-en* (accessed on 1 August 2016).

OECD (2015), Health at a Glance 2015: OECD Indicators, OECD Publishing, Paris.http://dx.doi.org/10.1787/health_glance-2015-en.

OECD (2014), *OECD Competition Assessment Reviews: Greece*, OECD Publishing, Paris, *http://dx.doi.org/10.1787/9789264206090-en.*

OECD (2011), *Competition Assessment Toolkit, Volume II: Guidance*, OECD Publishing, Paris, *www.oecd.org/daf/competition/45544507.pdf.*

OECD (2008), *Pharmaceutical Pricing Policies in a Global Market*, OECD Publishing, Paris, *http://dx.doi.org/10.1787/9789264044159-en.*

Pitruzzella, G. and G. Muscolo (2016), *Competition and Patent Law in the Pharmaceutical Sector: An International Perspective*, Kluwer Law International.

PPRI (2008), *Pharmaceutical Pricing and Reimbursement Information: France Pharma Profile*, Vienna, *.http://whocc.goeg.at*

Scherer, F. M (1967), "Market structure and the employment of scientists and engineers", *The American Economic Review*, 57(3), 524-531, *www.jstor.org/stable/1812118.*

SFEE (2016), Hellenic Association of Pharmaceutical Companies, *www.sfee.gr/category/contribution/economy* (accessed 23 August 2016).

Simoens, S., (2012), "A review of generic medicine pricing in Europe", *Generics and Biosimilars Initiative Journal (GaBI Journal), 1*(1), 8-12, *http://dx.doi.org/10.5639/gabij.2012.0101.004.*

UNCTAD (2015), *The role of competition in the pharmaceutical sector and its benefits for consumers.* UNCTAD, Geneva, *http://unctad.org/meetings/en/Contribution/CCPB_7RC2015_RTPharma_EC_en.pdf.*

Vogler, S. (2012), "The impact of pharmaceutical pricing and reimbursement policies on generics uptake: implementation of policy options on generics in 29 European countries: an overview" in *Generics and Biosimilars Initiative Journal (GaBI Journal)*, 1(2), 93-100, *http://dx.doi.org/10.5639/gabij.2012.0102.020.*

WHO Collaborating Centre for Pharmaceutical Pricing and Reimbursement Policies (2013), *Glossary of Pharmaceutical Terms*, WHO Collaborating Centre for Pharmaceutical Pricing and Reimbursement Policies, Vienna, *http://whocc.goeg.at/Literaturliste/Dokumente/MethodologyTemplate/PHIS%20Glossary_Update 2013_final_gesamt.pdf.*

WHO Collaborating Centre for Pharmaceutical Pricing and Reimbursement Policies (2008), "Pharmaceutical Pricing and Reimbursement Information: France Pharma Profile", Vienna, .

WHO (2015), *WHO Guidelines on Country Pharmaceutical Pricing Policies*. World Health Organization, Geneva, *http://apps.who.int/iris/bitstream/10665/153920/1/9789241549035_eng.pdf.*

WHO (2012), "Chapter 6: Pharmaceutical legislation and regulation", in Management Sciences for Health 2012, available at http://apps.who.int/medicinedocs/documents/s19583en/s19583en.pdf.

**Databases**

Eurostat, Annual detailed enterprise statistics for industry (NACE Rev. 2), Database [sbs_na_ind_r2], http://ec.europa.eu/eurostat (accessed 4 April 2016).

Eurostat, Annual detailed enterprise statistics for services (NACE Rev. 2), Database [sbs_na_dt_r2], http://ec.europa.eu/eurostat (accessed 4 April 2016).

*Chapter 7*

# Wholesale Trade

*The wholesale trade sector includes all major activities that form the supply chain of products before they reach the final consumer. Provisions restrictive to competition were identified between operators in the same market. For example, the organised wholesale trade of fruit, vegetables and meat products through the central markets of Athens, Thessaloniki and Patras operates on the basis of exclusivity clauses. In the fuel-trading sector, certain obligations included in exclusive supply agreements between wholesalers and retailers are safeguarded by law. Finally, much of the legislation covering the transportation of goods appears redundant or to have been horizontally replaced by newer legislation. Yet the level of regulatory uncertainty remains high even among the public administration officials charged with applying provisions and imposing fines.*

## 7.1. Definition and economic overview

According to the NACE definition, "wholesale is the resale (sale without transformation) of new and used goods to retailers, business-to-business trade, such as to industrial, commercial, institutional or professional users, or resale to other wholesalers, or involves acting as an agent or broker in buying merchandise for, or selling merchandise to, such persons or companies."[1]

The wholesale trade sector comprises the following codes: [2]

- wholesale on a fee or contract basis (NACE code 46.1);
- wholesale of agricultural raw materials and live animals (NACE code 46.2);
- wholesale of food, beverages and tobacco (NACE code 46.3);
- wholesale of household goods (NACE code 46.4);
- wholesale of information and communication equipment (NACE code 46.5);
- wholesale of other machinery, equipment and supplies (NACE code 46.6);
- other specialised wholesale[3] (NACE code 46.7); and
- non-specialised wholesale trade (NACE code 46.9).

The wholesale trade sector accounted for 5.6% of GDP in Greece in 2013, compared with a figure of 5.1% for the European Union on average. When measured in terms of employment, the sector represents 8.0% of the Greek economy while the corresponding figure for the European Union is 4.9% on average.

The value added of the wholesale sector in Greece amounted to EUR 8 billion in 2013, a value that has contracted by 9.7% on an annual basis since 2008 (Figure 7.1).

Figure 7.1. **Value added of wholesale trade (2008-2013)**

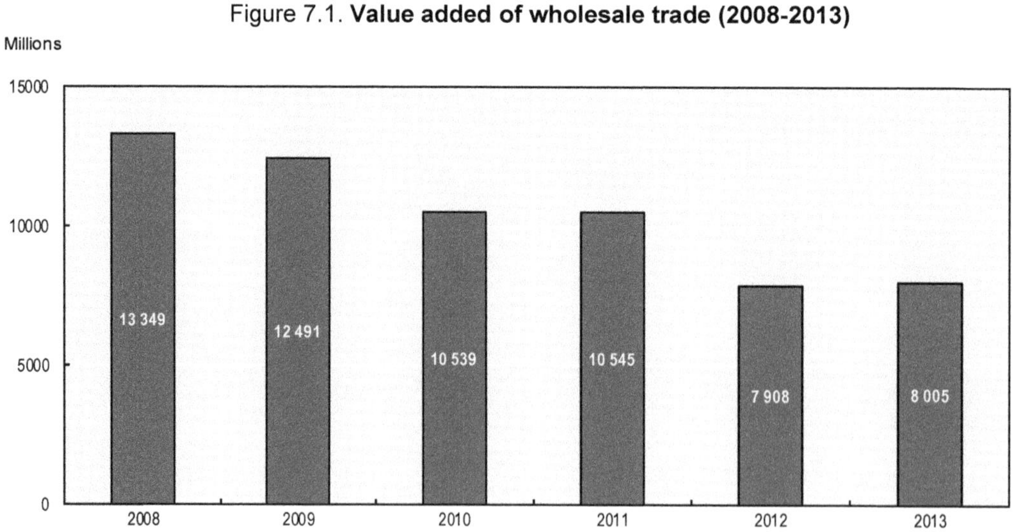


*Note*: Value added at factor cost

*Source*: Eurostat, Annual detailed enterprise statistics for industry (NACE Rev. 2, G), Database [sbs_na_dt_r2], *http://ec.europa.eu/eurostat* (accessed 24 August 2016).

Figure 7.2 compares the annual percentage changes of value added in the wholesale sector with GDP changes. Between 2010 and 2013, the sector's annual changes in value added fluctuated more than GDP changes, and significant contractions in 2010 and in 2012 were followed by minor expansions in 2011 and 2013.

Figure 7.2. **Percentage changes of value added of wholesale trade and GDP (2008-2013)**

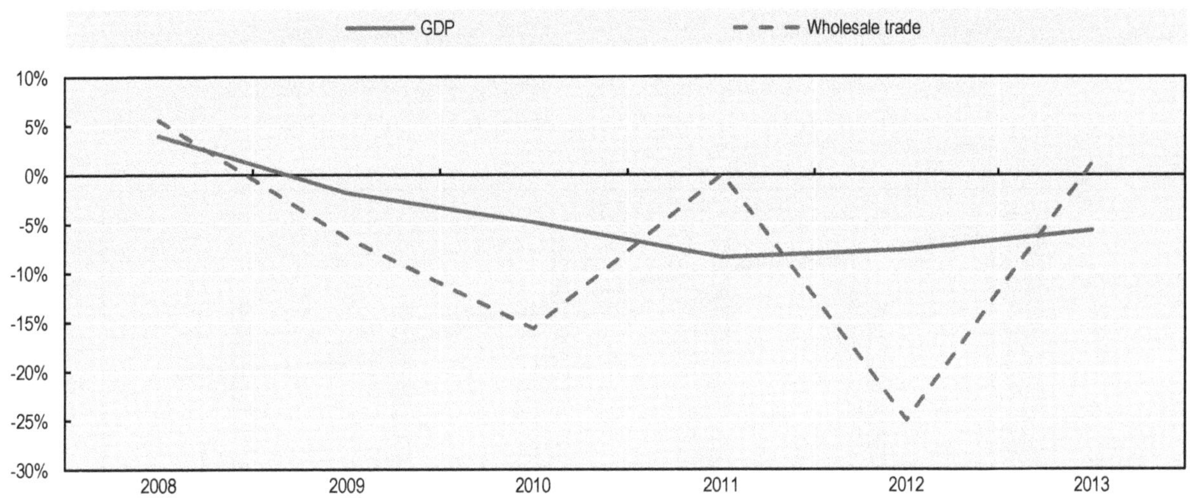


*Note*: Value added at factor cost; gross domestic product at market prices

*Source*: Eurostat, Annual detailed enterprise statistics for industry (NACE Rev. 2, G), Database [sbs_na_dt_r2], and GDP and main components, Database [nama_10_gdp], *http://ec.europa.eu/eurostat*(accessed 24 August 2016).

Figure 7.3 shows the structure of the value added of wholesale trade for each category. The top three categories (household goods; other specialised wholesale; and food, beverages and tobacco) make up almost 70% of total value added throughout the six-year period between 2008 and 2013, without any significant changes in their shares.

Figure 7.3. **Share of value added of wholesale trade per category in Greece (2008-2013)**

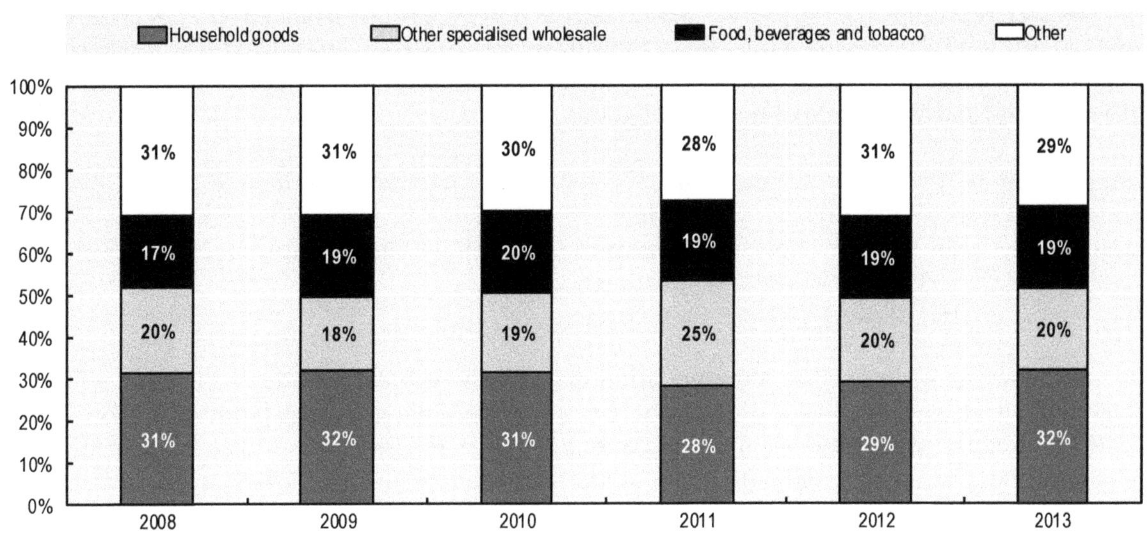


*Source*: Eurostat, Annual detailed enterprise statistics for industry (NACE Rev. 2, G), Database [sbs_na_dt_r2], *http://ec.europa.eu/eurostat* (accessed 24 August 2016).

Figure 7.4 depicts the turnover of wholesale trade across all sub-sectors in Greece. All followed a negative trend over the seven-year period 2008-2014, the two first categories suffering less compared to others. The turnover of other specialised wholesale and of food, beverages and tobacco fell by 4.4% and 6.5% respectively over the period.

Figure 7.4. **Turnover of wholesale trade per category in Greece (2008-2014)**

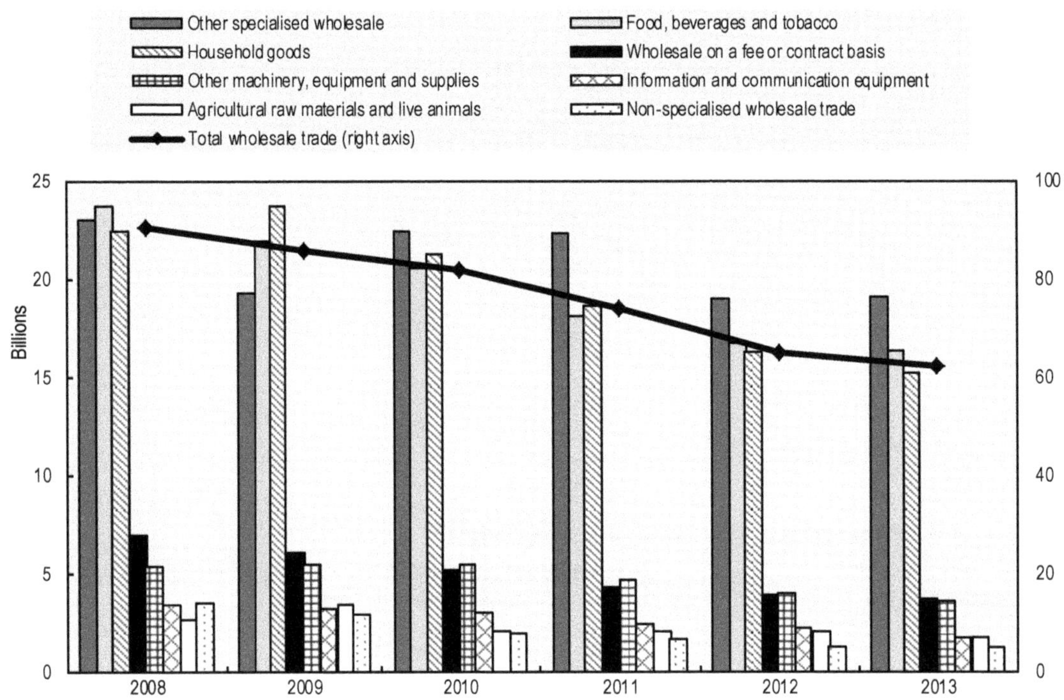


Note: Sales in EUR billions

*Source*: Eurostat, Annual detailed enterprise statistics for industry (NACE Rev. 2, G), Database [sbs_na_dt_r2], *http://ec.europa.eu/eurostat* (accessed 24 August 2016).

The number of companies in the wholesale sector fell by 11.5%, from 75 426 in 2008 to 66 782 companies in 2013, 43.4% of which operate in the sub-sectors of Other specialised wholesale (including, for instance, Wholesale of wood, construction materials and sanitary equipment and Wholesale of chemical products) and Wholesale of household goods.

Employment in the sector is important for the Greek economy as it amounts to 8% of total employment in Greece,[4] the highest single share in the economy throughout the period 2008-2013, despite a decrease in the number of persons employed from 350 080 in 2008 to 275 242 in 2013.

## 7.2. Overview of the legislation

Due to the nature of this sector, the regulation that affects wholesale trade can be found in multiple and diverse legislative texts. The process of mapping the relevant legislation therefore included provisions on product specifications, food hygiene, assembly, loading and piling, storage, distribution and transportation. Horizontal regulation, not directly related to the wholesale trade sector, such as licensing, fees, taxation, employment, company creation, national registries, and other matters were also reviewed.

 

Legislation rarely refers exclusively to the wholesale trade. On the contrary, during the review of legal texts we have observed that both wholesale and retail trade activities are covered by the same provisions, such as Law 4177/2013[5] on Rules on the trading of products and provision of services and Ministerial Decision A2-718/2014 on Codification of rules on the distribution and trading of products and provision of services.

The mapping of the legislation included 292 sector-specific laws and regulations, as well as horizontal legislation covering all sectors. Of the sector-specific legal texts:

- 12 laws and regulations are framework pieces of legislation, which can be related to the general activities covering wholesale trade activity, including general rules for the trading of products and rendering of services (DIEPPY), company creation, and registration obligations;
- 177 were product specific, with 125 covering the wholesale trade of agricultural products, i.e. fruit and vegetables, meat, poultry and fish (out of these, 19 covered wholesale trade through central markets) and 22 covering the wholesale trade of fuel;
- 42 pieces of legislation concerned the transportation and storage of goods; and
- 61 legal texts concerned taxation issues such as the imposition of excise duties on alcohol, fuel and tobacco products.

The legislation reviewed is sometimes redundant, since its requirements have become outdated by everyday practice, or more recent legislation, without being explicitly repealed. For example, legislation covering storage requirements in warehouses of certain products such as figs and raisins needs to be updated and directly linked to more recent provisions as they fail to take into account recent technological developments. This has in many cases caused regulatory uncertainty to businesses in or wishing to enter the market.

Another case of obsolete legislation addressed to all subsectors are the numerous references to the Market Code and Market Decrees, which are either left in old legislation or are still mentioned in the preamble of more recent legislation.[6] The regulatory uncertainty for potential new entrants in a market in this case could be severe since, in the past, violating these codes and decrees has led to significant fines.

Issues of misinterpretation of legal texts have also been found to affect public administration, especially when the relevant provisions had to be enforced by more than one competent authority.

OECD's view is that outdated and obsolete legislation should be explicitly abolished or amended to evolve into a comprehensive guide for businesses and individuals, to reduce uncertainty and so create a more attractive investment environment. More importantly, matters falling under the competency of more than one ministry should be unanimously agreed and better communicated. This need becomes imperative in cases where secondary legislation (Ministerial Decisions, Joint Ministerial Decisions or interpretative circulars) needs to be issued. For example, in the recent amendment of Law 1959/1991 on Road transports and communications, the Ministry of Infrastructure, Transport and Networks and the Ministry of Rural Development and Food, both competent for amending the secondary legislation ended up with a different interpretation of the new regime. Additional problems arise from the fact that regional authorities responsible for implementing the legislation, such as the Prefectural Directorates for Transportation, required specific guidelines on the matter, as interpretation of the legal amendments differed from one prefecture to the other, leading to differential treatment of economic operators.

In some cases, such as provisions regulating agreements between producers of agricultural products and wholesalers, or provisions on the licensing scheme of logistics centres, the provisions initially identified as problematic to competition were – discussions with the authorities revealed – a result of misplaced wording and not designed to have the adverse effect they did. Changing the wording to fit the intended policy maker's intentions is suggested in these cases. In other situations, provisions were found to lead to an administrative burden and should be reviewed by competent authorities.

The main restrictions identified in the sub-sectors of wholesale trade covered in this chapter, as traced in the Greek legislation, are described in detail in the following sections. Their harm to competition and recommendations are also set out. The benefits of these recommendations are estimated to amount to EUR 198 million. The OECD has considered whether recommendations would be expected to have an impact on either consumer benefit, through lower prices, or on economic activity, in terms of greater efficiency and additional revenue. In the former case, the framework described in Annex A was applied; in the latter, we have made a conservative assumption on an overall improvement in the efficiency of operation.

## 7.3. Agricultural, meat and fishery products

### *Economic overview of fruit and vegetable markets*[7]

The supply and distribution channels of agricultural products are organised at production, wholesale and retail levels. At the production level, the market is extremely fragmented. The average producer in Greece cultivates just 47 000m$^2$ (11.6 ac), when the EU average is 126 000m$^2$ (31.1 ac). Moreover, around 50% of the Greek producers own plots less than 20 000m$^2$ (4.9 ac).

The wholesale market is significantly more concentrated. Wholesalers operate either within the organised central markets or independently. The Central Markets of Athens (OKAA) with approximately 550 members and Thessaloniki (KATH) with approximately 280 members account for 15%-20% of the total number of distributed products. Wholesalers outside the central markets account for the remaining two thirds of the total market and operate both in the large cities and other urban areas across Greece. Wholesalers either purchase their products from the domestic market or they import them from abroad and sell them to retailers (with supermarkets being their largest customers), but also to street -market sellers, grocery stores, and restaurants.

Finally, at the retail level, consumers buy either from street markets (58% market share in year 2011, but steadily declining), supermarkets (32% market share and steadily increasing), and – to a lesser extent – from grocery stores or other corner shops (10%). In street markets, approximately half of the sellers are also producers themselves.

Organised wholesale markets aim to reduce the length and cost of transactions by concentrating them in a single location, easily accessible to operators and customers. These markets, either general or specialised, have the function of improving efficiency in the food-distribution chain and promote greater transparency by separating wholesale and retail functions in the distribution system, leading to clear price formation.

The benefits of central markets include better inspections, surveillance and quality controls. Storage under hygienic conditions and enhanced handling procedures are provided, including improved freezing, packing and processing of raw products.[8] In addition, handling operations reduce loading and unloading times, as well as repeated handling of goods between unloading and display. Innovation and new technology in methods of handling, storing and management are easier to be introduced and adopted in sites with a physical concentration of a large group of operators.

### *Historical background*

In the 1950s, the populations of Athens and Thessaloniki were growing rapidly. The Greek state sought to impose a surveillance mechanism on prices and mark-ups at the various levels of the market, especially for everyday goods such as bread, meat, fruit and vegetables, and pharmaceutical products. A series of market rules issued over the years and codified under Market Decree 7/2009[9] were adopted to eliminate profiteering, by determining food portions offered to the consumer, setting maximum prices and establishing maximum mark-ups, preventing wholesalers and retailers from making excess profits at the expense of consumers. The state decided to establish central markets and require that the wholesale trade of fruit and vegetables and later on, meat and fish products, take place in them, as a means of protecting public health and consumer safety.

Law 3475/1955 on the Processing of raw agricultural products and the establishment of state central markets required that the wholesale trade of these raw products could take place only within the central markets of Athens and Thessaloniki. In 1968, Patras Central Market was additionally established by Royal Decree 264/1968.

Wholesalers that operated at a distance of no less than two kilometres from the central markets could be granted a permission to continue operating, only by virtue of a Joint Ministerial Decision issued by the Ministers of Economy and Rural Development and Food. This was justified on the grounds that surveillance on the safety and hygiene conditions could easily be carried out by the competent authorities, together with price controls on the basis of Market Decrees. Moreover, the prices of goods sold by those wholesalers were not permitted to exceed the prices in the central market.

The policy maker's objective was to provide producers with transparency in wholesalers' prices, to protect consumers by setting specific standards on food hygiene, and to monitor the implementation of the rules. Moreover, the provisions aimed at safeguarding traffic and urban planning in overly populated areas.

Gradual steps have since been made towards the merger of central markets and offering a more complete range of products to the retail channel. In 1970, wholesalers of raw-meat products entered central markets and in 1998 the central market of Athens took the form of a state-owned société anonyme (SA) called Organisation of Athens Central Market (OKAA). In 2012, it absorbed the country's 11 fish markets, which continue to function as branches of the central market and became the Central Market and Fishery Organization. The market of Patras, was also absorbed in 2014, while in the same year, a retail-consumer market inside the central market was launched, in an effort to attract end consumers to the central markets.

Over time, wholesalers of meat products started operating and expanding their businesses outside the central markets, thanks to modern and technologically advanced infrastructure that allowed for a full range of processing and packaging services. In addition, urban planning, road infrastructure and state control mechanisms had grown to a level that allowed for a gradual disappearance of the need for higher regulatory intervention. The post-war necessity for price controls became significantly less important as time passed, while the expansion of resources and the significant growth of the market of fruit and vegetables made it impossible for the central markets to shelter all of the wholesalers within the Athens, Thessaloniki and Patras areas.

In an attempt to keep up with current circumstances, and to avoid any further problems created by the lack of available space within the central markets, a new law allowed wholesalers to continue functioning outside the markets. Article 35 of Law 3784/2009[10] required that these wholesalers were operating prior to the date that the new law entered into force.

In 2010, the European Commission opened case 2010/4090[11] against Greece for restrictions on the wholesale trade in the central markets. Wholesalers were finding it impossible to establish themselves in the Athens and Thessaloniki regions, whereas incumbents enjoyed a privileged situation and protection against new competitors. The Commission said that this could encourage collusion between wholesalers in the central markets, with potentially adverse effects for end consumers. It also found that the restrictions on establishing and obtaining a space applied by the Greek authorities could not be justified in the light of the fundamental principles of the freedom of establishment and the freedom to provide services.

In response to the European Commission's case, the state adopted Law 3982/2011,[12] abolishing the monopoly of central markets in the wholesale trade of raw fruit, vegetables and meat products.[13] Following this reform, wholesalers were not obliged to establish their activity within one of the central markets.

Moreover, an amendment of Market Decree 7/2009 was issued in 2011.[14] The new regime abolished regulated mark-ups on fresh fruits and vegetables, giving wholesalers and retailers an incentive to compete by freely pricing their products without constraints. This led to a significant drop in the relevant products' prices.[15]

The latest regulatory reform, Law 4235/2014,[16] introduced prefectural producer retail markets at which only producers of agricultural products can sell their raw produce directly to consumers. These markets were supposed to be subject to specific training and management requirements, and have been inactive as the Ministerial Decision specifying their functional details has not yet been issued.

***Central market exclusivity in organised wholesale trade and entry-exit requirements***

According to the legislation, only one central market may be established for each of the areas of Athens, Patras and Thessaloniki. The establishment of other state-controlled central markets, however, may be foreseen by virtue of a royal decree issued upon proposal from the Ministers of Rural Development and Commerce.

Given the legal framework on central markets and their importance in wholesale trade, their exclusive rights and entry and exit requirements have been thoroughly reviewed for this project. Since the central markets are a state-owned SA, matters related to their governance and operation are set at central-government level. The regulation of lease agreements for the premises leased to wholesalers is adopted by virtue of a Joint Ministerial Decision of the Ministers of Economy, Development and Tourism and Rural Development and Food. Following the OECD's competition assessment methodology, various provisions in the lease agreement requirements were identified as potentially harmful to competition under the present legislative regime.

However, it must be noted that none of the following provisions are harmful if the exclusivity of central markets in the organised wholesale trade is abolished.

- Requirements concerning the tendering procedure for a vacant space within the Central Market are based 60% on the bid price and 40% on the financial standing of the applicant, calculated in terms of profits and turnover, number of employees, transportation means, and so on. In addition, applicants are also rated on the basis of the relevance of their education, if any, in the fields of agronomy, veterinary, finance or fish science.
- Specific conditions of the lease agreement are also predetermined, such as the condition that the annual rent adjustment may not be lower than a specific threshold (at OKAA, this threshold

corresponds to the variation in the average consumer price index of the previous year, whereas at the Central Market of Thessaloniki or KATH, it is a flat 3%).

- On provisions covering the exit of a tenant, the Joint Ministerial Decision for OKAA treats similar cases differently. If the tenant of the premises is a company and is dissolved, then the lease agreement is terminated immediately without any prior notification or stipulation. If the company was formed by existing tenants of OKAA, however, and they wish to remain in the stores they occupied prior to the company's creation and continue trading independently, a change to the lease agreement is possible.
- Transferring the contractual lease agreement rights to another individual or entity is strictly regulated. For instance, should tenants transfer their rights from lease agreements to a company, then the shareholders are obliged to hold their participation of the company for at least one year after the transfer has taken place, without falling below a minimum of 30% of the total capital.
- In both central markets, if the lease agreement is amended, new tenants are obliged to pay a fee of EUR 10 000, plus VAT. However, in OKAA, this fee is not applicable in the following cases:
  - if the person is a spouse or relative of up to B grade of the departing tenant;
  - if the natural person or partner or shareholder departs due to retirement or death and is replaced by a relative or spouse of up to B grade;
  - if the departing tenant transfers shares without a change in the tax payer's identity (the company);
  - if the members of a shipping company want to continue the commercial activity in the same location, after this company has been dissolved.
- In KATH, the above exemption from paying the EUR 10 000 fee is valid in all cases that a company is set up between an existing tenant and a relative of up to B grade.

A provision was introduced at OKAA in 2014, allowing retail activities to take place in every part of the central market, even though the market was originally destined to facilitate wholesale-trade activities. Retail traders in the central market have thus different and more flexible market hours than the ones that function outside central markets.

*Harm to competition*

The exclusivity clause, which allows only one central market to exercise organised wholesale trade within a specific prefecture, may significantly limit competition. It creates an unclear framework to operators, such as wholesalers and producers, to form new, more flexible structures and introduce competitive forces into the market, possibly including other professionals, such as those engaged in logistics, packaging and food processing.

Restricting new wholesale markets could potentially eliminate the ability of wholesalers to innovate and producers to enter into wholesale-trade activities. According to the 2013 Hellenic Competition Commission sectoral study on fruit and vegetables,[17] this effect, together with inefficient quality-control management and producers' limited negotiating power has led to higher production costs in comparison with other countries in Southern Europe.

Since the organised wholesale trade may only be carried out through state central markets, transportation costs are higher in cases where a producer's site is located far from the market. In these cases, high costs are, at least partially, transferred to the retailer and finally, to the end consumer. Another result is the high risk of produce loss, which increases in the case of perishable products.

Additionally, according to the legal regime on stevedores (see 7.4 below) all loading-unloading work within the central markets has to be carried out by registered stevedores, which adds yet another cost eventually transferred to the final consumer.

The exclusivity clause on the organised wholesale trade to be carried out through central markets, when reviewed in combination with the criteria for entry or exit from the central markets, may deprive incumbents of incentives to make all efforts possible to meet their customers' needs, due to lack of competitive pressure from new entrants.

Provided that the exclusivity clause remains in the law, competition in the market of wholesale trade of raw fruit, vegetables and meat products may be harmed by the various restrictive provisions identified below.

- There may be a significant harm to competition, due to legislation favouring incumbents at the expense of new entrants. This imposes differential treatment on similar operators, burdening some of them through administrative and financial costs. The provision prevents the market from becoming more flexible and viable and reduces competition between existing suppliers.

- Provisions regarding the entry of new tenants create preferential treatment for larger entities. In addition, specific provisions on the termination of lease agreements and leaving the central market seem to favour incumbents.

- The provision on annual rent adjustments may limit wholesalers' contractual freedom to negotiate and imposes unjustified costs, potentially increasing prices to the end consumer.

- Restrictions on the ability of wholesalers to exit the market could also have negative effects on competition. In addition, the fees for amending or terminating the agreement seem to be applied differently between new and old tenants.

- The requirements for transferring the rights and obligations arising from a lease agreement are difficult to comply with, specifically the restriction on company structure. It limits the ability of old tenants to terminate their lease agreement and exit the market, since they may not find a new tenant willing to comply with the above requirements.

*Recommendations and benefits*

The OECD recommends lifting exclusivity in the establishment of organised wholesale markets and allowing private entities to enter the sector. New organised markets should be able to operate within the same region as the existing, state-owned central markets. In addition, producers should be allowed to participate in these markets.

As noted in a FAO report, "[i]n the legislation establishing many markets earlier this century, governments included an exclusivity clause. These made it illegal for anyone to either operate as a wholesaler outside the market or to establish a further market without approval. This was done to safeguard the investment in the central market. In today's legal, economic and social environment of free competition, such a provision would be now difficult for governments to introduce."[18]

Box 7.1. **Examples of similar facilities in other OECD countries**

**United Kingdom**

According to a Mayor of London report, in 2007 London had five principal wholesale food and flower markets:

- **New Spitalfields Market** for fruit and vegetables;
- **Smithfield Market** for meat and poultry, cheese, pies and other delicatessen goods;
- **Billingsgate Market** for fish;
- **New Covent Garden Market** for fruits, vegetables, flowers and plants, cheese, gourmet ingredients, and, by virtue of a House of Lords ruling, meat and fish;
- **Western International Market** for fruit, vegetables and flowers.

**Spain**

The Spanish **Mercasa** is a national company that manages the network of Spanish wholesale markets, together with respective city councils, and a dozen self-managed retail centres. In total, the Mercasa network of wholesale markets comprises 23 food estates across Spain. Its shareholders are Sociedad Estatal de Participaciones Industriales (SEPI) and Spain's Ministry of Agriculture, Fisheries and Food. Mercasa is one of the shareholders of **Mercabarna**, a facility operating 24 hours a day and housing more than 700 companies specialising in the distribution, preparation, import and export of fresh and frozen products.

Spain has 23 other central wholesale markets, two of which, **Mercalgeciras and Mercajerez** operate in the area of Cadiz.

The Spanish Competition Commission ruled that: "it is recommended that the Government suppresses the activity of central markets from the list of reserved activities of the municipality ( as provided for in Article 86.3 LBRL). The appearance of channels at least partially alternative to Mercas, that are not reserved for the public sector and therefore do not undertake other public objectives such as guarantee of supply, security, traceability or food quality, proves this point".

**Germany**

In the city of Berlin, two state-owned wholesale markets sell fruit and vegetables: Berliner Großmarkt and Fruchthof Berlin Verwaltungs.

**Australia**

Melbourne Market remains the only state-owned market, as control of the other five markets has been sold off to growers and traders over the past 15 years.

*Sources*:

UK - Mayor of London (2007), London Wholesale Markets Review, www.london.gov.uk/file/12723/download?token=j4mEZDd6.

Spain - www.mercasa.es/nosotros (accessed 17/10/2016) and www.cnmc.es/Portals/0/Ficheros/Promocion/Informes y Estudios Sectoriales/2013/CNC Inf%20prod%20perecederos%20indexado.pdf (accessed 17/10/2016).

Germany - *www.berliner-grossmarkt.de/en/wuns_en.asp?site=wuns* (accessed 17/10/2016).

Australia - www.agriculture.gov.au/SiteCollectionDocuments/ag-food/horticulture/code-conduct/submissions/central-markets-association-of-australia.pdf (accessed 17/10/2016).

The state must therefore adopt the position of providing for the ability of private, organised wholesale markets to be formed, since the conditions for a central market to be characterised as an "essential facility" are not met any longer.

Provided that urban planning and environmental regulations are respected, the possibility of other organised forms of wholesale trade should be permitted. This could lead to economies of scale and lower costs for operators, with the potential of attracting both sellers and buyers. Central markets allow producers and retailers to obtain full information on the range, varieties and quantities of produce marketed, packaged, stored and transported, the stocks available, quality of services, and market and price trends. Therefore, the creation of more than one organised wholesale trade centre in the same geographical area could further benefit consumers.

Indeed, there is no obvious rationale for concentrating the activities on a single site. Producers and retailers located far from this site may benefit from a local organised market, and new markets could be established, for instance, near producers' sites. This would limit transportation costs and could lead to lower product prices. Similar arguments hold also for retailers, especially in cities with widely dispersed retail areas.[19] The ability to create smaller, locally organised markets could also provide incentives for producers to create clusters and take an active role in organised wholesale trade activities. More flexible forms of wholesale trade could arise in conjunction with other type of services, such as manufacturing, packaging and logistics, with a possible positive effect on product quality, variety and prices.[20]

If central-market exclusivity is not removed, existing state-owned central markets' restrictive provisions should be abolished, so that incumbents and new entrants are treated equally in terms of entry and exit requirements, as detailed in Annex B.

Should central markets be liberalised, and private investors be allowed to organise similar forms of private central markets for wholesalers, the above recommendations for entry and exit requirements into wholesale central markets become redundant since market participants will have new choices if they wish to enter the market.

### ***Wholesale trade of seeds and propagating material***

#### *Types of trading enterprises*

##### *Description of the legal framework*

The legal framework for the requirements and the notification process of trading enterprises of seeds and propagating material is set by Joint Ministerial Decision 1153/16620/2014[21] and distinguishes between three categories of enterprises.

- **Type A**: enterprises with the ability to standardise (package, re-package, etc.) and trade (intra and extra EU), both wholesale and retail, seeds and propagating material of all types of products, as set out in Article 3 of Law 1564/1985.
- **Type B**: enterprises with the ability to trade, both wholesale and retail, seeds and propagating material, either locally produced or purchased from Type A trading enterprises, only in Greece.
- **Type C**: enterprises with the ability to standardise (package, re-package, etc.) and trade, both wholesale and retail, seeds and propagating material, either locally produced or purchased from Type A trading enterprises, only in Greece.

According to the relevant registry[22] of the Ministry of Rural Development and Food, 212 Type A enterprises, 2 676 Type B enterprises and 3 Type C enterprises are currently operating.

The objective of the provision is to set specific requirements for different types of trading enterprises, in order to facilitate controls.

*Harm to competition*

The restrictions on Type B and C trading enterprises aim to ensure they sell their products only in the domestic market, and that they acquire their products only from local producers or from Type A trading enterprises. This creates a geographical barrier to the ability of companies to market their goods, as well as limiting the number and range of their suppliers.

This restriction on trading products at an intra-EU level is inconsistent with the fundamental principles of EU law and the fundamental freedoms of the internal market, as stated in the Treaty on European Union and the Treaty on the Functioning of the European Union.[23]

As a result, this provision increases costs and restricts business strategies, by determining both the suppliers and the selling markets for Type B and C companies, leaving no room for business development.

*Recommendation and benefits*

The restriction on the ability to conduct both intra-EU and extra-EU trade should be abolished for Type B and C trading enterprises. By removing the barrier to choose suppliers and determine the markets for sales of their products, competition between incumbents would increase, as would incentives to enter the market. This would also mean that Type C category becomes obsolete, as it would be identical to Type A category.

*Minimum requirements*

*Description of the legal framework*

Joint Ministerial Decisions 1153/16620/2014[24] and 3967/41140/2012[25] set specific requirements for the notification of different types of seeds and propagating material enterprises, among which minimum requirements on land and buildings are included.

In order to begin operation, for example, it is foreseen that Type A nursery enterprises must cover land of at least 3 000m$^2$; Type B nursery enterprises must cover land of at least 1 000m$^2$; Type C nursery enterprises must have a tissue-culture lab of at least 25m$^2$; rootstock nurseries must cover land of at least 20 000m$^2$ in total and at least 5 000m$^2$ in part (in the case of multiple plots); and cutting-stock nurseries must cover land of at least 10 000m$^2$ in total and at least 5 000m$^2$ in part (in the case of multiple plots).

The objective of the provisions is to set requirements for the notification of operation of enterprises in the sector and the minimum requirements are required so as to ensure viable operation.

*Harm to competition*

Restrictive land and building requirements may lead to higher costs both for new entrants and incumbents, reducing competitive pressure as fewer operators may enter the market.

*Recommendation*

Abolish minimum requirements.

*Regulatory uncertainty*

*Description of the legal framework*

The legal framework of producing and trading enterprises[26] of seeds and propagating material requires the full-time employment of a "responsible scientist", in order to proceed with the notification of operation and meet specific requirements (Article 47 of Law 4384/2016). The objective of the provision is that the responsible scientist's presence guarantees:

- the high quality of seeds produced;
- compliance with phytosanitary conditions avoiding genetic contamination and ensuring the protection of biodiversity and the environment;
- compliance with the terms of the technical regulations; and
- avoidance of seed degradation and conformity with quality-control procedures.

This requirement for a responsible scientist raises operational costs through increased labour costs, but is considered justified in light of the provision's objective.

However, the more recent Law 4384/2016 introduces three exemptions.

1. Micro[27] producing or trading enterprises for seed and propagating material now have exemptions to employ a responsible scientist on part-time dependent work contract. The previous regulation, Presidential Decree 159/2014,[28] allowed both micro and small enterprises to employ part-time responsible scientists.
2. Micro Type A, Type B, and Vine nursery enterprises can employ their responsible scientist on part-time dependent work contracts or service contracts. Presidential Decree 159/2014 did not provide for a service contract.
3. Micro Type A, Type B, and Vine nursery enterprises with more than one production-trading facility in the same or neighbouring municipality are considered as one facility and thus can employ one responsible scientist for multiple locations. Presidential Decree 159/2014 did not foresee this.

The objective of these provisions is to facilitate market operation and adjust to the operating environment, by reducing labour costs for micro enterprises, and by introducing the option of service contract for nurseries. The provisions also take into account the fact that nursery enterprises usually have more than one set of fixed production-trading facilities (i.e plots) in close proximity to each other, and therefore can be supervised by the same responsible scientist.

*Harm to competition*

Both the implementation of part-time employment and the exemptions on contracts and facilities, as described above, are proportionate to the objective and justified, even though they create differential treatment between enterprises.

However, after the entry into force of Law 4384/2016, paragraphs 3 and 5 of Article 1 of Presidential Decree 159/2014 are now obsolete and have the potential to create regulatory uncertainty.

*Recommendation*

Explicitly repeal the provisions and introduce the necessary implementing legislation for Law 4384/2016.

### 7.4. Wholesale trade of solid, liquid and gaseous fuels and related products

In the Greek market, there are two groups of companies (Hellenic Petroleum and Motor Oil Hellas) that operate four refineries, which have a total refining capacity of 26.3 million tonnes per year.[29] Overall, the existing refining capacity in Greece is sufficient to meet domestic demand: in 2015, total domestic demand for petroleum products was 10.7 million tonnes.[30] The four refineries cover 90% of the oil demand in Greece, while the rest is imported by wholesale companies, for instance, during periods of high seasonal demand. Refiners may sell gasoline and other petroleum products (diesel, heating oil) directly to large final consumers such as trucking firms, industrial manufacturers and utilities or to independent (non-branded) retailers. The majority of refiners' gasoline sales are made to wholesalers.

At wholesale level, there is a greater number of economic operators, many of which belong to the same groups as the refineries, while others are independent. Wholesalers are allowed to import and export oil products and sell them to retail stations. Greek legislation divides licence holders into different categories depending on the type of product they sell.

Type A (gasoline, road diesel, heating diesel, fuel oil) licence holders may sell directly to final consumers, to retailers or to heating -oil retailers. According to data from the Hellenic Petroleum Marketing Companies Association, there are 23 such licensees with storage and distribution facilities throughout Greece.

Type B1 (marine fuel) licence holders may sell directly or indirectly to international marine bunkers and inland marine bunkers, using their own or hired sloops or fuel -transportation vehicles, whereas type B2 (aviation fuel) licence holders may sell to aviation companies using special sites and vehicles within airports. There are 29 such companies and among them, 14 also have type-A licences.

Type C (liquefied petroleum gas, LPG) licence holders sell bulk LPG directly to industrial and commercial clients (industries, manufacturers, etc.), hospitals, and houses or to automobile LPG retailers, while bottled LPG traders sell to distributors of bottled LPG and to retailers. There are 31 such companies, among whom four also have type-A licences.

Type D (asphalt) licence holders number 23, among whom seven also have type-A licences.

Finally, Greece has seen consolidation in the retail oil sector, partly due to mergers and the prolonged recession. In 2009, Hellenic Petroleum acquired BP's ground -fuels business in Greece. As a result, at the moment it has an extended network of 1 700 gas stations (900 under the EKO's brand and 816 under BP's brand). Later the same year, Motor Oil Hellas acquired the majority of Shell's activities in Greece and in 2015, it also acquired Cyclon Hellas network. It therefore controls a total of 1 350 petrol stations, including 450 petrol stations under the Avin brand, 200 stations under the Cyclon brand and approximately 700 stations under the Shell brand. In addition, mainly due to the prolonged recession the number of petrol stations has decreased from approximately 8 500 in 2005 to about 6 500 stations in 2015. Out of this total, only about 500 stations are unbranded, i.e. not selling under the brand held by a fuel wholesale company. Moreover, there are about 850 sellers of heating oil.

The strengthening of the wholesale market, combined with the removal of specific barriers that characterise the petroleum -refining industry may increase the competitive pressure and increase its efficiency for the benefit of the final consumer.

***Minimum storage spaces, minimum capital and letter of guarantee***

*Description of obstacles and policy maker's objective*

Minimum storage spaces are foreseen for all types of licence holders. As a general requirement applicable to all types of licences, storage spaces must be owned by the licence holders, leased by them, or conferred to them under exclusive-use rights. Moreover, the aforementioned lease or concession agreements must be of at least of the same duration as that of the licence, which, in the case of wholesale trade is five years.[31]

For Type A licence holders, the minimum capacity of the storage tanks used for petroleum products depends on their annual sales volume:

- up to 300 000MT 4 000$m^3$;
- from 300 000MT to 600 000MT 7 000$m^3$;
- over 600 000MT 13 000$m^3$.

In addition, there are a number of other provisions concerning storage requirements.

- Fuel wholesalers must register with the Ministry of Energy only the storage spaces sufficient to meet the minimum capacity requirement for obtaining a licence. Any additional storage spaces that they might own or lease, are not registered with the licensing authority. Instead, they are subject to another licence granted by another competent authority. The Ministry must register all fuel tanks regardless of any minimum storage requirements, to avoid cases where licence holders may conceal their actual storage spaces.

- All wholesalers of fuel are required to maintain quantities of fuel equal to at least five days of sales in their storage spaces.

- Wholesalers' storage spaces must be used for supplying consumers or retail licence holders in quantities equal to at least 30% of the annual sales in the administrative district where the establishments are placed.

- Biofuel distribution licence holders are required to have appropriate storage spaces of at least 100$m^3$ for storing biofuel and other renewable fuel. The capacity of their storage spaces may not be less than 1/100 of the quantity the licensee plans on trading annually nor less than 100$m^3$ per production site of the owner or contractual applicant for the licence.

- Law 3054/2002 requires liquid-gas licence holders to stock at least 30 000 refillable gas cylinders. However, Ministerial Decision Δ216570/2005 on Fuel trading licenses, exceptions, which was issued as a secondary legislation to the above law, raises that minimum to 50 000.

Minimum capital requirements are also imposed on all types of licence holders. More specifically, for Type A licence holders minimum capital based on sales volume the previous calendar year ranges from EUR 500 000 to EUR 1.5 million; for Types B and C, minimum capital is set at EUR 500 000. The above thresholds were initially higher, and were lowered in 2013 by Article 104 of Law 4172/2013[32] to foster competition and to avoid job losses due to the economic recession, according to the law's official recital.

The new law also provided for an alternative to the minimum capital requirement, i.e. a letter of guarantee or an insurance contract for specific risks, which was later specified by Article 55, paragraph 6 of Law 4223/2013[33] to require coverage in an amount equal to the operator's minimum capital. The alternative's purpose was to serve as a safety valve, in case any administrative fees were imposed on the licence holder on the basis of 1) not complying with the licence terms and requirements; 2) trading irregular fuel; 3) trading fuel after expiration of a licence or after a licence has been revoked; and 4) not keeping required safety reserves.

The relevant minimum capital requirement for Type D licence holders was abolished in 2014[34] following OECD recommendations. However, the law still contains a requirement to provide a letter of guarantee or insurance contract as an alternative, with the amount related to the now-abolished minimum capital requirement.[35]

Box 7.2. **Type ST licences**

According to Article 15 of Law 1571/1985[1], licences for the trade of oil products were divided in six categories. The general Type A Licence was granted for the entire Greek territory and for the marketing of all liquid fuel products, excluding liquid gas, and marine bunker and aircraft fuel. The special ST Licence was granted restrictively to companies that owned or leased storage spaces on the Aegean Islands and were established in the Aegean islands (except Crete, Rhodes and the Saronic Islands) for all products, as well as maritime oil and kerosene, but excluding liquid gas and heavy-oil products. As a prerequisite for obtaining the above licence, the law required companies to have a minimum registered capital of 15 million Greek drachmas (c. EUR 45 000); and own or lease storage space for at least 500m$^3$- 2 000m$^3$ of gasoline and other fuels.

Subsequently, Article 35 of Law 2008/1992 introduced a new paragraph to Article 15 of the 1985 law, which provided that: "petroleum-product wholesale companies, which have their establishments in remote areas, and were established before the entry into force of this Law, or companies that, at any given time were transformed from companies of the previous version, can obtain a Type A licence (except for an ST licence), regardless of whether they meet the conditions set by this article concerning minimum paid-up capital and minimum storage spaces".

A decade later, paragraph 4 of Article 23 of Law 3054/2002 stipulated: "Type A licences, issued in accordance to paragraph 7 of article 15 of Law 1571/1985, as introduced by Article 35 of Law 2008/1992, may be renewed as required by the provisions which applied before the entry into force of the present law."

In the introductory recital of that law, it was stipulated that: "Especially in the sensitive region of the Aegean Islands, special type ST licences were granted for survival reasons, by virtue of a special provision of law (Article 35 of Law 2008/1992). The holders of Type ST licences were also granted a Type A licence enabling them to trade in the entire Greek territory." For the same reasons, the law provided that those licences remain in force and could be renewed in accordance with the provisions that were in force at the time the Type ST licence was granted.

In this way the initial exclusive right granted by the state to wholesale fuel companies operating only in the remote areas, under less strict criteria for minimum capital and storage space than other companies elsewhere in Greece, was expanded and became valid for the entire Greek territory. Type ST licences only required a minimum capital of EUR 45 000, while all other licenses to trade fuel at a wholesale level required at least EUR 500 000 minimum capital (or an equal amount in a guarantee letter or insurance contract). For storage spaces, Law 3045/2002 requires a minimum of 4 000 m$^3$ capacity for a company to obtain the licence, whereas Type ST licence holders need a minimum capacity of only 500m$^3$.

1. Law 1571/1985 (Government Gazette 192).

*Objective of the law*

According to its official recital, the main objectives of Law 3054/2002 were the strengthening of competition, reform of the way that safety reserve stocks were kept to avoid harming competition, the establishment of control mechanism for the fuel supply chain in order to address smuggling and rigging, as well as enhancing transparency and efficiency for the benefit of consumers. The legislation also attempted a codification of multiple provisions that existed in the petroleum sector.[36]

The law also changed the compliance status of security reserve stocks to harmonise Greek law with EU legislation. It also introduced the possibility to use and access storage facilities of third parties, such as refineries or companies parties responsible for keeping security stocks.

Based on discussions with the competent authorities and Law 3054/2002's official recitals, as amended eight times since its introduction in 2002, minimum storage spaces and capital requirements are deemed important in order to ensure that the companies trading fuel retain a certain level of economic standing and credibility. This is related to the nature and value of the products traded and the fact that their activities could have negative implications on public and environmental safety. Reasons of higher public interest such as protecting energy policy and safety, and long-term energy planning, securing the sufficient function of the market to the consumers' benefits are also reported. Other reasons include maintaining a sufficient supply of fuel products to the market and eliminating potential risks of shortage.

For the provision requiring that the lease agreements between fuel wholesalers and property owners have at least the same duration as wholesalers' licences, OECD understands that the policy maker wished to protect licence holders by safeguarding lease agreements during the licence period.

On lease agreements for storage spaces and the obligation of licence holders to store at least 30% of their annual sales in the administrative district where they are based, the official recital of the law says that the policy maker's objective was to use all storage spaces across Greece at their maximum capacity and so avoid storage spaces sitting empty simply to comply with licence requirements. The team understands that the provision may be connected to the objective of ensuring fuel availability in the Greek islands (see Box 7.2 above).

*Harm to competition*

A company can begin wholesale trading of fuels, as long as the necessary logistics infrastructure (capital, network distribution, storage, collaboration with suppliers, etc.) is in place. Yet restrictions linked to licensing requirements, such as the basic condition of having sufficient storage spaces, might prove difficult for new entrants and so discourage their entry into the wholesale market. These restrictive provisions may hamper competition between operators in the fuel market and limit the number of new entrants, leading to higher fuel prices for consumers. As a result, strong incumbents may increase their market power.

Setting minimum storage spaces could also lead to high initial and operational costs both for new entrants and incumbents, reducing competitive pressure as fewer operators enter the market. It may also significantly reduce the number of suppliers involved in the local wholesale trade as a regional factor that increases the risk of creating local market power and reduce competitive action. Such requirements do not necessarily serve their stated purpose of protecting consumers and creditors from the risk posed by companies with limited financial standing and therefore a higher potential for insolvency.

The requirement that the minimum duration of storage spaces' lease agreements be equal to the duration of a wholesaler's licence could impede competition as it restricts wholesalers from changing storage spaces during the licence period. Such a restriction could make it difficult for wholesalers to lower their storage costs in the event that a cheaper storage space was found.

Specifically, the geographic restriction on the 30% use of "home" storage space limits business practices, increasing their costs and possibly restricting entry in certain geographic areas.

Minimum capital requirements impose, according to the OECD, a barrier to entry for new, especially small, entrants. Moreover, existing operators may also face difficulties in meeting the thresholds set by law, if the minimum is set too high.

The requirement obliging Type A, B1, B2 and C licence holders to have an insurance contract equal to the minimum capital requirement depending on the type of the licence in case of penalties from the competent authorities, constitutes a barrier to entry for wholesalers as it is often not feasible for insurance companies to cover such a risk, automatically limiting alternatives to minimum capital requirements or letters of guarantee.

Law 3054/2002 and Joint Ministerial Decision ΔΥδρογ.ΕΦ.5180086/2015 require Type D licence holders to file a letter of guarantee or an insurance contract of a value equivalent to the minimum share capital. Yet since minimum capital requirements have been abolished for this licence type, this requirement lacks a legal basis.

Type ST licence holders' right to trade in the entire Greek territory as Type A licence holders under lower threshold criteria is seen by the OECD as treating operators in the same market differently. This does not seem proportionate to meet the policy maker's objective. The favourable requirements attached to Type ST licences were, at the time they were granted, justified and proportionate to the policy maker's objective, since they were intended to provide incentives to wholesalers to supply fuel to islands and remote areas. However, granting Type ST licence holders an additional licence Type A valid for the entire Greek territory and then renewing those secondary licences automatically, imposes a differential treatment on wholesalers who enter and remain in the fuel market under a Type A licence scheme and so have to comply with far stricter criteria.

*Recommendations and benefits*

Abolishing the following provisions is expected to benefit both consumers and businesses.

The OECD makes the following recommendations on minimum storage requirements.

- The length of the storage space lease agreements should be disconnected from the length of the licence. An obligation that all storage spaces be registered with the General Secretariat of Energy should be introduced. At the moment, the law heavily regulates the storage spaces that wholesalers list to meet minimum storage requirements, but leaves completely unregistered any other storage spaces they may operate.

- Minimum storage capacity for Type A licence holders should be lowered, to include a lower previous calendar year's sales volume threshold.

- The minimum number of refillable cylinders required for bottled-gas wholesalers should be eased for new applicants wishing to enter the market

- The provision on minimum storage spaces for biofuel should be amended so that the requirement to hold a minimum capacity not less than 1/100 of the quantity requested by the applicant is removed.
- The geographic restriction requiring 30% use of storage spaces should be explicitly abolished for all licence holders

OECD makes the following recommendations on minimum capital requirements:

- Lower the minimum capital requirement for all types of licences to include a lower minimum capital threshold that moves in relation to sales volumes during the previous calendar year.
- The option of an insurance contract to replace capital requirements should be removed from the provision.
- The requirement of a letter of guarantee or insurance contract for Type D licence holders should be disconnected from the (now-abolished) provision on minimum capital requirements.
- Type ST licence holders should continue their activity under the minimum requirements set for this type of licence, when exercising their activity in the areas for which the Type ST licence was initially granted to them. However, for the rest of the Greek territory, Type A licences should be granted to them under the same conditions as all other Type A licence holders.

***Legal form***

*Description of the obstacle and policy maker's objective*

Legislation imposes the obligation that wholesale trade companies operate as SAs or any other similar legal structure. Based on the company-law provisions covering matters of corporate structure and liability, the only similar legal structure would appear to be limited liability company (LLC). The new form of private company (IKE) could potentially become another alternative, but this might be an arbitrary assumption, considering that IKE was established in 2012, whereas the law on fuel market dates from 2002. A wholesaler must therefore use the provisions of an SA or LLC to set up a company.

Since the SA form is subject to higher administrative, taxation and audit controls than all other legal forms, the policy maker's objectives such as regular functioning of the market, consumer safety and energy policy are deemed to be safeguarded.

*Harm to competition*

The determination of the legal form of the licensee interferes with the operator's freedom to decide on its investment structure and can impose higher costs for businesses already in the market. For example, Greek legislation imposes higher set-up and operational costs on SAs, as well as strict requirements, such as board decisions requiring prior approval by the Prefectural Directorates for Commerce.

*Recommendation and benefits*

The provision on the legal form of SAs could be amended to explicitly include LLCs and IKEs. Such a requirement has been set by the policy maker in an attempt to ensure that all licensees comply with their legal obligations, including that of transparency, which for SAs and LLCs was used to be implemented through publication in the Government Gazette. Nonetheless, since the obligation for certain corporate actions (such as amending the corporate seat or increasing the share capital) to be published in the Government Gazette was replaced with the general obligation for publication in the General Electronic Commercial Registry (GEMI),[37] all legal structures now appear on the same legal footing in terms of commercial publicity. Transparency is therefore safeguarded in the market and both public administration and third parties are aware of corporate actions.

The fact that SAs are highly controlled and their actions are subject to prior approval by the Prefectural Directorates ensures their compliance with Law 2190/1920 on SAs, but does not ensure the legality of their activities in terms of fuel legislation. Moreover, the argument that the policy maker intended to ensure a high level of conformity with the legal requirements by imposing the SA form is negated by the fact that the alternative legal structure, LLC, remains uncontrolled by the authorities.

***Exclusive fuel supply agreements between wholesalers and retailers***

*Duration of contracts*

Petrol-station types are based on ownership status.

- CODO (company owned, dealer operated) petrol stations are owned by wholesalers, operated by retailers either by lease agreement, representation agreement or sale agreement. Retailers operate as independent entrepreneurs and set the retail price.
- DODO (dealer owned, dealer operated) petrol stations are owned and operated by the retailer.
- COCO (company owned, company operated) petrol stations are owned by the wholesaler, which exercises full control in terms of its operation and prices. Operators and employees are employed by the wholesaler who can manage the pricing strategy at each stage of the supply chain.[38]

It is common practice for wholesalers and retailers to engage in exclusive co-operation agreements based upon which petrol stations functioning under the DODO structure procure fuel products exclusively from a specific wholesaler. Such vertical agreements are seen in EU Regulation 330/2010[39] as perhaps having an anticompetitive effect as they often include non-compete obligations. This type of obligation is also encountered in exclusive -supply fuel agreements, according to which, wholesalers forbid retailers to sell competitor brands. According to the EU Regulation and relevant Greek Law (4177/2012), the duration of such agreements should not exceed five years.

Greek legislation grants exemptions from this five-year limit when the fuel is sold by the buyer (retailer) in premises that belong to the supplier (wholesaler) or are leased to the latter by a third party, not connected in any way to the buyer (retailer).

In vertical agreements under a DODO structure, petrol stations are owned by the retailer. A recent Hellenic Competition Commission case[40] was issued following complaints by petrol-station owners engaging in exclusive supply agreements with wholesalers. The decision observed that wholesalers used a loophole in the legislation so that they could be exempt from the regulation by leasing petrol stations or land from retailers or from a person connected to them, and then signing an ancillary agreement to sublet the gas station or land to the retailer. In this way, they were able to prolong exclusive supply agreements for up to 20 years or more in some cases.

*Description of the obstacles and policy maker's objective*

The law prohibits exclusive supply agreements to last more than five years, with the possibility of renewing for an equivalent amount of time if one of the following conditions is met:

1. the wholesaler is the owner of the property or leasing it to the retailer;
2. the wholesaler is the owner of the property and conferring its use to the retailer; or
3. a third party, not connected in any way to the retailer, leases the property to the wholesaler who in turn subleases it to the retailer.

In all of the above cases, the duration of the exclusive agreement may last longer than the maximum regulated five years, but it may never exceed the duration of the lease agreement.

The law goes further in defining the framework of retailers' obligations in exclusive supply contracts, by demanding the mandatory placing of wholesalers' trademark on fuel transportation vehicles, regardless of whether they are owned by the retailer or leased from a third party. In addition, the law dictates that the cost for placing the wholesaler's trademark on the vehicle is to be paid either by the owner of the truck or, in the event that the truck has been obtained with a lease agreement or a bill of sale with an ownership reservation clause, by the renter or purchaser of the vehicle. The same obligation holds for other types of contracts.

An example of such an extensive description of the legal framework on the parties' obligations within exclusive supply agreements is Ministerial Decision A3/5262/2004 on the Function of petrol stations – obligations of fuel trading companies. The Ministry of Economy, Development and Tourism has confirmed that this particular decision is obsolete and that it was replaced by Article 115 of Ministerial Decision A2-718/2014 (DIEPPY). Yet the industry has recently reported that it has been used as the legal base for fining several wholesalers.

Box 7.3. **Consumer survey on fuel**

According to a study for the Executive Agency for Health and Consumers in 2014, most EU consumers reported not being loyal to a particular fuel brand or petrol station.

Only 13% and 10% of consumer survey respondents, respectively, indicated "sells my preferred brand" and "is at my preferred supermarket chain" as important considerations for their selection of a petrol station. According to the survey: "This suggests that most consumers were open to purchasing fuel from various retailers."

Price seems to be the critical factor in consumers' decision-making in terms of retailer selection: 68% of consumer survey respondents indicated "offers the lowest price" as an important consideration in their choice of a petrol station.

Aside from price, key factors in the selection of a particular petrol station include a convenient location (43%) and the offer of a loyalty card or membership scheme (22%). More in-depth key findings on the timing of fuel purchases and retailer selection reveal that almost half of the survey respondents say that they usually fill up their vehicle when the tank is nearly empty (46%), while 19% fill up whenever they see a good deal or see that prices have fallen; only 2% fill up on specific days of the week.

Finally, only 20% of responding EU-27 stakeholders[1] were of the opinion that it is easy for consumers in their country to compare the performance of branded fuels, generic/non-branded fuels, and fuels sold at supermarkets. Indeed, the majority of stakeholders (52%) reported that such comparisons are not at all easy.

1. Croatia was not yet a member of the EU when this study was commissioned.

*Source:* Executive Agency for Health and Consumers (2014), "Consumer market study on the functioning of the market for vehicle fuels from a consumer perspective", *http://ec.europa.eu/consumers/consumer_evidence/market_studies/vehicle_fuels/docs/study_en.pdf.*

OECD communications with the competent Ministries of Economy and of Energy point to the policy maker's objective being to safeguard consumers' right to be informed on the origin of fuel. However, there is insufficient evidence to suggest that consumers are aware of the differences between fuel products from different wholesalers.

*Harm to competition*

As a general observation, the identified provisions on exclusive agreements should be the subject of private negotiations between the parties.

The exemption regarding the duration of agreements could have a negative impact on competition. Vertical agreements containing non-compete clauses, such as the obligation of retailers to exclusively buy fuel from a specific wholesaler, which binds them for a long period of time, limit retailers' ability to switch to other wholesalers. As a result, larger wholesalers are able to lock in their customers and reduce smaller providers' opportunities to gain market share. This is particularly harmful for new entrants trying to establish a customer base. Competition is thus harmed at the wholesale level, with an adverse effect on consumers who may be deprived of a variety of products and choices.

By obliging retailers to place wholesalers' trademarks on their fuel transportation vehicles, the law grants wholesalers an advantage and deprives retailers of the right to negotiate.

The provision on the cost of placing the wholesaler's trademark on a fuel transportation vehicle can distort a wholesaler's choice between own account transportation and transportation for hire. As professional transport operators are liable for the cost of this provision, they may end up passing it on to wholesalers. Furthermore, wholesalers who use their own trucks for transporting their products pay the cost of placing the logo only once (when the vehicle is bought). Wholesalers without a privately owned fleet, on the other hand, may change transport operators and are therefore forced to bear the relevant cost more than once. Over time, wholesalers that own their own transportation vehicles may be more competitive than those that do not, as this reduced cost could potentially lead to cheaper products and therefore better market position.

*Recommendation and benefits*

Two of the three exemptions on the maximum duration of exclusive agreements should be amended to clearly prohibit any possibility for deviations from the policy maker's objective. More specifically, in cases 1) and 2) described above, the wording of the law must explicitly allow for such an extension only when the wholesaler has full ownership of the property, not bare ownership or usufruct. In this way, the law would prevent wholesalers from leasing the petrol station or land from the petrol station owner (i.e. retailer) and sub-leasing it back in order to benefit from exemptions in the maximum duration of an exclusivity agreement.

Abolishing retailers' obligations to place wholesalers' trademarks on their fuel transportation vehicles could lead to increased competition among wholesalers. Retailers and wholesalers should be allowed to decide on whether a wholesaler's trademark should be placed on transportation, allowing them to negotiate different, more favourable conditions and requirements. Consumers could benefit from any increased market diversity, as smaller brands and independent retailers affecting competition might emerge. Moreover, given the common enforcement practice and guidelines on vertical agreements,[41] competition authorities are able to assess ex post the effect of such agreements and their possible anti-competitive effects.[42] Thus, it may not be appropriate for the legislation to set strict ex -ante rules.

In addition, parties should be left free to negotiate the cost of placing wholesalers' trademarks. The provision requiring that the cost be paid by the owner of the truck or the renter or eventual purchaser of the vehicle should be abolished.

## 7.5. Transportation of goods

Reviewing the sector of wholesale trade requires an examination of the regulatory framework for freight transportation. In terms of the amount of cargo transported (tonnes per kilometre), almost all freight transportation in Greece is road transportation; the EU average is just over 75%.[43]

Road -haulage transport can be roughly categorised as transport on own account and transport for hire or reward.[44] Own -account transport is carried out by the individual or company owning private vehicles, whereas road haulage for hire or reward is transport carried out by a third party. Another intermediate category, freight forwarders and integrators may not own a fleet, but instead organise shipments on behalf of third parties.

Based on EU statistics,[45] the road -haulage market for transport for hire and reward in the EU comprises around 600000 enterprises, which have four employees on average; 80% of companies count fewer than 10 employees; and 99% have fewer than 50 employees.

In Greece, the total value of the domestic market for professional transport services has increased during the eight-year period 2001-2008 at an average annual growth rate of 8%.[46] During the five-year period 2009- 2013, the market showed an average annual decrease of around 7.5%. However, the market value slightly increased by 1.5% in 2014 by comparison to 2013, according to the same source.

ELSTAT counts 1 317 945 goods vehicles in Greece in 2014, 1 281 450 of which were vehicles used for transport on own account (so-called private trucks); road-freight transport trucks for hire or reward accounted for only 36 495 vehicles. According to the introductory recital of Law 3887/2010[47], among EU countries, Greece shows a large number of trucks used for own account compared to road -haulage trucks, whereas the per capita rate of private trucks in Greece is among the highest in Europe. This indicates that there may be too many private-use trucks operating in the market. As a market, road -haulage transport is poorly integrated in Greece, unable to achieve economies of scale without modernisation that would help move it towards being a logistics services chain.

Overall, wholesalers transport their goods either through privately owned vehicles or by hiring the services of transport operators, freight forwarders and integrators. According to industry sources, about 30% of wholesalers – mainly supermarket chains – transport goods using their own purpose vehicles.[48]

### *Framework for transport on own account*

Legislation on road transportation has changed significantly over the years. Law 1959/1991[49] on the licensing of trucks used for own account and Law 3887/2010[50] on road haulage are the main legislative texts and have both been partially amended by the more recent Laws 4233/2014[51] and 4336/2015.[52] The new laws do not replace the previous ones in their entirety, but rather amend some provisions, while leaving others in force. The new legislation also does not explicitly specify which provisions are being replaced and which remain in force.

Moreover, some of the provisions regulating the licensing of vehicles used for the transportation of agricultural products – which fall under the competency of the Ministry of Rural Development and Food – have entered into force, but the implementing legislation has not yet been amended accordingly. As a result, an unclear and ambiguous legal environment has emerged, not only for business operators, but also for the public administration.[53]

More specifically, Law 1959/1991 and Ministerial Decision A2/29542/5347/1991 on the Licensing of private-use trucks set a number of provisions covering the licensing scheme for own-account transportation. A series of requirements for acquiring one or more licences connected to an applicant's turnover were supposed to have been abolished by Law 4336/2015. However, a lack of direct reference to the old provisions – they are not explicitly abolished one by one – has created confusion as to the status of licensing.

The provisions on own-account transport vehicles also follow another horizontal amendment changing the threshold for heavy-duty vehicles from 4 to 3.5 tonnes. This may cause legal uncertainty, as legal texts mentioning both thresholds can be found. Greek legislation seems to have extended the maximum tonne threshold to apply also to non-professional operators for the number of vehicles over 3.5 tonnes they can use for own -account transportation, or as mentioned above, with regard to the delivery of goods to their customers.

It should be stressed that the legal regime on transportation for own account is rather complex, since Law 1959/2011, Legislative Decree 49/1968 and Royal Decree 281/1973, which codifies the second, have all remained in force, causing confusion and uncertainty. Since Law 1959/1991 is the main reference law, any newer legislation should explicitly replace the old framework, providing if necessary secondary legislation into detailed provisions on safety, security and hygiene measures to enter into force. Moreover, apart from 1959/2011, Law 3887/ 2010 is also regulating some aspects of the transportation for own account.

Specific recommendations on transport on own account can be found in Annex B.

***Framework for transport for hire or reward***

*History of the sector in Greece*

Before 1967, there was no national legal framework setting out the rules on granting licences for trucks used for transportation for hire or reward. It was left to the discretion of the competent Minister and it was often observed that requests for such licences were satisfied without prior controls. In 1967, Law 183/1967[54] allowed for the first time professional drivers with three years of experience to obtain licences. These permits were personal and non-transferable, and each driver had to pay 30000 drachmas (EUR 88) for the first tonne of the gross weight of the truck and 5000 drachmas (EUR 14) for each subsequent tonne.

In 1971 the State attempted to address the earlier uncontrolled licensing, and blocked the issuance of new licences to individuals by adopting Legislative Decree 1060/1971.[55] This new framework also provided for the creation of businesses dedicated to national and international transport. If trucks were not owned by such companies, they could only operate within a certain district. In 1971, the profession was effectively "closed" in terms of the number of licences for trucks used for hire or reward, and this freeze lasted until the liberalisation of the profession in 2010. Licence holders are considered by the state to have gained an intangible goodwill over the years, which is depicted in terms of taxation on the transfer of such licences.

The OECD index tracking the regulation of road-freight transportation shows that from 2000 to 2013 regulation in Greece was significantly relaxed. However, it remains among the most regulated in the European Union.

*Description of the obstacle and policy maker's objective*

At a European Union level, Regulation 1071/2009[56] establishes common rules concerning the conditions to be complied with as a road-transport operator. The regulation, which is applied in all EU member states including Greece, sets specific standards that road-transport operators must meet, such as the requirements for minimum financial standing to ensure their proper launch and administration. As a simple and cost-efficient method of meeting the requirement that road-transport companies demonstrate sound financial standing, Greek legislation adopted bank guarantees or professional -liability insurance.[57]

Road-haulage businesses that use vehicles or combinations of vehicles whose permissible laden mass does not exceed 3.5 tonnes are exempt from the regulation's provisions.

Provisions on the segmentation of transportation work between national and international transporters are considered abolished by Law 3887/2010, yet this has never been done explicitly, so they still appear in texts on legal databases.

*Recommendation*

Obsolete provisions should be removed explicitly from the body of legislation.

*Differential treatment among licence holders*

The regulatory framework is structured on the basis of a distinction between old and new licence holders for vehicles used for transport for hire and reward.

Such differences between operators licensed by the previous scheme and new operators are frequent in the legislation. This allows for incumbent operators to continue their activities for a reasonable transitional period before they have to comply with the new requirements. Such a practice is founded upon a basic principle that the state should avoid the deterioration of lawful licensees that have fulfilled all the requirements of the past regime by suddenly obliging them to abide by the new requirements. Allowing existing licence holders to operate under different obligations and requirements means treating incumbents differently to new entrants, significantly raising the costs for the latter. The provision does not seem to be justified on grounds of public interest.

In addition, the law introduces a difference between transport operators based upon their legal structure: transport companies functioning as an SA are required to file a letter of guarantee of EUR 9 000 for their first truck and EUR 5 000 for every additional truck, but for smaller legal forms, such as LLCs or personal companies, the letter of guarantee amount is higher – EUR 18 000 for the first truck and EUR 9 000 for every additional truck.

These requirements for financial guarantees are based in Regulation 1071/2009. The regulation does not, however, differentiate between legal forms.[58]

*Recommendation and benefits*

All distinctions between new and old licence holders should be abolished and licensees should all fall within the same framework, so as to avoid any regulatory uncertainty, or differential treatment between operators in the same market.

Distinctions in licensing requirements based on applicants' legal structures should be abolished and the thresholds set by Regulation 1071/2009, i.e. EUR 9 000 for the first vehicle and EUR 5 000 for each additional one should be applied uniformly to all legal structures and entrepreneurs.

As a general remark, all provisions deemed as obsolete and redundant must be explicitly abolished so that regulatory uncertainty, especially for existing operators, ceases.

*Operational restrictions on trailers*

A semi-trailer truck is the combination of a single truck tractor unit and one or more freight-carrying semi-trailers. Law 3446/2006[59] sets considerable restrictions on the ability of transport operators to use tractor units with different combinations of trailers or semi-trailers, whether owned by the operator or by third parties. Each tractor unit can transfer only up to two trailers or semi-trailers.

Intermodal freight transport involves the transportation of freight in an intermodal container or vehicle, using multiple modes of transportation (rail, ship, and truck), without any handling of the freight itself when changing modes. The method reduces cargo handling, and so improves security, reduces damage and loss, and allows freight to be transported faster. Multimodal transport (also known as combined transport) is the transportation of goods under a single contract, but performed with at least two different means of transport; the operator is liable (in a legal sense) for the entire transportation work, even though it is performed by different modes of transport (by rail, sea and road, for example). The operator does not have to possess all the means of transport, and in practice usually does not; the transport is often performed by sub-operators (referred to in legal language as "actual transport operators"). The operator responsible for the entire carriage is referred to as a multimodal transport operator.

The provision on the maximum number of trailers or semi-trailers that individual freelancers may place in circulation when executing national and international road transportation may have an adverse effect on individual freelancers' businesses. The regulation limits intermodal and multimodal transport and eliminates the possibility of any collaboration between two independent companies.

*Recommendation*

Operators should be able to use any number and combination of trailers and semi-trailers, in order to achieve greater flexibility, efficiency and possibly, economies of scale.

***Stevedores for land and port loading-unloading works***

*Description and policy maker's objective*

Until recently loading/unloading works in Greece were carried out by virtue of Legislative Decree 1254/1949.[60] In 2011, Law 3919/2011[61] on the Principle of professional freedom abolished all provisions in sectoral and horizontal legislation that required a licensing procedure to enter a market. Its principles were primarily destined to provide a comprehensive checklist on types of unjustifiable requirements in sectoral legislation that constituted a barrier to entry in the professions. These requirements, as laid out in Article 2, paragraph 2 of the law, included, for example, the setting of a minimum number of operators that may exercise a profession within a specific geographic area or throughout the Greek territory, or providing for an exclusive ability or restriction to provide some products to specific professional establishments.

Exemptions from this obligation had to be justified on public-interest grounds such as public health, environmental safety, consumer protection, urban planning and others, and any restriction had to be proportionate to the policy maker's objective, not discriminating directly or indirectly between businesses based on the country of establishment or, for individuals, in regards to their nationality.

For the profession of stevedores, several restrictive provisions regulated the licensing scheme, such as the obligation to have a professional "booklet". Moreover, the fees were determined at government stage, as they were approved by a special committee and further certified by a decision of the Minister of Labour. A first step in the direction of liberalising the profession was taken in 2012 following a decision by the Council of State[62] that ruled against the regulated stevedores' fees, as contradictory to Article 5 of the Greek Constitution on the right of economic freedom. Therefore regulated fees were abolished and the licensing of stevedores carrying out loading-unloading was replaced by a simple communication to the competent authority, accompanied by specific documentation proving the person's establishment in Greece or the EU, and their good condition to exercise the profession.

This effort has not been particularly successful, as the Hellenic Competition Commission noted in its information note on the sectoral review on fruit and vegetables,[63] which came to the conclusion that certain restrictions have remained in force. More specifically, it was found that wholesalers and other operators are limited in their choices of employees or external associates for loading-unloading activities.

Indeed, according to the legislative framework, all loading-unloading works both on the land and in ports, as well as all transfer and piling of goods or other movables must be carried out by workers belonging to the National Stevedores Registry, even in cases when the work is non-specialised, does not concern dangerous loads and products, or does not include operating machinery.

Exemptions from the above obligation are granted in the following cases.

- Loading of agricultural or farming and animal-feed products, fertilisers, agricultural supplies or other products that belong to producers being moved from the production site to storage spaces on behalf of the producers.
- Loading or unloading of products in sites of industrial production.
- Work carried out in the port zones of Piraeus and Thessaloniki.
- Work carried out by legal persons who, prior to the publication of Law 4093/2012, were acting as concessionaires or providers of port loading-unloading services provided that a training system on hygiene and safety for permanent personnel or such contractors, is in force.

*Harm to competition*

The framework on the obligatory hiring of stevedores registered in Type A Registry for non-specialised works imposes an extra financial burden on wholesalers, creating an artificial demand for this type of services. Given that a large volume of goods goes through ports and given their importance for trade, the restriction could have a far-reaching economic impact.

Exemptions from the general obligation tend to favour some operators over others, increasing operational costs. For instance, if the loading and unloading of agricultural products takes place in central markets, it is necessary to employ registered stevedores for this task. However, if the loading and unloading of the same products takes place where they are produced from the production site to storage spaces, on behalf of the producer, employing registered stevedores is not required. As a first observation, the wording of the exemption seems to be vague, as it is not clear up to which stage of the supply chain it applies, given that the term "storage spaces" may be interpreted broadly. Moreover, insofar as producers also sell directly to retailers, and therefore compete with wholesalers, the OECD's view is that this provision creates preferential treatment towards different operators. More specifically, producers engaged in the wholesale trade are favoured over wholesalers established in central markets, since they are not obliged to hire registered stevedores and their costs are therefore lower.

*Recommendation and benefit*

The mandatory hiring of stevedores registered in the Type A Registry for loading and piling work carried out on land or in ports should be abolished. Provisions providing exemptions from this obligation should then also be abolished for consistency. Business operators should be free to make use of their own workforce to carry out non -specialised loading, unloading, and piling works so that a level playing field for all competitors in the relevant market is created.

## Notes

1. For full definition, see *http://unstats.un.org/unsd/cr/registry/regcs.asp?Cl=27&Co=46&Lg=1&prn=yes*.

2. This chapter includes NACE code 46: "Wholesale trade, except of motor vehicles and motorcycles". It excludes Wholesale and retail trade and repair of motor vehicles and motorcycles (NACE code 45). The wholesale trade of products in Chapter 5 will not be re-examined in this chapter.

3. Other specialised wholesale categories include, among others, Sale of solid, liquid and gaseous fuels and related products (NACE code 46.71) and the Wholesale of wood, construction materials and sanitary equipment (NACE code 46.73).

4. EUROSTAT, total employment, persons aged from 15 to 64 years.

5. Law 4177/2013 on Rules regulating the purchase of products and provision of services (Government Gazette A'173/08.08.2013).

6. Market Code (Legislative Decree 136/1946) and the various Market Decrees issued as secondary legislation and codified under Market Decree 7/2009 have been replaced by Law 4177/2012 ibid and Ministerial Decision A2-718/2014, ibid (DIEPPY).

7. ICAP Group (2014), "Standardization: Packaging of raw fruit and vegetables" sectoral study *www.icap.gr/Default.aspx?id=1862&nt=149&lang=1.*

8. See Cadilhon J-J., Andrew P. Fearne, David R. Hughes & Paule Moustier (2003) *Wholesale Markets and Food Distribution in Europe: New Strategies for Old Functions*, *www.researchgate.net/publication/242172462_Wholesale_Markets_and_Food_Distribution_in_Europe_New_Strategies_for_Old_Functions.*

9. Market Decree 7/2009 (Official Gazette B'1388/2009), valid from 13 July 2009 on amending and codifying Market Decrees issued until 14 May 2009.

10. Law 3784/2009 on the Amendment of provisions of Law 703/77 on competition and other provisions (Government Gazette A'137/07.08.2009).

11. SG-Greffe (2011) D/2287/17.02.2011

12. Law 3982/2011 on the Simplification of licensing of technical professions and manufacturing activities (Official Gazette, A'143/17.06.2011)

13. See official response of the SG of Commerce on the matter of the exclusivity of central markets webcache.googleusercontent.com/search?q=cache:i0Ke0K_Lf4IJ:gge.gov.gr/wp-content/uploads/2011/08/287_EPISTOLH_KENTRIKHS_LAXANAGORAS_ATH_AN.doc+&cd=1&hl=el&ct=clnk&gl=fr.

14. Market Decree 03/2011 on Amending and completing the Market Decree 7/09 in relation to the rules of trading raw fruit and vegetables (Government Gazette, B'1502/2011)

15. See Genakos, Christos D., Pantelis Koutroumpis, Mario Pagliero (2014) "The Impact of Maximum Markup Regulation on Prices", Centre for Economic Policy Research, London, http://cepr.org/active/publications/discussion_papers/dp.php?dpno=10243.

16. Law 4235/2014 on the Administrative measures, procedures and sanctions on the field of food law (Official Gazette, A'32/11.02.2014).

17. Hellenic Competition Commission (2013), "Sectoral Study on Fruit and Vegetables", *www.epant.gr/img/File/parartima%20I%20oporokipeytika.pdf.*

18. Food And Agriculture Organization of the United Nations "*Managing Wholesale Markets*" *ftp://ftp.fao.org/docrep/fao/003/X3680E/X3680E00.pdf*

19. See, Tracey-White J.D., (1991), "Planning and environmental design criteria", in *Wholesale Markets: Planning and Design Manual*, FAO, Rome, *www.fao.org/docrep/t0521e/T0521E0g.htm#13.*

20. This would join up with EU policy aims. According to the Resolution of the Heads of the European Competition Authorities on the 21 December 2012, "where appropriate, farmers should be encouraged to form entities or organisations to create efficiencies in order to respond to market challenges in a pro-competitive way". "Resolution of the Heads of the European Competition Authorities: The Reform of the Common Agricultural Policy", 21 December 2012, *http://ec.europa.eu/competition/sectors/agriculture/resolution_nca_en.pdf.*

21. See Art.2, par.ε, στ, ζ of Joint Ministerial Decision 1153/16620/2014 on Requirements and start-up process of seeds, and enterprises producing and trading propagating material.

22. Ministry of Rural Development and Food, Registry, accessed 4 September 2016, *wwww.minagric.gr/pol_yliko/py_companies.aspx.*

23. "Consolidated versions of the Treaty on European Union and the Treaty on the Functioning of the European Union: Consolidated version of the Treaty on the Functioning of the European Union, Protocols – Annexes – Declarations annexed to the Final Act of the Intergovernmental Conference which adopted the Treaty of Lisbon, signed on 13 December 2007", *http://eur-lex.europa.eu/legal-content/EN/TXT/HTML/?uri=CELEX:12012E/TXT&from=EN.* More specifically, see Article 26 of the Treaty on the Functioning of the European Union: "The internal market shall comprise an area without internal frontiers in which the free movement of goods, persons, services and capital is ensured in accordance with the provisions of the Treaties".

24. See Art.3, par.β, γ, δ of Joint Ministerial Decision 1153/16620/2014, ibid.

25. See Art.8, par.γ of Joint Ministerial Decision 3967/41140/2012 on Requirements and start-up process of stock nurseries for the implementation of Regulations 1234/2007, 555/2008 and 436/2009.

26. Joint Ministerial Decision 1153/16620/2014 sets seven categories of producing and trading enterprises: Seed Producing; Nursery Type A; Nursery Type B; Nursery Type C; Seed and Propagating Material Trading Type A; Seed and Propagating Material Trading Type B; and Seed and Propagating Material Trading Type C.

27. According to EU Recommendation 2003/361, a micro enterprise is defined as an enterprise which employs fewer than 10 persons and whose annual turnover and/or annual balance sheet total does not exceed EUR 2 million, while a small enterprise is defined as an enterprise employing fewer than 50 persons and whose annual turnover and/or annual balance sheet total does not exceed EUR 10 million.

28. See Art.1, par.3,5 of Presidential Decree 159/2014 on Part-time employment of responsible scientist in small and micro enterprises of production and trade of seeds and propagating material and trade of fertilisers.

29. Danchev, Svetsolav and George Maniatis (2014), "The Refining Sector in Greece: Contribution to the Economy and Prospects", Foundation for Economic & Industrial Research (IOBE), Athens, *http://iobe.gr/docs/research/en/res_05_c_27062014_rep_en.pdf.*

30. *http://www.seepe.gr/site/* (accessed 20 October 2016).

31. According to Art.17, par.2 of Ministerial Decision Δ2/16570/2005 (Government Gazette B'1306/2005) on Fuel licences regulation.

32. Law 4172/2013 (Government Gazette A'176A/23.07.2013)

33. Law 4223/2013 (Government Gazette A'287/31.12.2013)

34. Sub-par. ΣΤ11 of par. ΣΤ of Art.1 of Law 4254/2014 (Government Gazette A'85/07.04.2014) states: "Requirements on minimum share capital and minimum storing spaces for asphalt trading licence holders (Type D) according to the provisions of Art. 6 of Law 3054/2002 are abolished."

35. Joint Ministerial Decision ΔΥδρογ.ΕΦ.5180086/2015 on Insurance coverage against risks or security deposit as requirements for the issuance of fuel trading licence further specifies the requirement.

36. Measures adopted included the overhaul of the licence system for activity in the petroleum-products sector; ensuring the possibility of company mergers and incentives for mergers; providing incentives for new storage facilities for petroleum products; strengthening mechanisms of market surveillance; the development of a suitable institutional framework for crisis in the market and to ensure transparency in the administration of storage areas in light of third parties to access essential facilities such as refinery storage areas.

37. See Art.2 of Law 4250/2014 on Administrative simplifications: Abolitions, Mergers of Legal Persons and Public Services –Amendment of Presidential Decree 318/1990 (A'161) and other provisions.

38. Polemis, Michael L. (2012), "Competition and price asymmetries in the Greek oil sector: an empirical analysis on gasoline market [sic]", *Empirical Economics* 43:789, *http://dx.doi.org/10.1007/s00181-011-0507-7.*

39. According to Art.1 (a) of Regulation 330/2010: "vertical agreement" means an agreement or concerted practice entered into between two or more undertakings each of which operates, for the purposes of the agreement or the concerted practice, at a different level of the production or distribution chain, and relating to the conditions under which the parties may purchase, sell or resell certain goods or services."

40. Hellenic Competition Decision 602/2015.

41. Whish R. & D. Bailey, *Competition Law*, Oxford University Press, Oxford, 2015.

42. According to OECD (1994), *Competition Policy and Vertical Restraints: Franchising Agreements*: "They would be prohibited only after an examination of the market conditions as to whether they substantially lessened competition. In Chrysler Australia (1975), the TPC cleared agreements where the distributor refrained from selling competing products (air conditioners)," p.118.

43. Eurostat "Freight transport statistics", data for 2013.

44. OECD Glossary of Statistical Terms, *https://stats.oecd.org/glossary/index.htm.*

45. Final Report from the Commission to the European Parliament Council on the State of the Union Road Transport Market, COM(2014) 222/14.4.2014, *http://ec.europa.eu/transport/modes/road/news/com(2014)-222_en.pdf*

46. ICAP (2016), "Leading sectors of the Greek economy", *http://dir.icap.gr/mailimages/e-books/Leading%20Sectors/2016_04_19_14_32_28/document.pdf.*

47. Law 3887/2010 on Road haulage (Government Gazette, A'174/30.09.2010).

48. According to industry sources.

49. Law 1959/1991 on Road transport (Government Gazette, A'123/05.08.1991).

50. Law 3887/2010 on Professional road transport (Government Gazette, A' 174/30.09.2010)

51. Law 4233/2014 on National Flight Coordination Authority (Government Gazette, A'22/29.01.2014)

52. Law 4336/2015 introducing pension provisions, ratifying the Financial Assistance Facility Agreement (FFA) launched under the European Stability Mechanism (ESM) framework and regulating the implementation of the Financing Agreement (MoU) (Government Gazette, A'94/2015)

53. According to communication with officials from the Ministry of Infrastructure, Transport and Networks.

54. Law 183/1967 on Granting licences to trucks and three-wheel vehicles for hire (Government Gazette A'195/10.11.1967)

55. Legislative Decree 1060/1971 on Organising road haulage carried out by trucks for hire (Government Gazette A'268/22.12.1971)

56. Regulation (EC) No. 1071/2009 on Establishing common rules concerning the conditions to be complied with to pursue the occupation of road transport operator and repealing Council Directive 96/26/EC

57. See recital (10) of Regulation (EC) No 1071/2009, ibid.

58. It should also be noted that at an EU level, the number of companies engaged in transport for hire are extremely small.

59. Law 3446/2006 on the Organisation and operation of vehicle traffic control authorities – reforms concerning passenger transport and other provisions (Government Gazette A'49/10.03.2006)

60. Legislative Decree 1254/1949 (Government Gazette, A'288/31.10.1949)

61. Law 3919/2011 on the Liberalisation of professions (Government Gazette A'32/02.03.2011).

62. Council of the State Decision No. 2451/2012

63. Hellenic Competition Commission (2013), "Sectoral Study on Fruit and Vegetables", *www.epant.gr/img/File/parartima%20I%20oporokipeytika.pdf.*

## References

Eurostat, Statistical classification of economic activities in the European Community, NACE Rev. 2

Tracey-White J. D. (1991), Wholesale Markets: Planning and Design Manual, Food and Agriculture Organization of the United Nations, *www.fao.org/docrep/t0521e/t0521e00.htm.*

## Databases

Eurostat, Annual detailed enterprise statistics for industry (NACE Rev. 2, G), Database [sbs_na_dt_r2], *http://ec.europa.eu/eurostat* (accessed 24 August 2016).

Eurostat, Employment and activity by sex and age, Database [lfsi_emp_a], *http://ec.europa.eu/eurostat* (accessed 1 September 2016).

Eurostat, GDP and main components, Database [nama_10_gdp], *http://ec.europa.eu/eurostat* (accessed 24 August 2016).

# ANNEX A

# Methodology

This study covers five sectors of the Greek economy. These are e-commerce, construction, media, wholesale trade and selected manufacturing sub-sectors not already reviewed in the first two Competition Assessment Projects. The manufacturing sub-sectors covered by the study are as follows, accompanied by the corresponding codes according to the Statistical Classification of Economic Activities in the European Community (NACE): paper and paper products (NACE code 17), printing and reproduction of recorded media (NACE code 18), chemicals and chemical products (NACE code 20), basic pharmaceutical products and pharmaceutical preparations (NACE code 21), rubber and plastic products (NACE code 22) and electrical equipment (NACE code 27). The sectors were selected, in consultation with the Ministry of Economy and the European Commission's SRSS, based on their value added and employment (2008-2013 averages).[1]

The assessment of laws and regulations in these sectors has been carried out in four stages. The present annex describes the methodology followed in each of these stages.

## Stage 1 – Mapping the sectors

The objective of Stage 1 of the project was to identify and collect all sector-relevant laws and regulations. As a prior condition, it was necessary to define the scope of the five sectors in detail. Whenever possible, we adopted a definition consistent with the NACE classification in order to ensure consistency with international practice and to facilitate comparisons with other European countries. However, this approach was not applicable to the definition of e-commerce, so for this sector, the definition was developed on the basis of NACE in conjunction with other sources, such as the OECD (Glossary of Statistics, Competition Committee 2000), European Commission Directives and implemented Greek laws, past competition -assessment sectoral studies of the Greek government and local business associations' codes of conducts.

The collection of the legislation relevant for the five sectors was conducted by the OECD team using a variety of sources. The NOMOS legal database[2] was the main tool used to identify the applicable legislation. This was complemented by the websites of relevant authorities, as well as industry and consumer associations. In addition, in order to ensure that all important pieces of legislation were covered by the study, input was solicited from all the competent line ministries and public bodies involved in the sectors, from the members of the High-level Committee (HLC) composed of senior government officials and from the industry.

Over the course of the project, the mapping of the legislation was refined, as additional pieces of legislation were discovered by the team or were issued by the authorities, while other pieces initially identified were found not to be relevant to the sectors. In total, 1,288 pieces of legislation were identified, including laws, ministerial decisions and circulars.

**Box A.1. OECD Competition Checklist**

Further competition assessment should be conducted if a piece of legislation answers 'yes' to any of the following questions:

**(A) Limits the number or range of suppliers**

This is likely to be the case if the piece of legislation:

1. grants exclusive rights for a supplier to provide goods or services
2. establishes a licence, permit or authorisation process as a requirement of operation
3. limits the ability of some types of suppliers to provide a good or service
4. significantly raises the cost of entry or exit by a supplier
5. creates a geographical barrier to the ability of companies to supply goods services or labour, or invest capital

**(B) Limits the ability of suppliers to compete**

This is likely to be the case if the piece of legislation:

1. limits sellers' ability to set the prices for goods or services
2. limits freedom of suppliers to advertise or market their goods or services
3. sets standards for product quality that provide an advantage to some suppliers over others or that are above the level that some well-informed customers would choose
4. significantly raises costs of production for some suppliers relative to others (especially by treating incumbents differently from new entrants)

**(C) Reduces the incentive of suppliers to compete**

This may be the case if the piece of legislation:

1. creates a self-regulatory or co-regulatory regime
2. requires or encourages information on supplier outputs, prices, sales or costs to be published
3. exempts the activity of a particular industry or group of suppliers from the operation of general competition law

**(D) Limits the choices and information available to customers**

This may be the case if the piece of legislation:

1. limits the ability of consumers to decide from whom they purchase
2. reduces mobility of customers between suppliers of goods or services by increasing the explicit or implicit costs of changing suppliers
3. fundamentally changes information required by buyers to shop effectively

*Source* : OECD (2011a).

For each of the sectors, the team collected data and information, covering industry trends and main indicators such as output, employment and prices. Input was solicited from industry associations, to improve the project team's understanding of the sectors and the challenges of the Greek market. An extremely important task begun during Stage 1 and continued through subsequent stages was the establishment of contact with the market through the main associations active in each sector. The interviews with market participants contributed to a better understanding of how the sectors under investigation work in practice and helped in the discussion of potential barriers deriving from the legislation or misinterpretation of specific provisions.

### Stage 2 – Screening of the legislation

The second stage of the project entailed screening the legislation to identify potentially restrictive provisions. Pieces of legislation transposing EU Directives were examined. EU Directives need transposition into national legislation and grant Member States the flexibility to impose additional requirements. Therefore, when transposing Directives, the national policy maker may establish a stricter regulatory framework than originally intended in the Directive (so-called gold-plating). These provisions, introduced at national level, were examined from a competition point of view. EU rules that are directly applicable in Greek legislation and require no further national legislation – i.e. Regulations – were not screened to assess if they restricted competition.

The legislation collected in Stage 1 was analysed using the framework provided by the OECD Competition Assessment Toolkit.[3] The Toolkit, developed by Working Party 2 of the OECD Competition Committee, provides a general methodology for identifying potential obstacles in laws and regulations. One of the main elements of the Toolkit is a Competition Checklist that asks a series of simple questions to screen laws and regulations with the potential to restrain competition unnecessarily.

Following the Toolkit methodology, the OECD team compiled a list of all the provisions that answered any of the questions in the checklist positively. The government experts received draft lists and were given an opportunity to comment, as were the members of the HLC.

### Stage 3 – Analysis of the selected provisions

The provisions carried forward to Stage 3 were investigated in order to 1) identify the objective of the policy maker; and 2) assess whether they could result in harm to competition.

The team researched the policy objectives in order to examine the proportionality of the selected provisions with the intended policy objective. An additional purpose in identifying the objectives was to prepare for the formulation of alternatives to existing regulations, when required, taking account of the objective of the specific provisions. The policy maker's objective was researched in the recitals of legislation, when applicable, or through discussions with the relevant public authorities.

The analysis of the harm to competition was carried out qualitatively and involved a variety of tools, including economic analysis, collection of background information on the sector and its regulation, and research into the regulation applied in other European countries. All provisions were analysed, relying on the guidance provided by the Toolkit. Interviews with market participants and with government experts complemented the analysis, by providing crucial information on the actual implementation and effects of the provisions.

### Stages 4 and 5 – Formulation of recommendations

The team developed draft recommendations for those provisions that were found to restrict competition. In this process, we relied on international experience whenever available. When it was not possible to identify in international practice examples of regulation with a lesser impact on competition, the team favoured alternatives that were less restrictive for suppliers, while still meeting the policy maker's initial objective. For instance, these could be policy changes likely to:

- lower barriers to entry into certain economic activities (e.g. when certain suppliers were prevented from engaging in related products or activities); and

- restrict the ability of suppliers to compete (e.g. restrictions to marketing and labelling).

The benefits from removing barriers to competition were analysed qualitatively and, whenever feasible and meaningful, quantitatively. Whenever feasible and appropriate for the analysis of the issue under consideration, the OECD team gathered data that could be used for the quantification of the effects. In these cases, the data were analysed using econometric techniques. In other cases, the expected impact of a lifting regulatory restriction was not modelled directly, for instance because of the lack of sufficient data. Therefore, the OECD team relied on the standard methodology of measuring the effect of policy changes on consumer surplus. In particular, as a result of data limitations, we followed the approach in OECD (2015), which derives a formula for changes in consumer benefits only when sector revenue and the average price effect of the restriction found are available. This is explained in Box A.2 below.

Draft recommendations were submitted to the Greek administration and SRSS. Recommendations were finalised following consultation with ministerial experts and stakeholders. In total, 356 recommendations were submitted to the Greek administration:

- E-commerce: 10;
- Construction: 42;
- Media: 68;
- Manufacturing and wholesale trade: 236, broken down into
- Pharmaceuticals: 54;
- Chemicals, rubber, paper, electrical equipment and printing: 48;
- Wholesale trade of other products: 134.

### Prioritisation of recommendations

In consultation with the Ministry of Economy and the European Commission's SRSS, the OECD prioritised the analysis of the e-commerce sector for the delivery of early recommendations in May 2016.[4] In addition, the OECD submitted early recommendations on the other sectors in July 2016.

### Co-operation with the Greek administration

Another important component of the project was to provide assistance in building up the competition -assessment capabilities of the Greek administration. The OECD organised four workshops during the course of the project, one for each of the stages. In Stage 1 of the project, we covered an introduction to competition and regulation, and provided an overview of the project and of our methodology in the mapping stage. In Stage 2, the team provided substantive training in the OECD Competition Assessment Toolkit that the team used to screen the legislation. In Stage 3, examples and applications of quantitative methods were presented. In Stage 4, OECD experts presented two topics relevant for the project: 1) the Product Market Regulation (PMR) index compiled by the OECD and policy analysis, which relies on this indicator; and 2) the OECD guidelines on fighting bid rigging in public procurement.

Box A.2. **Measuring changes in consumer surplus**

The effects of changing regulations can often be examined as movements from one point on the demand curve to another. For many regulations that have the effect of limiting supply or raising price, an estimate of consumer benefit or harm from the change from one equilibrium to another can be calculated. Graphically, the change is illustrated with a constant elasticity demand curve. Er shows the equilibrium with restrictive regulation; Ec shows the equilibrium point with competitive regulation. The competitive equilibrium is different from the restrictive regulation equilibrium in two important ways: lower price and higher quantity. These properties are a well-known result from many models of competition.

Figure A.1. **Changes in consumer surplus**

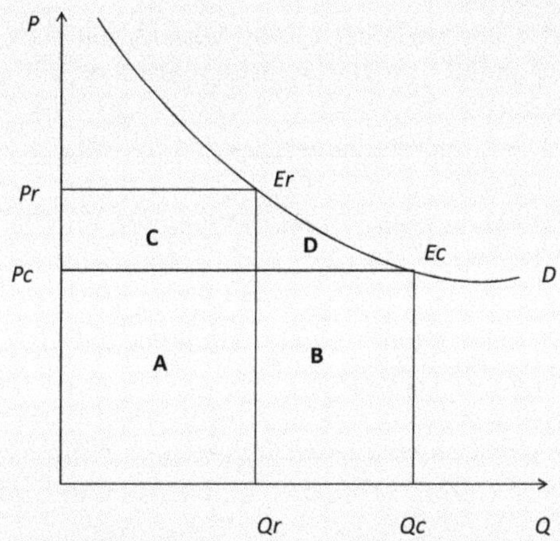


*Source:* OECD (2015).

Under the assumption of constant elasticity of demand, the equation for consumer benefit is:

$$CB = C + D \approx (P_r - P_c)Q_r + \frac{1}{2}(P_r - P_c)(Q_c - Q_r)$$

Where price changes are expected, a basic formula for such a standard measure of consumer benefit from eliminating the restriction is:

$$CB = \left(\rho + \frac{1}{2}\epsilon\rho^2\right)R_r$$

Where CB is standard measure of consumer harm; ρ is percentage change in price related to restriction; R is sector revenue; and ε is demand elasticity. When elasticity is not known, a relatively standard assumption is that |ε|=2. This value corresponds to more elastic demand than in a monopoly market, but is also far from perfectly elastic as in a competitive market. Under this assumption, the expression above is simplified as:

$$CB = (\rho + \rho^2)R_r$$

*Source*: OECD (2015).

Government experts made a significant contribution to the mapping of legislation by commenting on whether the regulations collected were comprehensive. Subsequently, close co-operation with government experts continued with the identification of the objectives of legislation in their sectors of expertise and discussion on the provisions identified by the OECD as restrictive on the basis of the Competition Assessment Checklist. A number of meetings and phone calls were held to discuss the provisions in detail, to understand to what extent they were implemented in practice and to provide feedback on the OECD's draft comments on the selected provisions.

The OECD regularly presented a status update on the project and its findings to the HLC of Secretaries General. In addition, the OECD requested individual meetings with all the members of the HLC to discuss the status of the work, including co-operation with their staff, and any preliminary views on the relevant legislation.

## Notes

1. The sub-sectors of manufacturing analysed by the OECD, whether in this study or in previous studies, account for 93% of the value added of manufacturing, based on 2008-2013 averages.

2. The NOMOS database is owned, operated and managed by Intrasoft International.

3. OECD (2011a), *Competition Assessment Toolkit: Principles*, OECD, *www.oecd.org/daf/competition/46193173.pdf*

   OECD (2011b), *Competition Assessment Toolkit: Guidance*, OECD, *www.oecd.org/daf/competition/45544507.pdf*

   OECD (2015), *Competition Assessment Toolkit: Operational manual*, OECD, *www.oecd.org/daf/competition/COMP_Toolkit_Vol.3_ENG_2015.pdf.*

4. For the e-commerce sector, time constraints resulting from the prioritisation of early recommendations led the team to merge stages 2 and 3. Screening and analysis of the legislation was conducted simultaneously, thus the list of Stage 2 was shorter and limited only to provisions that were already analysed in relation with the objective of the policy maker and the potential harm to competition.

## References

OECD (2015), *Competition Assessment Toolkit, Operational Manual*, OECD, Paris, *www.oecd.org/daf/competition/COMP_Toolkit_Vol.3_ENG_2015.pdf.*

OECD (2011a), *Competition Assessment Toolkit: Principles*, OECD, Paris, *www.oecd.org/daf/competition/46193173.pdf.*

OECD (2011b), *Competition Assessment Toolkit: Guidance*, OECD, Paris, *www.oecd.org/daf/competition/45544507.pdf.*

# ANNEX B

# Legislation screening by sector

## Sector: E-commerce

| No | No and title of Regulation | Article | Thematic category | Brief description of the potential obstacle | Keyword | Policy maker's objectives | Harm to competition | Recommendations | Competent Ministry / Authority |
|---|---|---|---|---|---|---|---|---|---|
| 1 | **Presidential Decree 131/2003 (Government Gazette A' 116/ 16.05.2003) on Specific aspects of information society services, notably electronic commerce** | Art.14 par.1 | E-commerce | The Presidential Decree implements Directive 2000/31/EC on E-commerce. In accordance with the Directive, it should relieve Internet Service Providers ("ISPs") of the obligation to monitor the legality of information they transmit or store when they: (a) act as a "mere conduit"; (b) perform "caching" services; or (c) provide a "hosting" service.<br><br>The Presidential Decree contains erroneous numbering in the text. As a result, hosting ISPs are not relieved of the obligation under these conditions, which constitutes wrongful implementation of the Directive. | Liability of ISPs | Implementation of art. 12-15 of Directive 2000/31/EC on E-commerce in relation with the limitation of ISPs obligation to monitor the information they transmit or store. | The wrongful implementation of the Directive has the effect of holding ISPs, including platforms hosting e-commerce traders, liable for the content and transactions conducted on their platforms.<br><br>This extended liability of Greek ISPs/platforms, which has been inadvertentlyintroduced in the Greek Law, creates legal uncertainty, and regulatory and compliance cost for e-commerce providers. | Align the PD with the Directive it implements by correcting the references in the text of Article 14 of the Presidential Decree to point to Articles 11, 12 and 13 instead of Articles 10, 11 and 12. | Ministry of Finance;<br>Ministry of Economy, Development and Tourism;<br>Ministry of Justice, Transparency and Human Rights;<br>Ministry of Infrastructure, Transport and Networks |
| 2 | **Law 2251/1994 on Consumer Protection (Government Gazette A' 191/ 16.11.1994) as amended and in force** | Art.1 par.4; Art.3 rec.1; Art.4θ par.1δ; Art.9α rec.α | Consumer Protection | The definition of consumer is not consistent across the core law on Consumer protection. "Consumer" is defined either as *an individual or legal entity that is the intended and final recipient of products and services (Art.1 par.4)*; or *as an individual acting for purposes that are wholly or mainly outside that individual's trade, business, craft or profession (Art.3 rec.1; Art.4θ par.1δ; Art.9α rec.α)*. | Definition of Consumer | Gradual implementation of various EU Directives on Consumer protection within the same law; widening of the consumer definition in relation with specific areas of consumer protection. | The lack of a uniform definition of consumer: (a) creates legal uncertainty concerning rights and obligations of consumers and suppliers and has to be examined on a case-by-case basis; (b) prevents e-commerce providers from applying automated processes in drafting the terms and conditions of use, offering standardised contracts etc.; (c) leads to regulatory and compliance costs for e-commerce providers.<br><br>In addition, the lack of clarity weakens the effectiveness of consumer protection law and burdens the enforcement system with the task of clarifying definitions on a case-by-case basis. | Adopt a uniform definition of consumer applicable across Law 2251/1994 on Consumer Protection. This should be done in the context of a broader review of and consultation on the law, given that Consumer Protection legislation is horizontal and applies beyond e-commerce. | Ministry of Economy, Development and Tourism;<br>Ministry of Justice, Transparency and Human Rights |
| 3 | **Law 2251/1994 on Consumer Protection (Government Gazette A' 191/ 16.11.1994) as amended and in force; in conjunction with the Civil Code** | Art.5 (Law 2251/ 1994); Art.534-561 (Civil Code) | Consumer Protection | Directive 1999/44/EC: (a) provides a common legal framework for legal guarantees, i.e. the legal protection of consumers if goods are faulty or do not meet the advertised standards, by requiring Member States to offer consumers a minimum level of protection; and (b) harmonises, to a lesser extent, the legal framework for commercial guarantees, i.e. additional optional warranties offered by the producer or the importer or the seller etc.<br><br>The provisions in the Directive provide for extended rights of consumers vis-à-vis sellers (repair, replacement, reduction in price etc.) in cases of non-conformity of goods with contract or advertisement by rendering the provision of legal guarantees compulsory for sellers. In contrast, the commercial guarantee is generally offered voluntarily by the guarantor (manufacturer, producer, seller etc.).<br><br>The provisions in the Directive have been transposed into Greek law in the form of amendments both to (existing) articles of the Greek Civil Code, to cover legal guarantee rights - thus applying not only to consumer goods, but also to all movable (and immovable) goods; and to Law 2251/1994 on Consumer protection, to cover commercial guarantee rights. Greek legislation has not used the discretion allowed by Art. 7, par. 2, to provide for shorter legal guarantees on second-hand goods. | Legal and Commercial guarantees | Dual implementation of Directive 1999/44/EC within the core law on Consumer protection and the Civil Code; ensuring additional protection to consumers. | The fragmentation of provisions on guarantees which are scattered in Consumer protection legislation and the Civil Code: (a) creates legal uncertainty concerning rights and obligations of consumers and suppliers; (b) prevents e-commerce providers from providing clear communications and applying automated processes in relation with legal and commercial guarantees; and (c) leads to regulatory and compliance costs for e-commerce providers.<br><br>Moreover, the implementation of the legal guarantee in the Civil Code has the – unintended – consequence that said provisions are applicable not only to business to consumer ("B2C") transactions, but also on transactions between businesses ("B2B) and consumers ("C2C"). This results in a potential barrier to C2C sales of goods on e-commerce platforms, including second-hand goods, which is the main platform for such transactions.<br><br>This ambiguity, together with the complex legal framework, results in unclear communication regarding commercial and legal guarantees, according to the competent authorities and consumer protection associations. In the end, consumers are ill informed, thus consumer confidence is not boosted and the objective of the legislator - for e-commerce, in particular - is not achieved. | A. Clarify the definitions and distinction between legal and commercial guarantees; define the rights of consumers connected to each of the above in Law 2251/1994; use the option provided for in Article 7 of Directive 1999/44/EC to consider a shorter duration of the legal guarantee for second-hand goods. This should be done in the context of a broader review of and consultation on the law, given that Consumer Protection legislation is horizontal and applies beyond e-commerce.<br><br>B. Launch a review of the Civil Code provisions taking into consideration the specificities of C2C and B2B transactions and the relevant legislative developments at EU level. | Ministry of Economy, Development and Tourism;<br>Ministry of Justice, Transparency and Human Rights |

## Sector: E-commerce

| No | No and title of Regulation | Article | Thematic category | Brief description of the potential obstacle | Keyword | Policy maker's objectives | Harm to competition | Recommendations | Competent Ministry / Authority |
|---|---|---|---|---|---|---|---|---|---|
| 4 | **Law 2251/1994 on Consumer Protection (Government Gazette A' 191/ 16.11.1994) as amended and in force** | Art.5 par.1 | Consumer Protection | This provision setting rights and obligations connected to commercial guarantees includes a definition of "supplier" as *the manufacturer and/or importer and/or any person purporting to be a producer by placing his name, trademark or other distinctive sign on the consumer goods.*<br><br>This definition is in conflict with other definitions in the same law (Art.1 par.4), that treat suppliers as *the legal entity or individual that supplies goods or services to the consumer, acting within his business or profession*.<br><br>Further, it is different from the definitions found in Directive 1999/44/EC which distinguishes between a producer and a seller (Art.1) and clearly links legal guarantees to sellers and commercial guarantees only to the entity that offers them (sellers and/or producers). | Commercial guarantee - Supplier definition | Discretionary implementation of Directive 1999/44/EC by virtue of an amendment of the core law on Consumer protection; ensuring additional protection to consumers by extending the circle of persons who should provide commercial guarantees. | The lack of a uniform definition of supplier creates legal uncertainty and confusion; leads to regulatory and compliance costs for e-commerce providers; and does not allow automated processes to be easily employed. | Adopt a uniform definition of supplier applicable across Law 2251/1994 on Consumer Protection and clarify the definitions of producer and seller in line with Directive 1999/44/EC. This should be done in the context of a broader review of and consultation on the law, given that Consumer Protection legislation is horizontal and applies beyond e-commerce. | Ministry of Economy, Development and Tourism;<br>Ministry of Justice, Transparency and Human Rights |
| 5 | **Law 2251/1994 on Consumer Protection (Government Gazette A' 191/ 16.11.1994) as amended and in force** | Art.5 par.4 | Consumer Protection | A commercial guarantee offered by the "*supplier*" is compulsory for "*durable*" products – and should be made available in writing, in Greek. This obligation is an additional requirement introduced in national legislation not provided in the corresponding Art.6 of Directive 1999/44/EC, which only requires that such guarantees, when voluntarily provided by specific offerers, be communicated to consumers under specific conditions. | Commercial guarantee - Durable products | Discretionary implementation of Directive 1999/44/EC in relation with commercial guarantees; ensuring additional protection to consumers in relation with durable products. | The obligations placed on Greek e-commerce providers in relation to commercial guarantees are more burdensome than intended in Directive 1999/44/EC. The provision sets the obligation of suppliers (as widely defined above and in practice including e-commerce providers, according to the Ministry) to provide a compulsory commercial guarantee for durable products. Said obligation is binding not only for the offerer of the commercial guarantee as foreseen by the Directive, but also to any final local supplier/ importer notwithstanding the fact that the original manufacturer might have not provided such guarantee. Local e-commerce providers need to bear the cost of the commercial guarantees (over and above what is offered by the original manufacturer/ supplier).<br><br>To the extent that similar requirements are not imposed on competitors abroad, there is the also potential for those requirements to hinder the ability of local providers to compete effectively. | Abolish compulsory commercial guarantee of durable products. The recommendation should be read in conjunction with the recommendation on clarifying legal guarantees in row 3. This should be done in the context of a broader review of and consultation on the law, given that Consumer Protection legislation is horizontal and applies beyond e-commerce. | Ministry of Economy, Development and Tourism;<br>Ministry of Justice, Transparency and Human Rights |
| 6 | **Law 2251/1994 on Consumer Protection (Government Gazette A' 191/ 16.11.1994) as amended and in force** | Art.5 par.4 rec.5 | Consumer Protection | "*Suppliers*" (according to the broad definition of the law) are required to offer a guarantee of such a duration that is reasonable and proportional to the expected life cycle of the product, irrespective of the guarantees given by the manufacturer. | Commercial guarantee - Duration | Discretionary implementation of Directive 1999/44/EC in relation with commercial guarantees; ensuring longer protection to consumers linked to commercial guarantees. | The obligations placed on Greek suppliers (as widely defined above and in practice including e-commerce providers according to the Ministry) on the duration of the commercial guarantee are more burdensome than intended in Directive 1999/44/EC. Local e-commerce providers need to bear the cost of the commercial guarantees (over and above what is offered by the original manufacturer/ supplier).<br><br>To the extent that similar requirements are not imposed on competitors abroad, there is the also potential for those requirements to hinder the ability of local providers to compete effectively. | Impose obligations linked to commercial guarantees only to the *offerer*, in line with the Directive. The recommendation should be read in conjunction with the recommendation on clarifying legal guarantees in row 3. This should be done in the context of a broader review of and consultation on the law, given that Consumer Protection legislation is horizontal and applies beyond e-commerce. | Ministry of Economy, Development and Tourism;<br>Ministry of Justice, Transparency and Human Rights |
| 7 | **Law 2251/1994 on Consumer Protection (Government Gazette A' 191/ 16.11.1994) as amended and in force** | Art.5 par.3 sub. par 3 | Consumer Protection | The provision requires that final "suppliers" repair, at their own cost, the product while it is covered by a commercial guarantee. This requirement applies even in cases where the manufacturer and/or producer does not offer such a guarantee . | Commercial guarantee - Repair | Discretionary implementation of Directive 1999/44/EC in relation with commercial guarantees; ensuring additional protection to consumers linked to commercial guarantees. | The obligations placed on Greek suppliers (as widely defined above and in practice including e-commerce providers according to the Ministry) on repairs are more burdensome than intended in Directive 1999/44/EC. Local e-commerce providers need to bear the cost of the commercial guarantees (over and above what is offered by the original manufacturer/ supplier).<br><br>To the extent that similar requirements are not imposed on competitors abroad, there is the also potential for those requirements to hinder the ability of local providers to compete effectively. | Impose obligations linked to commercial guarantees only to the *offerer*, in line with the Directive. The recommendation should be read in conjunction with the recommendation on clarifying legal guarantees in row 3. This should be done in the context of a broader review of and consultation on the law, given that Consumer Protection legislation is horizontal and applies beyond e-commerce. | Ministry of Economy, Development and Tourism;<br>Ministry of Justice, Transparency and Human Rights |

## Sector: E-commerce

| No | No and title of Regulation | Article | Thematic category | Brief description of the potential obstacle | Keyword | Policy maker's objectives | Harm to competition | Recommendations | Competent Ministry / Authority |
|---|---|---|---|---|---|---|---|---|---|
| 8 | **Ministerial Decision Z1-404/2001 (Government Gazette B' 827/ 28.06.2001) on Indication of products prices and adjustment of Greek law to Directive 1998/6/EC** | | Consumer Protection | Obsolete regulation: Ministerial Decision has been superseded by provisions in the Code on Marketing and Trading of Products and Services (ΔΙ.Ε.Π.Π.Υ.). | Obsolete | Obsolete | Obsolete, inactive or redundant legislation can be a regulatory barrier by creating legal uncertainty; and potentially raises the operating costs facing suppliers, for example legal costs. | Explicitly repeal | Ministry of Economy, Development and Tourism;<br>Ministry of Justice, Transparency and Human Rights |
| 9 | **Joint Ministerial Decision Z1-178/2001 (Government Gazette B' 255/ 09.03.2001) on Card transactions and harmonisation with Recommendation 97/489/EC** | | Consumer Protection | Obsolete regulation: Joint Ministerial Decision has been largely abolished by Law 3862/2010. | Obsolete | Obsolete | Obsolete, inactive or redundant legislation can be a regulatory barrier by creating legal uncertainty; and potentially raises the operating costs facing suppliers, for example legal costs. | Explicitly repeal | Ministry of Economy, Development and Tourism;<br>Ministry of Justice, Transparency and Human Rights |
| 10 | **Joint Ministerial Decision Γ5β/Γ.Π.οικ.20293/2016 (Government Gazette B' 787/ 23.03.2016) Designating the competent Authority for the accreditation of electronic pharmacies** | Art.4 | Product-related legislation | The Joint Ministerial Decision designates the industry association, Panhellenic Pharmaceutical Association ("PPA"), as the competent body for issuing the common logo of EU Regulation 699/2014 for e-shops selling medicinal products. It is further stipulated that the application for the PPA to issue the logo can be submitted by pharmacists. | Pharmacies | Designation of the Panhellenic Pharmaceutical Association, as the competent body for issuing the common logo for electronic pharmacies. | Whilst it appears that the intention is to allow all persons responsible for the operation of online pharmacies to apply and obtain the common logo of EU Regulation 699/2014, the language is ambiguous and open to interpretation; thus potentially restricting access to the process and to online trading (as permitted by the law in force). | Clarify the wording of Art. 4 of Joint Ministerial Decision Γ5(β)/ Γ.Π. οικ. 20293/ 2016, as regards the persons entitled to submit the application for the common logo of EU Regulation 699/2014 for online pharmacies. | Ministry of Economy, Development and Tourism;<br>Ministry of Health |

## Sector: Construction

| No | No and title of Regulation | Article | Thematic category | Brief description of the potential obstacle | Keyword | Policy maker's objectives | Harm to competition | Recommendations | Competent Ministry / Authority |
|---|---|---|---|---|---|---|---|---|---|
| 1 | **Law 4412/2016 (A 147)** | Art.2 par.1(7) | Designs | The definition of designs referred in the draft law, even though indicatively, to designs of works by civil engineers and not other types of engineers. Following OECD comments, the provision was amended in the voted law so that it does not refer any longer to civil engineers specifically. | Definitions | The provision aims at defining public designs . | The provision, in its initial form, could inadvertently exclude other categories of engineers. The text was amended following OECD comments. | The OECD has already commented on the draft law. No recommendation. | Ministry of Infrastructure, Transport and Networks; Ministry of Economy, Development and Tourism and Ministry of Health |
| 2 | **Law 4412/2016 (A 147)** | Art.2 par.3(15) | Designs | Categories of designs determined in the Annex of the law and related to CPV codes of the Directive 2014/24/EU might be re-determined on the basis of an MD. | Registries | There is no specific reference in the Official Recital of the Law. However, following communication with Ministry of Infrastructure and Ministry of Development it is our understanding that the provision aims at defining categories of public designs falling under the scope of the Directive and described at the CPV codes in the Annex of the 2014/24/EU Directive on Public procurement. | The categories of designers defined by the national legislation, including the forthcoming MD, should not be more restrictive than the list provided in the Directive 2014/24/EU. | The OECD has already commented on the draft law. No recommendation. | Ministry of Infrastructure, Transport and Networks; Ministry of Economy, Development and Tourism and Ministry of Health |
| 3 | **Law 4412/2016 (A 147)** | Art.22 par.1(γ) | Public works and designs | Contracting authorities are not obliged to use ESIDIS when its use would require special office equipment not provided generally to contracting authorities. | Tendering process | According to the Official Recital of EU Directive 2014/24/EU, in case special office equipment is necessary for the use of e - procurement, contracting authorities should not be obliged to use electronic means in tendering procedures. According to our understanding this provision was the result of a mutual agreement between member states until the gradual and broad application of e - procurement. | The EU Directive allows Member States to provide for exceptions to the use of e - procurement. In the spirit of the Directive, PC s / latest software programmes would not be considered as special equipment. We understand that customisation / interoperability are required for the existing platform to support public works and designs. | The OECD has already commented on the draft law. Guidelines should be issued to clarify the equipment in question and ensure that the provision does not restrict the broad implementation of e-procurement. | Ministry of Infrastructure, Transport and Networks; Ministry of Economy, Development and Tourism and Ministry of Health |
| 4 | **Law 4412/2016 (A 147)** | Art.45 par.3(ζ), par.4 par.5 | Public works and designs | Copy of the contract is kept for public contracts exceeding certain thresholds. The file of the procurement contract is also kept in an electronic database. The operation of the abovementioned database will be described in a future MD. | Monitoring | According to the official Recital of EU Directive 2014/24/EU, contracting authorities are obliged to keep records in the form of "file of the contract" in order to improve and ensure monitoring of the related tendering procedures and contracts. | According to par. 2 Art. 84 of the EU Directive, contracting authorities should be able to provide documentation and ensure the monitoring of public procurement contracts. Article 44 transposes the abovementioned article of the Directive. In order to increase transparency and improve the monitoring and planning of public works and designs, an electronic system should be implemented also for the copies of public procurement contracts below the thresholds of subpar z par.2 of art. 44. Otherwise, the lack of interoperability will be limiting information circulation. | The OECD has already commented on the draft law. The authorities should consider how to keep all the information on each contract in a single integrated system or make it easily accessible through interoperable systems. Electronic archiving of consolidated data shall improve tendering procedures, supervision and further planning of public works. | Ministry of Infrastructure, Transport and Networks; Ministry of Economy, Development and Tourism and Ministry of Health |
| 5 | **Law 4412/2016 (A 147)** | Art.47 par.1 | Public works and designs | Consultation with the economic operators takes place electronically. The invitation is made available on ESIDIS or the electronic page of the contracting authority.<br>In the voted law, following OECD comments the provision has been amended so that the invitation is made available both on ESIDIS and the electronic page of the contracting authority. | Electronic system | According to the Official Recital of the Law the provision aims at enhancing publicity and broad participation to the consultation. | In order to ensure broader participation in the consultation, economic operators should be properly informed about the call for consultation. By not specifying ESIDIS as the platform where all calls for consultation are published, the initial version of the provision risked compromising information circulation and thus competition. The provision was amended following OECD comments. | The OECD has already commented on the draft law. No recommendation. | Ministry of Infrastructure, Transport and Networks; Ministry of Economy, Development and Tourism and Ministry of Health |
| 6 | **Law 4412/2016 (A 147)** | Art.49 par.2 subpar.β | Public works | Preliminary works are provided in order to ensure maturity and faster initiation of the main work. | Preliminary works | According to the Official Recital of the Law preliminary works aim at ensuring the procuring of mature works. In addition, following communication with Ministry of Infrastructure and Ministry of Development as well as the wording of sub. b par. 2 of Article 49 it is our understanding that the provision aims at dealing with the phenomenon of delays in the initiation or completion of works due to works that need to be completed (e.g. archaeological works) and licences that need to be acquired before. These delays, especially in the case of completion, may initiate proceedings for termination of contracts and indemnification of the contractor by the contracting authority leaving, as well, works uncompleted. More specifically the abovementioned provision has as follows: "In order to ensure maturity of works and faster and uninterrupted execution of works...". It is, therefore, to our understanding that the provision aims at the definition of works and licences which are separate in nature and time of the work procured and do not fall within the liability of the contractor under the procured work. | In order to ensure broader participation in the consultation, economic operators should be properly informed about the call for consultation. By not specifying ESIDIS as the platform where all calls for consultation are published, the initial version of the provision risked compromising information circulation and thus competition. The provision was amended following OECD comments. | The OECD has already commented on this provision. The authorities should issue guidelines to clarify the definition of preliminary works and ensure a consistent approach is followed by contracting authorities. | Ministry of Infrastructure, Transport and Networks; Ministry of Economy, Development and Tourism and Ministry of Health |
| 7 | **Law 4412/2016 (A 147)** | Art.54 par.8 | Public works | A Ministerial Decision can set out the technical specifications for public works.<br>Following OECD comments, in the recital of the voted law it is stated that contracting authorities should focus on namely on what is to be achieved, rather than how it is to be done. | Tendering process | According to the Official Recital of the Law the provision aims at describing standardised or common technical specifications for categories of public works in order to be included or to be used as guidance when drafting a tender for calls. | According to the OECD guidelines on fighting bid rigging in public procurement, contracting authorities should design tender specifications and terms of reference focusing on functional performance, namely on what is to be achieved, rather than how it is to be done, in order to attract to the tender the highest number of bidders.<br><br>While the provision does not appear restrictive per se, authorities should bear in mind the above principle when implementing it. | The OECD has already commented on the draft law. No recommendation. | Ministry of Infrastructure, Transport and Networks; Ministry of Economy, Development and Tourism and Ministry of Health |

## Sector: Construction

| No | No and title of Regulation | Article | Thematic category | Brief description of the potential obstacle | Keyword | Policy maker's objectives | Harm to competition | Recommendations | Competent Ministry / Authority |
|---|---|---|---|---|---|---|---|---|---|
| 8 | **Law 4412/2016 (A 147)** | Art.73 par.8 | Public works and designs | The decision on the exclusion of an economic operator from a procurement procedure proceeds as follows: (i) the contracting authority issues a draft decision and sends it to a committee for an opinion; (ii) the committee receives the draft decision; (iii) the committee submits its opinion to the contracting authority; (iv) the contracting authority issues the final decision. Based on this provision, the committee submits its opinion within 30 days from (ii). | Sanctions | According to the Official Recital of the Law the provision aims at defining a deadline in order for the economic operator to be able to exercise its rights for prejudicial / judicial protection. | The provision does not describe a clear timeline for the decision excluding economic operators from procurement procedures. This creates uncertainty for the economic operators. | The OECD has already commented on the draft law. No recommendation. | Ministry of Infrastructure, Transport and Networks; Ministry of Economy, Development and Tourism and Ministry of Health |
| 9 | **Law 4412/2016 (A 147)** | Art.74 par.6 | Public works and designs | The decision on the exclusion of an economic operator from the procurement procedure should be notified to some contracting authorities. An electronic catalogue of excluded economic operators is kept in a database by the SPPA. | Electronic system | There is no specific reference in the Official Recital of the Law. However, following communication with Ministry of Infrastructure and Ministry of Development it is our understanding that the provision aims at making directly available to contracting authorities consolidated information on the exclusion of economic operators from the procurement procedure and enhance monitoring of procurement procedures. | According to the OECD recommendation on public procurement, authorities should "employ recent digital technology developments that allow integrated e-procurement solutions covering the public procurement cycle. Information and communication technologies should be used in public procurement to ensure transparency and access to public tenders, increasing competition, simplifying processes for contract award and management, driving cost savings and integrating public procurement and public finance information."<br><br>By not consolidating the information on excluded operators together with all the information related to a given tender and by not making it electronically accessible to contracting authorities competition is constrained. | The OECD has already commented on the draft law. The authorities should consider how to keep all the information on each contract in a single integrated system or make it easily accessible through interoperable systems. Electronic archiving of consolidated data shall improve tendering procedures, supervision and further planning of public works. | Ministry of Infrastructure, Transport and Networks; Ministry of Economy, Development and Tourism and Ministry of Health |
| 10 | **Law 4412/2016 (A 147)** | Art.86 par.6 | Designs | The initial wording of the provision in the draft law allowed the contracting authority to make a decision solely based on price or cost in cases where the technical specifications are clear/ simple. The law pre-defined some of the categories. The Minister of Infrastructure, Transport and Networks could determine the categories of works considered as simple or small.<br>Following OECD comments, the new provision does not provide for such decision by the Minister. | Bid criteria | According to the Official Recital of the Law the provision aims at introducing the most advantageous offer based on price criterion in tenders for certain categories of designs based on the complexity of the technical solution. | The criterion of the most advantageous offer could improve the quality of designs and, for higher value contracts, could avoid the award of a contract without any technical evaluation of the offer. However, in its initial form the provision was quite vague and may lead to differential treatment of similar works. | The OECD has already commented on the draft law. Guidelines should be issued to ensure uniform application of the provision by the contracting authorities. | Ministry of Infrastructure, Transport and Networks; Ministry of Economy, Development and Tourism and Ministry of Health |
| 11 | **Law 4412/2016 (A 147)** | Art.106 par.2(ε) | Public works and designs | The contracting authority may annul the tendering procedure in case the offer of the economic operator is not considered satisfactory.<br>Following OECD comments, the provision was amended in the voted law to include the word 'after specific justification'. | Tendering process | According to the Official Recital of the Law and following communication with Ministry of Infrastructure it is our understanding that the provision aims at leaving to the contracting authority the discretion to annul a tender in case an offer is not justifiably considered satisfactory. The provision reflects the superseding position of the contracting authority reserved for the latter and reflected in the overall philosophy of procurement procedures. | In the provision, the reasons why the contracting authority may require the annulment of the procedure remains vague and unclear. This could result in differential treatment of economic operators. The text was clarified following OECD comments. | The OECD has already commented on the draft law. No recommendation. | Ministry of Infrastructure, Transport and Networks; Ministry of Economy, Development and Tourism and Ministry of Health |
| 12 | **Law 4412/2016 (A 147)** | Art.136 par.7 | Public works and designs | The initial wording of the provision in the draft law was that the designer would participate as a technical advisor in the execution of the work.<br>Following OECD comments, in the new law the provision makes a specific reference to Article 144 describing the liability of the designer. | Monitoring | There is no specific reference in the Official Recital of the Law. However, following communication with Ministry of Infrastructure and Ministry of Development it is our understanding that the provision aims at ensuring and enhancing the efficient execution of the design, the completion of works according to said design and the effective monitoring of related works. | The provision in its initial form was unclear as to the liability of the designer -especially with regards to the timeline- in cases where a modification was needed. Clarifying the time limits of their responsibilities after the delivery of their designs provides bidders with incentives to submit truthful offers. In addition, legal uncertainty could reduce participation. | The OECD has already commented on the draft law. No recommendation. | Ministry of Infrastructure, Transport and Networks; Ministry of Economy, Development and Tourism and Ministry of Health |
| 13 | **Law 4412/2016 (A 147)** | Art.138 par.15 | Public works | The economic operator is obliged to send each trimester a report on the progress of works. | Electronic system | According to the Official Recital of the Law the provision aims at effective monitoring of works. | According to the OECD recommendation on public procurement, authorities should "employ recent digital technology developments that allow integrated e-procurement solutions covering the public procurement cycle. Information and communication technologies should be used in public procurement to ensure transparency and access to public tenders, increasing competition, simplifying processes for contract award and management, driving cost savings and integrating public procurement and public finance information."<br><br>The lack of an electronic monitoring of the progress could lead to inefficient execution of works and increase costs. | The OECD has already commented on the draft law. The authorities should consider how to keep all the information on each contract in a single integrated system or make it easily accessible through interoperable systems. | Ministry of Infrastructure, Transport and Networks; Ministry of Economy, Development and Tourism and Ministry of Health |

## Sector: Construction

| No | No and title of Regulation | Article | Thematic category | Brief description of the potential obstacle | Keyword | Policy maker's objectives | Harm to competition | Recommendations | Competent Ministry / Authority |
|---|---|---|---|---|---|---|---|---|---|
| 14 | **Law 4412/2016 (A 147)** | Art.143 | Public works and designs | The communication of the contracting authorities with the contractor is taking place via FAX, email, or by transmission of judicial and extrajudicial documents by a bailiff . | Electronic system | According to the Official Recital of the Law and following communication with Ministry of Infrastructure it is our understanding that the provision aims at providing methods for the swift and adequate communication of the contracting authority with the economic operator in order for the effective progress of works and the exercise of the latter's legal rights related to the contract. | According to the OECD recommendation on public procurement, authorities should "employ recent digital technology developments that allow integrated e-procurement solutions covering the public procurement cycle. Information and communication technologies should be used in public procurement to ensure transparency and access to public tenders, increasing competition, simplifying processes for contract award and management, driving cost savings and integrating public procurement and public finance information."<br><br>The lack of communication consolidation and electronic accessibility of all the information related to a given tender and the contracting authorities and contractors with all the information related to a given tender and made accessible electronically to contracting authorities. | The OECD has already commented on the draft law. The authorities should consider how to keep all the information on each contract in a single integrated system or make it easily accessible through interoperable systems. | Ministry of Infrastructure, Transport and Networks; Ministry of Economy, Development and Tourism and Ministry of Health |
| 15 | **Law 4412/2016 (A 147)** | Art.154 par.2 | Public works | The provision regulates emergency complementary works. In the draft law, the provision did not specify that the complementary works had to be 'unpredictable'.<br>Following OECD comments, this was made clear. | Definitions | According to the Official Recital of the Law the provision aims at defining and providing for complementary works which are considered urgent and unavoidable by reasonable care by the contracting authority, to be executed. | The provision on emergency complementary works should not be used to bypass the rules on complementary works. Following OECD comments, the definition of emergency complementary works was clarified. | The OECD has already commented on the draft law. No recommendation. | Ministry of Infrastructure, Transport and Networks; Ministry of Economy, Development and Tourism and Ministry of Health |
| 16 | **Law 4412/2016 (A 147)** | Art.52 par.7(ζ) and par.7(η) | Public works | The Minister approves common pricing for works according to their size and geographical area. Such pricing is binding for all contracting authorities. | Price lists | There is no Official Recital of the Draft Law. However, according to the Official Recital of codifying Law 3669/2008 and following communication with Ministry of Infrastructure and Ministry of Development it is our understanding that the provision aims at ensuring submission of credible offers. | According to the OECD guidelines for fighting bid rigging in public procurement, contracting authorities should use maximum reserve prices only if based on thorough market research and if officials are convinced they are competitive. In addition, the guidelines suggest that the reserve price should not be published but kept confidential. Predetermined price lists may facilitate co-ordination by acting as a focal points, i.e. bidders have an incentive to submit offers close to the maximum allowed. However, empirical evidence from Greek tenders indicates that this is not the case in practice. | Pricing for public works should be regularly updated. In addition, the issue of a Ministerial Decision may lead to delays and rigidities on the update of prices and the authorities should explore alternative means to set and publish prices. | Ministry of Infrastructure, Transport and Networks; Ministry of Economy, Development and Tourism and Ministry of Health |
| 17 | **Law 4412/2016 (A 147)** | Art.52 par.7(θ) | Public works | By provision of the call for tenders, the contracting authority may allow bidders to add 18% of their bid to allow for the general costs and profit for the specific contract. | Bid criteria | There is no specific reference in the Official Recital of the Law. However, according to the Official Recital of codifying Law 3669/2008 and following communication with the Ministry of Infrastructure it is our understanding that the provision sets a reasonable threshold for general costs and the contractor's profit in order for the contractor to execute only works of benefit to the work as well as to provide disincentive for the total redesign of works and for speculation. | It is not clear when the contracting authority can apply the 18% rate. | Provide guidance to the contracting authorities as to when it would be reasonable to add the 18% rate. | Ministry of Infrastructure, Transport and Networks; Ministry of Economy, Development and Tourism and Ministry of Health |
| 18 | **Law 4412/2016 (A 147)** | Art.52 par.8 (α - δα) | Designs | The provision provides to: (i) maximum unified price lists for designs; and (ii) a maximum rate of 15% of the budget for unforeseen expenses and technical services, which can be increased to 30% in cases where it is difficult to pre-determine the quantity of certain elements of the design. | Pricing | There is no specific reference in the Official Recital of the Law . However, according to the Official Recital of codifying Law 3669/2008 and following communication with Ministry of Infrastructure and Ministry of Development it is our understanding that the provision sets a reasonable threshold for unforeseen works in order for the contractor to execute only works of benefit to the work as well to provide disincentive for the total redesign of works and for speculation. | (i) According to the OECD guidelines for fighting bid rigging in public procurement, contracting authorities should use maximum reserve prices only if based on thorough market research and if officials are convinced they are competitive. In addition, the guidelines suggest that the reserve price should not be published but kept confidential. Predetermined price lists may facilitate co-ordination by acting as a focal points, i.e. bidders have an incentive to submit offers close to the maximum allowed. However, empirical evidence from Greek tenders indicates that this is not the case in practice. (ii) It increases the budget of the tender but does not appear to restrict competition among bidders. | (i) Pricing for designs should be regularly updated. In addition, the issue of a Ministerial Decision may lead to delays and rigidities on the update of prices and the authorities should explore alternative means to set and publish prices. (ii) No recommendation. | Ministry of Infrastructure, Transport and Networks; Ministry of Economy, Development and Tourism and Ministry of Health |
| 19 | **Law 4412/2016 (A 147)** | Art.76 | Public works | The pre-qualification of companies participating in a tendering process is based on the criteria used for their registration within the Registry of contractors. | Registries | According to the Official Recital of the Law, the Official Recital of codifying Law 3669/2008 and following communication with Ministry of Infrastructure and Ministry of Development it is our understanding that the provision aims at the classification of companies based on objective criteria and procedures at the level corresponding to their actual capabilities so as to avoid distortion of the market and in order to organise effectively the contractors' capacity. | Using registries as an obligatory mechanism of classification of operators can be restrictive. An operator may face lower direct and indirect (e.g. administration) costs by not participating in a registry – while still fulfilling the participation requirements. | The OECD recommends that class registration per se is not a requirement for participation in tenders, conditional that the operator can demonstrate fulfilling the same qualifications as those specified in the tender. | Ministry of Infrastructure, Transport and Networks; Ministry of Economy, Development and Tourism and Ministry of Health |

## Sector: Construction

| No | No and title of Regulation | Article | Thematic category | Brief description of the potential obstacle | Keyword | Policy maker's objectives | Harm to competition | Recommendations | Competent Ministry / Authority |
|---|---|---|---|---|---|---|---|---|---|
| 20 | **Law 4412/2016 (A 147)** | Art.76 par.1(ε) | Public works | Initial version of the provision in the draft law: When companies set up a consortium to participate in a tender, each company should participate in the consortium with a percentage that is no less than 25% of the estimated budget of the tender. If the tender includes more than one category of works, the aforementioned percentage is applicable to each category. Following OECD comments, in the final version in voted law the 25% requirement was removed. | Partnerships | According to the Official Recital of the Law, the Official Recital of codifying Law 3669/2008 and following communication with the Ministry of Infrastructure it is our understanding that the provision aims at ensuring substantial participation of the partners in the Joint Venture so that their participation according to their classification corresponds to their actual capabilities and avoid distortion of the market. | According to the OECD guidelines on fighting bid rigging in public procurement, contracting authorities should focus on what is to be achieved rather than how it is to be done. Bidders should be free to decide whether they set up partnership to bid and execute works. This OECD comment on the initial version of the law was incorporated in the final version of the article. | The OECD has already commented on this provision. No recommendation. | Ministry of Infrastructure, Transport and Networks; Ministry of Economy, Development and Tourism and Ministry of Health |
| 21 | **Law 4412/2016 (A 147)** | Art.76 par.2 | Public works | The call for tenders may determine that only a consortium of companies specialised in certain activities, or a partnership of technicians registered in the Registry of acquired experience may participate in the tendering process. | Partnerships | According to the Official Recital of the Law, the Official Recital of codifying Law 3669/2008 and following communication with the Ministry of Infrastructure it is our understanding that the provision aims at the participation of companies based on objective criteria and procedures at the level corresponding to their actual capabilities so as to avoid distortion of the market and in order to organise effectively contractors' capacity. | The provision grants discretion to contracting authorities to restrict potential participants from different registries. However, it is justified in light of the policy maker's objective. | No recommendation. | Ministry of Infrastructure, Transport and Networks; Ministry of Economy, Development and Tourism and Ministry of Health |
| 22 | **Law 4412/2016 (A 147)** | Art.95 par.2 | Public works | Submission of economic offer as a percentage discount on the price list for public works, as determined by contracting authorities. The discounts have to be submitted for each individual subgroup of works. The contracting authority will check that there are no sizeable differences between individual discounts. | Price lists | There is no specific reference in the official recital. According to the Official Recital of codifying Law 3669/2008, and following communication with the Ministry of Infrastructure, it is our understanding that the provision aims at addressing the phenomenon of abnormally low offers (excessive discounts). | A limit on the variation of the different discounts submitted by bidders restricts business strategies. For instance, a bidder might be able to offer a bigger discount in one category, but is prevented from doing so. The policy maker's objective could be achieved in alternative ways, including effective supervision, a well-functioning pricing system and ex-post mechanisms. | Given that the pricing system is being reviewed and that it may address the phenomenon of abnormally low offers, the need for this restriction should be assessed by the authorities. | Ministry of Infrastructure, Transport and Networks; Ministry of Economy, Development and Tourism and Ministry of Health |
| 23 | **Law 4412/2016 (A 147)** | Art.98 par.1(a) | Public works | All tendering processes are required to have their deadline set on a Tuesday. The new Law on Public Procurement increases the number of week days from one to two. | Tendering process | There is no specific reference as to the objective of the provision in the Official Recital of the Law. However, according to the Official Recital of codifying Law 3669/2008 and following communication with Ministry of Infrastructure and Ministry of Development it is our understanding that the provision aims at ensuring broader participation especially in islands where economic operators need to plan travelling in advance. Furthermore, since the opening of offers takes place on the same day of the last day of submission of offers, the provision aims at ensuring that the economic operators are able to be present to the relative procedure. | Bidders have an incentive to be present at the opening of all the offers. Given that offers are opened by the contracting authority upon the deadline of a tender, this means that bidders are likely to submit bids on the day of the deadline. This facilitates communication and deal-making among firms. | We understand that an electronic procurement system will be operational in April 2017. If this is not the case, the provision should be abolished. | Ministry of Infrastructure, Transport and Networks; Ministry of Economy, Development and Tourism and Ministry of Health |
| 24 | **Law 4412/2016 (A 147)** | Art.125 | Public works | In some cases, a tender is awarded following the submission of a single discount rate, instead of multiple discount rates. This case is as follows: approximate budget of up to EUR 60 000. | Price lists | There is no specific reference as to the objective of the provision in the Official Recital of the Law. However, according to the Official Recital of codifying Law 3669/2008 and following communication with Ministry of Infrastructure and Ministry of Development it is our understanding that for small (budget wise) works a single discount may be submitted so as to ensure flexibility and enhance broader participation. | According to the OECD guidelines for fighting bid rigging in public procurement, contracting authorities should use maximum reserve prices only if based on thorough market research and if officials are convinced they are very competitive. The provision has the intended objective of increasing participation through a simplified procedure and therefore it seems justified in light of the policy maker's objective. | No recommendation. | Ministry of Infrastructure, Transport and Networks; Ministry of Economy, Development and Tourism and Ministry of Health |
| 25 | **Law 4412/2016 (A 147)** | Art.126 | Public works | For some types of works, bids are based on a profit rate and general costs. The maximum profit rate bidders are allowed is set at 18%. | Bid criteria | There is no specific reference as to the objective of the provision in the Official Recital of the Law. However, according to the Official Recital of codifying Law 3669/2008 and following communication with Ministry of Infrastructure and Ministry of Development it is our understanding that the provision sets a reasonable threshold for unforeseen works in order for the contractor to execute only works of benefit to the work as well to provide disincentive for the total redesign of works and for speculation. | Setting a maximum rate can provide bidders with a focal point and result in higher bids. However, given the nature of works included in the scope of the provision (research, archaeological works) and the maximum budget allowed, this provision allows contracting authorities the necessary flexibility. | No recommendation. | Ministry of Infrastructure, Transport and Networks; Ministry of Economy, Development and Tourism and Ministry of Health |
| 26 | **Law 4412/2016 (A 147)** | Art.128 | Public works | The initial wording of the provision was that the award of a contract to a technical advisor or a special expert could be assigned by negotiated procedure without prior publication. Following OECD comments the provision was amended in the voted law so that it does include the publication to the contracting authority' s website. | Tendering process | There is no specific reference as to the objective of the provision in the Official Recital of the Law. However, according to the Official Recital of codifying Law 3669/2008 and following communication with Ministry of Infrastructure and Ministry of Development it is our understanding that the provision aims at the execution of works without delays and at the maintenance of flexibility in the award of contract to a technical advisor, necessary for the completion of works, in the exceptional case of technical uniqueness. | The provision in its initial form could inadvertently exclude categories of participants. The text was amended following OECD comments. | The OECD has already commented on the draft law. No recommendation. | Ministry of Infrastructure, Transport and Networks; Ministry of Economy, Development and Tourism and Ministry of Health |
| 27 | **Law 4412/2016 (A 147)** | Art.138 par.8 | Public works | According to the initial wording of the provision in certain cases, the contracting authority could impose an obligation for additional personnel on the contracting company, after the contract award. Following OECD comments, the provision was amended in the voted law so that the obligation was already described in the call for tenders. | Personnel | There is no specific reference in the Official Recital of the Law. However, according to the Official Recital of codifying Law 3669/2008 and following communication with Ministry of Infrastructure and Ministry of Development it is our understanding that the provision aims at encountering the phenomenon of excessively low offers (excessive discounts). Furthermore, since said provision is included in the tender for calls, it aims at ensuring the effective organisation of the contractor's capacity and execution of works and overall the submission of credible offers corresponding to the contractor's actual capabilities so as to avoid distortion of the market. | The provision in its initial form provided for the contracting authority to have the option to modify the staffing decisions of the contractor. According to the OECD guidelines on fighting bid rigging in public procurement, contracting authorities should define their requirements as clearly as possible in the tender. In addition, the guidelines suggest focusing on what is to be achieved rather than how it is to be done. The text was amended following OECD comments. | The OECD has already commented on the draft law. No recommendation. | Ministry of Infrastructure, Transport and Networks; Ministry of Economy, Development and Tourism and Ministry of Health |

## Sector: Construction

| No | No and title of Regulation | Article | Thematic category | Brief description of the potential obstacle | Keyword | Policy maker's objectives | Harm to competition | Recommendations | Competent Ministry / Authority |
|---|---|---|---|---|---|---|---|---|---|
| 28 | **Law 4412/2016 (A 147)** | Art.139 | Public works | Minimum requirements for a number of staff employed by the contracting company are subject to change following a decision by the contracting authority, if that is provided for in the call for tenders. Proof that said requirements are satisfied by the contracting company is provided in the form of a certificate. The satisfaction of said minimum requirements is proved by a certificate of payment of social security contributions. | Personnel | There is no specific reference in the new Official Recital of the new Law. However, according to the Official Recital of codifying Law 3669/2008 and following communication with Ministry of Infrastructure and Ministry of Development it is our understanding that the provision aims at encountering the phenomenon of excessively low offers (excessive discounts). Furthermore, since said provision is included in the tender for calls, it aims at ensuring the effective organisation of the contractor's capacity and execution of works and overall the submission of credible offers corresponding to the contractor's actual capabilities so as to avoid distortion of the market. | The provision sets minimum requirements for the participation in a tender. However, it seems justified in light of the policy maker's objective. | No recommendation. | Ministry of Infrastructure, Transport and Networks; Ministry of Economy, Development and Tourism and Ministry of Health |
| 29 | **Law 4412/2016 (A 147)** | Art.144 par.2 | Designs | When the design is considered more than 60% flawed the designer is declared to be revoked and the work is not executed upon his design. In those cases it is the responsibility of the contractor to select a new qualified designer. | Tendering process | There is no specific reference in the Official Recital of the new Law. However, according to the Official Recital of codifying Law 3669/2008 and following communication with Ministry of Infrastructure and Ministry of Development it is our understanding that the provision aims at ensuring the execution of works without delays in case there is a time gap between the initiation of works and the delivery of the design or in cases where during the process of execution of works the design needs amendments. | The provision can be used to award a design contract directly instead of resorting to a more open procedure. However, following communication with the Ministry it is our understanding that the establishment and operation of the technical board combined with the need for flexibility and completion of works seems to ensure transparency and due process. | No recommendation. | Ministry of Infrastructure, Transport and Networks; Ministry of Economy, Development and Tourism and Ministry of Health |
| 30 | **Law 4412/2016 (A 147)** | Art.145 | Public works | The provisions on execution and supervision of works do not make reference to an electronic system. | Electronic system | There is no specific reference as to the objective of the provision in the Official Recital of the Law. However, according to the Official Recital of codifying Law 3669/2008 and following communication with Ministry of Infrastructure and Ministry of Development it is our understanding that the provision aims at monitoring of works. | According to the OECD recommendation on public procurement, authorities should "employ recent digital technology developments that allow integrated e-procurement solutions covering the public procurement cycle. Information and communication technologies should be used in public procurement to ensure transparency and access to public tenders, increasing competition, simplifying processes for contract award and management, driving cost savings and integrating public procurement and public finance information." The lack of an electronic system supporting record keeping, invoicing, claims etc. can constrain information dissemination, efficiency and competition. | OECD has already commented on the draft law. The authorities should facilitate access and monitoring of all information related to the evolution of a given tender. Electronic archiving of consolidated data shall improve tendering procedures, supervision and further planning of public works. | Ministry of Infrastructure, Transport and Networks; Ministry of Economy, Development and Tourism and Ministry of Health |
| 31 | **Law 4412/2016 (A 147)** | Art.146 par.4 | Public works | The provision requires contractors to maintain a diary for the execution of works. The article does not mention any obligatory, or even optional, electronic maintenance of this service. | Electronic system | There is no specific reference as to the objective of the provision in the Official Recital of the Law. However, according to the Official Recital of codifying Law 3669/2008 and following communication with Ministry of Infrastructure and Ministry of Development it is our understanding that the provision aims at following the daily progress of works and enhance monitoring. | According to the OECD recommendation on public procurement, authorities should "employ recent digital technology developments that allow integrated e-procurement solutions covering the public procurement cycle. Information and communication technologies should be used in public procurement to ensure transparency and access to public tenders, increasing competition, simplifying processes for contract award and management, driving cost savings and integrating public procurement and public finance information."<br><br>By not consolidating the information on excluded operators together with all the information related to a given tender and by not making it electronically accessible to contracting authorities competition is constrained. | OECD has already commented on the draft law. The authorities should facilitate access and monitoring of all information related to the evolution of a given tender. Electronic archiving of consolidated data shall improve tendering procedures, supervision and further planning of public works. | Ministry of Infrastructure, Transport and Networks; Ministry of Economy, Development and Tourism and Ministry of Health |
| 32 | **Law 4412/2016 (A 147)** | Art.151 | Public works | Measurement of works that have been carried out is compiled jointly by the contractor and the supervisor. | Supervision | There is no specific reference as to the objective of the provision in the Official Recital of the Law. However, according to the Official Recital of codifying Law 3669/2008 and following communication with Ministry of Infrastructure and Ministry of Development it is our understanding that the provision aims at verifying in situ with the presence of the contractor of the execution and measurement of works by a supervisor competent for supervision of relative works. | According to the OECD recommendation on public procurement, authorities should "employ recent digital technology developments that allow integrated e-procurement solutions covering the public procurement cycle. Information and communication technologies should be used in public procurement to ensure transparency and access to public tenders, increasing competition, simplifying processes for contract award and management, driving cost savings and integrating public procurement and public finance information."<br><br>By not consolidating the information on excluded operators together with all the information related to a given tender and by not making it electronically accessible to contracting authorities competition is constrained. | OECD has already commented on the draft law. The authorities should facilitate access and monitoring of all information related to the evolution of a given tender. Electronic archiving of consolidated data shall improve tendering procedures, supervision and further planning of public works. | Ministry of Infrastructure, Transport and Networks; Ministry of Economy, Development and Tourism and Ministry of Health |
| 33 | **Law 4412/2016 (A 147)** | Art.154 par.2 | Public works | In the tenders according to Art. 125, contracting authorities can define the number and type of staff, equipment and materials; and approve the wage ceilings per specialisation and set differential wage ceilings based on performance. | Tendering process | There is no specific reference as to the objective of the provision in the Official Recital of the Law. However, according to the Official Recital of codifying Law 3669/2008 and following communication with Ministry of Infrastructure and Ministry of Development it is our understanding that the provision aims at ensuring the effective execution of works. | The provision is restrictive as it constraints firms' strategies. However, it is deemed proportionate to the policy maker's objective as a cost-monitoring mechanism. | No recommendation. | Ministry of Infrastructure, Transport and Networks; Ministry of Economy, Development and Tourism and Ministry of Health |

## Sector: Construction

| No | No and title of Regulation | Article | Thematic category | Brief description of the potential obstacle | Keyword | Policy maker's objectives | Harm to competition | Recommendations | Competent Ministry / Authority |
|---|---|---|---|---|---|---|---|---|---|
| 34 | **Law 4412/2016 (A 147)** | Art.166 par.1 | Public works | The initial version of the provision in the draft law provided for works with a budget above EU legislation thresholds, the contracting authority could require that bidders assign up to 30% of the total value of the works to subcontractors.<br>Following OECD comments, the new law does not contains such provision. | Subcontracting | There is no specific reference in the Official Recital of the Law. However, according to the Official Recital of codifying Law 3669/2008 and following communication with Ministry of Infrastructure and Ministry of Development it is our understanding that the provision aimed at ensuring that liability for the execution of the work remains with the contractor while ensuring effective execution of works and effective organisation of contractor's capacity. | This provision transposes Article 60 of Directive 2004/18/EC. Directive 2014/24/EC, replacing the 2004 Directive, contains no such restriction. As it stands, the provision grants to the contracting authority the competence to request that up to 30% of the value of the agreement be subcontracted. This may discriminate against economic operators that have the capabilities to provide the service or perform the work themselves. The text was amended following OECD comments. | The OECD has already commented on the draft law. No recommendation. | Ministry of Infrastructure, Transport and Networks; Ministry of Economy, Development and Tourism and Ministry of Health |
| 35 | **Law 4412/2016 (A 147)** | Still in force pursuant to Art.377 par.1(40) | Designs | Registration of an individual in the Registry of Designers and Design Offices is prohibited when the same individual is registered in the Registry of Acquired Experience (MEK). ) or employed by a company registered in MEEP[Art. 39 par. 2 of Law 3316/2005] | Registries | There is no specific reference in the Official Recital of the Law. However, following communication with the Ministry it is our understanding that the provision aims at defining cases where conflict of interest or of moral hazard would arise. | The provision could be restrictive. Not allowing engineers to register contemporaneously in both the Registry of Acquired Experience and the Registry of Designers and Design Offices makes switching more difficult (or costly) and decreases the flexibility individuals enjoy in building their specialisation and experience. | The OECD recommends that individuals are able to register contemporaneously in the Registry of Acquired Experience (M.E.K.) and the Registry of Designers. and Design Offices (MM). | Ministry of Infrastructure, Transport and Networks; Ministry of Economy, Development and Tourism and Ministry of Health |
| 36 | **Law 4412/2016 (A 147)** | Still in force pursuant to Art, 377 par. 1 (40) | Designs | Designing companies are prohibited from being affiliated with or being controlled - in any form - by companies registered in the Registry of Contractors (MEEP), Also from having as their scope non - design activities such as the execution of public works [Art. 39 par. 3 a and b subsection 2 of Law 3316/2005] | Registries | There is no specific reference in the Official Recital of the Law. However, following communication with the Ministry it is our understanding that the provision aims at defining cases where conflict of interest or of moral hazard would arise. | The provision could be restrictive. Allowing firms to engage in both the design and construction of public works may increase participation in both segments. Moreover, work execution and design may have important complementarities: experience in either activity can contribute towards a better end product. Prohibiting dual registration in the respective Registries could negate these potential benefits. Furthermore, not allowing participation in both markets can also restrict a firms' capacity to develop economies of scale and scope. However, given the possibility of problems phased in the monitoring of works the OECD understands that in order to avoid moral hazard and conflict of interest problems, economic operators should not be in any case able to bid for the design and execution of the same work – unless specified in the call for tenders. | The OECD recommends that companies engaging in the construction or design of public works should be allowed to register in the both Registries.<br>However, in order to avoid potential moral hazard and conflicts of interest, economic operators should not be allowed to bid (either directly or indirectly, relying on sub-contraction or lent experience) for the construction of a project that they have designed – unless explicitly provided for in the call for tenders. | Ministry of Infrastructure, Transport and Networks; Ministry of Economy, Development and Tourism and Ministry of Health |
| 37 | **Law 4412/2016 (A 147)** | Still in force pursuant to Art.377 par.1(40) | Designs | Registration in the Designers' Registry is done at the request of the person concerned. Individuals are classified in categories; and classes within each category. Designers may register in one or two categories, on the basis of their specialised scientific and technical knowledge, evidenced by their degree and field of study and their experience. They are also assigned a class within each category based on the field of study, experience in preparing public and private projects, experience in supervising design studies, and years since obtaining the relevant degree.<br>[Art.39, par.4 of Law 3316/2005] | Registries | There is no specific reference in the Official Recital of the Law. However, according to the Official Recital of codifying Law 3669/2008 and following communication with Ministry of Infrastructure and Ministry of Development it is our understanding that the provision aims at the classification of companies based on objective criteria and procedures at the level corresponding to their actual capabilities so as to avoid distortion of the market and in order to organise effectively the contractors' capacity. | The provision could be problematic as it does not seem to match the designers' professional rights to their ability to subscribe for 2/28 design categories. It is our understanding that designers -according to their University degree - could participate to more categories than this provision allows. This restricts entry and hence lowers competition within each designers' category. | OECD recommends that the number of categories in which designers may be registered should increase taking into account their professional rights. | Ministry of Infrastructure, Transport and Networks; Ministry of Economy, Development and Tourism and Ministry of Health |
| 38 | **Law 4412/2016 (A 147)** | Still in force pursuant to Art.377 par.1(40) | Designs | A company's classification within the Registry is dependent on the classification of the licensed designers who are either shareholders or permanent employees of the company. Said designers need to commit their 'degree' to the company; each designer can only commit/ register his degree with one designer company.<br>*[Art.39, par.4 of Law 3316/2005]* | Registries | There is no specific reference in the Official Recital of the Law. However, according to the Official Recital of codifying Law 3669/2008 and following communication with Ministry of Infrastructure and Ministry of Development it is our understanding that the provision aims at the classification of companies based on objective criteria corresponding to their actual capabilities. | The provision is linked to the system of registries. Segmenting the market into different categories could potentially limit competition. However, the framework is designed to ensure appropriate execution based on specialised professional knowledge. Therefore, the system in deemed proportionate. | No recommendation. | Ministry of Infrastructure, Transport and Networks; Ministry of Economy, Development and Tourism and Ministry of Health |
| 39 | **Law 4412/2016 (A 147)** | Still in force pursuant to Art.377 par.1(31) | Public works | Companies are allowed to participate in a tendering process only if they are registered in the Registry of contractors. Foreign companies may participate in a tendering process if an international tender takes place.<br>*[Art.80 par.1, Art.80 par.2 subpar.2, Art.80 par.4 of Law 3669/2008]* | Registries | Using registries as an obligatory mechanism of classification of operators can be restrictive. An operator may face lower direct and indirect (e.g. administration) costs by not participating in a registry – while still fulfilling the participation requirements. | Using registries as an obligatory mechanism of classification of operators can be restrictive. An operator may face lower direct and indirect (e.g. administration) costs by not participating in a registry – while still fulfilling the participation requirements. | The OECD recommends that class registration per se is not a requirement for participation in tenders, conditional that the operator can demonstrate fulfilling the same qualifications as those specified in the tender. | Ministry of Infrastructure, Transport and Networks; Ministry of Economy, Development and Tourism and Ministry of Health |

## Sector: Construction

| No | No and title of Regulation | Article | Thematic category | Brief description of the potential obstacle | Keyword | Policy maker's objectives | Harm to competition | Recommendations | Competent Ministry / Authority |
|---|---|---|---|---|---|---|---|---|---|
| 40 | **Law 4412/2016 (A 147)** | Still in force pursuant to Art.380 par.1(31) | Public works | If the body responsible to impose disciplinary sanctions does not issue its decision on an infringement within 18 months, the infringement lapses. The infringement may still be taken into account in disciplinary proceedings for another infringement that took place before the time when the limitation period of the former lapsed. [*Art.84 par.2, Art.84 par.3 of Law 3669/2008*] | Sanctions | There is no specific reference in the Official Recital of the Law. However, according to the Official Recital of codifying Law 3669/2008 and following communication with Ministry of Infrastructure and Ministry of Development it is our understanding that the provision aims at avoiding delays in the completion of works due to administrative delays and ensuring broad participation . | Legal uncertainty stemming from the discretion to take into account an infringement that has lapsed. | Abolish the provision allowing for a previous lapsed alleged infringement to be taken into consideration in future disciplinary proceedings. | Ministry of Infrastructure, Transport and Networks; Ministry of Economy, Development and Tourism and Ministry of Health |
| 41 | **Law 4412/2016 (A 147)** | Still in force pursuant to Art.380 par.1(31) | Public works | The body responsible to assess infringements and impose disciplinary sanctions is made up of public officials and representatives from the associations of contracting companies. [*Art.86 of Law 3669/2008*] | Sanctions | There is no specific reference in the Official Recital of the Law. However, according to the Official Recital of codifying Law 3669/2008 and following communication with Ministry of Infrastructure and Ministry of Development it is our understanding that the provision aims at giving the contractor's side representation in the decision making body deciding whether to impose sanctions on the contractor. The associations are representative ones. | There is a risk that the involvement of contractors may result in placing competitors, especially new entrants, at a disadvantage. However, given that the companies' representatives do not hold the majority in voting. The provision is deemed proportionate. | No recommendation. | Ministry of Infrastructure, Transport and Networks; Ministry of Economy, Development and Tourism and Ministry of Health |
| 42 | **Law 4412/2016 (A 147)** | Still in force pursuant to Art.380 par.1(31) | Public works | Individuals registered in the Registry of acquired experience may only work for one contracting company. The companies must maintain a minimum level of staff during its operations. [*Art.92 of Law 3669/2008*] | Registries | There is no specific reference in the Official Recital of the Law. However, according to the Official Recital of codifying Law 3669/2008 and following communication with Ministry of Infrastructure and Ministry of Development it is our understanding that the provision aims at the classification of companies based on objective criteria and procedures at the level corresponding to their actual capabilities. | The provision is linked to the system of registries. Segmenting the market into different categories could potentially limit competition. However, the framework is designed to ensure appropriate execution based on specialised professional knowledge. Therefore, the system is deemed proportionate. | No recommendation. | Ministry of Infrastructure, Transport and Networks; Ministry of Economy, Development and Tourism and Ministry of Health |
| 43 | **Law 4412/2016 (A 147)** | Still in force pursuant to Art.380 par.1(31) | Public works | The Committee for the Registry is responsible for the registration, registration renewal and classification of companies up to 5th class. The Minister of Infrastructure, Transport and Networks issues a decision for companies in classes 6 and 7, on advice from the Committee for the Registries. [*Art.92 par.3 subpar.4 of Law 3669/2008*] | Registries | There is no specific reference in the Official Recital of the Law. However, according to the Official Recital of codifying Law 3669/2008 and following communication with Ministry of Infrastructure and Ministry of Development it is our understanding that the provision aims at the classification of companies based on objective criteria and procedures at the level corresponding to their actual capabilities. | The provision is linked to the system of registries. Segmenting the market into different categories could potentially limit competition. However, the framework is designed to ensure appropriate execution based on specialised professional knowledge. Therefore, the system is deemed proportionate. | No recommendation. | Ministry of Infrastructure, Transport and Networks; Ministry of Economy, Development and Tourism and Ministry of Health |
| 44 | **Law 4412/2016 (A 147)** | Still in force pursuant to Art.380 par.1(31) | Public works | Companies are obliged to inform the administrator of the Registry of contractors for any upcoming change to their personnel and receive approval. [*Art.92 par.4 of Law 3669/2008*] | Registries | There is no specific reference in the Official Recital of the Law. However, according to the Official Recital of codifying Law 3669/2008 and following communication with Ministry of Infrastructure and Ministry of Development it is our understanding that the provision aims at the classification of companies based on objective criteria and procedures at the level corresponding to their actual capabilities. | The provision is linked to the system of registries. Segmenting the market into different categories could potentially limit competition. However, the framework is designed to ensure appropriate execution based on specialised professional knowledge. Therefore, the system is deemed proportionate. | No recommendation. | Ministry of Infrastructure, Transport and Networks; Ministry of Economy, Development and Tourism and Ministry of Health |
| 45 | **Law 4412/2016 (A 147)** | Still in force pursuant to Art.380 par.1(31) | Public works | Registration of companies in the Registry of contractors and registration renewal are approved by the Committee for the Registry. [*Art.94 par.1, Art.94 par.2 of Law 3669/2008*] | Registries | There is no specific reference in the Official Recital of the Law. However, according to the Official Recital of codifying Law 3669/2008 and following communication with Ministry of Infrastructure and Ministry of Development it is our understanding that the provision aims at the classification of companies based on objective criteria and procedures at the level corresponding to their actual capabilities. | The provision is linked to the system of registries. Segmenting the market into different categories could potentially limit competition. However, the framework is designed to ensure appropriate execution based on specialised professional knowledge. Therefore, the system is deemed proportionate. | No recommendation. | Ministry of Infrastructure, Transport and Networks; Ministry of Economy, Development and Tourism and Ministry of Health |
| 46 | **Law 4412/2016 (A 147)** | Still in force pursuant to Art.380 par.1(31) | Public works | Companies in the Registry of Contractors can apply to change class two years after the previous classification granting. [*Art.97 par.3 of Law 3669/2008*] | Registries | There is no specific reference in the Official Recital of the Law. However, according to the Official Recital of codifying Law 3669/2008 and following communication with Ministry of Infrastructure and Ministry of Development it is our understanding that the provision aims at the classification of companies based on objective criteria and procedures at the level corresponding to their actual capabilities. | This provision obliges a contractor to be part of a class for two years before he applies for a class change. This limits contractors' ability to upgrade classes in cases where they fulfil the formal criteria. hinders the operators' ability to compete within the market. This hinders contractors from participating in tenders, hence limiting competition. | No recommendation, provided that registration is not a pre-requirement for participating in tenders. | Ministry of Infrastructure, Transport and Networks; Ministry of Economy, Development and Tourism and Ministry of Health |
| 47 | **Law 4412/2016 (A 147)** | Still in force pursuant to Art.380 par.1(31) | Public works | In order for companies to be classified in a certain category and class they must keep their personnel unchanged for two years after the issuance of their registration certificate. [*Art.99 par.2(a)(vii) subpar.5, Art.99 par.2(c)(ii) subpar.4, Art.99 par.2(c)(iii) of Law 3669/2008*] | Registries | There is no specific reference in the Official Recital of the Law. However, according to the Official Recital of codifying Law 3669/2008 and following communication with Ministry of Infrastructure and Ministry of Development it is our understanding that the provision aims at the classification of companies based on objective criteria and procedures at the level corresponding to their actual capabilities. | This provision restricts firms' strategies regarding their personnel. However, it provides an additional safeguard of the viability of the Registry system. | No recommendation. | Ministry of Infrastructure, Transport and Networks; Ministry of Economy, Development and Tourism and Ministry of Health |
| 48 | **Law 4412/2016 (A 147)** | Still in force pursuant to Art.380 par.1(31) | Public works | Companies are allowed to participate in a tendering procedure only if they are registered in the Registry of contractors (MEEP). Limitations are provided as to their categorisation and their participation in tenders as well to a minimum obligation for staffing *(Art.100 of Law 3669/2008).* | Registry of contractors | There is no specific reference in the Official Recital of the Law. However, according to the Official Recital of codifying Law 3669/2008 and following communication with Ministry of Infrastructure and Ministry of Development it is our understanding that the provision aims at the classification of companies based on objective criteria and procedures at the level corresponding to their actual capabilities. | Using registries as an obligatory mechanism of classification of operators can be restrictive. An operator may face lower direct and indirect (e.g. administration) costs by not participating in a registry – while still fulfilling the participation requirements. | The OECD recommends that class registration per se is not a requirement for participation in tenders, conditional that the operator can demonstrate fulfilling the same qualifications as those specified in the tender. | Ministry of Infrastructure, Transport and Networks |
| 49 | **Law 4412/2016 (A 147)** | Still in force pursuant to Art.380 par.1(31) | Public works | Companies which are classified third class and above are obliged to have the form of an SA *(Art.100 par. 6 of Law 3669/2008).* | Registry of contractors | There is no specific reference in the Official Recital of the Law. However, according to the Official Recital of codifying Law 3669/2008 and following communication with Ministry of Infrastructure and Ministry of Development it is our understanding that the provision aims at the classification of companies based on objective criteria and procedures at the level corresponding to their actual capabilities. | This provision unnecessarily restricts the legal form a company can take from class 3 and above; hence limiting firm strategies. | Abolish the obligation for the legal form of a company from third class and above to be an S.A. and ensure in alternative ways the obligation that shares be registered to a natural person, | Ministry of Infrastructure, Transport and Networks |

## Sector: Construction

| No | No and title of Regulation | Article | Thematic category | Brief description of the potential obstacle | Keyword | Policy maker's objectives | Harm to competition | Recommendations | Competent Ministry / Authority |
|---|---|---|---|---|---|---|---|---|---|
| 50 | **Law 4412/2016 (A 147)** | Still in force pursuant to Art.380 par.1(31) | Public works | Companies are allowed to participate to tenders with regards to the budget of the contracting authorities and according to certain thresholds and their classification *(Art.102 of Law 3669/2008).* | Registry of contractors | There is no specific reference in the Official Recital of the Law. However, according to the Official Recital of codifying Law 3669/2008 and following communication with Ministry of Infrastructure and Ministry of Development it is our understanding that the provision aims at the classification of companies based on objective criteria and procedures at the level corresponding to their actual capabilities. | Using registries as an obligatory mechanism of classification of operators can be restrictive. An operator may face lower direct and indirect (e.g. administration) costs by not participating in a registry – while still fulfilling the participation requirements. | The OECD recommends that class registration per se is not a requirement for participation in tenders, conditional that the operator can demonstrate fulfilling the same qualifications as those specified in the tender. | Ministry of Infrastructure, Transport and Networks |
| 51 | **Law 4412/2016 (A 147)** | Still in force pursuant to Art.380 par.1(31) | Public works | Companies specialised in certain works are allowed to participate in a tendering procedure only if they are registered in the Registry of contractors (MEEP). Limitations are provided as to their categorisation, their legal status and their participation in tenders as well to a minimum obligation for staffing *(Art.103 of Law 3669/2008).* | Registry of contractors | There is no specific reference in the Official Recital of the Law. However, according to the Official Recital of codifying Law 3669/2008 and following communication with Ministry of Infrastructure and Ministry of Development it is our understanding that the provision aims at the classification of companies based on objective criteria and procedures at the level corresponding to their actual capabilities. | Using registries as an obligatory mechanism of classification of operators can be restrictive. An operator may face lower direct and indirect (e.g. administration) costs by not participating in a registry – while still fulfilling the participation requirements. | The OECD recommends that class registration per se is not a requirement for participation in tenders, conditional that the operator can demonstrate fulfilling the same qualifications as those specified in the tender. | Ministry of Infrastructure, Transport and Networks |
| 52 | **Law 4412/2016 (A 147)** | Still in force pursuant to Art.380 par.1(31) | Public works | Companies specialised in certain works are allowed to participate to tenders with regards to the budget of the contracting authorities and according to certain thresholds and their classification *(Art.104 of Law 3669/2008).* | Registry of contractors | There is no specific reference in the Official Recital of the Law. However, according to the Official Recital of codifying Law 3669/2008 and following communication with Ministry of Infrastructure and Ministry of Development it is our understanding that the provision aims at the classification of companies based on objective criteria and procedures at the level corresponding to their actual capabilities. | Using registries as an obligatory mechanism of classification of operators can be restrictive. An operator may face lower direct and indirect (e.g. administration) costs by not participating in a registry – while still fulfilling the participation requirements. | The OECD recommends that class registration per se is not a requirement for participation in tenders, conditional that the operator can demonstrate fulfilling the same qualifications as those specified in the tender. | Ministry of Infrastructure, Transport and Networks |
| 53 | **Law 4412/2016 (A 147)** | Still in force pursuant to Art.380 par.1(31) | Public works | Companies not registered in the Registry of contractors may participate in small scale works only if they are registered in Regional Registries. Partnership of a company registered in the Registry of Contractors with a company registered in the Regional Registries is not allowed .Companies are allowed to register in only one Regional Registry and a second neighbouring one. Registration in one of the regional registries of the Region of Attica is considered as registration for the whole Region *(Art.105 of Law 3669/2008).* | Regional Registries of contractors | There is no specific reference in the Official Recital of the Law. However, according to the Official Recital of codifying Law 3669/2008 and following communication with Ministry of Infrastructure it is our understanding that the provision aims at the classification of companies based on objective criteria and procedures at the level corresponding to their actual capabilities so as to avoid distortion of the market and in order to organise effectively the contractors' capacity. | This provision unnecessarily segments the market across different geographic areas; hence limiting competition. | Abolish regional registries. The Registry of Contractors could be modified accordingly. | Ministry of Infrastructure, Transport and Networks |
| 54 | **Law 4412/2016 (A 147)** | Still in force pursuant to Art.380 par.1(31) | Public works | Individuals are obliged to register in the registry of acquired experience. The articles describe how this system is implemented *(Arts. 107, 109,110 of Law 3669/2008).* | Registry of acquired experience | There is no specific reference in the Official Recital of the Law. However, according to the Official Recital of codifying Law 3669/2008 and following communication with Ministry of Infrastructure and Ministry of Development it is our understanding that the provision aims at the classification of companies based on objective criteria and procedures at the level corresponding to their actual capabilities. | The provision is linked to the system of registries. Segmenting the market into different categories could potentially limit competition. However, the framework is designed to ensure appropriate execution based on specialised professional knowledge. Therefore, the system is deemed proportionate. | No recommendation. | Ministry of Infrastructure, Transport and Networks |
| 55 | **Law 4014/2011 (A 209)** | 2 par. 2 b | Approval of environmental terms for the materialisation of a construction | Waste management works could be exempted from the procedure of the approval of environmental terms | Environmental terms | According to the Official Recital of Law 4067/2012 and amending Law 4315/2014 which clarified the abovementioned provisions, derogations from the general provisions on building regulations and approvals are allowed for operational / architectural reasons and only in case it does not undermine the natural and cultural environment. Derogations are approved by the Minister of Environment after a technical report on the integration into the urban planning | This provision sets a differential treatment between waste management works and all other works. However, it is our understanding that the provisions was meant to have a temporary character. Given the urgency of this provision when associated with public interest it is deemed proportionate. | OECD recommends a rephrasing of this provision with a clear sunset clause. | Ministry of Environment and Energy |
| 56 | **Law 4014/2011 (A 209)** | 2 par. 8 c | Approval of environmental terms for the materialisation of a construction | The duration of existing approvals at the date of the publication of law is extended until the completion of the 10 year duration if the terms under which the approvals were issued, have not changed. | Environmental terms | There is no specific reference in the Official Recital of the law. However, following communication with the Ministry it is our understanding that the provision aims at the approval of environmental terms for a duration corresponding to the work having environmental impact. | The provision sets unclear requirements with regards to extending environmental approvals of existing licenses in cases where the terms under which the existing ones were issued have not changed. This lack of clarity and specification in the definition creates uncertainty. Since the criteria are not well defined by the law, this kind of differentiation may entail extra costs to different suppliers. Following communication with the Ministry we understand that the criteria in question have been clarified with a Circular. | No recommendation. | Ministry of Environment and Energy |

## Sector: Construction

| No | No and title of Regulation | Article | Thematic category | Brief description of the potential obstacle | Keyword | Policy maker's objectives | Harm to competition | Recommendations | Competent Ministry / Authority |
|---|---|---|---|---|---|---|---|---|---|
| 57 | **Law 4014/2011 (A 209)** | 3 par 2 στ subpar 2 and 4 par. 3 στ | Approval of environmental terms for the materialisation of a construction | In the works co-funded by the EU and by the structural funds programs in case the competent authorities do not issue a decision on the approval within the deadlines provided the relevant work is considered to have the approval and the competent authority is obliged to issue the relevant administrative act. This is not the case for the rest of the works. | Environmental terms | There is no specific reference in the Official Recital of the law. However, following communication with the Ministry it is our understanding that the provision aims at accelerating procedures and avoiding multiple approvals by extending the duration of the approval of environmental terms when operators have already acquired approval for compliance. Overall it aims at avoiding duplication of procedures and delays in the acquiring of a new approval under the new regime (i.e. Law 4014/2011), nevertheless, evaluating, the satisfaction of the substantive conditions for acquiring of an approval under Law 4014/2011. | The provision discriminates in favour of works co-funded by the EU. However, given the public interest of these works the provision is deemed proportionate. | No recommendation. | Ministry of Environment and Energy |
| 58 | **Law 4014/2011 (A 209)** | 3 par. 4 | Approval of environmental terms for the materialisation of a construction | The Secretary General of the Ministry of Environment and Energy may decide on the extension of the decision time on the application for an approval for very complicated works following the opinion of the competent Directorate. This extension cannot exceed the initially provided timeline by a factor of two. | Environmental terms | There is no specific reference in the Official Recital of the law. However, following communication with the Ministry it is our understanding that the provision aims at accelerating procedures and avoiding multiple approvals when the procedures followed satisfy the objective of the approval of environmental terms. | The provision discriminates in favour of particularly complicated works However, following clarifications from the Ministry it is deemed proportionate. | No recommendation. | Ministry of Environment and Energy |
| 59 | **Presidential Decree 100/2010 (A 177) as amended by Law 4122/2013 (A 42)** | 5 par. 4 subpar.1 | Energy Efficiency of buildings | In order for a legal entity to be registered to the registry of energy supervisors at least one of the partners should be an energy inspector. | Registry of Energy supervisors | The provision aims at ensuring effective and substantial supervision by qualified operators as well ensure liability due to the high value of the protected good and the obligation of the State to reach certain targets on energy efficiency in the building sector. | It is unclear why the provision necessitates the equity stake of the energy inspector. The market could be more competitive and flexible if that was extended into having energy inspectors as employees of the registered company in question. | Clarify that the provision requiring the energy inspector to be a partner of the legal entity additionally allows an inspector to be, solely, an employee (and not, obligatory, a partner) of the company in question. | Ministry of Environment and Energy |
| 60 | **Law 3389/2005 (A 232)** | 6 par. 2 subpar. 1 | Public Private Partnerships | The provision of technical, consulting, legal or other services is on the basis of a decision by the competent authority notwithstanding any related provisions on the provision of such services. | Provision of services | Following communication with the Ministry it is our understanding that the provision aims at providing flexibility as well as avoiding delays in the award of the relevant contracts necessary for the execution of the Public Private Partnership contract. | The provision could inadvertently exclude categories of participants. Furthermore, the existence of new legislation on Public Procurement and Concessions creates legal uncertainty as to the application of the relevant regulatory framework. | Clarify in accordance to the new Law of Public Procurement and Concessions. | Ministry of Economy, Development and Tourism |
| 61 | **Law 3389/2005 (A 232)** | 6 par. 4 | Public Private Partnerships | The provision of financial, tax, technical, insurance, legal or other services is on the basis of a decision by the competent authority notwithstanding any related provisions on the provision of such services. | Provision of services | Following communication with the Ministry it is our understanding that the provision aims at providing flexibility as well as avoiding delays in the award of the relevant contracts necessary for the execution of the Public Private Partnership contract. | The provision could inadvertently exclude categories of participants. Furthermore, the existence of new legislation on Public Procurement and Concessions creates legal uncertainty as to the application of the relevant regulatory framework. | Clarify in accordance to the new Law of Public Procurement and Concessions. | Ministry of Economy, Development and Tourism |

## Sector: Media

| No | No and title of Regulation | Article | Thematic category | Brief description of the potential obstacle | Keyword | Policy maker's objectives | Harm to competition | Recommendations | Competent Ministry / Authority |
|---|---|---|---|---|---|---|---|---|---|
| 1 | **P.D 109/2010 Harmonisation with Directive 2010/13/EC** | art.23§3 | TV content | Announcements made in connection with TV programmes and with ancillary products directly derived from the latter as well as announcements made in connection with the rest of the activities of the TV broadcaster and of other enterprises belonging to the same corporate group which are active in the field of Media (informative or not) and they are related to informative or entertainment internet services, to production and distribution of music or/and audiovisual works and to technical training for providing services in the aforementioned sectors are exempt from the television advertising and teleshopping limits (20% within an hour). | TV advertising | It is our understanding that the provision aims to add more exceptions to the announcements whose duration is not calculated in the permitted, according to the Directive 2010/13/EU, time limit for television advertising spots and teleshopping spots (20% of an hour) . More specifically, the national provision aims to allow media corporate groups to take advantage of extra advertising time for all their products either stemming from the TV broadcaster or from other companies of the same corporate group. | The interpretation by this provision of the term "ancillary products" deriving from the Directive 2010/13/EU is too broad, allowing companies that belong to the same company group as the TV Broadcaster and offer services such as entertainment, music and film production and professional training to be advertised in excess of the permitted proportion of TV advertising and teleshopping spots. This provision implicitly raises advertising costs for all companies in the relevant markets that are not part of the particular media group in comparison to those that are. | The amendment of Article 23, paragraph 2 of Presidential Decree 109/2010 made by Article 6, Paragraph 8 of Law 4279/2014 should be abolished and the first version of the provision should be revived in line with Article 23, paragraph 2 of Directive 2010/13/EC. | Minister-SG of Information and Communication /Ministry of Culture and Sports |
| 2 | **L. 3548/2007 Public bodies' posts in the regional and local press and other provisions** | art. 2§1 (a), (b) | Publishing activities | The newspapers and magazines which are eligible for publishing public announcements are selected by the Minister who applies specific qualitative and quantitative requirements among which years of publication, number of sales and number of pages per edition are stated. | Newspapers qualified for public bodies advertising | According to the official recital, the provisions are necessary to demonstrate that a newspaper is known to the public, as well as the sustainability of the company that publishes it, and its independence. The ultimate aim is the widest possible publicity for state-paid announcements and the widest possible distribution of information. | Needs to be clarified whether the particular qualitative and quantitative requirements applied are excessive and restrict the number of eligible newspapers and magazines. Especially criteria that limit the provision of this particular service to existing publications while excluding new ones pose a direct barrier to entry by favouring incumbent businesses against newcomers. | The requirement for previous years of circulation (two years for daily newspapers and three years for weekly newspapers) should be abolished. Instead of this requirement, the necessary time for calculating the minimum number of printed and sold copies should be provided, a period that could range from six months to one-year maximum. | Minister-SG of Information and Communication |
| 3 | **L. 3548/2007 Public bodies' posts in the regional and local press and other provisions** | | Publishing activities | All the references to "publishing balance sheets" should be deleted. | Obsolete Regulation | Obsolete. | Obsolete, inactive or redundant legislation can be a regulatory barrier by creating legal uncertainty; and potentially raises the operating costs facing suppliers, for example legal costs. | Explicitly abolish. | Minister-SG of Information and Communication |
| 4 | **JMD 16682/2011 Determination of special pricing for the distribution of newspapers and magazines in the country** | art.1 | Publishing activities | The State guarantees special pricing for postal distribution of Press through competitive process . Only the newspapers and magazines which meet certain criteria set in the Minister's decision are eligible for the special pricing. These criteria include time of circulation and whether their owners are members (or potential members) of one specific Union (Hellenic Union of editors of periodical press - Ένωση Δημοσιογράφων Ιδιοκτητών Περιοδικού τύπου). Newspapers and magazines which are eligible for publishing state publications can also take advantage of the special pricing. | Pricing of newspapers distribution | The official recital states that the criteria are necessary for excluding advertising brochures or other commercial documents from taking advantage of the special postal pricing. Setting specific and strict criteria is considered the only way to stop the distortions that occurred prior to the amendment of the Joint Ministerial Decision. | Needs to be clarified whether the particular criteria applied are excessive and restrict the number of eligible newspapers and magazines, thus raising transport costs for some of the market players in favour of others. Especially criteria that limit the provision of this particular service to existing publications while excluding new ones pose a direct barrier to entry by favouring incumbent businesses against newcomers. This provision favours the same newspapers and magazines that are eligible for state publications and those whose owners are members of the Union of Journalists Owners of Periodical Press. | Abolish the requirements regarding an owner of a newspaper/magazine's membership or potential membership of the Hellenic Union of Editors of Periodical Press; the number of years of prior circulation before becoming eligible for preferential postal rates; and the compulsory requirement that the owner of a newspaper also be an editor and journalist. | Minister-SG of Information and Communication/ |
| 5 | **L. 2328/1995 Legal status of private TV broadcasters and of local radio, regulating issues of the TV-Radio market and other provisions** | art. 1 and art. 2 | Television broadcasting | L. 4339/2015 contains provisions that cover the issue of TV licensing. | Obsolete Regulation | Obsolete. | Obsolete, inactive or redundant legislation can be a regulatory barrier by creating legal uncertainty; and potentially raises the operating costs facing suppliers, for example legal costs. | Explicitly abolish. | Minister-SG of Information and Communication |
| 6 | **L. 2328/1995 Legal status of private TV broadcasters and of local radio, regulating issues of the TV-Radio market and other provisions** | art. 3 | Television broadcasting | P.D 109/2010 contains provisions that cover the issues of advertising and sponsorship. However, the content of paragraphs 15 to 18 is not found in PD 109/2010 and paragraph 1 is formulated in more general words. | Obsolete Regulation | Obsolete. | Obsolete, inactive or redundant legislation can be a regulatory barrier by creating legal uncertainty; and potentially raises the operating costs facing suppliers, for example legal costs. | Explicitly abolish. | Minister-SG of Information and Communication |

## Sector: Media

| No | No and title of Regulation | Article | Thematic category | Brief description of the potential obstacle | Keyword | Policy maker's objectives | Harm to competition | Recommendations | Competent Ministry / Authority |
|---|---|---|---|---|---|---|---|---|---|
| 7 | **L. 2328/1995 Legal status of private TV broadcasters and of local radio, regulating issues of the TV-Radio market and other provisions** | art. 1§12 | Television broadcasting | A TV licensed broadcaster cannot outsource the production or management of more than 30% of the programme monthly broadcasted to third parties. The latter does not exclude the possibility to assign production to independent producers. However, it should be clarified whether the provision is and up to what extent applicable because of art.11 par. 5 of L. 3592/2007 and art.14 par.4 L. 4339/2015 which states that the TV broadcasters can assign a specific part of their programme (without providing a particular portion) to audiovisual production companies or to independent audiovisual producers. | TV content | It is our understanding that the provision aims to the production of the majority of the programme by the TV licence holder itself. The production of a big portion of the programme may be used to abuse the regulations regarding the requirements fulfilled by the owners of TV licences which ensure plurality and objectivity. | This provision limits the choices of a broadcaster with regards to the sources of their broadcasted content without any clarification on the policy maker's objective that would justify this restriction; further, the lack of clarity with respect to the definition of "the independent producer" and to whether this provision is still in force, creates legal uncertainty and confusion, potentially rising operating costs facing TV broadcasters; Finally this provision by limiting the ability of the broadcasters to outsource only a small amount of their programme, limits competition in the upstream market of content providers. | Consolidate and streamline rules of Article 1, paragraph 12 of Law 2328/1995, Article 11, paragraph 5 of Law 3592/2007 and Article 14, paragraph 4 of Law 4339/2015, while defining which programming can be freely outsourced and to whom; any restrictions should be maintained only on the grounds of pluralism and transparency, and the requirements of EU law, notably the AVMS Directive. | Minister-SG of Information and Communication |
| 8 | **L 2328/1995 Legal status of private TV broadcasters and of local radio, regulating issues of the TV-Radio market and other provisions** | art. 6§6a | Radio Broadcasting | If the shares of an S.A which is a Radio licence holder are owned by another SA, the shares of the latter should be registered and owned by an individual. There is no possibility to be owned by another SA. This provision may be obsolete because of L. 3592/2007. | Radio Licensing | It is our understanding that this provisions aims to enhance the transparency and guarantee the pluralism regarding radio broadcasting. | As long as the rules of registered shares are enforced to all holding companies of media enterprises, there is not enough justification to enforce a particular corporate structure to a media group. The aim of transparency may still be pursued by applying the same rules to all holding companies up to the physical persons who own them. | The requirement that all shares be registered is justified by the policy maker's objective of protecting pluralism and objectivity in the media sector. If this condition is met, however, it removes any necessity to dictate the exact corporate structure of media organisations. This restriction should therefore be abolished. | Minister-SG of Information and Communication |
| 9 | **L 2328/1995 Legal status of private TV broadcasters and of local radio, regulating issues of the TV-Radio market and other provisions** | art. 6 and art. 7 | Radio broadcasting | The issue of Radio licensing is covered by the provisions of L. 3592/2007. | Obsolete Regulation | Obsolete. | Obsolete, inactive or redundant legislation can be a regulatory barrier by creating legal uncertainty; and potentially raises the operating costs facing suppliers, for example legal costs. | Explicitly abolish. | Minister-SG of Information and Communication |
| 10 | **L 2328/1995 Legal status of private TV broadcasters and of local radio, regulating issues of the TV-Radio market and other provisions** | art. 10 §1, 2, 3 | Motion picture, video and TV programme production, sound recording and music publishing activities | Only those who belong to the profession of the independent producer of audiovisual works can sign contracts between the intellectual property rights holders and TV broadcasters, advertisement companies, cinema companies or other relevant companies for the production of films, advertisements or audiovisual works whose duration is more than 2 min. The definition of Independent producer is linked to the definition of the producer of audiovisual works in Law 2121/1993 on Intellectual Property Rights. For exercising the profession, academic and experience qualifications are required as well as registration before the relevant professional chamber is needed. | Producer of audiovisual works | According to the official recital, this provision aims to secure the existence of the profession of the producer of audiovisual works. Therefore, it is our understanding that it aims to promote the interests of this particular profession. | This provision limits competition in the market of audio-visual productions by creating entry barriers to the production of audio-visual works and the profession of the producer of audiovisual works. The barriers include barriers in the assignment of IPRights to any potential investor, registration before the relevant professional chamber and a submission of numerous supportive documents that limit to great extent the access to the profession without proper justification on the side of the State for the necessity of such a restriction. | 1. Define the term independent producer of audio visual works in line with the Directive AVMS.<br>2. Abolish the compulsory registration of audio visual producers, audio visual production companies and their members/shareholders/managers before the professional Chamber in order to exercise the relevant profession or activity.<br>3. Abolish the provision of art.10 par. 1 Law 2328/1995. | Ministry of Culture and Sports/ Minister-SG of Information and Communication |
| 11 | **L 2328/1995 Legal status of private TV broadcasters and of local radio, regulating issues of the TV-Radio market and other provisions** | art. 10 §4 | Motion picture, video and television programme production, sound recording and music publishing activities | In case that someone is producer of audiovisual works or shareholder or member of a governing body of a company that produces audiovisual works, he/she cannot work for the public administration and be owner or shareholder or member of a governing body or employee of an advertising company. | Producer of audiovisual works | It was not possible to identify the objective of the specific provision. However, it is our understanding that it may aim to the objectivity of the programme produced and to the elimination of any interdependencies. | In connection to line No 10, this provision furthers restricts entry to the profession of the producer of audiovisual works. It is not clear what purpose it serves to exclude access to the profession from owners or shareholders or members of a governing body or employees of an advertising company. Furthermore it is not clear either why a restriction regarding Public Servants is needed here on top of what is already in force by the Code of Public Servants. | The ban on independent audiovisual producers participating in advertising and/or being employed in the public sector, as set out in Article 10, paragraph 4 of Law 2328/1995, should be explicitly abolished. Any eventual conflicts of interest may be treated within existing regulations such as applying Article 31 of the Code of Conduct for Public Administrative Employees by analogy. | Ministry of Culture and Sports/ Minister-SG of Information and Communication |

## Sector: Media

| No | No and title of Regulation | Article | Thematic category | Brief description of the potential obstacle | Keyword | Policy maker's objectives | Harm to competition | Recommendations | Competent Ministry / Authority |
|---|---|---|---|---|---|---|---|---|---|
| 12 | **L 2328/1995 Legal status of private TV broadcasters and of local radio, regulating issues of the TV-Radio market and other provisions** | art. 10§5 | Motion picture, video and television programme production, sound recording and music publishing activities | Audio visual production companies should be registered to a special section of the professional registry and (a) the unlimited liability partner/manager of personal liability production companies, (b) the manager of limited liability audio visual production companies (ΕΠΕ) who signs audio visual production agreements on behalf of the company and (c) the CEO of SA audio visual production companies, should be also registered with the professional Chamber and fulfil the relevant requirements. Moreover, the shares of audio visual production companies that have the structure of an SA, should be registered. | Producer of audiovisual works | It was not possible to identify the objective of the specific provision. However, in our understanding the provision aims to the enhancement of transparency. | See line No 10 for harm to competition regarding the obligation of the audiovisual production companies and their main partners/managers to be member of the Audiovisual producers registry; in addition, the obligation of S.A. audiovisual production companies to have their shares register, further increases administrative costs and hinders entry in the market to that extent. | Abolish the compulsory registration of audio visual producers, audio visual production companies and their members/shareholders/managers before the professional Chamber in order to exercise the relevant profession or activity. | Ministry of Culture and Sports/Minister-SG of Information and Communication |
| 13 | **L 2328/1995 Legal status of private TV broadcasters and of local radio, regulating issues of the TV-Radio market and other provisions** | art.13 §10,11 | Newspapers | Each person (legal entity or not) can be owner or member of a company or stockholder of a company owning up to 2 daily news newspapers that are published in Athens or Piraeus or Thessaloniki and they are distributed through Press Distribution Agencies, out of which one is published in the morning and the other in the afternoon/ up to one daily financial newspaper and up to one daily sports newspaper that are published in Athens, Piraeus or Thessaloniki / up to two daily regional newspapers but in different prefectures/ up to two not daily regional newspapers but in different prefectures / and to only one Sunday edition of a daily newspaper either with the same or similar title or as an independent newspaper (news or financial or sports). This restriction applies also for the spouse and the relatives up to 4th grade as long as they do not prove their independency (financial and entrepreneurship). | Cross ownership | It was not possible to identify the objective of the specific provision. However, in our understanding the provision aims to the enhancement of pluralism and of transparency. | It is not clear whether this provision has a net negative or a net positive effect to competition in the newspaper market. On one hand investment choices of potential investors are limited by particular restrictions on the number and type of newspaper ownership. On the other hand the provision prevents situations of over - concentration in the relevant market. In other words the objective of freedom of entrepreneurship should be counter balanced by the objective of pluralism. | 1. Streamline the provisions of Article 13, paragraph 10 and 11 of Law 2328/1995 and Articles 3 and 5 of Law 3592/2007. As part of this exercise, the correlation between a priori newspaper ownership restrictions in Law 2328/1995 and the media concentration rules of Article 3 of Law 3592/2007 should be reviewed. This to see if they can be combined and so focus more on the real impact of newspaper acquisition in the market and in the shaping of public opinion (i.e. apply criteria such as market share, daily circulation, share of newspaper supply in the market).<br>2. Specific criteria for the proof of financial and business independency of spouses and relatives before the competent administrative authorities and the courts should be provided.<br>3. References to press distribution agencies should be abolished. | Minister-SG of Information and Communication |
| 14 | **L 2328/1995 Legal status of private TV broadcasters and of local radio, regulating issues of the TV-Radio market and other provisions** | | Newspapers | where it is stated: "that are distributed by Press Agencies" -obsolete. | Obsolete Regulation | Obsolete. | Obsolete, inactive or redundant legislation can be a regulatory barrier by creating legal uncertainty; and potentially raises the operating costs facing suppliers, for example legal costs. | Explicitly abolish. | Minister-SG of Information and Communication |
| 15 | **L 1746/1988 Regulating the Institutions of Chambers** | art.24§3 sentence 2 and §8 sentence 2 | Radio/TV broadcasting | Provisions of L. 3592/2007 regulates the issue of TV/Radio ownership differently. | Obsolete Regulation | Obsolete. | Obsolete, inactive or redundant legislation can be a regulatory barrier by creating legal uncertainty; and potentially raises the operating costs facing suppliers, for example legal costs. | Explicitly abolish. | Minister-SG of Information and Communication |
| 16 | **L 1092/1938 On Press editors' obligations** | | Publishing activities | It should be clear which provisions have been abolished by art.1 of L. 2243/1994. | Obsolete Regulation | Obsolete. | Obsolete, inactive or redundant legislation can be a regulatory barrier by creating legal uncertainty; and potentially raises the operating costs facing suppliers, for example legal costs. | Explicitly abolish. | Minister-SG of Information and Communication |
| 17 | **L 1093/1938 On Journalists' Union** | art. 54 | Newspapers | According to the competent services (General Secretariat of Information and Communication) this provision is not in force. | Obsolete Regulation | Obsolete. | Obsolete, inactive or redundant legislation can be a regulatory barrier by creating legal uncertainty; and potentially raises the operating costs facing suppliers, for example legal costs. | Explicitly abolish. | Minister-SG of Information and Communication |
| 18 | **L 582/1945 On means of providing the Press with paper** | | Newspapers | According to the competent services (General Secretariat of Information and Communication) this law is not in force. | Obsolete Regulation | Obsolete. | Obsolete, inactive or redundant legislation can be a regulatory barrier by creating legal uncertainty; and potentially raises the operating costs facing suppliers, for example legal costs. | Explicitly abolish. | Minister-SG of Information and Communication |
| 19 | **L 3619/1956 On setting up and organizing the Union of owners of Daily Regional Newspapers** | art. 4 and art. 5§5, | Newspapers | It is not clear which laws and provisions regarding Unions of Owners of Newspapers are in force and valid. According to the competent services (General Secretariat of Information and Communication) this provisions are not in force. | Obsolete Regulation | Obsolete. | Obsolete, inactive or redundant legislation can be a regulatory barrier by creating legal uncertainty; and potentially raises the operating costs facing suppliers, for example legal costs. | Explicitly abolish. | Minister-SG of Information and Communication |

## Sector: Media

| No | No and title of Regulation | Article | Thematic category | Brief description of the potential obstacle | Keyword | Policy maker's objectives | Harm to competition | Recommendations | Competent Ministry / Authority |
|---|---|---|---|---|---|---|---|---|---|
| 20 | **L 1446/1984 Amendment and abolishment of the provisions relating to the Daily Regional Press** | art. 5 | Newspapers | More recent legal provisions cover the same issue. Namely, L. 3986/2011, art. 48. | Obsolete Regulation | Obsolete. | Obsolete, inactive or redundant legislation can be a regulatory barrier by creating legal uncertainty; and potentially raises the operating costs facing suppliers, for example legal costs. | Explicitly abolish. | Minister-SG of Information and Communication |
| 21 | **L 1004/1971 On the profession of Journalists** | art. 22§2 | Newspapers | More recent legal provisions cover the same issue. Namely L. 4339/2015 art. 55. | Obsolete Regulation | Obsolete. | Obsolete, inactive or redundant legislation can be a regulatory barrier by creating legal uncertainty; and potentially raises the operating costs facing suppliers, for example legal costs. | Explicitly abolish. | Minister-SG of Information and Communication |
| 22 | **L 433/1963 On the participation of foreigners in the Association of the correspondents of foreign Press in Greece** | | Newspapers | According to the competent services (General Secretariat of Information and Communication) this law is not in force. | Obsolete Regulation | Obsolete. | Obsolete, inactive or redundant legislation can be a regulatory barrier by creating legal uncertainty; and potentially raises the operating costs facing suppliers, for example legal costs. | Explicitly abolish. | Minister-SG of Information and Communication |
| 23 | **L 3757/1957 On amending L 3562/1956** | | Newspapers | According to the competent services (General Secretariat of Information and Communication) this provision is not in force. | Obsolete Regulation | Obsolete. | Obsolete, inactive or redundant legislation can be a regulatory barrier by creating legal uncertainty; and potentially raises the operating costs facing suppliers, for example legal costs. | Explicitly abolish. | Minister-SG of Information and Communication |
| 24 | **L 4286/1963 On the formation of the Union of Owners of Regional Press and other provisions** | art. 2, art 6§2, art.10 | Newspapers | It is not clear which laws and provisions regarding Unions of Owners of Newspapers are in force and valid. According to the competent services (General Secretariat of Information and Communication) this provisions are not in force. | Obsolete Regulation | Obsolete. | Obsolete, inactive or redundant legislation can be a regulatory barrier by creating legal uncertainty; and potentially raises the operating costs facing suppliers, for example legal costs. | Explicitly abolish. | Minister-SG of Information and Communication |
| 25 | **L 4070/2012 Regulating Electronic communications, Transport and Public Works and other provisions** | art. 80 (η) | TV Broadcasting | The Minister of Infrastructure, Transport and Networks has the option to remove the multiplex that has not been in sufficient use by the network provider as long as the content can be broadcasted by the other multiplexes managed by the network provider. | TV Networks | According to the official recital, the removal of the multiplex can be done only for reasons of public interest and more specifically for the better exploitation of public frequencies. | Broadcasting frequencies are a public resource and if a Network provider is making a limited use of this resource the state may reserve the right to remove the unused resources in favour of the public. The restrictive aspect of this provision has to do with the broad definition of "public interest" which in this case may lead to a wide variety of reasons why the State may end up removing a multiplex that is not being used sufficiently according to its own judgement by the network provider. There should be a more detailed justification on the technical level of the situations that can trigger such a unilateral action from the State. Otherwise, if left as it is, this general and wide statement creates legal uncertainty and disincentives for potential investors to enter the market in the future. This provision should also be viewed in connection to the number of licensed TV broadcasters in the market (both country-wide and local). A limited amount of licences may result into unused frequency bandwidth by the network provider due to limited demand. In conclusion, it should be clear by the provision that limited usage of multiplexes may be attributed to a) technical inefficiencies by the network provider or, b) limited demand by TV broadcasters due to market conditions and not due to limited licensing by the State. | The provision should be abolished or amended in order to provide a restrictive reference of the public-interest criteria that can trigger such unilateral action from the state, in accordance with Directive 2002/20/EC on licensing electronic communications networks and services. It should also be made clear that limited usage of multiplexes should be directly attributed to the network providers, such as cases of technical inefficiencies by the network provider or non-compliance with its licensing conditions. | Ministry of Infrastructure, Transport and Networks |
| 26 | **L 3801/2009 Regulating issues pertaining to employees with private law open-ended contracts and other provisions of organization and operation of Public Administration** | art.50 | Radio broadcasting | Radio stations owned by political parties represented in the Parliament that had been in function before the promulgation of L. 3592/2007, have the right to participate in the competitive tendering for radio licensing and they are considered legally functioning in the region they had been broadcasting until their licence is issued. | Radio Licensing | It was not possible to identify the objective of the specific provision. However, in our understanding the provision aims to legalise radio stations owned by political parties which could not prove or they were not in function before 1999. | This provision should be viewed together with all similar regulations listed here that allow for temporary renewal of broadcasting licences and the subsequent status of "legally operating" but not entirely "legal" broadcasters which lacks further legal justification. This type of provisions severely limit competition in the market of TV and Radio broadcasting. They are damaging competition because the market is essentially sealed from new entrants - since no new licences are available and the incumbent broadcasters have their expired licences renewed on a temporary basis. Therefore the only way for a potential new entrant to invest in the market is to acquire one of the existing firms that own one of the temporary licences. Further, the fact that these licences are only renewed on a temporary basis creates uncertainty in the market because it is very likely that under these circumstances, potential investment plans by incumbent and new entrant businesses are put on hold until a proper licensing procedure is launched and the rules are clearly stated. | 1. The provision should be abolished.<br>2. After completing the relevant technical analysis and issuing a map of frequencies, the authorities should launch tenders for each prefecture with a specific number of licences both for radio stations of informative and non-informative (music, sports) content. This will establish a stable investment environment with legal certainty and specific conditions known to all participants from the outset. All other provisions that insert derogations to the licensing procedure should be abolished.<br>3. Law 2328/1995 and Law 3592/2007 should be streamlined, so as to establish a definitive legal framework for radio licensing. | Minister-SG of Information and Communication/ |

## Sector: Media

| No | No and title of Regulation | Article | Thematic category | Brief description of the potential obstacle | Keyword | Policy maker's objectives | Harm to competition | Recommendations | Competent Ministry / Authority |
|---|---|---|---|---|---|---|---|---|---|
| 27 | **L 3021/2002 Restrictions on award of public contracts with individuals who are involved or participating in media companies and other provisions** | art. 8§1,2,3,5 | Radio broadcasting | Obsolete, because the issue of secondary placement of antennas of radio stations are covered by art. 64 of L. 4313/2014. | Obsolete Regulation | Obsolete. | Obsolete, inactive or redundant legislation can be a regulatory barrier by creating legal uncertainty; and potentially raises the operating costs facing suppliers, for example legal costs. | Explicitly abolish. | Minister-SG of Information and Communication/Ministry of Infrastructure, Transport and Networks |
| 28 | **L 3021/2002 Restrictions on award of public contracts with individuals who are involved or participating in media companies and other provisions** | art. 10§1, 2 | Radio Broadcasting | Obsolete, because art.20 par.1 of L.2644/1998 to which the provision makes reference has been abolished. Publishing of balance sheets has also been abolished. | Obsolete Regulation | Obsolete. | Obsolete, inactive or redundant legislation can be a regulatory barrier by creating legal uncertainty; and potentially raises the operating costs facing suppliers, for example legal costs. | Explicitly abolish. | Minister-SG of Information and Communication |
| 29 | **L 3905/2010 Reinforcement and Development of Film Art and other provisions** | art.7 | Film | Obsolete, because this provision describes a method of calculation of the amount granted to the Greek films which is based on article 5 which has been abolished by a recent law. | Obsolete Regulation | Obsolete. | Obsolete, inactive or redundant legislation can be a regulatory barrier by creating legal uncertainty; and potentially raises the operating costs facing suppliers, for example legal costs. | Explicitly abolish. | Ministry of Culture and Sports |
| 30 | **MD 198/64287/ 2003 (1812 B) Determination of the procedure and of all relevant documents for awarding the Greek identity certificate to a film production and for characterising fiction films, documentaries and animated films (long or short length) as Greek.** | | Film | MD 105396/2011 (2608 B) covers the same issue. | Obsolete Regulation | Obsolete. | Obsolete, inactive or redundant legislation can be a regulatory barrier by creating legal uncertainty; and potentially raises the operating costs facing suppliers, for example legal costs. | Explicitly abolish. | Ministry of Culture and Sports |
| 31 | **L 3592/2007 Concentration and Licensing of Mass Media Enterprises and Other Provisions** | | TV/Radio Broadcasting | In the law there are a lot of provisions and references to analogue TV which should be abolished, e.g.. art. 6, 7. | Obsolete Regulation | Obsolete. | Obsolete, inactive or redundant legislation can be a regulatory barrier by creating legal uncertainty; and potentially raises the operating costs facing suppliers, for example legal costs. | Explicitly abolish. | Minister-SG of Information and Communication |
| 32 | **L 3592/2007 Concentration and Licensing of Mass Media Enterprises and Other Provisions** | art. 5 §1,2 with conn to art 5. §5 | TV/Radio Broadcasting | It is prohibited to control more than one of the same kind of electronic media (TV/radio), meaning it is permitted to have up to 100% ownership of one TV licence and of one Radio licence (of informative content). | Cross ownership | It is our understanding that the provision aims to guarantee the pluralism and the objectivity of information. | Similarly to other provisions that regulates media ownership in a particular manner, It is not clear whether this provision has a net negative or a net positive effect to competition in the broadcasting (TV & Radio) market. On one hand investment choices of potential investors are limited by particular restrictions on the number and type of media ownership. On the other hand the provision prevents situations of over - concentration in the relevant market. In other words the objective of freedom of entrepreneurship should be counter balanced by the objective of pluralism. | We consider the restrictions to media ownership to be justified in light of the policy makers' objective of enhancing pluralism by preventing situations of over-concentration in the media sector. However, ownership and cross-ownership rules should be reviewed in combination with media concentration rules (as is done with newspapers), so as to conclude whether they can be updated to focus more on the real impact of media in the market and the shaping of public opinion (for instance, apply the criterion of audience share). | Minister-SG of Information and Communication |

## Sector: Media

| No | No and title of Regulation | Article | Thematic category | Brief description of the potential obstacle | Keyword | Policy maker's objectives | Harm to competition | Recommendations | Competent Ministry / Authority |
|---|---|---|---|---|---|---|---|---|---|
| 33 | **L 3592/2007 Concentration and Licensing of Mass Media Enterprises and Other Provisions** | art. 5 §3, 5 | TV/Radio Broadcasting | Control of a media enterprise of informative content exists when an individual or legal entity can influence the decisions taken by the enterprise. More specifically, it is considered control to exist in the following cases: a) having the status of owner, manager, member of a management body, partner, shareholder or have the right of voting in the shareholders' general meeting, being among the 10 shareholders with the largest amount of shares or voting rights and own individually or through another entity at least 1% of the capital of the media enterprise or b) holding the same capacity in both media enterprises or c) legal right to appoint or recall at least one member of the Administrative Board. | Media concentration rules | According to the official recital, this provision aims to promote pluralism, objective and equal information and competition. | It can be argued that the cut-off point of ownership of 1% of the capital of a media enterprise is too strict in an exercise to assess the control over the particular media company. It certainly not common in practise in assessing control in other sectors of the economy where more conventional criteria are followed (having the shareholders' majority for example). Here though as mentioned before the State aims not only to accommodate economic competition, the freedom of doing business and economic efficiency in general but also aims to fortify pluralism by promoting transparency in the ownership of media enterprises. | We consider the restrictions to media ownership to be justified in light of the policy makers' objective of enhancing pluralism by preventing situations of over-concentration in the media sector. However, Ownership and cross-ownership rules should be reviewed in combination with media concentration rules (as is done with newspapers), so as to conclude whether they can be updated to focus more on the real impact of media in the market and the shaping of public opinion (for instance, apply the criterion of audience share). | Minister-SG of Information and Communication |
| 34 | **L 3592/2007 Concentration and Licensing of Mass Media Enterprises and Other Provisions** | art. 5 §3 (b) | TV/Radio Broadcasting | It is prohibited for the spouse and the relatives up to the 3rd degree of an individual who has control of a media enterprise to control a second media enterprise of the same kind (TV or Radio) as long as it can be proved that there is unfair influence. This rule does not apply for spouses and relatives of non-Greek individuals who have shares of a media enterprise whose stocks are in EU or OECD member States Stock markets. | Media concentration rules | According to the official recital, this provision aims to promote pluralism, objective and equal information and competition. | This provision extends media ownership rules to close relatives of potential investors in the media sector in order to address a possible attempts of bypassing media ownership rules by fictitious transactions between relatives. Otherwise, similarly to other provisions that regulate media ownership in a particular manner, It is not clear whether this provision has a net negative or a net positive effect to competition in the broadcasting (TV & Radio) market. On one hand investment choices of potential investors are limited by particular restrictions on the number and type of media ownership. On the other hand the provision prevents situations of over - concentration in the relevant market. In other words the objective of freedom of entrepreneurship should be counter balanced by the objective of pluralism. | 1. Competent administrative authorities and the courts should be given specific criteria for the proof of unfair influence.<br>2. Abolish the exception currently in Article 5, paragraph 3(b) of Law 392/2007 provided for foreigners and Greek shareholders of companies registered in stock markets of EU and OECD member states. | Minister-SG of Information and Communication |
| 35 | **L 3592/2007 Concentration and Licensing of Mass Media Enterprises and Other Provisions** | art.5 §6 (b) | TV/Radio Broadcasting | The participation in media enterprises of non-informative content is permitted as long as there is: (i) participation in only one media enterprise of non-informative content and at the same time participation in one media enterprise of informative content of national or regional coverage or the participation in two media enterprises of non-informative content and no participation in a media enterprise of informative content and (ii) participation in not more than 15% of the licences of non-informative content that have been tendered in every region and up to 3 regions. | Cross ownership | According to the official recital, this provision aims to promote pluralism, objective and equal information and competition. | Similarly to other provisions that regulate media ownership in a particular manner, It is not clear whether this provision has a net negative or a net positive effect to competition in the broadcasting (TV & Radio) market. On one hand investment choices of potential investors are limited by particular restrictions on the number and type of media ownership. On the other hand the provision prevents situations of over - concentration in the relevant market. In other words the objective of freedom of entrepreneurship should be counter balanced by the objective of pluralism. | We consider the restrictions to media ownership to be justified in light of the policy makers' objective of enhancing pluralism by preventing situations of over-concentration in the media sector. However, ownership and cross-ownership rules should be reviewed in combination with media concentration rules (as is done with newspapers), so as to conclude whether they can be updated to focus more on the real impact of media in the market and the shaping of public opinion (for instance, apply the criterion of audience share). | Minister-SG of Information and Communication |

## Sector: Media

| No | No and title of Regulation | Article | Thematic category | Brief description of the potential obstacle | Keyword | Policy maker's objectives | Harm to competition | Recommendations | Competent Ministry / Authority |
|---|---|---|---|---|---|---|---|---|---|
| 36 | **L 3592/2007 Concentration and Licensing of Mass Media Enterprises and Other Provisions** | art. 5 §6 c | Radio Broadcasting | Until granting Radio broadcasting licences, it is permitted to participate in Radio stations of non-informative content as following: up to 5 radio stations in Attica, up to 3 in Thessaloniki, up to 1 in other regions. In any case, it is prohibited to participate in more than 5 radio stations of non-informative content in Greece and in up to 3 regions. | Cross ownership | It is our understanding that the provision aims to guarantee the pluralism and the objectivity of information. | Similarly to other provisions that regulate media ownership in a particular manner, It is not clear whether this provision has a net negative or a net positive effect to competition in the broadcasting (TV & Radio) market. On one hand investment choices of potential investors are limited by particular restrictions on the number and type of media ownership. On the other hand the provision prevents situations of over - concentration in the relevant market. In other words the objective of freedom of entrepreneurship should be counter balanced by the objective of pluralism. | We consider the restrictions to media ownership to be justified in light of the policy makers' objective of enhancing pluralism by preventing situations of over-concentration in the media sector. However, ownership and cross-ownership rules should be reviewed in combination with media concentration rules (as is done with newspapers), so as to conclude whether they can be updated to focus more on the real impact of media in the market and the shaping of public opinion (for instance, apply the criterion of audience share). | Minister-SG of Information and Communication |
| 37 | **L 3592/2007 Concentration and Licensing of Mass Media Enterprises and Other Provisions** | art.5§7 | TV broadcasting | Legally operating TV broadcasters of national coverage are considered those to which licences had been granted according to L. 1866/1989 (and then several law provisions gave extension to the validity of the licences). For the case of regional TV broadcasters, legally operating are those which were considered legal under L. 2644/1998 and maintained their legal status by several law provisions that have come in force over the years. | TV licensing | It is our understanding that the provision aims to clarify which TV broadcasters are considered legally operating and to provide them with legal security regarding their operation even though they do not have valid licences. | This provision should be viewed together with all similar regulations listed here that allow for temporary renewal of broadcasting licences and the subsequent status of "legally operating" but not entirely "legal" broadcasters which lacks further legal justification. This type of provisions severely limit competition in the market of TV and Radio broadcasting. They are severely damaging competition because the market is essentially sealed from new entrants - since no new licences are available and the incumbent broadcasters have their expired licences renewed on a temporary basis. Therefore the only way for a potential new entrant to invest in the market is to acquire one of the existing firms that own one of the temporary licences. Further, the fact that these licences are only renewed on a temporary basis creates uncertainty in the market and limits competition because it is very likely that under these circumstances, potential investment plans by incumbent and new entrant businesses are put on hold until a proper licensing procedure is launched and the rules are clearly stated. | At the moment, there is in progress one TV licensing procedure regarding TV broadcasters of terrestrial digital television broadcast of free-to-air content for national coverage and general content. However, these licences constitute only one of the types provided by the law (informative, non-general content, non informative, municipal, regional). The map of all types of TV licences available should be released so as the potential investors decide if and how they want to enter the market. The fact that licences are only renewed on a temporary basis creates uncertainty in the market and limits competition and therefore it should stop. | Minister-SG of Information and Communication |

## Sector: Media

| No | No and title of Regulation | Article | Thematic category | Brief description of the potential obstacle | Keyword | Policy maker's objectives | Harm to competition | Recommendations | Competent Ministry / Authority |
|---|---|---|---|---|---|---|---|---|---|
| 38 | **L 3592/2007 Concentration and Licensing of Mass Media Enterprises and Other Provisions** | art. 5§7 (b) | Radio broadcasting | Legally operating Radio broadcasters are considered those to which licences were granted according to PD 25/1988 (and other provisions) as well as those whose "legal status" has been recognised in several law provisions mainly on the basis that they have been operating since November 1998. | Radio Licensing | It is our understanding that the provision aims to clarify which Radio broadcasters are considered legally operating and to provide them with legal security regarding their operation without valid licences. | This provision should be viewed together with all similar regulations listed here that allow for temporary renewal of broadcasting licences and the subsequent status of "legally operating" but not entirely "legal" broadcasters which lacks further legal justification. This type of provisions severely limit competition in the market of TV and Radio broadcasting. They are severely damaging competition because the market is essentially sealed from new entrants - since no new licences are available and the incumbent broadcasters have their expired licences renewed on a temporary basis. Therefore the only way for a potential new entrant to invest in the market is to acquire one of the existing firms that own one of the temporary licences. Further, the fact that these licences are only renewed on a temporary basis creates uncertainty in the market and limits competition because it is very likely that under these circumstances, potential investment plans by incumbent and new entrant businesses are put on hold until a proper licensing procedure is launched and the rules are clearly stated. | 1. After completing the relevant technical analysis and issuing a map of frequencies, the authorities should launch tenders for each prefecture with a specific number of licences - both for radio stations of informative and non-informative (music, sports) content. This will establish a stable investment environment with legal certainty and specific conditions known to all participants from the outset. All other provisions that insert derogations to the licensing procedure should be abolished.<br>2. Law 2328/1995 and Law 3592/2007 should be streamlined, so as to establish a definitive legal framework for radio licensing. | Minister-SG of Information and Communication |
| 39 | **L 3592/2007 Concentration and Licensing of Mass Media Enterprises and Other Provisions** | art.5§10 | TV/Radio Broadcasting | It is prohibited to own media enterprises (TV. Radio, newspapers, magazines) as long as this ownership does not comply with the percentages provided in article 3 of L. 3592/2007 regarding concentration. This rule does not apply for foreign media enterprises and for Greek media enterprises that are listed in the stock markets of other EU member states or of OECD member countries. | Media concentration rules | It was not possible to identify the objective of the specific provision. However, in our understanding the provision aims to promote transparency and objective information. | Similarly to other provisions that regulate media ownership in a particular manner, it is not clear whether this provision has a net negative or a net positive effect to competition in the broadcasting (TV & Radio) market. On one hand investment choices of potential investors are limited by particular restrictions on the number and type of media ownership. On the other hand the provision prevents situations of over - concentration in the relevant market. In other words the objective of freedom of entrepreneurship should be counter balanced by the objective of pluralism. | Article 5, paragraph 10 of Law 3592/2007 should be abolished since it favours companies registered in stock markets of EU and OECD member states. | Minister-SG of Information and Communication |
| 40 | **L 3592/2007 Concentration and Licensing of Mass Media Enterprises and Other Provisions** | art.5§14 | TV/Radio Broadcasting | All the restrictions provided in art.5 regarding the ownership of media enterprises are applied only if the individuals or legal persons who own or participate in the media enterprises are Greek and only with regards their business activity in Greece. | Media concentration rules | It was not possible to identify the objective of the specific provision. However, in our understanding the provision aims to promote transparency and objective information. | The provision limits ownership regulations geographically to the Greek state. In other words, ownership rules apply for the enterprises owned within Greece by foreign nationals and any participation in foreign media companies is not accounted for towards filling the quotas of ownership rules (the same applies for Greek nationals who own or participate in foreign media companies). Other than that, similarly to other provisions that regulate media ownership in a particular manner, it is not clear whether this provision has a net negative or a net positive effect to competition in the broadcasting (TV & Radio) market. On the one hand investment choices of potential investors are limited by particular restrictions on the number and type of media ownership. On the other hand the provision prevents situations of over - concentration in the relevant market. In other words the objective of freedom of entrepreneurship should be counter balanced by the objective of pluralism. | We consider the restrictions to media ownership to be justified in light of the policy makers' objective of enhancing pluralism by preventing situations of over-concentration in the media sector. However, ownership and cross-ownership rules should be reviewed in combination with media concentration rules (as is done with newspapers), so as to conclude whether they can be updated to focus more on the real impact of media in the market and the shaping of public opinion (for instance, apply the criterion of audience share). | Minister-SG of Information and Communication |

## Sector: Media

| No | No and title of Regulation | Article | Thematic category | Brief description of the potential obstacle | Keyword | Policy maker's objectives | Harm to competition | Recommendations | Competent Ministry / Authority |
|---|---|---|---|---|---|---|---|---|---|
| 41 | **L 3592/2007 Concentration and Licensing of Mass Media Enterprises and Other Provisions** | art.5§16 | TV/Radio Broadcasting | The organisation and the operation as well as the control permitted of more than one media enterprises, electronic or not, can take place in the context of a group of media enterprises with common interests. In the framework of their common management and under the condition there is no harm to competition, TV and Radio stations which are controlled by the same people can: a) use or exchange the same sources (employees, infrastructure or other means to facilitate their operation), b) promote their programmes, services, activities using the same announcements, c) use the same programme sources such as audiovisual archive, make co-productions and sign contracts for common use of content. | TV advertising | According to the official recital, this provision aims to lead to economies of scale since it is permitted to the companies that belong to the same group to co-operate and exchange sources. | The core idea in this provision is not harmful to competition. On the contrary, being able to take advantage of possible economies of scale by a common use of resources within a media group that owns more than one media enterprises, improves the overall economic efficiency and releases resources that may be used in cost cutting and innovation. As an added note, in order to ensure a level playing field in the market, it should be made clear that these rules do not favour some competitors against others (e.g. line 1). | This provision is not harmful to competition apart from case b which should be in line with our recommendation of Line 1 and therefore it should be abolished. | Minister-SG of Information and Communication/Ministry of Culture and Sports |
| 42 | **L 3592/2007 Concentration and Licensing of Mass Media Enterprises and Other Provisions** | art. 8 §9 (στ) | Radio Broadcasting | In the case of a radio station that stops its operation or pauses it for o duration of at least 6 months or if there is a delay of 4 months to pay 1/3 of its employees or 1/3 of the total salary, the radio licence is recalled. After the application of half of the employees (1/3 should be journalists in case of radio station of informative content ), the radio licence is granted to the employees by the Minister in charge of the General Secretariat of Information and Communication. Under these circumstances, the amount of money for the minimum capital, the capital and the letter of guarantee is decided by the NCRTV and it can reach up to the 35% of the amount paid by the other Radio stations. | Radio bankruptcy | It was not possible to identify the objective of the specific provision. However, in our understanding the provision aims to avoid bulk dismissal of employees of radio stations in case the employees themselves can run the radio station. | This provision distorts market conditions in the radio broadcasting market. Normally, in any other industry, when a company goes bankrupt, it is usually driven into liquidation and this way resources are released (e.g. radio frequency) from an unsuccessful business for a new venture in the market. The provision in this case distorts the market by allowing bankrupt radio stations to operate on different terms to those of their non-bankrupt competitors with dubious results with regards to consumer welfare and to the job security of the former employees (now owners) of the radio station. | 1. Article 8, Paragraph 9 (στ) of Law 3592/2007 should be abolished.<br>2. After completing the relevant technical analysis and issuing a map of frequencies, the authorities should launch tenders for each prefecture with a specific number of licences both for radio stations of informative and non-informative (music, sports) content. This will establish a stable investment environment with legal certainty and specific conditions known to all participants from the outset. | Minister-SG of Information and Communication |
| 43 | **L 3592/2007 Concentration and Licensing of Mass Media Enterprises and Other Provisions** | art. 8 §14 | Radio Broadcasting | There is a requirement of a minimum number of full time employees -journalists, technicians and administration- that Radio stations of informative and non-informative content must have. This number is based on the population of the region. | Radio Licensing | According to the official recital, the provision aims to secure job positions as well as the smooth operation of Radio broadcasters. | Setting minimum employment requirements of the type imposed by this provision can be restrictive to competition and to the freedom of doing business. Imposing minimum requirements may create barriers to entry. Smaller companies may choose to operate on a smaller scale, but if this is not allowed by the legislation they will not be able to enter the market at all. This is a field that normally is not regulated by the State in most (if not all) other sectors of the economy. Due to this restriction Radio stations will tend to be extremely similar with each other in terms of employment structure and will not be able to manage their resources optimally. Eventually this may lead Radio broadcasters to operate on higher variable costs than they otherwise would, which in turn may lead to higher prices and less innovation in the market. | This provision should be explicitly abolished. | Minister-SG of Information and Communication |
| 44 | **L 3592/2007 Concentration and Licensing of Mass Media Enterprises and Other Provisions** | art.9 § A | Radio Broadcasting | Radio stations that participate in the competitive procedure for licensing get points because of their previous operation. These points increase following the number of years of operation and can be up to 120. | Radio Licensing | It is our understanding that the provision aims to boost the candidature of existent radio stations so as to secure their investment and the job positions. | This provision greatly distorts competition by treating incumbent businesses with more favourable terms in comparison to potential new entrants in the market (grandfather clause). The regulation lowers the probability of a new entrant to enter the market and may discourage some potential entrants and so reduce the number of participants in the market. | This provision should be explicitly abolished. | Minister-SG of Information and Communication |
| 45 | **L 3592/2007 Concentration and Licensing of Mass Media Enterprises and Other Provisions** | art.9 § A/4 | Radio broadcasting | Whereas there is a bonus of up to 120 points (depending on the years of operation) for the existent radio stations that participate in the competitive procedure for licensing in the region they broadcast, the same bonus is decreased by half (60 points) if the radio station participates in a competitive procedure for licensing in a different region than the one it used to broadcast. | Radio Licensing | It was not possible to identify the objective of the specific provision. However, in our understanding the provision aims to motivate the existent radio stations to remain at their region and maintain their premises and job positions. | This provision greatly distorts competition by treating incumbent businesses with more favourable terms in comparison to potential new entrants in the market (grandfather clause). The regulation lowers the probability of a new entrant to enter the market and may discourage some potential entrants and so reduce the number of participants in the market. | This provision should be explicitly abolished. | Minister-SG of Information and Communication |

## Sector: Media

| No | No and title of Regulation | Article | Thematic category | Brief description of the potential obstacle | Keyword | Policy maker's objectives | Harm to competition | Recommendations | Competent Ministry / Authority |
|---|---|---|---|---|---|---|---|---|---|
| 46 | **L 3592/2007 Concentration and Licensing of Mass Media Enterprises and Other Provisions** | art.9§ B | Radio Broadcasting | According to the competitive procedure for radio licensing, existing Radio stations to which administrative fines have been imposed because of breaching legal provisions referring to their operation, their content etc. get negative marks subject to the seriousness of the violation and the fine. | Radio Licensing | It is our understanding that the provision aims to guarantee that the Radio broadcasters that will be licensed are interested in the quality of their programme and obey the rules and regulations. | It is not harmful to competition if the state in a licensing procedure of a limited public resource such as the analogue radio frequencies reserves the right to evaluate the previous usage of this resource (positive or negative) as long as the evaluation criteria are clear and applicable to all players in the market. | The state should define and publish in advance all "positive" and "negative" criteria that are proportionate and applicable to all players in the market (incumbent and new entrants). | Minister-SG of Information and Communication |
| 47 | **L 3592/2007 Concentration and Licensing of Mass Media Enterprises and Other Provisions** | art.9 § ΣΤ | Radio Broadcasting | According to the competitive procedure for radio licensing, radio stations get points for the quality of their programme which is reviewed by the NCRTV. However, the law provides NCRTV with very vague criteria which apply only to the existing Radio stations. | Radio Licensing | According to the official recital, the provision aims to guarantee the qualitative level of the programme of radio stations and the fulfilment of the social mission of Radio broadcasting. | It is not harmful to competition if the state in a licensing procedure of a limited public resource such as the analogue radio frequencies reserves the right to evaluate the previous usage of this resource (positive or negative) as long as the evaluation criteria are clear and applicable to all players in the market. | The state should define and publish in advance all "positive" and "negative" criteria that are proportionate and applicable to all players in the market (incumbent and new entrants). | Minister-SG of Information and Communication |
| 48 | **L 3592/2007 Concentration and Licensing of Mass Media Enterprises and Other Provisions** | art. 12 | Radio Broadcasting | The law provides the competent Minister with the power to renew Radio licences for one time. The period and the amount of money due for the renewal are decided by the Minister. The same provision regarding TV licences is obsolete. | Radio Licensing | It was not possible to identify the objective of the specific provision. However, in our understanding this provision aims to allow the radio stations remain in operation if a new tender for licensing has not have been issued upon the expiration of the licences. | This provision severely limits competition in the market of Radio broadcasting. Under this provision the minister has the power to renew Radio licences for a long period of time (6 years the initial duration of the licence, plus another 6 years renewal by the minister) based on criteria which are not defined in advance and are well known to all players but are left to the discretion of the minister. Under an extreme scenario where all current licences get renewed the market may very well be sealed (for a period of 12 years) from new entrants since no new licences are available. In any case the fact that the criteria are not clearly stated in advance creates uncertainty and may work in favour of some Radio broadcasters over others. | The renewal of the Radio licences should not be left to the discretion of the Minister. Abolish the provision. | Minister-SG of Information and Communication |
| 49 | **L 2644/1998 Provisions for pay (subscription) radio and television** | art.1§2 | TV/Radio Broadcasting | According to competent authorities, the license is awarded by NCRTV instead of the Minister of Press and Media. | Obsolete Regulation | Obsolete. | Obsolete, inactive or redundant legislation can be a regulatory barrier by creating legal uncertainty; and potentially raises the operating costs facing suppliers, for example legal costs. | Explicitly abolish. | Minister-SG of Information and Communication |
| 50 | **L 2644/1998 Provisions for pay (subscription) radio and television** | art. 2§2 | TV/Radio Broadcasting | Only S.As with registered shares can hold a licence of Pay-Tv/Radio. Non Greek S.A.s have to declare registered shares unless a) they can prove high solvency and b) they have been in the market of media or of telecommunication for at least 3 years and c) according to the law of their country of origin they do not have to have registered shares; Or d) they have stocks in EU or OECD member states' stock markets (this applies also for Greek S.A.s). | Subscription TV/Radio | According to the official recital, the reason for the exclusion of companies that participate in the Stock market is the fact that the Stock market regulations require that a company complies with strict rules and conditions of operation, which also meet the requirements of transparency. Regarding the exception of foreign companies operating at least three years in the wider field of broadcasting or telecommunication services, the policy maker seeks to attract reliable and not occasionally active companies from abroad. | The exclusion of companies that participate in the Stock market is reasonable since it is indeed the case that Stock market regulations require that a company complies with strict rules and conditions of operation, which also meet the requirements of transparency. On the other hand the obligation of companies to have been in the market of media or of telecommunication for at least 3 years is unnecessary and hinders competition by creating barriers of entry to the relevant market especially for new formed companies that may otherwise have the financial capacity to invest in the industry. As a note there is no such restriction in the licensing procedures of free-to-air TV broadcasters and new companies may enter the market. | 1.The policy maker's objective to protect pluralism and objectivity in the media sector justifies the restrictions on share registration. If this condition is met, however, there is no point in going a step further and dictating the exact corporate structure of media organisations. The obligation to register shares easily allows regulators to trace ownership of media groups, if needed.<br>2.The high-solvency criterion for foreign companies should be abolished.<br>3. The requirement for foreign companies to have at least three years' previous presence in a media or telecommunications market should be abolished. | Minister-SG of Information and Communication |

## Sector: Media

| No | No and title of Regulation | Article | Thematic category | Brief description of the potential obstacle | Keyword | Policy maker's objectives | Harm to competition | Recommendations | Competent Ministry / Authority |
|---|---|---|---|---|---|---|---|---|---|
| 51 | **L 2644/1998 Provisions for pay (subscription) radio and television** | art. 2§3 | TV/Radio Broadcasting | Every S.A. can hold one licence for pay radio and TV by using the same technology and one more licence for the same content by using different technology. | Subscription TV/Radio | According to the official recital, the provision aims to avoid horizontal concentration in the field of broadcasting services. | The provision aims to avoid horizontal concentration. At the same time it harms competition by limiting the freedom of businesses to adopt new technologies and providing disincentives for innovation. Additionally, it limits competition within each different technological platform by forcing media enterprises to specialise in only two different technological platforms limiting this way the number of potential competitors within each technological platform. | 1. The restriction on the number of licences that a party using other technological methods of distribution than terrestrial can hold should be abolished.<br>2. The restriction on the number of delivery systems/means of distribution that a licensed pay-tv/radio broadcaster can use for transmitting its programming should be abolished. | Minister-SG of Information and Communication |
| 52 | **L 2644/1998 Provisions for pay (subscription) radio and television** | art.2 § 4 | TV/Radio Broadcasting | The holder of a pay TV-radio licence cannot hold a licence of free-to -air TV/Radio at the same time. The participation of a holder of pay TV/Radio in a company that owns one of the previous licences is legal only if there is no harm to competition. | Subscription TV/Radio | According to the official recital, the provision aims to avoid horizontal concentration in the field of broadcasting services. | Similarly to other provisions that regulate media ownership in a particular manner, It is not clear whether this provision has a net negative or a net positive effect to competition in the broadcasting (TV & Radio) market. On one hand investment choices of potential investors are limited by particular restrictions on the number and type of media ownership. On the other hand the provision prevents situations of over - concentration in the relevant market. In other words the objective of freedom of entrepreneurship should be counter balanced by the objective of pluralism. | Amend the provisions of Article 2, Paragraphs 4 and 5 of Law 2644/1998 so as to provide at least the same cross-ownership restrictions as those set out in Law 3592/2007. | Minister-SG of Information and Communication |
| 53 | **L 2644/1998 Provisions for pay (subscription) radio and television** | art.2 §5 | TV/Radio Broadcasting | The holder of licence of pay TV-radio, the shareholders as well as the shareholders of the shares of the owner cannot participate in more than two categories of media -TV, radio, newspapers - (magazines are not mentioned in the provision). | Subscription TV/Radio | According to the official recital, the provision aims to avoid horizontal concentration in the field of broadcasting services. | Similarly to other provisions that regulate media ownership in a particular manner, It is not clear whether this provision has a net negative or a net positive effect to competition in the broadcasting (TV & Radio) market. On one hand investment choices of potential investors are limited by particular restrictions on the number and type of media ownership. On the other hand the provision prevents situations of over - concentration in the relevant market. In other words the objective of freedom of entrepreneurship should be counter balanced by the objective of pluralism. However, given that L. 3592/2007 is in force and regulates the same issues (electronic media ownership) differently, there is legal uncertainty regarding its validity. | Amend the provisions of Article 2, Paragraphs 4 and 5 of Law 2644/1998 so as to provide at least the same cross-ownership restrictions as those set out in Law 3592/2007. | Minister-SG of Information and Communication |
| 54 | **L 2644/1998 Provisions for pay (subscription) radio and television** | art.3 § 1, 2, 3 | TV/Radio Broadcasting | Managers and suppliers of programmes to pay TV/radio have the obligation to be S.A.s and have registered (ονομαστικές) shares. Each manager and supplier cannot provide the owner of the pay TV/radio licence with more than 30% of the time of one month programme. Moreover, when they participate in other companies that provide programme, the total time of one month programme they can provide by using both capacities should not cover more than 40% of the time of one month programme. | Subscription TV/Radio | According to the official recital, the provision aims to avoid economic or other dependence of the holder of the licence from the manager or supplier of the programme. Moreover, it guarantees the political and cultural pluralism. Regarding, the participation in other companies, the official recital argues that the provision aims to avoid the circumvention of the first provision. | First, the obligation of managers and suppliers of Pay/TV to be SAs and have registered shares may come as a result from cross ownership restrictions that are listed here as well and from the general objective of the state to promote transparency in the media sector. It needs to be stressed though that these type of restrictions may be more relevant for the case of free to air broadcasters; they seem to be less relevant when it comes to subscription TV broadcasters and their programme suppliers where the consumers make their own decisions and the general public does not have free access to the product. Consequently any limitations to the owner of pay TV/radio licence regarding the source of their material hinders competition by not allowing an optimal allocation of resources. It may lead to increased costs, higher prices and limited consumer choice. | No recommendation is needed for the case of registered shares. However:<br>1. The compulsory corporate structure of an SA for suppliers should be abolished as other corporate structures can also guarantee the transparency required as long as they have to disclose their participants.<br>2. The limit on the hours of programming that can be supplied by one supplier should be abolished. | Minister-SG of Information and Communication |
| 55 | **L 2644/1998 Provisions for pay (subscription) radio and television** | art.3 § 4 | TV/Radio Broadcasting | The spouse or relatives up to the 4th grade of an individual who holds shares of a company of pay TV/radio or of a company which manages or supplies programmes for pay TV/radio cannot participate in companies of managers or suppliers of programmes unless they can prove that they are financially independent. | Subscription TV/Radio | According to official recital, since the status of the manager of the programme has the same value and importance as the status of the holder of pay TV or free-to air TV licence, the same restrictions should apply so as to avoid horizontal and vertical concentration in the field of broadcasting. | Cross ownership restrictions that are listed here as well and from the general objective of the state to promote transparency in the media sector. It needs to be stressed though that these type of restrictions may be more relevant for the case of free to air broadcasters; they seem to be less relevant when it comes to subscription TV broadcasters and their programme suppliers where the consumers make their own decisions and the general public does not have free access to the product. It is not well justified by the policy maker's objective why these restrictions should go beyond the general laws of competition. | The competent authorities should be provided with clear criteria so they can examine the "financial and business independence" of relatives in accordance with Article 3, Paragraph 4 of Law 2644/1998. | Minister-SG of Information and Communication |

## Sector: Media

| No | No and title of Regulation | Article | Thematic category | Brief description of the potential obstacle | Keyword | Policy maker's objectives | Harm to competition | Recommendations | Competent Ministry / Authority |
|---|---|---|---|---|---|---|---|---|---|
| 56 | **L 2644/1998 Provisions for pay (subscription) radio and television** | art. 3§6 | TV/Radio Broadcasting | Suppliers of TV programmes, their shareholders as well as the shareholders of the latter are not allowed to participate in companies that own licences of free-to-air Radio or companies that issue daily or not newspaper. | Subscription TV/Radio | According to official recital, since the status of the supplier of the programme has the same value and importance as the status of the owner of pay TV or free-to air TV licence, the same restrictions should apply so as to avoid horizontal and vertical concentration in the field of broadcasting. | Similarly to other provisions that regulate media ownership, it is not clear whether this provision has a net negative or a net positive effect to competition in the broadcasting (TV & Radio) market. On one hand investment choices of potential investors are limited by particular restrictions on the number and type of media ownership. On the other hand the provision prevents situations of over - concentration in the relevant market. In other words the objective of freedom of entrepreneurship should be counter balanced by the objective of pluralism. | Restrictions on the participation of suppliers in free-to-air broadcasters should be abolished (Article 3, Paragraph 6 of Law 2644/1998). | Minister-SG of Information and Communication |
| 0 | **L 2644/1998 Provisions for pay (subscription) radio and television** | art. 4 §1 | TV/Radio Broadcasting | The contracts signed between the owner of the licence and the manager of the programme are invalid if they have not been certified by the Minister in charge of the Secretariat of Information and Communication. | Subscription TV/Radio | According to the official recital, because of the importance of the co-operation between the owner of the licence and the manager or the supplier of the programme, their contracts should be checked. | This provision is clearly restrictive since it increases administrative costs for all affected businesses. Furthermore, it is not clear by the law under which terms the Minister may or may not certify a contract creating further legal uncertainty. | Abolish the compulsory verification of contracts between suppliers and pay-tv/radio licence holders should be abolished (Article 4, Paragraph 1 of Law 2644/1998). | Minister-SG of Information and Communication |
| 58 | **L 2644/1998 Provisions for pay (subscription) radio and television** | art. 9 §7 | TV/Radio Broadcasting | The owner of licence of pay TV/radio has to pay a fixed amount for the licence and a percentage of their revenues every year. This amount is provided by the law. However, it does not seem that it corresponds to a frequency or other state-owned source. | Subscription TV/Radio | According to the official recital, the provision aims to the collection of an amount of money for the enhancement of the supervisory role of NCRTV and for the development of the services of the national public broadcaster. | This provision harms competition by raising entry and operation costs for all new and incumbent Subscription TV/Radio broadcasters, potentially leading to limited suppliers in the market, higher prices and limited consumer choice. Meanwhile, IPTV and OTT fall under different regulatory regimes and they do not have to meet the same requirements and pay the same licensing fees. Therefore, an uneven playing field is created although all these providers offer similar products which are addressed to the same consumers. | 1. Update the one-off licence fee and annual fee paid by pay TV/radios, so as to correspond to new market conditions including IPTV and, if possible, OTT.<br>2. The distribution means of pay-tv/radio broadcasters should be streamlined to create a level playing field for pay TV, IPTV and OTT (where possible, and especially for the last). | Minister-SG of Information and Communication |
| 59 | **L 4389/2016 Urgent Provisions for the implementation of the Agreement for Financial Goals and Structural Reforms and other provisions** | art. 54 | TV/Radio Broadcasting | A Tax of 10% is imposed on the monthly bills for pay TV/radio (Affects only some players - the relevant market may not be defined properly). | Subscription TV/Radio | According to the official recital, the provision aims to the increase of the income of the state. | The 10% tax is only imposed to monthly bills of subscription TV/Radio broadcasters (using cable or Satellite technology) and are situated in Greece and not to Broadcasters situated in Foreign countries but who are able to sell subscription TV services by using IPTV technologies thus giving a competitive advantage to the latter group. | Streamline the provision (either expand or abolish) so as to create a level playing field for all competitors. | Minister-SG of Information and Communication |
| 60 | **L 4279/2014 Ratification of the purchase contract between the 1st Health Region of Attica, the General Tumour Hospital in Kifissia Agioi Anargyroi and the legal entity of private law Union of friends of the General Tumour Hospital in Kifissia Agioi Anargyroi and other provisions** | art.6§ 3, 4 | TV/Radio Broadcasting | Until granting TV and Radio licences, TV and Radio broadcasters with informative content can change their category of content to non-informative by submitting a declaration to NCRTV and continue their operation with their new content. | TV & Radio Licensing | It was not possible to identify the objective of the specific provision. However, in our understanding this provision aims to give the possibility to an existent enterprise which cannot afford the cost of a channel of informative content to turn to non informative. | This provision is not harmful to competition since it promotes the freedom of businesses to choose their own profile. Having said that, when a proper licensing procedure is launched and especially for the cases of limited resources like analogue FM Radio frequencies it is well justified for the State to distribute these frequencies in such a way that optimises access to different types of thematic Radio Stations. Under this assumption when a radio broadcaster is not able to broadcast the type of content according to the acquired licence, the State may reserve the right to revoke the licence in order to keep the thematic profile of the FM band constant. These restrictions are not that relevant any more for the case of TV broadcasters where the digital technology used allows for a much larger number of content providers than the analogue equivalent. | This provision needs to be abolished. | Minister-SG of Information and Communication |
| 61 | **MD Determination of the process for the aid of film producers and business using the special tax of art. 5 of L. 3905/2010** | | Motion picture, video and TV programme production, sound recording and music publishing activities | Obsolete, because art. 5 of L. 3905/2010 on which the MD is based has been abolished. | Obsolete Regulation | Obsolete. | Obsolete, inactive or redundant legislation can be a regulatory barrier by creating legal uncertainty; and potentially raises the operating costs facing suppliers, for example legal costs. | Explicitly abolish. | Ministry of Culture and Sports |
| 62 | **PD 235/2003 Terms and Conditions for Granting Licenses of establishing and operating a free-to-air radio broadcaster** | | Radio Broadcasting | L 3592/2007 provides new requirements for Radio licenses. Therefore, it seems that this PD should be revoked. | Obsolete Regulation | Obsolete. | Obsolete, inactive or redundant legislation can be a regulatory barrier by creating legal uncertainty; and potentially raises the operating costs facing suppliers, for example legal costs. | Explicitly abolish. | Minister-SG of Information and Communication |

## Sector: Media

| No | No and title of Regulation | Article | Thematic category | Brief description of the potential obstacle | Keyword | Policy maker's objectives | Harm to competition | Recommendations | Competent Ministry / Authority |
|---|---|---|---|---|---|---|---|---|---|
| 63 | **L 4173/2013 Establishment of the National Greek Broadcaster, ERT S.A** | art.2§11 | TV Broadcasting | ERT S.A is a provider of network and content for broadcasting its own programmes but also programmes of third parties. The competent Ministers provide ERT S.A with the frequencies for this use without payment. | TV Networks | It was not possible to identify the objective of the specific provision. However, in our understanding this provision aims to give the possibility to ERT S.A or to ERTnet as network provider to carry programmes of third parties. These programmes could be of public interest and therefore ERT can use the frequencies allocated to it for free. | This provision may be harmful to competition if the public broadcaster (ERT S.A.) is allowed to broadcast third party commercial programme providers (TV broadcasters). In this case the fact that ERTs network is provided by the state for free damages commercial network providers, who pay the state for their marketed frequencies (multiplexes). If the programmes broadcast by the network are considered as commercial , the provisions regarding all other broadcasters must apply (art.21 L. 4070/2012). | The phrase "third party" should be deleted, otherwise it should be further clarified in the law, in order to make sure that ERT cannot use its state-subsidised frequencies and premises to compete with commercial network providers. | Minister-SG of Information and Communication/Ministry of Infrastructure, Transport and Networks |
| 64 | **L 3905/2010 Reinforcement and Development of Film Art and other provisions** | art. 8 | Film/TV Broadcasting | Free-to-air TV stations and subscription TVs are required to spend 1,5% of their annual advertisement income and of their annual turnover, respectively, for film production. Moreover, whereas there is the possibility for the free-to-air TV stations to offer half of the amount that corresponds to the 1,5% to the Greek Film Centre for promotion and advertisement of films, there is not the same possibility for the subscription TV. | TV broadcasters and Film Industry | According to the official recital, this provision aims to the support of the film production by the TV broadcasters. | TV broadcasters are obliged to invest an amount in the local film industry, otherwise this amount will be deducted from them as a levy and will be paid to the state which in turn use it to finance film productions that are subsidised by the Greek Film Centre. This provision may distort the market against TV broadcasters and in favour of film producers by violating the freedom of the former to choose how to distribute their resources. It raises operation costs in the media sector (while at the same time providing a chance for new businesses or film makers to enter the market of film production). | 1. Pay-Tv broadcasters should also be allowed to opt to grant the Hellenic Film Centre free airtime for the advertisement and promotion of works of a total value that equals half the amount they are obliged to invest in the production of Greek films, thus reducing by half their obligation to invest directly in film production, similar to free-to-air TV broadcasters.<br>2. Both pay-tv broadcasters and free-to-air TV broadcasters' film-investment contributions should be calculated on the same basis according to their financial standing. | Ministry of Culture and Sports |
| 65 | **MD 84148/1376//1402/2005** | | TV Broadcasting/Film | Each professional related to the production of films or TV programmes should meet some requirements provided by the ministerial decision in order to obtain the license to exercise the profession. | Obsolete Regulation | The MD is based on art. 1 L. 358/1976 which was abolished by art 1 par. H(2) of L. 4254/2014. | Obsolete, inactive or redundant legislation can be a regulatory barrier by creating legal uncertainty, and potentially raises the operating costs facing suppliers, for example legal costs. | Explicitly abolish. | Ministry of Culture and Sports |
| 66 | **L 4313/2014 Regulation of Transport, Telecommunications and Public Works issues and other provisions** | art. 86§1 | Radio Broadcasting | The tender for radio licensing should be issued by 31.12.2015 and until then the radio stations are considered legally operating. | Radio Licensing | It is our understanding that the provision aims to give the radio stations an extension to their operation because the State has not issued the relevant tender. However, this tender must have been issued until 31.12.2015. Now it seems that the radio stations operate without any legal basis. | The lack of licence renewal OR the lack of a new tender that initiates a new licensing procedure creates legal uncertainty for all companies in the market as well as potential newcomers. | 1. After completing the relevant technical analysis and issuing a map of frequencies, the authorities should launch tenders for each prefecture with a specific number of licences both for radio stations of informative and non-informative (music, sports) content. This will establish a stable investment environment with legal certainty and specific conditions known to all participants from the outset. All other provisions that insert derogations to the licensing procedure should be abolished.<br>2. Law 2328/1995 and Law 3592/2007 should be streamlined, so as to establish a definitive legal framework for radio licensing. | Minister-SG of Information and Communication |

## Sector: Media

| No | No and title of Regulation | Article | Thematic category | Brief description of the potential obstacle | Keyword | Policy maker's objectives | Harm to competition | Recommendations | Competent Ministry / Authority |
|---|---|---|---|---|---|---|---|---|---|
| 67 | **L 2121/1993 Copyright law** | art. 55 §2, 58 | IPR | A. It is presumed that the collecting societies of IPRights or neighbouring rights "holders" represent all the beneficiaries and works they declare in writing that they have the right to. B. Regarding specifically the collection of equitable remuneration of performers of art. 49 L. 2121/1993, it is additionally presumed that the collecting society represents all the beneficiaries both national and international and for all their works. The first presumption may be overturned if the user proves before the Court that the collecting society does not represent the beneficiaries or works that it has declared in writing that it does. On the other hand, regarding the collection of fair compensation, where there is no obligation of the organisation for written declaration of representation, the user/broadcaster may not be able to overturn the presumption. | IPR Rights | It is our understanding that this provision aims to facilitate the protection of rights holders and the collection of royalties and notably of fair compensation provided in Art. 49 of Law 2121/1993 through collective organisations. | Users may face increased costs because they are obliged to pay equitable remuneration even if they broadcast audio and/or visual works not represented by the specific collecting society or even if they have not broadcasted works of specific rights holders. The reason for this distortion is the immense difficulty to prove before the courts which beneficiaries are or are not represented by Collecting societies collecting the equitable remuneration of Art. 49 Law 2121/1993. In addition, relevant Court proceedings are time-consuming and costly. | 1. It should be clarified either in the law or in a circular that the legal presumption of Art.55 par. 2 rec. 2 Law 2121/1993 is rebuttable and that users who opt for broadcasting specific works not represented by the collecting societies in the sense that their rights holders do not wish to receive the equitable remuneration may not be obliged to pay the relevant fees to collecting societies.<br>2. An independent alternative dispute resolution mechanism could be established (see also the option provided by art. 34 of Directive 2014/26/EU) so as to give users, collecting societies and rights holders the option to settle their disputes in a less time-consuming and costly procedure outside Courts. | Ministry of Culture and Sports |
| 68 | **472/157/23-04-2008 EETT (Hellenic Telecommunications and Post Commission) Administrative Regulation** | | Television broadcasting | Assignment of analogue frequencies to TV broadcasters | Obsolete Regulation | Obsolete. | Obsolete, inactive or redundant legislation can be a regulatory barrier by creating legal uncertainty; and potentially raises the operating costs facing suppliers, for example legal costs. | Explicitly abolish. | Ministry of Infrastructure, Transport and Networks |

The present recommendations do not include the assessment of Law 4339/2015 and of Joint Ministerial Decision 7577/2016 in relation to digital free-to-air TV licences, due to ongoing administrative and legal procedures.

## Sector: Chemicals and rubber, electrical equipment, paper and printing

| No | No and title of Regulation | Article | Thematic category | Brief description of the potential obstacle | Keyword | Policy maker's objectives | Harm to competition | Recommendations | Competent Ministry / Authority |
|---|---|---|---|---|---|---|---|---|---|
| 1 | **Law 4036/2012 "Circulation of plant protection products in the market, rational use and other provisions"** | art. 35 par. 1α, 1β and 1γ, par. 2 and par. 4 | Manufacturing and wholesale trade of plant protection products | a) Trade (wholesale and/or retail) of plant protection products is allowed only by specialised stores that have a "responsible scientist" (special requirements are set for him/her). A notification procedure is foreseen.<br>b) Sales are executed either by a "responsible scientist" and/or an "employee-salesperson" (special requirements are set for him/her) who has to be available at the time of selling. | Licensing | According to the official recital, the objective of the provision is to set requirements for the wholesale and retail trade of plant protection products. Following further communication with the Ministry, plant protection products are chemicals and their secure sustainable use and storage is necessary to reduce the risks and impact on human health and the environment, in line with in EU Directive 2009/128. They should be traded with caution and notifying a responsible scientist, as well as the presence of the latter or an employee-salesperson at the time of sale in specialised stores, guarantee their proper use.<br>In line with EU Directive 2009/128 (art. 6 par. 1). | No harm to competition has been identified. The requirements set are proportionate to the objective. | No recommendation for change. | Ministry of Interior and Administrative Reconstruction/ Economy, Development and Tourism / Finance/ Justice, Transparency and Human Rights / Rural Development and Food / Education, Research and Religious Affairs / Health |
| 2 | **Law 4036/2012 "Circulation of plant protection products in the market, rational use and other provisions"** | art. 35 par 1δ, and par. 5α | Manufacturing and wholesale trade of plant protection products | A prescription, issued by a scientist/professional who meets the criteria of a "responsible scientist" (but not necessarily is one), is a prerequisite for the selling of a plant protection product. Also, responsible for the proper execution of the prescription at the trading store is the "responsible scientist" and/or the "employee-salesperson". | Trading of products | According to the official recital, the objective of the provision is to set requirements of the wholesale and retail trade of plant protection products. Following further communication with the Ministry: a) plant protection products are chemicals and their secure sustainable use and storage is necessary to reduce the risks and impact on human health and the environment, in line with EU Directive 2009/128, and b) the electronic prescription system (not yet in force) is introduced in order to assure the proper use of plant protection products; in line with EU Directive 2009/128 (art. 1, 3 and 14 on sustainable use). | No harm to competition has been identified. The implementation of the prescription system, as well as the requirement for a scientist/professional, are proportionate to the objective. | Recommendation to start enforcing the electronic prescription system. | Ministry of Interior and Administrative Reconstruction/ Economy, Development and Tourism / Finance/ Justice, Transparency and Human Rights / Rural Development and Food / Education, Research and Religious Affairs / Health |
| 3 | **Law 4384/2016 "Agricultural co-operatives, forms of collective organisation of rural areas and other provisions. Amendment of Laws 4152/2013 on fertilisers and seeds and 4036/2012 on plant protection products"** | art. 48 par. 2δ | Manufacturing and wholesale trade of plant protection products | An exemption from prescription is granted for plant protection products that are to be used for plantations smaller than 1,000 $m^2$ and do not have the "hazard pictogram"; in these cases, electronic registration of the sales document is enough. Also, the "responsible scientist" who makes the sale is obliged to give instructions for the product's proper use. | Trading of products - Regulatory uncertainty | There is no official recital. However, following communication with the Ministry, this exemption is granted in order to facilitate market operation, taking into account a risk analysis for the selling of non-toxic plant protection products for use in small plantations. | No harm to competition has been identified from the exemption; it is proportionate to the objective. However, the fact that there is no mention of an employee-salesperson being also able to provide instructions for the proper use of plant protection products may create regulatory uncertainty. | Add the employee-salesperson in the wording of the provision. | Ministry of Interior and Administrative Reconstruction/ Economy, Development and Tourism / Finance/ Justice, Transparency and Human Rights / Rural Development and Food / Education, Research and Religious Affairs / Health |
| 4 | **Law 4036/2012 "Circulation of plant protection products in the market, rational use and other provisions"** | art. 47 par. γ and par. δ | Manufacturing and wholesale trade of plant protection products | Obligation for licence holders of plant protection products (including those with macro-organisms) to declare wholesale price lists and annual price changes to the Ministry of Rural Development and Food by March 31 of each year. A Retail Price Observatory is also founded. | Pricing | According to the official recital, the objective of the provision is to increase competitiveness and transparency in the trade of plant protection products. The Retail Price Observatory is inactive in practice. | Although, according to the Ministry, wholesale price levels are not publicly announced and therefore accessible to competitors, this process constitutes an administrative cost for the companies. Also, it may lead to price rigidities and harm competition.<br>Furthermore, with respect to the Retail Price Observatory, it may lead to price coordination between companies, price rigidities and increase administrative costs for daily updates. Price-list notifications cause price rigidity, discourage pricing flexibility in response to changes in market supply and demand conditions and reduce the transparency of discount policies available to all consumers. Eventually this leads to higher prices and lower quality and quantity offered by the suppliers, therefore reducing significantly the incentives and the ability to compete, resulting in consumer welfare loss. | Abolish the provisions. | Ministry of Interior and Administrative Reconstruction/ Economy, Development and Tourism / Finance/ Justice, Transparency and Human Rights / Rural Development and Food / Education, Research and Religious Affairs / Health |
| 5 | **Presidential Decree 159/2013 "Plant protection products trading and store functionality requirements"** | art. 7 par. 2 (referring to art. 5 par. 1ε and 3b and art. 6 par. 1α) and art. 7 par. 4α | Manufacturing and wholesale trade of plant protection products | Requirements for the wholesale trade notification of plant protection products are set:<br>a) art. 5 par. 1ε and 3β (also valid for art. 7 par. 2): the same person cannot be notified as a "responsible scientist" for more than one store and continuous presence is required<br>b) art. 6 par. 1α (also valid for art. 7 par. 2): For legal persons, the "responsible scientist" must have at least 20% capital share or he/she must be an employee with continuous presence at the store; also he/she cannot open a second store without employing another person as a "responsible scientist"<br>c) art.7, par. 4α: specific requirements for the storage of the wholesalers (see in conjunction with row 7). | Licensing - Raises cost of entry - Regulatory uncertainty | a) Following communication with the Ministry, plant protection products are chemicals and their secure sustainable use and storage is necessary to reduce the risks and impact on human health and the environment, in line with EU Directive 2009/128. They should be traded with caution and notifying a responsible scientist in the specialised stores guarantees their proper use.<br>b) Following communication with the Ministry, this requirement is introduced for control purposes, in order to ensure the responsible scientist's active involvement in the undertaking and presence at the store.<br>c) See art. 11 (in conjunction with row 7). | a) This provision is inactive and not implemented in practice and hence creates uncertainties in the business environment. Law 4036/2012 was amended in 2014, allowing for an employee-salesperson to also execute sales. The requirement for continuous presence of the responsible scientist is therefore superseded.<br>b) The requirement for minimum capital share restricts business practices. Also, the provision on the continuous presence of the responsible scientist is inactive and not implemented in practice and so creates uncertainties in the business environment (Law 4036/2012 was amended in 2014, allowing for an employee-salesperson to also execute sales).<br>c) See art. 11 (in conjunction with row 7). | a) Abolish the requirement according to which the responsible scientist notified for one store cannot be notified as a responsible scientist for another establishment.<br>b) Abolish the minimum capital share requirement, as well as the requirement for the continuous presence of the responsible scientist.<br>c) See art. 11 (in conjunction with row 7). | Ministry of Rural Development and Food |
| 6 | **Presidential Decree 159/2013 "Plant protection products trading and store functionality requirements"** | art. 9 par. 4 | Manufacturing and wholesale trade of plant protection products | Natural or legal persons who provide storage services for plant protection products intended for the wholesale trade are obliged to provide information on their clients/suppliers with whom they co-operate to the competent Regional authorities. | Trading of products - Regulatory uncertainty | There is no official recital. However, following communication with the Ministry, this requirement is set for record-keeping and control purposes, in line with Directive 1107/2009 (art. 67). | No harm to competition has been identified. The requirement is proportionate to the objective. | No recommendation for change. | Ministry of Rural Development and Food |

## Sector: Chemicals and rubber, electrical equipment, paper and printing

| No | No and title of Regulation | Article | Thematic category | Brief description of the potential obstacle | Keyword | Policy maker's objectives | Harm to competition | Recommendations | Competent Ministry / Authority |
|---|---|---|---|---|---|---|---|---|---|
| 7 | **Presidential Decree 159/2013 "Plant protection products trading and store functionality requirements"** | art. 11 par. 1α, 1ε, 1στ and 1η | Manufacturing and wholesale trade of plant protection products | Requirements for the storage of wholesale trade facilities are set.<br>a) par 1α: minimum surface of 100 m$^2$ of the storage facilities<br>b) par 1α: requirement to be on the ground floor<br>c) par 1ε: extra storage only in basement or half-basement<br>d) par 1στ: plant protection products must be kept separately from other agricultural inputs and classified in categories<br>e) par 1η: special room for unsuitable products | Licensing - Raises cost of entry | According to the Directive 2009/128, art. 13, "member states shall ensure that storage areas for pesticides for professional use are constructed in such a way as to prevent unwanted releases. Particular attention shall be paid to location, size and construction materials". Following communication with the Ministry, the objective of the provision is to meet these requirements; also it takes into account that plant protection products are flammable and easy access to emergency services should be guaranteed. | a, b and c) Restrictive surface and floor building requirements may act as barriers to entry and constraint suppliers' strategy and business practices. We understand from the competent authorities that they are not considered restrictive for current incumbents, however they may limit future entry.<br>d and e) No harm to competition identified, it is proportionate to the objective. | a, b and c) Abolish the provision.<br>d and e) No recommendation for change. | Ministry of Rural Development and Food |
| 8 | **Presidential Decree 159/2013 "Plant protection products trading and store functionality requirements"** | art. 12 par. 2β | Manufacturing and wholesale trade of plant protection products | If the "responsible scientist" leaves the trading company of plant protection products, a replacement has to be found and announced within 15 days, otherwise the Ministry removes the company from the registry. During this time, no sales are allowed. | Trading of products - Regulatory uncertainty | There is no official recital. However, following communication with the Ministry: a) plant protection products are chemicals and their secure sustainable use and storage is necessary to reduce risk and any impact on human health and the environment; they should therefore be traded with caution and notifying a responsible scientist in specialised stores guarantees their proper use, and b) the grace period takes into account the time that it might take to find a replacement, as well as the level of urgency to supply the professional user with the proper plant protection product. | This provision limits the ability of an enterprise to operate, without the responsible scientist, for more than 15 days. In principle, the restriction is proportionate to the objective. | No recommendation for change. | Ministry of Rural Development and Food |
| 9 | **Circular 7915/87546/2013 "Employment for the trading of plant protection products"** | | Manufacturing and wholesale trade of plant protection products | As the employment of a "responsible scientist" or certified "employee-salesperson" is a prerequisite for the selling of plant protection products, it is made clear that he/she can be employed either full-time or part-time. | Licensing | There is no official recital. Following communication with the Ministry, this requirement is set in order to facilitate market operation. | No harm to competition has been identified. The implementation of part-time employment is proportionate to the objective. | No recommendation for change. | Ministry of Rural Development and Food |
| 10 | **Circular 4016/41125/2014 "Notification procedure of pesticides trading and store functionality requirements"** | chapter 3.1 | Manufacturing and wholesale trade of plant protection products | The notification requirement for the trading of plant protection products also stands for the case of e-commerce sales. Therefore, the seller must also have a physical trading establishment/store, according to PD 159/2013. | Licensing - Regulatory uncertainty | There is no official recital. However, following communication with the Ministry, the objective of this provision is to clarify the requirements of operation in the case of online sales of plant protection products, so that secure sustainable use and storage is achieved. | The wording of this provision may create regulatory uncertainty, as it seems to be excluding trading companies that do not intend to execute sales in their physical establishment, but only sell online (e.g. by co-operating with logistic companies for the storage of their plant protection products). | Clarify that operators do not need to have a physical store but can co-operate with logistic companies for the storage of their plant protection products. | Ministry of Rural Development and Food |
| 11 | **Circular 4016/41125/2014 "Notification procedure of pesticides trading and store functionality requirements"** | chapter 3.3 and chapter 6.2.4 | Manufacturing and wholesale trade of plant protection products | Trade of plant protection products is forbidden by people not having the credentials set out in art. 35 of Law 4036/2012. | Licensing - Raises cost of entry | There is no official recital. However, following communication with the Ministry, plant protection products are chemicals and their secure sustainable use and storage is necessary to reduce risks and impact on human health and the environment, in line with EU Directive 2009/128. They should therefore be traded with caution and notifying a responsible scientist in specialised stores guarantees their proper use. | No harm to competition has been identified. The requirements set are proportionate to the objective. | No recommendation for change. | Ministry of Rural Development and Food |
| 12 | **Circular 4016/41125/2014 "Notification procedure of pesticides trading and store functionality requirements"** | chapter 8.1 | Manufacturing and wholesale trade of plant protection products | The trading store must be on the ground floor. Extra storage room can exist only in basement or half-basement. | Licensing - Raises cost of entry | According to EU Directive 2009/128, art. 13, "Member states shall ensure that storage areas for pesticides for professional use are constructed in such a way as to prevent unwanted releases. Particular attention shall be paid to location, size and construction materials". Following communication with the Ministry, the objective of the provision is to meet these requirements; it also takes into account that plant protection products are flammable and easy access for emergency services should be guaranteed. | Restrictive floor building requirements may act as barriers to entry and constraint suppliers' strategy and business practices. We understand from the competent authorities that they are not considered restrictive for current incumbents, however they may limit future entry. | Abolish the provision. | Ministry of Rural Development and Food |
| 13 | **Circular 4016/41125/2014 "Notification procedure of pesticides trading and store functionality requirements"** | chapter 8.6 | Manufacturing and wholesale trade of plant protection products | A specific floor plan for an establishment/store trading plant protection products is suggested. | Licensing - Raises cost of entry - Regulatory uncertainty | There is no official recital. However, following communication with the Ministry, the objective of the provision is to ensure safe storage of plant protection products. | This provision creates regulatory uncertainty. Even though it is indicative, it could be interpreted as a standard plan, with respect to building requirements, and thus may act as barrier to entry and restrict business activity. | Abolish the provision. | Ministry of Rural Development and Food |
| 14 | **Ministerial Decision 9497/104760/2014 "Prescription for the use of plant protection products"** | art. 2 par. 1 | Manufacturing and wholesale trade of plant protection products | Only a scientist/professional who meets the criteria to become a "responsible scientist" (but is not necessarily one) can prescribe a plant protection product via the electronic system. | Trading of products | There is no official recital. However, following communication with the Ministry: a) plant protection products are chemicals and their secure sustainable use and storage is necessary to reduce the risks and impact on human health and the environment, in line with EU Directive 2009/128, and b) the electronic prescription system (not yet in force) is introduced in order to assure the proper use of plant protection products; in line with EU Directive 2009/128 (art. 1, 3 and 14 on sustainable use). | No harm to competition has been identified. The requirement of a scientist/professional for the prescription is proportionate to the objective. | Recommendation to start enforcing the electronic prescription system. | Ministry of Rural Development and Food |

## Sector: Chemicals and rubber, electrical equipment, paper and printing

| No | No and title of Regulation | Article | Thematic category | Brief description of the potential obstacle | Keyword | Policy maker's objectives | Harm to competition | Recommendations | Competent Ministry / Authority |
|---|---|---|---|---|---|---|---|---|---|
| 15 | **Ministerial Decision 334/3099/2013 "Definition of terms and conditions for the registry of manufacturers of plant protection products"** | art. 2,3,4 | Manufacturing and wholesale trade of plant protection products | Registration requirements and procedure of registry for manufacturing companies of plant protection products are set, including:<br>a) 2c: being equipped with machinery and laboratories<br>b) 2d: having proper building infrastructure<br>c) 3 points 5 and 6: a need for mechanical engineer certifications<br>d) 3 point 7: a statement for quality control of all production, by each lot<br>e) 3 point 8: the employment of a "technical director". | Licensing - Raises cost of entry | There is no official recital. However, following communication with the Ministry, the provision aims to ensure that manufacturing of plant protection products is secure, taking into account that they can be toxic and/or flammable chemicals. | No harm to competition has been identified. The requirements are proportionate to the objective. | No recommendation for change. | Ministry of Rural Development and Food |
| 16 | **Ministerial Decision 10042/100536/2012 "Rules for the advertisement of plant protection products"** | art. 2 par. 2 | Manufacturing and wholesale trade of plant protection products | TV advertising of plant protection products is not allowed. Advertising on other media is allowed. | Advertising | There is no official recital. However, following communication with the Ministry, plant protection products are chemicals and their secure sustainable use is necessary to reduce the risks and impact on human health and the environment. Also, according to EU Regulation 1107/2009, art. 66 par. 3, member states may prohibit or restrict the advertising of plant protection products in certain media. | This provision limits freedom of suppliers to advertise their goods and limits their marketing strategies, thus it limits the ability of suppliers to compete. Also, taking into account the fact that advertisement in all other media is allowed, including internet, this restriction is disproportionate to the objective. | Abolish the provision. | Ministry of Rural Development and Food |
| 17 | **Circular 2012 "Guidelines for the advertisement of plant protection products"** | question 3 and 9 | Manufacturing and wholesale trade of plant protection products | It is forbidden to distribute, free of charge, samples of plant protection products in unapproved packages. | Advertising | There is no official recital. However, following communication with the Ministry, according to Regulation 1107/2009, art. 31, par 4i, "the authorisation requirements of plant protection products shall also include, where applicable, the packaging size and material", in order to assure quality of products and protection of professional users. | This provision limits freedom of suppliers to advertise or market their goods and may harm competition. However, this restriction is proportionate to the objective. | No recommendation for change. | Ministry of Rural Development and Food |
| 18 | **Ministerial Decision 10211/102084/2012 "Provisions on inspection of the production, storing or moving of pesticides without licence to be distributed in the Greek market destined to be used in another member state or third country"** | art. 2 par. 1 | Manufacturing and wholesale trade of plant protection products | A notification is needed when a company imports, produces, packages or stores plant protection products that do not have licence for distribution in the Greek market, but are destined to be used in another member state or third country. However, there are different terms: in the first case 5 days are needed, in the second, 10 days. | Trading of products | There is no official recital. However, following communication with the Ministry, the aim of the provision is to provide the Custom Authorities with enough time to handle plant protection products destined for third countries. | No harm to competition has been identified. The implementation of different terms (notification days) does not create differential treatment, as the products are destined to distinct markets. It is proportionate to the objective. | No recommendation for change. | Ministry of Rural Development and Food |
| 19 | **Ministerial Decision 10211/102084/2012 "Provisions on inspection of the production, storing or moving of pesticides without licence to be distributed in the Greek market destined to be used in another member state or third country"** | art. 2 par. 7 | Manufacturing and wholesale trade of plant protection products | Companies that have imported, produced, packaged or stored plant protection products that are not licensed for distribution in the Greek market, but destined for use in another member state or third country and which over a period of 2 years and 10 shipments controlled and found compliant with the regulatory framework, are entitled to a simplified procedure. | Trading of products | There is no official recital. However, following communication with the Ministry, the aim of the provision is to facilitate enterprises that have conformed with the legislation. | In principle, this provision creates differential treatment and may discourage enterprises. However, it is proportionate to the objective. | No recommendation for change. | Ministry of Rural Development and Food |
| 20 | **Law 4036/2012 "Circulation of plant protection products in the market, rational use and other provisions"** | art. 9 par. 6 | Manufacturing and wholesale trade of plant protection products | A fine is imposed only when the expiry date of a plant protection product has passed, as well as impermissible deviations in storage stability formulations are found. However, the only information available to the consumer is the expiry date on the label and thus he/she cannot find out that the product can still be used. | Trading of products - Shelf-life | There is no official recital. However, following communication with the Ministry, the aim of the provision is to protect suppliers, distributors and consumers from fine imposition, when plant protection products have expired but have no deviations in their storage stability formulations. | This provision affects the information required by buyers to shop effectively and thus limits the choices and the information available to them. In particular, the consumer is only aware of the expiry date on the label and he/she cannot find out that the product can still be used. There is unequal information available to the parties involved. | Abolish the provision. | Ministry of Interior and Administrative Reconstruction/ Economy, Development and Tourism / Finance/ Justice, Transparency and Human Rights / Rural Development and Food / Education, Research and Religious Affairs / Health |
| 21 | **Circular 3575/40028/2013 "Distribution to the market of plant protection products according to Regulation 547/2011"** | chapter 2 | Manufacturing and wholesale trade of plant protection products | Plant protection products whose circulation licences refer to storage stability formulation should indicate an expiry date on their labelling. | Trading of products - Shelf-life | There is no official recital. However, following communication with the Ministry, the aim of the provision is to comply with the labelling requirements as set out in EU Regulation 547/2011, "The following information shall be included clearly and indelibly on the packaging of plant protection products: ...where necessary, the expiry date for normal conditions of storage", as well as with the EU Regulation 1107/2009 on plant protection product authorisation. | No harm to competition has been identified. It is our understanding that according to international practice, the expiry date of a plant protection product usually equals the storage stability formulation study. | No recommendation for change. | Ministry of Rural Development and Food |
| 22 | **Ministerial Decision 1716/1999 "Plant protection product manufacturer and requirements for circulation of products"** | as a whole | Manufacturing and wholesale trade of plant protection products | Obsolete - Superseded by Law 4036/2012 on circulation of plant protection products in the market. | Regulatory uncertainty | This provision aims to set the requirements for plant protection product manufacturers and the circulation of their products. | Obsolete. | Explicitly repeal the provision. | Ministry of Rural Development and Food |
| 23 | **Presidential Decree 115/1997 "On approval, market distribution and control of plant protection products"** | as a whole | Manufacturing and wholesale trade of plant protection products | Obsolete - Directive 91/414 revoked by Regulation 1107/2009. | Regulatory uncertainty | This provision sets out the requirements on approval, market distribution and control of plant protection products. | Obsolete. | Explicitly repeal the provision. | Ministry of Rural Development and Food |
| 24 | **Ministerial Decision 85418/1988 "Techniques and methods for the control of plant protection products"** | as a whole | Manufacturing and wholesale trade of plant protection products | Obsolete - MD 5878/69892/2015 on technical procedures for chemical control of plant protection products. | Regulatory uncertainty | This provision sets out the techniques and methods for controlling plant protection products. | Obsolete. | Explicitly repeal the provision. | Ministry of Rural Development and Food |

## Sector: Chemicals and rubber, electrical equipment, paper and printing

| No | No and title of Regulation | Article | Thematic category | Brief description of the potential obstacle | Keyword | Policy maker's objectives | Harm to competition | Recommendations | Competent Ministry / Authority |
|---|---|---|---|---|---|---|---|---|---|
| 25 | **Law 4384/2016 "Agricultural co-operatives, forms of collective organisation of rural areas and other provisions. Amendment of Laws 4152/2013 on fertilisers and seeds and 4036/2012 on plant protection products"** | art. 47 | Manufacturing and wholesale trade of fertilisers | Amends Law 4152/2013 based on which PD 159/2014 and JMD 4166/51687/2014 allowed for part-time employment of the "responsible scientist". The provision now requires a full-time dependent work contract for the "responsible scientist", at every establishment. | Licensing - Raises cost of entry | There is no official recital. However, following communication with the Ministry, fertilisers are chemical products (with some, such as ammonium nitrate, having potentially explosive properties) and should be traded with caution. The responsible scientist therefore guarantees proper use and minimises risk of environmental burden and degradation (e.g. nitrate pollution, eutrophication). | The presence of a responsible scientist during business operating hours is justified to achieve the policy objective. However, a full-time dependent work contract may raise the labour cost of operation for smaller firms, which may not operate full-time. | Abolish the restriction on the full-time dependent work contract for the responsible scientist. | Ministry of Economy, Development and Tourism / Finance/ Rural Development and Food/ Justice/ Health/ Interior and Administrative Reconstruction/ Education, Research and Religious Affairs/ Labour, Social Insurance and Social Solidarity |
| 26 | **Joint Ministerial Decision 4166/51687/2014 "Amendment of JMD 9748/100747/2012 on prerequisites for licensing for Type A and B fertiliser companies"** | art. 1 par. 2α | Manufacturing and wholesale trade of fertilisers | Trade of fertilisers (Type A and B) is allowed only by natural or legal persons employing a "responsible scientist" (special requirements are set for him/her) who has to be present all opening hours. | Licensing - Raises cost of entry | There is no official recital. However, following communication with the Ministry, fertilisers are chemical products (with some, such as ammonium nitrate, having potentially explosive properties) and should be traded with caution. The responsible scientist therefore guarantees proper use and minimises risk of environmental burden and degradation (e.g. nitrate pollution, eutrophication). | This provision may raise the operational cost (labour cost). However, in principle, the notification of a responsible scientist is justified and proportionate to the objective. | No recommendation for change. | Ministry of Rural Development and Food/ Economy, Development and Tourism |
| 27 | **Joint Ministerial Decision 4166/51687/2014 "Amendment of JMD 9748/100747/2012 on prerequisites for licensing for Type A and B fertiliser companies"** | art. 1 par. 2 | Manufacturing and wholesale trade of fertilisers | A natural person trading fertilisers (Type A and B) meeting the requirements to be a "responsible scientist" cannot open a second branch without employing another person as a "responsible scientist". | Licensing | There is no official recital. However, following communication with the Ministry, fertilisers are chemical products (with some, such as ammonium nitrate, having potentially explosive properties) and should be traded with caution. The responsible scientist therefore guarantees proper use and minimises risk of environmental burden and degradation (e.g. nitrate pollution, eutrophication). | For natural persons, this provision restricts entry to the market only to those meeting the criteria to be a responsible scientist. Furthermore, the provision restricts operation to only one store and increases costs (labour costs). However, it is proportionate to the objective. | No recommendation for change. | Ministry of Rural Development and Food/ Economy, Development and Tourism |
| 28 | **Joint Ministerial Decision 4166/51687/2014 "Amendment of JMD 9748/100747/2012 on prerequisites for licensing for Type A and B fertiliser companies"** | art. 1 par. 3 | Manufacturing and wholesale trade of fertilisers | An exemption granted to micro or small fertiliser trading enterprises (Type A and B) allows the "responsible scientist" to be employed part-time and appropriately trained personnel to be employed additionally. | Licensing - Regulatory uncertainty | Recent Law 4384/2016, art.47, requires a full-time dependent work contract for the responsible scientist in order to assure proper use and trade of fertilisers. Therefore, this provision is no longer valid. Following communication with the Ministry, the objective of the provision was to reduce labour cost for micro or small fertiliser trading enterprises. | Obsolete (by Law 4384/2016). | Explicitly repeal the provision. | Ministry of Rural Development and Food/ Economy, Development and Tourism |
| 29 | **Presidential Decree 159/2014 "Part-time employment of Responsible Scientist in small and micro enterprises of production and trade of seeds and propagating material and trade of fertilisers"** | art. 2 par. 2 | Manufacturing and wholesale trade of fertilisers | In the case of micro or small fertiliser trading enterprises, a part-time "responsible scientist" has to be present at least two working days. | Trading of products - Regulatory uncertainty | Recent Law 4384/2016, art.47, requires a full-time dependent work contract for the responsible scientist in order to assure proper use and trade of fertilisers. Therefore, this provision is no longer valid. Following communication with the Ministry, the objective of the provision was to reduce labour cost for micro or small fertiliser trading enterprises. | Obsolete (by Law 4384/2016). | Explicitly repeal the provision. | Ministry of Rural Development and Food/ Economy, Development and Tourism |
| 30 | **Law 1565/1985 "Fertilisers"** | art. 4 par. 3β | Manufacturing and wholesale trade of fertilisers | The permit of operation (Βεβαίωση Συνδρομής των Νομίμων Προϋποθέσεων) for Type A and Type B trade enterprises is renewable and has a duration of five and three years respectively. | Licensing | There is no official recital. However, following communication with the Ministry, a specific duration of operation is set, because thorough and periodic checks of enterprises' operational requirements are necessary. | In principle, the requirement to renew the permit of operation is an administrative burden that could discourage potential entry. In addition, the provision also sets different duration for Type A and Type B enterprises, although both can make retail sales, thus it creates differential treatment and may discourage Type B enterprises. | Align the duration of both permits to five years. | Ministry of Economy, Development and Tourism/ Finance/ Justice, Transparency and Human Rights/ Rural Development and Food/ State |
| 31 | **Ministerial Decision 9748/100747/2012 "Determining the requirements and procedure for getting a licence for type A and B trade of fertilisers"** | art. 3 par. 5 and art. 7 | Manufacturing and wholesale trade of fertilisers | The permit of operation (Βεβαίωση Συνδρομής των Νομίμων Προϋποθέσεων) for Type A and Type B trade enterprises is renewable and has a duration of five and three years respectively. | Licensing | There is no official recital. However, following communication with the Ministry, a specific duration of operation is set, because thorough and periodic checks of enterprises' operational requirements are necessary. | In principle, the requirement to renew the permit of operation is an administrative burden that could discourage potential entry. In addition, the provision also sets different duration for Type A and Type B enterprises, although both can make retail sales, thus it creates differential treatment and may discourage Type B enterprises. | Align the duration of both permits to five years. | Ministry of Rural Development and Food |
| 32 | **Ministerial Decision 9748/100747/2012 "Determining the requirements and procedure for getting a licence for type A and B trade of fertilisers"** | art. 5α | Manufacturing and wholesale trade of fertilisers | If the "responsible scientist" leaves a Type A or B fertiliser trading company, a replacement has to be found and announced within one month, otherwise the Ministry will remove the company from the registry. During this time, sales cannot occur. | Trading of products | There is no official recital. However, following communication with the Ministry: a) fertilisers are chemical products (with some, such as ammonium nitrate, having potentially explosive properties) and should be traded with caution. The responsible scientist therefore guarantees proper use and minimises risk of environmental burden and degradation (e.g. nitrate pollution, eutrophication) and trade notification without his/her presence is not allowed and b) the grace period takes into account the time that it would take to find a replacement, as well as the level of urgency to supply the professional with the proper fertiliser. | This provision limits the ability of an enterprise to operate, without the responsible scientist, for more than one month. However, as the notification of a responsible scientist is justified, the restriction is proportionate. | No recommendation for change. | Ministry of Rural Development and Food |
| 33 | **Ministerial Decision 394199/5224/1999 "Licences of temporary circulation of new type of fertilisers without the designation "EC Fertiliser" imported from third countries and control of fertilisers designated "EC fertiliser"** | art. 4 | Manufacturing and wholesale trade of fertilisers | In case of trade of designated "EC fertiliser", accompanying documentation (e.g. quantity data, certification of qualitative and quantitative analysis of product etc.) must be submitted for every lot. | Trading of products - Regulatory uncertainty | There is no official recital. However, following communication with the Ministry, the aim of the provision is to be able to check the traded "EC fertilisers", in terms of formulation, labelling and packaging, in line with the EU Regulation 2003/2003 (art. 29). | It is our understanding that in practice, companies have the option to file an application as well as the required documentation for the quantities to be imported only once per semester, and not for every lot. The wording of this provision may therefore create regulatory uncertainty. | Review the provision to remove confusion and uncertainty for operators (e.g. the submission of files can be made once per semester). | Ministry of Rural Development and Food |

## Sector: Chemicals and rubber, electrical equipment, paper and printing

| No | No and title of Regulation | Article | Thematic category | Brief description of the potential obstacle | Keyword | Policy maker's objectives | Harm to competition | Recommendations | Competent Ministry / Authority |
|---|---|---|---|---|---|---|---|---|---|
| 34 | **Joint Ministerial Decision 3137/191/2012 "Classification of industries, professional laboratories and electricity generation activities according to the grades of disturbance as set out in decrees for urban planning"** | art. 5 (as amended by MD 48/5/2014) | Framework legislation | Low disturbance facilities legally existing and operating on April 4 of 2012 (date of adoption of Joint Ministerial Decision 3137/191/2012), which pursuant to Article 3 of this JMD are categorised as average disturbance, remain at low disturbance. | Grandfathering clause | There is no official recital. However after communication with the General Secretariat of Industry it is our understanding that the new rules on the classification of industries, professional laboratories and electricity generation activities, according to their disturbance, rate may place an undue burden of cost on incumbents who made their investments in production facilities and started operations under older rules, since the disturbance system is correlated with the land-use system. The rationale is that enterprises whose disturbance category moved from low to medium or high due to the JMD would have to relocate. | Grandfather clause: the incumbent businesses are allowed to continue operations under older rules, whereas new firms are subject to the newer, stricter, rules and regulations. Even if this provision was set in force to enable a smoother enactment of the new regulation, in practice it provides a different legal framework for existing businesses and for new entrants. However, we understand that the lack of such an exemption would cause major unrest in the market (i.e. relocation of manufacturing enterprises). | No recommendation for change. | Ministry of Economy, Development and Tourism/ Environment and Energy |
| 35 | **Ministerial Decision 15928/ΕΦΑ/1253/1987 "Filing of applications to OBI for the grant of patents or utility model certificates with OBI and keeping of record books"** | art. 3 | Framework legislation | The right to appear in person or file documents before the Hellenic Intellectual Property Organisation (OBI) is attributed to beneficiaries of patent applications, or utility model applications, or to their representative lawyer. | Licensing | It was not possible to identify the policy maker's objective. | This provision raises costs of entry and increases operational cost for suppliers. | Allow other professionals with the relevant technical background, i.e. engineers, to submit patent applications. In addition, accredited European Patent Attorneys should be eligible to file a patent application or represent a patent holder before the Organisation. | Ministry of Economy, Development and Tourism |
| 36 | **Presidential Decree 77/1988 "Implementing regulations of the Convention on the grant of European patents as ratified by Law 1607/1986"** | art. 19 | Framework legislation | The right to appear in person or file documents before the Hellenic Intellectual Property Organisation (OBI) is given solely to the beneficiary of a European application or a European patent or to their representative lawyer. | Licensing | It was not possible to identify the policy maker's objective. | This provision raises costs of entry and increases operational cost for suppliers. | Allow other professionals with the relevant technical background, i.e. engineers, to submit patent applications. In addition, accredited European Patent Attorneys should be eligible to file a patent application or represent a patent holder before the Organisation. | Ministry of Economy, Development and Tourism |
| 37 | **Ministerial Decision 1233/1991 and 172/1992 "Registration System for detergents and cleaning products"** | art. 5 | Manufacturing and wholesale trade of detergents | The General Chemical State Laboratory is the competent authority for the ex post control of detergent classification, labelling and quality. EU Regulation 648/2004 leaves room for discretion. | Regulatory uncertainty | There is no official recital. However it is our understanding that the objective is public health and consumer protection. | We investigated whether the framework in Greece was potentially more restrictive. The applicable legal framework is the same and we did not find any serious differences in the way this framework was applied. | No recommendation for change. | Ministry of Finance/ Economy, Development and Tourism |
| 38 | **Presidential Decree 111/2014 "Organizational Structure of the Ministry of Finance"** | art. 93, par. 3 (b), recital (γγ), (v) | Manufacturing and wholesale trade of detergents | The General Chemical State Laboratory is the competent authority for the control of detergents. EU Regulation 648/2004 leaves room for discretion. | Regulatory uncertainty | There is no official recital. However it is our understanding that the objective is public health and consumer protection. | We investigated whether the framework in Greece was potentially more restrictive. The applicable legal framework is the same and we did not find any serious differences in the way this framework was applied. | No recommendation for change. | Ministry of Finance/ Economy, Development and Tourism |
| 39 | **Joint Ministerial Decision 381/2005 "Determination of competent authority and of the control mechanisms, fees and penalties for the application of Regulation 648/2004 on detergents"** | art. 1 par. 1, art. 3 par.4 recital β | Manufacturing and wholesale trade of detergents | The Directorate of Raw Materials and Industrial Products of the General Chemical State Laboratory is the competent authority for the application of Regulation 648/2004 on detergents; According to art. 3, par. 4, if a detergent is not in compliance with the provisions of Regulation 648/2004, the Directorate of Raw Materials and Industrial Products should withdraw the detergent in question. The freezing and withdrawal of detergents from the market is imposed by the Directorate of Raw Materials and Industrial Products. | Limiting information to costumers | There is no official recital. However, it is our understanding that this provision aims to protect public health and the environment by allocating the responsibility of controls of detergents circulating in the market to the competent Directorate of the General Chemical State Laboratory. | We understand that withdrawal decisions are not currently published. This limits the information available to consumers as well as their ability to decide from whom they purchase. This is especially important when products are withdrawn on the grounds of public health protection. Finally, the publication of product withdrawal decisions promotes transparency and fosters competition. | Decisions of the Directorate of Raw Materials and Industrial Products of the General Chemical State Laboratory on withdrawal of detergents should be made public, in order to foster consumer protection, transparency and competition. | Ministry of Finance/ General Chemical State Laboratory |
| 40 | **Ministerial Decision A2/718/2014 "Rules for the Supply and Distribution of Products and the Provision of Services"** | art. 84, par. 3 and par. 5 | Manufacturing and wholesale trade of detergents | Selling detergents and cleaning products in bulk is forbidden. Penalties in case of violation of this provision. | Trading of products | There is no official recital. However, following communication with the General Chemical State Laboratory, it is our understanding that this provision aims to facilitate the control of the quality of detergents on grounds of consumer protection and traceability, since it is more difficult to control the composition and quality of chemical products traded in bulk. Additionally, packaged goods are easily more classified and labelled. | In general the prohibition of wholesale trade in bulk, when imposed for reason other than health and safety or if it does not derive from EU standards, restricts the ability of companies to exploit economies of scale and raises cost of operation. | Abolish the restriction of trading in bulk for the case of wholesale trade. | Ministry of Economy, Development and Tourism |
| 41 | **Ministerial Decision 1233/1991 and 172/1992 "Registration System for detergents and cleaning products"** | art. 6 par. 1 | Manufacturing and wholesale trade of detergents | Manufacturers of detergents need to obtain a special licence from the General Chemical State Laboratory. | Licensing | There is no official recital. However, it is our understanding that this provision aims to protect public health and the environment, as well as promote efficient controls of manufacturing facilities for detergents. | Manufacturers of detergents need to obtain a licence from the General Secretariat of Industry and a special licence from the General Chemical State Laboratory. In principle, multiplication of licences for an activity, if disproportionate to the public goal it serves, may be an entry barrier. However, the provision seems proportionate, since there are no direct effects on competition, only indirect ones. | No recommendation for change. | Ministry of Finance/ Economy, Development and Tourism |

## Sector: Chemicals and rubber, electrical equipment, paper and printing

| No | No and title of Regulation | Article | Thematic category | Brief description of the potential obstacle | Keyword | Policy maker's objectives | Harm to competition | Recommendations | Competent Ministry / Authority |
|---|---|---|---|---|---|---|---|---|---|
| 42 | **Ministerial Decision 1233/1991 and 172/1992 "Registration System for detergents and cleaning products"** | art. 6 par. 4 | Manufacturing and wholesale trade of detergents | Minimum surface of 100 $m^2$ for the establishment of a detergent-industry or professional laboratory. | Licensing | It was not possible to identify the objective of the specific provision. | Restrictive building requirements may raise barriers to entry and constrain suppliers' strategy and business practices.<br>We understand from the competent authorities that they are not considered restrictive for current incumbents, however it may limit future entry. | Abolish minimum surface requirements for manufacturing facilities of detergents. | Ministry of Finance/ Economy, Development and Tourism |
| 43 | **Ministerial Decision 1233/1991 and 172/1992 "Registration System for detergents and cleaning products"** | art. 6 par. 6 | Manufacturing and wholesale trade of detergents | Special licence is abolished or revoked if the ownership status of the manufacturing facility has changed. | Licensing | It was not possible to identify the objective of the specific provision. However, following communication with the General Chemical State Laboratory, it is our understanding that the objective is to ensure that a manufacturing facility is not run illegally by anyone other legal or natural person than its owner. | This provision can cause harm to competition, since it restricts entrepreneurship and business strategies. | Abolish. A notification procedure to competent authority could be established. | Ministry of Finance/ Economy, Development and Tourism |
| 44 | **Presidential Decree 205/2001 "Approval, marketing and control of biocides in harmonisation with Directive 98/8/EC"** | as a whole | Manufacturing and wholesale trade of biocides | Application procedure, terms and conditions for the approval of biocides. However, EU Regulation 528/2012 providing for the applicable procedures for approval of biocides is in force. Furthermore, the PD was incorrectly repealed with JMD 4616/52519/2016. | Regulatory uncertainty - Prevention of market entry | The objective of this provision is to abolish the previous approval system for biocides, since EU Regulation 528/2012 came into force. | Obsolete. Even though Law 1338/1983 allows for the transposition of EU legislation via MDs, the PD should be explicitly abolished by an act of equal or superior typical force, e.g. by another PD or by law, since this provision creates regulatory uncertainty. | The PD should be explicitly repealed by an act of equal or superior typical force. | Ministry of Rural Development and Food/ Health/ Economy, Development and Tourism |
| 45 | **Joint Ministerial Decision Δ.ΥΓ3α/Γ.Π.32221/2013 "Harmonisation of the Greek legislation with the EU legislation in the sector of production and circulation of medicinal products for human use in compliance with the Directive 2001/83/EC on the Community Code relating to medicinal products for human use as amended by the Directive 2011/62/EU as regards the prevention of the entry into legal supply chain of falsified medicinal products"** | art. 2 rec. 23, art. 9 par. 3 (b) | Manufacturing and wholesale trade of biocides | According to these provisions:<br><br>art. 2 rec. 23: name of the medicinal product: The name given to a medicinal product, which may be either an invented name or a common or scientific name, together with a trademark or the name of the manufacturer; the invented name shall not be liable to confusion with the common name, and<br><br>art. 9 par. 3: the application for authorisation shall be accompanied by the following particulars and documents: ... (b) name of the medicinal product.<br><br>According to EOF, since the authorisation is unique for each product, the trade mark accompanying the product, as part of its authorisation documents, is also unique.<br><br>This pharmaceutical provision may be applied for the licensing of biocides, in order to prevent producers from marketing products with different qualitative chemical composition in terms of active ingredients under the same brand name ("umbrella branding"). | Licensing - Trading of products | It was not possible to identify the objective of the specific provision. However, following communication with the National Organisation for Medicines, we understand that the objective is to avoid consumer confusion over different biocides and to protect public health. | If interpreted as preventing umbrella branding altogether, these provisions could hamper suppliers' ability to compete and prevent them from exploiting economies of scale in advertising. Developing a brand name, usually involves significant advertising expenses. If a firm cannot use the same brand name in different products with small additions (such as the clarification that the product is to be used for hands or for the floor), suppliers will have to invest more in brand development.<br>In addition, products authorised until recently were allowed to bear the same brand, despite the different chemical composition. The new interpretation of the provisions would block the entry of new products and possibly discriminate against some suppliers over others.<br>Furthermore, these provisions create differential treatment between biocides authorised by the National Organisation for Medicines and those authorised by the Ministry of Rural Development and Food, since the latter does not apply these provisions or any other regulation that impedes the authorisation of biocides with different qualitative chemical composition in terms of active ingredients under the same brand name.<br>Best practice suggests that there should be a single supervising authority of biocides, instead of responsibilities being split between two different authorities. | Clarify that this provision does not apply to biocides and that suppliers are allowed to use the same brand name, with the indication of the specific use of the product. | Ministry of Health/ National Organisation for Medicines |

## Sector: Chemicals and rubber, electrical equipment, paper and printing

| No | No and title of Regulation | Article | Thematic category | Brief description of the potential obstacle | Keyword | Policy maker's objectives | Harm to competition | Recommendations | Competent Ministry / Authority |
|---|---|---|---|---|---|---|---|---|---|
| 46 | **Legislative Decree 96/1973 "Marketing of pharmaceutical products"** | art. 10 par. 2 | Manufacturing and wholesale trade of biocides | The brand name of the pharmaceutical product must be changed upon any change in the active substance.<br><br>This pharmaceutical provision is also applied by National Organisation for Medicines for the licencing of biocides. | Licensing - Trading of products | It was not possible to identify the objective of the specific provision. However, following communication with the National Organisation for Medicines, we understand that the objective is to avoid consumer confusion over different disinfectants and to protect public health. | If interpreted as preventing umbrella branding altogether, these provisions could hamper suppliers' ability to compete and prevent them from exploiting economies of scale in advertising. Developing a brand name, usually involves significant advertising expenses. If a firm cannot use the same brand name in different products with small additions (such as the clarification that the product is to be used for hands or for the floor), suppliers will have to invest more in brand development.<br>In addition, products authorised until recently were allowed to bear the same brand, despite the different chemical composition. The new interpretation of the provisions would block the entry of new products and possibly discriminate against some suppliers over others.<br>Furthermore, these provisions create differential treatment between biocides authorised by the National Organisation for Medicines and those authorised by the Ministry of Rural Development and Food, since the latter does not apply these provisions or any other regulation that impedes the authorisation of biocides with different qualitative chemical composition in terms of active ingredients under the same brand name.<br>Best practice suggests that there should be a single supervising authority of biocides, instead of responsibilities being split between two different authorities. | Clarify that this provision does not apply to biocides and that suppliers are allowed to use the same brand name, accompanied by an indication of the product's specific use. | Ministry of Health/ National Organisation for Medicines |
| 47 | **Joint Ministerial Decision 4616/52519/2016 "Supplementary measures for the application of Regulation 528/2012 on marketing and use of biocidal products"** | art. 17 point (α) | Manufacturing and wholesale trade of biocides | This Joint Ministerial Decision repeals Presidential Decree 205/2001. Repealing PD 205/2001 in the light of the Regulation is necessary, however this cannot be done with a JMD. | Regulatory uncertainty | The objective of this provision is to abolish the previous approval system for biocides, since Regulation 528/2012 came into force. | Obsolete. Even though Law 1338/1983 allows for the transposition of EU legislation via Ministerial Decisions, the Presidential Decree should be explicitly abolished by an act of equal or superior typical force, e.g. by another presidential decree or by law, since this provision creates regulatory uncertainty. | The Presidential Decree should be explicitly repealed by an act of equal or superior typical force (see in conjunction with row 44). | Ministry of Economy, Development and Tourism/ Health/ Finance/ Rural Development and Food |
| 48 | **Joint Ministerial Decision 4616/52519/2016 "Supplementary measures for the application of Regulation 528/2012 on marketing and use of biocidal products"** | art. 18 par. 4 | Manufacturing and wholesale trade of biocides | According to this provision, since 1 September 2013, the following provisions apply to the marketing of biocides:<br><br>a. Law 721/1977, for biocides for which Ministry of Agricultural Development and Food is competent, and<br><br>b. Law 1316/1983 and MD 7723/1994, for biocides for which the National Organisation for Medicines is competent.<br><br>This provision is unclear, as it determines the applicable regulatory framework for the period before the entry of this JMD into force. | Regulatory uncertainty | There is no official recital. However, following communication with the Ministry of Rural Development and Food and National Organisation for Medicines, it is our understanding that the provision aims to comply with the requirements of Regulation 528/2012 (ex. determination of the competent national authorities etc.). | No harm to competition has been identified. However this provision creates regulatory uncertainty, as it defines the applicable legal framework retroactively since 1 September 2013 and cannot be abolished as that would leave a legal vacuum. | No recommendation for change. | Ministry of Economy, Development and Tourism/ Health/ Finance/ Rural Development and Food |
| 49 | **Circular 41936/1999 "Good Manufacturing Practice for disinfectants"** | art. 2 par. 2 points (α) and (β) | Manufacturing and wholesale trade of biocides | Provides for facility requirements for manufacturers of disinfectants (quarantine space and storage facilities for materials that are unsuitable for use). | Licensing | It was not possible to identify the objective of the specific provision. However, following communication with National Organisation for Medicines, it is our understanding that the objective is to protect public health by avoiding mixing with unsuitable products with those suitable for the market and their proper disposal. | No harm to competition has been identified. The requirements set are proportionate to the objective. | No recommendation for change. | National Organisation for Medicines |
| 50 | **Circular 41936/1999 "Good Manufacturing Practice for disinfectants"** | art. 2 par. 2 δ | Manufacturing and wholesale trade of biocides | Provides for facility requirements for manufacturers of disinfectants. Manufacturer should have separate storage spaces, where they can store samples of products for a year after their expiry date. | Licensing | It was not possible to identify the objective of the specific provision. However, following communication with National Organisation for Medicines, it is our understanding that the objective is to protect public health by storing samples that could be further examined if a problem arises when they are actually on the market. | No harm to competition has been identified. The requirements set are proportionate to the objective. | No recommendation for change. | National Organisation for Medicines |
| 51 | **Circular 41936/1999 "Good Manufacturing Practice for disinfectants"** | art. 4 | Manufacturing and wholesale trade of biocides | Manufacturers should avoid production of other products than disinfectants in the same facilities where disinfectants are manufactured. | Licensing | It was not possible to identify the objective of the specific provision. However, following communication with National Organisation for Medicines, we understand that the objective is to protect public health by preventing cross-contamination between different products produced in the same production facilities. | This provision may raise cost for manufacturers and limit their ability to provide goods, however it is proportionate to the objective, since manufacturers have the choice to produce different products in the same production line, if they apply a properly validated cleaning procedure. | No recommendation for change. | National Organisation for Medicines |
| 52 | **Circular 41936/1999 "Good Manufacturing Practice for disinfectants"** | art. 5 | Manufacturing and wholesale trade of biocides | Each manufacturing facility for disinfectants should have a specialised professional in charge (AEI/TEI graduate with the relevant specialisation). | Licensing | There is no official recital. However it is our understanding that the objective is to safeguard the quality and safety of products, thus protect public health and the consumers. | This provision raises labour cost for manufacturers, however it is proportionate to the objective. | No recommendation for change. | National Organisation for Medicines |

## Sector: Chemicals and rubber, electrical equipment, paper and printing

| No | No and title of Regulation | Article | Thematic category | Brief description of the potential obstacle | Keyword | Policy maker's objectives | Harm to competition | Recommendations | Competent Ministry / Authority |
|---|---|---|---|---|---|---|---|---|---|
| 53 | **Joint Ministerial Decision ΔΥΓ3α/ΓΠ. 132979/2005 "Adaptation of Greek legislation to Community Directives in cosmetics sector"** | art. 2 | Manufacturing and wholesale trade of cosmetics | This article provides a definition of cosmetics that is outdated and has not been aligned with EU Cosmetic Products Regulation (EC) No. 1223/2009. | Licensing | It was not possible to identify the objective of the specific provision. However, following communication with National Organisation for Medicines, we understand that the JMD's objective is to align Greek legislation in the cosmetics sector with the provisions of Directive 76/768/EEC and its subsequent amendments and it is not implemented in practice. | These definitions are not consistent with Regulation 1223/2009/EC (repealing Directive 76/768/EEC), which is followed in practice. Therefore, this obsolete provision could cause legal uncertainty to potential market entrants. | The provision should be amended, in line with Regulation 1223/2009/EC. | Ministry of Health |
| 54 | **Joint Ministerial Decision ΔΥΓ3α/ΓΠ. 132979/2005 "Adaptation of Greek legislation to Community Directives in cosmetics sector"** | Annexes | Manufacturing and wholesale trade of cosmetics | The annexes of the MD provide for lists of substances that are allowed or banned in the production of cosmetics. | Licensing | It was not possible to identify the objective of the specific provision. However, following communication with National Organisation for Medicines, we understand that the JMD's objective is to align Greek legislation in the cosmetics sector with the provisions of Directive 76/768/EEC and its subsequent amendments and it is not implemented in practice. | This obsolete provision may cause legal uncertainty. The lists should be amended in order to be aligned with the lists of substances banned or allowed for use in cosmetic products as those are included in the Annexes of EU Cosmetic Products Regulation (EC) 1223/2009/EC (repealing Directive 76/768/EEC). | The provision should be amended, in line with Regulation 1223/2009/EC. | Ministry of Health |
| 55 | **Joint Ministerial Decision ΔΥΓ3α/ΓΠ. 132979/2005 "Adaptation of Greek legislation to Community Directives in cosmetics sector"** | art. 20 par. 1α | Manufacturing and wholesale trade of cosmetics | The duration of the national licence for cosmetic products is 3 years. | Licensing | It was not possible to identify the objective of the specific provision. However, following communication with National Organisation for Medicines, we understand that the JMD's objective is to align Greek legislation in the cosmetics sector with the provisions of Directive 76/768/EEC and its subsequent amendments and it is not implemented in practice. | This obsolete provision may cause legal uncertainty since there is no national licensing procedure for cosmetics. Regulation 1223/2009/EC (repealing Directive 76/768/EEC) provides for a cosmetic product notification process and the exercise of internal controls on products circulating in the market by member states monitoring compliance with the Regulation. | Explicitly repeal the provision. | Ministry of Health |
| 56 | **Joint Ministerial Decision A6/2880/1980 "Rules on Good Manufacturing and Control of Cosmetics"** | art. 1 | Manufacturing and wholesale trade of cosmetics | This article provides a definition of cosmetics that is outdated and has not been aligned with EU Cosmetic Products Regulation (EC) No. 1223/2009. | Licensing | It was not possible to identify the objective of the specific provision from the relevant piece of legislation. Following communication with National Organisation for Medicines, we understand that the JMD is not implemented in practice. | The definition of cosmetics included in the MD shall be changed in order to be aligned with the definition included in EU Cosmetic Products Regulation (EC) No. 1223/2009. The MD provides for specific rules on Good Manufacturing Practices and Control of Cosmetics. Since 2013, the EU has published "Cosmetics - Good Manufacturing Practices (GMP) - Guidelines on Good Manufacturing Practices" (ISO 22716: 2007) as the harmonised standard for the GMP requirements of the EU Cosmetic Products Regulation (EC) No. 1223/2009. Since the MD has not been explicitly repealed, certain obligations for manufacturing and equipment may still apply and function as complementary to ISO-GMP. This may cause legal uncertainty. | Explicitly repeal the provision together with the entire JMD, given that EU Regulation is applicable. | Ministry of Health |
| 57 | **National Organisation for Medicines Circular 13898/2011 "On payment of fixed fee, readiness fee for medical devices and levy of 1% for cosmetics"** | par. 3b | Manufacturing and wholesale trade of cosmetics | A monthly levy of 1% on sales must be paid to the National Organisation for Medicines by persons responsible for placing cosmetic products in the market established in Greece or abroad (another member state or in a third country). | Licensing/ Fees | It was not possible to identify the objective of the specific provision from the relevant piece of legislation. However, we understand that these fees contribute to the funding of National Organisation for Medicines for the purposes of market surveillance and checking procedures. | A levy on the value of sales could lead to price distortion. The current scheme, which requires companies to pay a fee proportional to their sales, benefits from firms' marketing and brand building. Given the market surveillance purpose of the levy, it should not affect firms' price strategies and investment in innovation and quality. Given the market surveillance purpose of the levy, the latter should not affect price strategies and investment in innovation and quality by the firms. Equal competition terms and simultaneous coverage of the costs of cosmetic products surveillance would require a fee proportional to the number of products marketed by each firm and the number of units sold. | The administration should consider an alternative scheme based on the number of products marketed by each firm and the number of units sold. These fees must be directly related to the tasks and procedures they intend to fund. | National Organisation for Medicines |
| 58 | **Law 1316/1983 "Establishment, organisation and competence of the National Organisation for Medicines, the National Pharmaceutical Industry, the State Pharmaceutical Warehouse and other provisions"** | art. 11 par. 1ζ | Manufacturing and wholesale trade of cosmetics | This provision foresees the exclusion of cosmetics circulating in Greece from fees which apply to other categories and their replacement by a levy of 1% on the wholesale price. | Licensing/ Fees | It was not possible to identify the objective of the specific provision from the relevant piece of legislation. However, we understand that these fees contribute to the funding of National Organisation for Medicines for the purposes of market surveillance and checking procedures. | A levy on the value of sales could lead to price distortion. The current scheme, which requires companies to pay a fee proportional to their sales, benefits from firms' marketing and brand building. Given the market surveillance purpose of the levy, it should not affect firms' price strategies and investment in innovation and quality. Given the market surveillance purpose of the levy, the latter should not affect price strategies and investment in innovation and quality by the firms. Equal competition terms and simultaneous coverage of the costs of cosmetic products surveillance would require a fee proportional to the number of products marketed by each firm and the number of units sold. | The administration should consider an alternative scheme based on the number of products marketed by each firm and the number of units sold. These fees must be directly related to the tasks and procedures they intend to fund. | Ministry of Health |
| 59 | **National Organisation for Medicines Circular 92428/2009 "Legal circulation of cosmetic products"** | par. 1-3 | Manufacturing and wholesale trade of cosmetics | Labelling and package leaflet of cosmetic products must not include claims on antibacterial, antimicrobial or antiseptic use. Any such terms should be removed from the labelling and package leaflets of cosmetics. Suppliers wishing to market their products with antibacterial, antimicrobial or antiseptic claims must apply for a market authorisation pursuant to the biocides regulatory framework. | Licensing / Labelling | It was not possible to identify the objective of the specific provision from the relevant piece of legislation. However, following communication with National Organisation for Medicines, we understand that the Circular serves the need for dissemination of accurate information for reasons of protecting public health. | The provision treats interchangeable cosmetic products differently. Innovation in cosmetics has led to borderline products that combine characteristics of cosmetics and biocides. Greek legislation does not recognise primary and secondary functions of products, resulting in regulatory uncertainty with regard to their circulation in the market. Also, this provision may constitute a barrier to entry for new suppliers wishing to place their products in the Greek market thus limiting the variety of cosmetic products available to consumers. | Provision needs to be rephrased so as to recognise primary and secondary functions of products as foreseen in the EC Note for Guidance CA-Jul13-Doc.5.1.h and relevant EU documents concerning borderline products. | Ministry of Health/ National Organisation for Medicines |

## Sector: Chemicals and rubber, electrical equipment, paper and printing

| No | No and title of Regulation | Article | Thematic category | Brief description of the potential obstacle | Keyword | Policy maker's objectives | Harm to competition | Recommendations | Competent Ministry / Authority |
|---|---|---|---|---|---|---|---|---|---|
| 60 | **Legislative Decree 96/1973 "Trade of pharmaceuticals, dietary supplements and cosmetics"** | art. 7 par. 2 | Manufacturing and wholesale trade of cosmetics | A market authorisation for cosmetic products, as defined in art. 3, is granted to natural and legal persons that legally operate plants or factories, other than pharmaceutical ones. They ought to be adequately staffed, equipped and possess the required establishments for the proper manufacturing of products. | Licensing | It was not possible to identify the objective of the specific provision from the relevant piece of legislation. | The provision refers to Art. 3 of this Legislative Decree on the definition of cosmetics which has been abolished. In addition it refers to market authorisation for cosmetics that do not constitute a prerequisite for the circulation of cosmetics since a simplified procedure of notification is now followed pursuant to Art. 13 of EU Regulation 1223/2009. The provision is obsolete, it may cause legal uncertainty and prevent firms from entering the market or compete on equal terms. | Explicitly repeal the provision. | Ministry of Health |
| 61 | **Law 1316/1983 "Establishment, organisation and competence of the National Organisation for Medicines, the National Pharmaceutical Industry, the State Pharmaceutical Warehouse and other provisions"** | art. 11 par. 1γ | Manufacturing and wholesale trade of cosmetics | Fees for authorising the circulation of cosmetics (30,000 Drachma). | Licensing/ Fees | It was not possible to identify the objective of the specific provision. However, it is our understanding that the objective is to raise National Organisation for Medicines' revenues. Following communication with National Organisation for Medicines, we understand that the provision is not in practical use. | Obsolete legislation because cosmetics are not subject to market authorisation. In conjunction with par. 1ζ of the same article, this could apply only to products that do not circulate in Greece, i.e. the exported ones. For products circulating in Greece, this fee has been replaced with a 1% levy on the wholesale price of cosmetics for market surveillance reasons, which is not the case for exported cosmetic products. If applied, this could constitute an extra non-justified burden for domestically produced cosmetics that are to be exported. | Explicitly repeal the provision. | Ministry of Health |
| 62 | **Law 2960/2001 "National Customs Code"** | art. 81 par. 4 and 5 and art. 83 par. 2 | Manufacturing and wholesale trade of chemicals | Excise duty on isopropyl alcohol and exemption of excise duty if used for pharmaceutical products or for industrial use. | Taxation | It was impossible to identify the objective of this provision. | When isopropyl alcohol is only used as an industrial raw material, this provision constitutes harm to competition, as it raises the cost of operation, particularly for small firms, and may act as a barrier to entry. | Abolish the provision. | Ministry of Finance |
| 63 | **Ministerial Decision 811/337/2008 "Conditions of exemption from excise duties for isopropyl alcohol for industrial use"** | art. 1 - 7 | Manufacturing and wholesale trade of chemicals | Exemption of excise duty on isopropyl alcohol if used for pharmaceutical products or for industrial use. Denaturation procedure, marketing and bottling of denatured isopropyl alcohol. | Taxation | There is no official recital. However, it is our understanding that the objective can be found to the general legal practice according to which alcohols, used as raw material for industrial purposes, are exempted from excise duties if they are denatured. | The denaturation procedure is a costly, administratively complex and cumbersome process that needs to be followed by manufacturers in order to use isopropyl alcohol as a raw material. However, due to the complexity of the denaturation procedure, there are many manufacturers that prefer to bear the cost of the excise duty than follow the exemption procedure. This raises cost for some market participants compared to others. | Abolish the provision. | Ministry of Finance |
| 64 | **Ministerial Decision 812/338/2008 "Establishment and function of tax warehouses for isopropyl alcohol produced in Greece or imported by EU member states"** | as a whole | Manufacturing and wholesale trade of chemicals | Establishment and function of tax warehouses for isopropyl alcohol produced in Greece or imported by EU member states. | Taxation | There is no official recital. However, it is our understanding that the denaturing process must take place in a tax warehouse in order to ensure proper oversight of the denaturing process and prevent isopropyl alcohol on which excise duty has not been paid from being released into circulation and illegally sold for consumption. | The denaturation procedure is a costly, administratively complex and cumbersome process that needs to be followed by manufacturers in order to use isopropyl alcohol as raw material. However, due to the complexity of the denaturation procedure there are many manufacturers that prefer to bear the cost of the excise duty than follow the exemption procedure. This will raise cost for some market participants against others. | Abolish the provision. | Ministry of Finance |
| 65 | **Joint Ministerial Decision 3329/1989 "Regulations on production, storage and distribution of explosive material"** | art. 2 par. 2 recital (στ) | Manufacturing and wholesale trade of chemicals | Distances between the manufacturing facilities of explosives and other infrastructure of inhabited zones are calculated on the basis of a variable. This variable is the longest distance between any type of building applied to this facility according to the Regulation. | Licensing - Raises cost of entry | There is no official recital. However, it is our understanding that the objective is to set high safety standards. Distances between hazardous areas are shorter than those between a hazardous and a non-hazardous, so this variable actually coincides with the longer distance applied between hazardous and non-hazardous areas. | This provision raises costs, by imposing minimum distances. Furthermore, it makes it difficult for new entrants to find an appropriate area to locate their business. | Given the highly technical nature of this provision, we are unable to make an assessment. We recommend that the competent authorities review the provision, in consultation with representatives from the industry. | Ministry of National Defence/ Citizen Protection/ Economy, Development and Tourism/ Environment and Energy/ Interior and Administrative Reconstruction |
| 66 | **Joint Ministerial Decision 3329/1989 "Regulations on production, storage and distribution of explosive material"** | art. 22 par. 6 | Manufacturing and wholesale trade of chemicals | Steam generators in facilities manufacturing explosives can only be fuelled by diesel. | Licensing - Raises cost of entry | There is no official recital. However, following communication with the General Secretariat of Industry, it is our understanding that the objective is the protection of public and worker safety and the environment. Preference is given to fuels of low flammability risk, such as diesel, over those more dangerous, such as natural gas, which is more flammable and has a high risk of leakage. | This provision may restrict innovation and lead to inefficiency and higher cost, as it constrains suppliers' ability to choose their preferred production technology; however, this provision is proportionate to the objective. | No recommendation for change. | Ministry of National Defence/ Citizen Protection/ Economy, Development and Tourism/ Environment and Energy/ Interior and Administrative Reconstruction |
| 67 | **Joint Ministerial Decision 3329/1989 "Regulations on production, storage and distribution of explosive material"** | art. 30 par. 3 | Manufacturing and wholesale trade of chemicals | Employees holding responsible positions or positions that involve hazardous work should undergo at least two months training. | Licensing | There is no official recital. However, following communication with the General Secretariat of Industry, it is our understanding that internal training of employees that hold responsible positions or positions that involve hazardous work is necessary due to the high risk of their work. Thus, personnel in manufacturing facilities of explosives should be accustomed with the necessary safety regulations. | No harm to competition has been identified. It is proportionate to the objective. | No recommendation for change. | Ministry of National Defence/ Citizen Protection/ Economy, Development and Tourism/ Environment and Energy/ Interior and Administrative Reconstruction |
| 68 | **Joint Ministerial Decision 3329/1989 "Regulations on production, storage and distribution of explosive material"** | art. 30 par. 6 | Manufacturing and wholesale trade of chemicals | The Ministry of Industry should be notified of the appointment or dismissal or resignation of a facility's maintenance or production manager. | Licensing | There is no official recital. However, following communication with the General Secretariat of Industry, it is our understanding that this notification serves the objective of always having a responsible person who can immediately inform the competent authorities and take action in case of situations that might threaten public health or safety. | No harm to competition has been identified. It is proportionate to the objective. | No recommendation for change. | Ministry of National Defence/ Citizen Protection/ Economy, Development and Tourism/ Environment and Energy/ Interior and Administrative Reconstruction |

## Sector: Chemicals and rubber, electrical equipment, paper and printing

| No | No and title of Regulation | Article | Thematic category | Brief description of the potential obstacle | Keyword | Policy maker's objectives | Harm to competition | Recommendations | Competent Ministry / Authority |
|---|---|---|---|---|---|---|---|---|---|
| 69 | **Joint Ministerial Decision 3329/1989 "Regulations on production, storage and distribution of explosive material"** | art. 48 par. 3 | Manufacturing and wholesale trade of chemicals | In the laboratory of plants that produce explosives, the supervisor should hold a higher-education diploma in chemistry of chemical engineering. | Licensing | There is no official recital. However, following communication with the General Secretariat of Industry, it is our understanding that the objective is the protection of public and worker safety and the environment, since only a chemist or chemical engineer is able to undertake that kind of work. | No harm to competition has been identified. It is proportionate to the objective. | No recommendation for change. | Ministry of National Defence/ Citizen Protection/ Economy, Development and Tourism/ Environment and Energy/ Interior and Administrative Reconstruction |
| 70 | **Joint Ministerial Decision 3329/1989 "Regulations on production, storage and distribution of explosive material"** | art. 47 | Manufacturing and wholesale trade of chemicals | This provision provides for the procedure for explosives circulation approval. Obsolete, since explosives bear CE marking. | Licensing - Regulatory uncertainty | There is no official recital. However, following communication with the General Secretariat of Industry and the Ministry of Citizen Protection, it is our understanding that the objective is the protection of public and worker safety and the environment. The approval procedure also guarantees that explosives, which are extremely dangerous, are safe to circulate in the market. | Obsolete. This provision creates regulatory uncertainty and imposes extra cost to suppliers, taking into account that the circulation approval is no longer necessary, since explosives bear the CE marking, according to Regulation (EC) 765/2008. | Abolish the provision since it contradicts EU legislation. Further to this, Greece needs to transpose Directive 2014/28/EU on the harmonisation of the laws of the member states relating to the market availability and supervision of explosives for civil uses (it should have been transposed by 20 April 2016). Art. 41 of the Directive reiterates that explosives bear the CE marking. | Ministry of National Defence/ Citizen Protection/ Economy, Development and Tourism/ Environment and Energy/ Interior and Administrative Reconstruction |
| 71 | **Joint Ministerial Decision 3329/1989 "Regulations on production, storage and distribution of explosive material"** | art. 52 par. 2 | Manufacturing and wholesale trade of chemicals | This provision provides for penalties for producers, importers, traders of explosives that do not have an explosives circulation approval. | Licensing - Regulatory uncertainty | There is no official recital. However, following communication with the General Secretariat of Industry, it is our understanding that the objective is the protection of public and worker safety and the environment. Penalties safeguard the application of the approval procedure. | Obsolete. This provision creates regulatory uncertainty and imposes extra cost to suppliers, taking into account that the circulation approval is no longer necessary, since explosives bear the CE marking, according to Regulation (EC) 765/2008. | Abolish the provision since it contradicts EU legislation. Further to this, Greece needs to transpose Directive 2014/28/EU on the harmonisation of the laws of the member states relating to the market availability and supervision of explosives for civil uses (it should have been transposed by 20 April 2016). Art. 41 of the Directive reiterates that explosives bear the CE marking. | Ministry of National Defence/ Citizen Protection/ Economy, Development and Tourism/ Environment and Energy/ Interior and Administrative Reconstruction |
| 72 | **Joint Ministerial Decision 3329/1989 "Regulations on production, storage and distribution of explosive material"** | art. 53 par. 1α | Manufacturing and wholesale trade of chemicals | Buildings and facilities that at the time of publication of this Regulation had acquired a licence for establishment or building expansion or modernisation continue to fall under the provisions in force at the time of licensing. | Grandfathering clause | There is no official recital. However it is our understanding that the new Regulation may place an undue burden of cost on incumbents who made their investments in production facilities and started operations under older rules. | Grandfather clause: the existing businesses (incumbents) are allowed to continue operations under older rules, whereas new firms are subject to the newer, stricter, rules and regulations. These inequalities among old and new businesses can create cost differentials and act as a barrier to entry. | Abolish. Allow for a transitory period for older establishments and investigate a system of incentives to comply with the new legislation. | Ministry of National Defence/ Citizen Protection/ Economy, Development and Tourism/ Environment and Energy/ Interior and Administrative Reconstruction |
| 73 | **Presidential Decree 76/2010 "Harmonisation with Directive 2008/43/EC on the establishment of a system for the identification and traceability of explosives for civil uses"** | art. 14 recital (η) | Manufacturing and wholesale trade of chemicals | Manufacturers and traders of explosives should register in their books within five working days all data for recognition of explosives, followed by all relevant information, including the company's type of explosives. These data should be also registered on every invoice or consignment note. | Trading of products | There is no official recital. However it is our understanding that the objective of the provision is to protect public safety. | No harm to competition has been identified. However, this provision introduces an administrative burden for suppliers that is justified. | No recommendation for change. | |
| 74 | **Royal Decree 590/1968 "Regulations for health and safety in factories of lead accumulators"** | art. 2 par. 1 to 5 | Manufacturing and wholesale trade of electrical equipment | Special requirements on the ground surface and the width of corridors at the industrial plants or laboratories that produce accumulators. | Licensing - Raises cost of entry | There is no official recital. However, following communication with the Ministry of Labour and Social Security, it is our understanding that the objective of the requirement is to protect workers' safety in high risk activities and the environment. | Restrictive building requirements might raise barrier to entry and increase operational cost of suppliers; however, this provision is proportionate to the objective. | No recommendation for change. | Ministry of Health/ Labour |
| 75 | **Royal Decree 590/1968 "Regulations for health and safety in factories of lead accumulators"** | art. 3 | Manufacturing and wholesale trade of electrical equipment | Special requirements on the wall surface, the ceiling and the doors at industrial plants or laboratories that produce accumulators. | Licensing - Raises cost of entry | There is no official recital. However, following communication with the Ministry of Labour and Social Security, it is our understanding that the objective of the requirement is to protect workers' safety in high risk activities and the environment. | Restrictive building requirements might raise barrier to entry and increase operational cost of suppliers; however, this provision is proportionate to the objective. | No recommendation for change. | Ministry of Health/ Labour |
| 76 | **Royal Decree 590/1968 "Regulations for health and safety in factories of lead accumulators"** | art. 4 | Manufacturing and wholesale trade of electrical equipment | Special requirements on the ventilation at the industrial plants or laboratories that produce accumulators. | Licensing - Raises cost of entry | There is no official recital. However, following communication with the Ministry of Labour and Social Security, it is our understanding that the objective of the requirement is to protect workers' safety in high risk activities and the environment. | Restrictive building requirements might raise barrier to entry and increase operational cost of suppliers; however, this provision is proportionate to the objective. | No recommendation for change. | Ministry of Health/ Labour |
| 77 | **Royal Decree 590/1968 "Regulations for health and safety in factories of lead accumulators"** | art. 5 | Manufacturing and wholesale trade of electrical equipment | Special requirements on the lighting at the industrial plants or laboratories that produce accumulators. | Licensing - Raises cost of entry | There is no official recital. However, following communication with the Ministry of Labour and Social Security, it is our understanding that the objective of the requirement is to protect workers' safety in high risk activities and the environment. | Restrictive building requirements might raise barrier to entry and increase operational cost of suppliers; however, this provision is proportionate to the objective. | No recommendation for change. | Ministry of Health/ Labour |

## Sector: Chemicals and rubber, electrical equipment, paper and printing

| No | No and title of Regulation | Article | Thematic category | Brief description of the potential obstacle | Keyword | Policy maker's objectives | Harm to competition | Recommendations | Competent Ministry / Authority |
|---|---|---|---|---|---|---|---|---|---|
| 78 | **Royal Decree 590/1968 "Regulations for health and safety in factories of lead accumulators"** | art. 10 | Manufacturing and wholesale trade of electrical equipment | Special requirements on refectory facilities, with respect to the number of employees (over, or under 30 employees). | Licensing | There is no official recital. However, following communication with the Ministry of Labour and Social Security, it is our understanding that the objective of the requirement is to protect workers' safety in high risk activities and hygiene. | No harm to competition has been identified. Special requirements on refectory facilities are proportionate to the objective. | No recommendation for change. | Ministry of Health/ Labour |
| 79 | **Ministerial Decision 529/2000 "Marketing and installation of sockets and plugs"** | art. 3 | Manufacturing and wholesale trade of electrical equipment | A double requirement authorisation process (acquisition of ELOT quality mark and product registration with special registry kept at the General Secretariat of Industry) is required. ELOT quality mark is obligatory for the registration. | Licensing | The provision concerns specific electrical equipment destined for domestic use. Following communication with the competent Ministry, we were informed that the provision has been adopted for public interest purposes relevant to the safety of internal electrical installations. From our understanding, the registration process was deemed necessary for reasons of better monitoring by the competent authorities. | No harm to competition has been identified. The registration obligation is proportionate to the policy maker's objective. | No recommendation for change. | Ministry of Economy, Development and Tourism |
| 80 | **Ministerial Decision 529/2000 "Marketing and installation of sockets and plugs"** | art. 6 par. 1β and par. 3 | Manufacturing and wholesale trade of electrical equipment | The duration of the registration of electrical equipment is three years. Moreover, a registration fee is provided. After expiry of the three year period, the supplier has to renew the registration, whereas ELOT quality mark has no duration limit. | Licensing | It was not possible to identify the policy maker's objective. | ELOT certificate may be valid for a shorter or a longer time period than the three year registration. Therefore, should a product still comply with the ELOT certificate requirements after three years and the registration is not renewed, there is no threat to public safety. On the contrary, if the three year registration obligation has not lapsed, but the product is circulating in the market without being compliant with the ELOT mark, public safety will not be protected. Harm to competition is caused due to the costly and burdensome procedure of the renewal of the registration every three years and it may discourage new entrants or smaller operators. | The Ministry should review this provision, so that the duration of the registration and the duration of the ELOT certificate are aligned. The Ministry should introduce and electronic registry in this direction. | Ministry of Economy, Development and Tourism |

## Sector: Pharmaceuticals

| No | No and title of Regulation | Article | Thematic category | Brief description of the potential obstacle | Keyword | Policy maker's objectives | Harm to competition | Recommendations | Competent Ministry / Authority |
|---|---|---|---|---|---|---|---|---|---|
| 1 | **Legislative Decree 96/1973 "Trade of pharmaceuticals, dietary supplements and cosmetics"** | Art. 6, par. 2 | Wholesale Trade of Pharmaceuticals | The duration of the market authorisation for locally produced or imported pharmaceutical products is 2 to 5 years. | Licensing | It was not possible to identify the objective of the specific provision. Following communication with competent authorities, we understand that the provision is inactive. | The provision is inactive, it may cause legal uncertainty and prevent firms from entering the market or competing on equal terms. The equivalent EU legislation foresees a fixed 5 year duration of the market authorisation. Obsolete provision.<br>(Superseded by Dir. 2001/83/EC and JMD 32221/2013). | To be explicitly abolished. | Ministry of Health |
| 2 | **Legislative Decree 96/1973 "Trade of pharmaceuticals, dietary supplements and cosmetics"** | Art. 6, par. 4 | Wholesale Trade of Pharmaceuticals | The renewal of the market authorisation for locally produced or imported pharmaceutical products may be granted for 2 to 5 years. | Licensing | It was not possible to identify the objective of the specific provision. Following communication with competent authorities, we understand that the provision is inactive. | The provision is inactive, it may cause legal uncertainty and prevent firms from entering the market or competing on equal terms. The equivalent EU legislation foresees a fixed 5 year duration of the market authorisation. Obsolete provision.<br>(Superseded by Dir. 2001/83/EC and JMD 32221/2013). | To be explicitly abolished. | Ministry of Health |
| 3 | **Legislative Decree 96/1973 "Trade of pharmaceuticals, dietary supplements and cosmetics"** | Art. 6, par. 5 | Manufacturing and Wholesale Trade of Pharmaceuticals | Products included the Greek Pharmacopoeia (Ελληνικήν Φαρμακοποιΐαν) and products such as cotton and bandages are allowed to obtain and renew their market authorisation without the approval of State Laboratory for Medicines Control (KEEF). KEEF is the former national health organisation, which was abolished by art. 9 of Law 1316/1983. | Licensing | It was not possible to identify the objective of the specific provision. Following communication with competent authorities, we understand that the provision is not implemented in practice. | KEEF was abolished as an institution by Art. 9, par. 1 of Law 1316/1983. Its competences and obligations were passed to its successor, the National Organisation for Medicines (EOF). Despite becoming obsolete, this article has never been explicitly abolished. Therefore, the legal uncertainty caused by this law may harm competition. The State Laboratory for Medicines Control (KEEF) has been replaced by the Institute of Pharmaceutical Research and Technology (IFET), a subsidiary of EOF. | To be explicitly abolished. | Ministry of Health |
| 4 | **Legislative Decree 96/1973 "Trade of pharmaceuticals, dietary supplements and cosmetics"** | Art. 7, par. 1b | Manufacturing and Wholesale Trade of Pharmaceuticals | Domestic producers of pharmaceuticals are allowed to manufacture only a single product for each qualitative chemical composition in terms of active substance compared to products already circulating in the Greek market or abroad. This holds regardless of the quantitative composition and excipients of pharmaceuticals. | Licensing | It was not possible to identify the objective of the specific provision. Following communication with the National Organisation for Medicines (EOF), we understand that the provision is inactive and not implemented in practice. | This could substantially restrict the number of suppliers of pharmaceutical products in the market. This is an obsolete provision which could cause legal uncertainty to potential investors willing to enter the market. There is EU legislation in place which is followed. If applied this provision could limit the variety of products patients have access to (for example generics, co-marketed products, etc.). | To be explicitly abolished. | Ministry of Health |
| 5 | **Legislative Decree 96/1973 "Trade of pharmaceuticals, dietary supplements and cosmetics"** | Art. 8, par. 1 | Wholesale Trade of Pharmaceuticals | The market authorisation for imported pharmaceutical products of foreign countries is granted to the legal representatives of the companies, permanently residing in Greece. | Licensing / Import | It was not possible to identify the objective of the specific provision. Following communication with competent authorities, we understand that the provision is inactive. | The provision may lead to legal uncertainty as the permanent residence of the legal representative is not foreseen in the EU Directive 2001/83 and JMD 32221/2013. In addition, if enforced it would limit the choice of the representatives with regards to their residence. Economies of scale which could be achieved by the coverage of more than one market by the same legal representative is not allowed according to this provision. | The provision needs to be amended in order to allow for non-permanent residence of the legal representative. | Ministry of Health |
| 6 | **Legislative Decree 96/1973 "Trade of pharmaceuticals, dietary supplements and cosmetics"** | Art. 8, par. 2 | Manufacturing and Wholesale Trade of Pharmaceuticals | In order to license foreign pharmaceutical products in the Greek market, they ought to be significantly different from the existing ones or contain new active substances recognised as therapeutical in Greece. | Licensing / Import | It was not possible to identify the objective of the specific provision. However, in our understanding the objective of the provision was to protect and enhance domestic pharmaceutical production. Following communication with the National Organisation for Medicines (EOF), we understand that the provision is not implemented in practice. | This could substantially restrict the number of suppliers of pharmaceutical products in the market and reduce the incentives to compete. This is an obsolete provision which causes legal uncertainly. | To be explicitly abolished. | Ministry of Health |
| 7 | **Legislative Decree 96/1973 "Trade of pharmaceuticals, dietary supplements and cosmetics"** | Art. 8, par. 3 | Manufacturing and Wholesale Trade of Pharmaceuticals | Imported pharmaceutical products should be identical to those in their production country. | Licensing / Import | It was not possible to identify the objective of the specific provision. In our understanding the objective of the provision was to provide a safeguard by ensuring medicinal products' quality and protect public health. However, the concerns based on which the provision was introduced have now ceased to exist as Dir. 2001/83 and JMD 32221/2013 provide for a market authorisation procedure for imported medicines. Following communication with the National Organisation for Medicines (EOF), we understand that the provision is inactive and not implemented in practice. | The provision is inactive and may lead to legal uncertainty. If enforced, it may limit the diversity of products offered in the market and hamper the matching of patients' preferences. | To be explicitly abolished. | Ministry of Health |
| 8 | **Legislative Decree 96/1973 "Trade of pharmaceuticals, dietary supplements and cosmetics"** | Art. 9, par. 2 | Manufacturing and Wholesale Trade of Pharmaceuticals | Pharmaceutical products produced in Greece must have on the inside and outside package with capital letters and in an apparent way, the sign "Produced in Greece". | Licensing / Packaging | It was not possible to identify the objective of the specific provision. However, in our understanding the objective of the provision was to enhance domestic pharmaceutical production. Following communication with the National Organisation for Medicines (EOF), we understand that the provision is not implemented in practice. | The Ministry of Health and EOF acknowledge that the EMA QRD (Quality Review of Documents) template is rather followed in practice. If applied, this could distort the choices of patients who choose based on product origin rather than usage. This is an obsolete provision which could also affect the substitution and competition between similar medicines. | To be explicitly abolished. | Ministry of Health |
| 9 | **Legislative Decree 96/1973 "Trade of pharmaceuticals, dietary supplements and cosmetics"** | Art. 10, par. 2 | Manufacturing and Wholesale Trade of Pharmaceuticals | The brand name of the pharmaceutical product must mandatorily change upon any change or amendment in the active substance. | Licensing / Brand name | It was not possible to identify the objective of the specific provision. However, following communication with the National Organisation for Medicines (EOF), we understand that the objective is to avoid confusion within medical community and patients and to protect public health. | It could be restrictive if interpreted as impeding the development and improvement of active substances in pharmaceutical products. Read in conjunction with JMD 32221/2013, no harm to competition is identified. | No recommendation. | Ministry of Health |
| 10 | **Legislative Decree 96/1973 "Trade of pharmaceuticals, dietary supplements and cosmetics"** | Art. 12, par. 1 | Wholesale Trade of Pharmaceuticals | Wholesalers may sell pharmaceuticals to private clinics, on condition that a pharmacy operates within them. | Trading | It was not possible to identify the objective of the provision. However, following communication with the competent authorities, we understand that it is no longer in force. | This could disadvantage small private clinics choosing to operate without a pharmacy. In those cases, they may end up having a relatively lower number of suppliers and purchase pharmaceuticals in retail instead of wholesale price. | To be explicitly abolished. | Ministry of Health |

## Sector: Pharmaceuticals

| No | No and title of Regulation | Article | Thematic category | Brief description of the potential obstacle | Keyword | Policy maker's objectives | Harm to competition | Recommendations | Competent Ministry / Authority |
|---|---|---|---|---|---|---|---|---|---|
| 11 | **Legislative Decree 96/1973 "Trade of pharmaceuticals, dietary supplements and cosmetics"** | Art. 12, par. 2 | Manufacturing and Wholesale Trade of Pharmaceuticals | Representatives of pharmaceutical producers and importers are not allowed to sell or store products other than the ones they import or produce themselves. | Trading | It was not possible to identify the objective of the policy maker. According to Ministry of Health, this is an obsolete provision. Instead, JMD 32221/29-4-2013 (FEK B'1049) is followed, in compliance with Directive 2001/83/EC. Articles 102-115 of this JMD provide for a wide number of legal entities which may participate in the wholesale trade of pharmaceuticals. | The provision limits the ability of some suppliers to provide goods other than the ones that they import or produce. It therefore restricts them from engaging in trading of products of third parties, acting as agents. It reduces competition between suppliers, leading to less product variety and, possibly, higher prices. | To be explicitly abolished. | Ministry of Health |
| 12 | **Legislative Decree 96/1973 "Trade of pharmaceuticals, dietary supplements and cosmetics"** | Art. 13, par. 6 | Manufacturing and Wholesale Trade of Pharmaceuticals | Private clinics with more than 200 beds are obliged to have a pharmacy operating within their establishment. | Establishment | It was not possible to identify the policymaker's objective. However, following communication with the competent authorities, we understand that the objective of the policy maker may be outdated. | The provision is obsolete and may cause legal uncertainty. According to law 3846/2010, art. 27, par. 4, the obligation to have a pharmacy operating within their establishment applies to clinics with more than 60 beds, whereas those with up to 60 beds which do not have a pharmacy, are required to have a medicine storage room of at least 6 sq. metres. | To be explicitly abolished. | Ministry of Health |
| 13 | **Legislative Decree 96/1973 "Trade of pharmaceuticals, dietary supplements and cosmetics"** | Art. 14, par. 1 | Manufacturing and Wholesale Trade of Pharmaceuticals | Every pharmaceutical, dietary and cosmetic product is subject to pharmacological and hygiene controls, as well as controls based on Market Code and Market Decree provisions. | Market surveillance | It was not possible to identify the policy maker's objective. However, following communication with the competent authorities, we understand that the objective of the policymaker may be outdated. | The references to the Market Code and Market Decree, which are not in use anymore, may cause legal uncertainty. | Recommendation to abolish the reference to the Market Code and Market Decree. | Ministry of Health |
| 14 | **Legislative Decree 96/1973 "Trade of pharmaceuticals, dietary supplements and cosmetics"** | Art. 16, par. 6 | Manufacturing and Wholesale Trade of Pharmaceuticals | Scientific events organised or funded by pharmaceutical companies may be allowed upon prior approval by EOF. | Scientific events | It was not possible to identify the objective of the specific provision. However, following communication with EOF, we understand that the objective is to control pharmaceutical expenditure, to ensure compliance with ethical standards between health professionals and pharmaceutical companies, to control pharmaceutical expenditure and to assess the scientific nature of the events along with the proper implementation of their budget. | Given that the framework for the disclosure of transfers between pharmaceutical companies and medical practitioners is not enforced, the regulation of scientific events aims at achieving the objective of limiting these transfers. However, an ex-ante control mechanism may lead to delays for event organisers. | Recommendation to replace the prior approval requirement with a notification of scientific events to EOF. An ex-post control mechanism should be foreseen in law in order to complement the notification requirement. | Ministry of Health |
| 15 | **Legislative Decree 96/1973 "Trade of pharmaceuticals, dietary supplements and cosmetics"** | Art. 17, par. 3 | Wholesale Trade of Pharmaceuticals | Pharmaceutical warehouse representatives do not participate in the Pharmaceutical Pricing Committee. The members are officials of the Ministry of Health, EOF and other relevant authorities, representatives of the pharmacists' association, as well as employers in manufacturing and importing companies. | Pricing / Pricing Committee | The official recital of the policy objective could not be traced. | This may cause discrimination in the negotiation position between operators in the same market. Manufacturers also active at the wholesale level are currently represented in the committee, while wholesalers that are not vertically integrated are not. | To be amended in order to allow the participation of pharmaceutical warehouse representatives. | Ministry of Health |
| 16 | **Legislative Decree 96/1973 "Trade of pharmaceuticals, dietary supplements and cosmetics"** | Art. 17, par. 4 | Manufacturing and Wholesale Trade of Pharmaceuticals | For pharmaceutical products that get a new price, a 15% contribution on the wholesale price is calculated in order to set the new retail price. The 15% on the wholesale price is attributed to EOF. | Fees | It was not possible to identify the objective of the provision. However, according to our understanding, the fee was introduced in order to contribute to the funding of the National Organisation of Medicines (EOF) and reduce its reliance on the central budget. Following communication with EOF, we understand that the provision is not in force. | The provision is obsolete and may cause legal uncertainty and discourage potential investors. | To be explicitly abolished. | Ministry of Health / National Organisation for Medicines (EOF) |
| 17 | **Legislative Decree 96/1973 "Trade of pharmaceuticals, dietary supplements and cosmetics"** | Art. 17, par. 5b | Manufacturing and Wholesale Trade of Pharmaceuticals | Every business relevant to the pharmaceutical sector is obliged, if asked by the Minister of Health, following EOF's BoD opinion to complete its personnel with a percentage defined by the relevant Market Decree as personnel expenses. Any penalties are imposed based on art 19 par. 5 of law 96/1973. | Personnel costs | It was not possible to identify the objective of the specific provision. Following communication with competent authorities, we understand that the provision is not implemented in practice. | Obsolete article. However, as it has never been explicitly abolished it could create legal uncertainty. If applied this would distort the choices of pharmaceutical companies with regard to their management practices. Imposing higher personnel costs than firm's choice may distort competition and increase prices. | To be explicitly abolished. | Ministry of Health / National Organisation for Medicines (EOF) |
| 18 | **Legislative Decree 96/1973 "Trade of pharmaceuticals, dietary supplements and cosmetics"** | Art. 19, par. 4 | Manufacturing and Wholesale Trade of Pharmaceuticals | Any sanctions regarding pharmaceuticals' pricing are imposed based on the Market Code provisions. | Market surveillance / Sanctions | It was not possible to identify the objective of the specific provision. However, we understand that the aim is to ensure enforcement. | The references to the Market Code, which is not in use anymore, may cause legal uncertainty. | Recommendation to abolish the reference to the Market Code. | Ministry of Health |
| 19 | **Legislative Decree 96/1973 "Trade of pharmaceuticals, dietary supplements and cosmetics"** | Art. 19, par. 6 | Manufacturing and Wholesale Trade of Pharmaceuticals | In case of an second infringement for the same product, the licence is revoked for producers or their representatives. In case of a second infringement from pharmacists or licence holders of pharmaceutical warehouses or other stores, the licence is temporarily revoked for up to six months. In case of a relapse, the licence of the pharmacy or pharmaceutical warehouse is revoked permanently. | Market surveillance / Sanctions | It was not possible to identify the objective of the specific provision. Following communication with the Ministry of Health, we understand that the aim is to ensure the enforcement of legislation on the protection of public health, as well as prevent the observed persistent infringement of the law by enterprises. | Infringements by pharmacists of pharmaceutical warehouses licence holders are more flexible than those by producers or their representatives. Potential harm to competition may stem from the fact the pharmaceutical producers may also be warehouse licence holders. | Recommendation to amend the provision in order to impose the same penalties for the different categories of professionals. | Ministry of Health |
| 20 | **Law 1316/1983 "Establishment, organisation and competence of the National Organisation for Medicines, the National Pharmaceutical Industry, the State Pharmaceutical Warehouse and other provisions"** | Art. 11, par. 1στ | Manufacturing and Wholesale Trade of Pharmaceuticals | Contribution equal to 15% of the wholesale price (excluding any other fees which may be due) on the pharmaceutical products circulating in Greece. For cases where these pharmaceutical products are included in the categories of vaccines, the needs of armed forces or for the free provisions for humanitarian reasons, the governing body of EOF may reduce or nullify this contribution. | Fees | It was not possible to identify the objective of the specific provision. However, in our understanding the fee was introduced in order to contribute to the funding of the National Organisation for Medicines (EOF) and reduce its reliance on the central budget. Following communication with EOF, we understand that the provision is not implemented in practice. | This is an obsolete article without practical use and could create legal uncertainty. | To be explicitly abolished. | Ministry of Health |

## Sector: Pharmaceuticals

| No | No and title of Regulation | Article | Thematic category | Brief description of the potential obstacle | Keyword | Policy maker's objectives | Harm to competition | Recommendations | Competent Ministry / Authority |
|---|---|---|---|---|---|---|---|---|---|
| 21 | **Law 1316/1983 "Establishment, organisation and competence of the National Organisation for Medicines, the National Pharmaceutical Industry, the State Pharmaceutical Warehouse and other provisions"** | Art. 27, par. 5 | Manufacturing and Wholesale Trade of Pharmaceuticals | In case of mergers of pharmaceutical companies:<br>A. Production is permitted in the merged factories provided that each of them functions under the supervision of production managers and quality control personnel.<br>B. Production transfer between merged factories has to be authorised by EOF, which establishes the necessary conditions for quality control. | Licensing / Mergers | It was not possible to identify the objective of the specific provision. However, following communication with the Ministry of Health, we understand that the objective is to protect public health by ensuring safety of the medicines in manufacturing procedures. | This could intervene in the managerial choices on production facilities. If companies have been already authorised to operate and function, a potential re-authorisation of merged companies creates barriers to mergers and could therefore raise costs.<br>A. Effective supervision of manufacturing and quality control of pharmaceutical products is already foreseen as a requirement for the factories to obtain the Capability of Production licence. Any change in the supervision and quality control personnel is also shown in the Capability of Production licence. The provision, as stated, may lead to uncertainty concerning a potential duplication of the licensing process.<br>B. Since any change on the production line occurs a change in the Capability of Production licence the additional approval is redundant. | Provision needs to be rephrased in order to clearly state that both parts of it refer to the necessary amendments which need to be made in the Capability of Production licence and not another separate approval or licence by EOF. | Ministry of Health |
| 22 | **Law 1316/1983 "Establishment, organisation and competence of the National Organisation for Medicines, the National Pharmaceutical Industry, the State Pharmaceutical Warehouse and other provisions"** | Art. 32, par. 5a | Manufacturing and Wholesale Trade of Pharmaceuticals | For pharmaceuticals produced in Greece, the costs for the purposes of calculating prices cannot include the samples which are prescribed without EOF approval, costs of scientific events, expensive advertisement, fees of intermediaries, overpricing, etc. | Pricing | It was not possible to identify the objective of the specific provision. However, in our understanding, the provision applies to domestically produced medicines whose pricing is cost-plus. These aim at preventing high prices formation which would lead to higher public expenditure. | This may allow for different interpretations and could cause legal uncertainty of what cost-plus pharmaceuticals take into consideration as cost factors. For cases of pharmaceutical products priced through the cost-plus procedure, all cost components are set in tables (art. 10 MD 28408/2016) and are available to interested parties. | No recommendation. | Ministry of Health |
| 23 | **Law 1316/1983 "Establishment, organisation and competence of the National Organisation for Medicines, the National Pharmaceutical Industry, the State Pharmaceutical Warehouse and other provisions"** | Art. 32, par. 5b | Manufacturing and Wholesale Trade of Pharmaceuticals | If requested to do so by the Minister of Health and Welfare, pharmaceutical companies are obliged to recruit personnel when personnel costs are lower than those described in the relevant market decree. | Personnel costs | It was not possible to identify the objective of the specific provision. Following communication with competent authorities, we understand that the provision is not implemented in practice. | Obsolete article. However, as it has never been explicitly abolished it could create legal uncertainty. If applied this would distort the choices of pharmaceutical companies with regard to their management practices. Imposing higher personnel costs than firm's choice may distort competition and increase prices. | To be abolished. | Ministry of Health |
| 24 | **EOF Decision 6206/2009 "Standards for production of food supplements and foodstuffs intended for particular nutritional uses"** | Art. 5.9 | Manufacturing and Wholesale Trade of Food Supplements and Foodstuffs Intended for Particular Nutritional Uses | The weighing and sampling of raw materials should be carried out in separate rooms designed for that specific purpose. | Establishment | According to Art. 1 of the Circular, the objective is to ensure appropriate quality management and conformity with requirements of quality and purity with regard to food supplements and foodstuffs for particular nutritional uses. In addition, following communication with the Ministry of Health, we understand that the provision aims at ensuring particular quality control due to the specific nature of the products concerned. | It restricts suppliers' choices and imposes a strict limitation on their management practices. Various quality controls from GMP are already in place concerning the establishments, buildings and production facilities of pharmaceutical companies. | Make the provision less restrictive by removing the requirement for separate designated rooms; yet, ensuring quality control. | National Organisation for Medicines (EOF) |
| 25 | **Joint Ministerial Decision Υ1/Γ.Π.127962/2004 "Harmonisation of the Greek legislation with the Directive 2002/46/EC on the approximation of the laws of the Member States relating to food supplements"** | Art. 6, par. 3στ | Manufacturing and Wholesale Trade of Food Supplements | The labelling of food supplements should include the notification number to EOF and a statement that this number does not replace the market authorisation from EOF. | Licensing | It was not possible to identify the objective of the specific provision. However, according to the answer of Minister of Health in response to parliamentary questions, dated 12-08-2014, the objective of the provision is to protect consumers from consuming food supplements which are likely to impair or downgrade their state of health. In our understanding, the provision aims at informing consumers that food supplements are simply notified to EOF and are not subject to checks and authorisation before product launch. | Stating in each package of food supplements that these products do not hold a market authorisation by EOF may create the impression to the average consumer that these products are relatively uncontrolled or risky and therefore reduce their consumption propensity. This labelling requirement is additional to the ones foreseen by the EC Directive which this JMD is aligned to. | Recommendation to replace the current statement with the statement that product is not subject to market authorisation. | Ministry of Health / Economy, Development and Tourism |
| 26 | **Joint Ministerial Decision Υ1/Γ.Π.127962/2004 "Harmonisation of the Greek legislation with the Directive 2002/46/EC on the approximation of the laws of the Member States relating to food supplements"** | Art. 10, par. 1 | Manufacturing and Wholesale Trade of Food Supplements | This sets an obligation for the producer and/or the importer to pay a fee to EOF for each notification of a food supplement. For food supplements from EU countries the fee is reduced by 50% compared to those imported from third countries. | Licensing / Fees | It was not possible to identify the objective of the specific provision. However, we understand that these fees contribute to the funding of EOF for the purposes of checking procedures for firstly circulated products and market surveillance. | Bearing in mind that the fees are charged to the companies EOF oversees for the food supplements circulating in the Greek market, the doubled fee in the case of imports from third countries is justified for reasons of less work involved for food supplements of EU origin that are also subject to EU related control procedures. | No recommendation. | Ministry of Health / Economy, Development and Tourism |
| 27 | **Joint Ministerial Decision Υ1/Γ.Π.127962/2004 "Harmonisation of the Greek legislation with the Directive 2002/46/EC on the approximation of the laws of the Member States relating to food supplements"** | Annex 1 | Manufacturing and Wholesale Trade of Food Supplements | The list of minerals foreseen in the JMD 127962/2004 as eligible for the manufacture of food supplements do not include all the minerals defined in the EU Directive 2002/46/EC it transposes (as amended by EU Regulation 1170/2009). | Licensing / Ingredients | It was not possible to identify the objective of the specific provision. However, we understand that the objective is to protect public health. | This is not in line with the latest EU Regulation 1170/2009 which amended the Dir.2002/46/EC. Since the EU Regulation is directly applicable, this inconsistency may cause legal uncertainty. In its current form the provision may have an anti-competitive effect for firms in various EU countries marketing products which contain the minerals not included in the Greek text. These products may face a barrier to entry in the Greek market. | Recommendation to align the provision with the EU Directive 2002/46/EC as amended and in force. | Ministry of Health / Economy, Development and Tourism |

## Sector: Pharmaceuticals

| No | No and title of Regulation | Article | Thematic category | Brief description of the potential obstacle | Keyword | Policy maker's objectives | Harm to competition | Recommendations | Competent Ministry / Authority |
|---|---|---|---|---|---|---|---|---|---|
| 28 | **Joint Ministerial Decision Α2Ε/5478/1999 "Harmonising the national legislation to the relevant EU legislation on the sector of special nutrition food according to provisions of EU 89/398 EC and EU 96/84 EC of the European Parliament and the Council"** | Art. 6, par. 1 | Manufacturing and Wholesale Trade of Food Supplements and Foodstuffs Intended for Particular Nutritional Uses | For special nutrition purposes food products, which are not included in the categories foreseen in this piece of legislation, the person or company placing it in the market should inform EOF in written. While EU legislation requires them to submit only a labelling sample to the regulatory body (here EOF), this JMD also requires the submission of a sample of the product as circulated in the market, details concerning the producer, the composition and the appearance of the product and a special fee, as foreseen in the MD Υ6α/11094/97/4.3.98 (Β/235). | Licensing | It was not possible to identify the objective of the specific provision. However, we understand that the objective is to protect public health by ensuring food safety. | The MD Υ6α/11094/97/4.3.98 (Β/235), defining the fee to EOF, has been abolished. This may lead to legal uncertainty. The submission of these extra samples, information and fees may constitute a potential administrative burden, which may also increase costs to producers. | Change the MD in order to refer to the MD defining fees to EOF 139307/2005. | Ministry of Health / Economy, Development and Tourism |
| 29 | **Joint Ministerial Decision Υ3Ε/5497/1998 "Harmonisation of the Greek legislation with Directive 96/8/EC (as amended) on foods intended for use in energy-restricted diets for weight reduction"** | Art. 3, par. 1 | Manufacturing and Wholesale Trade of Foods Intended for Use in Energy-Restricted Diets for Weight Reduction | Companies placing in the market food products intended for energy-restricted diets for weight reduction should responsibly inform in written and communicate to EOF details concerning the manufacturer, packager, composition, presentation and labelling of the product and other information, according to specific instructions of EOF. The same applies to any modification of those elements. Fees apply for new circulation as well as each modification of the products. | Licensing | It was not possible to identify the objective of the specific provision. However, we understand that the objective is to protect public health by ensuring food safety. | The administrative procedures foreseen in this provision may create counter-incentives to market entry. However, it appears justified in light of the policy maker's objective. | No recommendation. | Ministry of Health / Economy, Development and Tourism |
| 30 | **Joint Ministerial Decision ΔΥΓ3α/Γ.Π 139307/2005 "Definition of fees in favour of National Organisation for Medicines (EOF)"** | Art. 1, par. 1 | Manufacturing and Wholesale Trade of Pharmaceuticals | Definition of fees in favour of National Organisation for Medicines (EOF) - Medicines for human use pay EUR 20,000 if they are firstly licensed in Greece and their active substance is known; EUR 20,000 if the request is based on bibliographic literature; and EUR 18,000 if the request is based on its well established use. | Licensing / Fees | It was not possible to identify the objective of the specific provision. However, in our understanding the fee was introduced in order to contribute to the funding of the National Organisation for Medicines (EOF) and reduce its reliance on the central budget. | Administrative cost which could be a barrier to entry. This is not a clear competition issue, but reciprocity should be ensured. | No recommendation. | Ministry of Health / Economy, Development and Tourism / Finance |
| 31 | **Joint Ministerial Decision ΔΥΓ3α/Γ.Π 139307/2005 "Definition of fees in favour of National Organisation for Medicines (EOF)"** | Art. 3, par. 1 | Manufacturing and Wholesale Trade of Pharmaceuticals | Definition of fees in favour of National Organisation for Medicines (EOF) - Medicines for human use pay EUR 40,000 if EOF is the reference country and a full file is submitted; EUR 30,000 in the cases of the simplified file for the licensing of a generic and for non-generic medicines with reference to the prototype; EUR 10,000 in the case of a simplified file following the consent for the use of the data of an already licensed medicine. | Licensing / Fees | It was not possible to identify the objective of the specific provision. However, in our understanding the fee was introduced in order to contribute to the funding of the National Organisation for Medicines (EOF) and reduce its reliance on the central budget. | Administrative cost which could be a barrier to entry. This is not a clear competition issue, but reciprocity should be ensured. | No recommendation. | Ministry of Health / Economy, Development and Tourism / Finance |
| 32 | **Joint Ministerial Decision ΔΥΓ3α/Γ.Π 139307/2005 "Definition of fees in favour of National Organisation for Medicines (EOF)"** | Art. 13 | Manufacturing and Wholesale Trade of Food Supplements | Notification fee for food supplements is EUR 600. | Licensing / Fees | It was not possible to identify the objective of the specific provision. However, we understand that these fees contribute to the funding of EOF for the purposes of market surveillance and checking procedures. | Administrative cost which could be a barrier to entry. This is not a clear competition issue, but reciprocity should be ensured. | No recommendation. | Ministry of Health / Economy, Development and Tourism / Finance |
| 33 | **Joint Ministerial Decision ΔΥΓ3α/Γ.Π 139307/2005 "Definition of fees in favour of National Organisation for Medicines (EOF)"** | Art. 29, par. 1 | Manufacturing and Wholesale Trade of Pharmaceuticals | Definition of fees in favour of National Organisation for Medicines (EOF) - For the inspection by EOF of third countries of medicines for human use pay EUR 7,000 per request and production unit for European countries, EUR 10,000 for countries outside Europe, and EUR 2,000 less in each case if market authorisation has been already requested in Greece. | Fees | It was not possible to identify the objective of the specific provision. However, we understand that these fees contribute to the funding of EOF for the purposes of market surveillance and checking procedures. | Administrative cost which could be a barrier to entry. This is not a clear competition issue, but reciprocity should be ensured. | No recommendation. | Ministry of Health / Economy, Development and Tourism / Finance |
| 34 | **Ministerial Decision 378812/1992 "Conditions governing the placing on the market, control and manufacture of veterinary medicinal products, immunological veterinary medicinal products and medicated feeding stuffs"** | Art. 50, par. 2 | Manufacturing and Wholesale Trade of Veterinary Medicinal Products | This article sets various criteria for the wholesale licensing of veterinary medical products, which are not clearly in line with the EU directive it transposes. For example, the person filing a request to EOF for the licensing has to have the Greek or EU citizenship, a degree of pharmacy or veterinary school and a work permit in Greece, to have completed the military service, clear penal precedent, to possess space for selling the products of at least 20 sq. metres, well lightened and equipped, a special storage room suitable for storing an adequate number of veterinary medical products, fridge or cool room for drugs which are affected by the temperature. In case the store sells medicines for human use as well, the space should be clearly separated. | Licensing | The objective of the MD is to set manufacturing, control and circulation conditions of veterinary medicinal products in compliance with Directives 81/851/EEC, 90/676/EEC, 90/677/EEC and 90/167/EEC. However, following communication with the competent Ministry of Rural Development and food, it is our understanding that the provision has been superseded by the Joint Ministerial Decision 282371/2006 and is therefore obsolete. | It sets an unjustified restriction on public health grounds and it is not in accordance with the relevant EU Directive. It imposes high entry costs and limits the number of suppliers due to the fact that it requires specific criteria to be met by the wholesaler. It limits product variety available in the market potentially leading to higher prices. | To be explicitly abolished. | Ministry of Rural Development and Food / Economy, Development and Tourism |

## Sector: Pharmaceuticals

| No | No and title of Regulation | Article | Thematic category | Brief description of the potential obstacle | Keyword | Policy maker's objectives | Harm to competition | Recommendations | Competent Ministry / Authority |
|---|---|---|---|---|---|---|---|---|---|
| 35 | **Ministerial Decision 378812/1992 "Conditions governing the placing on the market, control and manufacture of veterinary medicinal products, immunological veterinary medicinal products and medicated feeding stuffs"** | Art. 50, par. 4 & 5 | Manufacturing and Wholesale Trade of Veterinary Medicinal Products | Unlike the EU directive which this piece of legislation is based upon, these articles establish that the wholesalers of veterinary medicinal products may sell their products (not in the retail, only in the wholesale price) only to the following categories:<br>a) the public sector and legal entities of public law<br>b) wholesale stores of veterinary products<br>c) pharmacies and retail stores of veterinary products<br>d) farms, on condition that purchased products will be used only for their animals and not resale, and on condition that they have a licensed exclusively employed responsible private vet. The vet has to sign each purchase order, otherwise it is considered as illegal.<br>e) factories producing medicated feeding stuffs (only medicated premixes).<br>The holder of the licence has to be employed himself in his store. | Licensing | The objective of the MD is to set manufacturing, control and circulation conditions of veterinary medicinal products in compliance with Directives 81/851/EEC, 90/676/EEC, 90/677/EEC and 90/167/EEC. However, following communication with the competent Ministry of Rural Development and food, it is our understanding that the provision has been superseded by the Joint Ministerial Decision 282371/2006 and is therefore obsolete. | It sets an unjustified restriction on public health grounds and it is not in accordance with the relevant EU Directive. It imposes high entry costs for new suppliers impeding competition. | To be explicitly abolished. | Ministry of Rural Development and Food / Economy, Development and Tourism |
| 36 | **EOF Circular 17702/2016 "Organisation of scientific events"** | Par. II.B | Manufacturing and Wholesale Trade of Pharmaceuticals | Scientific events organised by pharmaceutical companies should not be organised at hospital or university venues. For this type of events a threshold of twenty-four (24) events per company per year applies. | Scientific events | The Circular's objective is to ensure compliance with ethical standards between health professionals and pharmaceutical companies, to control pharmaceutical expenditure and to assess the scientific nature of the events along with the proper implementation of their budget. | It restricts firms' ability to advertise and promote dissemination of scientific knowledge and development, as well as distort their marketing strategy. However, in light of the policymakers' objective, specific requirements which would provide the basis for the ex-post assessments, may be justified and should be foreseen. | No recommendation. | National Organisation for Medicines (EOF) |
| 37 | **EOF Circular 17702/2016 "Organisation of scientific events"** | Par. III.2 | Manufacturing and Wholesale Trade of Pharmaceuticals | A health professional may not be subsidised by EOF licensed companies more than 3 times a year for participation in scientific events or conferences organised abroad. At least two of them should be in Europe. | Scientific events | The Circular's objective is to ensure compliance with ethical standards between health professionals and pharmaceutical companies, to control pharmaceutical expenditure and to assess the scientific nature of the events along with the proper implementation of their budget. | It restricts firms' ability to advertise and promote dissemination of scientific knowledge and development, as well as distort their marketing strategy. However, in light of the policymakers' objective, specific requirements which would provide the basis for the ex-post assessments, may be justified and should be foreseen. | No recommendation. | National Organisation for Medicines (EOF) |
| 38 | **EOF Circular 17702/2016 "Organisation of scientific events"** | Par. IV | Manufacturing and Wholesale Trade of Pharmaceuticals | For the subsidy of watching online, in a group or individually, of a scientific event organised in Greece, a precondition is that the organiser should have obtained a permission by EOF for the event, including the streaming. If attending in a group, the expenses for the space and the equipment can be covered by the company producing EOF licensed products. Only coffee or refreshments are allowed to be served in group audiences. For online attending, personally or in group, of the scientific event organised abroad, a request should be submitted online to EOF. | Scientific events | The Circular's objective is to ensure compliance with ethical standards between health professionals and pharmaceutical companies, to control pharmaceutical expenditure and to assess the scientific nature of the events along with the proper implementation of their budget. | It restricts firms' ability to advertise and promote dissemination of scientific knowledge and development, as well as distort their marketing strategy. However, in light of the policymakers' objective, specific requirements which would provide the basis for the ex-post assessments, may be justified and should be foreseen. | No recommendation. | National Organisation for Medicines (EOF) |
| 39 | **Law 2519/1997 "Development and modernisation of National Health System, structure of health-care services, provisions on pharmaceuticals and other provisions"** | Art. 49, par. 1 | Manufacturing and Wholesale Trade of Pharmaceuticals | For prescription medicines licensed by EOF, promotion expenditures should not exceed the limits foreseen in the relevant Joint Ministerial Decision of the Minister of Development, the Minister of Finance and the Minister of Health and Welfare, after an EOF proposal, and based on the annual sales and the wholesale price. The definitions of promotion expenditure are also provided through similar decisions. | Promotion expenditure | It was not possible to identify the objective of the specific provision. However, following communication with EOF, the provision is necessary for the control of promotion expenditure. | It restricts firms' ability to advertise and promote dissemination of scientific knowledge and development, as well as distort their marketing strategy. However, it is justified in light of the policymakers' objective. | No recommendation. | Ministry of Health |

## Sector: Pharmaceuticals

| No | No and title of Regulation | Article | Thematic category | Brief description of the potential obstacle | Keyword | Policy maker's objectives | Harm to competition | Recommendations | Competent Ministry / Authority |
|---|---|---|---|---|---|---|---|---|---|
| 40 | **Joint Ministerial Decision Υ6α/28403/01/2002 "Expenditure of pharmaceutical firms related to promotion of pharmaceuticals"** | Art. 3α | Manufacturing and Wholesale Trade of Pharmaceuticals | This article defines the maximum promotion expenditure for prescription medicines as a share of the turnover of the pharmaceutical company:<br>1. 16% for turnover up to EUR 6 Million<br>2. 13% for turnover between EUR 6 Million and EUR 15 Million<br>3. 10% for turnover between EUR 15 Million and EUR 30 Million<br>4. 6% for turnover between EUR 30 Million and EUR 45 Million<br>5. 4% for turnover above EUR 45 Million<br><br>Promotion expenditure aiming at export promotion to third countries is excluded from the above percentages.<br><br>For pharmaceutical companies trading products of more than one pharmaceutical manufacturer, the calculation of the annual turnover will be split into the turnovers of products of each manufacturer, and considered as separate commercial entities. | Promotion expenditure | It was not possible to identify the objective of the specific provision. However, in our understanding the objective is to control pharmaceutical expenditure. | It restricts firms' ability to advertise and promote dissemination of scientific knowledge and development, as well as distort their marketing strategy. However, it is justified in light of the policymakers' objective. | No recommendation. | Ministry of Health |
| 41 | **EOF Circular 49393/2011 "Clarifications on the public advertisement of non-prescription medicine"** | Par. Γ | Manufacturing and Wholesale Trade of OTCs | OTCs aiming at the general public cannot be advertised in clinics, hospitals, health centres, diagnostic centres, etc. and anywhere else health services are provided. Specifically in pharmacies (which provide health services, but also conduct retail sales), only advertisement of OTCs is allowed, under certain conditions and guidelines (included in the two previous articles of this Circular). This advertisement may take the form of stands, screen displays, brochures, windows materials, and use material of clear advertising nature, where guidelines on the proper use of medicine shall be included. | Advertisement | It was not possible to identify the objective of the specific provision. However, following communication with the competent authorities, we understand that the policy maker does not consider pharmaceutical products as consumer goods falling as a result under more restrictive provisions than the general rules applied for consumer protection. | The provision does not take into account the new points of sale of General Sale Medicines (GEDIFA), as a sub-group of OTCs. The points of sale are defined in the MD Γ5(α)51194 (ΦΕΚ 2219 Β 2016), which does not explicitly regulate advertisement in those points; rather it makes reference to existing pharmaceutical legislation. As a result, advertisement in retail spaces other than pharmacies appears to not be regulated.<br>This limits the firms' ability to advertise; and interferes with their marketing strategies. | Recommendation to extend the provision in order to allow advertisement of OTCs in the points of sale, according to MD Γ5(α)51194 (ΦΕΚ 2219 Β 2016). | National Organisation for Medicines (EOF) |
| 42 | **EOF Circular 49393/2011 "Clarifications on the public advertisement of non-prescription medicine"** | Par. Γ | Manufacturing and Wholesale Trade of OTCs | Under no circumstance may the advertisement of OTCs in pharmacies be associated with the provision of benefits to the public, even of low pecuniary advantage, without excluding the samples and virtual samples of medicines. | Advertisement | It was not possible to identify the objective of the specific provision. However, following communication with the competent authorities, we understand that the policy maker does not consider pharmaceutical products as consumer goods falling as a result under more restrictive provisions than the general rules applied for consumer protection. | This restrict the ability to advertise the price discount and promotion. There is no equivalent EU legislation. Following Dir. 2001/83/EC, providing samples to the public is to be prohibited, while providing benefits is only prohibited to persons qualified to prescribe or supply the medicines. | Recommendation to reword the provision in order to allow the advertisement of price reductions/promotions as special case of benefits to the public. | National Organisation for Medicines (EOF) |
| 43 | **EOF Circular 49393/2011 "Clarifications on the public advertisement of non-prescription medicine"** | Par. Δ | Manufacturing and Wholesale Trade of OTCs | Any OTC advertisement should be submitted to EOF for approval. EOF will provide approval or suggestions for amendments within 30 days. | Advertisement | It was not possible to identify the objective of the specific provision. However, following communication with the competent authorities, we understand that the policy maker does not consider pharmaceutical products as consumer goods falling as a result under more restrictive provisions than the general rules applied for consumer protection. | According to EU Dir. 2001/83/EC (art. 97), it is up to Member Countries to regulate the system of approval of OTCs advertisements. It is proportionate to the objective, but it could cause legislative uncertainty if EOF does not provide an answer within 30 days. | Recommendation to reword the provision in order to explicitly provide that the lack of response corresponds to tacit approval. | National Organisation for Medicines (EOF) |
| 44 | **Joint Ministerial Decision οικ.146163/2012 "Measures and prerequisites for the management of medicinal waste deriving from health units"** | Art. 10, par. A2 | Manufacturing and Wholesale Trade of Pharmaceuticals | A fee and an insurance certificate is required for the provision of a licence for the collection and transport of hazardous health units waste. An organisation study of the collection and transport network is also required. | Hazardous waste management | The objective of the JMD is to ensure a high level of protection of human health and environment along with the implementation of prioritisation of waste management actions of Health Units as defined in Law 4042/2012. | This is an administrative procedure and not a clear competition issue. | No recommendation. | Ministry of Health / Finance / Environment and Energy |
| 45 | **Joint Ministerial Decision οικ.146163/2012 "Measures and prerequisites for the management of medicinal waste deriving from health units"** | Art. 20, par. 1β | Manufacturing and Wholesale Trade of Pharmaceuticals | The licence for the collection and transport of hazardous health units waste is included in the documents which should be submitted for the licence of trucks transporting this waste. | Hazardous waste management | The objective of the JMD is to ensure a high level of protection of human health and environment along with the implementation of prioritisation of waste management actions of Health Units as defined in Law 4042/2012. | Regulatory uncertainty concerning the possibility of specialisation of companies in only transporting waste. | Clarify that companies wishing to solely engage in the transporting of hazardous waste are subject to the same licence. | Ministry of Health / Finance / Environment and Energy |
| 46 | **Joint Ministerial Decision οικ.146163/2012 "Measures and prerequisites for the management of medicinal waste deriving from health units"** | Annex 1, part A, sections 1.2 & 1.3 | Manufacturing and Wholesale Trade of Pharmaceuticals | Foreseen special requirements concerning the packaging of waste, the bins, barrels, hospital boxes and any sort of packaging items. These include the colour of the plastic bags for each category, the way they should be tied, their labelling, etc. | Hazardous waste management | The objective of the JMD is to ensure a high level of protection of human health and environment along with the implementation of prioritisation of waste management actions of Health Units as defined in Law 4042/2012. | This may increase the cost of operations for firms. However, it is deemed to be justified on public health grounds. | No recommendation. | Ministry of Health / Finance / Environment and Energy |
| 47 | **Joint Ministerial Decision οικ.146163/2012 "Measures and prerequisites for the management of medicinal waste deriving from health units"** | Annex 1, part A, section 3.1.3 | Manufacturing and Wholesale Trade of Pharmaceuticals | For the storage of hazardous waste of purely infectious pharmaceutical products, storage spaces should be labelled, have a specific temperature, be painted inside out with high endurance colours, have non-slippery floor, be isolated, have a metallic door, etc. | Hazardous waste management | The objective of the JMD is to ensure a high level of protection of human health and environment along with the implementation of prioritisation of waste management actions of Health Units as defined in Law 4042/2012. | This may increase the cost of operations for firms. However, it is deemed to be justified on public health grounds. | No recommendation. | Ministry of Health / Finance / Environment and Energy |

## Sector: Pharmaceuticals

| No | No and title of Regulation | Article | Thematic category | Brief description of the potential obstacle | Keyword | Policy maker's objectives | Harm to competition | Recommendations | Competent Ministry / Authority |
|---|---|---|---|---|---|---|---|---|---|
| 48 | **Joint Ministerial Decision Η.Π.13588/725/2006 "Measures, prerequisites and restrictions for the hazardous waste management in compliance with the provisions Directive 91/689/EEC on hazardous waste"** | Art. 7, part B, par. 2.3.α | Manufacturing and Wholesale Trade of Pharmaceuticals | Insurance contracts should be of at least the following value of coverage:<br>- for distribution and restore operations (D1-D15 and R1-R13 categories): EUR 1 million annually for the establishments of the A1 category and EUR 0.5 million annually for the establishments of the A2 category of the JMD 15393/2332/5.8.2002 (B' 1022).<br>- for international transport: EUR 1 million annually<br>- for collection and transport: EUR 0.5 million annually. | Hazardous waste management | The objective of the JMD is to ensure a high level of environmental protection and public health, in particular by preventing and/or reducing production and waste hazard, and/ or recovery of the waste with the development and use of clean technologies not involving excessive costs. | Setting a minimum insurance value for the collection, transport and operations of these establishments restricts the choice of the insured entity and sets a fixed cost for them. The insured value does not depend on the quantity transported and could therefore have an adverse effect in the choice of the amount of waste managed. However, it is deemed proportionate to policymaker's objective. | No recommendation. | Ministry of Health / Economy, Development and Tourism / Finance / Interior and Administrative Reconstruction / Environment and Energy / Infrastructure, Transport and Networks / Shipping and Island Policy |
| 49 | **Ministerial Decision Α6/11920/1988 "Import, storage and distribution of pharmaceuticals active substances"** | Art. 5, par. 1 | Manufacturing and Wholesale Trade of Pharmaceuticals | The supply of active substances for the production of pharmaceutical products may be done only by pharmaceutical warehouse wholesalers, market authorisation holders (manufacturers and representatives) and representatives of foreign manufacturers of active substances. | Active substance / Trading | It was not possible to identify the objective of the specific provision. | This might cause legal uncertainty regarding the possibility and eligibility of Greek manufacturers of active substances to supply them to the market. It might constitute a barrier towards the creation of active substances factories. | Recommendation to be rephrased in order to include all manufacturers of active substances. | Ministry of Health |
| 50 | **Joint Ministerial Decision Δ.ΥΓ3α/Γ.Π.32221/2013 "Harmonisation of the Greek legislation with the EU legislation in the sector of production and circulation of medicinal products for human use in compliance with the Directive 2001/83/EC on the Community Code relating to medicinal products for human use as amended by the Directive 2011/62/EU as regards the prevention of the entry into legal supply chain of falsified medicinal products"** | Art. 74, par. 1 | Manufacturing and Wholesale Trade of Pharmaceuticals | Importers, manufacturers and distributors of active substances established in Greece shall register their activity with EOF. According to the Directive transposed through this MD, the registration form shall include, at least, the following : (i) name or corporate name and permanent address; (ii) the active substances which are to be imported, manufactured or distributed; (iii) particulars regarding the premises and the technical equipment for their activity. The MD sets additional requirements providing that the minimum necessary information to be submitted shall further include the name and address of the producer (in the case the latter is not the applicant), and the producer's Good Manufacturing Practice (GMP) certificate, if available, along with the countries where the active ingredient has been distributed. | Licensing | It was not possible to identify the objective of the specific provision. However, we understand that the objective is the traceability and the protection of public health. | Potential hurdle but proportionate and justified for reasons of traceability. | No recommendation. | Ministry of Health / Economy, Development and Tourism / Infrastructure, Transport & Networks |
| 51 | **Ministerial Decision 28408/2016 "Provisions on pharmaceuticals pricing"** | Art. 1, par. 2 | Manufacturing and Wholesale Trade of Pharmaceuticals | For pricing purposes, the provisions for pricing of generics also apply to the cases of article 12 of the JMD ΔΥΓ3α/Γ.Π.32221/2013 (Gov. Gazette 1049/B/29.4.2013). Article 12 refers to medicinal products circulating under a market authorisation which relies on the well established medicinal use of active substance and is supported by bibliographic literature. | Pricing | It was not possible to identify the objective of the specific provision. However, following communication with the Ministry of Health, we understand that medicinal products' pricing is strictly regulated for reasons of controlling pharmaceutical expenditure. | The provision creates legal uncertainty regarding the applicable rules for the pricing of bibliographic medicinal products as the provision contradicts Art. 2, par. 3 which provides that the price of bibliographic medicines is defined according to the pricing rules for reference medicinal products after the expiration of data protection period. | Abolish the provision. | Ministry of Health |
| 52 | **Ministerial Decision 28408/2016 "Provisions on pharmaceuticals pricing"** | Art. 3, par. 1 | Manufacturing and Wholesale Trade of Pharmaceuticals | The provision provides for regulated mark-ups for traders of pharmaceuticals ('φαρμακέμποροι'). | Pricing | It was not possible to identify the objective of the specific provision. However, following communication with the Ministry of Health, we understand that medicinal products' pricing is strictly regulated for reasons of controlling pharmaceutical expenditure. | This provision causes legal uncertainty with regard to the use of the term 'φαρμακέμποροι', which is not exactly referring to the definition of the wholesalers. Art. 1 of L.D. 363/1941 provides that 'φαρμακεμπορεία' (pharmaceuticals trading facilities) are renamed to 'φαρμακαποθήκες' (pharmaceuticals warehouses). | Rename '*φαρμακέμποροι*' (traders of pharmaceuticals) to '*χονδρέμποροι*' (pharmaceutical wholesalers). | Ministry of Health |
| 53 | **Ministerial Decision 28408/2016 "Provisions on pharmaceuticals pricing"** | Art. 4, par. 1-3 | Manufacturing and Wholesale Trade of Pharmaceuticals | A. Market authorisation holders and wholesalers may provide discounts/credit only on certain conditions regulated by law. For prescription drugs, discounts up to 10% and credit period of at least 2-months may be granted. Any discount must be stated in the invoices.<br>B. In case of infringement of the provision, the penalties of the Market Code will be imposed. | Pricing | It was not possible to identify the objective of the specific provision. However, following communication with the Ministry of Health, we understand that medicinal products' pricing is strictly regulated for reasons of controlling pharmaceutical expenditure. | A. Setting a maximum percentage discount for prescription drugs significantly inhibits firms' pricing strategies. However, given that the pricing framework throughout the value chain is strictly regulated, this provision is in line with the policy maker's objective.<br>B. References to Market Code cause legal uncertainty since the latter has been repealed. | A. No recommendation.<br>B. Abolish the reference to the Market Code. | Ministry of Health |
| 54 | **Ministerial Decision 28408/2016 "Provisions on pharmaceuticals pricing"** | Art. 5, par. 2 | Manufacturing and Wholesale Trade of Pharmaceuticals | The time period for price approval in generics and originator products differs (30 days for generics and 90 for originator products after the receipt of an application). | Pricing | It was not possible to identify the objective of the specific provision. However, following communication with the Ministry of Health, we understand that the objective is the increase of generic penetration in the market. | This provides for differential treatment in the entrance to the market between generics and originator medicines. This is not aligned to the EC Transparency Directive 89/105/EEC on price approvals, which this MD is referring to. However, it is in line with the amended proposal for a new Directive, adopted by the EC in 2013, aiming to reduce the time required for medicines pricing procedure at a national level. | No recommendation. | Ministry of Health |

## Sector: Pharmaceuticals

| No | No and title of Regulation | Article | Thematic category | Brief description of the potential obstacle | Keyword | Policy maker's objectives | Harm to competition | Recommendations | Competent Ministry / Authority |
|---|---|---|---|---|---|---|---|---|---|
| 55 | **Ministerial Decision 28408/2016 "Provisions on pharmaceuticals pricing"** | Art. 8, par. 1 | Manufacturing and Wholesale Trade of Pharmaceuticals | For the price revisions of generics, external reference pricing is applied. The price is defined at 65% of the average of the prices of the reference product in 3 EU member states whereas price increases are not allowed. When the reference product has not received a price in at least three EU member states, the prices of those generics will not be revised. | Pricing / Generics | It was not possible to identify the objective of the specific provision. However, following communication with EOF, we understand that the provision has been introduced for public health reasons and specifically as a safeguard for the so-called unique generics so that after any price revisions, their price would be viable in order to remain in the market. | This allows for differential treatment in the way prices are set when the product circulates in three or more countries. However, the provision is in line with the policymaker's objective. | No recommendation. | Ministry of Health |
| 56 | **Ministerial Decision 28408/2016 "Provisions on pharmaceuticals pricing"** | Art. 8, par. 3 | Manufacturing and Wholesale Trade of Pharmaceuticals | For generics, any price revision cannot result in a price drop exceeding 15% of the previous wholesale price. If the revised price of a generic results higher that the price of the reference product whose protection period has expired (off-patent), then the price of the reference product shall be revised to equal the revised generic price. | Pricing / Generics | According to the provision, the objectives are the promotion of the use of less expensive treatments, the protection of public health and the safeguarding of sufficient medicines' supplies. Following communication with EOF, the provision has been introduced to prevent severe reductions of generics' prices in view of implementing the policy to increase generic penetration in the market. | This provision sets a maximum reduction of 15% on the price of generics. When the re-pricing of off-patent products results in a price lower than the revised price of the generic, then the two prices are set equal. This could, in turn, limit the incentives of patients to choose generics over off-patent products. | Apply the maximum price reduction rule only when the resulting price of the generic is below that of the respective off-patent. | Ministry of Health |
| 57 | **Ministerial Decision 28408/2016 "Provisions on pharmaceuticals pricing"** | Art. 10, par. 1 | Manufacturing and Wholesale Trade of Pharmaceuticals | For medicinal products exclusively produced in Greece which cannot exactly correspond, as to their pharmacotechnical form or strength, to reference products circulating in the Greek market, pricing is cost-plus and based on tables specifying these costs. | Pricing / Domestic medicines | It was not possible to identify the objective of the specific provision. However, following communication with the Ministry of Health, we understand that the objective of the cost-plus pricing mechanism for domestically produced pharmaceuticals is to favour domestic products through pricing in order to promote R&D and stimulate domestic production to produce innovative domestic medicines. | This provision may lead to differential treatment in pricing, dependent upon the origin of the medicinal products. However, this pricing system could be justified in light of the policymakers' objective. | No recommendation. It would be advisable for the cost components taken into consideration to be publicly available and transparent, in line with the EU Transparency Directive. | Ministry of Health |
| 58 | **Ministerial Decision 28408/2016 "Provisions on pharmaceuticals pricing"** | Art. 10, par. 4 | Manufacturing and Wholesale Trade of Pharmaceuticals | For domestically produced medicinal products the maximum net profit margin is set at 8,5%. | Pricing / Domestic medicines | It was not possible to identify the objective of the specific provision. In our understanding these products are priced using a cost-plus pricing mechanism. | This is a cost-plus pricing mechanism. As a result, the authorities define a maximum profit rate. Products which do not fall under this category are generally priced based on the External Reference Pricing system, which sets a price cap. Setting a maximum net profit rate is consistent with the cost-plus pricing mechanism. | No recommendation. | Ministry of Health |
| 59 | **Ministerial Decision 28408/2016 "Provisions on pharmaceuticals pricing"** | Art. 11, par. 5 | Manufacturing and Wholesale Trade of Pharmaceuticals | If requested by the Ministry of Health or EOF, pharmaceutical manufacturers, representatives, importers, wholesalers, and pharmacists are obliged to provide them with information related to medicines, pursuant to article 30 of the Legislative Decree 136/1946 (Market Code). | Market surveillance | It was not possible to identify the objective of the specific provision. However, following communication with EOF, we understand that the aim is to allow the Ministry to be able to request information on pricing issues, especially in dealing with complaints. | The Market Code referred hereby has been abolished pursuant to Art. 48, par. 2 of Law 4177/2013. The paragraph causes regulatory uncertainty regarding the applicable framework and may confuse potential market investors. | It should be rephrased in order to eliminate any reference to the Market Code. | Ministry of Health |
| 60 | **EOF Circular 3154/2011 "Determination of supporting documents required for licensing capability production, packaging, repackaging, storage or checks on plants producing APIs for use in production of medicinal products for human or veterinary use"** | Par. A | Manufacturing and Wholesale Trade of Pharmaceuticals | The Circular provides for the necessary documents to be submitted and fees to be paid when filing an application with EOF for obtaining the Capability of Production licence, a packaging/repackaging licence, a storage licence or conduct checks on plants producing APIs for medicinal products for human use. The procedure requires that applicants have previously obtained an operation licence from the competent authority. | Licensing | It was not possible to identify the objective of the specific provision. Following communication with the Ministry of Health, we understand that the licence from the competent authority does not ensure compliance with the standards necessary for the production or packaging. Such a licence refers to energy and other building safety features. | This double licensing could create a barrier to entry and increase costs to firms. This is deemed to be proportionate to the policymakers' objective. | No recommendation. | National Organisation for Medicines (EOF) |
| 61 | **EOF Circular 3154/2011 "Determination of supporting documents required for licensing capability production, packaging, repackaging, storage or checks on plants producing APIs for use in production of medicinal products for human or veterinary use"** | Par. A | Manufacturing and Wholesale Trade of Veterinary Medicinal Products | The Circular provides for the necessary documents to be submitted and fees to be paid when filing an application with EOF for obtaining the Capability of Production licence, a packaging/repackaging licence, a storage licence or conduct checks on plants producing APIs for medicinal products for veterinary use. The procedure requires that applicants have previously obtained an operation licence from the competent authority. | Licensing | It was not possible to identify the objective of the specific provision. Following communication with the Ministry of Health, we understand that the licence from the competent authority does not ensure compliance with the standards necessary for the production or packaging. Such a licence refers to energy and other building safety features. | This double licensing could create a barrier to entry and increase costs to firms. This is deemed to be proportionate to the policymakers' objective. | No recommendation. | National Organisation for Medicines (EOF) |
| 62 | **Ministerial Decision Γ5(α)/οικ.88979/2015 "Provisions on pharmaceuticals pricing"** | Recital 1.v; Art. 4, par. 5; Art. 11, par. 5 | Manufacturing and Wholesale Trade of Pharmaceuticals | The Ministerial Decision contains several provisions referring to the Market Code. | Market surveillance | It was not possible to identify the objective of the specific provisions. However, we understand that the aim is to ensure enforcement. | The Market Code referred hereby has been abolished pursuant to Art. 48, par. 2 of Law 4177/2013. The references to the abolished Market Code may cause legal uncertainty. | It should be rephrased in order to eliminate any reference to Market Code. | Ministry of Health |
| 63 | **Ministerial Decision ΔΥΓ3(α)/οικ.104744/2012 "Process of implementing a system of reference prices for the drafting, amending and competing the prescription medicines catalogue"** | Art. 1, par. 4 | Manufacturing and Wholesale Trade of Pharmaceuticals | For each new medicinal product included in the positive list and reimbursable by Social Security Funds, the market authorisation holder shall pay to EOPYY a one-off contribution of EUR 2 000 per pharmaceutical form, strength and dosage. | Reimbursement | It was not possible to identify the objective of the specific provision. However, in our understanding the fee has been introduced in the context of controlling pharmaceutical expenditure. | The same contribution is foreseen in Law 3816/2010 in the amount of 4% of the producer price (ex-factory), and in art. 12, par. 4 of this law in the amount of EUR 2 000 for the first pharmaceutical strength and EUR 1 000 for its other strengths. Following consultations with the Ministry of Health and EOPYY, the MD is the one which seems to be practically applied. This may cause legal uncertainty. | No recommendation. | Ministry of Health |

## Sector: Pharmaceuticals

| No | No and title of Regulation | Article | Thematic category | Brief description of the potential obstacle | Keyword | Policy maker's objectives | Harm to competition | Recommendations | Competent Ministry / Authority |
|---|---|---|---|---|---|---|---|---|---|
| 64 | **Law 4052/2012 "Law of competency of Ministries of Health and Social Solidarity and Labour and Social Security for the application of Law "Approval of the Draft Financial Assistance Facility Agreement between the European Financial Stability Facility (EFSF), the Hellenic Republic and the Bank of Greece of the Memorandum of Understanding between the Hellenic Republic, the European Commission and the Bank of Greece and other provisions on the reduction of public debt and the rescue of the Greek economy" and other provisions"** | Art. 21, par. 2 | Manufacturing and Wholesale Trade of Pharmaceuticals | When new medicinal products of the same active substance and pharmaceutical form enter the market after the first generic product, prices are reduced by an additional 10% for new medicines which are not protected by a patent. | Pricing / Generics | It was not possible to identify the objective of the provision. Following communication with the National Organisation for Medicines (EOF), we understand that the provision is inactive and not implemented in practice. | The provision is obsolete may cause legal uncertainty to new entrants with regard to generics pricing. | To be explicitly abolished. | Ministry of Health |
| 65 | **Law 3816/2010 "Settlement of business and professional debts to credit institutions, provisions for the processing of economic behaviour data and other provisions"** | Art. 12, par. 1b | Manufacturing and Wholesale Trade of Pharmaceuticals | The Social Security Funds reimburse the cost of on-patent medicinal products circulating in Greece after 1.1.2012, only if they are reimbursed by Social Security Funds in 2/3 of EU Member States or in at least 12 EU Member States. In these Member States Social Security Funds reimburse the cost of these medicinal products following a Health Technology Assessment and provided that the Transparency Directive 89/105/EC is fully complied with. | Reimbursement | It was not possible to identify the objective of the specific provision. However, in our understanding the objective was to ensure that only already proven quality medicines are included in the positive list. | If on-patent medicinal products do not circulate already in a sufficiently large number of EU countries, or if they are not reimbursed, this provision substantially delays the entry of those medicines in the Greek market. An alternative scheme based on Health Technology Assessment which would require specialised knowledge and resources is already foreseen to be established by December 2017 (Art. 2.5.2 of Law 4336/2015). | No recommendation. | Ministry of Labour, Social Security and Social Solidarity / Health |
| 66 | **Law 3816/2010 "Settlement of business and professional debts to credit institutions, provisions for the processing of economic behaviour data and other provisions"** | Art. 12, par. 3a | Manufacturing and Wholesale Trade of Pharmaceuticals | For the inclusion of a medicinal product in the positive list an entry fee is set equal to 4% of the producer price (ex-factory) paid by the pharmaceutical companies or the market authorisation holders. | Reimbursement | It was not possible to identify the objective of the specific provision. However, in our understanding the fee has been introduced in the context of controlling pharmaceutical expenditure. | The same contribution is foreseen in Art. 1, par. 4 of the Ministerial Decision ΔΥΓ3(α)/οικ.104744/2012 in the amount of EUR 2 000 per pharmaceutical form, strength and dosage, and in art. 12, par. 4 of this law in the amount of EUR 2 000 for the first pharmaceutical strength and EUR 1 000 for each of its other strengths. Following consultations with the Ministry of Health and EOPYY, the MD is the one which seems to be practically applied. This may cause legal uncertainty. | Align provision with MD ΔΥΓ3(α)/οικ.104744/2012. | Ministry of Labour, Social Security and Social Solidarity / Health |
| 67 | **Law 3816/2010 "Settlement of business and professional debts to credit institutions, provisions for the processing of economic behaviour data and other provisions"** | Art. 12, par. 4 | Manufacturing and Wholesale Trade of Pharmaceuticals | For each new medicinal product included in the positive list, a one-off contribution of EUR 2 000 must be paid as entry fee for the first pharmaceutical strength and EUR 1 000 for each of its other strengths. | Reimbursement | It was not possible to identify the objective of the specific provision. However, in our understanding the fee has been introduced in the context of controlling pharmaceutical expenditure. | The same contribution is foreseen in Art. 1, par. 4 of the Ministerial Decision ΔΥΓ3(α)/οικ.104744/2012 in the amount of EUR 2 000 per pharmaceutical form, strength and dosage, and in art. 12, par. 3a of this law in the amount of 4% of the producer price. Following consultations with the Ministry of Health and EOPYY, the MD is the one which seems to be practically applied. This may cause legal uncertainty. | Align provision with MD ΔΥΓ3(α)/οικ.104744/2012. | Ministry of Labour, Social Security and Social Solidarity / Health |
| 68 | **Law 3816/2010 "Settlement of business and professional debts to credit institutions, provisions for the processing of economic behaviour data and other provisions"** | Art. 12, par. 5δ | Manufacturing and Wholesale Trade of Pharmaceuticals | The administrative penalty of exclusion from the positive list is imposed on market authorisation holders who fail to appear before the Negotiations' Committee established in EOPYY. | Reimbursement | It was not possible to identify the objective of the specific provision. | No harm to competition identified. | No recommendation. | Ministry of Labour, Social Security and Social Solidarity / Health |
| 69 | **Law 3580/2007 "Public procurement of bodies supervised by Ministry of Health and other provisions"** | Art. 3, par. ιζ; Art. 10, par. 3 | Manufacturing and Wholesale Trade of Pharmaceuticals | Medicinal products fall within the scope of Price Observatory. Price Observatory is a database aiming at controlling prices of products of Law 3580/2007. | Public procurement | It was not possible to identify the objective of the specific provisions. | Public tenders for the supply of pharmaceutical products are supervised by the Health Procurement Committee (EPY). According to these provisions medicinal products fall within the scope of the Price Observatory. The MD YA 08/31.5.2010 (GG 777/B/2010) foresees that the Price Observatory takes into consideration the lowest price achieved for the products referred therein. Following communications with EPY, we understand that in practice the pricing of medicinal products under tender follows the Price Bulletins rather than the prices announced at the Price Observatory. No harm to competition was identified. | No recommendation. | Ministry of Labour, Social Security and Social Solidarity / Health / Economy, Development and Tourism |

## Sector: Pharmaceuticals

| No | No and title of Regulation | Article | Thematic category | Brief description of the potential obstacle | Keyword | Policy maker's objectives | Harm to competition | Recommendations | Competent Ministry / Authority |
|---|---|---|---|---|---|---|---|---|---|
| 70 | **Law 4052/2012 "Law of competency of Ministries of Health and Social Solidarity and Labour and Social Security for the application of Law "Approval of the Draft Financial Assistance Facility Agreement between the European Financial Stability Facility (EFSF), the Hellenic Republic and the Bank of Greece of the Memorandum of Understanding between the Hellenic Republic, the European Commission and the Bank of Greece and other provisions on the reduction of public debt and the rescue of the Greek economy" and other provisions"** | Art. 21, par. 8 | Manufacturing and Wholesale Trade of Pharmaceuticals | Wholesale trade agreements between producers, representatives, importers and other licence holders are allowed upon the approval of EOF. The Ministers of Finance and Health shall determine the technical requirements of applying the agreement as well as any potential determination of retail price of the pharmaceutical products. | Trading | Following our communication with the Ministry of Health, EOF and the Public Health Procurement Authority, the provision is set out to be in accordance with the state policy for public health protection and effective controlling of the pharmaceutical expenditure. Wholesale trade agreements mainly refer to agreements for products to be circulated by companies not in possession of the market authorisation on behalf of MAHs. We understand that wholesale trade agreements should be approved by EOF in order to ensure the fulfilment of necessary requirements for the proper execution of the delegated task. | The provision establishes a permit system as a requirement for wholesale trade agreements. Possible harm to competition may be caused by possible delays for the admission of the agreement, whereas it may also prevent worthy applicants from entering the market and reduce thus patients' choices. However, it seems to be proportionate to policymaker's objective of ensuring health and quality control of pharmaceutical products. | No recommendation. | Ministry of Health / National Organisation for Medicines (EOF) |
| 71 | **Law 4052/2012 "Law of competency of Ministries of Health and Social Solidarity and Labour and Social Security for the application of Law "Approval of the Draft Financial Assistance Facility Agreement between the European Financial Stability Facility (EFSF), the Hellenic Republic and the Bank of Greece of the Memorandum of Understanding between the Hellenic Republic, the European Commission and the Bank of Greece and other provisions on the reduction of public debt and the rescue of the Greek economy" and other provisions"** | Art. 21, par. 5b | Manufacturing and Wholesale Trade of Pharmaceuticals | Prescription of pharmaceuticals must be made not on the basis of their brand name but on the basis of their active substance. | Prescription | According to our communication with the competent authorities, prescription of pharmaceuticals on the basis of their active substance was introduced after MoU suggestion. It is our understanding that the objective of the suggestion and subsequently the law was to increase generic penetration and reduce pharmaceutical expenditure that is caused from the Greek patients' choices for branded medicines. | No harm to competition identified. | No recommendation. | Ministry of Health |
| 72 | **Ministerial Decision A6 4171/1987 "Parallel imports of medicinal products from EU member states"** | Art. 2 | Wholesale Trade of Pharmaceuticals | Wholesalers may engage in parallel import of pharmaceutical products only upon the granting of a parallel import licence by EOF. The pharmaceutical product should be identical to another pharmaceutical product (the reference product) already licensed and circulating in Greece. | Parallel import | According to our communication with the competent authorities, we understand that the policymaker's objective is to protect public health and to effectively monitor the market. | The requirement that the pharmaceutical product is "identical", as opposed to the "sufficiently similar" requirement of the European Commission Communication COM(2003)839, could potentially limit the number of suppliers, the number of products and competition in the market. | The provision should be amended and be aligned with the wording of the European Commission Communication COM(2003)839, providing for products to be "sufficiently similar" ("επαρκώς ομοειδή") to the ones already circulating in Greece. This would also align it with the OECD (2014) recommendation on parallel import and similarity of products, avoiding thus any legal uncertainty which may arise from the existence of the identical requirement despite the recommendation. | Ministry of Health / National Organisation for Medicines (EOF) |
| 73 | **Ministerial Decision A6 4171/1987 "Parallel imports of medicinal products from EU member states"** | Art. 3, par. 2 | Wholesale Trade of Pharmaceuticals | The parallel import licence is valid for 5 years and only under the condition that the pharmaceutical product is still licensed both in Greece and the member state of origin. | Parallel import | It was not possible to identify the objective of the provision. However, from our communication with EOF, we understand that the objectives of the provision consist in the protection of public health and the traceability of the products. | The provision could potentially limit the number of suppliers as it connects the licence granted in Greece to the licence granted in the member state of origin. This sets out a stricter rule compared to the European Commission Communication COM(2003)839, which does not link the two. | Rephrase the provision so that the parallel import licence may be valid irrespective of the validity of the market authorisation of the product in the member state of origin and Greece. | Ministry of Health / National Organisation for Medicines (EOF) |
| 74 | **Ministerial Decision A6 4171/1987 "Parallel imports of medicinal products from EU member states"** | Art. 6 | Wholesale Trade of Pharmaceuticals | The person licensed to engage in parallel import may package the product in Greece only if he has the necessary licence for packaging granted by EOF according to the Presidential Decree 883/86. | Parallel import | It was not possible to identify the objective of the provision. | The legislation cited cannot be traced. Therefore this provision may create legal uncertainty. | Amend the provision in order to refer to the specific piece of legislation defining the required licence. | Ministry of Health / National Organisation for Medicines (EOF) |

## Sector: Pharmaceuticals

| No | No and title of Regulation | Article | Thematic category | Brief description of the potential obstacle | Keyword | Policy maker's objectives | Harm to competition | Recommendations | Competent Ministry / Authority |
|---|---|---|---|---|---|---|---|---|---|
| 75 | **Presidential Decree 88/2004 "Organisation and operation requirements for pharmaceutical warehouses"** | Art. 2, par. 1 | Wholesale Trade of Pharmaceuticals | Pharmaceutical warehouses may only have up to one additional supporting establishment in a different and independent building. This has to be situated within the same prefecture. | Establishment / Warehouses | It was not possible to identify the policymaker's objective. However, following communication with the competent authorities, it is our understanding that the obligation was adopted in order to safeguard product safety and hence protect patient health, especially with regard to susceptible pharmaceuticals. | On the one hand, the provision sets a geographical barrier to the ability of warehouses to establish more than one economic unit (additional branches) within the same prefecture, creating thus an artificial scarcity in the market and discouraging operators from engaging in competition. It also creates a geographical barrier regarding the ability of warehouses to establish a supporting unit outside the same prefecture, limiting their freedom to operate and function in the way that they deem appropriate and more profitable. This reduces the number of suppliers and limits patients' options. Similar situations arise in other sectors where this type of restriction does not exist. | To be abolished. | Ministry of Health |
| 76 | **Ministerial Decision Υ6α/οικ. 22261/2002 "Advertisement of OTCs"** | Art. 1, par. 4 | Manufacturing and Wholesale Trade of OTCs | The part of the written advertisement of OTCs noting "Το Υπουργείο Υγείας και Πρόνοιας και ο Εθνικός Οργανισμός Φαρμάκων συνιστούν" (The Ministry of Health and the National Organisation for Medicines suggest) must have specific letter font and colour. | Advertisement | Following our communication with the competent authorities it is our understanding that the objective of the provision was to ensure patients' information and safeguard the diligent use of pharmaceuticals. To this aim, letter font and colour are important. | Proportionate to the policymaker's objective. | No recommendation. | Ministry of Health |
| 77 | **Ministerial Decision Γ5/οικ.28408/2016 "Provisions on pharmaceuticals pricing"** | Art. 1, par. 5 | Manufacturing and Wholesale Trade of Pharmaceuticals | When the co-marketing agreement is declared to EOF by all involved Market Authorisation Holders, pharmaceutical products with different brand names circulating under co-marketing agreements get the same lowest price. | Pricing | It was not possible to identify the policymaker's objective. Following communication with competent authorities we understand that the aim of the provision is to avoid possible confusion of patients when they choose co-marketed medicines. | When the maximum prices for the co-marketed products determined by EOF differ, the provision eliminates this difference and removes any residual price competition between co-marketed products. | To be abolished. | Ministry of Health / National Organisation for Medicines (EOF) |
| 78 | **Law 2166/1993 "Incentives for business development, amendments in the direct and indirect taxation and other provisions"** | Art. 26, par. 2 | Wholesale Trade of Pharmaceuticals | A licence to set up a pharmaceutical warehouse may be granted to companies having the form of Société Anonyme or Limited Liability Company. | Licensing | It was not possible to identify the policymaker's objective. | By not clarifying the eligibility to set up pharmaceutical warehouses by legal forms of companies other than Société Anonyme or Limited Liability Companies, the provision may discourage new investors willing to enter the market. | Rephrase the provision in order to include all legal forms of companies. | Ministry of Health |
| 79 | **Law 5607/1932 "Codification and amendment of pharmaceutical legislation"** | Art. 11, par. 5 | Wholesale Trade of Pharmaceuticals | The licensed pharmacist cannot participate in pharmaceutical warehouse companies from the day he retires. | Licensing | It was not possible to identify the policymaker's objective. | The provision is not in use and can create legal uncertainty. | To be explicitly abolished. | Ministry of Health |
| 80 | **Law 5607/1932 "Codification and amendment of pharmaceutical legislation"** | Art. 11, par. 6 | Wholesale Trade of Pharmaceuticals | A licensed pharmacist that has completed at least 35 years in running a pharmaceutical warehouse, is more than 65 years old, and has a child enrolled in a university programme of pharmaceutical studies, is entitled to a licence extension of up to seven years. During these years the pharmaceutical warehouse shall function by another pharmacist in charge. | Licensing | It was not possible to identify the policymaker's objective. | The provision is not in use and can create legal uncertainty. If applied it would provide for a preferential treatment of a sub-group of pharmacists. | To be explicitly abolished. | Ministry of Health |
| 81 | **Law 5607/1932 "Codification and amendment of pharmaceutical legislation"** | Art. 12, par. 2 | Wholesale Trade of Pharmaceuticals | In co-located pharmaceutical warehouses pharmacists in charge of them are equally responsible for any violation of the legislation. | Operation / Warehouses | Following our communication with the Ministry of Health, we understand that the objective of the policymaker was to secure public safety and public health through enhanced responsibility of pharmacists. | The provision is proportionate to the public policy objective. | No recommendation. | Ministry of Health |
| 82 | **Law 5607/1932 "Codification and amendment of pharmaceutical legislation"** | Art. 12, par. 2 | Wholesale Trade of Pharmaceuticals | In co-located warehouses the responsible pharmacists must be present while exercising their duties. | Operation / Warehouses | Following our communication with the Ministry of Health, we understand that the objective of the policymaker was to secure public safety and public health through enhanced responsibility of pharmacists. | The provision is proportionate to the public policy objective. | No recommendation. | Ministry of Health |

## Sector: Pharmaceuticals

| No | No and title of Regulation | Article | Thematic category | Brief description of the potential obstacle | Keyword | Policy maker's objectives | Harm to competition | Recommendations | Competent Ministry / Authority |
|---|---|---|---|---|---|---|---|---|---|
| 83 | **Law 5607/1932 "Codification and amendment of pharmaceutical legislation"** | Art. 17, par. 1 | Wholesale Trade of Pharmaceuticals | Article 17 of Law 5607/1932, as subsequently replaced as a whole by Article 6 of Law 328/1976, provided in paragraph 1 that:<br>A. Pharmaceutical warehouses or pharmacies may only take the legal form of a personal or limited partnership company.<br>B. Only pharmacists can participate in personal or limited partnership pharmaceutical warehouse companies. The licensed pharmacist must participate by at least 50% in the capital, profits and losses of the company.<br>C. The pharmacist may participate in at most one more pharmaceutical warehouse company under the condition that the licence has been issued in the name of the other pharmacist.<br>D. The pharmaceutical warehouse company must be set up only through a notarial deed.<br>E. Existing pharmaceutical warehouse companies at the time the law entered into force (1932) functioning without the participation of pharmacists were allowed to continue functioning under the condition that new members non-pharmacists enter the company and their duration was not renewed.<br><br>In implementing MoU obligations based on previous OECD recommendation (OECD 2014 Competition Assessment Reviews: Greece), Laws 4254/2014 and 4336/2015 respectively replaced and abolished Article 6 of Law 328/1976, which had replaced the original Article 17. | Licensing | It was not possible to identify the policymakers' objective. However, following communication with the Ministry of Health, we understand that the purpose of imposing these restrictions was to safeguard public health through the enhanced responsibilities of pharmacists (taking into consideration that pharmacists, by profession, are presumed to run the warehouse not only with a purely economic objective, but also from a pharmacist's professional viewpoint). Moreover, this takes into consideration that if non-pharmacists own the warehouses, the independence of employed pharmacists might be influenced by managerial decisions in a direction that it does not promote public health. | A. The legal uncertainty caused by subsequent replacements of pre-existing provisions results in legal and compliance costs for businesses.<br><br>B. If applied, the provision would provide for numerous restrictions in the ownership and managerial rules of pharmaceutical warehouses. | To be explicitly abolished. | Ministry of Health |
| 84 | **Law 5607/1932 "Codification and amendment of pharmaceutical legislation"** | Art. 17, par. 2 | Wholesale Trade of Pharmaceuticals | Article 17 of Law 5607/1932, as subsequently replaced as a whole by Article 6 of Law 328/1976, provided in paragraph 2 that all contracts signed in the name of the pharmaceutical warehouse company should be signed by the licence holder pharmacist, who is mandatorily director of the company. Substitution of the director by another person by virtue of a general or special Power of Attorney is prohibited.<br>Article 6 of Law 328/1976, which had replaced the original Article 17, was abolished by Law 4336/2015. | Operation / Warehouses | It was not possible to identify the policymakers' objective. However, following communication with the Ministry of Health, we understand that the purpose of imposing these restrictions was to safeguard public health through the enhanced responsibilities of pharmacists (taking into consideration that pharmacists, by profession, are presumed to run the warehouse not only with a purely economic objective, but also from a pharmacist's professional viewpoint). Moreover, this takes into consideration that if non-pharmacists own the warehouses, the independence of employed pharmacists might be influenced by managerial decisions in a direction that it does not promote public health. | A. The legal uncertainty caused by subsequent replacements of pre-existing provisions results in legal and compliance costs for businesses.<br><br>B. If applied, the provision would provide for numerous restrictions in the ownership and managerial rules of pharmaceutical warehouses. | To be explicitly abolished. | Ministry of Health |
| 85 | **Law 5607/1932 "Codification and amendment of pharmaceutical legislation"** | Art. 17, par. 7 | Wholesale Trade of Pharmaceuticals | Article 17 of Law 5607/1932, as subsequently replaced as a whole by Article 6 of Law 328/1976, provided in paragraph 7 that restrictions concerning the pharmaceutical warehouse companies (excluding the ones on the personal responsibility of the licence holder pharmacist and the company form) do not apply to co-operations between spouses or blood relatives or relatives by marriage.<br>Article 6 of Law 328/1976, which had replaced the original Article 17, was abolished by Law 4336/2015. | Operation / Warehouses | It was not possible to identify the policymaker's objective. | A. The legal uncertainty caused by subsequent replacements of pre-existing provisions results to legal and compliance costs for businesses.<br><br>B. If applied, the provision would exempt specific operators from the requirements set out for wholesalers' legal entities. It would set higher costs for some suppliers compared to others. | To be explicitly abolished. | Ministry of Health |
| 86 | **Law 1965/1991 "Amending and completing the provisions on the National Organisation for Medicines and other provisions"** | Art. 9, par. 8 | Manufacturing and Wholesale Trade of Pharmaceuticals | For pharmaceutical industries or laboratories to be permitted to co-locate in the same industrial area they should be already legally functioning for a minimum of five years. This co-location is subject to prior opinion of EOF and under the condition that each of them shall function independently under its own responsible producers and quality controls. | Licensing | Following communication with the competent authorities, it is our understanding that the provision was based on the assumption that co-location can only be safely done between experienced operators. Moreover, the prior opinion of EOF ensures the quality and technical requirements of the new establishment. | Taking into consideration that the function of industries or laboratories is licensed based on specific requirements, this additional control on behalf of the competent authority is not justified on public safety grounds and it is not proportionate to the policymaker's objective. Moreover, the five year threshold provides for a preferential treatment towards incumbents and restricts mergers of new operators in the market. | Recommendation to abolish the 5-year threshold and the requirement for the prior opinion of EOF. | Ministry of Health / National Organisation for Medicines (EOF) |
| 87 | **Law 1965/1991 "Amending and completing the provisions on the National Organisation for Medicines and other provisions"** | Art. 9, par. 9 | Manufacturing and Wholesale Trade of Pharmaceuticals | Importers, producers and representatives, are allowed to import, store, trade and distribute pharmaceutical and diagnostic products produced or imported by them or on behalf of third parties only by using their own fleet and according to the provisions set in the law. | Transportation | This provision takes into account the safety of pharmaceuticals transportation and the need for traceability of a cargo carrying medicines. | The provision restricts the freedom of suppliers in choosing the transport method for their products. It is not justified on public safety grounds and is not proportionate to the policymaker's objective. | Recommendation to abolish the requirement for own use trucks. It could be specified that trucks must comply with specific safety requirements. | Ministry of Health |

## Sector: Pharmaceuticals

| No | No and title of Regulation | Article | Thematic category | Brief description of the potential obstacle | Keyword | Policy maker's objectives | Harm to competition | Recommendations | Competent Ministry / Authority |
|---|---|---|---|---|---|---|---|---|---|
| 88 | **Ministerial Decision ΔΥΓ3(α)/οικ.104744/2012 "Process of implementing a system of reference prices for the drafting, amending and competing the prescription medicines catalogue"** | Art. 2, par. 5 | Manufacturing and Wholesale Trade of Pharmaceuticals | A pharmaceutical product may be exceptionally listed in the ATC5 category (rather than the initial classification in the ATC4 category). In this case, it can be reimbursed for the entire amount of its retail price. | Reimbursement | There is no official recital. Following communication with the Ministry of Health, we understand that the criteria for including products in ATC5 are strict and take into consideration public health issues (e.g. uniqueness of the product, non-interchangeability of the products, etc.). | The provision may lead to favourable treatment towards specific market authorisation holders, that have the resources to develop pharmaceuticals similar to others in terms of therapeutical value, yet quite different in terms of form and appearance. The restriction is considered to be appropriate to the policymakers' objective. | No recommendation. | Ministry of Health |

## Sector: Wholesale trade

| No | No and title of Regulation | Article | Thematic category | Brief description of the potential obstacle | Keyword | Policy maker's objectives | Harm to competition | Recommendations | Competent Ministry / Authority |
|---|---|---|---|---|---|---|---|---|---|
| 1 | **Presidential Decree 219/1991 "On Commercial Representatives in compliance with Directive 86/653/EEC"** | art. 1 par. 3b | Commercial Representation | A commercial representative/ agent may appoint sub - representatives only within the seat of his establishment or in other cities, only within the geographical sector of his activity. | Representation | Protect producers from fraud and combat illicit trade phenomena. | Though the provision sets out a restriction that may in most cases result from the business practise of representation agreements, however, it may overly restrict the ability of parties to decide differently on an ad hoc basis according to their needs, especially with regard to commercial representation within small areas where the appointment of a sub- representative outside those areas may be deemed necessary. Restricts the flow of goods/ services within a specific geographical area reduces the number of suppliers and denying product choice to customers. | Abolish. | Ministry of Economy, Development and Tourism |
| 2 | **Joint Ministerial Decision 3508/2011 "Terms and conditions of the function of commercial exhibitions and exhibition centers in Greece"** | | Commercial Exhibitions | Obsolete | Licence requirement exemption | There is no official recital | Obsolete | Clarify explicitly which provisions are abolished and which ones are still in force. | Ministry of Economy, Development and Tourism / Interior and Administrative Reconstruction / Environment and Energy |
| 3 | **Ministerial Decision of MD K1-1480/2014 terms and conditions for the suitability of exhibitions** | art. 2 par. 2b | Commercial Exhibitions | Exhibition spaces functioning since April 1997 have to comply with certain minimum requirements concerning height (minimum 4 metres in at least 75% of their total surface and minimum 3 metres for the rest of the surface) and floor durability (500 kg / $m^2$) | Grandfathering | There is no official recital. However, according to our communication with the competent Ministry, the provision may be amended | The provision protects incumbent suppliers from competition as it sets different criteria for them compared to new ones, protecting them from competition. | Abolish | Ministry of Economy, Development and Tourism / Interior and Administrative Reconstruction / Environment and Energy |
| 4 | **Ministerial Decision of MD K1-1480/2014 terms and conditions for the suitability of exhibitions** | art. 3 par. 1a | Commercial Exhibitions | Commercial exhibitions and exhibition centres of total surface not exceeding 1 000 $m^2$ are exempt from the penalty system for functioning without a suitability licence | Licence requirement exemption | The official recital of the policy objective could not be found. However, according to our understanding from communication with the competent authorities, the suitability licensing system has been destined to protect the urban environment and public safety, therefore, small establishments were exempt due to their small impact on both urban environment and public health and safety | The provision unjustifiably discriminates between suppliers, granting an exception for some of them from the authorisation system and raising thus the costs of those not falling within the exeption. This may lead to lower intensity of competitive pressure in the market as it discourages potential entrants and reduces the number of participants over time. | Abolish | Ministry of Economy, Development and Tourism / Interior and Administrative Reconstruction / Environment and Energy |
| 5 | **Law 3054/2002 "Organisation of fuel market"** | art. 5 par. 2 | Wholesale trade of fuel | Fuel retail licence holders, when buying fuel directly from a refinery either individually or as members of a supply co-operative or association, must file a declaration of art. 8 of law 1599/1986 stating that they are not under an exclusive supply agreement with a wholesaler, nor bearing the trademark of such a wholesaler. | Exclusive agreements | There is no official recital. However, according to our communication with the competent Ministries, we were informed that the provision was adopted to monitor the retailers' obligations towards wholesalers and safeguard the application of the exclusive agreement provisions on the side of the retailer. | Though the provision tries to monitor wholesalers and retailers relations holding accountable the retailers that breach their obligations towards wholesalers, it is deemed proportionate to the policy maker's objective. | No recommendation. | Ministry of Finance / Economy, Development and Tourism/ Environment and Energy |
| 6 | **Law 3054/2002 "Organisation of fuel market"** | art. 5A par. 1, art. 6 par. 1 | Wholesale trade of fuel | A licence for the distribution of fuel/ biofuel is granted to SAs or similar legal forms seated in a member state of the EU, or to Collective Agricultural Associations of law 4015/2011. | Licensing | There is no official recital. However, it is our understanding that the possible policy maker's objective would be to limit the possibility for an enterprise lacking the necessary financial standing to enter the fuel market. | Given that the law imposes various security measures on the viability and credibility of the licence holder, limiting the legal form of the entity is deemed unnecessary. | The provision should be made more flexible to include LLCs and Private Companies (I.K.E). | Ministry of Finance / Economy, Development and Tourism/ Environment and Energy |
| 7 | **Law 3054/2002 "Organisation of fuel market"** | art. 5A par. 3 | Wholesale trade of fuel | Biofuel distribution licence holders are obliged to have appropriate storage spaces of at least 100 $m^3$ for storing biofuel and other renewable fuel. | Storage capacity | There is no official recital. However, it is our understanding that the possible policy maker's objective is to ensure the sufficient supply of the specific product in the market. | The provision is proportionate to the policy maker's objective and it is consistent with the recommendation on capacity of biodiesel storage spaces. | No recommendation. | Ministry of Finance / Economy, Development and Tourism/ Environment and Energy |
| 8 | **Law 3054/2002 "Organisation of fuel market"** | art. 5A par. 4 | Wholesale trade of fuel | The cost for placing the biofuel wholesaler's trademark on the vehicle is paid by the owner of the truck, or, in the event that the truck has been leased with a lease agreement or a bill of sale with an ownership reservation clause, the cost is paid by the tenant or buyer of the vehicle accordingly. | Advertising | It was not possible to identify the policy maker's objective, however we assume that the reasoning is to ensure that the consumer is adequately informed. Following communication with the competent Ministry we were informed that the provision may be subject to amendments. | The provision intervenes into private matters between contracting parties, limiting their freedom to negotiate on the contractual terms. | Abolish. | Ministry of Finance / Economy, Development and Tourism / Environment and Energy |
| 9 | **Law 3054/2002 "Organisation of fuel market"** | art. 6 par. 5a (aa) | Wholesale trade of fuel | The minimum capital of type A fuel companies depending on the sales volume of the previous calendar year is as follows:<br>Up to 300 000 M.T. - EUR 500 000 capital<br>From 300 000 M.T. to 600 000 M.T. - EUR1m capital<br>Greater than 600 000 M.T. - EUR 1.5m capital. | Minimum capital requirement | There is no official recital. However, it is our understanding that the possible policy maker's objective would be to limit the possibility for an enterprise lacking the necessary financial capacity to enter the fuel market. Moreover security of supply is also safeguarded. | The provision sets a minimum capital requirement obligation as an alternative to filing a letter of guarantee or having an insurance contract. The provision sets a high cost for new entrants and also a high cost for existing wholesalers. Some of the current wholesalers may not be able to satisfy the requirement every year given the economic situation of Greece and may be driven off market. | Lower the minimum capital requirement in order to minimize entry costs for new businesses and to minimize operating costs to existing ones. | Ministry of Finance /Economy, Development and Tourism / Environment and Energy |
| 10 | **Law 3054/2002 "Organisation of fuel market"** | art. 6 par. 5a (aa) | Wholesale trade of fuel | The minimum capital of Type B1 fuel companies is EUR 500 000. | Minimum capital requirement | There is no official recital. However, it is our understanding that the possible policy maker's objective would be to limit the possibility for an enterprise lacking the necessary financial capacity to enter the fuel market. Moreover security of supply is also safeguarded. | The provision sets a minimum capital requirement obligation as an alternative to filing a letter of guarantee or having an insurance contract. It may set a high cost for new entrants however it is deemed proportionate to the policy maker's objective due to the sensitive nature of the product for tax avoiding reasons. | No recommendation. | Ministry of Finance / Economy, Development and Tourism/ Environment and Energy |

## Sector: Wholesale trade

| No | No and title of Regulation | Article | Thematic category | Brief description of the potential obstacle | Keyword | Policy maker's objectives | Harm to competition | Recommendations | Competent Ministry / Authority |
|---|---|---|---|---|---|---|---|---|---|
| 11 | **Law 3054/2002 "Organisation of fuel market"** | art. 6 par. 5a (aa) | Wholesale trade of fuel | The minimum capital of Type B2 fuel companies is EUR 500 000. | Minimum capital requirement | There is no official recital. However, it is our understanding that the possible policy maker's objective would be to limit the possibility for an enterprise lacking the necessary financial capacity to enter the fuel market. Moreover security of supply is also safeguarded. | The provision sets a minimum capital requirement obligation as an alternative to filing a letter of guarantee or having an insurance contract. It may set a high cost for new entrants however it is deemed proportionate to the policy maker's objective due to the sensitive nature of the product for tax avoiding reasons | No recommendation. | Ministry of Finance / Economy, Development and Tourism/ Environment and Energy |
| 12 | **Law 3054/2002 "Organisation of fuel market"** | art. 6 par. 5a (aa) | Wholesale trade of fuel | The minimum capital of Type C companies is EUR 500 000. | Minimum capital requirement | There is no official recital. However, it is our understanding that the possible policy maker's objective would be to limit the possibility for an enterprise lacking the necessary financial capacity to enter the fuel market. Moreover security of supply and consumer safety is also safeguarded. | The provision sets a minimum capital requirement obligation as an alternative to filing a letter of guarantee or having an insurance contract. It may set a high cost for new entrants however it is deemed proportionate to the policy maker's objective due to the sensitive nature of the product | No recommendation. | Ministry of Finance / Economy, Development and Tourism/ Environment and Energy |
| 13 | **Law 3054/2002 "Organisation of fuel market"** | art. 6 par. 5a (bb) | Wholesale trade of fuel | All companies applying for any type of fuel licence must have an insurance contract or file a letter of guarantee to compensate for any penalties that may be imposed by the competent authorities, due to (i) not complying with the licence terms and requirements, (ii) trading irregular fuel, (iii) trading fuel after expiration of the licence or after the licence has been revoked, (iv) not keeping the necessary safety reserves. The amount of the insurance or letter of guarantee equals the amount of the minimum capital requirement depending on the type of the licence. | Insurance | It was not possible to identify the policy maker's objective, however, following communication with the competent authorities, it is our understanding that the reasoning is to protect the state from any distortions caused by the inability of the operators to pay the penalties imposed to them. | Connecting the insurance contract to a future and unpredictable event such as the imposition of a penalty to the licence holder has led to the requirement not to be in practical use | The provision should be amended to abolish the requirement for an insurance contract for all types of companies. Moreover, for type D licence holders the requirement for a letter of guarantee or insurance contract should be disconnected from the (abolished provision on) minimum capital requirement. | Ministry of Finance / Economy, Development and Tourism/ Environment and Energy |
| 14 | **Law 3054/2002 "Organisation of fuel market"** | art. 6 par. 5b | Wholesale trade of fuel | storage spaces used by the licence holders must be privately owned by them, leased by them, or their use must be conferred to them exclusively. The lease or concession agreement must be of at least the same duration as the licence. | Storage | It was not possible to identify the policy maker's objective, however our assumption is that the law maker focused on protecting the licence holder by safeguarding the continuation of the lease agreement during the period for which the licence is in force. | The requirement for the lease or concession agreement to be of at least the same duration as the licence causes an unjustifiable burden to both parties and limits their ability to freely decide on the duration of the lease agreement. In any case, any changes in storage locations should be notified to the authorities, ensuring thus the need for market surveillance and monitoring. | The provision should be amended so as to disconnect the lease agreement duration from the duration of the licence. Moreover, it should be stipulated that all storage spaces are registered with the General Secretariat of Energy. | Ministry of Finance / Economy, Development and Tourism/ Environment and Energy |
| 15 | **Law 3054/2002 "Organisation of fuel market"** | art.6 par.5b | Wholesale trade of fuel | For type A licence holders, the minimum capacity of the storage spaces used for petroleum products depends on their sales volume:<br>Up to 300 000MT - 4 000m$^3$<br>From 300 000MT to 600 000MT- 7 000m$^3$<br>Over 600 000MT - 13 000m$^3$ | Storage | Possible policy maker's objective would be to limit the possibility for an enterprise lacking the necessary storage spaces for the sufficient supply of the market to become a licence holder. | Restrictive provision setting high costs for market participants, potentially restricting entry. Note that the law specifies for a minimum quantity of fuel to be always available thereby ensuring commercial viability. | Amend the provision to include a smaller introductory category in order to stipulate possible entrance from new investors. | Ministry of Finance / Economy, Development and Tourism/ Environment and Energy |
| 16 | **Law 3054/2002 "Organisation of fuel market"** | art.6 par.5b | Wholesale trade of fuel | For type B1 licence holders, the minimum capacity of storage spaces used must be over 5 000m$^3$. | Storage | Possible policy maker's objective would be to limit the possibility for an enterprise lacking the necessary storage spaces for the sufficient supply of the market to become a licence holder. | The provision sets a minimum storage capacity obligation. It may set a high cost for new entrants however it is deemed proportionate to the policy maker's objective due to the sensitive nature of the product for tax avoiding reasons. | No recommendation. | Ministry of Finance / Economy, Development and Tourism/ Environment and Energy |
| 17 | **Law 3054/2002 "Organisation of fuel market"** | art.6 par.5b | Wholesale trade of fuel | For type B2 licence holders, the minimum capacity of the storage spaces used must be over 5 000m$^3$. | Storage | Possible policy maker's objective would be to limit the possibility for an enterprise lacking the necessary storage spaces for the sufficient supply of the market to become a licence holder. | The provision sets a minimum storage capacity obligation. It may set a high cost for new entrants however it is deemed proportionate to the policy maker's objective due to the sensitive nature of the product for tax avoiding reasons. | No recommendation. | Ministry of Finance / Economy, Development and Tourism/ Environment and Energy |
| 18 | **Law 3054/2002 "Organisation of fuel market"** | art.6 par.5b | Wholesale trade of fuel | For type C licence holders, the minimum capacity of the storage spaces used must be over 500m$^3$. | Storage | Possible policy maker's objective would be to limit the possibility for an enterprise lacking the necessary storage spaces for the sufficient supply of the market to become a licence holder. | The provision sets a minimum storage capacity obligation. It may set a high cost for new entrants however it is deemed proportionate to the policy maker's objective due to the sensitive nature of the product for tax avoiding reasons. | No recommendation. | Ministry of Finance / Economy, Development and Tourism/ Environment and Energy |
| 19 | **Law 3054/2002 "Organisation of fuel market"** | art. 6 par. 5c | Wholesale trade of fuel | The cost of placing the wholesaler's trademark is paid by the owner of the vehicle or, in the case of a lease agreement or bill of sale with an ownership reservation clause, the cost is paid by the tenant or the buyer of the vehicle accordingly. | Exclusive agreements | There is no official recital. | Restrictive provision imposing a financial burden on professional transporters compared to wholesalers who engage in fuel transportation activities using privately owned vehicles. The parties should be left to decide freely on such a term. | Abolish the obligation the cost to be paid by the tenant or the buyer. | Ministry of Finance / Economy, Development and Tourism/ Environment and Energy |
| 20 | **Law 3054/2002 "Organisation of fuel market"** | art. 6 par. 5d | Wholesale trade of fuel | Liquid gas licence holders must have at least 30 000 refillable gas cylinders. | Equipment | There is no official recital. However, it is our understanding that the possible policy maker's objective would be to limit the possibility for an enterprise lacking the necessary storage capacity for the sufficient supply of the market to become a licence holder. | Restrictive provision setting high costs for market participants, potentially restricting entry. | Amend the provision to lower the minimum number of cylinders thus entry costs for new applicants willing to enter the market. | Ministry of Finance / Economy, Development and Tourism/ Environment and Energy |
| 21 | **Law 3054/2002 "Organisation of fuel market"** | art. 6 par. 6c | Wholesale trade of fuel | storage spaces of fuel licence holders must be used for at least 30% of the annual sales in the administrative district where the licence holder's establishments are placed. | Geographical restriction | According to the official recital of the law, the policy maker's objective was to make use of all storage spaces throughout Greece at their maximum capacity and avoid having storage spaces empty just for complying with licence requirements. | Restrictive provision limiting remote businesses flexibility to compete in other geographic areas where they do not have storage capacity. | Abolish the 30% threshold. | Ministry of Finance / Economy, Development and Tourism/ Environment and Energy |

## Sector: Wholesale trade

| No | No and title of Regulation | Article | Thematic category | Brief description of the potential obstacle | Keyword | Policy maker's objectives | Harm to competition | Recommendations | Competent Ministry / Authority |
|---|---|---|---|---|---|---|---|---|---|
| 22 | **Law 3054/2002 "Organisation of fuel market"** | art. 7 par. 2 | Wholesale trade of fuel | Gas station owners under exclusive agreements with wholesalers must display the wholesaler's trademark on a clearly evident spot on the container vehicles they use. | Exclusive agreements | There is no official recital. However, following communication with the competent Ministry, we understand that the provision is adopted to monitor and safeguard consumer information on the origin of the fuel. | Restrictive provision that intervenes in private matters. The parties should be left to decide freely on such a term. | Abolish the obligation for the vehicles bearing the trademark of the wholesales. | Ministry of Finance / Economy, Development and Tourism/ Environment and Energy |
| 23 | **Law 3054/2002 "Organisation of fuel market"** | art. 7 par. 2 | Wholesale trade of fuel | The cost for the placement of the wholesaler's trademark is paid by the owner of the vehicle, while in the case of a lease agreement or a bill of purchase with ownership reservation clause, the cost is paid by the tenant or the buyer of the vehicle, accordingly. | Exclusive agreements | There is no official recital. | Restrictive provision imposing a financial burden on professional transporters compared to wholesalers who engage in fuel transportation activities using privately owned vehicles. The parties should be left to decide freely on such a term. | Abolish. | Ministry of Finance / Economy, Development and Tourism/ Environment and Energy |
| 24 | **Law 3054/2002 "Organisation of fuel market"** | art. 7 par. 4 | Wholesale trade of fuel | The gas station owner under an exclusive agreement with a wholesaler, is obliged to place on an evident spot of his gas station, the wholesaler's trademark. | Exclusive agreements | There is no official recital. However, following communication with the competent Ministry, we understand that the provision is adopted to monitor the retailers' obligation to place the wholesaler's trademark on the gas station. Additionally, it protects consumer information regarding the origin of the fuel. | The provision that intervenes in private matters, however it seems to be proportionate to the policy maker's objective. | No recommendation. | Ministry of Finance / Economy, Development and Tourism/ Environment and Energy |
| 25 | **Law 3054/2002 "Organisation of fuel market"** | art. 9 par. 2 | Wholesale trade of fuel | Liquid gas bottling licence holders may engage in bottling liquid gas only for liquid gas trading licence holders . | Supply restriction | There is no official recital. However, following communication with the competent Ministry, we understand that the provision facilitates the safe and effective distribution of the product to final consumers or retailers. Traceability reasons were also reported. | The provision seems restrictive but proportionate for security and traceability reasons. | No recommendation. | Ministry of Finance / Economy, Development and Tourism/ Environment and Energy |
| 26 | **Law 3054/2002 "Organisation of fuel market"** | art. 9 par. 2 | Wholesale trade of fuel | Liquid gas bottling licence holders are allowed to refill only the refillable bottles that belong to those liquid gas licence holders with whom they have signed an agreement. | Supply restriction | There is no official recital. However, following communication with the competent Ministry, we understand that the provision facilitates the safe and effective distribution of the product to final consumers or retailers. Traceability reasons were also reported. | The provision seems restrictive but proportionate for security and traceability reasons. | No recommendation. | Ministry of Finance / Economy, Development and Tourism/ Environment and Energy |
| 27 | **Law 3054/2002 "Organisation of fuel market"** | art. 9 par. 2 | Wholesale trade of fuel | Liquid gas bottling licence holders are not allowed to bottle or distribute non bottled or bottled liquid gas on their account or for third parties, who are not liquid gas trade licence holders. | Supply restriction | There is no official recital. However, following communication with the competent Ministry, we understand that the provision facilitates the safe and effective distribution of the product to final consumers or retailers. Traceability reasons were also reported. | The provision seems restrictive but proportionate for security and traceability reasons. | No recommendation. | Ministry of Finance / Economy, Development and Tourism/ Environment and Energy |
| 28 | **Law 3054/2002 "Organisation of fuel market"** | art. 15 par. 8a (bb) | Wholesale trade of fuel | The GPS installation cost is paid by the owner of the vehicle, while in case of a lease agreement or bill of purchase with an ownership retention clause, the cost is paid by the tenant or the buyer of the vehicle, accordingly. | Determination of agreement terms | There is no official recital. | Restrictive provision imposing a financial burden on the transporter and raising his costs compared to wholesalers who engage in fuel transportation activities using privately owned vehicles. The parties should be left to decide freely on such a term. | Abolish the obligation the cost to be paid by the tenant or the buyer of the vehicle. | Ministry of Finance / Economy, Development and Tourism/ Environment and Energy |
| 29 | **Law 3054/2002 "Organisation of fuel market"** | art. 15 par. 8c | Wholesale trade of fuel | Quality and quantity electronic assurance systems may be used in the private or public use containers or vessels (such as tankers and sloops), privately owned or leased, of the wholesalers or retailers and biofuel traders. | Smuggling | There is no official recital. However, it is our understanding that the policy maker's objective was to combat smuggling and illicit trade of fuel. | The provision as it stands, does not oblige or provide incentives for wholesalers or retailers to install an electronic assurance system. Illicit trade has a negative effect on the market and on competition. | The authorities should review the voluntary nature of the obligation when the following conditions are satisfied: (i) the GPS system on vessels and tanker trucks is operational; and (ii) the inflow-outflow system currently mandatory on vessels is operational. | Ministry of Finance / Economy, Development and Tourism/ Environment and Energy |
| 30 | **Law 3054/2002 "Organisation of fuel market"** | art. 15 par. 8c | Wholesale trade of fuel | The installation cost for the quality and quantity assurance system is paid by the owner of the vehicle, while in case of a lease agreement or bill of purchase with an ownership retention clause, the cost is paid by the tenant or the buyer of the vehicle, accordingly. | Determination of agreement terms | There is no official recital. However, it is our understanding that the policy maker's objective was to combat smuggling and illicit trade of fuel. | Restrictive provision imposing a financial burden on the transporter and raising his costs compared to wholesalers who engage in fuel transportation activities using privately owned vehicles. The parties should be left to decide freely on such a term. | Abolish. | Ministry of Finance / Economy, Development and Tourism/ Environment and Energy |
| 31 | **Law 3054/2002 "Organisation of fuel market"** | art. 15A par. 5b | Wholesale trade of fuel | The capacity of the storage spaces for biodiesel may not be less than 1/100 of the requested quantity nor less than 100 $m^3$ per production unit of the owner or contractual applicant for the allocation. | Storage | There is no official recital. However, following communication with the competent Ministry we understand that the possible policy maker's objective would be to limit the possibility of an enterprise lacking the necessary storage spaces to enter the market. | Restrictive provision setting high costs for market participants, potentially restricting entry | Abolish the requirement for capacity of storage spaces not to be less than 1/100 of the requested quantity. | Ministry of Finance / Economy, Development and Tourism/ Environment and Energy |

## Sector: Wholesale trade

| No | No and title of Regulation | Article | Thematic category | Brief description of the potential obstacle | Keyword | Policy maker's objectives | Harm to competition | Recommendations | Competent Ministry / Authority |
|---|---|---|---|---|---|---|---|---|---|
| 32 | **Law 3054/2002 "Organisation of fuel market"** | art 23 par. 4 | Wholesale trade of fuel | Type A' licences issued according to par. 7 art. 15 law 1571/1985 (192A) as this was added with art. 35 law 2008/1992 (16A) as well as type ST' licences issued according to art. 5 of law 1769/1988 (66A) and art. 24 of law 2008/1992 (154A) may be renewed according to the provisions that were in force before the present law is introduced. The present provision is implemented retrospectively since law 3054/2002. | Licence requirement exemption | According to our communication with the competent Ministry it is our understanding that this provision was introduced to provide incentives to wholesalers trading under licence type ST' to continue trading fuel in the islands, granting them the right to trade in the entire Greek territory under less strict criteria compared to the rest of type A' licence holders. | Given the fact that Type ST' capital and storage requirements are substantially lower, the provision introduces a preferential treatment towards type ST' licence holders, as opposed to all the other type A' licence holders trading in the Greek territory, causing harm to competition since it leads to an artificial elimination of equal competition terms among players in the same relevant market. | Amend the provision so that the first sentence regarding type A' licences that were granted according to par. 7 art. 15 of law 1571/1985 may be renewed only once according to the provisions that were in force before law 3054/2002 was introduced. After the expiration of the renewed licences, the renewal shall have to be based on the type A' licence criteria set in the law for the businesses operating in Greek mainland. If the state grants new type ST' licences to promote efficient supply of the islands and remote areas the minimum requirements should be aligned with the minimum requirements to obtain type A' licences. | Ministry of Finance / Economy, Development and Tourism/ Environment and Energy |
| 33 | **Law 4177/2013 "Rules on the trading of products and rendering of services"** | art. 29 par. 1 | Wholesale trade of fuel | By exemption, the duration of the exclusive supply agreement between wholesaler and gas station holder may be longer than 5 years, but it may never exceed the duration of the lease agreement:<br>i) if the gas station holder leases the property from the wholesaler<br>ii) if the wholesaler grants the use of the gas station to the gas station holder<br>iii) if the wholesaler leases the property from a third party, not connected in any way with the gas station holder. | Exclusive agreements | There is no official recital. However, following communication with the competent Ministry, we understand that the provision is adopted to monitor retailers' obligations towards wholesalers and it is further justified on the basis of pricing transparency issues and lower prices to the consumer. | The provision allows for exceptions in the duration of the exclusive supply agreements, by connecting contractual duration with property ownership. However, the exceptions i and ii are described in such a way that do not guarantee that the wholesaler is the owner of the property. This may lead to exclusive contracts more than five years that are not in the spirit of the law. Thus retailers are restricted from switching suppliers. | The provision should be amended for cases (i) and (ii) to explicitly allow for such an extension only when the wholesaler has full ownership of the property, not bare ownership or usufruct. | Ministry of Economy, Development and Tourism |
| 34 | **Ministerial Decision A2-718/2014 "Codification of Rules on the distribution and trading of products and rendering of services"** | art. 115 par. 1.1 | Wholesale trade of fuel | Retailers of a) liquid fuel and/or b) liquid gas exclusively for the movement of vehicles through pumps (AUTOGAS) and/ or c) compressed gas (CNG), since they are under an exclusive agreement with a wholesaler, are obliged to place on an apparent spot of their gas station the wholesaler's trademark, or, their trademark or the trademark of the co-operation or the consortium in which they participate. | Exclusive agreements | There is no official recital. However, following communication with the competent Ministry, we understand that the provision is adopted to monitor the retailers' obligation to place the wholesaler's trademark on the gas station. Additionally, it protects consumer information regarding the origin of the fuel. | The provision is justified. | No recommendation. | Ministry of Economy, Development and Tourism |
| 35 | **Ministerial Decision A2-718/2014 "Codification of Rules on the distribution and trading of products and rendering of services"** | art. 115 par. 1.2 | Wholesale trade of fuel | Retailers that are not under an exclusive agreement with wholesalers either concerning liquid fuel or AUTOGAS, or compressed gas (CNG), are prohibited from placing in any spot of their gas station trademarks of wholesalers. They are also prohibited from placing trademarks of wholesalers on the pumps. | Exclusive agreements | There is no official recital. However, following communication with the competent Ministry, we understand that the provision is adopted to ensure consumer information regarding the origin of autogas or CNG in those cases where there is no exclusive supplier. | The provision is justified. | No recommendation. | Ministry of Economy, Development and Tourism |
| 36 | **Ministerial Decision A2-718/2014 "Codification of Rules on the distribution and trading of products and rendering of services"** | art. 115 par. 1.3 | Wholesale trade of fuel | If retailers that are not under liquid fuel exclusive agreements with wholesalers, place on their gas stations signs that advertise products, other than wholesalers' fuel products (such as lubricants), these signs must be smaller than the trademark sign, and must be placed at a distance of less than three meters from that sign. Also, the type of the product appear on these signs in an apparent way. | Exclusive agreements | There is no official recital, however, following communication with the competent Ministry, our understanding is that the policy maker's objective was to avoid consumer confusion as to the origin of the fuel and the origin of the lubricants. | The provision is justified. | No recommendation. | Ministry of Economy, Development and Tourism |

## Sector: Wholesale trade

| No | No and title of Regulation | Article | Thematic category | Brief description of the potential obstacle | Keyword | Policy maker's objectives | Harm to competition | Recommendations | Competent Ministry / Authority |
|---|---|---|---|---|---|---|---|---|---|
| 37 | **Ministerial Decision Α2-718/2014 "Codification of Rules on the distribution and trading of products and rendering of services"** | art. 15 par. 1.4.1 | Wholesale trade of fuel | If the retailer is under an exclusive agreement with a wholesaler concerning liquid fuel, whereas for the AUTOGAS he does not have an exclusive wholesaler, he must place on an apparent spot of the gas station the trademark of the wholesaler with whom he has an exclusive agreement for liquid fuel, whereas for the autogas he must place either his trademark or the trademark of the co-operation or consortium in which he participates, in the spot of the retail sale sign. | Exclusive agreements | There is no official recital, however, following communication with the competent Ministry, our understanding is that the policy maker's objective was to avoid consumer confusion as to the origin of the liquid fuel and the origin of the autogas. | The provision is justified. | No recommendation. | Ministry of Economy, Development and Tourism |
| 38 | **Ministerial Decision Α2-718/2014 "Codification of Rules on the distribution and trading of products and rendering of services"** | art. 115 par. 1.4.2 | Wholesale trade of fuel | If the retailer does not have an exclusive agreement for liquid fuel with a wholesaler while he receives the autogas exclusively by a specific wholesaler, he must place his trademark for the liquid fuel or the trademark of the co-operation or consortium in which he participates, while for the liquid gas, he must place the wholesaler's trademark in the spot of the retail sale sign. | Exclusive agreements | There is no official recital, however, following communication with the competent Ministry, our understanding is that the policy maker's objective was to avoid consumer confusion as to the origin of the liquid fuel and the origin of the autogas. | The provision is justified. | No recommendation. | Ministry of Economy, Development and Tourism |
| 39 | **Ministerial Decision Α2-718/2014 "Codification of Rules on the distribution and trading of products and rendering of services"** | art. 115 par. 1.4.3 | Wholesale trade of fuel | If the retailer is under an exclusive agreement with a wholesaler for liquid fuel and an exclusive agreement for AUTOGAS with another wholesaler, he must place the trademark of the wholesaler from whom he buys the liquid fuel, while for autogas, he must place the wholesaler's trademark, in the spot of the retail sale sign. | Exclusive agreements | There is no official recital, however, following communication with the competent Ministry, our understanding is that the policy maker's objective was to avoid consumer confusion as to the origin of the liquid fuel and the origin of the autogas. | The provision is justified. | No recommendation. | Ministry of Economy, Development and Tourism |
| 40 | **Ministerial Decision Δ216570/2005 "Licences Regulation"** | art.17 | Wholesale trade of fuel | A different licence duration is provided for fuel wholesaler (5 years) and a different licence duration (4 years) for the import or supply of fuel directly from distilleries. | Licensing | There is no official recital. | The provision sets a discrimination in the licence obtaining process between operators in the retail fuel market. Thus, it imposes a higher cost for retailers who import or purchase fuel directly from distilleries, as opposed to the cost of wholesalers whose licence duration lasts one year longer. However, the provision seems justified considering the stricter licensing criteria imposed on wholesalers. | Align the duration of the licences to 5 years for all cases. | Ministry of Environment and Energy |
| 41 | **Ministerial Decision Δ216570/2005 "Licences Regulation"** | art.20 par. 2 | Wholesale trade of fuel | Liquid gas type C licence holder is restricted from selling gas products to liquid gas bottling licence holders, if the product is not destined to be bottled for him. | Supply restriction | There is no official recital. However, following communication with the competent Ministry, we understand that the provision was adopted for traceability reasons. | The provision seems restrictive but proportionate for security and traceability reasons. | No recommendation. | Ministry of Environment and Energy |
| 42 | **Ministerial Decision Δ216570/2005 "Licences Regulation"** | art. 21 | Wholesale trade of fuel | Heating oil trading licence holders shall not engage in wholesale activities unless they have storage spaces of minimum capacity 80m$^3$. | storage | There is no official recital. However, it is our understanding that the possible policy maker's objective would be to limit the possibility for an enterprise lacking the necessary storage spaces to enter the fuel market. | The provision seems restrictive but is proportionate to the policy maker's objective. | No recommendation. | Ministry of Environment and Energy |
| 43 | **Ministerial Decision Δ216570/2005 "Licences Regulation"** | art. 21d | Wholesale trade of fuel | Heating oil trading licence holders may not distribute kerosene bulk to the wholesale or retail channels. | Supply restriction | There is no official recital however we understand that the provision was adopted for safety reasons. | The provision may increase costs but it is justified in light of the policy maker's objective. | No recommendation. | Ministry of Environment and Energy |
| 44 | **Ministerial Decision Δ216570/2005 "Licences Regulation"** | art. 22b | Wholesale trade of fuel | Bottled gas distributors may only buy gas only from licence C holders. | Supply restriction | There is no official recital. However, following communication with the competent Ministry, we understand that the provision was adopted for traceability reasons. | The provision is proportionate to the intended purpose. | No recommendation. | Ministry of Environment and Energy |
| 45 | **Ministerial Decision Δ216570/2005 "Licences Regulation"** | Annex 3 point 7 | Wholesale trade of fuel | The minimum number of bottles for liquid fuel license holders must be 50 000. | Equipment | There is no official recital. However, it is our understanding that the possible policy maker's objective would be to limit the possibility for an enterprise lacking the necessary storage spaces to enter the fuel market. | Restrictive provision setting high costs for entering the market. Moreover, legal uncertainty is caused by the fact that this provision is contradictory to the provision of law 3054/2002 that explicitly sets the minimum number of bottles to 30.000. | Amend the provision to lower the minimum number of cylinders in order to minimize entry costs for new applicants. | Ministry of Environment and Energy |
| 46 | **Ministerial Decision Δ216570/2005 "Licences Regulation"** | art. 22d | Wholesale trade of fuel | Bottled gas is not to be distributed from the distribution licence holder to other bottled gas distributor licence holders. | Supply restriction | There is no official recital however we understand that the provision was adopted for safety reasons. | The provision is proportionate to the intended purpose. | No recommendation. | Ministry of Environment and Energy |
| 47 | **Ministerial Decision Α3/5262/2004 "Function of gas stations- Obligations of fuel trading companies"** | art. 1 par.4 | Wholesale trade of fuel | Independent gas station holders are not allowed to place in any point of their establishment commercial signs of a wholesale fuel trader by which fuel products of these companies are advertised. | Advertising | There is no official recital, however, following communication with the competent Ministry, our understanding is that the policy maker's objective was to safeguard fuel traceability and consumer information. | The provision is considered by the competent authorities to have been replaced by art. 115 of Ministerial Decision A2-718/2014. | Explicitly abolish. | Ministry of Economy, Development and Tourism |
| 48 | **Ministerial Decision Α3/5262/2004 "Function of gas stations- Obligations of fuel trading companies"** | art. 1 par.4 | Wholesale trade of fuel | Independent gas stations holders are not allowed to place on their gas pumps trademarks of fuel wholesalers. | Advertising | There is no official recital, however, following communication with the competent Ministry, our understanding is that the policy maker's objective was to safeguard fuel traceability and consumer information. | The provision is considered by the competent authorities to have been replaced by art. 115 of Ministerial Decision A2-718/2014. | Explicitly abolish. | Ministry of Economy, Development and Tourism |
| 49 | **Ministerial Decision Α3/5262/2004 "Function of gas stations- Obligations of fuel trading companies"** | art. 1 par. 6 | Wholesale trade of fuel | Wholesalers cannot provide fuel to gas stations, either directly or through a third party, when these gas stations use the trademark of another wholesaler. | Supply restriction | There is no official recital, however, following communication with the competent Ministry, our understanding is that the policy maker's objective was to safeguard fuel traceability and consumer information. | The provision is considered by the competent authorities to have been replaced by art. 115 of Ministerial Decision A2-718/2014. | Explicitly abolish. | Ministry of Economy, Development and Tourism |

## Sector: Wholesale trade

| No | No and title of Regulation | Article | Thematic category | Brief description of the potential obstacle | Keyword | Policy maker's objectives | Harm to competition | Recommendations | Competent Ministry / Authority |
|---|---|---|---|---|---|---|---|---|---|
| 50 | **Presidential Decree 11/2007 "Definition of wastage percentage on aromatic hydro carbonates"** | art. 3 par. 2 | Wholesale trade of fuel | When an amount of fuel is naturally eliminated while it is stored in tax warehouses or other repositories, VAT is imposed on the wastage while an exemption from the excise duty imposition is claimed. | Taxation | There is no official recital. | The provision may impose an unjustified cost to operators and hence limit entry in the market and have a negative impact on competition . | Abolish. | Ministry of Environment and Energy/ Finance |
| 51 | **Ministerial Decision Α3/5262/2004 "Function of gas stations- Obligations of fuel trading companies"** | art. 1 par. 3.1 | Wholesale trade of fuel | Gas station owners under exclusive agreements with wholesalers must place on an evident spot of their gas station the wholesaler's trademark. | Exclusive agreements | There is no official recital. However, following communication with the competent Ministry we understand that the policy maker's objective was to safeguard consumer's information on the origin of the fuel. | The provision is considered by the competent authorities to have been replaced by newer legislation. | Explicitly abolish. | Ministry of Economy, Development and Tourism |
| 52 | **Ministerial Decision Α3/5262/2004 "Function of gas stations- Obligations of fuel trading companies"** | art. 1 par. 3.1 | Wholesale trade of fuel | Right under or next to the sign of the wholesaler's trademark, the gas station must place a sign according to art. 83A of the Codified Market Decree 14/1989 with the fuel retail prices. | Obsolete | There is no official recital. However, following communication with the competent Ministry we understand that the policy maker's objective was to safeguard consumer's information on the prices. | The provision is considered by the competent authorities to have been replaced by newer legislation. | Explicitly abolish. | Ministry of Economy, Development and Tourism |
| 53 | **Ministerial Decision Α3/5262/2004 "Function of gas stations- Obligations of fuel trading companies"** | art. 1 par. 4.2 | Wholesale trade of fuel | Independent gas stations functioning under the special sign "A.Π" are not allowed to place in any spot of their establishment signs of wholesalers advertising their products through the specific gas station. | Advertising | There is no official recital. However, following communication with the competent Ministry we understand that the policy maker's objective was to safeguard consumer's information concerning fuel origin. | The provision is considered by the competent authorities to have been replaced by newer legislation. | Abolish. | Ministry of Economy, Development and Tourism |
| 54 | **Ministerial Decision Α3/5262/2004 "Function of gas stations- Obligations of fuel trading companies"** | art. 1 par. 4.2 | Wholesale trade of fuel | Independent gas stations are not allowed to place advertising trademarks of wholesalers on their gas pumps. | Advertising | There is no official recital. However, following communication with the competent Ministry we understand that the policy maker's objective was to safeguard consumer's information concerning fuel origin. | The provision is considered by the competent authorities to have been replaced by newer legislation. | Abolish. | Ministry of Economy, Development and Tourism |
| 55 | **Ministerial Decision Α3/5262/2004 "Function of gas stations- Obligations of fuel trading companies"** | art. 1 par. 6 | Wholesale trade of fuel | Wholesalers are prohibited from distributing fuel, either directly or through third parties, to gas stations that have placed trademarks of other wholesalers on their establishments. | Supply restriction | There is no official recital. However, it is our understanding that the provision is adopted to monitor the retailers' obligation to place the wholesaler's trademark on the gas station. Additionally, it protects consumer information concerning fuel origin. | The provision is considered by the competent authorities to have been replaced by newer legislation. | Abolish. | Ministry of Economy, Development and Tourism |
| 56 | **Joint Ministerial Decision ΔΥδρογ./Ε/Φ.5/180086/2015 "Insurance coverage against risks or security deposit as requirement for fuel trading licences"** | art. 1 par. 1 | Wholesale trade of fuel | The amount of the letter of guarantee for type A fuel companies depends on the sales volume of the previous calendar year as follows:<br>Up to 300 000 M.T. - 500 000 EUR<br>From 300 000 M.T. up to 600 000 M.T. - EUR 1 000 000<br>Higher than 600 000 M.T. - 1 500 000 EURO. | Guarantee | It was not possible to identify the policy maker's objective, however, following communication with the competent authorities, it is our understanding that the reasoning is to protect the state from any distortions caused by the inability of the operators to pay the penalties imposed to them. | The provision may limit the ability of new entrants to become active in the market. Moreover it may impose a high operational cost for incumbents. It should be further noted that the law should not be connecting the filling of the letter of guarantee or insurance contract to a future and unpredictable event of the imposition of a penalty to the licence holder. | Amend the provision to introduce a lower threshold consistent with the new minimum capital requirement. | Ministry of Finance / Economy, Development and Tourism/ Environment and Energy |
| 57 | **Joint Ministerial Decision ΔΥδρογ./Ε/Φ.5/180086/2015 "Insurance coverage against risks or security deposit as requirement for fuel trading licences"** | art. 1 par. 1 | Wholesale trade of fuel | The amount of the letter of guarantee that Type B1 (tax free shipping fuel) licence holders have to deposit is EUR 500 000. | Guarantee | It was not possible to identify the policy maker's objective, however, following communication with the competent authorities, it is our understanding that the reasoning is to protect the state from any distortions caused by the inability of the operators to pay the penalties imposed to them. | The provision is proportionate to the policy maker's objective given the sensitive nature of the product, however it should be noted that the law should not be connecting the filling of the letter of guarantee or insurance contract to a future and unpredictable event of the imposition of a penalty to the licence holder. | No recommendation. | Ministry of Finance / Economy, Development and Tourism/ Environment and Energy |
| 58 | **Joint Ministerial Decision ΔΥδρογ./Ε/Φ.5/180086/2015 "Insurance coverage against risks or security deposit as requirement for fuel trading licences"** | art. 1 par. 1 | Wholesale trade of fuel | The amount of the letter of guarantee that Type B2 (tax free aviation fuel) licence holders have to deposit is EUR 500 000. | Guarantee | It was not possible to identify the policy maker's objective, however, following communication with the competent authorities, it is our understanding that the reasoning is to protect the state from any distortions caused by the inability of the operators to pay the penalties imposed to them. | The provision is proportionate to the policy maker's objective given the sensitive nature of the product, however it should be noted that the law should not be connecting the filling of the letter of guarantee or insurance contract to a future and unpredictable event of the imposition of a penalty to the licence holder. | No recommendation. | Ministry of Finance / Economy, Development and Tourism/ Environment and Energy |
| 59 | **Joint Ministerial Decision ΔΥδρογ./Ε/Φ.5/180086/2015 "Insurance coverage against risks or security deposit as requirement for fuel trading licences"** | art. 1 par. 1 | Wholesale trade of fuel | The amount of the letter of guarantee that Type C (liquid gas licence holders have to deposit is EUR 500 000. | Guarantee | It was not possible to identify the policy maker's objective, however, following communication with the competent authorities, it is our understanding that the reasoning is to protect the state from any distortions caused by the inability of the operators to pay the penalties imposed to them. | The provision is proportionate to the policy maker's objective given the sensitive nature of the product, however it should be noted that the law should not be connecting the filling of the letter of guarantee or insurance contract to a future and unpredictable event of the imposition of a penalty to the licence holder. | No recommendation. | Ministry of Finance / Economy, Development and Tourism/ Environment and Energy |
| 60 | **Joint Ministerial Decision ΔΥδρογ./Ε/Φ.5/180086/2015 "Insurance coverage against risks or security deposit as requirement for fuel trading licences"** | art. 1 par. 1 | Wholesale trade of fuel | The amount of the letter of guarantee that Type D (asphalt) licence holders have to deposit is EUR 500 000. | Guarantee | The policymaker's objective was to provide for an alternative to the obligation of minimum capital requirement. Hence, the height of amount mentioned in the letter of guarantee is aligned with the minimum capital amount. | The measure is not consistent with the abolition of licence D minimum capital requirement however should not be abolished due to legal uncertainty reasons since these business use crude oil as raw material to produce asphalt. | No recommendation. | Ministry of Finance / Economy, Development and Tourism/ Environment and Energy |
| 61 | **Joint Ministerial Decision ΔΥδρογ./Ε/Φ.5/180086/2015 "Insurance coverage against risks or security deposit as requirement for fuel trading licences"** | art. 1 par. 7, 8, 9 | Wholesale trade of fuel | Insurance contract details for all licence holders. | Insurance | The policymaker's objective was to provide for an alternative to the obligation of minimum capital requirement. | Connecting the insurance contract to a future and unpredictable event such as the imposition of a penalty to the licence holder has led to the requirement not to be in practical use. | Abolish. | Ministry of Finance / Economy, Development and Tourism/ Environment and Energy |

## Sector: Wholesale trade

| No | No and title of Regulation | Article | Thematic category | Brief description of the potential obstacle | Keyword | Policy maker's objectives | Harm to competition | Recommendations | Competent Ministry / Authority |
|---|---|---|---|---|---|---|---|---|---|
| 62 | **Joint Ministerial Decision A8/oικ26374/2079/2014 "Defining the requirements and details for the distribution of fuel by licence holders according to law 3054/2002"** | art. 2 par. 2 | Wholesale trade of fuel | The toll fee for transferring fuel shall be calculated and paid in addition to the fee corresponding to the transport service. | Determination of agreement terms | There is no official recital. It is our understanding that the provision aims at protecting the professional transport operators from unforeseen fluctuations in toll payments. | The provision sets a restriction in the determination of the transportation fee, as it imposes that the toll fee is calculated separately. As a result, the final client would not know in advance the actual cost and would not have all the information to choose among competing transport operators. However, it is good practice to fully specify in the contract (especially if it is a long-term agreement) the cost elements that may vary and are outside the control of the transport operator. | No recommendation. | Ministry of Environment and Energy / Finance / Infrastructure, Transport and Networks |
| 63 | **Joint Ministerial Decision A2-818/2014 "Approval of the Regulation on Lease agreements of the Organisation of Central Markets and fisheries of Athens SA"** | art. 3 par. 1B | Wholesale trade of agricultural products | Applicants for a lease agreement within the central market may file additional documentation proving that the potential tenant or the potential tenant company's legal representative (when the tenant is a legal person), has been trained on a subject relevant to Agronomy or Veterinary science, Fish science or Finance in an educational institution of Greece or abroad. | Lease agreements | There is no official recital, however, following communication with the competent Ministry, we were informed that the policymaker's objective was to motivate new scientists that wish to enter the market. | The provision may place at a disadvantage some potential new entrants compared with others. | Conditional on the abolition of exclusivity of central markets, no recommendation. | Ministry of Economy, Development and Tourism, Ministry of Rural Development and Food |
| 64 | **Joint Ministerial Decision A2-818/2014 "Approval of the Regulation on Lease agreements of the Organisation of Central Markets and fisheries of Athens SA"** | art. 3 par. 1B | Wholesale trade of agricultural products | Applicants for a lease agreement may provide any document proving their prior occupation in the wholesale or retail sector of plant or animal products or fisheries. Indicatively the applicant may have worked as an employee, director or member of the Board of Directors or as partner in a business with a relevant activity. | Lease agreements | There is no official recital. It is our understanding that the objective is to assign more points to experienced applicants. | The provision may place at a disadvantage some potential new entrants compared with others. However, it is considered proportionate to the objective. | No recommendation. | Ministry of Economy, Development and Tourism / Rural Development and Food |
| 65 | **Joint Ministerial Decision A2-818/2014 "Approval of the Regulation on Lease agreements of the Organisation of Central Markets and fisheries of Athens SA"** | art. 4 I2b | Wholesale trade of agricultural products | The applicants are rated based on their turnover<br>Wholesalers of plant products:<br>Average Turnover in € / Points<br>50000 - 400000 / 20<br>400001 - 1000000 / 30<br>1000001 – 2000000 / 40<br>above 2000001 / 50 | Lease agreements | There is no official recital. It is our understanding that the policy maker considers larger applicants to be more trustworthy. Therefore, the objective is to assign more points to more trustworthy applicants. | The provision may place at a disadvantage some potential new entrants compared with others. However, it is considered proportionate to the objective. | No recommendation. | Ministry of Economy, Development and Tourism / Rural Development and Food |
| 66 | **Joint Ministerial Decision A2-818/2014 "Approval of the Regulation on Lease agreements of the Organisation of Central Markets and fisheries of Athens SA"** | art. 4 I2b | Wholesale trade of agricultural products | Wholesalers of animal products and fisheries:<br>Average Turnover in € / Points<br>100000 - 650000 / 20<br>650001 - 1500000 / 30<br>1500001 - 3000000 / 40<br>above 3000001 / 50 | Lease agreements | There is no official recital. It is our understanding that the policy maker considers larger applicants to be more trustworthy. Therefore, the objective is to assign more points to more trustworthy applicants. | The provision may place at a disadvantage some potential new entrants compared with others. However, it is considered proportionate to the objective. | No recommendation. | Ministry of Economy, Development and Tourism / Rural Development and Food |
| 67 | **Joint Ministerial Decision A2-818/2014 "Approval of the Regulation on Lease agreements of the Organisation of Central Markets and fisheries of Athens SA"** | art. 4 I2b | Wholesale trade of agricultural products | Profits:<br>Accounting profit before taxes and depreciations divided by the average turnover / Points<br>5 - 10% / 10<br>10.01 - 20% / 30<br>above 20.01% / 50 | Lease agreements | There is no official recital. It is our understanding that the policy maker considers profit rates as an indicator of trustworthiness. | The provision may place at a disadvantage some potential new entrants compared with others. However, it is considered proportionate to the objective. | No recommendation. | Ministry of Economy, Development and Tourism /Rural Development and Food |
| 68 | **Joint Ministerial Decision A2-818/2014 "Approval of the Regulation on Lease agreements of the Organisation of Central Markets and fisheries of Athens SA"** | art. 4 par. 2Bi | Wholesale trade of agricultural products | Applicants with a prior training in Agronomy-Veterinary -Fish science -Sea cultivation or finance are rated as follows:<br>Training in an object relevant to Agronomy- Fish science- Veterinary or finance:<br><br>Level of training / Points<br>Master's Degree / 100<br>University or High School Degree / 50<br>Degree not relevant or no degree / 0 | Lease agreements | There is no official recital. | The provision may place at a disadvantage some potential new entrants compared with others. However, it is considered proportionate to the objective. | No recommendation. | Ministry of Economy, Development and Tourism /Rural Development and Food |
| 69 | **Joint Ministerial Decision A2-818/2014 "Approval of the Regulation on Lease agreements of the Organisation of Central Markets and fisheries of Athens SA"** | art. 4 par. 2 Bi | Wholesale trade of agricultural products | Applicants with a prior occupation at a relevant activity are rated as follows:<br>Prior occupation at a relevant activity:<br>Duration of the prior occupation / Points<br>0 - 5 / 20<br>Above 5- up to 15 / 40<br>Higher than 15 - up to 25 / 70<br>above 25 / 100 | Lease agreements | There is no official recital. | The provision may place at a disadvantage some potential new entrants compared with others. However, it is considered proportionate to the objective. | No recommendation. | Ministry of Economy, Development and Tourism /Rural Development and Food |
| 70 | **Joint Ministerial Decision A2-818/2014 "Approval of the Regulation on Lease agreements of the Organisation of Central Markets and fisheries of Athens SA"** | art. 4 par. 5 | Wholesale trade of agricultural products | Any annual adjustment of the rent is provided in the lease agreement and it may not be lower than the variation in the average Consumer Price Index of the previous year. | Lease agreements | There is no official recital, however, following communication with the competent Ministry, we were informed that the provision depicts the usual practice followed during lease agreements providing for an annual raise of the rent. | The provision sets a minimum adjustment in the rent, depending on the change in the general price index, should the parties choose to amend the annual rent. However, it does not capture other factors which may affect the rent, such as the conditions on the specific product market (e.g. fruits and vegetables) or market demand for stalls in the central market. | Conditional on the abolition of exclusivity of central markets, no recommendation. | Ministry of Economy, Development and Tourism /Rural Development and Food |

## Sector: Wholesale trade

| No | No and title of Regulation | Article | Thematic category | Brief description of the potential obstacle | Keyword | Policy maker's objectives | Harm to competition | Recommendations | Competent Ministry / Authority |
|---|---|---|---|---|---|---|---|---|---|
| 71 | **Joint Ministerial Decision A2-818/2014 "Approval of the Regulation on Lease agreements of the Organisation of Central Markets and fisheries of Athens SA"** | art. 5 par. 3 | Wholesale trade of agricultural products | If the tenant of the premises is a company and it is dissolved, then the lease agreement is terminated immediately without any prior notification or stipulation. By exception, if the specific company had been formed by old tenants of OKAA SA that wish to remain in the OKAA stores that they possessed prior to the set up of the company and trade independently, the amendment of the lease agreement is feasible. | Lease agreements | There is no official recital, however, following communication with the competent Ministry, we have been informed that this provision was destined to provide an incentive for companies mergers so that they become more competitive. | The provision unjustifiably discriminates between old tenants that had established a relationship with OKAA SA through individual lease agreements, and new tenants that enter OKAA SA through the form of a new company. | Conditional on the abolition of exclusivity of central markets, no recommendation. | Ministry of Economy, Development and Tourism /Rural Development and Food |
| 72 | **Joint Ministerial Decision A2-818/2014 "Approval of the Regulation on Lease agreements of the Organisation of Central Markets and fisheries of Athens SA"** | art. 5 par. 5 | Wholesale trade of agricultural products | If a tenant transfers his rights from the lease agreement to a company, the shareholders of the company are obliged to participate in it for at least 1 year with a minimum of 30% share. | Lease agreements | There is no official recital, however, following communication with the competent Ministry we were informed that the policymaker's objective was to inhibit the formation of companies that engage in money laundering purposes. | Overly restrictive agreement that sets barriers to exit to those wholesalers that want to end their commercial relationship with OKAA and confer the keeping of the lease agreement terms to a company. The wholesaler may have difficulties in entering into such an agreement, when the members of the new company must adhere to a binding clause that their participation in it will last for at least one year. | Conditional on the abolition of exclusivity of central markets, no recommendation. | Ministry of Economy, Development and Tourism /Rural Development and Food |
| 73 | **Joint Ministerial Decision A2-818/2014 "Approval of the Regulation on Lease agreements of the Organisation of Central Markets and fisheries of Athens SA"** | art. 6 par. 1 | Wholesale trade of agricultural products | In case the lease agreement is amended, the new tenant must pay a fee. For the Central Market of Athens, the fee for a store lease agreement amendment is EUR 10 000, plus VAT. | Lease agreements | There is no official recital, however, following communication with the competent Ministry we were informed that this provision is a means to restrict illicit commercial practises along with maintaining the commercial value of the property and securing financial flows to the Organisation. | The provision sets barrier to exit for wholesalers that wish to terminate their lease agreement. Overly restrictive provision not justifiable by reasons of public interest, and not proportionate to the policy maker's objective. | Conditional on the abolition of exclusivity of central markets, no recommendation. | Ministry of Economy, Development and Tourism /Rural Development and Food |
| 74 | **Joint Ministerial Decision A2-818/2014 "Approval of the Regulation on Lease agreements of the Organisation of Central Markets and fisheries of Athens SA"** | art. 6 par. 2 | Wholesale trade of agricultural products | The fee for the lease agreement amendment may not be paid a) by a relative of up to B'grade or spouse to the departing tenant b) if the natural person or partner or shareholder depart due to retirement or death and is replaced by a relative of up to B' grade or spouse c) if the departing tenant transfers shares without change in the tax payer identity (the company), d) if the members of the sailing company want to continue the commercial activity in the same spot, after it has been dissolved. | Lease agreements | There is no official recital. | This exception allows the wholesaler to avoid paying the exit fee of 10.000 euros in specific cases of succession in the lease agreement. This preferential treatment is unjustifiable and discriminatory distorting competition between similar players in the market. | Conditional on the abolition of exclusivity of central markets, no recommendation. | Ministry of Economy, Development and Tourism /Rural Development and Food |
| 75 | **Joint Ministerial Decision A2-818/2014 "Approval of the Regulation on Lease agreements of the Organisation of Central Markets and fisheries of Athens SA"** | art. 13 par. 3 | Wholesale trade of agricultural products | Retail activities may take place in every part of the Central Market. | Central Markets | There is no official recital. | Retailers who operate within the central markets take advantage of the central markets' operating favourable provisions for wholesalers in the central market. For example, they can operate every Sunday. This creates an unequal treatment to other retailers and hence it is anticompetitive. | Conditional on the abolition of exclusivity of central markets, no recommendation. | Ministry of Economy, Development and Tourism /Rural Development and Food |
| 76 | **Joint Ministerial Decision A2-565/2012 "Regulation on the lease agreements of Athens and Thessaloniki Central Market"** | art. 3B | Wholesale trade of agricultural products | The applicants for a lease agreement within the central market may file additional documentation proving that the potential tenant or the potential tenant company's legal representative if the tenant is a legal person, has been trained on a subject relevant to Agronomy or Finance in an educational institution of Greece or abroad. | Lease agreements | There is no official recital, however, following communication with the competent Ministry, we were informed that the policymaker's objective was to motivate new scientists that wish to enter the market. | The provision may place at a disadvantage some potential new entrants compared with others. | Conditional on the abolition of exclusivity of central markets, no recommendation. | Ministry of Economy, Development and Tourism /Rural Development and Food |
| 77 | **Joint Ministerial Decision A2-565/2012 "Regulation on the lease agreements of Athens and Thessaloniki Central Market"** | art. 3B | Wholesale trade of agricultural products | Applicants may also provide any document proving the prior occupation at the wholesale or retail sector of plant or animal products or fisheries. Indicatively the applicant may have worked as an employee, director or member of the Board of Directors or as partner in a business with a relevant objective. | Lease agreements | There is no official recital. It is our understanding that the objective is to assign more points to experienced applicants. | The provision may place at a disadvantage some potential new entrants compared with others. However, it is considered proportionate to the objective. | No recommendation. | Ministry of Economy, Development and Tourism /Rural Development and Food |
| 78 | **Joint Ministerial Decision A2-565/2012 "Regulation on the lease agreements of Athens and Thessaloniki Central Market"** | art. 4 par 2b | Wholesale trade of agricultural products | The applicants are rated based on their turnover<br>Wholesalers of plant products:<br>Average Turnover in € / Points<br>0-400000 / 6<br>400001-1000000 / 7<br>1000001 - 2000000 / 9<br>above 2000001 / 13 | Lease agreements | There is no official recital. It is our understanding that the policy maker considers larger applicants to be more trustworthy. Therefore, the objective is to assign more points to more trustworthy applicants. | The provision may place at a disadvantage some potential new entrants compared with others. However, it is considered proportionate to the objective. | No recommendation. | Ministry of Economy, Development and Tourism /Rural Development and Food |
| 79 | **Joint Ministerial Decision A2-565/2012 "Regulation on the lease agreements of Athens and Thessaloniki Central Market"** | art. 4 par 2b | Wholesale trade of agricultural products | Wholesalers of animal products and fisheries:<br>Average Turnover in € / Points<br>0-650000 / 6<br>650001-1500000 / 7<br>1500001 - 3000000 / 9<br>above 3000001 / 13 | Lease agreements | There is no official recital. It is our understanding that the policy maker considers larger applicants to be more trustworthy. Therefore, the objective is to assign more points to more trustworthy applicants. | The provision may place at a disadvantage some potential new entrants compared with others. However, it is considered proportionate to the objective. | No recommendation. | Ministry of Economy, Development and Tourism /Rural Development and Food |

## Sector: Wholesale trade

| No | No and title of Regulation | Article | Thematic category | Brief description of the potential obstacle | Keyword | Policy maker's objectives | Harm to competition | Recommendations | Competent Ministry / Authority |
|---|---|---|---|---|---|---|---|---|---|
| 80 | **Joint Ministerial Decision A2-565/2012 "Regulation on the lease agreements of Athens and Thessaloniki Central Market"** | art. 4 par 2b | Wholesale trade of agricultural products | Percentage on the average annual turnover / Points<br>0-5% / 6<br>5.1-10% / 9<br>above 10.1% / 13 | Lease agreements | There is no official recital. It is our understanding that the policy maker considers larger applicants to be more trustworthy. Therefore, the objective is to assign more points to more trustworthy applicants. | The provision may place at a disadvantage some potential new entrants compared with others. However, it is considered proportionate to the objective. | No recommendation. | Ministry of Economy, Development and Tourism /Rural Development and Food |
| 81 | **Joint Ministerial Decision A2-565/2012 "Regulation on the lease agreements of Athens and Thessaloniki Central Market"** | art. 4 par 2b | Wholesale trade of agricultural products | Turnover related to loans:<br>Average annual turnover percentage / Points<br>0-30% / 13<br>31-50% / 7<br>51-80% / 3<br>81-100 % / 2<br>above 101% / 0 | Lease agreements | There is no official recital. It is our understanding that the policy maker considers larger applicants to be more trustworthy. Therefore, the objective is to assign more points to more trustworthy applicants. | The provision may place at a disadvantage some potential new entrants compared with others. However, it is considered proportionate to the objective. | No recommendation. | Ministry of Economy, Development and Tourism /Rural Development and Food |
| 82 | **Joint Ministerial Decision A2-565/2012 "Regulation on the lease agreements of Athens and Thessaloniki Central Market"** | art. 4 par 2b | Wholesale trade of agricultural products | Number of employees / Points<br>0-1 / 6<br>2-5 / 8<br>6-10 / 10<br>above 11 / 13 | Lease agreements | There is no official recital. It is our understanding that the policy maker considers larger applicants to be more trustworthy. Therefore, the objective is to assign more points to more trustworthy applicants. | The provision may place at a disadvantage some potential new entrants compared with others. However, it is considered proportionate to the objective. | No recommendation. | Ministry of Economy, Development and Tourism /Rural Development and Food |
| 83 | **Joint Ministerial Decision A2-565/2012 "Regulation on the lease agreements of Athens and Thessaloniki Central Market"** | art. 4 par 2b | Wholesale trade of agricultural products | Transportation vehicles<br>Number / Points<br>1 / 7<br>2-3 / 10<br>above 4 / 13 | Lease agreements | There is no official recital. It is our understanding that the policy maker considers larger applicants to be more trustworthy. Therefore, the objective is to assign more points to more trustworthy applicants. | The provision may place at a disadvantage some potential new entrants compared with others. However, it is considered proportionate to the objective. | No recommendation. | Ministry of Economy, Development and Tourism /Rural Development and Food |
| 84 | **Joint Ministerial Decision A2-565/2012 "Regulation on the lease agreements of Athens and Thessaloniki Central Market"** | art. 4 par 2b | Wholesale trade of agricultural products | Refrigerators:<br>Square metres / Points<br>up to 20 m2 / 7<br>21-50 m2 / 9<br>above 51 / 13 | Lease agreements | There is no official recital. It is our understanding that the policy maker considers larger applicants to be more trustworthy. Therefore, the objective is to assign more points to more trustworthy applicants. | The provision may place at a disadvantage some potential new entrants compared with others. However, it is considered proportionate to the objective. | No recommendation. | Ministry of Economy, Development and Tourism /Rural Development and Food |
| 85 | **Joint Ministerial Decision A2-565/2012 "Regulation on the lease agreements of Athens and Thessaloniki Central Market"** | art. 4 par 2b | Wholesale trade of agricultural products | Building capacity (packaging - storage):<br>Square metres / Points<br>0-1000 / 7<br>1001-5000 / 10<br>above 5001 / 13 | Lease agreements | There is no official recital. It is our understanding that the policy maker considers larger applicants to be more trustworthy. Therefore, the objective is to assign more points to more trustworthy applicants. | The provision may place at a disadvantage some potential new entrants compared with others. However, it is considered proportionate to the objective. | No recommendation. | Ministry of Economy, Development and Tourism /Rural Development and Food |
| 86 | **Joint Ministerial Decision A2-565/2012 "Regulation on the lease agreements of Athens and Thessaloniki Central Market"** | art. 4 par. 6 | Wholesale trade of agricultural products | Any annual rent adjustment provided in the lease agreement shall not be lower than 3%. | Lease agreements | There is no official recital, however, following communication with the competent Ministry, we were informed that the provision depicts the usual practice followed during lease agreements providing for an annual raise of the rent. | The provision sets a minimum adjustment in the rent, depending on the change in the general price index, should the parties choose to amend the annual rent. However, it does not capture other factors which may affect the rent, such as the conditions on the specific product market (e.g. fruits and vegetables) or market demand for stalls in the central market. | Conditional on the abolition of exclusivity of central markets, no recommendation. | Ministry of Economy, Development and Tourism /Rural Development and Food |
| 87 | **Joint Ministerial Decision A2-565/2012 "Regulation on the lease agreements of Athens and Thessaloniki Central Market"** | art. 7 par. 1 | Wholesale trade of agricultural products | A fee of EUR 10000 plus VAT is paid for amending the lease agreement as to the person of the tenant. | Lease agreements | There is no official recital, however, following communication with the competent Ministry we were informed that this provision is a means to restrict illicit commercial practises along with maintaining the commercial value of the property and securing financial flows to the Organisation. | The provision sets barrier to exit for wholesalers that wish to terminate their lease agreement. Overly restrictive provision not justifiable by reasons of public interest, and not proportionate to the policy maker's objective. | Conditional on the abolition of exclusivity of central markets, no recommendation. | Ministry of Economy, Development and Tourism /Rural Development and Food |
| 88 | **Joint Ministerial Decision A2-565/2012 "Regulation on the lease agreements of Athens and Thessaloniki Central Market"** | art. 7 par. 1 | Wholesale trade of agricultural products | If a company is set up between an existing tenant and a relative of up to B' grade, there is no obligation to pay for the amendment fee. | Lease agreements | There is no official recital. | This exception allows the wholesaler to avoid paying the exit fee of EUR 10 000 in specific cases of succession in the lease agreement. This preferential treatment is unjustifiable and discriminatory distorting competition between similar players in the market. | Conditional on the abolition of exclusivity of central markets, no recommendation. | Ministry of Economy, Development and Tourism /Rural Development and Food |
| 89 | **Joint Ministerial Decision 158825/2003 "Setting the special fee paid by operators in the State fish markets-obligations by professionals"** | art. 1 Ab | Wholesale trade of agricultural products | A 0.5% fee is imposed on the value of raw fisheries coming from aquaculture and are brought to the fish market for control and packaging and do not fall under case Aa . | Fees | There is no official recital. However, following communication with the competent Ministry, it is our understanding that the 0.5% fee corresponds to a series of services provided to the wholesalers by the Central Markets such as control and packaging of products destined for export, ensuring the hygiene and safety of the products. It also allows retailers to make use of the OKAA infrastructure such as storage, transportation and freezing. | The provision imposes a fee on fish coming from aquaculture units. For the fee to be reciprocal it should be imposed on the quantity of the fisheries and not their value. | Amend provision to adjust the fee to be corresponding to the volume of the fisheries. | Ministry of Finance / Rural Development and Food |
| 90 | **Law 3475/1955 "On the standardisation of raw agricultural products and the establishment of central and local markets"** | art. 6 par. 1 | Wholesale trade of agricultural products | Only one Central Market is allowed to be established in Athens and Thessaloniki. | Central Markets | There is no official recital. According to our understanding following communication with the competent Ministry, the objective of the policy maker was to safeguard hygiene and public safety. | The provision cannot be justified on competition grounds, or on public interest grounds. Opening up the market can only benefit consumers, increase economic activity and enhance consumer welfare. | Abolish the exclusivity clause and further amend the provision to allow for private organised wholesale markets to be established in the entire Greek territory. | Ministry of Economy, Development and Tourism /Rural Development and Food |
| 91 | **Law 3475/1955 "On the standardisation of raw agricultural products and the establishment of central and local markets"** | art. 6 par. 2 | Wholesale trade of agricultural products | Central Markets may be established in other areas outside Athens and Thessaloniki only by virtue of a royal decree issued upon relevant proposal of the Ministers of Rural Development and Commerce. | Central Markets | There is no official recital. | The provision is justified on the grounds that Central Markets are state owned and the law making process for the issuance of a royal (nowadays presidential) decree requires for a proposal by the competent Minister. | No recommendation. | Ministry of Economy, Development and Tourism /Rural Development and Food |

## Sector: Wholesale trade

| No | No and title of Regulation | Article | Thematic category | Brief description of the potential obstacle | Keyword | Policy maker's objectives | Harm to competition | Recommendations | Competent Ministry / Authority |
|---|---|---|---|---|---|---|---|---|---|
| 92 | **Royal Decree 746/1969 "Legal form, administration, management and functional organisation of the Central Fruit and Vegetables Market of Patras"** | art. 1 par. 3b | Wholesale trade of agricultural products | The Central Market of Patras establishments are available to wholesalers situated only in the prefecture of Patras, whereas they are also available to Agricultural Co-operations and producers from all over Greece. | Central Markets | There is no official recital. | Sets a geographical restriction to wholesalers established in other areas to enter the central market of Patras. | Conditional on the abolition of exclusivity of central markets, no recommendation. | Ministry of Economy, Development and Tourism /Rural Development and Food |
| 93 | **Royal Decree 746/1969 "Legal form, administration, management and functional organisation of the Central Fruit and Vegetables Market of Patras"** | art. 15 par. 2 | Wholesale trade of agricultural products | Wholesale trade in Patras prefecture to retailers is only allowed through the Central Market of Patras. | Central Markets | There is no official recital. | Sets an unjustified restriction for wholesalers to trade outside the central market of Patras. Limits participation in the market and establishes a geographical barrier to entry. | Abolish the geographical restriction. | Ministry of Economy, Development and Tourism /Rural Development and Food |
| 94 | **Law 3955/2011 "Unified Registry for traders of agricultural products, supplies and inputs and other provisions"** | art. 4 par. 4 | Wholesale trade of agricultural products | Sellers of agricultural products deposit an additional letter of guarantee, of annual duration. | Guarantee | There is no official recital. | The provision raises the cost of entry. | Abolish. | Ministry of Rural Development and Food |
| 95 | **Law 3955/2011 "Unified Registry for traders of agricultural products, supplies and inputs and other provisions"** | art. 3 par. 1 | Wholesale trade of agricultural products | Natural and legal persons registered with the Registry of Agricultural Exploiting Businesses are not obliged to register with the Registry for Sellers of Agricultural Products if they only sell products produced by themselves. | Registration | Policymaker's objective was to allow producers that are already registered with the National Registry for Producers of agricultural products to avoid the extra burden of registering to a second registry. | The provision is proportionate to the objective of the policy maker. | No recommendation. | Ministry of Rural Development and Food |
| 96 | **Joint Ministerial Decision 230/20798/2012 "Substitution of documentation of art. 4 of Law 3955/11 (Registration with the Unified Registry for sellers of Agricultural Products, Supplies and Inputs)"** | art. 2 par. 3 | Wholesale trade of agricultural products | A certificate by the Commercial and Industrial Chamber of Commerce is required for the registration. | Chamber of Commerce | There is no official recital, however, it is our understanding that during the law making, the registration with the Chambers of Commerce was obligatory and therefore this provision was consistent with the general obligation imposed by other legislation. | Since the provision is not compatible with law 3955/2011 as amended by law 4235/2014, it must be explicitly abolished because it creates legal uncertainty. | Abolish. | Ministry of Interior and Administrative Reconstruction/ Rural Development and Food |
| 97 | **Joint Ministerial Decision 230/20798/2012 "Substitution of documentation of art. 4 of Law 3955/11 (Registration with the Unified Registry for sellers of Agricultural Products, Supplies and Inputs)"** | art. 2 par. 5 | Wholesale trade of agricultural products | Wholesalers registered with the Organisation of Central Market of Athens SA (O.K.K.A. A.E.) and with the Central Market of Thessaloniki SA (K.A.O. A.E.) are exempt from filing a security deposit. | Central Markets | There is no official recital. However, it is our understanding that wholesalers already active in the market through the Central Markets, are considered to have complied with guarantee measures imposed by the Organisation of Central Markets and will be less prone to financial instability risks. | The provision imposes a differential treatment towards wholesalers trading within the central markets, and it therefore discriminates in favour of them, creating a higher entry cost to the ones outside the Central Markets. | Abolish. | Ministry of Interior and Administrative Reconstruction/ Rural Development and Food |
| 98 | **Joint Ministerial Decision 230/20798/2012 "Substitution of documentation of art. 4 of Law 3955/11 (Registration with the Unified Registry for sellers of Agricultural Products, Supplies and Inputs)"** | art. 2 par. 7 | Wholesale trade of agricultural products | A new letter of guarantee is deposited if the amounts declared by the seller exceed by EUR1000 the previous year's amounts. | Guarantee | There is no official recital. | The provision imposes a barrier to entry for new entities that are interested in entering the market. Moreover, it imposes a high cost to the ones already exercising the activity. Connecting the amount of the letter of guarantee to the value of the products purchased by the wholesaler discourages companies to grow economically and compete with each other, and minimises consumer choice. | Abolish. | Ministry of Interior and Administrative Reconstruction/ Rural Development and Food |
| 99 | **Ministerial Decision 225/2014 "Deposit of security letter for the registration of sellers of agricultural products with the Unified Registry of Sellers of Agricultural Products, Supplies and Inputs of Law 3955/2011"** | art. 1 par. 1 | Wholesale trade of agricultural products | Sellers of agricultural products must deposit a letter of guarantee of 10% on the value of the products provided in art. 1 par 1 of law 3955/2011 | Guarantee | There is no official recital, however following communication with the competent Ministry, we understand that the provision may be repealed or amended due to problems of application. | The provision imposes a barrier to entry for new entities that are interested in entering the market. Moreover, it imposes a high cost to the ones already exercising the activity. Connecting the amount of the letter of guarantee to the value of the products purchased by the wholesaler discourages companies to grow and compete. | Abolish. | Ministry of Rural Development and Food |
| 100 | **Ministerial Decision 225/2014 "Deposit of security letter for the registration of sellers of agricultural products with the Unified Registry of Sellers of Agricultural Products, Supplies and Inputs of Law 3955/2011"** | art. 1 par. 1 | Wholesale trade of agricultural products | In case the seller started his commercial activity after the 31st December the letter of guarantee deposited is 10% on the value of the purchases of agricultural products made during the activity until the deposit of the guarantee. The maximum amount is EUR 150000. | Guarantee | There is no official recital, however following communication with the competent Ministry, we understand that the provision may be repealed or amended due to problems of application. | The provision imposes a barrier to entry for new entities that are interested in entering the market. Moreover, it imposes a high cost to the ones already exercising the activity. Connecting the amount of the letter of guarantee to the value of the products purchased by the wholesaler discourages companies to grow and compete. | Abolish. | Ministry of Rural Development and Food |

## Sector: Wholesale trade

| No | No and title of Regulation | Article | Thematic category | Brief description of the potential obstacle | Keyword | Policy maker's objectives | Harm to competition | Recommendations | Competent Ministry / Authority |
|---|---|---|---|---|---|---|---|---|---|
| 101 | **Ministerial Decision 225/2014 "Deposit of security letter for the registration of sellers of agricultural products with the Unified Registry of Sellers of Agricultural Products, Supplies and Inputs of Law 3955/2011"** | art. 1 par. 2 | Wholesale trade of agricultural products | The next day after the expiry of the letter of guarantee, sellers must deposit a new letter of guarantee to replace the one that expired, following a recalculation based on 10% of the value of purchases from the 1st January until the 31st of December of the year preceding the year that the letter of guarantee expired. | Guarantee | There is no official recital, however following communication with the competent Ministry, we understand that the provision may be repealed or amended due to problems of application. | The provision imposes a barrier to entry for new entities that are interested in entering the market. Moreover, it imposes a high cost to the ones already exercising the activity. Connecting the amount of the letter of guarantee to the value of the products purchased by the wholesaler discourages companies to grow and compete. | Abolish. | Ministry of Rural Development and Food |
| 102 | **Ministerial Decision 225/2014 "Deposit of security letter for the registration of sellers of agricultural products with the Unified Registry of Sellers of Agricultural Products, Supplies and Inputs of Law 3955/2011"** | art. 1 par. 3 | Wholesale trade of agricultural products | Traders that own private establishments similar to their trading activity, such as standardisation establishments, packaging establishments, freezing or storage establishments, that are free of legal claims, and whose total value according to the VAT clearance statement of the previous year is at least twice of the value of the letter of guarantee that they are obliged to file, are obliged to file a letter of guarantee that is half in value from the one in par 1 and 2. | Guarantee | There is no official recital, however following communication with the competent Ministry, we understand that the provision may be repealed or amended due to problems of application. | The provision treats favourably those entities that own private establishments only if these establishments are used for accommodating activities that are similar to their trading activity. It imposes thus a differential treatment between operators in the same market, as it sets higher costs for the ones that lack such establishments, or those that may own establishments that are not relevant with their trading activity. | Abolish. | Ministry of Rural Development and Food |
| 103 | **Ministerial Decision 225/2014 "Deposit of security letter for the registration of sellers of agricultural products with the Unified Registry of Sellers of Agricultural Products, Supplies and Inputs of Law 3955/2011"** | art. 1 par. 4 | Wholesale trade of agricultural products | The bank granting the letter of guarantee must explicitly resign from any objection provided by law and must declare that, in any event that the letter of guarantee forfeits, it will deposit the claimed account. | Guarantee | There is no official recital, however following communication with the competent Ministry, we understand that the provision may be repealed or amended due to problems of application. | The provision imposes a barrier to entry for new entities that are interested in entering the market. Moreover, it imposes a high cost to the ones already exercising the activity . | Abolish. | Ministry of Rural Development and Food |
| 104 | **Ministerial Decision 225/2014 "Deposit of security letter for the registration of sellers of agricultural products with the Unified Registry of Sellers of Agricultural Products, Supplies and Inputs of Law 3955/2011"** | art. 2 par. 5 | Wholesale trade of agricultural products | Exemptions from the obligation of depositing a letter of guarantee:<br><br>a) Wholesalers of agricultural products registered with the Organisation of Central Market and Fisheries and with the organised municipal markets of Ioannina, Herakleio, Larissa, Volos and Chania<br>b) Sellers of agricultural products that during the periods provided in art. 1 par. 1 above, have purchased agricultural products of a value up to EUR120000<br>c) Natural or legal persons who mediate in the purchase of agricultural products according to par. 3 of art.1 of law 3955/2011, and are obliged to issue a tax notice. | Guarantee | There is no official recital, however following communication with the competent Ministry, we understand that the provision may be repealed or amended due to problems of application. | The provision discriminates between wholesalers, excluding from the obligation of filing a guarantee on the basis of geographical and production criteria. This may lead to a distortion of competition as it creates a counter- incentive for wholesalers who want to purchase greater amounts of products. | Abolish. | Ministry of Rural Development and Food |
| 105 | **Ministerial Decision 225/2014 "Deposit of security letter for the registration of sellers of agricultural products with the Unified Registry of Sellers of Agricultural Products, Supplies and Inputs of Law 3955/2011"** | art. 2 par. 7 | Wholesale trade of agricultural products | A new letter of guarantee is filed during the next year, if there is a change in the data. For filling a new letter of guarantee in case of an increase, the amount must exceed EUR1000 the amount of the previous letter of guarantee. | Guarantee | There is no official recital, however following communication with the competent Ministry, we understand that the provision may be repealed or amended due to problems of application. | The provision discriminates between wholesalers, excluding from the obligation of filing a guarantee on the basis of geographical and production criteria. This may lead to a distortion of competition as it creates a counter- incentive for wholesalers who want to purchase greater amounts of products. | Abolish. | Ministry of Rural Development and Food |
| 106 | **Joint Ministerial Decision 323306/2007 "Measures of implementation of Regulations 178/02 & 882/04 on feed safety & controls"** | art. 21 par. 4 | Wholesale trade of agricultural products | In case of disagreement with the decision of the competent authority an objection may be filed if the volume of the product exceeds 5 tonnes. | Penalty system | There is no official recital, however following communication with the competent Ministry, we understand that the provision may be repealed. | The provision discriminates between operators relating the importance of the penalty imposed with the amount of the product. | Abolish. | Ministry of Economy, Development and Tourism/ Rural Development and Food |
| 107 | **Joint Ministerial Decision 340668/2008 "Additional measures for the implementation of Regulations 183/2005 and 141/2007 of the European Council and the Council on the determination of the requirements for feed hygiene"** | art. 12a | Wholesale trade of agricultural products | The approval by the authorities of the Prefectures to the feed business operators is granted without prejudice to the granting of establishment licences. | Licensing | There is no official recital, however following communication with the competent Ministry, we understand that the provision may be repealed due to legal uncertainty reasons. | A double authorisation scheme may protect incumbents from competition, or cause long delays for the issuance of both licences. | Abolish. | Ministry of Economy, Development and Tourism/ Rural Development and Food |

## Sector: Wholesale trade

| No | No and title of Regulation | Article | Thematic category | Brief description of the potential obstacle | Keyword | Policy maker's objectives | Harm to competition | Recommendations | Competent Ministry / Authority |
|---|---|---|---|---|---|---|---|---|---|
| 108 | **Joint Ministerial Decision 263233/2008 "Determination of fees for official controls in feed and amendment of Joint Ministerial Decision 323306/2007"** | art. 6 | Wholesale trade of agricultural products | Fees are increased by 20% per year in case of infringement of the legal provisions regarding feed safety and 10% in any other case of infringement, even though a detailed penalty system is provided in Joint Ministerial Decision 323306/2007. | Fees | There is no official recital, however following communication with the competent Ministry, we understand that the provision may be repealed. | Introduces excessive and unreasonable costs and may discourage potential investors. | Abolish. | Ministry of Economy, Development and Tourism/ Rural Development and Food |
| 109 | **Joint Ministerial Decision 2533.63997/2013 "Additional measures regarding the authorized trader of raw vegetables in accordance with art. 12 Regulation (EU) 543/2011"** | art. 4 par. 4 | Wholesale trade of agricultural products | Obligation to hire an agronomist of University degree in Agronomy or a technology agronomist of technological Institute. | Professional qualifications | The policymaker's objective was to safeguard that the high quality product control required for the specific activity will be carried out by specialised personnel. | Proportionate to the public policy objective. | No recommendation. | Ministry of Rural Development and Food/ Finance/ Infrastructure, Transport and Networks/ Economy, Development and Tourism |
| 110 | **Ministerial Decision 2787/57103/2013 "Presentation and wholesale trade of fisheries in the State Fish Markets"** | art. 1 par. 2a | Wholesale trade of agricultural products | i) Raw fisheries from aquaculture units that are transported for wholesale purposes in the country or in another member state or in a third country through establishments that have been approved according to the current veterinary provisions<br>ii) raw products that come from the collective fishing transported for wholesale purposes to another member state or third country through units that have been approved according to the current veterinary provisions<br>iii) shellfish transported for wholesale purposes in the country or another member state or third country through units that have been approved according to the current veterinary provisions<br>iv) frozen, semi processed and preserved in brine<br>v) productions of aquatic organisations<br>vi) sponges<br>are exempt from the obligatory presentation and wholesale through the State Fish Markets and from paying the special fee. | Fees | The objective of the provision was to facilitate the circulation of products that have already been processed by approved establishments that carry out the production, manufacturing or packaging of these products. | The provision is proportionate to the policymaker's objective. | No recommendation. | Ministry of Rural Development and Food |
| 111 | **Ministerial Decision 2787/57103/2013 "Presentation and wholesale trade of fisheries in the State Fish Markets"** | art. 1 par. 3a | Wholesale trade of agricultural products | In Fish markets within the Regional Unit of Kalymnos and Chios, the presentation and wholesale of raw fisheries through the Fish market is obligatory only for the products brought to these islands. | Central Markets | The exception provided is set out to facilitate the circulation and distribution of fisheries in those areas where it is not possible for the producer to reach a Central Fish Market. The nature of the products is taken into consideration in addition to inadequate sea transport structures and high transportation costs. | Justified on grounds concerning the nature of the product. | No recommendation. | Ministry of Rural Development and Food |
| 112 | **Ministerial Decision 2787/57103/2013 "Presentation and wholesale trade of fisheries in the State Fish Markets"** | art. 1 par. 3b | Wholesale trade of agricultural products | In Fish markets within the Regional Unit of Evros, Evoia, Kavala, Chania the presentation and wholesale of raw fisheries through the Fish Market is not obligatory when these goods are destined to the islands of Samothrace, Skyros, Thasos and Gavdos. | Central Markets | The exception provided is set out to facilitate the circulation and distribution of fisheries in those areas where it is not possible for the producer to reach a Central Fish Market. The nature of the products is taken into consideration in addition to inadequate sea transport structures and high transportation costs. | Justified on grounds concerning the nature of the product. | No recommendation. | Ministry of Rural Development and Food |
| 113 | **Ministerial Decision 2787/57103/2013 "Presentation and wholesale trade of fisheries in the State Fish Markets"** | art. 1 par. 3c | Wholesale trade of agricultural products | Regarding raw fisheries coming from the collective fishing sector that are unloaded within the Regional Unit of Aitoloakarnania or Evros or Evoia or Preveza or Kalymnos or Chania or Chios, the presentation and wholesale in the Fish market functioning in the Regional Unit is not obligatory only in the case that these products are transported for wholesale purposes to the representative of the ship-owner in one of the fish markets of Piraeus, Nea Michaniona, Patras, Kavala. | Central Markets | The exception provided is set out to facilitate the circulation and distribution of fisheries in those areas where it is not possible for the producer to reach a Central Fish Market. The nature of the products is taken into consideration in addition to inadequate sea transport structures and high transportation costs. | Justified on grounds concerning the nature of the product. | No recommendation. | Ministry of Rural Development and Food |
| 114 | **Royal Decree 869/1966 "On the legal form, management, administration and organisation of the function of the central market of Thessaloniki"** | art. 15 par. 5 | Wholesale trade of agricultural products | Sub leasing of stores within the market or hiring personnel through participation in the business is not allowed. Wholesalers are allowed to hire a partner choosing from the already established ones in the Central Market. | Central Markets | There is no official recital. | Obsolete provision creating regulatory uncertainty. | Conditional on the abolition of exclusivity of central markets, no recommendation. | Ministry of Rural Development and Food/ Economy, Development and Tourism |
| 115 | **Royal Decree 869/1966 "On the legal form, management, administration and organisation of the function of the central market of Thessaloniki"** | art. 15 par. 6 | Wholesale trade of agricultural products | Sheltered spaces can be leased for short periods preferably to individual producers wishing to distribute their own production to consumers. Associations of producers or wholesalers of vegetables may also lease the spaces in case there is availability. | Central Markets | There is no official recital. | The provision grants preferential treatment to producers and is probably outdated. | Conditional on the abolition of exclusivity of central markets, no recommendation. | Ministry of Rural Development and Food/ Economy, Development and Tourism |

## Sector: Wholesale trade

| No | No and title of Regulation | Article | Thematic category | Brief description of the potential obstacle | Keyword | Policy maker's objectives | Harm to competition | Recommendations | Competent Ministry / Authority |
|---|---|---|---|---|---|---|---|---|---|
| 116 | **Presidential Decree 406/1998 "Central Athens Market Organisation change of legal form to SA and approval of its articles of association"** | art. 12 par. 2 | Wholesale trade of agricultural products | Members of the Board of Directors shall not, without permission of the General Assembly either on their own account or for third parties, acts relevant to the purposes of the Central Market of Athens SA or participate as partners or be members of the Board of Directors, officials, employees or representatives of companies that are active in similar activities as the Central Market or that are in a contractual relationship with the Central Market. | Central Markets | There is no official recital, however it is our understanding that the objective is to safeguard the integrity of the Board of Directors' members. | The provision is proportionate to the policy maker's objective. | No recommendation. | Ministry of Rural Development and Food/ Economy, Development and Tourism |
| 117 | **Joint Ministerial Decision 412/ 8932/2012 "Control of the Greek meat market in relevance to the origin and keeping of the monthly meat balances"** | art. 10 par. 3 | Wholesale trade of agricultural products | Individual imported portions of 500 gr distributed to the consumer are exempt from the special ELOGAK contribution. | Fees | There is no official recital. However, following our communication with the competent Ministry it is our understanding that for packaged standardised food imported by other Member states and are distributed directly to the final consumer, no traceability controls are carried out and such a fee would be considered as a tax on import. | The provision may discriminate between standardised packaged meat products in individual portions of 500gr and standardised packaged meat products in individual portions of more than 500gr, increasing the costs for some entities. | Abolish. | Ministry of Rural Development and Food / Finance / Interior and Administrative Reconstruction |
| 118 | **Joint Ministerial Decision 412/ 8932/2012 "Control of the Greek meat market in relevance to the origin and keeping of the monthly meat balances"** | art. 10 par. 3 | Wholesale trade of agricultural products | Meat products destined for export or destined to be sold to another member state are exempt from the special ELOGAK contribution. | Fees | Following communication with the competent Ministry, it is our understanding that the exemption from paying the fee is justified by the fact that no controls are exercised on the exported products. | The provision is proportionate to the policymaker's objective. | No recommendation. | Ministry of Rural Development and Food / Finance / Interior and Administrative Reconstruction |
| 119 | **Ministerial Decision A2-718/2014 "Codification of Rules on the distribution and trading of products and rendering of services"** | art. 42 | Wholesale trade of agricultural products | Wholesalers buying raw fruit and vegetables from producers before these are harvested, must sign an agreement whereby the production, purchase price and total value of the production is agreed. The invoice for the sale of the production is issued upon the signing of the agreement and the agreement is attached to the invoice. | Determination of agreement terms | Following communication with the competent Ministry, it is our understanding that the provision was adopted to protect farmers from any breach of the contractual obligations by wholesalers or manufacturers. | The provision is proportionate to the policymaker's objective. | No recommendation. | Ministry of Economy, Development and Tourism |
| 120 | **Ministerial Decision A2-718/2014 "Codification of Rules on the distribution and trading of products and rendering of services"** | art. 44 par. 1 | Wholesale trade of agricultural products | The process of evaluating the transactions between producers and traders is carried out either before the standardisation process on the total amount sold, or after the standardisation process distinctively by category on the total amount sold. | Determination of agreement terms | Following communication with the competent Ministry, it is our understanding that the policy maker's objective was not to impose any restrictions between wholesalers and producers. | As the provision is, it creates a rather binding rule for the formation of the contractual terms between farmers and wholesalers or manufacturers. It makes thus difficult for both parties to decide on the way that the value of the products will be decided and may lead to higher prices to the consumer. | Amend recommendation to explicitly allow for the ability of parties to decide on the evaluation of the production by category at any stage of the standardisation process. | Ministry of Economy, Development and Tourism |
| 121 | **Ministerial Decision A2-718/2014 "Codification of Rules on the distribution and trading of products and rendering of services"** | art. 53 par. 2b | Wholesale trade of agricultural products | Trading and circulating bulk edible oil is obligatorily carried out through containers suitable for food circulation according to Regulation 852/2004 "on food hygiene". In addition, producers only are allowed to use tanker trucks for this purpose. | Determination of agreement terms | There is no official recital. However, following communication with the competent Ministry officials, the objective was to ensure product safety and facilitate better and more efficient controls. | The provision sets a restriction in the transportation of bulk oil for wholesalers as opposed to producers, limiting their ability to choose the transportation means of their products. | Amend provision to permit the bulk trading of edible oil to be carried out with tanker trucks between wholesalers and to provide for extensive controls on food hygiene and food safety to be exercised. | Ministry of Economy, Development and Tourism |
| 122 | **Law 3730/2008 "Protection of minors from smoke and alcohol, smoking prohibition, doctors' issues etc."** | art. 2 par. 1z, par. 6 | Wholesale trade of tobacco | Tobacco products cannot be advertised or promoted inside commercial shops or sanitary interest shops (KYE). Especially with regard to hypermarkets, tobacco products are allowed to be placed inside closed displays. | Restriction in sales | There is no official recital. | The provision allowing hypermarkets to place tobacco products in closed displays is interpreted by the authorities as a ban on the same practice by other types of retailers. This creates legal uncertainty for wholesalers on whether and how they can sell their tobacco products to all types of retailers. | Clarify that all retailers allowed to sell tobacco products can place the products in closed displays. | Ministry of Health |
| 123 | **Circular 1012668/590/198/0014/ΠΟΛ.1250 /18.9.1998 "Directions on the implementation of Circular 1000887/2569/3/ΠΟΛ.1004/2.1.19 97 AYO as this has been amended and is in force, concerning the function of tax warehouses"** | art. 2 par. 7 | Tax | If the tax warehouse establishment was not initially declared to the tax registry as an establishment, it must be registered with the tax authority Registry through the process of filling an amendment declaration, within 10 days from the notification of the tax warehouse licence. | Licensing | There is no official recital. However, according to our understanding, the policy maker's objective is to ensure market surveillance. | According to our understanding, the simplified procedure may be used to by pass the licensing of the warehouse-some operators may benefit from the preferential treatment. However, due to market surveillance and market monitoring reasons, the provision is deemed proportionate to the policy maker's objective. | No recommendation. | Ministry of Finance |

## Sector: Wholesale trade

| No | No and title of Regulation | Article | Thematic category | Brief description of the potential obstacle | Keyword | Policy maker's objectives | Harm to competition | Recommendations | Competent Ministry / Authority |
|---|---|---|---|---|---|---|---|---|---|
| 124 | **Circular 1012668/590/198/0014/ΠΟΛ.1250 /18.9.1998 "Directions on the implementation of Circular 1000887/2569/3/ΠΟΛ.1004/2.1.1997 ΑΥΟ as this has been amended and is in force, concerning the function of tax warehouses"** | art. 2 par. 7 | Tax | Any change in the activity of the warehouse keeper must be declared within ten days from the notification of the tax warehouse licence,<br>If the warehouse keeper uses the warehouse for keeping third parties' goods, he must declare this activity concerning the specific establishment, unless he has already done so in the past. Should the tax warehouse be established in the company seat or in already existing branch building of the company and these establishments have already been declared to the Registry, a declaration for change is not required. | Licensing | There is no official recital. However, according to our understanding, the policy maker's objective is to ensure market surveillance. | According to our understanding, the simplified procedure may be used to by pass the licensing of the warehouse-some operators may benefit from the preferential treatment. However, due to market surveillance and market monitoring reasons, the provision is deemed proportionate to the policy maker's objective. | No recommendation. | Ministry of Finance |
| 125 | **Circular 1012668/590/198/0014/ΠΟΛ.1250 /18.9.1998 "Directions on the implementation of Circular 1000887/2569/3/ΠΟΛ.1004/2.1.1997 ΑΥΟ as this has been amended and is in force, concerning the function of tax warehouses"** | art. 2 par. 9 | Tax | The tax warehouse licence may be revoked either upon request of the tax warehouse keeper or the tax authority, for reasons such as not depositing the annual administrative cost. | Licensing | There is no official recital. | The provision may cause regulatory uncertainty, as it is not possible to identify the "annual administrative cost" that the provision refers to. | The provision should be amended to explicitly refer to the components of the "administrative cost" and the relevant provisions. | Ministry of Finance |
| 126 | **Circular 1012668/590/198/0014/ΠΟΛ.1250 /18.9.1998 "Directions on the implementation of Circular 1000887/2569/3/ΠΟΛ.1004/2.1.1997 ΑΥΟ as this has been amended and is in force, concerning the function of tax warehouses"** | art. 2 par. 10 | Tax | In case a tax warehouse functions in the same establishment with a warehouse under customs' surveillance, this establishment must be adequately constructed in order for the tax control to be feasible. | Storage | There is no official recital. | The term "adequate" allows for a broad discretion to be exercised by the competent authority and may also create regulatory uncertainty leading to a harm in competition. | The provision must be amended to explicitly refer to the applicable legislation, e.g. by product. However, this should not introduce any new restrictions for businesses, e.g. minimum height of buildings. | Ministry of Finance |
| 127 | **Ministerial Decision ΔΕΦΚ Α 5010479 ΕΞ/2014 "Installation and control of the complete input- output surveillance systems in tax warehouses"** | art. 14 par. 3 | Tax | The responsibilities of the input - output system installation licence holder for the correct and continuous function of the system and the correct data input and update, do not exempt the approved storer or the director of the tax storage space for any tax obligations or penalties that may be imposed during controls from the competent authorities. | Penalty system | There is no official recital. | Concerning the liability of the tax warehouse keeper for the correct and continuous function of the system, the provision is very strict and not proportionate to the policy maker's objective. | Amend the provision to hold the tax warehouse keeper responsible only for the data input and update. | Ministry of Finance |
| 128 | **Law 1642/1986 "On the implementation of VAT and other provisions"** | art.21a par. 12 | Tax | The keeper of a tax warehouse is equally and entirely responsible for the tax pending when he is not the owner of the goods that exit the tax warehouse. | Penalty system | There is no official recital, however it is our understanding that the objective is to avoid tax evasion phenomena. | The provision sets an exception for specific operators potentially raising their costs, however it is deemed proportionate to the policy maker's objective. | No recommendation. | Ministry of Finance |
| 129 | **Ministerial Decision Φ883/ 530/ 1990 "Terms for granting licence to approved storers"** | art. 2 par. 1c | Tax | The approved storer must keep C' category books. An exemption is provided for producers and manufacturers and the ones carrying out transfers to other member states or carry out exports to third countries. | Book keeping | There is no official recital, however it is our understanding that the policy maker's objective was to ensure the diligent function of tax warehouse keepers with regard to their tax obligations. | The provision sets out an exception for specific operators potentially raising their costs, however it is deemed proportionate to the policy maker's objective. | No recommendation. | Ministry of Finance |

## Sector: Wholesale trade

| No | No and title of Regulation | Article | Thematic category | Brief description of the potential obstacle | Keyword | Policy maker's objectives | Harm to competition | Recommendations | Competent Ministry / Authority |
|---|---|---|---|---|---|---|---|---|---|
| 130 | **Ministerial Decision Φ883/ 530/ 1990 "Terms for granting licence to approved storers"** | art. 4Aa I | Tax | Producers or manufacturers of energy products must deposit a guarantee of 4% of the excise duty paid during the past year.<br><br>Producers of biofuels must deposit a guarantee of 4% of the excise duty corresponding to the products circulated during the past year.<br><br>Producers and manufacturers of energy products deposit a security of 4% on the total excise duty paid during the past year, consisting of 2% of financial and 2% of other type of guarantee with a minimum of EUR 235000 if they receive ready products not used for their production activity but for commercial purposes.<br><br>Simple owners of energy products deposit a security of 4% on the total excise duty paid during the past year, consisting of 2% financial and 2% of other type of guarantee with a minimum of EUR 235000.<br><br>Simple owners of biofuels pay a security of 4% on the total excise duty tax corresponding to the goods distributed during the past year, consisting of 2% financial and 2% of other type of guarantee with a minimum of EUR 20000. | Security deposit | There is no official recital. However, following our communication with the competent Ministry, it is our understanding that the objective of the policy maker is to ensure payment of tax obligations and avoid tax evasion phenomena. The provision differentiates between producers and simple owners of the products as to the amount of security deposit that they have to pay. | The provision sets out different guarantee amount thresholds for different operators in the same market. May lead to higher costs for some storers and may hamper competition between operators, lowering competitive pressure in the market. However, given that producers of energy products are considered to be credible operators with big financial standing, the amount of guarantee is deemed proportionate. The lower amounts paid by biofuel producers/ manufacturers/ owners as opposed to energy products producers/ manufacturers and owners is justified considering that operators in the biofuels market are smaller entities. Moreover, biofuels are not to be placed in immediate consumption. | No recommendation. | Ministry of Finance |
| 131 | **Ministerial Decision Φ883/ 530/ 1990 "Terms for granting licence to approved storers"** | art. 4a AIII | Tax | Producers, manufacturers or holders of additives classified as Σ.Ο. 3811 1100, 3811 1190, 3811 1900 and 3811 9000, deposit a guarantee of 4% of the excise duty paid during the past year with a minimum of financial security of EUR 10000. | Security deposit | There is no official recital. However, following our communication with the competent Ministry, it is our understanding that the objective of the policy maker is to provide incentives to small and medium entities and biofuel products' penetration in the market. | The provision sets out different guarantee minimum amount thresholds for producers, manufacturers or holders of additives. However, the differentiation is proportionate to the policymaker's objective since producers of additives are smaller operators than refineries. | No recommendation. | Ministry of Finance |
| 132 | **Ministerial Decision Φ883/ 530/ 1990 "Terms for granting licence to approved storers"** | art. 4b I | Tax | Producers or manufacturers of tobacco products deposit a guarantee of 8% of the excise duty paid during the past year with a minimum of EUR 235000.<br><br>For professional workshops producing industrialised tobacco the minimum guarantee amount is 8% of the excise duty paid during the past year with a minimum of EUR 20000.<br><br>When a tax warehouse functions outside the manufacturing establishments an additional guarantee of 50% of the excise duty corresponding to the stored goods is deposited. The amount of the guarantee is recalculated every three months, at least, based on a control carried out in the warehouse. | Security deposit | There is no official recital. However, following our communication with the competent Ministry, it is our understanding that the objective of the policy maker is to provide incentives to small and medium entities. | The provision sets out different guarantee amount thresholds for different operators in the same market. However it is deemed proportionate to the policy maker's objective since professional tobacco workshops have a low production volume and therefore the minimum guarantee deposited may be lower than that of the rest of producers or manufacturers. | No recommendation. | Ministry of Finance |
| 133 | **Ministerial Decision Φ883/ 530/ 1990 "Terms for granting licence to approved storers"** | art. 4c I | Tax | Producers or manufacturers of alcohol and alcoholic products deposit a guarantee of 4% on the excise duty paid during the past year with minimum of EUR 14000 if the produced or received amounts did not exceed 10000 litres.<br><br>This amount is increased by EUR 7000 for every 5000 litres of alcohol received with a maximum of EUR 180000.<br>For intermediate products the guarantee is EUR 7000.<br><br>When a tax warehouse functions besides the production site, an additional 4% guarantee is deposited, corresponding to the excise duty of the stored goods. The guarantee is recalculated every three months, at least, following controls of the competent authorities. | Security deposit | There is no official recital. However, following our communication with the competent Ministry, it is our understanding that the objective of the policy maker is to provide incentives to small and medium entities. | The provision sets out different guarantee minimum amount thresholds for producers and manufacturers of alcohol and alcoholic products. However, the differentiation is proportionate to the policymaker's objective since producers are smaller operators than wholesalers and their production volume may easily be monitored and controlled by tax authorities before they enter consumption. | No recommendation. | Ministry of Finance |

## Sector: Wholesale trade

| No | No and title of Regulation | Article | Thematic category | Brief description of the potential obstacle | Keyword | Policy maker's objectives | Harm to competition | Recommendations | Competent Ministry / Authority |
|---|---|---|---|---|---|---|---|---|---|
| 134 | **Ministerial Decision Φ883/ 530/ 1990 "Terms for granting licence to approved storers"** | art. 4c I | Tax | Producers of wine and products coming from the process of brewing apart from wine and beer, the minimum guarantee amount is EUR 1000 until a quantity of 100000 litres of finished product. This amount is increased by EUR 1000 for every additional amount of 100000 litres with a maximum of EUR 40000. | Security deposit | There is no official recital. However, following our communication with the competent Ministry, it is our understanding that the objective of the policy maker is to provide incentives to small and medium entities. | The provision is proportionate to the policy maker's objective. | No recommendation. | Ministry of Finance |
| 135 | **Ministerial Decision Φ883/ 530/ 1990 "Terms for granting licence to approved storers"** | art. 4c II | Tax | Simple owners of alcohol and alcohol products deposit a guarantee of 15% on the excise duty paid during the past year consisting of 7% financial and 8% other form with a minimum of EUR180000, if the person is not an ethyl alcohol trader. The minimum amount of EUR 180000 is reduced to EUR 35000 in the case of intermediate products<br>For wine and beverages produced through brewing, the minimum amount is EUR 5000. | Security deposit | There is no official recital. | The provision sets different guarantee minimum amount thresholds between wholesalers and manufacturers/producers of alcohol and alcoholic products. However, the differentiation is proportionate to the policymaker's objective since wholesalers store large volume of products. Therefore, any late payment of the corresponding excise duty for these products may impose a higher risk to the market and to the state revenue. | No recommendation. | Ministry of Finance |
| 136 | **Ministerial Decision Φ883/ 530/ 1990 "Terms for granting licence to approved storers"** | art. 4c II | Tax | Traders of ethyl alcohol and distilled products deposit a minimum guarantee of EUR 470000. The safety deposit must be financial. | Security deposit | There is no official recital. | The provision sets different guarantee amount thresholds for different operators in the same market. However, it is deemed proportionate to the policymaker's objective since the amount of minimum guarantee corresponds to the amount of excise duty and VAT imposed on ethyl alcohol. | No recommendation. | Ministry of Finance |
| 137 | **Ministerial Decision Φ883/ 530/ 1990 "Terms for granting licence to approved storers"** | art. 4c I | Tax | For ethyl alcohol and distilled products in tax warehouses that are sealed by the Tax authority, even if there is no constant presence of the authority, the minimum amount of EUR 470000 is limited to EUR 235000. | Security deposit | There is no official recital. However, it is our understanding that the provision aimed at limiting the amount of the guarantee in cases where the presence of a tax authority is considered as safeguarding the storage procedure. | The provision sets different guarantee amount thresholds for different operators in the same market. However, it is deemed proportionate to the policymaker's objective since the specific warehouses are subject to more strict controls and supervision by the tax authorities. | No recommendation. | Ministry of Finance |
| 138 | **Ministerial Decision Φ883/ 530/ 1990 "Terms for granting licence to approved storers"** | art. 4c I | Tax | Producers of ethyl alcohol and distilled products have to meet the minimum deposit requirements as traders when they purchase finished goods not for their production process but for trading purposes. | Security deposit | There is no official recital. | The provision is proportionate to the policymaker's objective since producers acting as wholesalers must be subject to the obligations of wholesalers given that they are competing operators in the same market. | No recommendation. | Ministry of Finance |
| 139 | **Ministerial Decision Φ883/ 530/ 1990 "Terms for granting licence to approved storers"** | art. 4c I | Tax | Regarding intermediate products the amount of guarantee is EUR 7000. | Security deposit | There is no official recital. | The provision sets out different guarantee amount thresholds for different operators in the same market. However, the provision is proportionate to the policymaker's objective. | No recommendation. | Ministry of Finance |
| 140 | **Ministerial Decision Φ883/ 530/ 1990 "Terms for granting licence to approved storers"** | art. 4d I | Tax | Producers or manufacturers of beer deposit a guarantee of 4% on the excise duty paid during the past year<br><br>If there is a tax warehouse besides the production site, an additional guarantee is deposited amounting to 4% of the excise duty corresponding to the stored goods. The amount of the guarantee is recalculated every three months, at least, based on controls carried out by the competent authorities. | Security deposit | There is no official recital. However, following our communication with the competent Ministry, it is our understanding that the objective of the policy maker is to provide incentives to small and medium entities. | The provision sets out different guarantee minimum amount thresholds for producers and manufacturers of alcohol and alcoholic products. However, the differentiation is proportionate to the policymaker's objective since producers are smaller operators than wholesalers and their production volume may easily be monitored and controlled by tax authorities before they enter consumption. | No recommendation. | Ministry of Finance |
| 141 | **Ministerial Decision Φ883/ 530/ 1990 "Terms for granting licence to approved storers"** | art. 4d II | Tax | Simple owners of beer deposit a guarantee of 15% of the excise duty paid during the past year consisting of 7% financial and 8% of security of other form with a minimum of EUR 47000. | Security deposit | There is no official recital. | The provision sets out different guarantee minimum amount thresholds between wholesalers and manufacturers/producers of alcohol and alcoholic products. However, the differentiation is proportionate to the policymaker's objective since wholesalers store large volume of products. Therefore, any late payment of the corresponding excise duty for these products may impose a higher risk to the market and to the state revenue. | No recommendation. | Ministry of Finance |
| 142 | **Ministerial Decision Φ883/ 530/ 1990 "Terms for granting licence to approved storers"** | art. 4d II | Tax | Producers or manufacturers deposit a guarantee of 15% of the excise duty paid during the past year consisting of 7% financial and 8% of security of other form with a minimum of EUR 47000 in case they receive ready products for trading purposes. | Security deposit | There is no official recital. However, following our communication with the competent Ministry, it is our understanding that the objective of the policy maker is to provide incentives to small and medium entities. | The provision is proportionate to the policymaker's objective since producers acting as wholesalers must be subject to the obligations of wholesalers given that they are competing operators in the same market. | No recommendation. | Ministry of Finance |

## Sector: Wholesale trade

| No | No and title of Regulation | Article | Thematic category | Brief description of the potential obstacle | Keyword | Policy maker's objectives | Harm to competition | Recommendations | Competent Ministry / Authority |
|---|---|---|---|---|---|---|---|---|---|
| 143 | **Ministerial Decision Φ883/ 530/ 1990 "Terms for granting licence to approved storers"** | art. 4e I | Tax | Producers or manufacturers that do not have an annual activity in the production/ manufacturing of alcohol and energy products including bio- fuel deposit a guarantee of 4% on the excise duty corresponding to the products that, by declaration of the applicant, will be produced or manufactured during the first year of their activity, with a minimum of EUR 70000 for alcohol products.<br>For beer tax warehouses the minimum amount is reduced toEUR 20000.<br>For intermediate products tax warehouse the minimum amount is reduced to EUR 10000<br>For wine and products produced through brewing apart from wine and beer, the minimum guarantee is reduced to EUR 3000. | Security deposit | There is no official recital. However, following our communication with the competent Ministry, it is our understanding that the objective of the policy maker is to provide incentives to small and medium entities. | The provision is deemed justified considering the policy maker's objective. | No recommendation. | Ministry of Finance |
| 144 | **Ministerial Decision Φ883/ 530/ 1990 "Terms for granting licence to approved storers"** | art. 4e II | Tax | Producers or manufacturers of industrial tobacco deposit a guarantee of 8% on the excise duty corresponding to the products that by declaration will be produced or manufactured during the first year of the activity with a minimum of EUR 235000 and for professional workshops EUR 20000. | Security deposit | There is no official recital. However, following our communication with the competent Ministry, it is our understanding that the objective of the policy maker is to provide incentives to small and medium entities. | The provision is deemed justified considering the policy maker's objective. | No recommendation. | Ministry of Finance |
| 145 | **Ministerial Decision Φ883/ 530/ 1990 "Terms for granting licence to approved storers"** | art. 4e IV | Tax | Simple owners of industrial tobacco products deposit a guarantee that is equal to the minimum amounts provided for simple owners of tobacco products. | Security deposit | There is no official recital. | The provision is deemed justified considering the policy maker's objective. | No recommendation. | Ministry of Finance |
| 146 | **Ministerial Decision Φ883/ 530/ 1990 "Terms for granting licence to approved storers"** | art. 4e V | Tax | Producers or manufacturers or owners of additives classified as Σ.Ο. 3811 1100, 3811 1190, 3811 1900 and 3811 9000, deposit a guarantee of 4% of the excise duty corresponding to the products that by declaration will be produced, manufactured or distributed with a minimum amount of EUR 10000. | Security deposit | There is no official recital. However, following our communication with the competent Ministry, it is our understanding that the objective of the policy maker is to provide incentives to small and medium entities. | The differentiation is proportionate to the policymaker's objective. | No recommendation. | Ministry of Finance |
| 147 | **Ministerial Decision Φ883/ 530/ 1990 "Terms for granting licence to approved storers"** | art. 4 C | Tax | Guarantees are reduced by 30% if the approved storer is holder of an Approved Economic Operator certificate type AEOS for purposes of safety or security or type AEOF for customs simplification purposes and safety and security. | Security deposit | There is no official recital. | The amount of guarantee required for this type of repositors, is lower than the amount provided for the regular ones. Authorised economic operators have been licenced on a more strict procedure and are considered as more capable of compensating beneficiaries in the event of product damage. Therefore, the lower threshold on the amount of guarantee seems reasonable and proportionate. | No recommendation. | Ministry of Finance |
| 148 | **Law 2960/2001 "Greek Customs Code"** | art. 25 par. 7 st | Tax | Security paid for the assurance of the levies, taxes and various fees to the State for the goods stored in temporary warehouses and customs repositories. No security needs to be paid when the warehouse or repository is used by a Public Entity (N.Π.Δ.Δ). | Security deposit | There is no official recital. | The provision grants a preferential treatment to entities functioning under the legal form of a Public Entity. This exception raises the costs of some suppliers relative to others, lowering the intensity of competitive pressure in the market. | The provision should be amended to abolish the exemption for public entities (N.Π.Δ.Δ) in cases where public entities compete with private entities. | Ministry of Finance |
| 149 | **Ministerial Decision B1/ουκ. 38810/3156/2014 "Financial capacity of businesses as a requirement for the issuance of a transport operator licence"** | art. 3a | Transport-logistics-warehousing | New road transport operators functioning under the form of an SA have to prove their financial standing through a letter of guarantee or a note of permanent deposit of EUR 9000 for the first vehicle and EUR 5000 for every additional vehicle. | Security deposit | There is no official recital. However, following communication with the competent Ministry, it is our understanding that the policy maker's objective is to allow only operators with the appropriate financial standing to enter the market, so that their proper launching and administration is secured. Moreover, based on our communication we have concluded that the provision may be amended so as to equality treat new and old licence holders . | The measure is proportionate to the policy maker's objective and it is in alliance with Regulation EC 1071/2009. However, due to equal treatment reasons of all road transport operators, as mentioned in the recital no (6) of Reg. EU 1071/2009, there should be no discrimination between legal forms in the amount of guarantee deposited. | The provision should be amended to include all legal forms without distinguishing between old and new. | Ministry of Infrastructure, Transport and Networks |
| 150 | **Ministerial Decision B1/ουκ. 38810/3156/2014 "Financial capacity of businesses as a requirement for the issuance of a transport operator licence"** | art. 3b | Transport-logistics-warehousing | New road transport operators functioning under a legal form different than SAs have to prove their financial standing through a letter of guarantee or a note of permanent deposit of EUR 18000 for the first vehicle and EUR 9000 for every additional vehicle. | Security deposit | There is no official recital. However, following communication with the competent Ministry, it is our understanding that the policy maker's objective is to allow only operators with the appropriate financial standing to enter the market, so that their proper launching and administration is secured. Moreover, based on our communication we have concluded that the provision may be amended so as to equally treat new and old licence holders . | The provision may constitute a barrier to entry for small suppliers, as it may entail extra cost for them. Moreover, it may limit investments and reduce the number of suppliers over time. Due to equal treatment reasons of all road transport operators, as mentioned in the recital no (6) of Reg. EU 1071/2009, there should be no discrimination between legal forms in the amount of guarantee deposited. | Abolish. | Ministry of Infrastructure, Transport and Networks |

## Sector: Wholesale trade

| No | No and title of Regulation | Article | Thematic category | Brief description of the potential obstacle | Keyword | Policy maker's objectives | Harm to competition | Recommendations | Competent Ministry / Authority |
|---|---|---|---|---|---|---|---|---|---|
| 151 | **Ministerial Decision B1/οικ. 38810/3156/2014 "Financial capacity of businesses as a requirement for the issuance of a transport operator licence"** | art. 4a | Transport-logistics-warehousing | Old transport operators have to prove their financial standing through a bank account balance certificate or a copy of their bank account issued up to one week prior to the application for the licence. The amounts covered must be EUR 9000 for the initial "old" licence granted for trucks used for hire or reward and EUR 5000 for every additional "old" licence. | Security deposit | There is no official recital. However, following communication with the competent Ministry, it is our understanding that the policy maker's objective is to allow only operators with the appropriate financial standing to remain in the market, so that their proper launching and administration is secured. Moreover, based on our communication we have concluded that the provision may be amended so as to equally treat new and old licence holders. | The provision discriminates between new and old transporters, granting a preferential treatment towards the latter, reducing thus competition. | Abolish. | Ministry of Infrastructure, Transport and Networks |
| 152 | **Ministerial Decision B1/οικ. 38810/3156/2014 "Financial capacity of businesses as a requirement for the issuance of a transport operator licence"** | art. 4b | Transport-logistics-warehousing | Old transport operators functioning under the form of an SA have to prove their financial standing through a bank letter guarantee or a note of permanent deposit of EUR 9000 for the first truck used for hire or reward with an "initial licence" and EUR 5000 for every additional truck used for hire or reward with an "initial licence".<br>If the transport operator functions under another legal form, the amount required is EUR 18000 for the first truck used for hire or reward with an "initial licence" and EUR 9000 for every additional truck used for hire or reward with an "initial licence". | Security deposit | There is no official recital. However, following communication with the competent Ministry, it is our understanding that the policy maker's objective is to allow only operators with the appropriate financial standing to remain in the market, so that their proper launching and administration is secured. Moreover, based on our communication we have concluded that the provision may be amended so as to equally treat new and old licence holders. | The provision discriminates between new and old transporters, granting a preferential treatment towards the latter, reducing thus competition. | Abolish. | Ministry of Infrastructure, Transport and Networks |
| 153 | **Ministerial Decision B1/οικ. 38810/3156/2014 "Financial capacity of businesses as a requirement for the issuance of a transport operator licence"** | art. 6 par. 1 | Transport-logistics-warehousing | Letters of guarantee and notes of permanent deposit filed by transport operators to prove their financial standing according to Ministerial Decision B1/13082/1410/2012 are still valid. | Security deposit | There is no official recital. However, following communication with the competent Ministry, it is our understanding that the policy maker's objective is to allow only operators with the appropriate financial standing to remain in the market, so that their proper launching and administration is secured. Moreover, based on our communication we have concluded that the provision may be amended so as to equally treat new and old licence holders. | The provision seems to discriminate between new and old transporters, granting a preferential treatment towards the latter reducing competition in the market. | Abolish. | Ministry of Infrastructure, Transport and Networks |
| 154 | **Ministerial Decision T 6525/421/A0019/2000 "Requirements, terms and functional procedures of warehouses or places destined to accommodate the temporary repository of goods under the management of legal or natural persons, other than the Customs authorities"** | art. 14 par. 3a | Transport-logistics-warehousing | For temporary repositories placed at the entrance of ports and airports where a customs' authority is seated, the guarantee height is 1% on the total taxes and duties paid for the products stored in the temporary repository during the past calendar year. A 3% guarantee is provided for repositories located elsewhere. | Security deposit | It was not possible to identify the objective of the provision. However, it is our understanding that the provision aims at ensuring product safety as well as the ability of the operator to pay for compensation in case any damages might be incurred. | The provision requires for a guarantee to be deposited, in order to ensure compensation of the beneficiaries in the event of product damage. It seems reasonable and proportionate. | No recommendation. | Ministry of Finance |
| 155 | **Ministerial Decision T 6525/421/A0019/2000 "Requirements, terms and functional procedures of warehouses or places destined to accommodate the temporary repository of goods under the management of legal or natural persons, other than the Customs authorities"** | art. 14 par. 3b | Transport-logistics-warehousing | For temporary repositories that do not fall under par. A, the guarantee is 3% on the taxes and duties paid for the goods stored in the temporary repository during the past calendar year. | Security deposit | It was not possible to identify the objective of the provision. However, it is our understanding that the provision aims to ensure product safety and the ability of the operator to pay for compensation in case any damages might be incurred. | The provision discriminates between economic operators, based on the location of the repository. However, the different amount of guarantee seems reasonable as the presence of the customs authority safeguards that the storage of products is conducted according to the legal requirements. | No recommendation. | Ministry of Finance |
| 156 | **Ministerial Decision T 6525/421/A0019/2000 "Requirements, terms and functional procedures of warehouses or places destined to accommodate the temporary repository of goods under the management of legal or natural persons, other than the Customs authorities"** | art. 14 par. 3c | Transport-logistics-warehousing | For repositories placed at the entrances of ports and airports, where a customs' office is present, when administrators of the temporary repositories are holders of an Authorised Economic Operator "AEOS" certificate for security and protection or holders of a type "AEOF" certificate for customs' simplifications, security and protection, the height of the guarantee is 0.50% of the taxes and duties paid for the goods stored in the temporary repository during the past calendar year. | Security deposit | It was not possible to identify the objective of the provision. However, it is our understanding that the provision aims to ensure product safety and the ability of the operator to pay for compensation in case any damages might be incurred. | The amount of guarantee required for this type of repositors, is lower than the amount provided for the regular ones. Authorised economic operators have been licenced on a more strict procedure and are considered as more capable of compensating beneficiaries in the event of product damage. Therefore, the lower threshold on the amount of guarantee seems reasonable and proportionate. | No recommendation. | Ministry of Finance |
| 157 | **Ministerial Decision T 6525/421/A0019/2000 "Requirements, terms and functional procedures of warehouses or places destined to accommodate the temporary repository of goods under the management of legal or natural persons, other than the Customs authorities"** | art. 14 par. 3c | Transport-logistics-warehousing | When administrators of temporary repositories placed outside the entrances of ports and airports are holders of an Authorised Economic Operator "AEOS" certificate for security purposes and protection or type "AEOF" for customs' simplifications and security and protection, the height of the guarantee is 1.5% of the taxes and duties paid for the goods stored in the repository during the past calendar year. | Security deposit | It was not possible to identify the objective of the provision. However, it is our understanding that the provision aims to ensure product safety and the ability of the operator to pay for compensation in case any damages might be incurred. | The provision discriminates between economic operators, based on the location of the repository. However, the different amount of guarantee seems reasonable as the presence of the customs authority safeguards that the storage of products is conducted according to the legal requirements. | No recommendation. | Ministry of Finance |

## Sector: Wholesale trade

| No | No and title of Regulation | Article | Thematic category | Brief description of the potential obstacle | Keyword | Policy maker's objectives | Harm to competition | Recommendations | Competent Ministry / Authority |
|---|---|---|---|---|---|---|---|---|---|
| 158 | **Joint Ministerial Decision 18532/2014 "Supply hours of stores (Supermarkets) and Retail Hyper Markets in the centre of Athens"** | art. 1 par. 2 | Transport-logistics-warehousing | Raw fisheries may be supplied to Varvakeios Market in hours different than all other stores. | Security deposit | There is no official recital. However, following communication with the competent Ministry we were informed that the objective of the provision was to allow for perishable products to be distributed to stores in different hours than other products. | The provision seems to discriminate between products in terms of store supply hours. However, considering the perishable nature of fisheries, such a discrimination seems reasonable. Considering that the Ministerial Decision was released for the year 2014, due to legal uncertainty reasons we suggest that it is updated for the upcoming year. | No recommendation. | Ministry of Infrastructure, Transport and Networks/ Environment and Energy/ Interior and Administrative Reconstruction |
| 159 | **Ministerial Decision A2/29542/5347/1991 "Licensing of private use trucks according to Law 1959/2001"** | Chapter C par. 2 | Transport-logistics-warehousing | Only one licence per applicant is granted to agricultural businesses. Granting of more licences requires for a certificate by the competent Directorate of Agriculture proving the existence of the business and the necessity for the circulation of more than one trucks used for own account. | Transport/ Licensing | There is no official recital. However, according to our communication with the competent Ministry, it is our understanding that the provision is considered to be abolished. | Legal uncertainty. If the provision is in force, it is considered as introducing a barrier to entry for agricultural businesses that want to obtain more than one licence. | Abolish. | Ministry of Infrastructure, Transport and Networks |
| 160 | **Ministerial Decision A2/29542/5347/1991 "Licensing of private use trucks according to Law 1959/2001"** | Chapter D par. 3 | Transport-logistics-warehousing | A business with gross income of 16 000 000 drachmas corresponding to any given period during the previous year, may circulate one or more own account trucks of gross weight of 40 tonnes. | Transport/ Licensing | There is no official recital. | Following communication with the competent Ministry, this provision has been abolished by law 4336/2015. However, it should be explicitly abolished as it creates regulatory uncertainty. | Explicitly abolish. | Ministry of Infrastructure, Transport and Networks |
| 161 | **Ministerial Decision A2/29542/5347/1991 "Licensing of private use trucks according to Law 1959/2001"** | Chapter D par. 3 | Transport-logistics-warehousing | Temporary licences become finalised if the gross income of the business is 1 000 000 drachmas for every tonne of gross weight of the trucks used for own account within any given period during the temporary licence<br>For example: a business that wants to turn the temporary licences of its trucks used for own account of 40 tonnes gross weight to final licences must file a certificate by the Tax authority certifying that during that given period the gross income was 40 000 000 drachmas. | Transport/ Licensing | There is no official recital. | Following communication with the competent Ministry, this provision has been abolished by law 4336/2015. However, it should be explicitly abolished as it creates regulatory uncertainty. | Explicitly abolish. | Ministry of Infrastructure, Transport and Networks |
| 162 | **Ministerial Decision A2/29542/5347/1991 "Licensing of private use trucks according to Law 1959/2001"** | Chapter D par. 3 | Transport-logistics-warehousing | If the business' s gross income is less than the thresholds set, temporary licences are revoked and they turn into final licences of trucks used for own account of total gross weight equal to the height of the gross income.<br>For example if the said business has gross income of 24000000 drachmas instead of 40000000 drachmas then the temporary licences will turn into final private trucks licences of total gross weight of 24 tonnes, while the other licences will be removed. | Transport/ Licensing | There is no official recital. | Following communication with the competent Ministry, this provision has been abolished by law 4336/2015. However, it should be explicitly abolished as it creates regulatory uncertainty. | Explicitly abolish. | Ministry of Infrastructure, Transport and Networks |
| 163 | **Ministerial Decision A2/29542/5347/1991 "Licensing of private use trucks according to Law 1959/2001"** | Chapter D par. 5 | Transport-logistics-warehousing | If the applicant engages in more activities, a specialised private truck licence of gross weight of more than 3500 kgs is granted only if the gross income deriving both by the temporary and the final licences apply to the specific activities or activity that the specialised truck is destined for. | Transport/ Licensing | There is no official recital. | Following communication with the competent Ministry, this provision has been abolished by law 4336/2015. However, it should be explicitly abolished as it creates regulatory uncertainty. | Explicitly abolish. | Ministry of Infrastructure, Transport and Networks |
| 164 | **Ministerial Decision A2/29542/5347/1991 "Licensing of private use trucks according to Law 1959/2001"** | Chapter D par. 6 | Transport-logistics-warehousing | One final licence for an own account truck may be granted to trucks of gross weight of over 3500kgs by exemption to the provisions of par. 3 of the present Chapter, to industrial or contracting businesses provided that they will also file an authorisation licence or a contracting decree, and only if within any given period during the past financial year they had gross income of at least 20000000 drachmas. | Transport/ Licensing | There is no official recital. | Following communication with the competent Ministry, this provision has been abolished by law 4336/2015. However, it should be explicitly abolished as it creates regulatory uncertainty. | Abolish. | Ministry of Infrastructure, Transport and Networks |
| 165 | **Ministerial Decision A2/29542/5347/1991 "Licensing of private use trucks according to Law 1959/2001"** | Chapter D par. 7a | Transport-logistics-warehousing | Only industrial or manufacturing companies that engage in the production of oil and spent oil products are entitled to a licence for a truck used for own account for the specific oil products. | Transport/ Licensing | There is no official recital. | The provision does not seem to concern wholesalers. | No recommendation. | Ministry of Infrastructure, Transport and Networks |
| 166 | **Ministerial Decision A2/29542/5347/1991 "Licensing of private use trucks according to Law 1959/2001"** | Chapter D par. 7b | Transport-logistics-warehousing | Only industrial or manufacturing industries engaged in the production of concrete are entitled to trucks used for own account for the transport of concrete. | Transport/ Licensing | There is no official recital. | The provision does not seem to concern wholesalers. | No recommendation. | Ministry of Infrastructure, Transport and Networks |

## Sector: Wholesale trade

| No | No and title of Regulation | Article | Thematic category | Brief description of the potential obstacle | Keyword | Policy maker's objectives | Harm to competition | Recommendations | Competent Ministry / Authority |
|---|---|---|---|---|---|---|---|---|---|
| 167 | **Ministerial Decision A2/29542/5347/1991 "Licensing of private use trucks according to Law 1959/2001"** | Chapter D par. 8a | Transport-logistics-warehousing | A licence for distributing drinking water can only be granted to one vehicle of gross weight up to the maximum limit. The truck is allowed to circulate only within the area of the prefecture in which the applicant is seated. | Transport/ Licensing | Following communication with the competent Ministry, we understand that the initial objective of the provision was to ensure that areas lacking a water network would not suffer from water shortage. However, according to the competent Ministry, the provision has become redundant and it is deemed necessary to issue an explanatory circular or to explicitly abolish the provision. | The provision sets an unjustifiable restriction in the number of transportation means that a wholesaler could use in order to transport drinking water. Moreover it imposes a geographical barrier restricting the circulation of drinking water by the said entities outside the area of their seat. Since the competent Ministry has confirmed that this provision is no longer in force, due to reasons of regulatory uncertainty it should be explicitly abolished. | Abolish. | Ministry of Infrastructure, Transport and Networks |
| 168 | **Ministerial Decision A2/29542/5347/1991 "Licensing of private use trucks according to Law 1959/2001"** | Chapter D par. 8c | Transport-logistics-warehousing | If the applicant is a licence holder for a container truck used for own account for the transportation of drinking water of any gross weight based on older provisions, a new licence shall not be granted. | Transport/ Licensing | Following communication with the competent Ministry, we understand that the initial objective of the provision was to ensure that areas lacking a water network would not suffer from water shortage. However, according to the competent Ministry, the provision has become redundant and it is deemed necessary to issue an explanatory circular or to explicitly abolish the provision. | The provision sets an unjustifiable restriction in the number of transportation means that a transport businesses could use in order to engage in the transportation of drinking water. Moreover it imposed a geographical barrier restricting the circulation of drinking water by the said entities outside the area of their seat. Since the competent Ministry has confirmed that this provision is no longer in force, due to reasons of regulatory uncertainty it should be explicitly abolished. | Abolish. | Ministry of Infrastructure, Transport and Networks |
| 169 | **Ministerial Decision A2/29542/5347/1991 "Licensing of private use trucks according to Law 1959/2001"** | Chapter D par. 8d | Transport-logistics-warehousing | Own account container trucks for drinking water may by exemption be used in areas that belong in the same or adjacent Prefectures to the Prefecture that the truck is based, by decision of the competent Prefect/s and given that these areas do not have a watering network and the population is in need of drinking water supplies. | Transport/ Licensing | Following communication with the competent Ministry, we understand that the initial objective of the provision was to ensure that areas lacking a water network would not suffer from water shortage. However, according to the competent Ministry, the provision has become redundant and it is deemed necessary to issue an explanatory circular or to explicitly abolish the provision. | The provision sets an unjustifiable restriction in the number of transportation means that a transport businesses could use in order to engage in the transportation of drinking water. Moreover it imposed a geographical barrier restricting the circulation of drinking water by the said entities outside the area of their seat. Since the competent Ministry has confirmed that this provision is no longer in force, due to reasons of regulatory uncertainty it should be explicitly abolished. | Abolish. | Ministry of Infrastructure, Transport and Networks |
| 170 | **Ministerial Decision A2/29542/5347/1991 "Licensing of private use trucks according to Law 1959/2001"** | Chapter E par. 1 | Transport-logistics-warehousing | The issued licences of trucks of used for own account should stipulate the goods and the materials that will be transported. In case of products referred to as "domestic products or products of general commerce", such products should be named in summary by the competent Tax Authority and be similar. | Transport/ Licensing | The objective of the provision was to allow the roadside control officials to verify whether the private use truck is illegally performing a third party transaction. | While the provision constitutes an administrative burden, we have no evidence of competition distortion. | No recommendation. | Ministry of Infrastructure, Transport and Networks |
| 171 | **Ministerial Decision A2/29542/5347/1991 "Licensing of private use trucks according to Law 1959/2001"** | Chapter D par. 3 | Transport-logistics-warehousing | One or more licences are granted for the use of own account trucks with total gross weight equal to the wholesaler's gross income divided by 400000 rounded up to the closest round number. | Transport/ Licensing | There is no official recital. | Following communication with the competent Ministry, this provision is considered to be abolished by law 4336/2015. However, due to the fact that it discriminated between economic operators on the basis of their gross income, it should be explicitly abolished as it creates regulatory uncertainty. | Explicitly abolish. | Ministry of Infrastructure, Transport and Networks |
| 172 | **Royal Decree 281/1993 "On the codification in a unified document of the provisions of legislative decree 49/1968 "on granting of circulation licence to trucks of private use" and legislative decrees 833/1971 and 1268/1972 amending and completing it"** | art. 1 par. 2a | Transport-logistics-warehousing | Goods transferred by trucks used for own account must either belong to the business or to the professional, or sold to them, bought by them, or leased through leasing agreements. | Transport/ Licensing | There is no official recital. However, it is our understanding that the policy maker did not exclude lease agreements in purpose. Following communication with the competent Ministry, the specific provision intended to include all possible means of property use acquisition. | The provision does not include the case of regular lease agreements for the acquisition of the products transferred, but seems to provide only for the possibility to sign a leasing agreement. It therefore restricts market entry and eliminates applicants, creating artificial scarcity. Must be amended as to explicitly include lease agreements. | The provision should be amended to include all forms of ownership. | Ministry of Infrastructure, Transport and Networks |
| 173 | **Royal Decree 281/1993 "On the codification in a unified document of the provisions of legislative decree 49/1968 "on granting of circulation licence to trucks of private use" and legislative decrees 833/1971 and 1268/1972 amending and completing it"** | art. 2 par. 8 | Transport-logistics-warehousing | The fee paid is limited to 1/3 regarding trucks used for own account that belong to agricultural, farming, poultry, bee keeping and silk worm growing, fishing businesses, forest workers, resin collectors, members or not of agricultural-forestal co-operations or forest businesses. | Fees | There is no official recital. However, following communication with the competent Ministries, we understand that the policymaker's objective was to facilitate the transport of agricultural products within the general framework of promoting agricultural activity. | The provision discriminates between operators based on the category of the products transferred, granting a preferential treatment to agricultural products' transportation. Within the general framework of promoting farming and agricultural activities and operators engaging in these activities, the exemption can be justified. | No recommendation. | Ministry of Infrastructure, Transport and Networks |
| 174 | **Law 1959/1991 "On road transports, communications and other provisions"** | art. 1 par. 2a | Transport-logistics-warehousing | Goods transferred by trucks used for own account must belong to the business or professionals, or they must be sold, bought, leased by leasing agreement, produced, excavated, manufactured or repaired by them and they must be necessary to fit their functional needs. | Transport/ Licensing | There is no official recital. However, following communication with the competent Ministry, our understanding is that the intention of the policy maker was not to exclude regular lease agreements from the scope. | The provision may lead to high costs as it excludes the ability of the wholesaler to lease the goods by regular lease agreements. | The provision should be amended to include lease agreements. | Ministry of Infrastructure, Transport and Networks |
| 175 | **Law 1959/1991 "On road transports, communications and other provisions"** | art. 2 par. 2 | Transport-logistics-warehousing | Granting of only one licence for a truck used for own account is allowed to trucks of 3500 kgs maximum gross weight. | Transport/ Licensing | There is no official recital. However, following communication with the competent Ministry, our understanding is that the provision was not destined to restrict the granting of more licences for trucks above 3,500kgs but to specify the terms of licence granting between different categories of trucks. | No harm to competition was identified. | No recommendation. | Ministry of Infrastructure, Transport and Networks |

## Sector: Wholesale trade

| No | No and title of Regulation | Article | Thematic category | Brief description of the potential obstacle | Keyword | Policy maker's objectives | Harm to competition | Recommendations | Competent Ministry / Authority |
|---|---|---|---|---|---|---|---|---|---|
| 176 | **Law 1959/1991 "On road transports, communications and other provisions"- Also art. 2 par. 2 RD 281/1973 "Private use trucks licensing"** | art. 2 par. 2 | Transport-logistics-warehousing | The contribution paid to the State is limited by one third (1/3) for trucks that belong to agricultural, farming, poultry, beekeeping, silk worm growing, fishing businesses, forest workers, resin collectors that are either members of agricultural-forest co-operations or acting independently as well as trucks exploited by Ο.Δ.Δ.Υ.or trucks that belong to forest businesses . | Transport/ Licensing | There is no official recital. However, following communication with the competent Ministry it is our understanding that the objective of the provision was to promote agricultural activities . | Since farmers will be transferring solely their own production, the exemption granted is proportionate to the policymaker's objective to promote agricultural activities. Moreover, since non professional farmers will be transferring solely their own production, for reasons of equal treatment of operators in the same market, the provision should not discriminate between professional and not professional farmers. | No recommendation. | Ministry of Infrastructure, Transport and Networks |
| 177 | **Law 1959/1991 "On road transports, communications and other provisions"** | art. 2 par. 2 | Transport-logistics-warehousing | Farmers that are not mainly occupied with the farming profession may get only one licence for a truck used for own account of maximum gross weight up to 2500 kgs, or net weight up to 1300 kgs, under the condition that their income derives from any agricultural activity . | Transport/ Licensing | There is no official recital. | Given that non professional farmers' production volume shall not exceed specific amounts, the provision is justified. | No recommendation. | Ministry of Infrastructure, Transport and Networks |
| 178 | **Law 1959/1991 "On road transports, communications and other provisions"** | art. 2 par. 3a | Transport-logistics-warehousing | Licences for trucks used for own account of gross weight over 3500 kgs are exclusively granted for the purposes of exercising a profitable profession or running a business, including agricultural, farming, poultry, silk worm growing, beekeeping, fishing, foresting, as well as forest workers or resin collectors that may or not be members of agricultural co-operations or foresting businesses, under the condition that the exercised profession or business has such a transport load that is absolutely necessary to use a truck. | Transport/ Licensing | There is no official recital. | The provision does not impose a restriction to competition. | No recommendation. | Ministry of Infrastructure, Transport and Networks |
| 179 | **Law 1959/1991 "On road transports, communications and other provisions"** | art. 2 par. 3b (aa) | Transport-logistics-warehousing | During the licence granting, a lump sum contribution is paid to the State and it is calculated:<br>For closed carriage trucks 140000 drachmas, increased by sixteen (16) drachmas/ kg for gross weight exceeding 3500 kgs. | Transport/ Licensing | There is no official recital. | Following communication with the competent Ministry, this provision introduces the obligation of businesses to pay a fee to the state as a requirement to obtain the licence . | No recommendation. | Ministry of Infrastructure, Transport and Networks |
| 180 | **Law 1959/1991 "On road transports, communications and other provisions"** | art. 2 par. 3b (bb) | Transport-logistics-warehousing | For trucks with open carriage, the contribution is 80.000 drachmas, increased by 16 drachmas/kg for gross weight over 3500 kgs. | Transport/ Licensing | There is no official recital. | Following communication with the competent Ministry, this provision introduces the obligation of businesses to pay a fee to the state as a requirement to obtain the licence . | No recommendation. | Ministry of Infrastructure, Transport and Networks |
| 181 | **Law 1959/1991 "On road transports, communications and other provisions"- Also art. 2 par. 3c of RD 281/1973 "Private use trucks licensing"** | art. 2 par. 3c | Transport-logistics-warehousing | Licences for trucks used for own account are final and are granted once the function of the business or the exercise of the profession of the applicant (natural or legal person or consortium) is realised and the applicant has achieved gross income of one million (1000000) drachmas, at least, for every tonne of gross weight of the truck, within any given time period during the past twelve months prior to the filling of the application for the licence. | Transport/ Licensing | There is no official recital. | Following communication with the competent Ministry, this provision has been abolished by law 4336/2015. However, it should be explicitly abolished as it creates regulatory uncertainty for new businesses. | Explicitly abolish. | Ministry of Infrastructure, Transport and Networks |
| 182 | **Law 1959/1991 "On road transports, communications and other provisions"- Also art. 2 par. 3d of RD 281/1973 "Private use trucks licensing"** | art. 2 par. 3d | Transport-logistics-warehousing | Businesses that belong to natural or legal persons or consortiums and have functioned within the last twelve months prior to the filling of the application for a private truck licence, are considered as newly set up businesses. Should these businesses have achieved within the above time frame a gross income of at least one million (1000000) drachmas/tonne of gross weight, then they are licenced based on par. 3c above. However, if they did not have this gross income they are entitled to temporary licences for own account trucks of gross weight over 3500 kgs with one year duration. | Transport/ Licensing | There is no official recital. | Following communication with the competent Ministry, this provision has been abolished by law 4336/2015. However, it should be explicitly abolished as it creates regulatory uncertainty. | Explicitly abolish. | Ministry of Infrastructure, Transport and Networks |
| 183 | **Law 1959/1991 "On road transports, communications and other provisions" and RD 281/1973 art. 4 par. 1h** | art. 4 par. 1 point η | Transport-logistics-warehousing | In the event that the professional or the company exercise exclusively trade without engaging in the production of goods, they are prohibited from transferring their products or goods and objects from the production site directly to the customer. This prohibition is imposed on trucks used for own account of gross weight over 3.5 tonnes. | Transport/ Licensing | There is no official recital. However, following communication with the competent Ministry, it is our understanding that the policy maker's objective was to distinguish between wholesalers and professional transport operators. | The provision limits wholesalers' freedom to distribute their products with the transportation means of their choice, potentially increasing their costs. Following communication with the competent Ministry, we understand that the provision may be abolished. | Abolish. | Ministry of Infrastructure, Transport and Networks |

## Sector: Wholesale trade

| No | No and title of Regulation | Article | Thematic category | Brief description of the potential obstacle | Keyword | Policy maker's objectives | Harm to competition | Recommendations | Competent Ministry / Authority |
|---|---|---|---|---|---|---|---|---|---|
| 184 | **Law 1959/1991 "On road transports, communications and other provisions"** | art. 7 | Transport-logistics-warehousing | The total gross weight of self powered trucks or vehicle combinations of the above mentioned transport businesses, during the time of their set up and function, must be at least one hundred and ten (110) tonnes or the number of trucks used for own account they contribute by use or by ownership must be at least ten (10). | Transport/ Licensing | There is no official recital. However, according to our communication with the competent Ministry, it is our understanding that the provision is considered to be abolished. | Following communication with the competent Ministry, this provision has been abolished by law 3887/2010. However, it should be explicitly abolished as it creates regulatory uncertainty discouraging new businesses willing to enter the market. | Explicitly abolish. | Ministry of Infrastructure, Transport and Networks |
| 185 | **Law 1959/1991 "On road transports, communications and other provisions"** | art. 14 par. 1 | Transport-logistics-warehousing | Individual freelancers that execute national and international road transportations may place into circulation up to two trailers or semi trailers, for every towing vehicle they possess. | Transport/ Licensing | There is no official recital, however, following communication with the competent Ministry, we were informed that the objective of the provision was destined to provide an incentive to the merger of transport entities and the creation of larger ones. However, it is in our understanding that this restriction may be amended. | The provision limits individual freelancers' operation. For instance, the business model of an operator may be to transport trailers to and from a set place, such as a port. Moreover it may raise cost for some operators against others since it limits operational freedom to acquire more trailers per tractor. | Abolish. | Ministry of Infrastructure, Transport and Networks |
| 186 | **Law 1959/1991 "On road transports, communications and other provisions"** | art. 15 par. 1 | Transport-logistics-warehousing | Road transport operators that during the publication of the law are engaged in international or national transports may chose to be included either in the category of national road transports or in the category of international road transports. | Transport/ Licensing | There is no official recital. | Following communication with the competent Ministry, this provision has been abolished by art. 2 par. 5 of law 3887/2010. However, it should be explicitly abolished as it creates regulatory uncertainty discouraging new businesses willing to enter the market. | Explicitly abolish. | Ministry of Infrastructure, Transport and Networks |
| 187 | **Law 1959/1991 "On road transports, communications and other provisions"** | art. 15 par. 2 | Transport-logistics-warehousing | Changing category from national to international road transport and vice versa is possible at any time. | Transport/ Licensing | There is no official recital. | Following communication with the competent Ministry, this provision has been abolished by art. 2 par. 5 of law 3887/2010. However, it should be explicitly abolished as it creates regulatory uncertainty discouraging new businesses willing to enter the market. | Explicitly abolish. | Ministry of Infrastructure, Transport and Networks |
| 188 | **Law 1959/1991 "On road transports, communications and other provisions"** | art. 15 par. 2 | Transport-logistics-warehousing | However, if an international road transporter changes from international to national transport category prior to a period of at least 3 years following his initial classification or his transfer to the national transport category, he must mandatorily remain in the national transport category for at least 5 years. | Transport/ Licensing | There is no official recital. | Following communication with the competent Ministry, this provision has been abolished by art. 2 par. 5 of law 3887/2010. However, it should be explicitly abolished as it creates regulatory uncertainty discouraging new businesses willing to enter the market. | Explicitly abolish. | Ministry of Infrastructure, Transport and Networks |
| 189 | **Law 1959/1991 "On road transports, communications and other provisions"** | art.15 par.5 | Transport-logistics-warehousing | It is prohibited for international transport companies to carry out national road transports. | Transport/ Licensing | There is no official recital. | This provision is no longer in force. Law 4233/2014 allowed for national transport operators to carry out international transports, and vice versa. It may cause legal uncertainty that may discourage new entrants in the relevant market. | Explicitly abolish. | Ministry of Infrastructure, Transport and Networks |
| 190 | **Law 1959/1991 "On road transports, communications and other provisions"** | art.15 par.5 | Transport-logistics-warehousing | It is prohibited for national transport companies to carry out international transports. | Transport/ Licensing | There is no official recital. | This provision is no longer in force. Law 4233/2014 allowed for national transport operators to carry out international transports, and vice versa. It may cause legal uncertainty that may discourage new entrants in the relevant market. | Explicitly abolish. | Ministry of Infrastructure, Transport and Networks |
| 191 | **Joint Ministerial Decision A9/οιχ/16954/1248 "Classification of Private use trucks up to 8 tonnes to beekeeping businesses"** | art. 1 par. 1.1 | Transport-logistics-warehousing | The provision exempts bee keeping businesses from the gross turnover thresholds provided by law 1959/1991 for trucks used for own account. | Transport/ Licensing | There is no official recital. However, it is our understanding that the provision was set out to enhance small agricultural activities such as beekeeping. | Since the provision is not compatible with law 4336/2015, it may cause legal uncertainty that may inhibit new entrants and lead to unequal treatment among competitors during controls by the competent authorities. | Abolish. | Ministry of Rural Development and Food |
| 192 | **Ministerial Decision A2/29542/5347/1991 "Licensing of private use trucks according to Law 1959/2001"** | Chapter B 1a | Transport-logistics-warehousing | Goods transferred with trucks used for own account must either belong to the business or to the professional, or sold, bought, leased through leasing agreements. | Transport/ Licensing | There is no official recital. However, it is our understanding that the policy maker did not exclude lease agreements in purpose. Following communication with the competent Ministry, the specific provision intended to include all possible means of property use acquisition. | The provision does not include the case of regular lease agreements for the acquisition of the use of a product, but seems to provide only for the possibility to sign a leasing agreement. It therefore restricts market entry and eliminates applicants, creating artificial scarcity. Must be amended as to explicitly include lease agreements. | Must be amended as to explicitly include lease agreements. | Ministry of Infrastructure, Transport and Networks |
| 193 | **Ministerial Decision A2/29542/5347/1991 "Licensing of private use trucks according to Law 1959/2001"** | Chapter B 1b | Transport-logistics-warehousing | If the professional or business is exclusively engaged in trading activities, transferring goods from the production site directly to the customer is prohibited if the products are to be transferred with own account trucks of over 4000 kgs. | Transport/ Licensing | There is no official recital. However, following communication with the competent Ministry, it is our understanding that the policy maker's objective was to distinguish between wholesalers and professional transport operators. | The provision limits commercial entities' freedom to provide their products or services with the transportation means of their choice hence raising costs by not allowing economies of scale. | Abolish. | Ministry of Infrastructure, Transport and Networks |
| 194 | **Ministerial Decision A2/29542/5347/1991 "Licensing of private use trucks according to Law 1959/2001"** | Chapter B 1c | Transport-logistics-warehousing | Trucks for own account transport of over 4000 gross weight must be driven by the professional or by business staff who must have a driver's licence or by a professional driver who has been employed with an employment agreement. | Transport/ Licensing | There is no official recital | The provision may raise the cost of operation (labour cost). Since it is the company's responsibility to safeguard the quality of the product and the safety of the transport, the company should be allowed to decide on the nature of the labour agreement. | The provision should be amended to include all types of employment or work contracts. | Ministry of Infrastructure, Transport and Networks |

## Sector: Wholesale trade

| No | No and title of Regulation | Article | Thematic category | Brief description of the potential obstacle | Keyword | Policy maker's objectives | Harm to competition | Recommendations | Competent Ministry / Authority |
|---|---|---|---|---|---|---|---|---|---|
| 195 | **Ministerial Decision A2/29542/5347/1991 "Licensing of private use trucks according to Law 1959/2001"** | Chapter C par. 2 | Transport-logistics-warehousing | Natural or legal persons are entitled only one licence for trucks used for agricultural purposes<br>A certificate issued by the competent Farming Directorate is needed for more licences to be granted to the same person, ascertaining that the specific business of the applicant must have two or more trucks used for own account, for the purposes of his activity.<br>The applicant must file a solemn declaration stating that he has no other truck used for own account of this category. | Transport/ Licensing | There is no official recital. However, following our communication with the competent Ministries, it is our understanding that the provision has not been typically abolished and both competent Ministries agree with the explicit repeal of it. | Following communication with the competent Ministry, this provision has been abolished by art. 2 par. 5 of law 3887/2010. However, it should be explicitly abolished as it creates regulatory uncertainty discouraging new businesses willing to enter the market. | Explicitly abolish. | Ministry of Infrastructure, Transport and Networks |
| 196 | **Ministerial Decision A2/29542/5347/1991 "Licensing of private use trucks according to Law 1959/2001"** | Chapter C par. 2b (dd) | Transport-logistics-warehousing | For professional own account trucks additional evidence is required to prove that the specific vehicle of the applicant is absolutely necessary for the business, in case the transport work of the business is not apparent, due to the nature of the products, the frequency of the transportations and the volume of the transported goods in comparison to the type of the own account truck. | Transport/ Licensing | There is no official recital. However, following our communication with the competent Ministries, it is our understanding that the provision has not been typically abolished and both competent Ministries agree with the explicit repeal of it. | Following communication with the competent Ministry, this provision has been abolished by law 4336/2015. However, it should be explicitly abolished as it creates regulatory uncertainty for new businesses that want to enter the relevant market. | Explicitly abolish. | Ministry of Infrastructure, Transport and Networks |
| 197 | **Ministerial Decision A2/29542/5347/1991 "Licensing of private use trucks according to Law 1959/2001"** | Chapter D par. 2d | Transport-logistics-warehousing | For the granting of an own account truck over 4000kgs licence a certificate of the competent Agriculture Directorate is required certifying the existence of the agricultural business and the necessity for an own account truck of gross weight over 4000kgs. | Transport/ Licensing | There is no official recital. However, following our communication with the competent Ministries, it is our understanding that the provision has not been typically abolished and both competent Ministries agree with the explicit repeal of it. | Following communication with the competent Ministry, this provision has been abolished by law 4336/2015. However, it should be explicitly abolished as it creates regulatory uncertainty for new businesses that want to enter the relevant market. | Explicitly abolish. | Ministry of Infrastructure, Transport and Networks |
| 198 | **Ministerial Decision A2/29542/5347/1991 "Licensing of private use trucks according to Law 1959/2001"** | Chapter D par. 3 | Transport-logistics-warehousing | After filling the documentation required, the competent transport authority grants one or more temporary own account truck licences of total gross weight that equals the result of the division of the gross income to the number 400 000 rounded by the closest whole number. For example a business that has had a gross income of 16 000 000 drachmas within any given time during the past fiscal year may circulate one or more own account trucks of 40 tonnes gross weight. | Transport/ Licensing | There is no official recital. | Following communication with the competent Ministry, this provision has been abolished by law 4336/2015. However, it should be explicitly abolished as it creates regulatory uncertainty discouraging new businesses that want to enter the relevant market. | Explicitly abolish. | Ministry of Infrastructure, Transport and Networks |
| 199 | **Ministerial Decision A2/29542/5347/1991 "Licensing of private use trucks according to Law 1959/2001"** | Chapter D par. 3 | Transport-logistics-warehousing | Temporary licences become final if the same business has 1 000 000 drachmas gross income for every ton of gross weight of its private use trucks within any given time during which the temporary licence was valid.<br>For example, the business mentioned as an example may turn the 40 tonnes gross weight private use trucks temporary licences to final, if it files a tax authority certificate stating that during this period it had 40 000 000 drachmas gross income. | Transport/ Licensing | There is no official recital. | Following communication with the competent Ministry, this provision has been abolished by law 4336/2015. However, it should be explicitly abolished as it creates regulatory uncertainty regarding costs therefore discouraging new businesses that want to enter the relevant market. | Explicitly abolish. | Ministry of Infrastructure, Transport and Networks |
| 200 | **Ministerial Decision A2/29542/5347/1991 "Licensing of private use trucks according to Law 1959/2001"** | Chapter D par. 3 | Transport-logistics-warehousing | If the gross income is less than 1 000 000 drachmas for every ton of gross weight of the truck, then the temporary licences are revoked and they become final own account trucks licences for gross weight that equals the gross income of the business<br>For example, if the business has a gross income of 24 000 000 instead of 40 000 000 then the final licences will turn to own account trucks of 24 tonnes gross weight while the other licences will be revoked. | Transport/ Licensing | There is no official recital. | Following communication with the competent Ministry, this provision has been abolished by law 4336/2015. However, it should be explicitly abolished as it creates regulatory uncertainty regarding costs therefore discouraging new businesses that want to enter the relevant market. | Explicitly abolish. | Ministry of Infrastructure, Transport and Networks |
| 201 | **Ministerial Decision A2/29542/5347/1991 "Licensing of private use trucks according to Law 1959/2001"** | Chapter D par. 5 | Transport-logistics-warehousing | In case the applicant (natural or legal person or consortium or society of heirs) has a business that exercises different activities, the specialised own account truck licence for over 3500kgs gross weight is allowed, if the gross income provided for both the temporary and final licences exist for the particular activity or activities that the specialised truck will be used for. | Transport/ Licensing | There is no official recital. | Following communication with the competent Ministry, this provision has been abolished by law 4336/2015. However, it should be explicitly abolished as it creates regulatory uncertainty regarding costs therefore discouraging new businesses that want to enter the relevant market. | Explicitly abolish. | Ministry of Infrastructure, Transport and Networks |

## Sector: Wholesale trade

| No | No and title of Regulation | Article | Thematic category | Brief description of the potential obstacle | Keyword | Policy maker's objectives | Harm to competition | Recommendations | Competent Ministry / Authority |
|---|---|---|---|---|---|---|---|---|---|
| 202 | **Ministerial Decision A2/29542/5347/1991 "Licensing of private use trucks according to Law 1959/2001"** | Chapter D par. 6 | Transport-logistics-warehousing | By exemption to what is mentioned in par. 3, one (1) final licence for trucks used for own account of over 3500 tonnes may be granted to an industrial or contracting business if in addition to the documentation mentioned in par. 2 a licence or contractor's degree is filed, accordingly and if, within any given time during the past financial year the gross income was at least 20 000 000 drachmas. | Transport/ Licensing | There is no official recital. | Following communication with the competent Ministry, this provision has been abolished by law 4336/2015. However, it should be explicitly abolished as it creates regulatory uncertainty. | Abolish. | Ministry of Infrastructure, Transport and Networks |
| 203 | **Ministerial Decision A2/29542/5347/1991 "Licensing of private use trucks according to Law 1959/2001"** | Chapter D par. 7a | Transport-logistics-warehousing | For specialised trucks used for hire or reward of gross weight over 3500 kgs, apart from the documentation provided in par. 2, for containers used to transfer specific types of oil the licence for the own account truck is granted only to industrial or manufacturing businesses that produce such types of oil. | Transport/ Licensing | There is no official recital. | The provision does not seem to affect wholesalers. | No recommendation | Ministry of Infrastructure, Transport and Networks |
| 204 | **Ministerial Decision A2/29542/5347/1991 "Licensing of private use trucks according to Law 1959/2001"** | Chapter D par. 7b | Transport-logistics-warehousing | For specialised trucks used for own account of gross weight over 3 500 kgs, apart from the documentation provided in par. 2, for container trucks transferring ready concrete the licence for trucks used for own account of this category is granted only in industrial or manufacturing businesses that produce ready concrete. | Transport/ Licensing | There is no official recital. However we understand that the restriction exists to safeguard the quality of the produced concrete. | The provision does not seem to concern wholesalers. | No recommendation | Ministry of Infrastructure, Transport and Networks |
| 205 | **Ministerial Decision A2/29542/5347/1991 "Licensing of private use trucks according to Law 1959/2001"** | Chapter D par. 8a | Transport-logistics-warehousing | Drinking water container truck licences is granted to the applicant only for one vehicle of gross weight that does not exceed the maximum limit and with a right to circulate only within the prefecture where the applicant is seated. | Transport/ Licensing | Following communication with the competent Ministry, we understand that the objective of the provision was to ensure that areas lacking a water network would not suffer from water shortage. | The provision sets an unjustifiable restriction in the number of transportation means that a transport businesses could use in order to engage in the transportation of drinking water. Moreover it imposed a geographical barrier restricting the circulation of drinking water by the said entities outside the area of their seat. Since the competent Ministry has confirmed that this provision is no longer in force, due to reasons of regulatory uncertainty it should be explicitly abolished. | Explicitly abolish. | Ministry of Infrastructure, Transport and Networks |
| 206 | **Ministerial Decision A2/29542/5347/1991 "Licensing of private use trucks according to Law 1959/2001"** | Chapter D par. 8c | Transport-logistics-warehousing | In case the applicant owns an own account container truck of any gross weight, is not allowed to get a new licence. | Transport/ Licensing | Following communication with the competent Ministry, we understand that the objective of the provision was to ensure that areas lacking a water network would not suffer from water shortage. | The provision sets an unjustifiable restriction in the number of transportation means that a transport businesses could use in order to engage in the transportation of drinking water. Moreover it imposed a geographical barrier restricting the circulation of drinking water by the said entities outside the area of their seat. Since the competent Ministry has confirmed that this provision is no longer in force, due to reasons of regulatory uncertainty it should be explicitly abolished. | Explicitly abolish. | Ministry of Infrastructure, Transport and Networks |
| 207 | **Ministerial Decision A2/29542/5347/1991 "Licensing of private use trucks according to Law 1959/2001"** | Chapter D par. 8d | Transport-logistics-warehousing | By exemption, the circulation of own account container trucks for drinking water is allowed in areas of the same or adjacent prefecture where the vehicle is seated by decision of the competent Prefect/ Prefects under the condition that these areas lack a watering network and the citizens are in need of drinking water. | Transport/ Licensing | Following communication with the competent Ministry, we understand that the objective of the provision was to ensure that areas lacking a water network would not suffer from water shortage. | The provision sets an unjustifiable restriction in the number of transportation means that a transport businesses could use in order to engage in the transportation of drinking water. Moreover it imposed a geographical barrier restricting the circulation of drinking water by the said entities outside the area of their seat. Since the competent Ministry has confirmed that this provision is no longer in force, due to reasons of regulatory uncertainty it should be explicitly abolished. | Explicitly abolish. | Ministry of Infrastructure, Transport and Networks |
| 208 | **Ministerial Decision A2/29542/5347/1991 "Licensing of private use trucks according to Law 1959/2001"** | Chapter E par. 1 | Transport-logistics-warehousing | The goods and materials that are allowed to be transferred must be written on the licences of the trucks used for own account, as mentioned in the certificate of the tax authority. | Transport/ Licensing | The objective of the provision was to allow the roadside control officials to verify whether the private use truck actually transfers goods related to the business activity and not illegally performing a third party transaction. | While the provision may constitutes an administrative burden, we have no evidence of competition distortion. | No recommendation. | Ministry of Infrastructure, Transport and Networks |
| 209 | **Ministerial Decision A2/29542/5347/1991 "Licensing of private use trucks according to Law 1959/2001"** | Chapter E par. 1 | Transport-logistics-warehousing | If the licence holder is an industrial or manufacturing business, the raw materials produced by them must also be mentioned on the licence for the truck used for own account. | Transport/ Licensing | The objective of the provision was to allow the roadside control officials to verify whether the private use truck actually transfers goods related to the business activity and not illegally performing a third party transaction. | While the provision may constitutes an administrative burden, we have no evidence of competition distortion on the relevant market. | No recommendation. | Ministry of Infrastructure, Transport and Networks |
| 210 | **Ministerial Decision A2/29542/5347/1991 "Licensing of private use trucks according to Law 1959/2001"** | Chapter E par. 1 | Transport-logistics-warehousing | When products under the term "domestic or general commerce products" are sold, these must be mentioned by the competent tax authority and they must be of the same category. | Transport/ Licensing | The objective of the provision was to allow the roadside control officials to verify whether the private use truck is illegally performing a third party transaction. | While the provision may constitutes an administrative burden, we have no evidence of competition distortion on the relevant market. | No recommendation. | Ministry of Infrastructure, Transport and Networks |
| 211 | **Law 3887/2010 "Road transports"** | art. 2 par. 4 | Transport-logistics-warehousing | International road transports must be carried out by trucks used for hire or reward of over 3.5 tonnes. | Transport/ Licensing | There is no official recital. However, following communication with the competent Ministry, we understand that the provision was set out to safeguard a high quality of services provided at the level of international transports. | The provision sets a restriction on the type of trucks allowed to carry out international transport limiting professional operators' freedom of choice concerning the type of vehicles they will chose. | Abolish. | Ministry of Infrastructure, Transport and Networks |

## Sector: Wholesale trade

| No | No and title of Regulation | Article | Thematic category | Brief description of the potential obstacle | Keyword | Policy maker's objectives | Harm to competition | Recommendations | Competent Ministry / Authority |
|---|---|---|---|---|---|---|---|---|---|
| 212 | **Law 3887/2010 "Road transports"** | art. 2 par. 7 a | Transport-logistics-warehousing | Transport businesses already functioning under a different legal form other than the one provided by the specific law, may continue to function under this legal form for ten years since the transitional period provided in art. 14 par. 1 . | Transport/ Licensing | There is no official recital. However, it is our understanding that the policymaker's objective was to be consistent with the principle of the justified trust of the persons subject to administrative rules, that the regime will only be amended in their favour and not against them. In the specific case, the provision was set out to grant a transitionary period to entities whose economic operation had been organised on the basis of the previous regime. | The provision creates a differential treatment and constitutes grandfathering clause for companies already operating and may benefit for a large time period from the favourable treatment granted to them. However, for reasons of prudent regulation and safeguarding the justified trust to the state, the provision is deemed justified. | No recommendation. | Ministry of Infrastructure, Transport and Networks |
| 213 | **Law 3887/2010 "Road transports"** | art. 2 par. 10a | Transport-logistics-warehousing | "Old transport business" is considered the one already in possession of a licence of a truck used for hire or reward during the expiration of the transitional period of art. 14 par. 1. | Transport/ Licensing | There is no official recital. However, following communication with the competent Ministry, we understand that the distinction between old and new entities is attributed to consistency with the provisions set out in Ministerial Decision B1/38810/3156/2014/ (B'1809). | The provision grants a preferential treatment towards old operators, creating a grandfathering clause. It therefore raises the cost of new suppliers relative to incumbents, possibly protecting them from competition, as they may profit from different terms for proving their credibility. | Abolish. | Ministry of Infrastructure, Transport and Networks |
| 214 | **Law 3887/2010 "Road transports"** | art. 2 par. 10b | Transport-logistics-warehousing | "Old transport business" for the purposes of the law is considered the one getting for the first time a licence for a truck used for hire or reward after the expiration of the transitional period of art. 14 par. 1 and consists exclusively by old transporters or has been formed as a result of a change in the company name, entrance or exit of an old partner, transformation, merger, dissolution, selling of, or buy off of old transporters. | Transport/ Licensing | There is no official recital. However, following communication with the competent Ministry, we understand that the distinction between old and new entities is attributed to consistency with the provisions set out in Ministerial Decision B1/38810/3156/2014/ (B'1809). | The provision grants a preferential treatment towards old operators, creating a grandfathering clause. It therefore raises the cost of new suppliers relative to incumbents, possibly protecting them from competition, as they may profit from different terms for proving their credibility. | Abolish. | Ministry of Infrastructure, Transport and Networks |
| 215 | **Law 3887/2010 "Road transports"** | art. 2 par. 10c | Transport-logistics-warehousing | "Old transport business" for the purposes of the law, is considered the natural person acquiring for the first time a licence for a truck used for hire or reward after the expiration of the transitional period of art. 14 par. 1 either through parental grant, donation and transfer by a relative up to second grade or spouse, or through inheritance. | Transport/ Licensing | There is no official recital. However, following communication with the competent Ministry, we understand that the distinction between old and new entities is attributed to consistency with the provisions set out in Ministerial Decision B1/38810/3156/2014/ (B'1809). | The provision grants a preferential treatment towards old operators, creating a grandfathering clause. It therefore raises the cost of new suppliers relative to incumbents, possibly protecting them from competition, as they may profit from different terms for proving their credibility. | Abolish. | Ministry of Infrastructure, Transport and Networks |
| 216 | **Law 3887/2010 "Road transports"** | art. 2 par. 11 | Transport-logistics-warehousing | "New transport business" for the purposes of the law is the one acquiring a licence for a truck used for hire or reward for the first time after the expiration of the transitional period of art. 14 par. 1 and does not belong to the categories described under art. 2 par. 10. | Transport/ Licensing | There is no official recital. However, following communication with the competent Ministry, we understand that the distinction between old and new entities is attributed to consistency with the provisions set out in Ministerial Decision B1/38810/3156/2014/ (B'1809) . | The provision grants a preferential treatment towards old operators, creating a grandfathering clause. It therefore raises the cost of new suppliers relative to incumbents, possibly protecting them from competition, as they may profit from different terms for proving their credibility. | Abolish. | Ministry of Infrastructure, Transport and Networks |
| 217 | **Law 3887/2010 "Road transports"** | art. 3 par. 2b | Transport-logistics-warehousing | An SA or LLC can be set up to execute national, international, special or prefectural transports, through contribution of a privately owned truck used for hire or through a leased one. This lease agreement may include a driver on a fee under the terms and conditions of pd 91/1988 by predetermined compensation calculated on the basis of the distance, according to the contractual terms concerning the transport work determined by the transport company. | Transport/ Licensing | Following our communication with the competent Ministry, it is our understanding that the provision is no longer in force, as the lease of the trucks is regulated by Directive 2006/1/EC. | The provision describes in detail how the compensation will be set in the lease agreement. It overly restricts the freedom of transport business to choose the terms of the lease agreement and the terms of the employment agreement (since this may also be covered in the lease agreement) thus reducing their ability to compete. | Abolish the sentence starting "under the terms and conditions of p.d 91/1988…". | Ministry of Infrastructure, Transport and Networks |
| 218 | **Law 3887/2010 "Road transports"** | art. 8 | Transport-logistics-warehousing | In case the transport companies that were set up based on art. 3 are dissolved, the trucks used for hire or reward that belonged to them together with the corresponding truck licence are passed on to their shareholders or partners, without any tax obligation described in art. 10 par. 1 (after creditors have been satisfied). | Transport/ Licensing | Following communication with the competent Ministry, it is our understanding that the provision is destined to provide an incentive to transport companies to merge and form larger and more competitive entities. Moreover, the objective was to grant the ability to shareholders to acquire the trucks owned by company after its dissolution. | No harm to competition was identified. | No recommendation. | Ministry of Infrastructure, Transport and Networks |
| 219 | **Law 3887/2010 "Road transports"** | art. 11 par. 1 | Transport-logistics-warehousing | The toll cost must mandatorily be calculated and deposited in addition to the transportation fare that has been agreed, and the toll payment receipt shall be mentioned separately. | Transport/ Licensing | There is no official recital. It is our understanding that the provision aims at protecting the professional transport operators from unforeseen fluctuations in toll payments. | No harm to competition was identified, as it helps in the transparency of contractual terms. | No recommendation. | Ministry of Infrastructure, Transport and Networks |
| 220 | **Joint Ministerial Decision 9944/734/2014 "Amending the Joint Ministerial Decision 14366/416/9-5-2013 "National Stevedores Registry- defining the documentation for the exercise of the profession of land and port stevedore""** | art. 2 par. 1 | Transport-logistics-warehousing | All loadings/ unloadings carried out on the land or in ports, irrespectively of the legal status under which the place of loading/ unloading is used, as well as all transfer and piling of goods or other moveables must be carried out by workers registered with the National Stevedores' Registry. | Registration | There is no official recital. | The obligatory hiring of stevedores in Registry Type A for non-specialised works may impose an extra financial burden to wholesalers, creating an artificial demand for this type of services. | Abolish the obligation to use exclusively stevedores registered with type A Registry. | Ministry of Infrastructure, Transport and Networks |

## Sector: Wholesale trade

| No | No and title of Regulation | Article | Thematic category | Brief description of the potential obstacle | Keyword | Policy maker's objectives | Harm to competition | Recommendations | Competent Ministry / Authority |
|---|---|---|---|---|---|---|---|---|---|
| 221 | **Joint Ministerial Decision 9944/734/2014 "Amending the Joint Ministerial Decision 14366/416/9-5-2013 "National Stevedores Registry- defining the documentation for the exercise of the profession of land and port stevedore""** | art. 2 par. 2 | Transport-logistics-warehousing | The following activities are exempt from the obligations set in the Ministerial Decision<br>a) Loading of agricultural or farming and animal feed products, fertilisers, agricultural supplies or other products that belong to producers from the production site to storage places on account of the producers<br>b) loading or unloading of products in industrial production sites<br>c) loading/ unloading works by legal persons that acted before publication of law 4093/2012 as concessionaires or providers of port loading/ unloading services, under the condition that there is a training system in matters of hygiene and security of the permanent personnel or contractors, when this system is carried out by a recognised operator. Employees of the above legal persons are considered as equal to the ones mentioned in par. 4 sub par. IA 7 of law 4093/2012 only if their employment or contractual relationship is in force for the exercise of the company activity, without any geographical restrictions. | Registration | There is no official recital. | The exception is not justified on public interest grounds and it imposes extra costs for some suppliers relevant to others, granting a preferential treatment. | Abolish. | Ministry of Labour and Social Security / Shipping |
| 222 | **Joint Ministerial Decision 9944/734/2014 "Amending the Joint Ministerial Decision 14366/416/9-5-2013 "National Stevedores Registry- defining the documentation for the exercise of the profession of land and port stevedore""** | art. 3 par. 1a | Transport-logistics-warehousing | The National Stevedores Registry includes:<br>a) Registry A (Entry): Stevedores that execute loading/ unloadings for operating all loads, apart from the specialised or dangerous loads and apart from operating machinery or vehicles used for loading/ unloading and specialised loading/ unloading work. | Registration | There is no official recital. | No harm to competition was identified. | No recommendation. | Ministry of Labour and Social Security, Ministry of Shipping |
| 223 | **Ministerial Decision 460/15662/2013 "General Unified Work Regulation for carrying out land loading/ unloading works"** | art. 1 par. 5 | Transport-logistics-warehousing | By exemption, the following works may not be carried out by workers that have the certificate of paragraph 4 subparagraph IA 7 of art. 1 of Law 4093/2012<br>a) Loading of agricultural or farming and animal feed products, fertilisers, agricultural supplies or other products that belong to producers from the production site to storage places on account of the producers<br>b) loading or unloading of products in industrial production sites<br>c) art. 40 par. 4c of law 4144/2013. | Exemption from obligation | There is no official recital. | The exception is not justified on public interest grounds and it imposes extra costs for some suppliers relevant to others, granting a preferential treatment. | Abolish. | Ministry of Labour and Social Security, Ministry of Shipping |
| 224 | **Law 4093/2012 "Approval of the Midterm Framework of Fiscal Strategy for 2013-2016 - Emergency Measures for the implementation of law 4046/2012 and the Midterm Framework of Fiscal Strategy 2013-2016"** | art. 1 IA 7 par. 1 | Transport-logistics-warehousing | All loading/ unloading of goods or other movable objects independently of the legal status of the loading, unloading, transportation and piling site (such as central markets, ports, etc.) are carried out by workers that have the certificate of par. 4. The port zones of Piraeus and Thessaloniki are exempt. | Exemption from obligation | There is no official recital. | The obligatory hiring of stevedores in Registry Type A for non-specialised works may impose an extra financial burden to wholesalers, creating an artificial demand for this type of services. | Abolish the obligation to use exclusively stevedores registered with type A Registry. | Ministry of Labour and Social Security, Ministry of Shipping |
| 225 | **Law 4093/2012 "Approval of the Midterm Framework of Fiscal Strategy for 2013-2016 - Emergency Measures for the implementation of law 4046/2012 and the Midterm Framework of Fiscal Strategy 2013-2016"** | art. 1 IA 7 par. 2 | Transport-logistics-warehousing | By exemption, the following works may not be carried out by workers that have the certificate of paragraph 4<br>a) Loading of agricultural or farming and animal feed products, fertilisers, agricultural supplies or other products that belong to producers from the production site to storage places on account of the producers<br>b) loading or unloading of products in industrial production sites<br>c)loadings or unloadings by legal persons that prior to the publication of this law were acting as concessionaires or providers of port loading/ unloading services as long as there is a training system on hygiene and safety issues of the permanent personnel or any contractors, by a recognised body. These employees for the entire duration of their contract are considered as equal to the ones mentioned in par. 4 for exercising the company activity without any geographical limitations. | Exemption from obligation | There is no official recital. | The exception is not justified on public interest grounds and it imposes extra costs for some suppliers relevant to others, granting a preferential treatment. | Abolish. | Ministry of Labour and Social Security, Ministry of Shipping |

## Sector: Wholesale trade

| No | No and title of Regulation | Article | Thematic category | Brief description of the potential obstacle | Keyword | Policy maker's objectives | Harm to competition | Recommendations | Competent Ministry / Authority |
|---|---|---|---|---|---|---|---|---|---|
| 226 | **Law 4093/2012 "Approval of the Midterm Framework of Fiscal Strategy for 2013-2016 - Emergency Measures for the implementation of law 4046/2012 and the Midterm Framework of Fiscal Strategy 2013-2016"** | par. IE 4bb | Transport-logistics-warehousing | Businesses and professionals not engaged in transportations, exercising a business or a profession in Greece may rent trucks used for own account from other transport businesses and professional non transporters that exercise a business or profession in Greece, without any limitation in the gross weight of the vehicle. In this case, the truck's transportation work leased must be the same as the transportation work of the lessor. | Licensing | There is no official recital. However, following our communication with the competent Ministry, it is our understanding that the policy maker's objective was to ensure safety of transportation means and road safety. | Since the licence granted for the own account truck corresponds to a broad range of products, the wording of the provision seems to be more restrictive than the objective of the policy maker. It limits freedom of businesses as regards the transportation of their products, possibly leading to high costs and barriers to entry. | Amend the provision to allow for products similar to the ones mentioned in the licence, or suitable to meet the requirements of the licence. | Ministry of Infrastructure, Transport and Networks |
| 227 | **Law 3446/2006 "Organisation and function of the traffic of vehicles controlling authorities-Provisions on passengers' transportation etc."** | art. 3 par. 2A | Transport-logistics-warehousing | Trucks (conducting either transport for hire or on own account) or their combinations having the shape of a platform may transfer a load up to two vacant trailers or semi trailers with platform shaped coachwork within a distance of 20 km from and to the Piraeus port and 10km from and to the rest of the ports. | Geographical restriction | According to our communication with the competent Ministry, it is our understanding that the objective of the provision was to facilitate especially transportation carried out in the islands. It is recognised as introducing an exceptional treatment but it is justified as proportionate, as it applies only to small distance transports of loads being unloaded from ships. Reasons of avoidance of negative impact on the road safety are also mentioned. | Due to reasons of public safety the provision is deemed proportionate to the policy maker's objective. No harm to competition is identified. | No recommendation. | Ministry of Infrastructure, Transport and Networks |
| 228 | **Law 3446/2006 "Organisation and function of the traffic of vehicles controlling authorities - Provisions on passengers' transportation etc."** | art. 3 par. 2A | Transport-logistics-warehousing | The restriction imposed on trucks or their combinations having the shape of a platform transferring a load up to two vacant trailers or semi trailers with platform shaped coachwork within a distance of 20 km from and to the Piraeus port and 10km from and to the rest of the ports is also applicable to own account trucks and their combinations. | Restriction in the exercise of profession | According to our communication with the competent Ministry, it is our understanding that the objective of the provision was to facilitate especially transportation carried out in the islands. It is recognised as introducing an exceptional treatment but it is justified as proportionate, as it applies only to small distance transports of loads being unloaded from ships. Reasons of avoidance of negative impact on the road safety are also mentioned. | Due to reasons of public safety the provision is deemed proportionate to the policy maker's objective. No harm to competition is identified. | No recommendation. | Ministry of Infrastructure, Transport and Networks |
| 229 | **Law 3446/2006 "Organisation and function of the traffic of vehicles controlling authorities - Provisions on passengers' transportation etc."** | art. 3 par. 2A | Transport-logistics-warehousing | The restriction imposed on trucks or their combinations having the shape of a platform transferring a load up to two vacant trailers or semi trailers with platform shaped coachwork within a distance of 20 km from and to the Piraeus port and 10 km from and to the rest of the ports is also applicable to trucks used for hire or reward, and their combinations. | Restriction in the exercise of profession | According to our communication with the competent Ministry, it is our understanding that the objective of the provision was to facilitate especially transportation carried out in the islands. It is recognised as introducing an exceptional treatment but it is justified as proportionate, as it applies only to small distance transports of loads being unloaded from ships. Reasons of avoidance of negative impact on the road safety are also mentioned. | Due to reasons of public safety the provision is deemed proportionate to the policy maker's objective. No harm to competition is identified. | No recommendation. | Ministry of Infrastructure, Transport and Networks |
| 230 | **Ministerial Decision B1/13 082/1410/ 2012 "Proof of the financial standing for the issuance of Road transport operator licence"** | entire MD | Transport-logistics-warehousing | For the issuance of the road transport operator licence for SAs, companies must have a minimum capital and reserves of EUR 9000 for the first vehicle and EUR 5000 euros for every additional vehicle. For company types other than SAs, companies must have a minimum capital and reserves of EUR 18000 for the first vehicle and EUR 9000 for every additional vehicle. To prove the financial standing of the transport business, a letter of guarantee is filed from a bank seated and legally functioning in a member state. The letter of guarantee must cover entirely the amounts required for the issuance of the road transport operator licence. | Minimum capital requirement | There is no official recital. However, following communication with the competent Ministry, the entire Ministerial Decision is considered to have been abolished. | Obsolete provision creating regulatory uncertainty related with high potential entry costs. | Explicitly abolish. | Ministry of Infrastructure, Transport and Networks |
| 231 | **Law 4302/2014 "Issues of supply chain and other provisions"** | art. 1e | Transport-logistics-warehousing | Storage and distribution centre: the total number of establishments, sheltered or not, including the parking spaces for all types of vehicles, that exclusively accommodate the exercise of one or more main supply chain activities. Such establishments must be autonomous, in the sense that they must not function within the same space as the industrial or manufacturing or retail or farming activity by the same person and accommodate this activity. | Activity restriction | Following our communication with the competent Ministries, the objective of the provision was not to restrict the exercising of multiple activities within the same establishment, but to set out comprehensive definitions of logistics centres, for purposes of clarity regarding their licensing requirements. | No recommendation for change. | No recommendation. | Ministry of Infrastructure, Transport and Networks |
| 232 | **Law 4302/2014 "Issues of supply chain and other provisions"** | art. 8 par. 1 | Transport-logistics-warehousing | All storage and distribution centres that are not classified under category A´ of law 4014/2011 are exempt from obtaining a licence (both for establishment and function) whether they have mechanical equipment or not. | Licensing | Following our communication with the competent Ministries, the objective of the provision was not to restrict the exercising of multiple activities within the same establishment, but to set out comprehensive definitions of logistics centres, for purposes of clarity regarding their licensing requirements | No recommendation for change. | No recommendation. | Ministry of Infrastructure, Transport and Networks |
| 233 | **Law 4302/2014 "Issues of supply chain and other provisions"** | art. 8 par. 2 | Transport-logistics-warehousing | For the installation or extension or upgrading of the storage and Distribution centres that, irrespectively of whether they have mechanical equipment or not, fall under the subcategory A2 of law 4014/2011, the licensing authority must issue a licence. | Licensing | Following our communication with the competent Ministries, the objective of the provision was not to restrict the exercising of multiple activities within the same establishment, but to set out comprehensive definitions of logistics centres, for purposes of clarity regarding their licensing requirements. | No recommendation for change. | No recommendation. | Ministry of Infrastructure, Transport and Networks |

## Sector: Wholesale trade

| No | No and title of Regulation | Article | Thematic category | Brief description of the potential obstacle | Keyword | Policy maker's objectives | Harm to competition | Recommendations | Competent Ministry / Authority |
|---|---|---|---|---|---|---|---|---|---|
| 234 | **Ministerial Decision Β1/οικ.7397/786/2012 "Defining the height of the contribution paid to the State for the purposes of granting and renewal of Road transport operator licences of law 3887/2010"** | art. 2 par. 1 | Transport-logistics-warehousing | The contribution to the state is set to EUR 500 for transport businesses that have an A.O.M. according to law 3887/2010, for every vehicle owned or leased which is used for the road transports. | Fees | Following communication with the competent Ministry, the provision is set to relate the administrative cost of the state required for the issuance of a licence. Similar requirements are met in the national legislation of other member states. | No recommendation for change. | No recommendation. | Ministry of Infrastructure, Transport and Networks |
| 235 | **Royal Decree 361/1964 "Exempting the owners of small manufacturing workshops or warehouses from the obligation to obtain an establishment or operation licence"** | art 1 par.1 | Transport-logistics-warehousing | Owners of warehouses with total capacity of 1000 $m^3$ are exempt from the obligation to obtain a licence under Law ΔΚΣΤ'/1912 "on the terms of establishing Industrial Factories". | Licensing | There is no official recital. | The provision is obsolete and should be explicitly abolished due to legal uncertainty reasons that may discourage the entry of new businesses and limit the competitive powers in the market. | Explicitly abolish. | Ministry of Economy, Development and Tourism |
| 236 | **Royal Decree 361/1964 "Exempting the owners of small manufacturing workshops or warehouses from the obligation to obtain an establishment or operation licence"** | art 1 par. 2b | Transport-logistics-warehousing | Warehouses or storage shops for explosive materials of quantity over 20 kgs, warehouses and gas stations storage gas or liquid gas over 100 kgs, paraffin oil or alcohol over 300 kgs and oil over 6 tonnes if there is no oil pump and other relevant establishments<br>do not fall under the exemption of art. 1 par. 1. | Licensing | There is no official recital. | The provision is obsolete and should be explicitly abolished due to legal uncertainty reasons that may discourage the entry of new businesses and limit the competitive powers in the market. | Abolish. | Ministry of Economy, Development and Tourism |
| 237 | **Royal Decree 361/1964 "Exempting the owners of small manufacturing workshops or warehouses from the obligation to obtain an establishment or operation licence"** | art 1 par. 2c | Transport-logistics-warehousing | Warehouses and storage shops for explosive or flammable materials irrespectively of the quantities stored, do not fall under the exemption of art. 1 par. 1 if their building is wooden or flammable. | Licensing | There is no official recital. | The provision is obsolete and should be explicitly abolished due to legal uncertainty reasons that may discourage the entry of new businesses and limit the competitive powers in the market. | Abolish. | Ministry of Economy, Development and Tourism |
| 238 | **Ministerial Decision Ε1γ/10871/1961 "Warehouses for storage semi processed-non processed leather"** | art. 1c | Transport-logistics-warehousing | Warehouses storage semi processed - non processed leather are not allowed to be established along the length of the national roads or at a distance less than 300m vertically of the national road axis. | Geographical restriction | There is no official recital, however, according to our communication with the competent Ministry, it is our understanding that the objective of the policy maker was to safeguard public safety, given that the activity of the specific warehouses requires for strict measures due to hygiene reasons. | The provision may restrict the businesses freedom of establishment. We understand that some warehouses are located outside the scope of general city plan. Based on communication with the authorities, we understand that these warehouses need some special regulation, such as the provision in question. | No recommendation. | Ministry of Health |
| 239 | **Ministerial Decision Ε1γ/10871/1961 "Warehouses for storage semi processed-non processed leather"** | art. 1c | Transport-logistics-warehousing | Warehouses may function along the length of the national roads or at a smaller than 300m distance from the national roads axis, if the local circumstances allow that exemption, under the condition that these warehouses are located around legally functioning slaughterhouses or within existing industrial zones. | Geographical restriction | There is no official recital, however, according to our communication with the competent Ministry, it is our understanding that the objective of the policy maker was to safeguard public safety, given that the activity of the specific warehouses requires for strict measures due to hygiene reasons. | The provision may restrict the businesses freedom of establishment. We understand that some warehouses are located outside the scope of general city plan. Based on communication with the authorities, we understand that these warehouses need some special regulation, such as the provision in question. | No recommendation. | Ministry of Health |
| 240 | **Presidential Decree 03/1924 "Working terms in figs processing workshops and warehouses"** | art. 4 | Transport-logistics-warehousing | The height of the storage rooms for figs must not be less than 4m. | Establishment requirements | There is no official recital. | The provision is obsolete and should be explicitly abolished due to legal uncertainty reasons that may discourage the entry of new businesses and limit competition in the market. | Abolish. | Ministry of Labour |
| 241 | **Presidential Decree 03/1924 "Working terms in figs processing workshops and warehouses"** | art. 5 | Transport-logistics-warehousing | The floors of figs warehouses' must be made of paraffined wood. | Establishment requirements | There is no official recital. | The provision is obsolete and should be explicitly abolished due to legal uncertainty reasons that may discourage the entry of new businesses and limit competition in the market. | Abolish. | Ministry of Labour |
| 242 | **Royal Decree 05/1923 "Rules on hygiene and cleanliness of raisin warehouses"** | art. 4 | Transport-logistics-warehousing | The height of the raisin warehouses must not be lower than 3m. | Establishment requirements | There is no official recital. | The provision is obsolete and should be explicitly abolished due to legal uncertainty reasons that may discourage the entry of new businesses and limit competition in the market. | Abolish. | Ministry of Labour |
| 243 | **Royal Decree 05/1923 "Rules on hygiene and cleanliness of raisin warehouses"** | art. 5 | Transport-logistics-warehousing | The floor of the warehouses must be wooden and covered by a non hydroscopic material. | Establishment requirements | There is no official recital. | The provision is obsolete and should be explicitly abolished due to legal uncertainty reasons that may discourage the entry of new businesses and limit competition in the market. | Abolish. | Ministry of Labour |
| 244 | **Law 4072/2012 "Improvement of investment environment-New Company type-Trademarks- Real Estate Agents- Issues concerning Shipping, ports and fishing and other provisions"** | art. 51 | Framework Legislation | The Private Company (IKE) set up process is carried out through the One Stop Shop as described in art. 5A law 3853/2010, even if a licence for the function of the business is required. | Company set up | The policymaker's objective was to simplify the set up procedure for the new company type. However, there is no evidence that the objective was to exclude other company types from the simplification procedure, rather than gradually initiate the abolition of the lengthy set up procedure for them. | The set up of other legal forms that wish to engage in sanitary interest activities is facilitated through the previous complex and timely system. These companies cannot benefit from the cost and time savings of the one stop shop system. Higher costs for some company types, not justifiable for public safety reasons | The provision should be amended to explicitly provide for the ability of all legal forms independently of their sanitary interest activity to be set up through the One Stop Shop. | Ministry of Economy, Development and Tourism |

## Sector: Wholesale trade

| No | No and title of Regulation | Article | Thematic category | Brief description of the potential obstacle | Keyword | Policy maker's objectives | Harm to competition | Recommendations | Competent Ministry / Authority |
|---|---|---|---|---|---|---|---|---|---|
| 245 | **Law 4072/2012 "Improvement of investment environment- New Company type- Trademarks- Real Estate Agents- Issues concerning Shipping, ports and fishing and other provisions"** | art. 282 par. 2 | Framework Legislation | Only the ability of transformation of Limited Proprietorships (EE) into Private Proprietorships (OE) is provided. | Company set up | It was not possible to identify the policymaker's objective. | Legal uncertainty caused by the fact that the transformation of a Private Proprietorship into Limited Proprietorship is not explicitly provided in the law while the previous regime granted this ability. | The provision should be amended to explicitly provide for Private Proprietorships (OE) to be allowed to transform into Limited Proprietorships (EE). | Ministry of Economy, Development and Tourism |
| 246 | **Law 4384/2016 "Agricultural co-operatives, forms of collective organisation of rural areas and other provisions. Amendment of Laws 4152/2013 on fertilisers and seeds and 4036/2012 on plant protection products"** | art. 47 | Wholesale trade of seeds and propagating material | a) Seed and propagating material enterprises (producing and/or trading) are obliged to employ a full-time "responsible scientist", at every production / trading facility, via dependent work contract.<br>b) An exemption is granted to micro seed and propagating material producing or trading enterprises: the "responsible scientist" can be employed via part-time dependent work contract.<br>c) An exemption is granted to micro Nursery Type A or B or Vine Nursery enterprises: the "responsible scientist" can be employed via part-time dependent work contract or via service contract.<br>d) Micro Nursery Type A or B or Vine Nursery enterprises with more than one production / trading facility in the same or neighbouring municipality, are considered as one facility and thus can employ one "responsible scientist". | Licensing - Raises cost of entry | a) There is no official recital. However, following communication with the Ministry, the notification of a responsible scientist is necessary as it guarantees that high quality seeds are produced, there is compliance with the phytosanitary conditions to avoid genetic contamination and to protect biodiversity and the environment, the terms of the Technical Regulations are met, there is no seed degradation and quality control procedures are followed.<br>b) There is no official recital. However, following communication with the Ministry, the exemption is granted in order to facilitate market operation and adjust to the operating environment by reducing labour costs.<br>c) There is no official recital. However, following communication with the Ministry, the exemption is granted in order to facilitate market operation.<br>d) According to the official recital, nursery enterprises usually have more than one fixed production / trading facilities. Based on their size and proximity, it is possible to be supervised by the same responsible scientist. | a) This provision may raise the cost of operation (labour cost), however, in general principle, the requirement of notification of a responsible scientist is justified and proportionate to the objective.<br>b) In principle, the implementation of the part-time employment is proportionate to the objective, although it creates differential treatment between different size of enterprises. Note: prior JMD 1153/16620/2014 provided for part-time employment of the responsible scientist for both micro and small enterprises and PD 159/2014 provided the implementation terms/details.<br>c) This provision may seem to create differential treatment between the several categories of enterprises, however, it is justified and proportionate to the objective.<br>d) This exemption is justified and proportionate to the objective. | a-d) No recommendation. | Ministry of Interior and Administrative Reconstruction/ Economy, Development and Tourism / Finance/ Justice, Transparency and Human Rights / Rural Development and Food / Education, Research and Religious Affairs / Health |
| 247 | **Presidential Decree 159/2014 "Part-time employment of Responsible Scientist in small and micro enterprises of production and trade of seeds and propagating material and trade of fertilisers"** | art. 1 par. 3 | Wholesale trade of seeds and propagating material | In the case of micro or small seed and propagating material producing enterprises, the "responsible scientist", employed part-time, has to be present at least: 20 hours per week for Seed Producing and Nursery Type C enterprises and 10 hours per week for Nursery Type A and B enterprises. | Licensing - Regulatory uncertainty | Recent Law 4384/2016, art.47, grants an exemption for the part-time employment of the responsible scientist only to micro seed and propagating material producing or trading enterprises. Therefore, this provision is no longer valid and thus creates regulatory uncertainty. Following communication with the Ministry, the objective of the provision was to reduce labour cost for micro or small seed and propagating material producing enterprises. | This provision is obsolete and creates regulatory uncertainty. | Explicitly repeal the provision and introduce the implementing legislation for Law 4384/2016. | Ministry of Rural Development and Food |
| 248 | **Presidential Decree 159/2014 "Part-time employment of Responsible Scientist in small and micro enterprises of production and trade of seeds and propagating material and trade of fertilisers"** | art. 1 par. 5 | Wholesale trade of seeds and propagating material | In the case of micro or small seed and propagating material trading enterprises, the "responsible scientist", employed part-time, has to be present at least 20 hours per week for Seed and Propagating Material Trading Type A, B and C enterprises. | Licensing - Regulatory uncertainty | The recent Law 4384/2016, art.47, grants an exemption for the part-time employment of the responsible scientist only to micro seed and propagating material producing or trading enterprises. Therefore, this provision is no longer valid and thus creates regulatory uncertainty. Following communication with the Ministry, the objective of the provision was to reduce labour cost for micro or small seed and propagating material producing enterprises. | This provision is obsolete and creates regulatory uncertainty. | Explicitly repeal the provision and introduce the implementing legislation for Law 4384/2016. | Ministry of Rural Development and Food |
| 249 | **Presidential Decree 159/2014 "Part-time employment of Responsible Scientist in small and micro enterprises of production and trade of seeds and propagating material and trade of fertilisers"** | art. 1 par. 6 | Wholesale trade of seeds and propagating material | In the case of a micro or small seed and propagating material producing and trading enterprise holding more than one type of licence, it can have the same "responsible scientist" in maximum two types of enterprises. | Licensing - Raises cost of entry - Regulatory uncertainty | It was not possible to identify the objective of the specific provision. However, it is our understanding that the provision aims on the one hand to facilitate operation for the micro or small enterprises and on the other hand to facilitate control for the requirement of the responsible scientist. | Setting a restriction for the same responsible scientist in maximum two types of enterprises raises the cost of operation (labour cost). Also, this provision is obsolete, since recent Law 4384/2016, art.47, grants an exemption for the part-time employment of the responsible scientist only to micro seed and propagating material producing or trading enterprises. | Abolish | Ministry of Rural Development and Food |
| 250 | **Joint Ministerial Decision 1153/16620/2014 "Requirements and start up process of seeds and propagating material producing and trading enterprises"** | art. 2 par. στ | Wholesale trade of seeds and propagating material | Type B trading enterprises can only sell seeds and propagating material in Greece; also, they cannot import, but they can only trade products either locally produced or purchased from Type A trading enterprises. | Licensing - Trading of products | It was not possible to identify the objective of the specific provision. However, it is our understanding that the provision aims to set specific requirements for different types of enterprises, in order to facilitate control. | This provision limits the number and range of suppliers and creates a geographical barrier to the ability of enterprises to supply their goods. It leaves no room for economies of scale for the trading enterprises, increases costs and restricts their business strategies, by determining both their suppliers and the markets for selling their products. | Abolish the restriction on intra-EU and extra-EU trade. | Ministry of Finance / Rural Development and Food |
| 251 | **Joint Ministerial Decision 1153/16620/2014 "Requirements and start up process of seeds and propagating material producing and trading enterprises"** | art. 2 par. ζ | Wholesale trade of seeds and propagating material | Type C trading enterprises can only sell seeds and propagating material in Greece; also, they cannot import, but they can only trade products either locally produced or purchased from Type A trading enterprises. | Licensing - Trading of products | It was not possible to identify the objective of the specific provision. However, it is our understanding that the provision aims to set specific requirements for different types of enterprises, in order to facilitate control. | This provision limits the number and range of suppliers and it creates a geographical barrier to the ability of enterprises to supply their goods. It leaves no room for economies of scale for the trading enterprises, increases costs and restricts their business strategies, by determining both their suppliers and the markets for selling their products. | Abolish the restriction on intra-EU and extra-EU trade. Consequently, this would mean that Type C category becomes obsolete, as it would be exactly similar to Type A category. | Ministry of Finance / Rural Development and Food |
| 252 | **Joint Ministerial Decision 1153/16620/2014 "Requirements and start up process of seeds and propagating material producing and trading enterprises"** | art. 3 | Wholesale trade of seeds and propagating material | Seed and propagating material enterprises (all types of article 2) are obliged to employ a "responsible scientist" (special requirements are set); he/she can be employed full-time or part-time. In case of part-time employment, appropriately trained personnel has to be employed who follows the instructions of the "responsible scientist". | Licensing - Raises cost of entry | There is no official recital. However, following communication with the Ministry, the exemption is granted in order to facilitate market operation and adjust to the operating environment by reducing labour costs. | No harm to competition has been identified. The implementation of part-time employment is proportionate to the objective. | No recommendation | Ministry of Finance / Rural Development and Food |

## Sector: Wholesale trade

| No | No and title of Regulation | Article | Thematic category | Brief description of the potential obstacle | Keyword | Policy,maker's objectives | Harm to competition | Recommendations | Competent Ministry / Authority |
|---|---|---|---|---|---|---|---|---|---|
| 253 | **Joint Ministerial Decision 1153/16620/2014 "Requirements and start up process of seeds and propagating material producing and trading enterprises"** | art. 3 par. α | Wholesale trade of seeds and propagating material | Specific requirements are set for the operation of Seed Producing enterprises:<br>a) "responsible scientist" full-time or "responsible scientist" part-time with trained personnel following his/her instructions<br>b) proper infrastructure<br>c) lab is required; exemption for potatoes<br>d) conservation room for stocks<br>e) specialised technical personnel. | Licensing - Raises cost of entry | a) There is no official recital. However, following communication with the Ministry, the notification of a responsible scientist is necessary as it guarantees that high quality seeds are produced, there is compliance with the phytosanitary conditions to avoid genetic contamination and to protect biodiversity and the environment, the terms of the Technical Regulations are met, there is no seed degradation and quality control procedures are followed.<br>b-e) There is no official recital. However, following communication with the Ministry, the requirements are set in order to ensure proper standardization, packaging, storage and laboratory testing. | a) This provision may raise the cost of operation (labour cost); however, in general the requirement of a responsible scientist is justified and proportionate to the objective.<br>b-e) No harm to competition has been identified. The requirements set are proportionate to the objective. | No recommendation. | Ministry of Finance / Rural Development and Food |
| 254 | **Joint Ministerial Decision 1153/16620/2014 "Requirements and start up process of seeds and propagating material producing and trading enterprises"** | art. 3 par. β | Wholesale trade of seeds and propagating material | Specific requirements are set for the operation of Nursery Type A enterprises:<br>a) "responsible scientist" full-time or "responsible scientist" part-time with trained personnel following his/her instructions<br>b) special soil characteristics are set<br>c) proper infrastructure and machinery<br>d) land of at least 3,000 m$^2$ | Licensing - Raises cost of entry | a) There is no official recital. However, following communication with the Ministry, the notification of a responsible scientist is necessary as it guarantees the identification of varieties, the suitability of the nursery fields and the quality of plants for sale.<br>b and c) There is no official recital. However, following communication with the Ministry, the requirements are set in order to ensure plant health.<br>d) There is no official recital. However, following communication with the Ministry, the land requirement is set in order to ensure viable operation. | a) This provision may raise the cost of operation (labour cost); however, in general the requirement of a responsible scientist is justified and proportionate to the objective.<br>b and c) No harm to competition has been identified. The requirements set are proportionate to the objective.<br>d) Restrictive land requirements may act as barriers to entry. We understand from the competent authorities that it is not considered restrictive for current incumbents, however they may limit future entry. | a), b) and c) No recommendation.<br>d) Abolish the provision. | Ministry of Finance / Rural Development and Food |
| 255 | **Joint Ministerial Decision 1153/16620/2014 "Requirements and start up process of seeds and propagating material producing and trading enterprises"** | art. 3 par. γ | Wholesale trade of seeds and propagating material | Specific requirements are set for the operation of Nursery Type B enterprises:<br>a) "responsible scientist" full-time or "responsible scientist" part-time with trained personnel following his/her instructions<br>b) special soil characteristics are set<br>c) proper infrastructure and machinery<br>d) land of at least 1000 m$^2$ | Licensing - Raises cost of entry | a) There is no official recital. However, following communication with the Ministry, the notification of a responsible scientist is necessary as it guarantees the identification of varieties, the suitability of the nursery fields, the quality of plants for sale and plant health, as well as integrated plant protection system.<br>b and c) There is no official recital. However, following communication with the Ministry, the requirements are set in order to ensure plant health.<br>d) There is no official recital. However, following communication with the Ministry, the land requirement is set in order to ensure viable operation. | a) This provision may raise the cost of operation (labour cost); however, in general the requirement of a responsible scientist is justified and proportionate to the objective.<br>b and c) No harm to competition has been identified. The requirements set are proportionate to the objective.<br>d) Restrictive land requirements may act as barriers to entry. We understand from the competent authorities that they are not considered restrictive for current incumbents, however they may limit future entry. | a), b) and c) No recommendation.<br>d) Abolish the provision. | Ministry of Finance / Rural Development and Food |
| 256 | **Joint Ministerial Decision 1153/16620/2014 "Requirements and start up process of seeds and propagating material producing and trading enterprises"** | art. 3 par. δ | Wholesale trade of seeds and propagating material | Specific requirements are set for the operation of Nursery Type C enterprises:<br>a) "responsible scientist" full-time or "responsible scientist" part-time with trained personnel following his/her instructions<br>b) special soil characteristics are set<br>c) proper infrastructure and machinery<br>d) tissue-culture lab characteristics are set (25 m$^2$ etc.). | Licensing - Raises cost of entry | a) There is no official recital. However, following communication with the Ministry, the notification of a responsible scientist is necessary as it guarantees control of the accompanying certified material documents, performance of sampling to carry out soil testing and water, quality control of plants for sale, plant health, as well as implementation of integrated plant protection system.<br>b and c) There is no official recital. However, following communication with the Ministry, the requirements are set in order to ensure plant health.<br>d) There is no official recital. However, following communication with the Ministry, the building requirement is calculated based on size of needed equipment. | a) This provision may raise the cost of operation (labour cost); however, in general principle, the requirement of a responsible scientist is justified and proportionate to the objective.<br>b and c) No harm to competition has been identified. The requirements set are proportionate to the objective.<br>d) Restrictive building requirements, in terms of size, may act as barriers to entry. We understand from the competent authorities that they are not considered restrictive for current incumbents, however they may limit future entry. | a), b) and c) No recommendation.<br>d) Abolish the provision. | Ministry of Finance / Rural Development and Food |
| 257 | **Joint Ministerial Decision 1153/16620/2014 "Requirements and start up process of seeds and propagating material producing and trading enterprises"** | art. 3 par. ε | Wholesale trade of seeds and propagating material | Specific requirements are set for the operation of Seed and Propagating Material Trading Type A enterprises:<br>a) "responsible scientist" full-time or "responsible scientist" part-time with trained personnel following his/her instructions<br>b) proper storage and standardization facilities and machinery<br>c) lab for seeds' purity, germination. | Licensing - Raises cost of entry | a) There is no official recital. However, following communication with the Ministry, the notification of a responsible scientist guarantees plant health, proper storage, implementation of integrated plant protection system and quality control of products to be sold.<br>b and c) There is no official recital. However, following communication with the Ministry, the requirements are set in order to ensure proper standardization, packaging and storage. | a) This provision may raise the cost of operation (labour cost), however, in general principle, the requirement of a responsible scientist is justified and proportionate to the objective.<br>b and c) No harm to competition has been identified. The requirements set are proportionate to the objective. | No recommendation. | Ministry of Finance / Rural Development and Food |
| 258 | **Joint Ministerial Decision 1153/16620/2014 "Requirements and start up process of seeds and propagating material producing and trading enterprises"** | art. 3 par. στ | Wholesale trade of seeds and propagating material | Specific requirements are set for the operation of Seed and Propagating Material Trading Type B enterprises:<br>a) "responsible scientist" full-time or "responsible scientist" part-time with trained personnel following his/her instructions<br>b) proper storage facilities. | Licensing - Raises cost of entry | a) There is no official recital. However, following communication with the Ministry, the notification of a responsible scientist guarantees plant health, proper storage, implementation of integrated plant protection system and quality control of products to be sold.<br>b) There is no official recital. However, following communication with the Ministry, the requirements are set in order to ensure plant health and proper storage. | a) This provision may raise the cost of operation (labour cost); however, in general principle, the requirement of a responsible scientist is justified and proportionate to the objective.<br>b) No harm to competition has been identified. The requirements set are proportionate to the objective. | No recommendation. | Ministry of Finance / Rural Development and Food |

## Sector: Wholesale trade

| No | No and title of Regulation | Article | Thematic category | Brief description of the potential obstacle | Keyword | Policy maker's objectives | Harm to competition | Recommendations | Competent Ministry / Authority |
|---|---|---|---|---|---|---|---|---|---|
| 259 | **Joint Ministerial Decision 1153/16620/2014 "Requirements and start up process of seeds and propagating material producing and trading enterprises"** | art. 3 par. ζ | Wholesale trade of seeds and propagating material | Specific requirements are set for the operation of Seed and Propagating Material Trading Type C enterprises:<br>a) "responsible scientist" full-time or "responsible scientist" part-time with trained personnel following his/her instructions<br>b) proper storage and standardization/processing facilities and machinery<br>c) lab for seeds' purity, germination. | Licensing - Raises cost of entry | a) There is no official recital. However, following communication with the Ministry, the notification of a responsible scientist guarantees plant health, proper standardization, packaging and storage and quality control of products to be sold.<br>b and c) There is no official recital. However, following communication with the Ministry, the requirements are set in order to ensure proper standardization, packaging and storage. | a) This provision may raise the cost of operation (labour cost); however, in general principle, the requirement of a responsible scientist is justified and proportionate to the objective.<br>b and c) No harm to competition has been identified. The requirements set are proportionate to the objective. | No recommendation. | Ministry of Finance / Rural Development and Food |
| 260 | **Joint Ministerial Decision 1153/16620/2014 "Requirements and start up process of seeds and propagating material producing and trading enterprises"** | art. 4 par. 3 and art. 7 | Wholesale trade of seeds and propagating material | The permit of operation (Βεβαίωση Συνδρομής των Νομίμων Προϋποθέσεων) of seed and propagating material producing or trading enterprises is renewable and has five years duration. | Licensing | There is no official recital. However, following communication with the Ministry, a specific duration of operation is set, because thorough and periodical checks of enterprises operation requirements are necessary. | No harm on competition grounds has been identified. In principle, the requirement to renew the permit of operation is an administrative burden that could discourage potential entry. | No recommendation. | Ministry of Finance / Rural Development and Food |
| 261 | **Joint Ministerial Decision 1153/16620/2014 "Requirements and start up process of seeds and propagating material producing and trading enterprises"** | art. 5 par. 1 | Wholesale trade of seeds and propagating material | If the "responsible scientist" leaves the seed and propagating material producing or trading enterprises, a replacement has to be found and announced in three months, otherwise the Ministry writes off the company from the registry. During this time, sales occur. | Licensing | There is no official recital. However, following communication with the Ministry: a) the notification of a responsible scientist is necessary as it guarantees that high quality seeds are produced, there is compliance with the phytosanitary conditions to avoid genetic contamination and to protect biodiversity and the environment, the terms of the Technical Regulations are met, there is no seed degradation and quality control procedures are followed, and b) the grace period takes into account the time that would take to find a replacement, as well as the distinctive characteristics of the sector. | This provision limits the ability of an enterprise to operate, without the responsible scientist, for more than three months. However, as the notification of a responsible scientist is justified, the restriction is proportionate. | No recommendation. | Ministry of Finance / Rural Development and Food |
| 262 | **Law 1564/1985 "Organisation of production and trade of seeds and propagating material"** | art. 8 | Wholesale trade of seeds and propagating material | A plant breeder has the exclusive right to produce, trade or transfer his/her propagating material. He/she can apply for a plant creation certificate, granted by the Ministry Rural Development and Food. In this case, protection rights last for up to 18 years for vines, fruit and artificial trees and up to 15 years for all the rest. However, according to Regulation 2100/1994, the EU plant variety right should in principle have a life of at least 25 years (at least 30 years for vine and tree species). | Exclusive rights | There is no official recital. However, following communication with the Ministry, the aim of the provision is to stimulate the breeding and development of new varieties. | No harm to competition has been identified. Both procedures exist in parallel, with the EU superseding the national one. | No recommendation. | Ministry of Interior and Administrative Reconstruction/ Economy, Development and Tourism / Finance/ Justice, Transparency and Human Rights / Rural Development and Food |
| 263 | **Joint Ministerial Decision 3967/41140/2012 "Requirements and start up process of stock nurseries for the implementation of Regulations 1234/2007, 555/2008 and 436/2009"** | art. 6 par. 2δ, par. 2ε and par. 5 | Wholesale trade of seeds and propagating material | Specific requirements are set for the beginning of operation of stock nurseries:<br>a) employment of a "technical supervisor" is necessary<br>b) rootstock nurseries and cutting stock nurseries may employ a "technical supervisor" on a part-time basis, if the land is maximum 20000 and 10000 $m^2$, respectively; also, he/she can be employed at maximum five stock nurseries, which cannot be larger than 100000 $m^2$ in total<br>c) the "technical supervisor" cannot be employed at a stock nursery if he/she is employed elsewhere, at the public or private sector; there is an exemption in the case of micro enterprises<br>d) stock nurseries' permit of operation is renewable and has a duration of five years. | Licensing - Raises cost of entry | a) There is no official recital. However, following communication with the Ministry, the notification of a technical supervisor guarantees plant health, proper standardization, proper production and quality control of products to be sold.<br>b) There is no official recital. However, following communication with the Ministry, the exemption is granted in order to facilitate market operation and adjust to the operating environment by reducing labour costs. The land requirements are set in order to ensure viable operation.<br>c) It was not possible to identify the objective of the specific provision.<br>d) There is no official recital. However, following communication with the Ministry, a specific duration of operation is set, because thorough and periodical checks of enterprises operation requirements are necessary. | a) This provision may raise the cost of operation (labour cost), however, in general principle, the requirement of a technical supervisor is justified and proportionate to the objective.<br>b) In principle, the implementation of the part-time employment is proportionate to the objective, although it creates differential treatment between different size of enterprises.<br>c) This provision is contradictory to the concept of part-time employment, may raise the cost of operation (labour cost) and creates differential treatment between different size of enterprises.<br>d) No harm on competition grounds has been identified. In principle, the requirement to renew the permit of operation is an administrative burden that could discourage potential entry. | a) No recommendation for change.<br>b) No recommendation for change.<br>c) Abolish the provision.<br>d) No recommendation for change. | Ministry of Economy, Development and Tourism / Rural Development and Food |
| 264 | **Joint Ministerial Decision 3967/41140/2012 "Requirements and start up process of stock nurseries for the implementation of Regulations 1234/2007, 555/2008 and 436/2009"** | art. 8 | Wholesale trade of seeds and propagating material | Specific requirements are set for the beginning of operation of stock nurseries:<br>a) the land must meet special characteristics and not be used for vine cultivation for at least ten years<br>b) if the land is leased, the contract must have at least ten years duration<br>c) minimum land sizes are set: rootstock nurseries at least 20000 $m^2$ in total and at least 5000 $m^2$ in part, and cutting stock nurseries at least 10000 $m^2$ in total and at least 5000 $m^2$ in part<br>d) in a distance of 20 m. there cannot be vine cultivation<br>e) special soil and water characteristics are set. | Licensing - Raises cost of entry | a, d and e) There is no official recital. However, following communication with the Ministry, the requirements are set in order to ensure plant health.<br>b) There is no official recital. However, following communication with the Ministry, the duration is set in order to ensure operation of the lessee.<br>c) There is no official recital. However, following communication with the Ministry, the land requirements are set in order to ensure viable operation. | a, d and e) No harm to competition has been identified. The requirements set are proportionate to the objective.<br>b) No harm to competition has been identified, given that from our understanding based on communication with the competent authorities, this type of cultivations require for at least 10 years; therefore the provision seems proportionate.<br>c) In principle, restrictive land requirements may act as barriers to entry. We understand from the competent authorities that they are not considered restrictive for current incumbents, however they may limit future entry. | a, b, d and e) No recommendation for change.<br>c) Abolish the provision. | Ministry of Economy, Development and Tourism / Rural Development and Food |

## Sector: Wholesale trade

| No | No and title of Regulation | Article | Thematic category | Brief description of the potential obstacle | Keyword | Policy maker's objectives | Harm to competition | Recommendations | Competent Ministry / Authority |
|---|---|---|---|---|---|---|---|---|---|
| 265 | **Joint Ministerial Decision 3967/41140/2012 "Requirements and start up process of stock nurseries for the implementation of Regulations 1234/2007, 555/2008 and 436/2009"** | art. 12 | Wholesale trade of seeds and propagating material | Stock nurseries are obliged to renew notification of operation, in case of change in the name of the SA or in the case of change in the name of the enterprise due to change in company entity or shareholders' composition. | Licensing | It was not possible to identify the objective of the specific provision. | This provision increases cost of operation and restricts business strategies. | Notification should be renewed only in case of change of the tax identification number. In case of change in the name of the enterprise, the last one should just inform the competent authority. | Ministry of Economy, Development and Tourism / Rural Development and Food |

# ORGANISATION FOR ECONOMIC CO-OPERATION AND DEVELOPMENT

The OECD is a unique forum where governments work together to address the economic, social and environmental challenges of globalisation. The OECD is also at the forefront of efforts to understand and to help governments respond to new developments and concerns, such as corporate governance, the information economy and the challenges of an ageing population. The Organisation provides a setting where governments can compare policy experiences, seek answers to common problems, identify good practice and work to co-ordinate domestic and international policies.

The OECD member countries are: Australia, Austria, Belgium, Canada, Chile, the Czech Republic, Denmark, Estonia, Finland, France, Germany, Greece, Hungary, Iceland, Ireland, Israel, Italy, Japan, Korea, Latvia, Luxembourg, Mexico, the Netherlands, New Zealand, Norway, Poland, Portugal, the Slovak Republic, Slovenia, Spain, Sweden, Switzerland, Turkey, the United Kingdom and the United States. The European Union takes part in the work of the OECD.

OECD Publishing disseminates widely the results of the Organisation's statistics gathering and research on economic, social and environmental issues, as well as the conventions, guidelines and standards agreed by its members.

OECD PUBLISHING, 2, rue André-Pascal, 75775 PARIS CEDEX 16
(24 2016 02 1 P) ISBN 978-92-64-26637-7 – 2017

www.ingramcontent.com/pod-product-compliance
Ingram Content Group UK Ltd.
Pitfield, Milton Keynes, MK11 3LW, UK
UKHW051457290926
15471UKWH00008B/1252

9 789264 266377